A Multilateral Convention for Tax

Series on International Taxation

VOLUME 80

Series Editors

Prof. Ruth Mason, University of Virginia School of Law
Prof. Dr Ekkehart Reimer, University of Heidelberg

Introduction & Contents

The Series on International Taxation deals with a wide variety of topics in the global tax arena. The authors include many of the field's leading experts as well as talented newcomers. Their expert views and incisive commentary have proven highly useful to practitioners and academics alike.

Objective

The volumes published in this series are aimed at offering high-quality analytical information and practical solutions to international tax practitioners.

Readership

Practitioners, academics and policy makers in international tax law.

Frequency of Publication

2-3 new volumes published each year.

The titles published in this series are listed at the end of this volume.

A Multilateral Convention for Tax

From Theory to Implementation

Edited by

Sergio André Rocha
Allison Christians

Wolters Kluwer

Published by:
Kluwer Law International B.V.
PO Box 316
2400 AH Alphen aan den Rijn
The Netherlands
E-mail: international-sales@wolterskluwer.com
Website: www.wolterskluwer.com/en/solutions/kluwerlawinternational

Sold and distributed by:
Wolters Kluwer Legal & Regulatory U.S.
7201 McKinney Circle
Frederick, MD 21704
United States of America
E-mail: customer.service@wolterskluwer.com

ISBN 978-90-411-9428-2

e-Book: ISBN 978-90-411-9429-9
web-PDF: ISBN 978-90-411-9430-5

Editors

Sergio André Rocha is a Tenured Professor of Tax Law and Public Finance at the Rio de Janeiro State University, Brazil.

Allison Christians, H. is a Heward Stikeman Chair in Taxation Law at the McGill University.

Contributors

Andrea Laura Riccardi Sacchi holds a Ph.D. (cum laude) from *Universität de Valencia*, Spain and is a member of the Tax Advisory to the Directorate General at *Dirección General Impositiva*, Ministry of Economic and Finance, Uruguay. **Cristián Billardi** is an Interim Associate Professor of Tax Law at the University of Buenos Aires (U.B.A., Argentina) and a Postgraduate Professor in different Latin American countries and Italy. He holds a Ph.D. from the UNIPA-Italy. He is an active member of the AAEF and the Associazione Italiana per il Diritto Tributario Latinoamericano. He is also an academic member of the ABDT. He is incharge of the editorial of *Revista Diritto e Pratica Tributaria Internazionale* (www.dpti.it) and is a Studio Uckmar Associate Professor (c.billardi@uckmar.com).

Gisele Barra Bossa is a Ph.D. Student. She holds a Master's and an LL.M. in Legal and Economic Science from the Coimbra University (PT). She is a judge at the Brazilian Administrative Tax Court of Appeals (September 2017-May 2021). She is a lawyer. The author can be contacted at bossa.gisele@gmail.com.

Guillermo O. Teijeiro holds an LL.B. (summa cum laude) from La Plata University; an LL.M. from the Harvard Law School (HLS), and is a Visiting Scholar HLS-ITP; he is a Professor of International Tax Law, Master Program in Taxation, Argentine Catholic University (UCA); a Member of the Academic Council, UTDT Master Program in Taxation; and a Member of Teijeiro & Ballone Abogados.

Marcus Livio Gomes is a Tax Law Professor at the Rio de Janeiro State University.

Natalia Pushkareva is a Scientific Guest at the Max Planck Institute for Tax Law and Public Finance.

Michell Przepiorka holds a Master's in International Tax Law at the Instituto Brasileiro de Direito Tributário (IBDT). He has a specialization in International Tax Law and in Brazilian Tax Law at IBDT. He is a lawyer. The author can be contacted at przepiorka@tpa.adv.br.

Nathalie Bravo, Ph.D., LL.M. and tax adviser for international tax law and transfer pricing matters at PwC in Vienna, Austria. She completed the Doctoral Program in International Business Taxation (DIBT) at the Institute for Austrian and International Tax Law, WU (Vienna University of Economics and Business). Her doctoral project titled 'A Multilateral Instrument for Updating the Tax Treaty Network' was published in the doctoral series of the IBFD and awarded the DOC Fellowship of the Austrian Academy of Sciences and the Wolfgang Gassner Prize 2019 granted by the Austrian branch of the International Fiscal Association. The author can be contacted at nathalie.bravo@pwc.com.

Ramon Tomazela Santos, Ramon Tomazela holds a Ph.D. and a Master's in Tax Law from the University of São Paulo and a Master's (LL.M.) in International Taxation from the Vienna University of Economics and Business (WU). He is partner at Mariz de Oliveira e Siqueira Campos Advogados. The author can be contacted at ramon.tomazela@marizadvogados.com.br.

Ricardo García Antón is Assistant Professor of International and European Tax Law at Tilburg University (Fiscal Institute Tilburg).

Rita Calçada Pires, is an Associate Professor at NOVA School of Law (Universidade NOVA de Lisboa). She is a Tax Referee at the Tax Arbitration Centre (CAAD) and a member of the Academic Committee of the European Association of Tax Law Professors.

Vanessa Arruda Ferreira, is a managing principal at IBFD in Amsterdam, Netherlands. She holds a doctoral degree in International Tax Law from the University of Amsterdam (Netherlands) and a Master's in Tax Law at Université Paris 1 Panthéon-Sorbonne, Paris (France). She received her Bachelor's in Law from Universidade Católica de Pernambuco, Recife (Brazil) and is registered at the Brazilian Bar since 2003.

Summary of Contents

Table of Contents

Introduction

Allison Christians

Base erosion and profit-shifting—BEPS—has by now become perhaps the most recognizable acronym ever to be formulated for international taxation, with major recognition not only among tax experts and researchers but also across general news and social media circles. BEPS and the overwhelming public appetite for reform measures to curb it have together been the impetus for the most forceful multilateral initiative to coordinate tax regimes on a worldwide basis since the dawn of modern income taxation at the turn of the 20th century. In devising this landmark initiative, the Organisation for Economic Cooperation and Development (OECD) laid out three tiers of norms in the form of "minimum standards," "recommendations," and "best practices" to be operationalized in both OECD and non-OECD member states via multiple soft and hard law mechanisms: the former embedded in guidance, commentary, and reports, and the latter in the form of the Multilateral Convention to Implement Tax Treaty Related Measures to Prevent Base Erosion and Profit Shifting (MLI).

Styled as an innovative and even pathbreaking mechanism to work alongside the complex network of the world's estimated 3,000 existing income tax conventions, most of which are bilateral, the MLI may be a lesser-known acronym among the general population, but it has become a symbol of an emerging phase of increased multilateral cooperation in taxation. Yet whether the subject fulfills its symbolism is a matter of debate. Some see the MLI as momentous and revolutionary with impacts redounding to nations of all means and levels of geopolitical influence; others see it fulfilling more of a mechanical role that primarily continues an ongoing flow of limited policy coordination under the guidance of the same institutions and processes that have long dominated policy space in international tax, namely the key member states of the OECD.

This book seeks to illuminate both perspectives in an effort to bring to life the hopes and the realities of the current era of multilateral tax cooperation. Bringing together authors from multiple countries with varying perspectives who analyze the MLI from multiple angles across the spectrum of the theoretical to the practical, the book provides first, a comprehensive analysis of the design and goals of the multilateral convention as a treaty and an institutional framework, second, an overview of the structure of the MLI and its take-up across the globe to date, and third, a set of assessments on the various substantive topics covered by the convention with a view toward implementation and impact of its subject matter across jurisdictions and regions. The book is accordingly organized into three parts. The first part examines the role and nature of the MLI as an instrument of law and as a progression of the coordinative efforts of the past; the second provides a detailed examination of the structure of the MLI as well as a comparative survey of its adoption by states to date; the third considers the substantive implementation of the MLI with a series of in-depth analyses from a variety of jurisdictional and regime-based perspectives. Each part is discussed in turn.

PART I THE PURPOSE, NATURE, AND SIGNIFICANCE OF THE MLI

This Part begins with the *first chapter* by *Rita Calçada Pires*, in which she places the MLI in institutional and historical context, tracing the line of decision-making by key geopolitical actors to first establish a need for reform, then define the content of such reforms, and then deliver the reforms with some innovative and some less than innovative mechanisms. The chapter makes a persuasive case that the MLI is not really a revolution in tax lawmaking but rather a soft evolution from one stage to the next in an established succession of geopolitical relationships. Drawing upon the themes of sovereignty, autonomy, institutions, and international relations, the chapter examines the ways in which the BEPS project releveled the MLI as an implementation tool. Pires notes that the agenda-setting and institutional organizing of expertise and tasks continued a long history of powerful sovereigns leading the world to consensus with the prioritization of policy goals and rationales of those countries held intact even as the group of countries invited to join in at the implementation stage grew exponentially.

Pires lays out a set of assumptions about the network of rules, norms, institutions, and laws that effectively make up what is referred to as the international tax law system, even though she argues that the characterization is misapplied: countries are less nodes in a network than independent entities, attracting for some purposes and repelling for others. The result, as the chapter visualizes through a series of useful figures and diagrams, is a commanding group of coordinating regimes coming under constant pressure by an equally impactful range of unilateral lawmaking designed mainly to exploit or undermine any such coordination. All countries are participants in this schizophrenia, as Pires characterizes it, but the result is that the aspirations to multilateralism are not met as in practice, some countries are ever-present and influential at all stages of the development of consensus norms and rules, while others are habitually excluded until later or even end stages of each coordination cycle.

The analysis is sobering for those who look at the MLI, and the OECD's move towards inclusiveness of nonmember countries, as opportunities for a significant shift in the ways countries undertake policymaking in the area of taxation. Pires does not see that shift yet established by the MLI, yet she illuminates the seeds for its future development.

The discussion by Rita Calçada Pires provides useful background for the two chapters that follow, by *Vanessa Arruda Ferreira* and *Nathalie Bravo* respectively, each of which considers the multilateral nature of the MLI as an instrument governed by public international law.

The MLI was by all accounts a novelty to many international tax law scholars: an international agreement to be agreed by multiple parties, yet with immediate effect only on the basis of stand-alone treaties, most of which are bilateral; a text that framed a new direction for international taxation yet that was meant to coexist with and not override these other agreements, some of which date back several decades. The legal workings and implications of the MLI might still seem mysterious to those whose daily work is impacted by it, and there is as yet no jurisprudence regarding its legal nature or ultimate effect on the bilateral treaties coming within its scope.

In *Chapter 2, Vanessa Arruda Ferreira* takes a detailed look at the legal nature of the MLI in the language of the Vienna Convention on the Law of Treaties, examining the MLI's legal status as a treaty first, then a multilateral treaty, and then a "successive" treaty, but ultimately not a "subsequent" treaty. She examines the implications of the status of the MLI in each of these terms, including the interpretation of its terms in the context of their relationship to the bilateral treaties they modify, as well as the rules and principles governing the modification of the terms and termination of the MLI itself.

In *Chapter 3, Nathalie Bravo,* in turn, provides historical and comparative analysis that will serve as useful guidance for the perplexed, finding precedents for its unique structure and application within a range of regimes including world trade and human rights, and analyzing the ways in which the MLI adheres to and departs from these examples. Bravo explains that while multilateralism does not necessarily imply complete uniformity, the MLI promotes uniform interpretation in structure and purpose. She shows that the nature of the MLI as a multilateral instrument derives from the common interests of the parties that signed it, and that this nature is distinct from its scope and application in any particular case. Scholars in other areas have taken note of the MLI as an important development in the international legal sphere, with lessons to be learned not only within but also well beyond taxation law.

Together, these two chapters paint a picture of the international tax regime as a complex latticework of bilateral agreements united by an overlying framework that is and will remain under construction for the foreseeable future, if not permanently, yet grounded in a set of well-established governing principles and rules. A century ago, a small group of experts designed the tax treaty models that are still reflected in today's treaties. Some of these experts hoped that their bilateral approach, a necessity given incompatible policy preferences of the great powers of their day, was nevertheless temporary. They anticipated and hoped a fully multilateral tax treaty could be forged as bilateral negotiations replicated and converged over time, and that this multilateral treaty would replace its bilateral precedents. Despite its historic significance, the MLI is not their envisioned agreement; Bravo's chapter establishes that those original hopes remain unrealized because the MLI firmly continues the tradition of bilateralism in tax.

However, Bravo nevertheless concludes that the MLI has great potential as a means to achieving convergence across the distinct nodes of the network going forward. Ferreira's chapter in turn confirms that public international law rules in general, and the Vienna Convention in particular, provide the necessary ground rules to allow for such convergence.

My coeditor *Sergio André Rocha* furthers the foregoing discussion in *Chapter 4*, in which he asks whether multilateralism—at least as that term is thought to be embodied within the mechanism of the MLI—is the only valid way to achieve tax rule coordination across countries, and further whether the goal of such coordination is itself fully valid. Rocha examines the purported goals to be achieved by tax multilateralism by examining the developments of the past decade against the idea of the risk society—roughly defined as the collective, globally scaled, and cumulative social, environmental, political, economic risks people create through their actions and interactions with each other. He argues that the risk society in which we currently find ourselves across the globe requires a new approach to taxation. He therefore outlines a set of working principles for such approach and considers the work of the OECD on BEPS and the MLI in light of these observations.

Reviewing the main features of the MLI through this lens and from the perspective of one of the countries that has not yet signed on to the MLI, namely Brazil, Rocha shows that upon examination we can see that tax multilateralism is not always truly multilateral, while unilateralism, even as it is being discouraged by key policymakers, is still possible, is an equally valid approach, and can even be multilateral in its own way. In critiquing tax multilateralism, Rocha takes issue with the priorities of the leading OECD nations, finding them essentially colonial in nature, and argues that we should not be so eager to attach the label of multilateralism to what has been produced from efforts that by design appear to inure mostly to the benefit of their architects. In the past, that was the world's most developed countries, and Rocha argues that this status quo is fully maintained throughout the BEPS process. He concludes his forceful argument by advocating a more thoughtful and tailored approach to the idea of multilateralism, and cautions against an instinctual acceptance of the idea without careful consideration of a countries' specific tax coordination needs and possible solutions.

Rocha's cautions are well-advised as the book continues to an in-depth analysis of the content and implementation of the MLI.

PART II STRUCTURE AND ADOPTION

In this Part, the first chapter examines the structure of the MLI. This useful overview is followed by two chapters that survey the MLI's take-up to date.

Ramon Tomazela Santos sets the stage in *Chapter 5* with a detailed examination of the structure and components of the MLI. The chapter serves as a comprehensive explanation of the four main parts of the MLI, namely the minimum standards and optional additional coordinative enhancements aimed at hybrid mismatches, treaty abuse, permanent establishments, and dispute resolution. In addition to providing a thorough overview of the MLI, Tomazela provides a brief critical analysis of the main provisions. His insights are echoed and revisited in the chapters that follow.

In *Chapter 6, Andrea Laura Riccardi Sacchi* surveys the use of the MLI to implement the BEPS minimum standards by 32 Latin American and Caribbean countries. She notes that most of these countries had little or no role in the formulation of the OECD's BEPS initiative. Nine of the studied countries are nonmembers of the Inclusive Framework, none of which has signed on to the MLI, but even among the 23 countries that are Inclusive Framework Members, only 11 have signed the MLI to date. She analyzes the breadth of coverage of the MLI signatories and the rationales for the different choices made by Latin American and Caribbean countries with respect to the MLI.

In addition to its insightful analysis of the substantive degree of involvement and take-up by Latin American and Caribbean countries in the MLI including the work leading up to its formulation, this chapter provides valuable resources to researchers in the form of tabular data analyzing the development of the Latin and Caribbean bilateral tax treaty network by decade from 1940 through 2021, the membership of these countries in the OECD, G20, and Inclusive Framework, and their status in relation to the MLI.

The chapter concludes with a cautionary note. Sacchi observes that the rapid implementation by Latin American and Caribbean countries of BEPS measures in general, and the MLI in particular, has been rushed to the point that it has prevented countries from taking the opportunity to examine and potentially revisit their past tax treaty policy. The MLI's overlay design has the effect of entrenching past policy even if there are good reasons for change, but the OECD's leadership and timeframe on BEPS left insufficient time for reflection of the policy considerations unique to Latin American and the Caribbean.

In *Chapter 7, Natalia Pushkareva* surveys the 95 covered tax agreements that had been registered as of March 2021 with an article-by-article comparison of the agreed terms. Focusing its analysis especially on the differences between developed and developing countries, the chapter provides detailed insights and analysis of the trends to date, showing that countries fall into distinct categories with respect to their embrace of the different articles and that these groupings shift from article to article. Overall, the MLI signatories fall into demonstrably "more compliant" and "less compliant" groupings, with distinct policy stances revealed in the process. For example, it will probably not surprise too many readers to observe that despite the enthusiasm of the United States and a few other countries for mandatory arbitration of tax disputes, this provision is among those least accepted by the signatories, together with such optional provisions as the restriction of the rights of parties to tax their own residents in Article 11 (referred to as "saving clauses," following the U.S. precedent); the anti-abuse rule for permanent establishments situated in the third jurisdiction in Article 10, and the rules for transparent entities in Article 3.

In laying out her detailed analysis of each country's respective stance on each of the MLI articles, Pushkareva demonstrates just how much divergence the MLI actually allows across treaties and across jurisdictions. Providing the reader with a set of detailed comparison tables showing the take-up of various of the MLI elements by the 95, this chapter will be of great interest to those seeking to visualize the degree of harmonization being achieved in its adoption to date and to understand some of the impetus for divergence. It will also provide a resource going forward as countries continue to adjust their approach to their tax treaties within and beyond the provisions of the MLI.

The broad comparative surveys provided by Sacchi and Pushkareva are followed in the next Part with focused studies on the workings of the MLI in relation to specific regimes and within specific jurisdictions in the four chapters that follow.

PART III IMPLEMENTATION IN PRACTICE: PRECEDENTS, CHALLENGES, AND PROSPECTS FOR UNIFORMITY

Guillermo O. Teijeiro begins the detailed examination of MLI implementation in *Chapter 8* with his analysis of the MLI in light of existing general anti-avoidance regimes (GAARs) and specific anti-avoidance regimes (SAARs). Teijeiro calls the MLI a "new GAAR treaty" and examines its potential collision with domestic GAAR parallels, precedents, and practices from the perspective of Argentina. As one of the earliest signatories to the MLI and a country with deep experience with domestic and treaty-based GAARs, the obstacles to coherent implementation and the immediate need for coordinating and organizing principles encountered by Argentina are impactful and will serve as valuable guidance to other states facing similar rule harmonization challenges.

Beginning his exploration with an analysis of Argentina's various domestic and international general and specific anti-avoidance regimes, Teijero outlines the scope of application of these rules in domestic and international contexts. He then considers existing conflicts among these various regimes and introduces a path to facilitate their harmonious co-existence resolution in the form of ordering principles. Having laid out his proposed approach, Teijero examines the likely impact in light of administrative and judicial precedent as well as Argentina's experiences with limitation of benefit clauses in its treaty network.

Marcus Livio Gomes continues the theme of GAARs and the MLI in *Chapter 9*, in which he examines the content and effect of Article 7 of the MLI, namely the anti-abuse provisions and in particular the principal purpose test (PPT). Gomes conceptualizes the PPT as a general anti-avoidance rule that in some states will run parallel to domestic rules designed to address the same phenomena. The chapter examines the similarities among the PPT and its domestic GAAR counterparts in Australia, Canada, South Africa, and the United Kingdom, starting with an exploration of the parameters of the concept of avoidance as it is being developed by the MLI through the PPT. There may be historical differences in approach as between common law and civil law systems. The PPT can be read to embody the common requirements across systems, even if there are distinguishing requirements that will no doubt continue, creating costs in the form of taxpayer certainty.

In undertaking his analysis, Gomes shows that across domestic regimes, GAARs are not purely subjective tests, and that modern legislation tends toward including objective tests, in an effort to reduce the amount of discretionary administrative power. Gomes considers this trend likely to be replicated in the implementation of the PPT. In support of his argument, he lays out a comparative analysis of the various requirements in domestic GAARs including a "scheme" and a tax benefit or advantage and examines the likely overlap of coverage with the PPT. He then considers the claim that finding a tax avoidance purpose is a wholly subjective exercise and points to the trend toward discerning purpose from objective considerations including the results and effects of the scheme in question as evidence to the contrary. On the other hand, Gomes also notes that it is not so clear that the apparently objective aspects of GAARs and by extension the PPT, are in fact objective. For this inquiry, he aims at the reasonableness requirement in determining the rationale of a scheme, and the analysis of the legislator's intent in determining an underlying policy of a provision. While these might be characterized as more objective tests, Gomes concludes that there remains a significant risk of material divergence in approach across states which will impede the MLI's quest to broadly transplant divergent national systems with a harmonized multilateral approach.

In *Chapter 10*, *Michell Przepiorka* and *Gisele Barra Bossa* analyze the impact of the MLI from the perspective of one of the countries that has not signed it, namely Brazil. Brazil's decision not to sign to date seems in conflict with its intention to join the OECD membership, a process which requires Brazil to sign on to OECD norms and standards. These include the arm's-length standard and the general preference for residence over source-based taxation as it plays out within the provisions of the OECD model convention, in particular in its embodiment of the permanent establishment concept. This concept, the authors note, dates back to 19th-century-era treaties among a few European countries, after which the League of Nations effectively transformed it into a global consensus by crafting the first model treaties with the permanent establishment threshold a key element.

Brazil has long stood apart from the norms and standards promulgated by the League's successor, the OECD. It has done so in the form of safeguarding its source tax base by, *inter alia*, adopting lower thresholds to the taxation of nonresidents and using fixed margins in its transfer pricing regime. The authors note that Brazil is expected to abandon its unique deviations from the standards set out by the OECD over the past several decades, even as the OECD itself introduces measures that look suspiciously like the Brazilian approach. The specter of Brazil and the OECD crossing paths in their respective tax policy evolutions is a notable phenomenon in contemporary tax relations that ought to prompt many studies for the foreseeable future.

In line with these positioning moves, the authors note that Brazil's recent treaty negotiations evidence an intent to align with the MLI in practice if not by formal signature, and also to go along with the international trend toward the taxation of the digitalized economy, including by way of (ostensibly temporary) digital services taxes, even if this is not a particularly strong national policy preference. The authors point to Brazil's treaty relations with Singapore and Switzerland as evidence of Brazil's soft adherence to the MLI. The combination of shifting standards on the permanent establishment and the expansion of withholding to cover advertising services paid to highly digitalized firms are two markers of effective multilateralism even though on paper, Brazil stands formally outside of the MLI. In this way, Brazil's approach echoes that of the United States: in the digitalized economy negotiations surrounding a global minimum tax for certain multinational firms, the clear message has been that the U.S. position on the matter will remain unilateral yet be seen to "coexist" with whatever consensus is reached by the rest of the world. Meanwhile, that consensus itself being largely shaped by U.S. policy preferences. As a nonmember of the OECD, Brazil has never had the opportunity to influence the member states in the same way as the United States, but Przepiorka and Bossa's chapter suggests there may yet be room in tax multilateralism for Brazil's unique approach.

In *Chapter 11, Ricardo Garcia Anton* examines whether the MLI can deliver uniformity of tax norms across states given its hallmark feature, namely, its flexibility. Since states can and do take different approaches to both the number of treaties to be covered by the MLI, the specificity of its application in each such agreement, and the non-self-executing nature of its key provisions, Anton argues for caution in drawing conclusions about the ultimate success of the MLI just yet. Focusing on the treaty abuse protections laid out in Article 7(1) with a particular eye toward the distinct approaches taken by developed and developing countries, he analyzes a series of gaps and inconsistencies in application and interpretation that will prove challenging to the goal of harmonization. Among these are inconsistencies in the burden of proof standards among MLI and domestic law terms within and across states, incompatible definitions and applications of economic substance rules, and varying hierarchies of legal standards between MLI and domestic law special and general anti-abuse regimes.

Anton lays out a particularly vivid application of the difficulty ahead in his analysis of the Canadian case of *Alta Energy v. the Queen*, 2020 FCA 43, in which a transfer of shares from a Canadian company to a Luxembourg Holding company, which resulted in no taxable gain, was quickly followed by a sale by the Luxembourg company to a third party at a large gain, all of which was free of Canadian tax under the Canada-Luxembourg tax treaty. As Anton notes, the Canadian courts could find no abuse of the treaty in question, and it is difficult to determine whether or how the analysis should differ if the (subsequently agreed) MLI treaty abuse provisions would have applied in addition or instead of the domestic GAAR provision since the Federal Court of Appeal ultimately concluded that the relevant treaty terms "speak for themselves." Anton concludes that despite the gaps and inconsistencies, overall, the addition of treaty abuse provisions in the MLI point toward greater norm harmonization going forward, and that experience will be the best teacher.

In our *final chapter, Cristián Billardi* invites us to look to the future: will the MLI truly deliver uniform tax norms, or will merely open new avenues of tax avoidance and potentially lead to new cycles of tax negotiation? The chapter begins with the observation that the effort to curb tax avoidance has arisen because many of the European states that were long exporters of capital and technology, and therefore strongly concerned with the preservation of taxation by residence states, suddenly found their interests more closely aligned with those states that have traditionally been capital and technology importers, and thus concerned with the preservation of taxation at source. The change in perspective has illuminated a longstanding incoherence in the concept of "aggressive tax planning" in those states that have long been engaged actively—not to say aggressively—in using their tax regimes to lure capital by means that now must be eschewed.

Billardi analyzes the implications of this evolution by examining the goals and scope of the MLI in the context of the development of global norms surrounding the codification and sanction of aggressive tax planning, notably in the context of the European Union's Anti-Tax Avoidance and DAC6 Directives. He analyzes some difficult areas of divergence and asymmetry surrounding the definition of the concept including with respect to the intended scope of coverage, the burden of proof standards, the assignment of responsibilities among taxpayers and their advisers, and coordination across the pluralistic legal regimes and institutions of the international tax system.

Billardi points out that the latter problem brings up latent challenges inherent to running soft norms and hard rules in parallel without the benefit of formalized multilateral agreements or institutions to assign policy- and decision-making power in a mutually acceptable way. The conceptual imprecision of aggressive tax planning rules and their uneasy relationship to the purposes and the terms of the MLI in all of their uncoordinated splendor are but a symptom of these unresolved problems, as Billardi argues throughout his chapter. The risk is that if these asymmetries and divergences are absorbed into the pluralistic order, they will simply become a new ground for the continuation of forum and rule shopping by taxpayers and their advisers. Closing with thoughtful reflection, Billardi mirrors the main concerns expressed by the authors throughout this volume when he notes that the entire intention of the BEPS plan will be for naught if tax competition and tax uncertainty continue apace, simply in a different place or form. The terrain will have shifted but ultimately not undergone the transformation expected of a multilateral overhaul.

PART I The Purpose, Nature, and Significance of the MLI

CHAPTER 1

Multilateralism, Multilateralism, Who Is Sovereign after All? Tax Sovereignty after BEPS Multilateral Instrument

Rita Calçada Pires

Rita Calçada Pires places the Multilateral Instrument (MLI) in institutional and historical context, tracing the line of decision-making by key geopolitical actors to first establish a need for reform, then define the content of such reforms, and then deliver the reforms with some innovative and some less than innovative mechanisms. The chapter argues that the MLI is not really a revolution in tax lawmaking but rather an evolution from one stage to the next in an established succession of geopolitical relationships. Drawing upon the themes of sovereignty, autonomy, institutions, and international relations, the chapter examines the ways in which the base erosion and profit shifting (BEPS) project developed the MLI as an implementation tool.

1 TO BEGIN WITH: MIRROR, MIRROR ON THE WALL, WHAT AND WHY AM I ASKING WHO IS SOVEREIGN AFTER ALL?

1.1 BEPS, MLI, And Questioning If a Real Change Is Coming: Fundamental Questions

Going through the Organisation for Economic Co-operation and Development (OECD)/G20 BEPS Project (BEPS Project) tends to be a voyage where the observer is inclined to focus his attention on the various *Action Plans* reports, its normative solutions, and the eventual loopholes that still exist due to lack of consensus on the solutions provided or the ongoing analysis of the specific subject. Even when the analysis is specifically directed to Action 15 and the MLI, as this book is, a macro approach is still needed.

What I consider a macro approach is a result of *zooming out* on the specificities of the MLI. The analysis is oriented toward the generated impact on the international tax law arena by a different type of application instrument; one involving an enlarged community of States. Its inevitability comes from the fact that to understand the wider impact of a transformation, it is necessary to comprehend what exactly was modified, what was not, and what is still necessary to address as a step to fulfill the main objectives of an adequate and effective regime.

The starting point is the recognition that the BEPS project is complex and multilayered, an ambitious project that challenges the way international tax law is understood and designed. As a multifaceted project, its analysis must have a double lens: one that is able to *zoom in* and analyze specific approaches and solutions to problems that originated the need for action, and another that is able to *zoom out* and provide the designed architecture of a system that generates impact on the current international tax regime and national tax law, as well as the equilibrium of those two different arenas.

This chapter analyzes the BEPS project through a mirror, with an attempt to understand the challenges created by its complete architecture to tax sovereignty, specifically assessing the fact that the MLI provides the format in which major transformations are presented, determined, and applied. The focus is on the equilibrium between the *international tax regime and international tax actions v. national tax authority/sovereignty*.

To map the reflection, some guiding questions are presented, and possible answers are offered. The attempt is to provide *food for thought* to feed the global discussion about what kind of international tax regime exists and what type of transformations are occurring, while also identifying the long road ahead toward a well-adjusted regime.

Addressing MLI and its actual impact requires answering the following questions:

- Is MLI a reproduction of an international tax revolution?
- Is tax sovereignty diminished by MLI?
- Can MLI guarantee an equilibrium between the need for international cooperation, tax sovereignty, and global tax justice?
- From now on, following the MLI process, will tax sovereignty be affected by a new way of designing international tax law?
- Will MLI, as a new instrument within the application of the international tax regime, be strong enough to lead a substantial transformation on how international tax law is designed?

The questions above may raise some conflicting issues. On the one hand, states may wish to establish their own tax options, without considering other interests (e.g., economic, political, social, or environmental). On the other hand, the undeniable economic interdependence between jurisdictions and territories urges a conciliatory approach between tax regimes. It is a significant and schizophrenic tension, one between individuality, shared needs, and collective belonging. This tension highlights considerations on the status quo of the international tax arena, while also providing space to understand the options ahead.

1.2 What to Have in Mind While Questioning: Assumptions About the Current Context of the International Tax Arena

To meet scientific objectivity while also providing a clear path toward what is presented, this chapter is written having in mind some prior assumptions These assumptions provide a common ground that influences the proposed answers to the previously listed questions. Those assumptions will now be presented. It should be kept in mind that throughout this identification process and its reasoning, some of the responses will already become discernible.

1.2.1 First Assumption: An International Tax Regime Currently Exists, but Not an International Tax System

International Tax Law gave birth to an international regime made of tax rules that balance hard law (Tax Agreements) with a majority of soft law (e.g., OECD Transfer Pricing Guidelines). Fundamental principles include the benefits principle and the single tax principle: source and residence divide their tax powers while only one should ultimately be able to effectively tax. The creation and development of this international tax regime take place through *Soft Governance* (e.g., OECD, United Nations (UN), European Union (EU)), enhanced by tax cooperation between Tax Authorities.

So far, an international tax system has never existed. Until now, political will has not accepted it, delaying the connection it has with the transformation of tax powers and tax rules. Even if it is acknowledged that the effective and fair approach to deal with the existing tax gap would be via an international tax system, it is not a central political aim "*Because global justice would require global sovereignty.*"[1]

However, a regime is not a system. A system demands more from the components of a regime. It goes beyond interconnection, thus demanding a specific International Governance Structure:[2] one that designs, interprets, applies, and controls tax rules while arbitrating tax conflicts and enforcing the adequate solution. To be a full international tax system, a global tax should also be a necessary instrument. If this combination of factors does not exist, then there is a regime, not a system.

1. Thomas Nagel, *The Problem of Global Justice*. 33 Philosophy & Public Affairs 113, 147 n. 2 (2005), quote from p. 122.
2. About what Governance Structure means and implies, e.g., Kenneth W. Abbott & Duncan Snidal, *Hard and Soft Law in International Governance*. 54 International Organization 421, 456 (2000); Lewis A. Kornhauser, *Governance Structures, Legal Systems, and the Concept of Law*. 79 Chicago-Kent Law Review 355, 381 (2004).

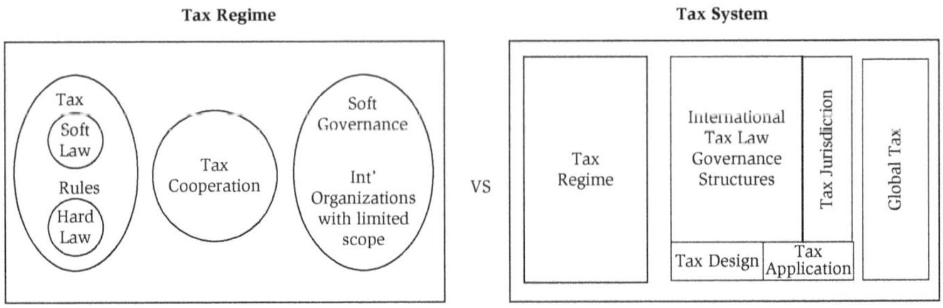

The international tax regime is made of flexible procedures, nonlinear processes, dynamic approaches, and responses, and is dominantly led by developed OECD countries. Many agreed standards contain *opt-out clauses* and are primarily fulfilled by soft law with no guarantee of effectiveness.

The lack of widespread acceptance of tax arbitration is also significant. It is still seen as a threat to tax sovereignty, which demonstrates why an international judicial tax structure is also nonexistent. Besides a Mutual Agreement Procedure contained in tax agreements, not many states have incorporated—both nationally and in those same tax agreements—tax arbitration mechanisms to deal with international tax conflicts. Moreover, within the international tax regime, there is no structure that resembles the World Trade Organization (WTO) panels.

If no judicial governance structures exist, considering a global tax is more complicated.[3] Even though the creation of a global tax was sometimes considered throughout international tax history, that discussion never resulted in a sufficiently developed project for a global tax,[4] and one is not foreseen in the future either—even regionally. The EU Common Consolidated Corporate Tax Base proposal (CCCTB) is entirely different from an EU tax. The CCCTB still maintains its distance from that approach, strictly dealing with the definition of the profitable taxes and the distribution of taxable profit through the Member States that have significant economic allegiance, based on an apportionment formula and proportional to that *economic allegiance*.[5]

It is thus reasonable to affirm that an international tax regime existed before the BEPS Project.[6] After the BEPS project, a transformed international tax regime was born. Nonetheless, an international tax regime and not an international tax system. The BEPS project creates substantive adjustments to prior international tax standards while

3. About the topic, Richard M. Bird, *Are Global Taxes Feasible?* (February 18, 2018). Rotman School of Management Working Paper No. 3006175 SSRN Electronic Journal. https://papers.ssrn.com/sol3/papers.cfm?abstract_id=3006175 (last visited April 30, 2021).
4. Besides XX Century UN attempts at sea resources taxation, at the Leaders' Summit on Climate (April 2021) the Shipping Industry and International Chamber of Shipping (ICS) have proposed a global taxation on carbon emissions. https://www.internationaltaxreview.com/article/b1rjhcgqrzdvr4/this-week-in-tax-shipping-industry-calls-for-global-carbon-tax (last visited April 30, 2021).
5. For details, COM (2016) 685 final, October 25, 2016, Proposal for a Council Directive on a *Common Corporate Tax Base* and COM (2016) 683 final, October 25, 2016, Proposal for a Council Directive on a *Common Consolidated Corporate Tax Base (CCCTB)*.
6. *Infra* 2.2.

promoting acceptance of part of those adjustments within the network of tax agreements through MLI. However, it also depends on unilateral acceptance by tax jurisdictions of many other tax rules that require national incorporation. The BEPS project still provides many soft law proposals, approaches, and recommendations, thus continuing a traditional procedure.

It is relevant to acknowledge that the BEPS project is still part of the *Soft Governance* model that has guided international tax relations since the 1920s. The OECD takes the *chairman* status, even if a renewed approach is started. The OECD partners with G20 (and not G7 or G8), aiming at improving the type of cooperation implemented and adding a more global approach through an *Inclusive Framework*.

However, even if the BEPS project is an undisputable evolution, many unilateral positions and tax measures have taken place during the BEPS project era (e.g., Foreign Account Tax Compliance Act (FACTA) on the US; India's digital tax levy). This negatively impacts the desired consensus on major substantial aspects—transparency and exchange of information; and digital economy connecting factors—and significantly influences the way the international cooperation model reacts and develops itself. International tax practice continues to reveal tax power fragmentation. The international tax arena is increasingly about multilevel and multilayer *Soft Governance*, with an increasing wide space occupied by *Informal Governance*.[7] With multiple levels, actors, stakeholders, and instruments, it becomes arduous to create an International Tax Law Governance Structure that is able to fulfill both the conditions and functions required by a *World Tax Organization*.[8]

7. Many International Law authors, dealing with the way international power, structures and actors, present these ideas about fragmentation of public power and rise of private actors, being corporate sector, civil society or digital platforms. E.g., Philipp Pattberg, *The Institutionalization of Private Governance: How Business and Nonprofit Organizations Agree on Transnational Rules*. 18 Governance 589, 610 (2005); Sebastian Botzem & Jeanette Hofmann, *Transnational Governance Spirals: The Transformation of Rule-Making Authority in Internet Regulation and Corporate Financial Reporting*. Critical Policy Studies 18, 37 (2010); Francis Fukuyama, *Governance: What Do We Know, and How Do We Know It?*. 4 Annual Review of Political Science 89,105 n. 19 (2016); Carey Doberstein, *Designing Collaborative Governance Decision-Making in Search of a "Collaborative Advantage."* 18 Public Management Review 819, 841 (2016); Robert Gorwa, *What Is Platform Governance?*. 22 Information, Communication & Society 854, 871 (2019). Even though International Tax Law has its own specificities, as Avi-Yonah stated, international tax law is International Law. Reuven S. Avi-Yonah, *International Tax as International Law* (Cambridge University Press 2007).
8. About the possibility and desirability of a World Tax Organization, e.g., Frances M. Horner, *Do We Need an International Tax Organization?*. 24 Tax Notes International 179 (October 8, 2001); Arthur J. Cockfield, *The Rise of the OECD as Informal "World Tax Organization" Through National Responses to e-commerce Tax Challenges*. 8 Yale Journal of Law and Technology n. 1 (2006) and Dale Pinto & Adrian Sawyer, *Building Bridges Between Revenue Authorities. Would a World Tax Organization Be a Key Facilitator?*. Journal of Applied Law and Policy 25, 40 (2011). Also, Wolfgang Obenland, *Options for Strengthening Global Tax Governance*, Freidrich Ebert Stiftung, November 20, specifically pp. 8-11, https://library.fes.de/pdf-files/iez/12958.pdf (last visited April 30, 2021), presenting either a strengthening the UN Committee of Experts, Upgrading the UN Committee of Experts, creating a functional commission under auspices of ECOSOC, establish a global convention on tax and a treaty body or Establish a new international organization.

1.2.2 Second Assumption: Tax Sovereignty as Responsibility and Sharing Tax Powers

This chapter does not aim to define tax sovereignty, nor to debate the various approaches to the concept, either based on political science and international relations.[9] The purpose of this assumption is to present the concept of sovereignty as it is understood by the author, providing a guide to understand the type of ideas offered throughout the chapter. It should be kept in mind the intrinsic link between the concept of tax sovereignty and how it influences the way tax cooperation is understood and how tax competition is assessed.[10]

Following the approach provided by Peter Dietsch,[11] sovereignty is seen as Responsibility.

Even acknowledging the typology of approaches provided by Stephen Krasner,[12] sovereignty, and therefore tax sovereignty, is more than *Domestic Sovereignty*; it also goes beyond *Westphalian Sovereignty* and integrates more elements than the traditional *International Legal Sovereignty*. All these models lack full awareness of the multiple elements that build tax sovereignty. These approaches are limited since they do not recognize the utmost importance of tax solidarity as a necessary step toward guaranteeing national sovereignty within an overarching economic interdependence arena.

Thus, to accomplish national political options and satisfy tax revenue necessities, while also guaranteeing the ability to accomplish high levels of tax compliance and effectively collect the corresponding fair share, a substantial convergence and cooperation must exist. Only if all ends meet at the beginning of the tax procedure will it be possible to diminish the tax gap, and suffocate aggressive tax planning schemes as well as their negative impact on sovereignty, public finances, and fair share. Moreover, the beginning of the tax procedure is the design of tax rules.

Contemporary tax sovereignty should be all about *Shared Sovereignty*.

---

9. For that, consider, e.g., Wm. A. Dunning, *Jean Bodin on Sovereignty*. 11 Political Science Quarterly 82, 104, n. 1 (1896); Peggy B. Musgrave, *Sovereignty, Entitlement, and Cooperation in International Taxation*. 26 Brooklyn Journal of International Law. (2001); Stephen D. Krasner, *Rethinking the Sovereign State Model*. 27 Review of International Studies 17, 42 (2001); Allison Christian, *Sovereignty, Taxation and Social Contract*. 18 Minnesota Journal of International Law 99, 153 n. 245 (2009); Allison Christians, *Human Rights at the Borders of Tax Sovereignty*. (Working Draft, NYU, Spring 2017); Laurens van Apeldoon, *International Taxation and the Erosion of Sovereignty*, 215-230 in Peter Dietsch & Thomas Rixen (eds) *Global Tax Governance* (ECPR Press 2016); *Tax Sovereignty and the Concept of Fiscal Rule-Making in the Countries of Central and Eastern Europe. Conference Proceedings* (Marina Sentsova et al. (eds), Voronezh State University, Faculty of Law 2018); Luis Calderon Gomez, *Transcending "Tax" Sovereignty and Tax Standardization: Three Questions*. 44 The Yale Journal of International Law, 191, 226, n. 1 (2020).
10. Dealing with the links within those three elements, Diane M. Ring, Democracy, *Sovereignty and Tax Competition: The Role of Tax Sovereignty in Shaping Tax Cooperation*. 9 Florida Tax Review 555, 596 (2009).
11. Peter Dietsch, *Catching Capital. The Ethics of Tax Competition*, specifically 167-187 (Oxford University Press 2015).
12. Stephen D. Krasner, *Rethinking the Sovereign State Model*. 27 Review of International Studies 17, 42 (2001); Stephen D. Krasner, *Pervasive Not Perverse: Semi-Sovereigns as the Global Norm*. 30 Cornell International Law Journal 653, 659 (2007).

It is no longer possible to present the myth of complete national individuality. The State no longer has an absolute and per se power. No longer the State is able to patronizingly suppress its national options as a personal option and in a nonsignificant way. No longer the State is able to dispense its sovereign powers only when and how a result of an unavoidable pressure. Rather, tax sovereignty implies a double composition:

- First element: Responsibility and Shared Sovereignty as self-preservation.
- Second element: Responsibility and Shared Sovereignty as integrity, assigning an ethical approach to tax design, interpretation, application, and control.

At present, tax sovereignty is increasingly sharing responsibility for tax decisions and tax actions, as states have a responsibility that comes with an intrinsic ethical value that should be blended with tax technical instruments and international commitments.[13] States are ethical agents, and so, State options and actions cannot be seen only as sourced by internal democratic power. Rather it needs to be assumed that Sate options and actions are revelations of what *should be*, not only of what *can be*.

1.2.3 *Third Assumption: Global Tax Justice Is, Indeed, a Global Goal*

When analyzing the relationship between power relations and the global redistribution of tax revenue, Patrik Emblad calls for a *breaking with sovereignty*. The author states that an analysis of tax sovereignty must be expurgated from a narrower and more formal sense that blinds the capacity to make tax powers function with what he calls economic-ideological forces. Overall, this openness is what allows for a re-centered concept of sovereignty that makes it possible to set aside preconceived ideas of how international tax order must be structured, opening up to what should be the adequate international tax structure.[14]

Establishing tax sovereignty as responsibility and as shared tax powers imply recognizing that global tax justice is an essential element of tax sovereignty. Addressing international tax law, and specifically tax sovereignty, without assuming the existence and the necessity of an ethical goal is denying the very essence of the system itself, thus disabling a balanced tax ecosystem. Moreover, a tax ecosystem is meant at national, regional, and global levels, all integrated and fully functional. In other words, a coherent and fair tax regime.

As Yariv Brauner wrote, "the sovereign operates within the confines of a system, with ethics and perhaps other fundamental bases, which one may view as potentially

13. Providing an insightful approach, Hans Gribnau, *The Integrity of the Tax System after BEPS: A Shared Responsibility*. 2017 Erasmus Law Review 12, 28 n. 1 (2017).
14. Patrik Emblad, *Breaking with Sovereignty. An Essay on Power Relations and Global Redistribution of Tax Revenue*. Copenhagen Business School Law Research Paper Series No. 20-14, Special issue I: International Tax Challenges for Developing Countries, https://research.cbs.dk/en/publications/breaking-with-sovereignty-an-essay-on-power-relations-and-global- (last visited April 30, 2021).

constraining its absolute powers,"[15] which denotes accepting and acting on the fact that a State is just one State among other States, being limited on its freedom and its action by the freedoms and actions of other States.

The allocation of taxes must be fair and tax revenue distribution must be equitable. It must provide both inter-taxpayer equity and inter-nation equity. Recapping the title of WILDE's 2017 book,[16] it should guarantee that the tax pie is fairly distributed.

Indeed, tax sovereignty is relevant at a national level, promoting the type of society taxpayers can contribute to. Tax sovereignty permits income redistribution, while also assisting economic and social decisions. However, tax sovereignty is also relevant at regional and global levels, which means that a fine-tuned balance must be established between national economic and social interests and a worldwide tax fair share.[17] As Tsilly Dagan states, "not only cosmopolitanism but political justice too requires that a justifiable cooperative regime must improve (or at least not worsen) the welfare of the least well-off citizens in all cooperating states. I explain that cooperation alone is no guarantee of improved welfare and that certain transfer payments between rich and poor countries might be required to ensure this."[18,19]

Unfortunately, the history of international relations and tax law practice has been based on individuality, promoting free space for crystallization of the principle of tax competition.

This chapter does not intend to discuss the positive and negative aspects stemming from the use of taxes as public instruments to create investment-friendly environments and provide safe harbors for economic activities. Rather, what is necessary to point out is the fact that tax competition is an international tax law pillar; a core fundamental principle of action that is diametrically opposed to the other international tax principle of tax cooperation. Additionally, it should also be recognized that within the international tax regime, tax competition has been frequently used as harmful tax competition, even if the designation and rhetoric of so many of those tax rules do not identify themselves with that negative impact.

Tax competition has enabled the development of race to the bottom approaches and relevant losses on public revenues. Data from international tax history demonstrates that tax competition has not produced a fair and equal distribution of tax

---

15. Yariv Brauner, *An Essay on BEPS, Sovereignty, and Taxation*, 73-93 in Sergio André Rocha & Allison Christians (eds), *Tax Sovereignty in BEPS Era* (Kluwer Law International 2017), quote from p. 78.
16. Maarten Floris de Wilde, *Sharing the Pie. Taxing Multinationals in a Global Market* (IBFD 2017). Related to this subject, specifically, 51-91.
17. Providing a strong link to a universal international law of human dignity, the McDougall-Lasswel-Chen theory could be part of the reasoning. Myres S. McDougal et al., *Human Rights and World Public Order: The Basic Policies of an International Law of Human Dignity* (Yale University Press 1980).
18. Tsilly Dagan, *International Tax and Global Justice*. 18 Theoretical Inquiries in Law 1, 35 n. 1 (2017).
19. Arguing in favor of inclusivity of less affluent countries, but also establishing a normative framework that provides those countries differentiated taxing rights dependent on the level of development, Ivan Ozal, *Two Accounts of International Tax Justice*. XXXIII Canadian Journal of Law & Jurisprudence 317, 339 n. 2 (2020).

burdens and tax revenues. It is far from allowing a balanced use of taxes and has rather been used as an instrument to merely adjust productivity, economic and social national infrastructures, and competencies.[20] Precisely due to tax competition, taxpayers throughout the globe have been exploring BEPS actions, creating the current tax gap that minimizes tax equality and strengthens the necessity of more tax pressure. It is enabling an increase of sovereign debts levels and, in the end, the conviction that tax cooperation is indispensable and that a shortage of traditional tax sovereignty is a price necessary to pay in order to create obstacles to aggressive tax planning/tax avoidance schemes.[21,22]

This status quo makes it relevant to acknowledge, as Arthur J. Cockfield does, that "a challenge for international tax regime is hence that different countries have different collective understandings of justice and morality. This has become more apparent in an era of increasing protectionism, nationalism, and populism. In this environment, countries more obviously pursue their own visions of national interest—potentially at the expenses of global welfare."[23] In order to break the chain, global tax fairness becomes an essential part of how tax sovereignty is interpreted and applied. It is this global tax fairness that allows a re-balancing of interests and a fruitful retraction of tax competition,[24] while also providing for a determination for current value creation and allocation of economic benefits.[25]

1.2.4 Fourth Assumption: Economic Allegiance Is Stronger Than Political Allegiance

The principle of prioritization of substance over form unavoidably makes the argument for valuing economic allegiance as more relevant than political allegiance. Economic

20. Also, about this discussion, William Vleck, *Offshore Finance and Global Governance. Disciplining the Tax Nomad* (Palgrave Macmillan 2017).
21. Aligned with the idea, Allison Christians, *BEPS and the Power to Tax*, 3-27 in Sergio André Rocha & Allison Christians (eds), *Tax Sovereignty in BEPS Era* (Kluwer Law International 2017)—specifically p. 4—presents the conflict between an optimistic theory of cooperative convergence of sovereign equals and the opportunistic self-dealing and ruthless competition. On a different mindset, sustaining that cooperative rhetoric is overrated and that cannot be expected from States to cooperate automatically, specifically when their welfare and collective good is negatively impacted, Tsilly Dagan, *BRICS: Theoretical Framework and the Potential of Cooperation*, 15–32, in Yariv Brauner & Pasquale Pistone (eds), *BRICS and the Emergence of International Tax Coordination* (IBFD 2015), specifically pp. 23–32.
22. Also, to keep in mind that international approaches to capital export neutrality and capital import neutrality measures have been delivering scope for unbalanced distribution of tax bases and tax revenues which tend to attract unilateral tax measures, most of the time, presented in the format of harmful tax competition, either with harmful tax practices or special tax regimes that may be assessed as harmful. Which indicate that a transformational approach should occur.
23. Arthur J. Cockfield, *Shaping International Tax Law and Policy in Challenging Times*. 54 Stanford Journal of International Law 223, 240 n. 2 (2018), quote from p. 240.
24. Defending a *Code of Conduct of Taxation*, Richard Murphy, (http://www.taxresearch.org.uk/Documents/TaxCodeofConductFinal.pdf (last visited April 30, 2021)). Also promoting a code of conduct of taxation and broadening of the BEPS-Agenda, Irene Burgers & Irma Mosquera, *Corporate Taxation and BEPS: A Fair Slice for Developing Countries?*. 2017 Erasmus Law Review 29, 47 n. 1 (2017), quote from p. 45.
25. Following the wording of *ibid.*, p. 46.

allegiance is all about substance, global tax justice, sharing tax powers, and multilateralism. On the contrary, political allegiance is all about form, individual/national competition, imposing tax powers, and unilateralism.

Even if political allegiance has been dominating taxation worldwide since the 1920s, if one analyzes the key characteristic of international taxation, one finds that economic allegiance *should be* the option. It is the criteria that reveal where value is created, which means where the tax base arises. Instead, political allegiance is born out of *Westphalian* tax sovereignty and diplomatic approaches to international relations. Some might call it allegiance by choice and by political and economic interests. Others might call it egoism or, at least, unfair connection criteria.[26]

The League of Nations report by four economists indicated the economic allegiance path as desirable, providing proof of its necessity and defending full tax powers to economic allegiance jurisdiction, even with recognition of the necessity to value the link to the place of residence.[27] However, even if a combination was the approach by political choice, political allegiance became the core of territorial connections and a significant foundation of contemporary international tax law as known. In this scenario, economic and State practices lead to a well-recognized paradox: within an integrated and globalized economy, too much tax sovereignty develops less tax sovereignty.[28] From tax practice, what States want is not what they obtain. What was generated was a schizophrenic personality: an aggressive competitor actively negotiating and seeking to implement actions as an ethical cooperator. Using Allison Christians' words, *certainty is favored over accuracy*.

Even if wrong, harmful tax competition exists and is still established and promoted worldwide.[29] This practice explains why criticism is part of many contemporary analyzes. But mainly, it demonstrates what is wrong.

Maintaining this international paradigm as it is—a schizophrenic paradigm, as shown—while designing and applying international tax standards is the equivalent of choosing only a palliative care. If solutions are needed, to guarantee a cure for tax spillovers, then a new paradigm must be agreed upon, and that new approach can only be based on new rules for tax allocation. Indeed, it seems to be a revolution. Nevertheless, what is needed is not a painkiller that soothes the disease, but rather a cure for an outdated and insufficient international tax regime. It is essential to build a resilient and fair international tax regime, one that is able to ensure that taxes are effectively paid according to a fair share.[30]

---

26. Using *mercenary behavior by the State*, Allison Christians, *Putting the Reign Back in Sovereign*. 40 Pepperdine Law Review 1373, 1414 n. 5 (2013), quote from p. 1377.
27. League of Nations, Economic and Financial Commission, *Report on Double Taxation, Submitted to the Financial Committee by Professors Bruins, Einaudi, Seligman and Sir Josiah Stamp*, April 5, 1923, especially pp. 20-27 and 39.
28. Sergio André Rocha, *The Other Side of BEPS: Imperial Taxation and International Tax Imperialism*, 179–200 in Sergio André Rocha & Allison Christians (eds) *Tax Sovereignty in BEPS Era* (Kluwer Law International 2017), specifically, p. 199.
29. Allison Christians, *BEPS and the Power to Tax*, 3-23 in Sergio André Rocha & Allison Christians (eds), *Tax Sovereignty in BEPS Era* (Kluwer Law International 2017), specifically p. 13.
30. Also, William Vleck, *Offshore Finance and Global Governance. Disciplining the Tax Nomad* (Palgrave Macmillan 2017), specifically, p. 54.

Being a game-changer means addressing economic allegiance at its core. Considering the type of socio-economic globalized and mobile world we live in, this goes directly to the heart and soul of the value creation processes, either through digital value-chains[31] or global wealth chains.[32]

I fully agree with Allison Christians' statement that "this principle accords with the idea that income is a creature not of human industry alone but of the collective efforts, through generations, within the institution of the Nation-State and beyond it, through pluralistic international orders."[33] That is why, when considering a core transformation fully based on economic allegiance, it tends to suggest the substitution of the unity principle—one residence, one source. Considered as an undeniable substantial connection to the territory, economic allegiance strongly encourages accepting more than one residence and more than one source. It demands shared taxation and shared revenues, which means inter-nation fair share and equity on sharing the tax pie.

To be noted, this is something not effectively addressed by BEPS and it is something that has been haunting the OECD and many States throughout the world, including the EU Member States.[34]

1.2.5 Fifth Assumption: Tax Sovereignty Creates Impact on Tax Legitimacy, Yet Is a Different Concept

As part of its *Westphalian* and *International* powers, a State may choose what type of taxation to impose and the amount subject to it. But while defining the scope of tax sovereignty, from the tax sovereignty concept the State is also dealing with the concept of tax legitimacy. Not the other way around.[35] It is all about the power to do and the power to impose, which means deciding within an environment of what *could* and what *could not* be done.

---

31. About the necessity of rethinking the unity principle and the option for a value creation chain approach, my 2009 Ph.D. thesis, *Tributação internacional do rendimento empresarial gerado através do comércio electrónico. Desvendar mitos e construir realidades* (Almedina 2011) and Rita Calçada Pires, *Uncovering A Brave New World On Taxation: Income From Digital Economy* 43–60 *in International Taxation: New Challenges*, (University of Minho—School of Law 2017).
32. Considering also the idea, Siobhan Airey, *Taxation Untapped: The Potential of the UN Sustainable Development Goals to Promote Progressive International Tax Reform*, UCD Working Papers in Law, Criminology & Socio-Legal Studies, Research Paper No. 6/2020, p. 7. Presenting the concept and exploring the challenges, e.g., Leonard Seabrooke and Duncan Wigan, *The Governance of Global Wealth Chains*. 24 Review of International Political Economy 1, 29 n. 1 (2017).
33. Allison Christians, *BEPS and the Power to Tax*, 3-23 in Sérgio André Rocha & Allison Christians (eds), *Tax Sovereignty in BEPS Era* (Kluwer Law International 2017), quote from p. 12.
34. It is also the explanation why Member States/Council have been resisting to approve both CCCTB proposal and Digital Taxation package proposal. As Yariv Brauner states: "The deeper issue is that there is no agreement on common principles regarding tax jurisdiction." Yariv Brauner, *An Essay on BEPS, Sovereignty, and Taxation* 73-93, in Sergio André Rocha & Allison Christians (eds), *Tax Sovereignty in BEPS Era* (Kluwer Law International 2017), quote from p. 82.
35. As stated by Thomas Nagel, *The Problem of Global Justice*. 33 Philosophy & Public Affairs 113, 147 n. 2, specifically pp. 145-147.

However, if tax sovereignty is *Responsibility*, then when a State is deciding about which tax actions and tax rules are to be undertaken, that same State must decide considering what *should* and what *should not* be done. Decisions based on what *could* and what *could not* be done should no longer exist. Rather, decisions must be made contemplating what *should* and what *should not* be done. Tax decisions are a choice, not an imposition. A choice of what *should* and what *should not* be for a specific tax rule, within a tax regime and the overall national tax system. Conceiving tax sovereignty as *Responsibility* and as containing an ethical and moral gene involves creating an impact on the concept of tax legitimacy due to responsibility, ethical action, and global tax justice as part of the way an individual State reasons and acts.

National powers tend to act under the assumption that their tax sovereignty allows protection of their tax system. As Yariv Brauner mentioned, "sovereignty is often used in international tax discourse as a hand grenade to shut down difficult discussion."[36] Tracking the causes, the answer is mainly because shared revenues are not a national ambition and taxes are the most relevant State budget revenue to guarantee public action. It is true that States, individually considered, have the necessity of gathering enough resources to provide the financing social states or any type of State that may exist. However, the last decades suggest—as the BEPS project argues—that an active tax competition scenario is not facilitating the fulfillment of that aim; rather, it is bringing unbalanced and dangerous loss of significant tax revenues while attempting tax equity.

I do not agree that legitimacy is only a matter of perception.[37] Tax history tends to reveal it, but I cannot accept that an international tax regime could address tax legitimacy as such. International tax legitimacy implies an active and global participation; one that does not endorse what was designed by some, but rather one that divides responsibility and decision. It is a natural consequence of the above concept of sovereignty as responsibility with global tax justice as an essential component.

Bearing this in mind, it is believed that instead of adopting *mercenary behavior*,[38] the States must meet their interests in a balanced way and base their choice of tax regimes and tax measures on what *should* or *should not* be done. This comprises self-restraint as a choice toward an active and responsible type of tax cooperation.[39] If this type of commitment is understood and accepted, then trust can grow within the

36. Yariv Brauner, *An Essay on BEPS, Sovereignty, and Taxation* 73-93 in Sergio André Rocha & Allison Christians (eds) *Tax Sovereignty in BEPS Era* (Kluwer Law International 2017), quote from p. 73.
37. Around this notion, demonstrating how BEPS project is still reflecting the dominance of few over many more, Sissie Fung, *The Questionable Legitimacy of the OECD/G20 BEPS Project.* 10 Erasmus Law Review 76, 88 n. 2 (2017).
38. Using Allison Christians's expression. Allison Christians, *Putting the Reign Back in Sovereign.* 40 Pepperdine Law Review 5 (2013), p. 1377.
39. About a parallel approach, consider the *Theory of Jurisdictional Reasonableness* by Cedric Ryngaert, *The Concept of Jurisdiction in International Law,* 50-75 in Alexander Orakhelashvili (ed.) *Research Handbook on Jurisdiction and Immunities in International Law* (Elgar Publishing 2015).

international tax regime, favoring the standardization of tax rules. And the so-called substantial multilateralism may have a chance of becoming the new normal.[40]

Additionally, an element to consider is that international tax legitimacy is born of national tax legitimacy, and a top-to-bottom approach is not possible while actively lacking legitimacy. Consequently, as stated by Tsilly Dagan, if and:

> when States initiate multilateral cooperation to restore their legitimacy, they each entrust the multilateral regime with the authority to act on their behalf so as to enable them to provide their constituents with justice. This is the sine qua non for their legitimacy. They incorporate their otherwise impaired individual coercive power into a collective regime that encompasses more power than the sum of its components' power.[41]

As a consequence, global fairness must be present in each stage of international action and international standards. Otherwise, the expected outcomes that motivate international cooperation will not be achieved.

1.2.6 Sixth Assumption: Tax Governance as an Instrument of Tax Sovereignty and, Therefore, Distinct from It

As tax sovereignty is not tax legitimacy, tax sovereignty is also not tax governance. Instead, the latter is an instrument of tax sovereignty. Tax globalization developed into tax governance, creating a larger arena of actors and actions that go beyond the State territory and powers. The State is no longer just a State or a self-isolated territory. Rather, the State is integrated into a network of stakeholders and influencers and must participate in it either individually, through informal platforms, or through international organizations where it is a member.

Tax Governance does not only influence a State individually. As Peter Dietsch and Thomas Rixen stated, "governance is global governance if the reach of the principles, norms, rules, and procedures is global or at least international. [And] Global tax governance thus consists of the set of institutions governing issues of taxation that involve cross-border transactions or have other international implication."[42]

Contemporary tax governance is born out of a necessity to create order out of international tax chaos generated by different tax regimes and tax rules throughout the world. Moreover, as previously stated, until now, the international tax arena is based on the *prisoner's dilemma*: States navigate global tax governance by trying to build an

40. *Infra* 1.2.10. Also, about the positive impact of multilateralism, Kimberley Brooks, *The Potential of Multilateral Tax Treaties*, 211-236 in Michael Lang et. al. (eds) *Tax Treaties: Building Bridges Between Law and Economics* (IBFD 2010).
41. Tsilly Dagan, *International Tax and Global Justice*. 18 Theoretical Inquiries in Law 1, 35 n. 1 (2017), quote from p. 31.
42. Peter Dietsch & Thomas Rixen, *Global Tax Governance: What It Is and Why It Matters*, 1-23 in Peter Dietsch & Thomas Rixen (eds) *Global Tax Governance* (ECPR Press 2016), quote from p. 3.

(im)possible balance between tax competition and tax cooperation, while adopting tax rhetoric that moves from *sharing tax power* to *imposing tax power*.[43]

Nowadays, global tax governance is dominated mostly by those States that *have* economic power and are home to very competitive economies. Those are the strongest voices within established international organizations. Even if BRICS are acquiring recognition as relevant agents,[44] they still lack presence within the core design of the regime and its modifications.[45] In addition to BRICS, non-OECD countries are also spectators. Even if asked to join in, they do not achieve the quality of full-right members and thus do not share an active part of the procedure. The international tax regime is still dominated by OECD members—and, among them, by a few—presenting a difficult inter-nation equality, while managing the prisoner's dilemma.[46]

To note, the BEPS project was individually started by OECD. The definition of the problem, the quantification of the impact, the determination of the core problems, and a delineation of the questions and necessities that should be satisfied by each action were all established within the scope of the OECD decision and action. The *Addressing Base Erosion and Profit Shifting Report* and *Action Plan on Base Erosion and Profit Shifting*, both from 2013, are OECD materials, decisions, and priorities.

Even if the G20 became part of the process and Brazil, Russia, India, China, and South Africa (BRICS) were integrated as participants, not all other countries that are non-OECD and non-G20 members could have an active participation within the process, including being active members of working groups. Following OECD data, in 2015, "under the OECD/G20 BEPS Project, over 60 countries delivered 15 Actions to tackle tax avoidance, improve the coherence of international tax rules and ensure a more transparent tax environment (BEPS package)."[47] Even within those 60 participating countries, it has never been very clear how other non-G20 countries would be called on to participate in the process. It was by invitation only, which made those participants simple observers of what was decided by working groups. It is also relevant to highlight that the *2015 BEPS package was endorsed by the G20*.[48] Endorsement is not the same as designing and deciding.

The *Inclusive Framework* was created in 2016 after the main options were designed and presented through those 15 BEPS project reports that were mentioned

43. Providing criticism on discursive power and global governmentally, specifically considering tax nomads and the global attempt to override them, William Vleck, *Offshore Finance and Global Governance. Disciplining the Tax Nomad* (Palgrave Macmillan 2017), e.g., p. 21 onwards. Also providing a very clear insight on the topic, Arthur J. Cockfield, *Shaping International Tax Law and Policy in Challenging Times*. 54 Stanford Journal of International Law 223. 240 n. 2 (2018).
44. As seen by the BEPS Project procedures—the G20, instead of G8, and the *Inclusive Framework*.
45. About this legitimacy aspect of BEPS, e.g., Irma Johana Mosquera Valderrama, *Legitimacy and the Making of International Tax Law: The Challenges of Multilateralism*. 37 World Tax Journal 343, 382 n. 3 (2015); Sissie Fung, *The Questionable Legitimacy of the OECD/G20 BEPS Project*. 10 Erasmus Law Review 76, 88 n. 2 (2017).
46. About the topic with specific proposal, Thomas Rixen, *Institutional Reform of a Global Tax Governance: A Proposal*, 325-349 in Pieter Dietsch & Thomas Rixen (eds), *Global Tax Governance. What Is Wrong With it and How to Fix It* (ECPR Press, 2016).
47. https://www.oecd.org/tax/beps/flyer-inclusive-framework-on-beps.pdf (last visited April 30, 2021).
48. OECD/G20 (2020) *Inclusive Framework on BEPS Progress report*. July 2019-July 2020, p. 2.

above. It started with 82 members and the latest data indicates 135 countries, including 66 developing countries and 14 observer organizations.[49] Until today, only within Action 1—taxing digital economy—was the *Inclusive Framework* asked to actively *join* the discussion (2018-2020). Maybe this can be explained due to a consensus not having been achieved during the prior process and given the fact that India (a BRIC) recently decided to unilaterally impose a digital tax model. In the context of this new role of the *Inclusive Framework*, it should also be noted that working parties and groups are carrying out the technical work under the guidance of the *Inclusive Framework Steering Group*, a selective group of 24 countries.[50,51]

This description shows how complex global tax governance is becoming and how it involves almost impossible equilibriums. It is all about political will. Any transformations or revolutions on how international tax law is designed, interpreted, applied, and controlled will always be about what may reveal as a change of heart in political will.

In such a scenario, building trust is a difficult process, mediated by unilateral approaches, reactions, and counterreactions, regional mitigation of tax differences, improvement of mechanisms creating entanglement of techniques and information by Tax Authorities, i.e., improving Tax Cooperation, but still maintaining and preserving Tax Competition.

1.2.7 Seventh Assumption: Tax Rhetoric Is Not as Valuable as Tax Practices

Since tackling aggressive tax planning became a nuclear action worldwide, political narratives have taken a responsibility discourse, closing doors to those who are noncooperative tax havens and multinationals that restrain themselves from Corporate Social Responsibility or Corporate Moral Agency. This is reflected in national political agendas and the BEPS project rhetoric as well.

However, it is necessary to go beyond tax rhetoric and concentrate on what is effectively a result of international and national decisions. As Tim Buttner and Matthias Thiemann demonstrate, "due to a decrease in the OECD's capacity to effectively bring about technocratic solutions, the authority of the OECD is increasingly relying on political maneuvering and rhetoric."[52] This way of acting emphasizes how to analyze facts. Statements must be considered as nuclear. The analysis must include how tax

49. *Ibid.*
50. As of April 2021, the *Inclusive Framework Steering Group* is chaired by Germany, co-chaired by China and Nigeria, having more 11 members from the *Committee of Fiscal Affairs* and 10 BEPS Associates members. https://www.oecd.org/tax/beps/steering-group-of-the-inclusive-framework-on-beps.pdf (last visited April 30, 2021).
51. Presenting Inclusive Framework as a momentous event in international tax governance, but also recognizing its legitimacy failure on first stages of tax standards design, Allison Christians, *BEPS and the New International Order*. 2016 Brigham Young University Law Review 1603, 1647 (2017), specifically p. 1645.
52. Tim Buttner & Matthias Thiemann, *Breaking Regime Stability? The Politicization of Expertise in the OECD/G20 Process on BEPS and the Potential Transformation of International Taxation*. 7 Accounting, Economics, and Law: A Convivium 1, 16 n. 1 (2017).

practices are designed, how they are implemented, and how they integrate a complete balance of the interests of economic actors. It must not be a matter of language. It is all about performance based on prior rhetoric.[53]

1.2.8 *Eighth Assumption: International Tax Regime as a Permanent Work In Progress*

An international tax regime is not analyzed as being a closed reality crystallized by political discourse. Instead, due to tax practices and its inherent international tax rhetoric, an international tax regime should be characterized as an open reality, described as a permanent work in progress.

Considering international tax history in an abridged way, it is possible to summarize international tax as follows:

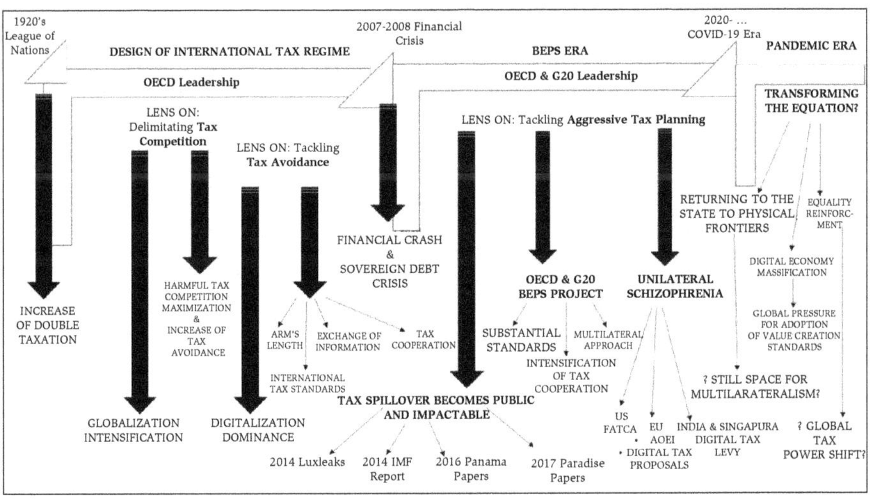

Even from a simplified perspective, some central intrinsic characteristics are present:

- Throughout decades, there is always one dominant organization leading the development of an international tax regime: first the League of Nations, afterward, the OECD.
- The OECD work is dominated more by reaction than creation. The reaction is born out of the actions of economic agents[54] and their tax practices.
- Material issues have been growing throughout the years, making almost all of the tax arena a subject of international tax law. Indeed, double taxation is no

53. *See infra* 1.2.10.
54. Economic agents as corporations, wealthy individuals, some States unilaterally and other international organizations. LuxLeaks and Panama Papers presented relevant inputs from Civil Society, specifically, the international consortium of journalists.

longer the main concern, with there being many other more relevant pressures such as double non-taxation, aggressive tax planning, digital economy taxation, and hybrid-mismatching.

- Procedural subjects have also expanded. From a simple indication to use mutual agreement procedure, they evolved into tax arbitration and a more complex network to provide assistance in the collection. Additionally, a change occurs from exchange of information by demand toward automatic exchange of information.
- From simple soft law instruments, the OECD has been building a strong set-up of standardization on main international taxation topics—transfer pricing, exchange of information, and other ways of improving tax cooperation (e.g., tax transparency and tax administration competencies).
- Even with the BEPS project, the *prisoner's dilemma* is always part of the international tax regime organization, its design, implementation, and application. It is revealed on the *fast-forward* and *pause* stages within the international community when core transformations occur. It is exposed by FATCA, a unilateral instrument that amplifies U.S. tax sovereignty[55] while increasing obligations and limitations on other States, economic agents, and individuals. It is also visible in the fact that the United States is not a current signatory of MLI. And it is shown in the lack of consensus on digital taxation, the transformation of source rules, and subsequent delimitation of tax powers.
- Questions arise during the COVID-19 era and the State's financial and territorial efforts. In order to contain the pandemic, public spending is at high pressure. It may have a bearing on how the OECD is going to be able to ensure the multilateralization of international tax law and how new pressures will push forward the modification of the international tax law agenda.[56]

This micro-identification helps clarify that multilateralism born out of the BEPS project is still in its infancy. Moreover, too many interrogations surround it, questioning the possibility of it being clearly considered as a powerful tool that, from now on, would be the optimal and practical choice to provide international tax law standards. After looking at the *supra* macro-overview of the international tax law regime throughout the years, having in mind the core moments and instruments and its underlying dilemma, it stands out the intrinsic bilateral approach on building hard law instruments and how complex the revolution of multilateralism use is. What is desired is that multilateralism stops *sometimes* being an option—an exception—but rather the new normal way to design and implement international tax law standards. This would mean, according to ARAÚJO, that tax exceptionalism would become a creature of the past.[57]

55. Using Allison Christians' expression. Allison Christians, *Putting the Reign Back in Sovereign*. 40 Pepperdine Law Review 5 (2013), p. 1397.
56. *Infra* 3.5.
57. Hélio Eduardo de Paiva Araújo, *Multilateralism Versus Exceptionalism in International Tax: Would the Multilateral Instrument Be a Reconciliation?*. 7 *Revista Direito Tributário Internacional Atual* 182, 203 (2020).

Overall, how many years did the OECD take to determine the automatic exchange of information as the preferable choice? How many years did the OECD take to include arbitration in the model convention? How many years and which countries complied immediately with those changes? If a description of international tax law development may be considered as appropriate, it is the one that outlines the international tax regime as a reality made of evolutions and not revolutions—until now.

1.2.9 *Ninth Assumption: Cooperation Is Not the Same as Harmonization or Uniformization*

Even if international tax standards exist, as well as a complex and multi-linked network of tax agreements, one cannot characterize the contemporary international tax regime as one of tax harmonization or tax uniformization. So far, the international tax regime is one where cooperation leads to tax coordination only.

Tax sovereignty still means having specific tax rules and the ability to create them at will. Tax sovereignty also still means different tax rules worldwide, which means no uniformization.

Indeed, with some types of international tax standards (such as transfer pricing and exchange of information) one may question if tax harmonization exists due to the implementation and application of OECD standards across many jurisdictions. However, the concept of tax harmonization does not appear to be compatible with its creation by an international organization such as the OECD, which has no power to establish the set rules and, if not integrated within a State's tax law, to enforce it.[58] This is the main reason why no international tax harmonization exists. The only account for tax harmonization worldwide is the regional tax harmonization within the EU.[59]

Therefore, the existence of international tax coordination is merely observed through tax cooperation, even if coordination is made via a MLI and not a bilateral one. It also means that unless States bond themselves through an international tax authority with effective powers, no international tax harmonization is possible.

It is relevant to consider that the type of instrument used to accomplish the international tax negotiation and to spread international tax standards has not had, as per the current international tax regime, an impact on the relationship model between tax jurisdictions. If tax uniformity was desired, eliminating the differences between the tax rules worldwide would require a legitimate and democratic international authority capable of leading the process of design, interpretation, application, control, and dispute resolution. None of that exists, even if multilateralism is the option. Additionally, if international tax harmonization would be the option, the abovementioned

58. Differently, defending that most rules comprising international taxation are very close to being de facto harmonized, Yariv Bauner, *An International Tax Regime in Crystallization*. 56 Tax Law Review 259, 328 (2003).
59. Exploring the costs on unilateral tax measures, bilateral treaties and multilateral tax agreements toward protecting the Welfare State, Tsilly Dagan, *The Costs of International Tax Cooperation*. University of Michigan, John M. Olin Center for Law & Economics, Research Paper No. 02-07. https://papers.ssrn.com/sol3/papers.cfm?abstract_id=315373 (last visited April 30, 2021).

international tax authority would also be needed to enforce the harmonized options, should these not be voluntarily integrated and applied by States.[60,61]

Consequently, for now, multilateralism is a way of achieving extended international tax coordination, allowing for an easier and efficient means to improve international tax standards through the already existing bilateral tax treaties and their rules—nothing more.

1.2.10 Tenth Assumption: Procedural Multilateralism Is Not Substantial Multilateralism

Multilateralism is a necessary instrument within an international tax regime.[62] As Thomas Nagel wrote, "traditional model of international organizations based on treaties between sovereign States has been transcended."[63] From a limited bilateral scope, multilateralism becomes a stronger instrument toward better global tax justice. It is part of core procedures, fostering tax cooperation, while also contributing to an enhanced and more legitimate tax coordination. However, multilateralism is not a single layer concept, which suggests that it cannot always support both those targets.

Multilateralism has two distinct approaches: formal multilateralism and substantial multilateralism,[64] which demand different kinds of components and create different types of regimes.

Formal multilateralism stands for procedural action. It is a sequence of arrangements oriented toward achieving consensus. It is not about the content of the tax rules that are to be integrated within tax agreements. Rather, formal multilateralism is aimed at procedures, techniques, practices, and methods. As Garcia Antón explains, it is a *club diplomacy*.[65]

In contrast, substantial multilateralism is based on substance. It is grounded on material decisions born out of a democratic decision-making process while creating, interpreting, and applying international tax standards. It implies worldwide participation at all moments—design, interpretation, application, and control. It is based on inter-nation equity and, therefore, "one that unmistakably requires a greater cession of

60. Pushing for further development on existing institutions or new ones established, Wolfgang Obenland, *Options for Strengthening Global Tax Governance*, Freidrich Ebert Stiftung, November 2016. http://library.fes.de/pdf-files/iez/12958.pdf (last visited April 30, 2021).
61. Denying value of harmonization in international tax law, defending tax deharmonization, Seteven A. Dean, *More Cooperation, Less Uniformity: Tax Deharmonization and the Future of the International Tax Regime*. 84 Tulane Law Review 125, 164 (2009).
62. With same opinion, e.g., Allison Christians, *BEPS and the Power to Tax*, 3-27 in Sergio André Rocha & Allison Christians (eds), *Tax Sovereignty in BEPS Era* (Kluwer Law International 2017), specifically p. 3.
63. Thomas Nagel, *The Problem of Global Justice*. 33 Philosophy & Public Affairs 113, 147 n. 2 (2005), quote from p. 139.
64. Also assuming the distinction, Natalia Quiñones, *The Birth of a New International Tax Framework*, 165-177 in Sergio André Rocha & Allison Christians (eds), *Tax Sovereignty in BEPS Era* (Kluwer Law international 2017), specifically pp. 170-172.
65. Gárcia Anton. *The 21st Century Multilateralism in International Taxation: The Emperor's New Clothes?*. 8 World Tax Journal 147, 192 n. 2 (2016).

sovereignty by all nations, in favor of peer-review bodies and, hopefully, an international dispute resolution body."[66]

Substantial multilateralism should be considered to achieve global tax justice. This model can integrate as many tax jurisdictions as possible throughout the design, interpretation, application, *and* control of international tax standards. Only through substantial multilateralism can an effective equilibrium between all tax interests be accomplished, allowing the implementation of global tax justice and not just regional or local tax justice.[67]

Bearing in mind these 10 assumptions, the following section will address MLI as it currently exists as of April 2021 and analyzes how it relates to tax sovereignty and how it also reflects modifications within the international tax regime.

2 THE MIRROR GIVEN ANSWER: FROM FAIRYTALE TO REALITY, SAGA OF A *SOFT EVOLUTION*

2.1 Tax Sovereignty Now

2.1.1 How the BEPS MLI Changes the International Tax Regime

The international discussion of how the international tax regime is created, developed, and applied did not start with the BEPS project. Considerations regarding how the international tax regime was developed have already been shared.[68] Moreover, the debate regarding bilateral versus multilateral tax agreements is extensive.[69] It is not the aim of this chapter to analyze the arguments on both sides. Notwithstanding, it is acknowledged that before the BEPS project, only rare, regional, and simplified cases of tax multilateralism existed.

Until now and worldwide, bilateral tax agreements were always the preferred hard law instrument. To provide an effective network capable of addressing global mobility—and therefore multilocation—this choice demanded multiple bilateral negotiations that translated into multiple bilateral agreements. This was how double taxation was supposed to be eliminated and, progressively, how specific anti-abuse clauses would be added to those agreements to raise obstacles to tax avoidance, while also providing better ways to improve tax coordination.

66. Natalia Quiñones, *The Birth of a New International Tax Framework*, 165-177 in Sergio André Rocha & Allison Christians (eds), *Tax Sovereignty in BEPS Era* (Kluwer Law International 2017), specifically pp. 170-172.
67. Presenting the necessarily multilevel justice on multilateralism cooperation, Tsilly Dagan, *International Tax Justice*. 18 Theoretical Inquiries in Law 32, 34 n. 1 (2017), specifically, pp. 32-34.
68. *Supra* 1.2. 8. Additionally, for a relatively recent sum up, e.g., Ruth Manson, *The Transformation of International Tax*. 114 The American Journal of International Law 353, 402 n. 3 (2020).
69. About it, e.g., Nathalie Bravo, *A Multilateral Instrument for Updating the Tax Treaty Network* (IBFD 2020), specifically, pp. 36-54; Kimberley Brooks, *The Potential of Multilateral Tax Treaties*, 211-236 in Michael Lang et. al., (eds), *Tax Treaties: Building Bridges Between Law and Economics* (IBFD 2010).

Nowadays, bilateral tax agreements are seen as relevant mechanisms that are consistent with tax sovereignty. They are common and believed to include a process whereby States, by choice and within a balanced negotiation, create limitations to sovereignty on a voluntary basis.

Apart from the bilateral agreements, the OECD and the UN have provided answers to a balance within various States interests by creating soft law instruments, based on guidelines, recommendations, and similar instruments, that may be integrated by OECD Member States at a national level, while also aiming to be recognized by the third Member States.

When the BEPS project presented its Action 15, it demonstrated that to produce substantive outcomes, an MLI would be an effective and innovative tool, in comparison to depending on thousands of bilateral tax treaties renegotiations.[70]

Based on these points, MLI is seen as a procedural approach to implement the BEPS project. Considering the categories presented in section 1.2.10, MLI is Formal Multilateralism. This means that it is not, by itself, a way of reformulating the design, interpretation, application, *and* control of the international tax regime. Rather, it is an innovative way—following the wording of the OECD—of facilitating a speedy action. Additionally, it is an instrument to guarantee a coordinated and synchronized modification of tax rules contained in bilateral tax agreements, thereby aiming for a coordinated application of previously designed tax rules. Because it is not a complete approach, the MLI is only procedural multilateralism and not substantial multilateralism.

Considering a *legislative* process, which mirrors the way the OECD deals internally with the discussion and creation of international tax standards, four successive stages exist.

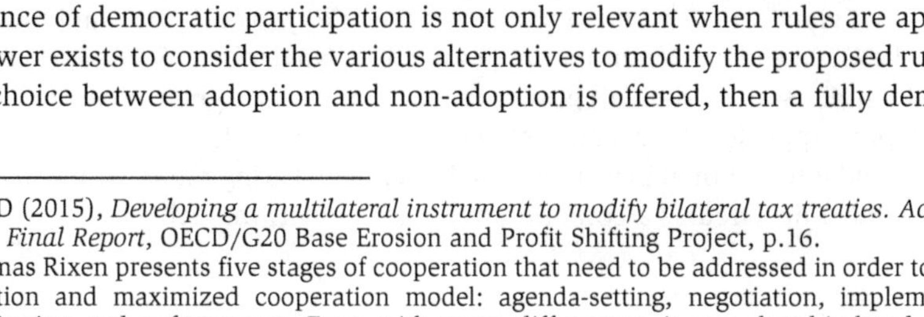

A truly democratic process demands full participation during all the phases.[71] The importance of democratic participation is not only relevant when rules are approved. If no power exists to consider the various alternatives to modify the proposed rules, and only a choice between adoption and non-adoption is offered, then a fully democratic

70. OECD (2015), *Developing a multilateral instrument to modify bilateral tax treaties. Action 15 – 2015 Final Report*, OECD/G20 Base Erosion and Profit Shifting Project, p.16.
71. Thomas Rixen presents five stages of cooperation that need to be addressed in order to create a function and maximized cooperation model: agenda-setting, negotiation, implementation, monitoring and enforcement. Even with some differences, it goes hand-in-hand with the proposed stages and the necessity to guarantee participation in all of those stages, as a necessity if full legitimacy, acceptance and efficacy is the objective. Thomas Rixen, *Institutional Reform of a Global Tax Governance: A Proposal*, 325-349 in Peter Dietsch and Thomas Rixen (eds), *Global Tax Governance. What Is Wrong With it and How to Fix It* (ECPR Press 2016), specifically p. 333.

process is nonexistent. A fully democratic process also implies full participation during the discussion and decision making of the specific substantive tax rules. The first stage of this process represents the core where democracy is fully bloomed. From an international perspective, it is also the stage where inter-nation equity can be accessible and actively recognized. It is also essential for the process to include the moment where control over the adequate application is made. Legitimate accountability is indispensable to achieve global tax inclusivity.

From a careful analysis of MLI, it is not possible to affirm that it represents the above-described approach. As Irma Mosquera Valderrama concluded, either from an input and output, legitimacy requirements are not met.[72] *MLI continues a mere diplomatic path, being a formal/procedural multilateralism instrument, rather than a substantial/material multilateralism tool.* Indeed, the MLI text contains international tax standards. However, these standards were previously designed to be contained within MLI, not as part of the design of the MLI itself. Moreover, these standards were designed by the OECD for the G20, who subsequently endorsed those options.

The call to the G20 for the launch of the BEPS project was a democratic enlargement tactic to attract BRICS and their leading economies into the process and, with that, to promote the appeal of the *Inclusive Framework*, constituted by so many States that are not part of the G20 or the OECD. Indeed, the BEPS Project represents an enlargement of the number of States and their interests that are present *in the application* of the renewed international tax regime. Although the type of substantial solutions provided was previously dominated by OECD members within their technical choices, those members participated in the discussions and designed the action plan in 2013. Even if non-OECD G20 members may have been present in the designation of the project— OECD/G20 BEPS—one can question their proactiveness within the working groups and the technical design of the solutions. What is safe to say is that the G20 approved the plan and supported the outcomes. Additionally, the *Inclusive Framework* (the platform that makes MLI an active instrument) was only created in 2016, after the 2015 BEPS outputs were presented.[73] Moreover, not all of the OECD members have accepted the MLI and integrated it into their legal jurisdiction (e.g., the United States), which demonstrates that consensus is not naturally incorporated in the outcomes.

To fully understand the characterization of MLI, it is also necessary to objectively *compare BEPS and MLI rhetoric with BEPS and MLI contents and practice.*

At first glance, the *wording used within the BEPS project* is very ambitious. It was said by the G20 Leaders Communiqué (adopted on November 16, 2014) that the BEPS Action Plan aims at modernizing international tax rules. When presented, the 2013 BEPS Report appealed to a comprehensive action plan, providing countries with domestic and international instruments to better align taxing rights with real economic activity. OECD declared as a commitment, in particular, the delivery of:

72. Irma Johana Mosquera Valderrama, *Legitimacy and the Making of International Tax Law: The Challenges of Multilateralism*. 37 World Tax Journal 343, 382 n. 3 (2015). Even if published in 2015, and even if *Inclusive Framework* was afterward created, the conclusions still are maintained, for MLI scope is at application of standards, having no impact on prior stages.

73. *Supra* 1.2.6.

"a global and comprehensive action plan based on in-depth analysis of the identified pressure areas with view to provide concrete solutions to realign international standards with the current global business environment. This will require some "out of the box" thinking as well as ambition and pragmatism to overcome implementation difficulties, such as the existence of current tax treaties."[74] It expressly stated that *"indeed, incremental approaches may help curb the current trends but will not respond to several of the challenges governments face.*[75,76]

The BEPS Action Plan also continues with the same wording, highlighting that "new international standards must be designed to ensure the coherence of corporate income taxation at the international level."[77]

However, when a more committed analysis of the chosen wording is made, to understand what type of action it supports, one finds words that merely encapsulate amendments rather than a comprehensive change.

Considering the BEPS project main pressure areas, the wording comprehends:[78]

- *improvements*;
- *clarification*;
- *broader*;
- *updated*;
- *revision as a complement to previous*;
- *realignment*;
- *restor*ation.

Thus, when substantive analysis is made about options, regimes, and procedures, even though the abstract BEPS rhetoric is ambitious, BEPS practice forces an adjustment of the mindset. What was born from BEPS was not a revolution; rather, every single international tax principle and standard was maintained. The international tax standards were modified to broaden and densify the impact of anti-abuse and artificiality. They were not recreated nor revolutionized.[79,80]

This chapter does not seek to undermine the indisputable value of the BEPS project or denounce an attempt to improve the function of an international tax regime.

74. OECD (2013), *Addressing Base Erosion and Profit Shifting*, p. 10.
75. OECD (2013), *Addressing Base Erosion and Profit Shifting*, pp. 8 and 51.
76. About incremental and radical changes within international tax regime, Tim Buttner & Matthias Thiemann, *Breaking Regime Stability? The Politicization of Expertise in the OECD/G20 Process on BEPS and the Potential Transformation of International Taxation*. 7 Accounting, Economics, and Law: A Convivium 1, 16 n. 1 (2017).
77. OECD (2013), *Action Plan on Base Erosion and Profit Shifting*, p. 13.
78. OECD (2013), *Addressing Base Erosion and Profit Shifting*, p. 10 and OECD (2013), *Action Plan on Base Erosion and Profit Shifting*, pp. 14, 18, 19, 22.
79. Taking as an example Action 7—Prevent the artificial avoidance of PE status, the Action Plan revealed that due to the difficulty of achieving consensus and practical difficulties, no new model or system should be created, rather a mere correction of flaws was to be the option. "Alternative income allocation systems, including formula-based systems, are sometimes suggested. However, the importance of concerted action and the practical difficulties associated with agreeing to and implementing the details of a new system consistently across all countries mean that, rather than seeking to replace the current transfer pricing system, the best course is to directly address the flaws in the current system, in particular with respect to returns related to intangible assets, risk and over-capitalisation. Nevertheless, special measures, either within

Indeed, the BEPS project is of paramount relevance to tackle aggressive tax planning by building stronger cooperation between tax authorities and deepening the coordination of tax systems. However, until now, it is not revolutionary as far as the modifications provided are concerned, nor does it fully accomplish global tax justice principles.[81] If Action 1 was effectively concretized, following the value chain creation criteria and its impact on the territoriality principle, then the BEPS project would have been much closer to groundbreaking. But it is well known that an abandonment of the Permanent Establishment (PE) rule for digital taxation is contested precisely because it is revolutionary and not a mere enhancement.

This conforms with the *wording used specifically for the MLI.* At first glance, it was said that "interested Parties will develop a MLI designed to provide an innovative approach to international tax matters, reflecting the rapidly evolving nature of the global economy and the need to adapt quickly to this evolution."[82] Even currently, the OECD website dedicated to the MLI points that:

> the Multilateral Instrument offers concrete solutions for governments to close loopholes in international tax treaties by transposing results from the BEPS Project into bilateral tax treaties worldwide. The MLI allows governments to implement agreed minimum standards to counter treaty abuse and to improve dispute resolution mechanisms while providing flexibility to accommodate specific tax treaty policies.[83]

But when a more careful analysis of the chosen wording is conducted, the 2013 Action Plan presents the MLI as an instrument committed to a swift implementation of BEPS measures and outputs.[84] Even when characterizing MLI as innovative—as it is—it is merely procedural. The outputs were designed and decided on another platform, while some are not even part of MLI content. Since the beginning of the process, BEPS outputs were thought of as following various procedures to be incorporated as international standards. Some would be recommendations regarding domestic law provisions. Some would be changes to the Commentary of the Model Tax Convention and to the Transfer Pricing Guidelines.[85] Some would be encapsulated into a MLI. MLI was thought to be one of the instruments, one dedicated to guaranteeing a way to rapidly and smoothly address the need to change many bilateral agreements. Not

or beyond the arm's length principle, may be required with respect to intangible assets, risk and over-capitalisation to address these flaws." OECD (2013), *Action Plan on Base Erosion and Profit Shifting*, p. 20.

80. Also defending this approach, Yariv Brauner, *An Essay on BEPS, Sovereignty, and Taxation*, 73-93 in Sergio André Rocha & Allison Christians (eds), *Tax Sovereignty in BEPS Era* (Kluwer Law International 2017), p. 84.
81. Considering the same output, Laurens van Apeldoorn, *BEPS, Tax Sovereignty and Global Justice*. 21 Critical Review of International Social and Political Philosophy 478, 499 n. 4 (2018).
82. OECD (2013), *Action Plan on Base Erosion and Profit Shifting*, p. 24.
83. https://www.oecd.org/tax/treaties/multilateral-convention-to-implement-tax-treaty-related-measures-to-prevent-beps.htm (last visited April 30, 2021).
84. OECD (2013), *Action Plan on Base Erosion and Profit Shifting*, p. 23.
85. *Ibid.*

more.[86] consequently, *MLI may only represent the tool through which the BEPS project provides modernization of international tax negotiation procedures.*

It is valuable to consider that the 2015 *Action 15—Final Report* concentrated its analysis on the desirability and feasibility of the MLI as a procedure to encapsulate BEPS outputs and effectively address the necessary change of bilateral tax agreements.[87] Another pertinent feature is the MLI *opt-out clause* and the multiple reservations available. Providing the possibility to adopt or *opt-out* of relevant transformations is a weakness of the aimed transformations. While it may be considered flexibility, given the number of possible reservations in Article 28, one may ask what stays after all reservations have been considered. The need to gather consensus brought flexibility to the MLI, but this came with a price: the weakening of the substantial upgrade, which demonstrates that the modification provided by MLI is not as effective as it was presented by the BEPS *want-to-be rhetoric.*

Nevertheless, it is also necessary to highlight the topic of legitimacy. As previously presented, the *Inclusive Framework* was created only in 2016, after the working groups delivered 15 reports, including one about the MLI (2014/2015). Both content and procedures of the MLI were already designed. Thus, even if OECD rhetoric presented that the *Inclusive Framework* "was established to ensure interested countries and jurisdictions, including developing economies, can participate on an equal footing in the development of standards on BEPS related issues, while reviewing and monitoring the implementation of the OECD/G20 BEPS Project,"[88,89] the equality of developing countries is not fully established. As Irma Mosquera defended:

> "the so-called equal footing for developing countries is not a reality, once they are latecomers in the discussion, and, as a consequence, they have little capacity and probably less knowledge on the topic than developed countries ... Moreover, the participation in discussion of the multilateral instrument and in the inclusive framework will not solve the problem of the lack of participation of developing countries in the setting of the agenda and the content of the BEPS Actions."[90]

The discussion above comprises of two main ideas:

- Idea 1: MLI can only be characterized as an upgrade to the international tax regime techniques. It does not provide substantial transformations to the

86. "Changes to the OECD Model Tax Convention are not directly effective without amendments to bilateral tax treaties. If undertaken on a purely treaty-by-treaty basis, the sheer number of treaties in effect may make such a process very lengthy, the more so where countries embark on comprehensive renegotiations of their bilateral tax treaties. A multilateral instrument to amend bilateral treaties is a promising way forward in this respect." OECD (2013), *Action Plan on Base Erosion and Profit Shifting*, p. 24.
87. OECD (2015), *Developing a multilateral instrument to modify bilateral tax treaties*, pp. 18-23.
88. https://www.oecd.org/tax/beps/flyer-inclusive-framework-on-beps.pdf (last visited April 30, 2021).
89. About the necessity to overcome a global tax governance monopoly held by small number of rich countries, pushing into a meaningful participation by countries that have been excluded, Allison Christians, *BEPS and the New International Tax Order*. 2016 Brigham Young University Law Review 1063 (2017).
90. Irene Burgers & Irma Mosquera, *Corporate Taxation and BEPS: A Fair Slice for Developing Countries?*. 29 Erasmus Law Review 29, 47 n. 1 (2017), specifically p. 38.

international tax regime. *Undeniably, the BEPS project generated modernization in some previous international tax rules, leading to a substance upgrade. However, this did not occur within an MLI creation procedure.*
- Idea 2: The *BEPS project chronology and MLI procedure reveal that the schizophrenic paradigm of tax competition and tax coordination still exists* within the international tax regime and continues to be a core pattern.

Overall, a *true revolution within the international tax regime, led by a MIL, would imply a fully democratic process*, managed by an international organization or platform closer to the scope of the UN rather than that of the OECD.[91] A full democratic process demands that all States are active participants in the various sequential stages of creation, modification, and control of the international tax regime, rather than only one or some of those stages.

2.1.2 What Is Still Missing? Justification for a Soft Evolution Characterization and Not a Revolution

Considering the discussion above, the MLI does not revolutionize the international tax regime. Rather, the MLI represents a different and more effective way of changing the negotiating process, integrating adjustments on the various bilateral agreements of the Member States of the MLI. This means that the *MLI provides a Soft Evolution and not a Revolution.*[92]

Multilateralism is not capable of transforming the DNA of international tax regime on its own, even if it is an innovative procedure in OECD. For a true revolution to take place, multilateralism is needed, but it would have to be part of a wider process. As such, multilateralism cannot be a buzzword used indistinctly and without considering, as Tsilly Dagan does, that if established as a rule and not as an exception, multilateralism must contribute to global tax justice, for "a multilateral regime established through cooperation is justified in promoting justice if and only it improves (or at least does not worsen) the welfare of the least well-off in all cooperating States. Consequently, a multilateral agreement that pursues harmonization will only be valid if it ensures domestic justice in all States involved."[93] This finality of multilateralism, being part of its essence, would lead the way to another indisputable transformation.

The international tax regime revolution would imply a change of the international tax paradigm: from one based on the *prisoner's dilemma* to one that fully accomplishes cooperation as the founding element leading the way the international

91. Defending a predominant role for UN, *ibid.*, p. 39.
92. Also, in this direction, Rifat Azam, *Ruling the World: Generating International Tax Norms in the Era of Globalization and BEPS*. L Suffolk University Law Review 517, 586 n. 4 (2017); Dirk M. Broekhuijsen, *A Multilateral Tax Treaty: Designing An Instrument to Modernize International Tax Law*. 2017, Leiden University Repository, https://scholarlypublications.universiteitleiden.nl/handle/1887/57407 (last visited April 30, 2021).
93. Tsilly Dagan, *International Tax and Global Justice*. 18 Theoretical Inquiries in Law 1, 35 n. 1 (2017), p. 34.

tax regime would be designed, interpreted, applied, and controlled. As stated by Calderon Gomez:

> *"reformers are vastly underestimating the breadth and depth of the necessary concessions of sovereignty needed for effective and realistic tax standardization."* With this in mind, tax competition needs to be reconsidered and, as the above-mentioned author defends, *"instead of seeking shallow cooperation through standardization (i.e., setting arbitrary limits on which kinds of competition are to be forbidden and which are encouraged), we should perhaps strive for real cooperation in comprehensive tax structures through which the harm of tax competition is comprehensively addressed."*[94]

However, the tax competition paradigm is strong and permanently evolving and adapting. Some authors[95] affirm that nowadays we are already faced with a third type of tax competition, one that is oriented toward defining the distributive rules which will create higher tax revenues. This almost indicates a hopeless scenario in terms of the abolishment of the prisoner's dilemma. Although in order to guarantee the inexistence of unilateral approaches or sustainable harmful tax practices, the tax competition paradigm would need to be blocked. If tax competition is silenced, then this would lead to a complete transfiguration of the contemporary international tax paradigm, which, by itself, would be considered a revolution. From an objective perspective, if such a transformation occurred, it would mean that many international tax standards would be substituted for new ones. Consequently, three immediate transformations would be necessary: first, an effective increase of participants throughout the design process of international tax standards, second, the incorporation of value creation into rules about international tax competencies and third, following Andrew Baker and Richard Murphy,[96] defending the case for an international moral harm convention.

Considering the first topic—increasing the amount of participants throughout the design process of international tax standards—this would mean not only assuming multilateralism as a procedure but also as a substantive canon, one capable of equilibrating the interests of various States and the need to build a consensus around fair share on the taxing rights and worldwide distribution of tax revenues. This would also mean creating a path toward effective global tax legitimacy and inter-nation equity to ensure global tax justice. In this scenario, the OECD would have to be transformed in a way to incorporate other tax jurisdictions. Otherwise, the UN could start leading global tax matters. As a third option, a new Global Tax Organization would need to be created.[97] Overall, the design of international tax standards—i.e. choice of elements,

94. Luis Calderon Gomez, *Transcending* "Tax" *Sovereignty and Tax Standardization: Three Questions*. 45 The Yale Journal of International Law 191, 226 n. 1 (2020), quotations from p. 224 and p. 226.
95. Hugh Ault, *Tax Competition and Tax Cooperation: A Survey and Reassessment*, 1-14 in Jérôme Monsenego & Jan Bjuvberg (eds), *International Taxation in a Changing Landscape: Liber Amicorum in Honor of Bertil Wiman* (Kluwer Law International 2019); Ruth Manson, *The Transformation of International Tax*. 114 The American Journal of International Law 353, 402 n. 3 (2020).
96. Andrew Baker & Richard Murphy, *The Political Economy of "Tax Spillover:" A New Multilateral Framework*. 10 Global Policy 178, 192 n. 2 (2019).
97. About this possibility, *supra* n. 8.

criterion, and substantial rules—would have to be based on full global participation. As such, the current MLI would have to be transformed to reflect those deep changes.

Considering the second topic—incorporating value creation into rules about international tax competencies—it would mean accepting the establishment of alternative rules for those factual situations where traditional ones are unfit. The place where the value is created would no longer be rhetoric and abstract suggestion; rather, it would effectively be a tangible economic criterion included in tax agreements and national tax rules. Addressing the insufficiency of the PE rule as well as the unity principle would be considered without political barriers. It would maybe even mean going further than coordination, adopting an international tax harmonization fast track. This would be the way to dissolve the significant differences between tax jurisdiction regimes and effectively stop international tax competition as a meaningful element in the mindset of international tax relationships.

Considering the third topic, the idea is to create pressure against tax competition, using the transparency principle and a specific instrument to demonstrate the existence of tax spillover and create visible international accountability. As proposed by Andrew Baker and Andrew Murphy, it is necessary to review self-assessments of tax spillover, which are much more prone to manipulation and *tax-image-washing*. Therefore, a neutral multilateral agency using a common assessment framework could generate unbiased data to allow for multilateral surveillance or peer review. It would use the so-called shaming process and unfavorable comparisons with peers to create the basis for symbolic judgments.[98]

These three transformations would revolutionize the international tax regime and represent a completely different approach toward international taxation. These transformations would not be a mere adaptation, update, or improvement, as the MLI encapsulates. As such, they would not be an evolution, but rather provide a revolution that makes a path to an international tax system possible.[99]

In comparison with the approaches above, the MLI does not entail enough elements that are capable of representing a true revolution. Even if material changes exist and the MLI embodies a new way for the OECD to incorporate modifications into tax agreements, all the updates reveal continuity. The coordination path remains. No harmonization or uniformization effectively happens. The unity principle is still the rule. No active plural sources of income can exist. An arm's-length principle endures. No common consolidated taxation is promoted. In many cases, form maintains prevalence over substance. No value chain creation was effectively amended, even if it still is a possibility provided by action 1 on digital taxation. And if continuity is the characteristic, no revolution may effectively take place.

Naturally, evolution may occur with the BEPS project and standards, particularly within MLI. But the type of transformation is not sufficiently groundbreaking to be characterized as a revolution. As stated, what exists cannot be categorized as a revolution; rather, it is a soft evolution. The same type of soft governance persists. Even

98. Following wording and thought of Andrew Baker & Richard Murphy, *The Political Economy of "Tax Spillover:" A New Multilateral Framework*. 10 Global Policy 178, 192 n. 2 (2019).
99. *Supra* 1.2.1. for the elements of an international tax system.

if through MLI and *Inclusive Framework* there seems to be an improvement on global tax justice, progress is still inadequate. To emphasize, MLI is procedural/formal multilateralism. Within MLI, global participation is requested on the application, effectively not on the creation. And this ultimate aspect makes all the difference.

Considering this, *no overwhelming transformation takes place for tax sovereignty*. Material adjustments and acceptance of a specific new procedure for modifying the bilateral tax agreements network occur, but not so intense as to revolutionize national taxation options. Indeed, creating an MLI that is a substitute for bilateral tax negotiations is remarkably different from previous international tax procedures. It is widening the scope of participants by accommodating more States (i.e. not just OECD members) and providing for a wider network with less time-consuming negotiations. It elevates the levels of democratic legitimacy but nevertheless does not transform the current principles and rules of international standards creation. As it is, no transformation has occurred in the *design* of the international tax regime. As no paradigm revolution has occurred, States still use tax unilaterally as an effective powerful tool to act on and depend upon.

2.2 Tax Sovereignty Tomorrow

Even if no international tax revolution was produced by MLI, the soft evolution may indicate future transformations. Not all revolutions are born out of only one moment. Many are the result of several soft attempts.

Following that thought, a future analysis may be useful. After all, the MLI modified the status quo. Can one interpret this as a signal of future transformation for the international tax regime?

For the short and medium term, if MLI acceptance continues to increase, multilateralism becomes a successful international standard. This may also signify an open door toward a more democratic and participatory international tax regime. Adopting multilateralism as a stable and expected international standard procedure may make the choice of substantial multilateralism a reality. This would mean that global tax justice would become part of the international tax agenda and the enhancement of the legitimacy procedures would encompass the organization of the international tax regime. Moreover, tax sovereignty would be transformed reveal itself as responsibility.

Within this context, it is necessary to acknowledge the pressure that can be applied by civil society. At first glance, as Allison Christians remarks, "the Inclusive Framework might facilitate the participation of stakeholders beyond member country government representatives and private sector tax professionals, namely the nongovernmental sector."[100] But a wider perspective could be valuable. For instance, by examining the 2014 LuxLeaks, the 2016 Panama Papers, and the 2017 Paradise Papers scandals, one can acknowledge, as Oei and Ring do, that those "data leaks can be a

100. Allison Christians, *BEPS and the New International Order*. 2016 Brigham Young University Law Review 1603, 1647 (2017), specifically p. 1645.

valuable source of information to governments and can function as a 'free audit' [but also] that leaks can pressure governments, taxpayers, and elites to undertake systematic legal reform."[101] Leak-driven tax law, in a more coordinated way, is still relevant if political will becomes more pressured by civil society, including not only nongovernmental organizations, but also media, consumers, and taxpayers.

If this scenario would manifest, the international tax regime could be enriched, allowing convergence to an international tax system in the long term. This would involve a combination of procedures and substance united with a higher legitimacy achieved through global participation.[102] Maybe a utopia, yet a tax sovereignty dream. The first stage would be joint accomplishment. On the one hand, global tax justice and value creation would become basic principles guiding the design, interpretation, application, and control of the international tax regime. On the other hand, the axe would be laid on the rules of how the global tax revenue pie is shared.[103] Unfortunately, there are not enough elements to admit this as a real possibility.

Indeed, political rhetoric, and specifically BEPS rhetoric, indicates recognition of value creation as an objective. Having both MLI and *Inclusive Framework* represents a significant indication. However, as previously demonstrated, rhetoric is one thing, and tax practice is another.

As a first stage, political will must clearly endorse the new paradigm, which requires a big transformation. It demands a new type of global tax governance, one based on a transformed mindset: from competition to negotiation,[104] while demanding new societal and economical choices. In this scenario, tax would stop being understood and used unilaterally as a political instrument aiming to influence the choices of economic agents. It would imply that tax sovereignty would exclude taxation as a public policy instrument and adopt tax neutrality as the way tax legislators would create tax rules. The abandonment of tax neutrality would only exist if a global option for non-neutrality occurred, either from a coordinated or a harmonized option. In this case, as it happens in some regions where monetary policy is no longer a public policy

101. Oei, Shu-Yi & Ring, Diane M., *Leak-Driven Law*. 65 UCLA Law Review 532, 618 n. 3 (2018).
102. Natalia Quiñones presents a new international tax Framework based on multilateralism as the way to set international tax standards, combined with automatic exchange of information and peer-review system. All these elements would need to lead toward common principles, common standards and common regulatory bodies. The birth of a new international tax framework and the role of developing countries would be secured by a global representativity and a set of bodies able to develop that legitimacy and reproduce it. Natalia Quiñones, *The Birth of a New International Tax Framework*, 165-177 in Sergio André Rocha & Allison Christians (eds), *Tax Sovereignty in BEPS Era* (Kluwer Law International) 2017, from p. 165 onwards.
103. With an opposite position, defending tax policy as an area of domestic decision making, implying the improvement of tax competition, therefore, urging fight-back BEPS project objectives and implications, Jason J. Fichtner & Adam N. Michel, *The OECD's Conquest of the United States: Understanding the Costs and Consequences of the BEPS Project and Tax Harmonization*. (March 17, 2016) MERCATUS RESEARCH, George Manson University, 2016 https://www.mercatus.org/publications/government-spending/oecd's-conquest-united-states-understanding-costs-and-consequences (last visited April 30, 2021).
104. Exploring the undesirable distributional effects of a multilateral agreement, Tsilly Dagan, *The Costs of International Tax Cooperation*. Research Paper No. 02-07, University of Michigan, John M. Olin Center for Law & Economics, pp. 23-25.

to be used unilaterally, tax policy would also be limited in the ways it could be designed and interpreted.

However, no signs of that approach are being detected. Even the EU, a global case study on economic integration still does not have a sufficiently stabilized tax regime, despite having specific infrastructures for compliance and enforcement. Within the EU, harmful tax practices still exist and are maintained. Even if the European Court of Justice (ECJ) tries to create negative harmonization, and even if the European Commission (EC) is attacking tax regimes and tax rulings through State-Aid regulation. Among its 27 members, a collective oriented toward the same type of development and society—the social European model—taxation is still a full-size problem. Considering the number of active States taxing worldwide, the creation of a platform for guaranteeing the active participation of everyone in the design, interpretation, application, and control of tax standards can only be a task of extreme complexity. Considering the only worldwide platform that includes all States, one wonders: is the UN an adequate and effective organization for that purpose? And if not an existing global organization, but a different platform, would it really be sufficient to guarantee compliance with the global fair share?

If consensus would continue to be the rule, the functioning of that platform—whichever format it would have and apart from its intrinsic complexities—would also be subject to blockage, either by minorities or by the most powerful States. But if not consensus, how would global acceptance be built within the international tax regime? The EU is an example of how tax unanimity as a rule blocks the possibility of building a tax regime for direct taxation. Within the EU Member States, no significant transformations have occurred and a majority rule is unwanted.[105,106]

The lack of technical knowledge by some under-developed and developing countries is also a problem that challenges the dynamic participation of all tax jurisdictions in the design of the international tax regime. Even considering the OECD and UN specific programs to empower Tax Administrations—e.g. OECD Forum on Tax Administration, OECD Joint International Taskforce on Shared Intelligence and Collaboration, or UN Inter-Agency Task Force on Financing for Development—those results still aren't ideal. Both organizations keep deepening the task forces' work, responsibilities, and outcomes, aiming at better results.[107] This enables creating true

105. In 2019, EC tried to change the unanimity rule, COM (2019) 8 final, January 15, 2019, Communication from the Commission to the European Parliament, the European Council and the Council. *Towards a more efficient and democratic decision making in EU tax policy*.
106. Take as an example the EC proposal on corporate income taxation. Since 2001 it is being discussed and present as a relevant necessity and adequate regime, and still in 2021 no revolution was agreed. Even if a denser approach was present in 2011 and was modified and completed in 2016. *See supra* n. 5.
107. For example UN Inter-Agency Task Force on Financing for Development is developing the use of TADAT—Tax Administration Diagnostic Assessment Tool—in order to guide high-level decisions on tax administration reform efforts (United Nations, Inter-agency Task Force on Financing for Development, *Financing for Sustainable Development Report 2020* (New York: United Nations, 2020), available from: https://developmentfinance.un.org/fsdr2020). OECD Forum on Tax Administration produced a statement "Multilateral strategic plan on mutual

legitimacy in the process, as it raises obstacles to the technical discussion. Because the idea is not only to ensure that all tax jurisdictions have a seat at the design stage. The adequate procedure is to allow every tax jurisdiction to be one tax jurisdiction among equals, which unfortunately still seems very far away.

Besides all the challenges included in creating a functioning legitimate process for the design and interpretation of the international tax standards, as written above, the axe would also need to be laid on the rules of how the global tax revenue pie is shared. This means being open to question the contemporary dominance of residence taxation and fully incorporate value creation as a solid criterion for distributing tax powers worldwide and allocating tax revenues after collection. BEPS Action 1 results are still not impressive, for no practical agreement exists, only tendencies and attempts.

Even if value creation is taken as the path that must exist for taxing the digital economy, BEPS Action 1 still has not obtained a viable and consensual solution that could be an international tax standard. Even if the *Inclusive Framework* was brought as a reliable platform to achieve consensus, Action 1 is still all about rhetoric and no material decision. This is precisely because it implies the abandonment of an old international tax standard while accepting a new and very different one.

Indeed, Action 1, 2018-2020 activity, is a good example of the enlargement of the OECD working groups to include other States: those who are members of the *Inclusive Framework*. It tends to create a more legitimate process, even with the difficult challenges referred to above. However, the present work is attempting to achieve a result that wasn't obtained in OECD tax jurisdictions over the years.[108] A consensus had still not been achieved in prior Action 1 reports, including G20 members. The division between Pillar 1 and Pillar 2 seems to emphasize the deadlock.[109] Guiding taxing rights by the value creation factor is agreed, but no agreement is achieved when a specific tax rule is to be designed, precisely because it implies an overriding of the classical standard and the creation of a new one that unbalances the opportunity/choice to tax and not tax big tech corporations that are incorporated in countries that export those technologies and business models through digital platforms. That serves as a marketplace. The same countries create most of the obstacles to consensus. It is mainly all about tax powers, tax collection, and consequently, about not losing the already characterized *Westphalian* tax sovereignty.

---

agreement procedures: a vision for continuous map improvement" where it is recognized the need to "collectively improve in order to meet the needs of both governments and taxpayers and so assure the critical role of those procedures in the global tax environment, and that this can best be accomplished through the collaborative work of the MAP Forum in accordance with this Multilateral Strategic Plan" (https://www.oecd.org/tax/forum-on-tax-administration/publications-and-products/map-strategic-plan.pdf last visited April 30, 2021).

108. OECD commentaries stated that a server could be a PE, insisting on validity of a physical rule for a digital economy. For a critical analysis, Rita Calçada Pires, *supra* n. 31.

109. OECD (2020), *Statement by the OECD/G20 Inclusive Framework on BEPS on the Two-Pillar Approach to Address the Tax Challenges Arising from the Digitalisation of the Economy—January 2020*; OECD (2020), *Tax Challenges Arising from Digitalisation—Report on Pillar One Blueprint*; OECD (2020), *Tax Challenges Arising from Digitalisation—Report on Pillar Two Blueprint*.

3 MIRROR, MIRROR ON THE WALL, STILL DON'T KNOW WHO THE SOVEREIGN OF IT ALL IS!

Considering the above discussion, to close this chapter, it is necessary to provide explicit answers to the questions listed at the beginning.

3.1 Is MLI a Reproduction of an International Tax Revolution?

Considering all the elements presented above, one can only answer *NO*. Facts suggest MLI as being a specific *change of heart,* a very particular one, similar to a precise surgical intervention, containing exact objectives and limited to a clear-cut intervention.

MLI cannot be characterized as an instrument containing a deep commitment and transformation of how the international tax regime is cumulatively designed, interpreted, applied, *and* controlled. What the BEPS MLI represents is a new way to modify bilateral agreements, generating the same effect as a simultaneous renegotiation of thousands of bilateral agreements: procedural/formal innovation.

It cannot be forgotten that material adjustments to the bilateral agreements´ rules were not part of the MLI process itself.[110] Those were created by a separate procedure, becoming part of the content of the MLI after consensus was reached about those substantial rules. This is why it is stated that substantial outputs originated from a different method and through a different procedure. This was demonstrated by the existence of a particular BEPS action (Action 15), distinct from others.

Also, it should not be forgotten that the OECD is always the epicenter of the process, with the G20 acting as a subsequent endorsement platform. And if the *Inclusive Framework* is currently gaining ground and having more impact,[111] it still remains unclear if it is going to be innovative and effective enough to act as an incentive to the creation of viable alternatives.

Consequently, the MLI is an example of formal multilateralism aligned with an effective determination of simultaneous renegotiations of existing bilateral agreements. As such, it cannot provide a revolution for the international tax regime, whilst not transforming its contents.

In fairness, the MLI represents a different and more effective way of negotiating adjustments on various bilateral agreements. Through this achievement, the tax sovereignty of developed/OECD members and of non-OECD members are effectively impacted. On the one hand, non-OECD members gain a visible platform in the international tax regime, while extending the gains on technical know-how. On the other hand, an increase in the number of voices through the G20 and the *Inclusive Framework* may reveal itself as a means to enable the propagation of the OECD's perspectives and standards, as it can lead to significant improvements in tackling

110. *Supra* 1.2.6.
111. Either by the growing number of members and due to Action 1 work on the two established pillars.

non-OECD members' rules that facilitate aggressive tax planning schemes. But indeed, this is still a precarious model. Nonmembers will have to trust that OECD members will act according to their ethical rhetoric. OECD members will also have to trust non-OECD members' commitment to use BEPS and MLI as a step forward on global tax cooperation instead of tax competition.

This demonstrates that *the MLI embodies only a Soft Evolution rather than a revolution in the international tax regime.*

3.2 Is Tax Sovereignty Diminished by MLI?

The answer should be *NO* if tax sovereignty is seen as responsibility.

Even if one assumes a *Westphalian* concept, the MLI being an example of formal multilateralism with *opt-out clauses* and reservations, the flexibility is guaranteed to address national specificities. MLI is oriented toward effectiveness of the negotiation process, not as an instrument to supplant tax sovereignty, and that is stated in the 2015 Report: "A multilateral instrument can address treaty-based BEPS issues while respecting sovereignty autonomy in tax matters."[112]

However, a *YES* should be the case if the substantive modifications to bilateral tax agreements provided by MLI were not designed by States that welcome and become signatory members of the MLI. If the State did not actively participate in the design of those adjustments, then tax sovereignty will be diminished. Nonetheless, it should be emphasized: this occurs through the inadequate process of design and not through the inadequate process of the application stage while using the MLI as an instrument.

3.3 Can MLI Guarantee an Equilibrium Between the Need for International Cooperation, Tax Sovereignty, and Global Tax Justice?

Fighting back aggressive tax planning as a multi-localized activity connects as many tax systems as possible. MLI provides a platform made of many tax jurisdictions, more than just OECD members. It should be considered that MLI is undeniably a good instrument as it ensures the synchronized adjustments that should be incorporated in the numerous bilateral tax agreements.

However, the type of transformations projected by BEPS' other actions imply many other incorporations that are not integrated into the MLI. Some changes need to occur within national tax systems, and on those, MLI does not have an influence. The fact that MLI is flexible means that no uniformization occurs. Each signatory State will choose how to incorporate the minimum standard and if more than that is accepted. It is even possible to have a pessimist approach as Joseph Morley.[113] The author states that:

112. OECD (2015), *Developing a multilateral instrument to modify bilateral tax treaties*, p. 16.
113. Joseph Morley, *Why the MLI Will Have Limited Direct Impact on Base Erosion Profit Sharing*. 39 Northwestern Journal of International Law and Business 225, 2019.

> "the MLI ultimately does not require jurisdictions to commit to eliminating double non-taxation scenarios, nor does it provide a mandatory enforcement mechanism for ensuring double non-taxation is eliminated without producing double taxation. In fact, very little of the MLI is mandatory, and it is worth considering the reality that many of the signees have not adopted some of the most impactful provisions of the MLI. Thus, the MLI largely continues to rely on the voluntary actions of the nations involved in it to address and eliminate double non-taxation scenarios. As voluntary resolution of double non-taxation scenarios may conflict with the policies of many developing tax jurisdictions as well as those that generate the highest tax revenue, the MLI is unlikely to significantly reduce BEPS by itself. Because it relies on voluntary cooperation between tax jurisdictions on addressing BEPS, the MLI will generally be ineffective at reducing BEPS.

Additionally, MLI works toward a better equilibrium of global tax voices in the context of international tax dialogue. As declared by the 2013 Report,[114] the BEPS project and all its actions should be developed in consultation with all stakeholders, including the business community and civil society. All of it represents more legitimacy. But it can never be compared to national instruments of democratic legitimacy. The BEPS project and MLI are OECD work, which was endorsed by the G20.

Moreover, to fully integrate global tax justice into the international tax regime, the type of transformations required are much more dense and profound than those that an instrument of formal multilateralism can produce.

Considering all these elements, the answer is not an easy one. MLI is, indeed, an instrument that can improve tax cooperation and global tax legitimacy. Yet, it is not a self-sufficient instrument that can fully accomplish global tax justice and accommodate tax sovereignty as responsibility. This holds true despite being a formal MLI and also if it would be transformed into a substantial MLI. As indicated, other relevant material challenges need to be addressed.

3.4 From Now On, Following MLI Process, Will Tax Sovereignty Be Compressed by a New Way of Designing International Tax Law?

Very much likely, *NO*.

MLI, as it is, does not tend to diminish tax sovereignty. If no transformations occur to the process, and formal multilateralism is adopted as the new procedure to provide effective global renegotiations of existing bilateral treaties, it seems accurate to think that tax sovereignty will not be compressed. Even if, while intensifying cooperation, coordination is also densified.

However, no pattern is effectively created by the MLI. Within the *Preamble of the mandate for the development of a multilateral instrument on tax treaty measures to tackle BEPS*, even if valuing the MLI was born of an innovative procedure, "they recognize that the Group is not a formal or informal OECD body and therefore participation of non-OECD members in the Group does not create, and cannot be

114. OECD (2013), *Addressing Base Erosion and Profit Shifting*, p. 51.

interpreted to create, a precedent in the context of OECD procedures for the participation of nonmembers in OECD activities." This statement rapidly dissolves the enthusiasm of believing that, from now on, the international tax regime will always be revised by a MLI.

As previously written, the MLI seems to be a precise surgical intervention inside the international tax regime.[115]

If this is the reaction to formal multilateralism, one can imagine how much harder establishing substantial multilateralism as a pattern would be and, as consequence, accepting a long-lasting global platform, as *Inclusive Framework*, outside the BEPS project—especially one oriented toward revolutionizing the international tax regime into an international tax system. Unilateralism and bilateralism already tried to implement an international regime oriented toward achieving an adequate balance between cooperation and competition, without success. The perception of taxpayers, observers, and academics is one of failure and skepticism.[116] Isn't the BEPS project based on that assessment?

Unless political will is transformed, no substantial modification will exist and only adjustments will continue to occur. As William Vleck recognizes, "whether or not it is hypocritical, the language of sovereignty and the concept for sovereignty as non-intervention frames diplomatic exchange on issues of international taxation."[117] Considering recent events, for the most relevant standards, international tax practice has been generated through an alternate clash/equilibrium between the OECD and the EU, via the EC or the ECJ. Some call it the *Brussels/Luxemburg effect* or the *Paris effect*.[118]

Thus, to allow an adequate transformation on how to design, interpret, apply, *and* control international tax standards, the following points must be considered:

- on the one hand, the OECD is not currently a sufficient international organization that leads the international tax regime, as it lacks global tax justice with its format and procedures;
- on the other hand, many of the current international tax standards about distribution of taxing rights and global allocation of tax revenues are not adequate and should effectively be transformed, providing a consensus that has not been possible until now. Bearing in mind all these elements, the answer is not optimistic. For now, it does not seem probable.

115. Presenting as explanation for the negative reaction toward generalizing multilateralism, MNEs lobbying, Reuven S. Avi-Yonah & Haiyan Xu, *Evaluating BEPS*, 97-124 in Sergio André Rocha & Allison Christians (eds), *Tax Sovereignty in BEPS Era* (Kluwer Law International 2017), p. 121.
116. For example, Allison Christians, *BEPS and the Power to Tax*, 3-27, in Sergio André Rocha & Allison Christians (eds), *Tax Sovereignty in BEPS Era* (Kluwer Law International 2017), p. 27.
117. William Vleck, *Offshore Finance and Global Governance: Disciplining the Tax Nomad* (Palgrave Macmillan 2017), p. 27.
118. Anu Bradford, *The Brussels Effect*. 107 Northwestern University Law Review 1 (2015); Lilian V. Faulhaber, *The Luxemburg Effect: Patent Boxes and the Limits of International Cooperation*. 101 Minnesota Law Review 1641 (2017); Ruth Manson, *The Transformation of International Tax*. 114 The American Journal of International Law 353, 402 n. 3 (2020).

3.5 Will MLI, as a New Instrument for the Application of International Tax Regime, Be Strong Enough to Lead a Substantial Transformation on How International Tax Law Is Designed?

It is tempting to say *NO*.

Considering the discussion above, there seem to be too many obstacles to overcome.

Indeed, the MLI can be an inspiration for the transformative path that is needed. Nevertheless, it does not contain the holistic approach that is needed. It is only formal multilateralism, even though it can serve the purpose of starting an active pressure on existing powers to initiate a true revolution. This is only possible if MLI demonstrates outcomes globally accepted and integrated because of this procedural approach.[119]

The *wildcard* in this reasoning is the transformations due to COVID-19. The global pandemic throughout 2020 and 2021 has surprised the possible results provided by the MLI mindset. Nationalism and encouragement of national frontiers as health requirements disturb this new approach. Global access to vaccines is being challenged with inequality. Divisions between developed and under-developed or developing countries appear to have increased. Sovereignty appears to have been reinforced alongside the *Westphalian* concept, increasing the distance toward sovereignty as responsibility. Transformations of the priorities and the types of processes are currently being managed.[120]

However, the UN and the European Parliament have made statements to fight back that tendency provided by the COVID-19 pandemic. Even if no reference to taxation is made, a compromise toward multilateralism is recommended, anticipating the UN statement on the same aspect.[121] It is stated that:

---

119. Outcomes that revel gains to signatory states, acknowledge either by them or by those states that chose not to participate.
120. *See* Rasmus Corlin Christensen & Martin Hearson, *The New Politics of Global Tax Governance: Taking Stock a Decade after the Final Crisis*. 26 Review of International Political Economy 1068, 1088 n. 5 (2019).
121. Following the special session on *The future we want, the UN we need: reaffirming our collective commitment to multilateralism*, United Nations General Assembly approved Resolution A/RES/75/1, September 21, 2020—Declaration on the commemoration of the 75th anniversary of the United Nations, where is stated: "5. Our challenges are interconnected and can only be addressed through reinvigorated multilateralism. As we meet, the coronavirus disease (COVID-19) pandemic continues to reverberate around our world. In a matter of weeks, the pandemic manifested itself as the largest global challenge in the history of the United Nations. It has not only caused death and serious illness, but also global economic recession, increased poverty, anxiety and fear. It has put enormous pressure on our societies, economies and health systems. While none of us have been left untouched, people in vulnerable situations and the most vulnerable countries have been the hardest hit. The COVID-19 pandemic has reminded us in the most powerful way that we are closely interconnected and only as strong as our weakest link. Only by working together and in solidarity can we end the pandemic and effectively tackle its consequences. Only together can we build resilience against future pandemics and other global challenges. Multilateralism is not an option but a necessity as we build back better for a more equal, more resilient and more sustainable world. The United Nations must be at the center of our efforts. 6. Strengthening international cooperation is in the interest of both nations and peoples. The three pillars of the United Nations—peace and security, development and human rights—are equally important, interrelated and interdependent. We have come far in 75

> the coronavirus pandemic 2020 has exacerbated global geopolitical trends, including the struggle to uphold multilateralism in a climate of growth nationalisms, protectionism and rising great power competition. At the same time, it has demonstrated the need for multilateral cooperation for effective mitigation of cross-border threats, including health crisis. [Recognizing also that,] as coronavirus leaves parts of the world more fragile and vulnerable, it also precipitates the need for reformed multilateral system "fit for purpose" and able to address the challenges of the future. Thinking through new practices to enrich multilateralism will be important for the future development of international cooperation.[122,123]

The acceptance of multilateralism as a necessary tool to deal with inter-nation relationships may be a hopeful sign. However, even if no taxation is present in these declarations, one wonders if they will help improve international tax multilateralism.

---

years but much more remains to be done. We have the tools and now we need to use them. The 2030 Agenda for Sustainable Development is our road map and its implementation a necessity for our survival. Urgent efforts are required. Therefore, we are not here to celebrate. We are here to take action. Guided by the purposes and principles of the Charter, we are here to ensure the future we want and the United Nations we need."

122. European Parliament, *The future of multilateralism and strategic partnerships*. EPRS Ideas Paper. Toward a more resilient EU, Elena Lazarou, PE 652.071—September 2020.

123. Presented to the G20 in June 2020, Homi Kharas, Dennis J. Snower & Sebastian Strauss present an initiative concerning *The Future of Multilateralism and Global Governance. The Future of Multilateralism: Towards a Responsible Globalization that Empowers Citizens and Leaves no One Behind*. It is said: "Recently, however, disaffection with globalization and current forms of global governance has emerged, threatening the very edifice of the rules-based multilateral order, partly because of competing economic models that have opened up issues of fairness and of the distribution of the costs and benefits of maintaining the existing multilateral system. The political discontent with multilateralism, most notably in the United States, is associated with the failure of the post-Bretton Woods system to stem the tide of slow growth, rising inequality, rising migration, social fragmentation and job insecurity associated with technological change, offshoring and automation. Many of the world's biggest challenges are not a result of disagreements about how to cooperate, but a profound loss of direction about why to cooperate in the first place. A sense of multilateralism creeping beyond the boundaries set by the principle of subsidiarity has created a backlash of populism, protectionism, and nationalism. The core goals and values of multilateralism have been forgotten, and a growing number of governments lack the domestic backing required to forge stronger multilateral ties. Unfortunately, while stakeholders debate the merits of global cooperation, the window of opportunity to address a myriad of inherently globalized problems—such as climate change, financial fragility, and pandemics--is closing and important institutions like the WTO can no longer carry out core functions of trade dispute resolution. ... While COVID-19 is holding up a magnifying glass to deep- and hard-set structural problems in the global governance architecture, even before its emergence the world was already fast approaching irreversible thresholds and tipping points on several global challenges, most notably in the realms of climate change and artificial intelligence.3 The window of opportunity to address some of these problems is closing; the catastrophe brought on by COVID-19 has only added greater urgency to the need for a multilateralism that can deal with the huge dangers that lie ahead." Within the proposal, the creation of a specific Working Group to deal with multilateralism is proposed. It would have the goal to present the *G20 Principles for Sustainable Multilateralism*, described as principles that will respond to the existing challenges and opportunities. If those emerge, and considering the *Inclusive Framework* present mandate, wonder if it can pre-determine how still active BEPS activities are performed. https://www.g20-insights.org/policy_briefs/the-future-of-multilateralism-responsible-globalization-that-empowers-citizens-and-leaves-no-one-behind/ (last visited April 30, 2021).

In the first place, doubts arise due to the wording chosen by the mentioned organizations: these declarations affirm that multilateralism needs reform. If so, how are BEPS' MLI and its *Inclusive Framework* presented as innovative and such a *good practice*?

The pandemic also raises the question of the increased need for tax revenues. Public action was transformed, and immense pressure was created on the public health system and vaccination system, or on financial support to economic activities that were severely affected by the requirements of continuous lockdowns and health measures. Keeping this in mind, and considering the experience of previous sovereign debt crisis, taxation will be even more desired and necessary on a global scale. Maybe that compression will ultimately increase pressure on political actors and states to start accepting the need to change the basic international tax standards, perhaps starting with a consensus on how to tax the digital economy.

Some positive signs came from *The Made in America Tax Plan*, an US President tax initiative, with a goal to:

> make American companies and workers more competitive by eliminating incentives to offshore investment, substantially reducing profit shifting, countering tax competition on corporate rates, and providing tax preferences for clean energy production. Importantly, this tax plan would generate new funding to pay for a sustained increase in investments in infrastructure, research, and support for manufacturing, fully paying for the investments in the American Jobs Plan over a 15-year period and continuing to generate revenue on a permanent basis.[124]

It is a national tax plan with principles aligned by BEPS project objectives, particularly those that will endorse rules to reducing profit shifting and eliminating incentives to offshore investment,[125] ending the race to the bottom around the world,[126] and requiring all corporations to pay their fair share.[127] Nonetheless, it is a

124. U.S. Department of Treasury, *The Made in America Tax Plan*, April 2021. https://home.treasury.gov/system/files/136/MadeInAmericaTaxPlan_Report.pdf https://home.treasury.gov/system/files/136/MadeInAmericaTaxPlan_Report.pdf(last visited April 30, 2021).
125. "Reducing profit shifting and eliminating incentives to offshore investment. The enactment of a country-by-country minimum tax aims to substantially curtail profit shifting by U.S. multinational corporations. By tackling the profit shifting of foreign multinational companies out of the U.S. tax base, the plan works to level the playing field between multinational companies headquartered in the United States and foreign countries. The President's plan would also eliminate the tax laws embedded in the 2017 TCJA that incentivize the offshoring of assets." *Ibid.*, p. 1.
126. "Ending the race to the bottom around the world. Countries too often compete for multinationals' business by reducing corporate tax rates which makes it difficult for the United States and other countries to meet revenue needs. The President's plan provides a strong incentive for nations to join a global agreement that implements minimum tax rules worldwide through the denial of U.S. deductions on related party payments to foreign corporations residing in a regime that has not implemented a strong minimum tax. This aspect of the plan is designed to help level the playing field between foreign and U.S. companies." *Ibid.*, p. 2.
127. "Requiring all corporations to pay their fair share. To ensure that large, profitable companies pay a baseline amount of taxes, the President's plan would impose a minimum tax on firms with large discrepancies between income reported to shareholders and that reported to the IRS. It would also provide the IRS with resources to pursue large corporations who do not meet their tax obligations, reversing a trend toward fewer corporate audits." *Ibid.*, p. 2.

unilateral initiative. Reactions from OECD staff were immediate.[128] G20 finance ministers provided several endorsements as well.[129]

However, no certainties exist. Rhetoric is yet to be fulfilled by consensus toward international tax standards. Delimitating where the international tax regime is going is almost impossible. One could incorporate Voltaire's Doctor Pangloss spirit and believe that even when everything is being questioned, there will be light. Or one could refer to the Murphy's Law spirit and believe that tax competition is stronger than global tax justice—as it always has been—so no possible breach of the traditional prisoner's dilemma will be strong enough to overcome it.

From MLI to where? It will mainly depend on where the mindsets and mentalities of the political class lead, how political power acknowledge tax sovereignty, how it accepts it as responsibility, and how it immunizes itself to MNEs' interests and pressures.

I wish I could predict which path will be chosen. Even with so many doubts and disbeliefs, I hope it is toward the cure of the *schizophrenic paradigm*. I hope political power opts for tax sovereignty as responsibility and develops an innovative work toward intensive tax cooperation. But hope is not very different from rhetoric without practice.

Does anyone have a crystal ball?

---

128. OECD Secretary-General, Ángel Gurría, *An overhaul of the global tax system can wait no longer*, The Guardian, April 29, 2021 (https://www.theguardian.com/business/2021/apr/29/overhaul-global-tax-system-covid-economy-trade-war?CMP=Share_iOSApp_Other (last visited April 30, 2021)). In here, the Secretary-General state that "*the biggest change, however, stems from the US decision to call time on the 'race to the bottom' … Biden's plan is to tighten this rule considerably, bring the minimum rate to 21% and advocate for a worldwide move in that direction to limit tax competition between countries.*" OECD director of Center for Tax Policy, Pascal Saint-Amans, also reacted to The Guardian, stating that "*What the US has put on the table … [is saying] we want the rest of the world to follow, we kill tax havens. The game is over. Let's move to a minimum agreed level. Countries want a solution. They want to get out of controversies and want to move on.*" (https://www.theguardian.com/business/2021/apr/08/biden-proposes-global-reforms-to-end-profit-shifting-to-tax-havens (last visited April 30, 2021)).
129. For example https://www.breakingnews.ie/business/germany-and-france-see-global-tax-deal-in-reach-after-us-pledge-1107183.html and https://www.theguardian.com/business/2021/apr/07/g20-global-minimum-corporate-tax-rate-finance-ministers-us-avoidance (both last visited April 30, 2021).

CHAPTER 2

The Multilateral Convention from a Public International Law Perspective

Vanessa Arruda Ferreira

Vanessa Arruda Ferreira further considers the multilateral nature of the MLI as an instrument governed by public international law. This chapter analyses the legal nature of the MLI in the language of the Vienna Convention on the Law of Treaties, affirming the MLI's legal status as a treaty first, then a multilateral treaty, and then a 'successive' treaty, but ultimately not a 'subsequent agreement regarding the interpretation of the treaty [bilateral tax treaty] or the application of its provisions' as defined in the Vienna Convention. The chapter examines special public international law rules applicable to multilateral treaties, the interaction between the MLI and related bilateral tax treaties and specific issues arising from the interpretation of the MLI itself.

1 INTRODUCTION

The signature of the Multilateral Convention to Implement Tax Treaty Related Measures to Prevent Base Erosion and Profit Shifting (BEPS)[1] (also referred to as 'Multilateral Instrument' or 'MLI', and hereinafter referred to as 'Multilateral Convention') was acknowledged by international tax practitioners as a major and innovative event that marked 'a new turning point in tax treaty history'.[2] The implementation of the BEPS

1. *Multilateral Convention to Implement Tax Treaty Related Measures to Prevent Base Erosion and Profit Shifting,* https://www.oecd.org/tax/treaties/multilateral-convention-to-implement-tax-treaty-related-measures-to-prevent-BEPS.pdf.
2. Words of the OECD Secretary-General, Angel Gurría, in OECD, *Multilateral Instrument – Information Brochure May 2020,* https://www.oecd.org/tax/treaties/multilateral-instrument-BEPS-tax-treaty-information-brochure.pdf.

Project treaty-related measures through coordinated action impacting more than 1,650 tax treaties[3] proved to be a challenging test from an international tax view. Yet, when it comes to the assessment, interpretation and application of the Multilateral Convention, interpreters must resort to the public international law principles codified[4] in the Vienna Convention on the Law of Treaties (VCLT)[5] ('Vienna Convention')—the so-called treaty on treaties.[6] Not surprisingly, the development of the Multilateral Convention enabling countries to modify their bilateral tax treaties and implement BEPS treaty-related measures resulted from the work accomplished in BEPS Action 15 by a group of international tax law *and* public international law experts.[7] Indeed, as much as international tax lawyers frequently dealing with tax treaties are familiar with the law of treaties, the Multilateral Convention did push tax experts' boundaries towards a more unfamiliar area of public international law, such as the governance of multilateral and successive treaties.

This chapter investigates how public international law rules the Multilateral Convention and its interaction with the related bilateral tax treaties (i.e., the 'covered tax agreements' as defined by the Multilateral Convention[8]). Section 2 starts by discussing the nature of the Multilateral Convention under public international law by

3. By May 2020, over 2,800 treaties had been listed, leading up to over 1,680 matched agreements (*Ibid.*).
4. 'The law of treaties is defined as the body of rules on the concept of a treaty, on how it is made, brought into force, amended, terminated and how it generally operates. The Vienna Convention on the Law of Treaties (hereinafter "Vienna Convention (1969)") is an international agreement applicable to treaties concluded between states and generally codifies the most important rules of the law of treaties. The International Court of Justice (ICJ), as well as international and national courts and tribunals, generally follow the approach that the Vienna Convention (1969) (or at least some of its rules) represents customary international law on the law of treaties and is, therefore, considered one of the most relevant sources of law on the operation of international treaties.' (Vanessa Arruda Ferreira, *Chapter 21: The Vienna Convention on the Law of Treaties* in Roy Rohatgi on International Taxation: Volume 1 Principles (Ola Ostaszewska & Belema Obuoforibo eds., IBFD 2018), s. 21.1.
5. *Vienna Convention on the Law of Treaties (1969)*, https://legal.un.org/ilc/texts/instruments/english/conventions/1_1_1969.pdf.
6. 'Although the Vienna Convention on the Law of Treaties ("VCLT") does not occupy the whole ground of the law of treaties, it covers the most important areas and is the indispensable starting point for any description of the law. For good reason, the VCLT has been called the treaty on treaties' (Anthony Aust, *Vienna Convention on the Law of Treaties (1969)* (Max Planck Encyclopedia of Public International Law 2006), http://opil.ouplaw.com/view/10.1093/law:epil/9780199231690/law-9780199231690-e1498, para. 1).
7. OECD, *Explanatory Statement to the Multilateral Convention to Implement Tax Treaty Related Measures to Prevent Base Erosion and Profit Shifting*, https://www.oecd.org/tax/treaties/explanatory-statement-multilateral-convention-to-implement-tax-treaty-related-measures-to-prevent-BEPS.pdf, para. 5.
8. 'The term "Covered Tax Agreement" means an agreement for the avoidance of double taxation with respect to taxes on income (whether or not other taxes are also covered): i) that is in force between two or more: A) Parties; and/or B) jurisdictions or territories which are parties to an agreement described above and for whose international relations a Party is responsible; and ii) with respect to which each such Party has made a notification to the Depositary listing the agreement as well as any amending or accompanying instruments thereto (identified by title, names of the parties, date of signature, and, if applicable at the time of the notification, date of entry into force) as an agreement which it wishes to be covered by this Convention' (*See supra* n. 1, Article 2(1)).

assessing its possible qualification not only as a 'treaty' (*see* 2.1.) but also as a 'multilateral treaty' under the Vienna Convention and the consequences therefrom (*see* 2.2.). Further, it analyses the Multilateral Convention as a 'successive treaty relating to the same subject matter' according to the Vienna Convention (*see* 2.3.) and questions its role as a 'subsequent agreement regarding the interpretation of the treaty or the application of its provisions' (*see* 2.4.).

In section 3, the chapter continues by covering the application and interpretation of the Multilateral Convention under public international law. This section initially explores the special rules for multilateral treaties in the Vienna Convention and the relevant deviations in the specific case of the Multilateral Convention (*see* 3.1.). It further explains how principles of public international law determine the interaction between the Multilateral Convention and related bilateral tax treaties (*see* 3.2.) and discusses interpretation issues, such as the role of relevant material in the interpretation of the Multilateral Convention (*see* 3.3.1.), the interpretation of terms not defined in the Multilateral Convention (*see* 3.3.2.) and the issues resulting from the policy choice of having the Multilateral Convention in two equally authoritative language versions without a prevailing text (*see* 3.3.3).

2 QUALIFICATION OF THE MULTILATERAL CONVENTION UNDER PUBLIC INTERNATIONAL LAW

2.1 The Multilateral Convention as a 'Treaty'

The Vienna Convention defines a treaty as 'an international agreement concluded between States in written form and governed by international law, whether embodied in a single instrument or in two or more related instruments and whatever its particular designation'.[9] The term 'treaty' is meant to cover all forms of international agreements that are concluded in writing between states. In this sense, international agreements that are not a single formal instrument (e.g., exchanges of notes) or single instruments in daily use that are not formal instruments (e.g., a memorandum of understanding) are covered by this definition.[10]

However, not all written international agreements concluded between states and governed by international law are designated as 'treaty' in their own texts. Other terms may be used instead, such as 'convention', 'act', 'agreement', 'instrument', 'pact', 'declaration', or even uncommon terms like 'compact' or 'concordat'.[11] The different terms used do not impact the qualification of an international agreement as a 'treaty' since the definition in Article 2(1)(a) of the Vienna Convention stipulates that the

9. *See supra* n. 5, Article 2(1)(a).
10. ILC, *Draft Articles on the Law of Treaties with Commentaries (1966)* (UN 2005), https://legal.un.org/ilc/texts/instruments/english/commentaries/1_1_1966.pdf, commentary on Article 2(1)(a).
11. Anthony Aust, *Modern Treaty Law and Practice* (Cambridge University Press 2000), 24.

particular designation used is not relevant for qualification purposes.[12] Indeed, what is decisive for the qualification of a written agreement as a 'treaty' is whether the negotiating states intend it to create binding obligations under international law[13] as opposed to other agreements that would not be governed by those rules, although concluded between states.[14] It is thus for the negotiating states to decide whether they want the agreement to be governed by international law or not; or, as directly put by Anthony Aust, 'whether they will conclude a treaty or something else'.[15] In addition, some international agreements may not fall within the definition of 'treaty' in the Vienna Convention either because they are not concluded in a written form or not concluded between states. For instance, this is the case in oral or tacit agreements,[16] agreements concluded between states and other subjects of international law (e.g., international organizations) or between such other subjects of international law.

It is thus important to assess whether an international agreement can be qualified as a 'treaty' as defined by the Vienna Convention. The consequence of an international agreement not meeting the requirements of a 'treaty' in the sense of Article 2(1)(a) of the Vienna Convention is that it does not fall within the scope of that convention – although it continues to be subject to rules in the Vienna Convention to which it would anyway be subject to under international law.[17] This is clearly stated by Article 3 of the Vienna Convention, which covers 'international agreements not within the scope of the present Convention'.

12. '(...) in itself the name does *not* determine the status of the instrument; what is decisive is whether the negotiating states intend the instrument to be (or not to be) binding in international law. Thus, just as one should never judge a book by its cover, one should never assume that the name given to an international instrument automatically indicates its status either as a treaty or as a MOU [memorandum of understanding]. Although it is reasonable to assume that an instrument called a treaty, agreement or a convention is a treaty, one should nevertheless examine the text to make *quite* sure' (*see supra* n. 11, p. 20).
13. *See supra* n. 11, p. 17.
14. States may contract with each other governed by domestic law if the subject matter is exclusively commercial, such as the purchase of commodities in bulk (*see supra* n. 11, p. 26). *See also* the example by Lord McNair of a contract executed between the UK government and the Argentine government for the purchase of chilled beef that was not governed by public international law but by the terms of the contract itself and, thus, would not be a treaty (Lord McNair, *The Law of Treaties* (Oxford University Press 1961), 4-5). In this respect, Nathalie Bravo also adds that '(...) nothing prevents states from deciding that such a transaction should be governed by public international law instead of private law and, thus, from agreeing to establish a treaty instead of a contract' (Nathalie Bravo, *A Multilateral Instrument for Updating the Tax Treaty Network* (IBFD 2020), s. 1.2).
15. *See supra* n. 11, p. 17.
16. 'While the Commission considered that in the interests of clarity and simplicity the present articles on the general law of treaties must be confined to agreements in written form, it recognized that oral international agreements may possess legal force and that certain of the substantive rules set out in the draft articles may have relevance also in regard to such agreements' (*see supra* n. 10, Article 3, commentary (3)).
17. Article 3(b) of the Vienna Convention. Besides, this article also indicates that the fact that these agreements fall outside the scope of the Vienna Convention does not affect the legal force of such agreements or the application of the convention to the relations of states under international agreements to which other subjects of international law are also parties (*see supra* n. 5, Article 3(a)(c)).

It is not difficult to conclude that, as a written international agreement concluded between states and creating obligations under international law, the Multilateral Convention can be qualified as 'treaty' in the sense of the Vienna Convention – even if designated as 'convention' in its text or also often referred to as an 'instrument.' As a 'treaty', the Multilateral Convention is subject to the rules of the Vienna Convention as much as the bilateral tax treaties it intends to modify; in other words, they are all equally considered tax treaties subject to the law on treaties.[18]

2.2 The Multilateral Convention as a 'Multilateral' Treaty

In public international law, a treaty qualifies as a 'multilateral treaty' when it is concluded between three or more parties.[19] The term 'multilateral' in this sense simply relies on a certain number of states being party to an international agreement. Lord McNair (as well as other subsequent international tax law scholars) regrets this approach of public international law, in the sense that it merely relies on the number of contracting parties for such qualification, without considering the content and obligations created by the agreement.[20] In his view, a better approach would be to consider as multilateral treaties those 'containing three or more "sides" or "parties" in this sense and creating obligations between each possible pair or some of them'.[21] This is not, however, the approach of public international law.

While bilateral treaties are more common than multilateral ones in the field of international taxation, other policy areas of international law such as human rights and the law of the sea, commonly rely on multilateral treaties.[22] Still, some regional multilateral treaties that promote the avoidance of double taxation exist, such as the Convention between the Nordic Countries for the Avoidance of Double Taxation with Respect to Taxes on Income and on Capital (the Nordic Convention), the Agreement

18. Some scholars have the position that the Multilateral Convention is not a *tax* treaty in the same sense as the covered bilateral tax treaties are, because it does neither achieve or aim to achieve the avoidance of double taxation nor does it allocate taxing rights to the contracting states by itself. Rather, the Multilateral Convention would be qualified as framework agreement for the modification of bilateral tax treaties, due to its dual nature deriving from a mix of procedural and substantive rules (Yariv Brauner, *McBEPS: The MLI – The First Multilateral Tax Treaty that Has Never Been*, 46 Intertax 1 (Alphen aan den Rijn 2018), 6-17; Werner C. Haslehner, *A Multilateral Interpretation of the Multilateral Instrument (and Covered Tax Agreements)?*, 74 Bulletin for International Taxation 4/5 (IBFD 2020), s. 1.2). This discussion is nevertheless irrelevant for the present discussion, as the qualification as 'treaty' and application of the Vienna Convention rules do not depend on whether the treaty is regarded as having *tax* as its subject or not.
19. *See supra* n. 11, p. 15.
20. *See supra* n. 14, Lord McNair, 30.
21. *Ibid.*
22. Rita Szudoczky & Daniel Blum, *Chapter 5: Unveiling the MLI: An Analysis of Its Nature, Relationship to Covered Tax Agreements and Interpretation in Light of the Obligations of Its Parties*, in International and EU Tax Multilateralism: Challenges Raised by the MLI (Ana Paula Dourado ed., IBFD 2020), s. 5.2.1. 'Whereas investment is an area truly reluctant to adopt multilateral instruments of governance, fields such as human rights, the Law of the Sea and climate change are likely to be regulated thorough multilateral instruments' (Ricardo García Antón, *The 21st Century Multilateralism in International Taxation: The Emperor's New Clothes?*, 8 World Tax Journal (IBFD 2016), s. 3.1).

among the Governments of the Member States of the Caribbean Community for the Avoidance of Double Taxation and Prevention of Fiscal Evasion (the CARICOM Agreement), the Regime for the Avoidance of Double Taxation and the Prevention of Fiscal Evasion of the Andean Community (the Andean Community treaty) and the Rules for the Avoidance of Double Taxation and for Assistance in Tax Matters among the Member States of the West African Economic and Monetary Union.

These regional multilateral tax treaties were all concluded to replace bilateral and previous regional multilateral tax treaties existing in these regions and became the only international agreements ruling the allocation of taxing rights between the countries involved.[23] The fact that the domestic tax systems of the signatories of these regional multilateral tax treaties are (or were at the time of the signature) generally uniform is considered a reason for such multilateral agreements to exist and be successful.[24] Indeed, it seems that the higher the level of uniformity and harmonization between countries, the more likely are the chances for a multilateral treaty to be successfully concluded. In fact, many multilateral treaties exist in areas of interest for the international community where, in principle, conflicts do not arise among states, as in the case of humanitarian law and environmental law.[25]

The Multilateral Convention so far signed by 95 countries[26] – and still counting – undoubtedly qualifies as a multilateral treaty under public international law and, consequently, joins the list of current multilateral treaties in the field of international taxation. The public international law practice of qualifying a treaty as multilateral merely based on the number of signatories is however also criticized by international tax scholars as a 'minimalistic approach.'[27] In this respect – and in the same direction as Lord McNair's position on the ideal assessment of multilateralism on the basis of content and obligations created – Rita Szudoczky and Daniel Blum advocate that 'it cannot be inferred from the actual obligations and rights of the parties to the MLI

23. *See supra* n. 14, Nathalie Bravo, s. 1.4.5.
24. 'Most probably, a multilateral agreement concerning all of these matters was reached because the domestic tax systems of the contracting states were uniform, or were uniform at the time the multilateral tax treaty was first negotiated. In this sense, as the member countries of the Andean Community had adopted the territorial principle in their domestic tax systems, Decision 578 was based on source taxation. Contrastingly, as the Nordic countries were members of the OECD, their multilateral tax treaty was modeled after the OECD Model and, thus, is based on residence taxation. Uniformity was also found in the domestic systems of the CARICOM countries, although the decision to give preference to source-based taxation in their multilateral convention seems to be in conflict with their domestic tax systems and traditions. Scholars claim that one of the main reasons why multilateral tax treaties have been successful in certain regions is precisely the uniformity of the domestic tax systems of the contracting states' (*see supra* n. 14, Nathalie Bravo, s. 1.4.5).
25. *See supra* n. 14, Nathalie Bravo, s. 1.2.
26. Status as of 18 February 2021 (https://www.oecd.org/tax/treaties/beps-mli-signatories-and-parties.pdf, accessed on 17 March 2021).
27. 'The term "multilateral" can refer to this factual circumstance, i.e. how many states (or other international actors) are party to an international agreement. In this minimalist definition, multilateralism has a pure technical meaning. (...) the term multilateralism can be understood in different ways depending on its theoretical and ideological background. First, in the most minimalist approach, it simply refers to the number of states participating in an act of international coordination, i.e. if it is more than two, we are dealing with a multilateral act or instrument.' (*see supra* n. 22, Rita Szudoczky & Daniel Blum, s. 5.2.1).

[multilateral instrument] that there is a core multilateral commitment between the parties which they can only change with the consent of all the other parties' and therefore 'in a substantive sense, the MLI [multilateral instrument] lacks an essential multilateral feature'.[28] The fact that the Multilateral Convention has bilateral rather than multilateral effects and that it does not constitute a single body of coherent and identical rules to which all, or at least the great majority of the parties have comprehensively subscribed is also seen as emphasizing its hybrid nature.[29]

However, from the perspective of public international law, the mere fact that a treaty signed by more than two states modifies bilateral agreements does not per se remove its nature as a multilateral treaty. The Vienna Convention is rather flexible in respect of the methods states can use to amend their treaties and, in areas other than international taxation, multilateral treaties have already modified bilateral treaties without this having an impact on their nature - e.g., the European Convention on Extradition, the Agreement on Mutual Legal Assistance between the European Union and the United States, the European Convention on the Repatriation of Minors, and even the United Nations Convention on Transparency in Treaty-based Investor-State Arbitration, which, similarly to the Multilateral Convention, modified a considerable number of bilateral investment treaties by using the *lex posterior* principle of Article 30 of the Vienna Convention.[30]

On the other hand, many international tax scholars propose the assessment of the Multilateral Convention as a multilateral treaty based on more complex indicators, such as the elimination of global inequalities, inclusiveness, fairness and legitimacy,[31] or even international tax coordination over tax competition or unilateralism[32] - thus

---

28. *See supra* n. 22, Rita Szudoczky & Daniel Blum, s. 5.4. They also add: 'In addition, because of its objective - implementing the tax treaty-related BEPS recommendations in the network of existing bilateral treaties - the MLI essentially preserves the bilateral nature of international tax relations. The limited objective of the MLI prevents it from going beyond the boundaries of the BEPS Project. Therefore, the MLI - no matter how many and how great the variety of signatories it eventually attracts - cannot remedy the deficiencies of the decision-making process under the BEPS Project which have failed to ensure equal say for non-OECD/G20 - mostly developing - countries' (*see supra* n. 22, Rita Szudoczky & Daniel Blum, s. 5.4).
29. 'The MLI is not truly multilateral by its nature. It is a hybrid between a multilateral and a bilateral instrument. (...) The numerous opt-ins, opt-outs and reservations have instigated the necessary flexibility to obtain sufficient political support, but at the price of not only making the entire enterprise extremely burdensome and complex, but also very bilateral in nature. The strongest multilateral characteristic of the MLI, in addition to its name, is that states were forced to determine a given position with regard to all of the other participating states on certain key issues, instead of distinguishing their position according to their bilateral needs. One swallow, however, does not make a summer' (Daniel W. Blum, *The Relationship Between the OECD Multilateral Instrument and Covered Tax Agreements: Multilateralism and the Interpretation of the MLI*, 72 Bulletin for International Taxation 3 (IBFD 2018), s. 2.2).
30. *See supra* n. 14, Nathalie Bravo, s. 1.5.1.
31. 'In contrast to this minimalist approach, commentators argue that certain value-based criteria must be included in the concept of multilateralism, be it the inclusiveness and fairness of the decision-making process or even the pursuance of substantive normative ideals which should govern not only the process but also the content of the legal instruments which result from the multilateral coordination of international tax relations' (*see supra* n. 22, Rita Szudoczky & Daniel Blum, s. 5.2.1).
32. 'Furthermore, from a different angle, multilateralism in international taxation may mean the reform of substantive international tax rules in a truly inclusive multilateral framework that

adding more teleological layers to multilateralism. Regardless of the approach taken in international tax law or even by critical scholars of public international law, the Multilateral Convention eventually qualifies as a multilateral treaty by the applicable public international law rules, for it is a treaty concluded by more than two states. This conclusion is important because once qualified as a multilateral treaty, the agreement becomes subject to the special rules of the Vienna Convention that are tailored for multilateral treaties, such as Article 40 on the amendment of multilateral treaties or Article 58 on the suspension of the operation of a multilateral treaty by agreement between certain of the parties only (for details, *see* 3.1.).

2.3 The Multilateral Convention as a 'Successive Treaty Relating to the Same Subject Matter'

Article 30 of the Vienna Convention governs the rights and obligations of states who are parties to 'successive treaties relating to the same subject matter.' The rules in Article 30 are however subject to Article 103 of the Charter of the United Nations,[33] which states that in the event of a conflict between the obligations of the members of the United Nations under the Charter and their obligations under any other international agreement, their obligations under the Charter prevail. This means that irrespective of the rules prescribed in Article 30 of the Vienna Convention for solving conflicts between conflicting successive treaties, the Charter of the United Nations must always be observed and will override other incompatible obligations held by United Nations members in other international agreements.[34] As a result, except for the superiority of the Charter of the United Nations for United Nations members, successive treaties on the same subject matter must follow the guidance in Article 30 of the Vienna Convention for solving incompatibility of treaties – these rules are discussed in detail in section 3.2 of this chapter.

---

leads to increased coordination in the field of international tax law and the creation of global international tax rules, as opposed to the pursuance of particular national interest in domestic tax policy or in tax treaty policy in bilateral relations with other states. In this perspective, the emphasis is on the fact that multilateralism favours international tax coordination over tax competition. Tax competition, on the one hand, may follow from domestic law measures which aim at providing preferential treatment to certain groups of taxpayers in order to attract business and investment to a certain country. The pursuance of such tax policy can be described as unilateralism, which constitutes the reverse of multilateralism' (*See supra* n. 22, Rita Szudoczky & Daniel Blum, s. 5.2.1).

33. 'Subject to Article 103 of the Charter of the United Nations, the rights and obligations of States Parties to successive treaties relating to the same subject matter shall be determined in accordance with the following paragraphs' (*see supra* n. 5, Article 30(1)).
34. This is clearly confirmed by the Commentaries on the Vienna Convention: 'But the position of the Charter of the United Nations in modern international law is of such importance, and the States Members of the United Nations constitute so large a part of the international community, that it appeared to the Commission to be essential to give Article 103 of the Charter special mention and a special place in the present article. Therefore, (...) it decided to recognize the overriding character of Article 103 of the Charter with respect to any treaty obligations of Members' (*see supra* n. 10, commentary on Article 26 (current Article 30), para. 3).

For now, the relevant question is whether the Multilateral Convention is subject to the rules prescribed in Article 30 of the Vienna Convention for being (1) a successive treaty in respect of the bilateral treaties therein covered; and (2) related to the same subject matter of such bilateral treaties.

Determining the order of treaties for the purpose of this rule has been an object of debate among scholars in respect of the date to be taken as a reference point – e.g., date of conclusion, adoption, ratification or entry into force.[35] In the case of multilateral treaties, there is even the additional difficulty that there could be different relevant dates for different states, since contracting states may accede after the treaty has been concluded or entered into force.[36] According to public international law scholars, to determine treaty succession, the relevant date of the adoption of the text[37] and not that of its entry into force must be observed.[38] In practice, the notifications listing the bilateral tax treaties signatories of the Multilateral Convention wish to modify allows the identification of the 'earlier' treaties without major problems. However, issues may arise in cases where the parties to the Multilateral Convention have expanded their list by notifying a tax treaty that was adopted after the Multilateral Convention; in such cases, the Multilateral Convention could not be considered a 'later' treaty under the rules of the Vienna Convention – but the rights and obligations in this 'earlier' multilateral treaty may still prevail in case-specific rules allowed by 30(2) of the Vienna Convention are implemented in later treaties (*see* details in 3.2.).[39]

The second point that must be assessed is whether the Multilateral Convention relates to the same subject matter of the covered bilateral treaties. Most public international law scholars agree that the expression 'relating to the same subject matter' should be construed strictly[40] and, therefore, should 'not cover cases where a general treaty impinges indirectly on the content of a particular provision of an earlier treaty.'[41] It is undeniable that the Multilateral Convention does not merely 'impinge

35. *See supra* n. 14, Nathalie Bravo, s. 3.3.2.
36. *Ibid.*
37. According to Article 9 of the Vienna Convention '1. The adoption of the text of a treaty takes place by the consent of all the States participating in its drawing up except as provided in para. 2. 2. The adoption of the text of a treaty at an international conference takes place by the vote of two thirds of the States present and voting, unless by the same majority they shall decide to apply a different rule' (*See supra* n. 5, Article 9).
38. Ian Sinclair, *The Vienna Convention on the Law of Treaties* (Manchester University Press 1984), 98; *see supra* n. 11, p. 204; see, however, a different view (i.e., date of conclusion) brought forward by Pauwelyn from a review of the official records of the Vienna Conference, *see supra* n. 14, Nathaly Bravo, s. 3.3.2.
39. In this respect but proposing a different solution, Nathaly Bravo states that 'the Multilateral Instrument also needs to supersede the Covered Tax Agreement that entered into force after the Multilateral Instrument. This is the only possible solution that can be adopted so that the Multilateral Instrument can still achieve its object and purpose of modifying tax treaties that were concluded after the Multilateral Instrument entered into force and that were notified as Covered Tax Agreements. As a consequence, despite the explanations found in the Explanatory Statement, the term "supersede" in the notification clauses cannot be equated with the *lex posterior* principle. Otherwise, the Multilateral Instrument will, in some cases, fail to produce the desired effect of modifying Covered Tax Agreements' (*see supra* n. 14, Nathaly Bravo, s. 3.8). Whether this is in line with public international law is debatable.
40. *See supra* n. 38, p. 98; *see supra* n. 11, p. 204; *see supra* n. 14, Nathalie Bravo, s. 3.3.2.
41. *See supra* n. 38, p. 98.

indirectly on the content of the bilateral tax treaties'; conversely, it deals with the core subject matters of these agreements by adjusting the allocation of taxing rights among states and implementing anti-BEPS measures, both central topics that are also part of the object and purpose of these bilateral agreements. Indeed, Nathalie Bravo agrees that 'the fact that they relate to the same subject matter is not debatable: not only do they deal with the allocation of taxing rights between the parties, but the object and purpose of the Multilateral Instrument is actually to update the content of the Covered Tax Agreements to implement measures that counter BEPS practices'.[42] She further adds: 'it is clear that the provisions of the Multilateral Instrument and the provisions of the Covered Tax Agreements would apply to the same set of facts or actions. This means that the test of sameness would be satisfied, even if sameness is interpreted in a strict manner as suggested by conservative scholars'.[43] In this regard, the Organisation for Economic Co-operation and Development (OECD) not only recognizes in its Explanatory Statement to the Multilateral Convention to Implement Tax Treaty Related Measures to Prevent BEPS (Explanatory Statement)[44] that the Multilateral Convention deals with the same subject matter of the covered bilateral tax treaties,[45] but it also concludes that the compatibility clauses in the Multilateral Convention do reflect the rules on the application of successive treaties relating to the same subject matter in Article 30(3) of the Vienna Convention.[46]

Because the Multilateral Convention is a successive treaty relating to the same subject matter of the bilateral tax treaties therein covered, the rights and obligations resulting from the interaction of these treaties must be governed by the rules in Article 30 of the Vienna Convention – on the application of these rules to the Multilateral Convention, *see* 3.2.

2.4 The Multilateral Convention as a 'Subsequent Agreement Regarding the Interpretation of the Treaty or the Application of Its Provisions'

One topic that frequently triggers some debate is whether the Multilateral Convention could qualify as a 'subsequent agreement between the parties regarding the interpretation of the treaty or the application of its provisions', as described in Article 31(3)(a) of the Vienna Convention. In other words, whether the Multilateral Convention could

42. *See supra* n. 14, Nathalie Bravo, s. 3.5.1.4.
43. *Ibid.*
44. *See supra* n. 7.
45. 'Where the provisions of the [Multilateral] Convention may conflict with existing provisions *covering the same subject matter*, however, this conflict is addressed through one or more compatibility clauses which may, for example, describe the existing provisions which the Convention is intended to supersede, as well as the effect on Covered Tax Agreements that do not contain a provision of the same type' (*see supra* n. 44, para. 15) (emphasis added).
46. 'The approach described in the last bullet of the previous paragraph is intended to reflect the ordinary rule of treaty interpretation, as reflected in Article 30(3) of the Vienna Convention on the Law of Treaties, under which an earlier treaty between parties that are also parties to a later treaty will apply only to the extent that its provisions are compatible with those of the later treaty' (*see supra* n. 44, para. 16).

be considered a subsequent agreement between the parties regarding the interpretation of the bilateral tax treaties covered therein or application of their provisions. In such case, the Multilateral Convention would be an element to be taken into account together with the context for the interpretation of such bilateral tax treaties under the general rule of interpretation of Article 31 of the Vienna Convention.[47] This possibility has been considered - although not necessarily advocated for - by some scholars.[48] The Multilateral Convention indeed is an international agreement concluded between parties in cases where both parties have opted into the same provisions.

However, this proposition encounters an obstacle in the fact that only interpretative agreements are considered within the scope of Article 31(3) of the Vienna Convention. The Commentaries on the Vienna Convention indeed only refer to subsequent agreements 'regarding the interpretation of the treaty' or 'agreement as to interpretation of a provision' and concludes that 'an agreement as to the interpretation of a provision reached after the conclusion of the treaty represents an authentic interpretation by the parties which must be read into the treaty for purposes of its interpretation'.[49] In this sense, Sir Ian Sinclair refers to subsequent agreements indeed as agreements for the interpretation of treaties as opposed to those signed to modify or terminate a treaty.[50] In addition, he comments that 'it is rarely that one comes across subsequent agreements between the parties bearing upon the interpretation of a treaty which they have concluded' and concludes that, for this reason, state practice tends to rely more on 'subsequent practice'.

In the same direction, Frank Engelen expressly excludes amending or modifying treaties as subsequent agreements:

> [P]ursuant to Article 31(3)(a) VCLT [Vienna Convention on the Law of Treaties], only agreements that are interpretative in character may be taken into account, together with the context. If a subsequent agreement between the parties cannot reasonably be reconciled with the text of the treaty, it has the effect of modifying the treaty and therefore has no role to play in the application of the general rule of interpretation, but rather comes under the general rule regarding the amendment of treaties embodied in Article 39 VCLT, which provides that a treaty may be amended by agreement between the parties on the condition that the agreement complies with the rules laid down in Part II of the Vienna Convention concerning the conclusion and entry into force of treaties.[51]

47. Article 31(1) and (3) of the Vienna Convention reads as follows: '1. A treaty shall be interpreted in good faith in accordance with the ordinary meaning to be given to the terms of the treaty in their context and in the light of its object and purpose. 2. (...) 3. There shall be taken into account, together with the context: (a) any subsequent agreement between the parties regarding the interpretation of the treaty or the application of its provisions; (b) any subsequent practice in the application of the treaty which establishes the agreement of the parties regarding its interpretation; (c) any relevant rules of international law applicable in the relations between the parties' (*See supra* n. 5, Article 31(1) and (3)).
48. *see supra* n. 22, Rita Szudoczky & Daniel Blum, s. 5.3.3.2; *see supra* n. 29 s. 2.2.
49. *See supra* n. 10, commentary on Article 27 (current Article 31), para. 14.
50. 'Let us consider first the case of subsequent agreements. it follows naturally from the proposition that the parties to a treaty are legally entitled to modify the treaty or indeed to terminate it that they are empowered to interpret it' (*see supra* n. 38, p. 136).
51. Frank Engelen, *Interpretation of Tax Treaties under International Law* (IBFD 2004), p. 220.

The restrictive definition of subsequent agreements to only include interpretative agreements and exclude amending and modifying agreements is logical, in the sense that the purpose of the rule in Article 31(2)(a) of the Vienna Convention is the use of such agreements for the interpretation of the earlier treaties; a subsequent agreement that amends of modifies earlier treaties cannot assist in interpreting what such earlier treaties intended to mean in the first place.

The requirement of this interpretative character thus poses obstacles for the qualification of the Multilateral Convention as a subsequent agreement in the sense of Article 31(3)(a) of the Vienna Convention. However, it should be noted that this article refers to agreements regarding the interpretation of the treaty *or the application of its provisions*. In this sense, Daniel Blum argues that 'the OECD's description of the second category of compatibility clauses to "*change the application* of an existing provision" (emphasis added) could back this hypothesis, while, at the same time, strictly limiting the relevance of the hypothesis to those scenarios in which it was the intention of the parties to alter the application of an already existing provision, not only in the future, but also de facto retroactively'[52] – he cites as an example for such retroactive change Article 6 of the Multilateral Convention on the preamble,[53] though the present author finds this retroactive effect debatable.

The author however does not view the reference to 'the application of its provisions' as a way to include changes to the application of provisions. This interpretation would conflict with the underlying logic of Article 31(3)(a) of the Vienna Convention, which, as already stated, aims to help interpret the meaning of the earlier treaty provision so that changes to the provision should not help in this regard. The author believes that the interpretation of Article 31(3)(a) of the Vienna Convention that would be in line with its purpose is the one in the sense that subsequent agreements regarding the application of treaty provisions refer to agreements clarifying or explaining the application of provisions of earlier treaties, rather than agreements changing their provisions. A good example of agreements that would certainly qualify as subsequent agreements regarding the interpretation of the tax treaties are the well-known agreements under mutual agreement procedure. The interpretative character of these agreements is emphasized by Article 25(3) of the OECD Model when indicating that 'the competent authorities of the contracting states shall endeavour to resolve by mutual agreement any difficulties or doubts arising as to the interpretation or application of the Convention'.[54]

52. *See supra* n. 29, s. 2.2.
53. 'There is one particular provision of the MLI that might serve as an illustrative example of the foregoing theoretical deliberations: the change of the preamble under article 6 of the MLI could be understood to be such a binding subsequent agreement on the treaty's interpretation in the sense of article 31(3)(b) of the VCLT. The OECD itself seems to back this assumption when it states in the Explanatory Statement that in interpreting an undefined term, a CTA's context should be considered "as reflected in the preamble modified by Article 6". In other words, the OECD assumes that the change of the preamble pursuant to article 6 of the MLI has a de facto retroactive effect; otherwise it could never have any effect on the way the CTA's context is meant to be understood' (*see supra* n. 22, Rita Szudoczky & Daniel Blum, s. 5.3.3.2).
54. OECD, *Model Tax Convention on Income and on Capital: Condensed Version 2017* (OECD 2017), https://doi.org/10.1787/mtc_cond-2017-en, Article 25(3).

As a result, the author is of the opinion that the Multilateral Convention cannot be qualified as a subsequent agreement between the parties regarding the interpretation of the bilateral tax treaties covered therein or application of their provisions.

3 APPLICATION AND INTERPRETATION OF THE MULTILATERAL CONVENTION UNDER PUBLIC INTERNATIONAL LAW

The qualification of the Multilateral Convention as a multilateral and successive treaty relating to the same subject matter triggers the application of special rules in the Vienna Convention. The following sections address the application and interpretation of the Multilateral Convention on the basis of these specific rules governing the lifecycle of multilateral treaties (*see* 3.1.), the interaction of successive treaties with the related treaties on the same subject matter (*see* 3.2.) and specific topics on interpretation of treaties (*see* 3.3.).

3.1 Lifecycle of Multilateral Treaties: Selected Special Rules in the Vienna Convention and Relevant Deviations in the Multilateral Convention

As explained in section 2.2, the fact that the Multilateral Convention is a multilateral treaty triggers the application of special rules in the Vienna Convention on several aspects of the modus operandi of this type of treaty. The first special rules address the amendment and modification of multilateral treaties. While the general rule on the amendment treaties is found in Article 39 of the Vienna Convention, Article 40 brings special rules concerning the amendment of multilateral treaties and Article 41 the rules on agreements modifying multilateral treaties between certain of the parties only. Multilateral treaties may therefore be altered through an amending procedure or through a modification procedure. While the former is concerned only with the amendment *stricto sensu* of a multilateral treaty – that is, where the intention is to conclude a formal agreement between the parties generally for modifying the treaty between them all – the latter procedure is used to draw up an agreement between certain parties only for the purpose of modifying the treaty between themselves alone.[55] The amendment of multilateral treaties seeks universality; that is, that all parties to the multilateral treaty approve and ratify the amendment agreement.[56] The main difference between these two procedures is therefore the number of parties involved, although in practice this can become unclear, as it may be that only some of the parties to a multilateral treaty approve and ratify its amendment, while it may also be that all of the parties to a multilateral treaty decide to carry out the modification.[57]

Indeed, the commentaries to the Vienna Convention acknowledge that:

55. *See supra* n. 10, commentary on Article 36 (current Article 40), para. 6.
56. *See supra* n. 14, Nathaly Bravo, s. 5.2.
57. *See supra* n. 14, Nathaly Bravo, s. 5.2. While states may have an intention to conclude an amendment that eventually is ratified only by some parties, thus becoming an *inter se* modification, a situation may also arise where two or more parties set the intention of

> [T]he growth of multilateral treaties having a very large number of parties has made it virtually impossible to limit the amending process to amendments brought into force by an agreement entered into by all the parties to the original treaty; and has led to an increasing practice of bringing amending agreements into force as between those States willing to accept the amendment, while at the same time leaving the existing treaty in force with respect to the other parties to the earlier treaty.[58]

Consequently, as pointed out by Sir Ian Sinclair, in practice, states deviate from the rule of customary international law that a treaty may not be revised without the consent of all parties, and amending treaties to a multilateral treaty may also end up creating two categories of states each bound to different obligations.[59]

Even if an amendment of a multilateral treaty may end up becoming a modification, and vice-versa, the initial intention of the parties of either engaging in an amendment or a modification procedure will eventually determine whether the states must follow the rules in Article 40 or 41 of the Vienna Convention. One of the main differences between the procedures is that Article 40 of the Vienna Convention requires every party to be notified of the proposal to amend the multilateral treaty and that each party has the right to take part in the decision as to an action, if any, to be taken in regard to the proposal and the negotiation and conclusion of any agreement designed to amend the treaty.[60] This may sometimes be difficult to comply with in practice due to doubts as to whether the successor states have inherited rights and obligations under the original treaty.[61]

Article 40 of the Vienna Convention is however a residual rule that applies to multilateral treaties unless the treaty provides otherwise – the same residual rule applies to the general rules on the general amendment of treaties in Article 39 of the Vienna Convention. This means that multilateral treaties may provide in their own text the procedural rules for their amendment, which would prevail over the residual rules in the Vienna Convention. These types of provisions vary extensively; while some deal with all steps of the amendment procedure, others may be much less detailed.[62] The Multilateral Convention has one article ruling the amendment of this agreement (Article 33), which states the following: '1. any party may propose an amendment to this Convention by submitting the proposed amendment to the Depositary. 2. A Conference of the Parties may be convened to consider the proposed amendment in accordance with paragraph 3 of Article 31 (Conference of the Parties).' Article 31(3) of the Multilateral Convention provides more details in respect of the notification procedure to be followed by the depositary, who must inform the parties about the amendment proposal, and convene a conference of the parties if one-third of the parties

negotiating an inter se modification that is eventually accepted by all parties, thus operating a formal amendment (*see supra* n. 38, p. 107).

58. *See supra* n. 10, commentary on Article 36 (current Article 40), para. 1.
59. *See supra* n. 38, p. 106.
60. *See supra* n. 5, Article 40(2).
61. *See supra* n. 38, p. 108.
62. *See supra* n. 14, Nathaly Bravo, s. 5.5.1.

support the proposal within six calendar months, counted from the date of the communication.

The question is whether the rules in Articles 33 and 31(3) of the Multilateral Convention may be considered detailed enough or whether the states will need to apply the residual rules of the Vienna Convention. Nathaly Bravo assessed how sufficient these rules are for this purpose by comparing these provisions with Article 12 of the Optional Protocol to the 1989 Convention that was assessed by the UN Office of Legal Affairs as 'very detailed' for dealing with most of the steps of an amendment procedure. She concluded that Articles 33 and 31 of the Multilateral Convention do not expressly deal with all the relevant steps of the amendment procedure and, therefore, the conference of the parties must apply the residual rules of the Vienna Convention as set out in Articles 39 and 40, or agree to apply a different amendment procedure.[63] However, the notification provided for in Article 31(3) ensures that all parties and signatories that could be affected by changes to the provisions of the Multilateral Convention are aware of the initiation of a review procedure, which goes in line with the special rules in Article 40 of the Vienna Convention.

Regarding the modification of multilateral treaties, Article 41 of the Vienna Convention states that an agreement to modify the treaty may be concluded between two or more parties if it (1) is not prohibited by the treaty, (2) does not affect the enjoyment by the other parties of their rights under the treaty or the performance of their obligations, and (3) does not relate to a provision derogation from which is incompatible with the object and purpose of the treaty as a whole. Also, the parties in question must notify the other parties of their intention to conclude the agreement and of the modification to the treaty for which it provides – unless the treaty otherwise provides. There is no provision in the Multilateral Convention that expressly refers to the modification of the Multilateral Convention in the sense of Article 41 of the Vienna Convention (Article 30 of the Multilateral Convention refers to the possibility of subsequent modifications but in respect of the bilateral tax treaties therein covered); neither has a provision prohibiting it. Provided that states follow the requirements in Article 41 of the Vienna Convention, the Multilateral Convention may be the object of future modifications treaties between certain parties only.

Conditions of invalidity, termination and suspension of operation of treaty special rules also exist for multilateral treaties. First, two main differences exist between termination and suspension of operation of a treaty in respect of multilateral treaties: while the former is definitive and requires consent from all parties, the latter is temporary and consent is required only between the parties involved. Similar to Article 41 of the Vienna Convention on the *inter se* modification of multilateral treaties, Article 58 brings a special rule on the suspension of the operation of a multilateral treaty (or some of its provisions) by agreement between only some of the parties. It states that two or more parties to a multilateral treaty may conclude an agreement to suspend the operation of provisions of the treaty temporarily and as between themselves alone, if the possibility of such a suspension is provided for or not prohibited by

63. *See supra* n. 14, Nathaly Bravo, s. 5.5.1.

the treaty and it does not affect the enjoyment by the other parties of their rights under the treaty, or the performance of their obligations is not incompatible with the object and purpose of the treaty. A notification similar to the one in Article 41 is required unless the treaty otherwise provides. The suspension of operation of a treaty is not dealt with in the Multilateral Convention, neither to specify rules nor to prohibit it, so that states are free to do it subject to the conditions in Article 58 of the Vienna Convention.

An interesting aspect concerning multilateral treaties is that the Vienna Convention does not include rules on the termination of these treaties through a per se agreement; that is, the termination of the multilateral treaty only between certain parties – as it foresees for modification and suspension of operation of treaty provisions. This would mean that, for example, some of the parties to the Multilateral Convention would be able to conclude an agreement *inter se* for the suspension of operation of the treaty between themselves only but not to terminate it between themselves only. According to Sir Ian Sinclair, 'the Commission appears to have taken the view that *inter se* agreements of this nature should be excluded'.[64] Indeed, the Commentary on the Vienna Convention indicates that, unlike the amendment of a treaty, termination deprives all parties of their rights and therefore requires consent from all of them.[65] However, the author agrees with Sir In Sinclair in the sense that the premise on which this conclusion is based seems to be flawed, as some parties to a multilateral treaty may decide by an *inter se* agreement to terminate the treaty in their *inter se* relations without impacting the rights and obligations of the other parties in the multilateral treaty.[66] As a result, nothing could oppose the termination of the multilateral treaty by agreement between some of the parties only. He also adds that this absence in the Vienna Convention 'may be considered another lacuna in the scheme drawn up by the Commission and endorsed by the Conference'.[67] It may be argued that such a clause foreseeing the possibility of termination of a multilateral treaty by agreement between some of the parties only would not be necessary in view of the possibility of parties to withdraw from a multilateral treaty – which has the effect of terminating that treaty for the withdrawing parties. However, the difference is that termination through an *inter se* agreement would offer the possibility of terminating the multilateral treaty between certain parties only while keeping the treaty effective for these parties in their relations with the other remaining parties not taking part in the agreement.

In respect of the withdrawal from the Multilateral Convention, it has been raised that an important deviation exists in respect of the residual rules in the Vienna Convention on the topic (i.e., Articles 42, 54, 56 and 70). Article 37(2) of the Multilateral Convention determines that 'in cases where this Convention has entered into force with respect to all Contracting Jurisdictions to a Covered Tax Agreement before the date on which a Party's withdrawal becomes effective, that Covered Tax

64. *See supra* n. 38, p. 185.
65. *See supra* n. 10 commentary on Article 51 (current Article 54), para. 3.
66. *See supra* n. 38, p. 185.
67. *Ibid.*

Agreement shall remain as modified by this Convention'. This means that the provisions of the bilateral tax treaties signed by the withdrawing state and modified through the Multilateral Convention remain modified, even after the withdrawal becomes effective. The withdrawal would thus have effects only in respect of bilateral tax treaties that have not been modified through the Multilateral Convention; that is, tax treaties listed by one of the parties in respect of which the Multilateral Convention did not enter into force because the other parties either did not list the tax treaties or did not complete the ratification process of the Multilateral Convention before the withdrawal became effective.[68] This has been detected as an important deviation from the Vienna Convention residual rules, according to which the withdrawing party is freed from its obligation to perform the treaty towards the rest of the parties, while under the MLI the withdrawing state would not be released from its obligation to apply the instrument in all cases.[69] The Explanatory Statement confirms that the effects of the withdrawal are forward-looking only and thus could not reverse the modifications made to bilateral tax treaties covered by the Multilateral Convention.[70] It also explains that 'this approach replicates the approach taken in amending protocols to bilateral tax treaties in which the bilaterally agreed amendments cannot be unilaterally reversed by means of withdrawal from the protocol'.[71] If states want to be freed from the modifications of the Multilateral Convention, they would need to either agree on modification of the multilateral treaty or simply renegotiate the relevant bilateral tax treaties.

However, it should be noted that the effect of withdrawing from a treaty according to Article 70(1) of the Vienna Convention is not only one of releasing the parties from any obligation further to perform the treaty, but also one of not affecting any right, obligation or legal situation of the parties created through the execution of the treaty prior to its termination (or withdrawal).[72] The question is whether it would be possible to interpret the modifications promoted by the Multilateral Convention as rights, obligations or a legal situation created prior to the withdrawal. If the answer to this question is yes, it means that such modifications would indeed not be affected by the withdrawal according to Article 70(1)(b) of the Vienna Convention, and Article 37 of the Multilateral Convention would simply apply this approach rather than deviate from the Vienna Convention rules.

The same question regarding the effect of withdrawal from the Multilateral Convention has been asked in respect of termination of this treaty. The Multilateral Convention does not set out specific rules concerning its termination. Nevertheless, the Multilateral Convention can be terminated on the basis of Article 54 of the Vienna Convention if all parties agree to that. The effects of termination of a treaty and withdrawal from a treaty are the same according to Article 70 of the Vienna Convention, so that parties are released from any obligation further to perform the treaty, but

68. *See supra* n. 14, Nathaly Bravo, s. 5.6.1.
69. *Ibid.*
70. *See supra* n. 7, para. 353.
71. *Ibid.*
72. *See supra* n. 5, Article 70(1)(b).

are also bound to any right, obligation or legal situation created through the execution of the treaty prior to its termination. In this respect, Nathaly Bravo supports that 'if, for the treaty makers, the effects established in Article 70 are undesirable in the event of withdrawals, those effects should also be undesirable in the event of the termination of the instrument'[73] and that also applying the same effects of Article 37 of the Multilateral Convention for termination would mean that modifications promoted by the Multilateral Convention would also remain after the termination becomes effective.

Other special rules for multilateral treaties exist in the Vienna Convention, such as the ones in Articles 69 and 70 of the Vienna Convention specifying that the effects of the invalidity of a state's consent to be bound by a multilateral treaty are ruled by the article on the consequences of invalidity of a treaty (Article 69) and apply in the relations between that state and the parties to the treaty and that the consequences of the termination of a treaty in Article 70 apply between a state and each of the other parties to the multilateral treaty in case a state denounces or withdraws from that treaty. Also, Article 55 of the Vienna Convention brings the special rule that a multilateral treaty does not terminate by reason only of the fact that the number of the parties falls below the number necessary for its entry into force unless otherwise provided by the treaty. This rule was brought in the Vienna Convention with the purpose of solving doubts that could arise on whether a treaty would continue valid and effective in this scenario. In the absence of a resolution, the rule is therefore that there is no presumption of termination of the multilateral treaty if the number of parties falls below the one necessary for its entry into force (in case of the Multilateral Convention, five signatories).

3.2 Principles of Public International Law Governing the Interaction Between the Multilateral Convention and Bilateral Tax Treaties

The Explanatory Statement often refers to the Multilateral Convention as a treaty modifying (rather than amending) covered bilateral tax treaties and that 'it will be applied alongside existing tax treaties, modifying their application in order to implement the BEPS measures'.[74] Two remarks must first be made in respect of this explanation. First, throughout the Explanatory Statement, the OECD refers to the Multilateral Convention as 'modifying' the covered bilateral tax treaties. This modification should not be confused with the modification of treaties dealt with in Article 41 of the Vienna Convention, which refers to agreements between certain parties only of a multilateral treaty for the purpose of modifying such multilateral treaty but between themselves alone (*see* 3.1.). It seems the OECD used the term 'modify' in the Explanatory Statement in its common sense (i.e., to alter or change something) and not in the specific sense of Article 41 of the Vienna Convention.

The second point is that the Explanatory Statement instructs both the Multilateral Convention and the covered bilateral tax treaties to be read alongside each other,

73. *See supra* n. 14, Nathaly Bravo, s. 5.6.2.
74. *See supra* n. 7, para. 13.

without explaining the reason behind this approach. The need for both treaties to be read, as the OECD says, 'alongside' is that both treaties are effective and both deal with the same subject matter (*see* 2.3.). In other words, because an earlier treaty (bilateral tax treaty) and a successive treaty (the Multilateral Convention) deal with the same subject matter and neither of them have been terminated, they both apply and need to be checked when the subject matter arises. This is however only the start of a process in the application of these treaties. The reading of the two treaties alongside each other may on one hand reveal that provisions may be in line to confirm or complement each other, but may also show that rights and obligations in one treaty would infringe the other treaty provisions, resulting in a conflict[75] between provisions. The question is how to address the latter case, that is, how to determine which provision prevails, since both treaties are valid and effective.

Besides the possibility of trying to avoid conflict of treaties through a harmonious interpretation of the applicable provisions,[76] the proposed solution by public international law is given by the principle of *lex posterior derogat legi posteri* (or simply *lex posterior*), which finds partial expression in the concept that 'when all parties to an earlier treaty are parties also to the later treaty, the earlier treaty applies only to the extent that its provisions are compatible with those of the later treaty'.[77] This principle is reflected in Article 30 of the Vienna Convention dealing with rights and obligations of states who are parties to 'successive treaties relating to the same subject matter'. As explained in section 2.3, except in respect of superiority of the Charter of the United Nations for the United Nations members and the specific rules, successive treaties on the same subject matter must follow the guidance in Article 30 of the Vienna

75. In this respect, 'Aufricht has held that "conflict between an earlier and a later treaty arises if both deal with the same subject matter in a different manner and if at least one State is party to both treaties". This approach inspired Sir Waldock when he drafted article 30 of the Vienna Convention dealing with the application of successive treaties relating to the same subject matter. In the Yearbook of the International Law Commission (ILC) of 1964, he indicated, with regard to conflicts of treaty provisions, that the "idea conveyed by that term was that of a comparison between two treaties which revealed that their clauses, or some of them, could not be reconciled with one another". More recently, some scholars have given special relevance to the object and purpose of treaties for defining conflicts of treaties. They have postulated that a conflict of treaties also exists when the "higher aim" that parties ascribe to one of the treaties is undermined due to the application of the other treaty. This definition seems to respond to the restrictive definition of Jenks that, as illustrated above, can result in the nullification of the object and purpose of one of the treaty provisions. (...) Conflicts of treaties also arise when a new treaty provision is enacted with the aim of changing an existing treaty provision. Conflicts of treaty provisions do not always result from the inadvertent work of treaty makers; sometimes, they are deliberately created to replace old treaty provisions with the text of new ones. To resolve a conflict of treaties, a third provision (different to the provisions that conflict) or a principle of interpretation is required.' (*See supra* n. 14, Nathalie Bravo, s. 3.2).
76. 'Given that there is an accepted presumption against conflicts of treaty provisions that stems from the premise that new treaty provisions are in conformity with pre-existing norms of international law, most of the time, conflicts of treaties are avoided through a harmonious interpretation of the applicable provisions. Such a harmonizing interpretation intends to obtain a compatible reading of the provisions in conflict if it can be understood from the treaties that this was the intention of the parties. Nevertheless, cases of conflicts of treaties may still arise if the interpreter cannot achieve a harmonious reading of the provisions' (*Ibid.*).
77. *See supra* n. 38, p. 96.

Convention for solving incompatibility of treaty provisions. The article reads as follows:

1. Subject to Article 103 of the Charter of the United Nations, the rights and obligations of States Parties to successive treaties relating to the same subject matter shall be determined in accordance with the following paragraphs.
2. When a treaty specifies that it is subject to, or that it is not to be considered as incompatible with, an earlier or later treaty, the provisions of that other treaty prevail.
3. When all the parties to the earlier treaty are parties also to the later treaty but the earlier treaty is not terminated or suspended in operation under article 59, the earlier treaty applies only to the extent that its provisions are compatible with those of the later treaty.
4. When the parties to the later treaty do not include all the parties to the earlier one: (a) as between States Parties to both treaties the same rule applies as in paragraph 3; (b) as between a State party to both treaties and a State party to only one of the treaties, the treaty to which both States are parties governs their mutual rights and obligations.
5. Paragraph 4 is without prejudice to article 41, or to any question of the termination or suspension of the operation of a treaty under article 60 or to any question of responsibility which may arise for a State from the conclusion or application of a treaty the provisions of which are incompatible with its obligations towards another State under another treaty.[78]

In brief, the rules determine that the later treaty generally prevails when there is incompatibility of provisions, which is the pure application of *lex posterior* principle, except in cases where the incompatibility or the superiority of the earlier treaty is stated in the treaty, therefore creating an exception to *lex posterior*.[79] Indeed, the Commentaries on the Vienna Convention acknowledge that 'treaties not infrequently contain a clause intended to regulate the relation between the provisions of the treaty and those of another treaty or of any other treaty relating to the matters with which the treaty deals' and that 'the clause has necessarily to be taken into account in appreciating the priority of successive treaties relating to the same subject-matter'.[80] The commentaries also indicate that, in many cases, clauses inserted in treaties for the purpose of determining the relation of their provisions to those of other treaties entered into by the contracting states may do no more than confirm the general rules of priority contained in Article 30(3) and (4) of the Vienna Convention (i.e., the *lex posterior* principle).[81] However, other clauses may implement the exception allowed in Article 30(2) of the Vienna Convention by stating that the provision is not incompatible with, or that it is not to affect, their obligations under the earlier treaty.

78. *See supra* n. 5, Article 30.
79. Ian Sinclair summarizes the rules as follows '(a) if a treaty says that it is subject to or is not to be considered as incompatible with another treaty, that other treaty will prevail; (b) as between parties to a treaty who become parties to a later, inconsistent, treaty, the earlier treaty will apply only where its provisions are not incompatible with the later treaty; (c) as between a party to both treaties and a party to only one of them, the treaty to which both are parties will govern the mutual rights and obligations of the states concerned' (*See supra* n. 38, p. 94).
80. *See supra* n. 10, commentary on Article 26 (current Article 30), para. 2.
81. *See supra* n. 10, commentary on Article 26 (current Article 30), para. 4.

These clauses regulating 'the relation between the provisions of the treaty and those of another treaty or of any other treaty relating to the matters with which the treaty deals' are referred to as conflict or compatibility clauses. Compatibility clauses may relate to existing treaties or future treaties.[82] If one of the conflicting treaties provides for compatibility clauses, those compatibility clauses prevail over the *lex posterior* principle in Article 30 of the Vienna Convention. This means that, following the *lex posterior* principle, the Multilateral Convention provisions that are not compatible with earlier bilateral tax treaties therein covered prevail, unless otherwise stated by the compatibility clauses in the Multilateral Convention.

In this sense, the Explanatory Statement mentions the *lex posterior* principle when referring to one of the compatibility clauses by stating that 'the approach described in the last bullet of the previous paragraph is intended to reflect the ordinary rule of treaty interpretation, as reflected in Article 30(3) of the Vienna Convention on the Law of Treaties, under which an earlier treaty between parties that are also parties to a later treaty will apply only to the extent that its provisions are compatible with those of the later treaty'.[83] It also clarifies that the compatibility clauses indeed define the relationship between the provisions of the Convention and Covered Tax Agreements in objective terms.[84]

The Multilateral Convention has four types of compatibility clauses regulating the relation between its provisions and those of covered bilateral tax treaties. These clauses indicate that the Multilateral Convention provisions (1) apply 'in place of' provisions in the bilateral tax treaties (i.e., it replaces an existing provision if one exists, and does not apply if a provision does not exist); (2); 'applies to' or 'modifies' provisions in the bilateral tax treaties (i.e., it changes the application of an existing provision without replacing it, and therefore cannot apply if a provision does not exist); (3) apply 'in the absence of' a provision in the bilateral tax treaties (i.e., it only applies in if no provision is in place); or (4) apply 'in place of or in the absence of' provisions in the bilateral tax treaties (i.e., it applies in all cases[85]). The compatibility clauses must be read together with the notification clauses (and the actual notifications made by the parties), as they

82. The BEPS Action 15 Final Report referred to the possibility of including obedience clauses in the Multilateral Convention stipulating that parties shall not conclude agreements in contradiction with the multilateral treaty, but such clauses were eventually not included in the Multilateral Convention (OECD, *Developing a Multilateral Instrument to Modify Bilateral Tax Treaties – Action 15: 2015 Final Report* (OECD 2015), https://www.oecd.org/tax/developing-a-multilateral-instrument-to-modify-bilateral-tax-treaties-action-15-2015-final-report-9789264241688-en.htm, 35-36).
83. *See supra* n. 7, para. 16.
84. *See supra* n. 7, para. 15.
85. The compatibility clauses that determine that a provision of the Multilateral Convention applies 'in place of or in the absence of' a bilateral tax treaty provision will always apply, regardless of whether a provision exists or not in the bilateral tax treaty and of whether all the parties made the corresponding notification: 'If all Contracting Jurisdictions notify the existence of an existing provision, that provision will be replaced by the provision of the Convention (to the extent described in the relevant compatibility clause). Where the Contracting Jurisdictions do not notify the existence of a provision, the provision of the Convention will still apply. If there is in fact a relevant existing provision which has not been notified by all Contracting Jurisdictions, the provision of the Convention will prevail over that existing provision, superseding it to the extent that it is incompatible with the relevant provision of the Convention. If there is no existing

ensure clarity about existing provisions that are within the scope of compatibility clauses.[86] For example, in the case of Multilateral Convention provisions that apply 'in place of' (as indicated in (1)), the notification provision states that the provision will apply only in cases where all states make a notification with respect to the existing provision of the bilateral tax treaty.[87] As indicated by Nathaly Bravo, although these notifications made in accordance with the notification clauses are not found in common treaty law practice, they not only ensure that parties agree on which provisions of their treaties are or are not subject to modification (also allowing stakeholders to know relatively easily which provisions are modified), but they also have a constitutive effect, which means that only if all the parties to a bilateral tax treaty produce the respective notification will the provision of the Multilateral Convention modify the relevant provision.[88]

The compatibility clauses do regulate the relation between the Multilateral Convention provisions and those of the covered bilateral tax treaties by stating that the former replace, change the application of, supplement or supersede the latter. At a first glance, they do not seem to deviate from the general principle of *lex posterior*, as it happens in the case of 'subject to' clauses as described in Article 30(2) of the Vienna Convention. This means that the provisions of the Multilateral Convention generally prevail over the conflicting provisions of the covered bilateral tax treaties - either by replacing or modifying them - thus following the *lex posterior* principle. However, a closer look at the provisions that apply 'in the absence of' a provision in the bilateral tax treaties (as described in (3) above) reveals a deviation from (or at least a limitation to) the *lex posterior* principle, since the Multilateral Convention provisions in this case apply only if no provision exists in the bilateral tax treaty. In other words, if a provision exists in the earlier bilateral treaty on a subject matter, the later Multilateral Convention provision on this subject matter will not apply. However, this becomes a more theoretical deviation of the *lex posterior* principle, since in practice where the earlier bilateral treaty clauses exist and are allowed to remain applicable by the Multilateral Convention itself instead of the later provision in this multilateral treaty is because such provisions do conflict.[89]

A more concrete deviation from or limitation of the *lex posterior* clause may happen because of the notifications made by the parties. For example, in case of the

provision, the provision of the Convention will, in effect, be added to the Covered Tax Agreement' (*See supra* n. 7, para. 15).

86. 'To ensure clarity and transparency about the application of the Convention, where a provision supersedes or modifies specific types of existing provisions of a Covered Tax Agreement, Parties are generally required to make a notification specifying which Covered Tax Agreements contain provisions of that type. It is expected that Parties would use their best efforts to identify all provisions that are within the objective scope of the compatibility clause. It is therefore not intended that Parties would choose to omit some relevant provisions while listing others. The effect of these notifications varies depending on the type of compatibility clause that applies to that provision' (*See supra* n. 7, para. 15).
87. *See supra* n. 7, para. 15.
88. *See supra* n. 14, Nathalie Bravo, s. 3.8.
89. This however become only a theoretical deviation of the *lex posterior* principle, since in practice where the earlier bilateral treaty clauses remain applicable is because they are in line with the provision in the Multilateral Convention, that is, no incompatibility exists.

compatibility clauses that prescribe that a provision of the Multilateral Convention applies 'in place of' a bilateral tax treaty provision (as described in (1) above), and only some of the parties include a notification with respect to the existing provision (as required by the notification clauses), the provision of the Multilateral Convention does not replace the provision of the earlier bilateral tax treaty. This means that the earlier (and conflicting) treaty provision - and not that of the later treaty provision - will apply. The same result occurs in the case of provisions of the Multilateral Convention that 'apply to' or 'modify' a provision of a bilateral tax treaty (as described in (2) above) and only some or none of the parties notify that the provision exists. In such a case, according to the notification clauses, the provision of the Multilateral Convention will not apply or modify the provision of the earlier tax treaty.[90]

A deviation from the *lex posterior* principle may also exist if in future treaties the signatories decide to include a 'subject to' type of clause as allowed by Article 30(2) of the Vienna Convention, in reference to the earlier Multilateral Convention. In such case, the earlier provision of the Multilateral Convention would apply. In fact, since the Multilateral Convention did not include obedience clauses,[91] this may be the only way of allowing conflicting provisions of the Multilateral Convention to apply instead of future conflicting treaty provisions.[92]

Besides the possibility of introducing specific provisions in the later treaty to implement special rules and deviate from the *lex posterior* principle, the *lex specialis derogat legi generali* (or simply *lex specialis*) principle may also be considered as an alternative solution for conflicts between treaty provisions. This principle has been widely recognized in public international law literature,[93] but because it is not referred to in Article 30 of the Vienna Convention (neither in the Multilateral Convention nor Explanatory Statement) as a possible deviation from the *lex posterior* principle, one may question how and when it would be applicable. According to Sir Ian Sinclair, the concept of a specific norm of conventional international law prevailing over a more general norm (even in the case where the general norm is a later norm), which the *lex specialis* stands for, can be regarded as raising primarily a question of interpretation.[94] Some scholars and international courts accept the application of the *lex specialis* principle to solve conflicts of treaties provisions when the *lex posterior* principle leads

90. In case the proper notifications are made, the provisions in the Multilateral Convention will 'apply to' or 'modify' the application of an existing provision in the bilateral tax treaty without replacing it. Although this is not a deviation from the *lex posterior* principle, some interpretation efforts are needed when reading the provisions together for producing a harmonious result. In this respect but going into a different direction concerning the applicability of the *lex posterior* rule in this case, Nathaly Bravo supports the idea that 'the provisions of the Multilateral Instrument containing this type of compatibility clause do not deal with exactly the same subject matter as the provisions of the Covered Tax Agreements; they only deal with a related matter' (*see supra* n. 14, Nathalie Bravo, s. 3.8).
91. *See supra* n. 82.
92. For a different position, *see supra* n. 39.
93. *See supra* n. 38, p. 96.
94. *Ibid.*

to unacceptable results and its application needs to be determined on a case-by-case basis.[95]

However, the *lex specialis* is a principle that is not always easy to apply in practice, for it is hard for interpreters to determine which treaty is general or specific. Some may even advocate that the *lex specialis* principle is more appropriate in cases of conflicting provisions within the same regime or even within the same treaty.[96] Outside this scope, the use of the principle alone by courts is rather limited. In this sense, the author agrees with Nathaly Bravo that there seems to be no room for the applicability of the *lex specialis* for solving conflicts between the Multilateral Convention and covered bilateral tax treaties since both treaties most likely have the same degree of generality.[97]

3.3 The Interpretation of the Multilateral Convention: Issues under Public International Law

Articles 31-33 of the Vienna Convention constitute a general expression of principles of customary international law on treaty interpretation.[98] In this respect, it should be noted that the interpretation of tax treaties follows the principles of interpretation of treaties in international law[99] and, therefore, should also guide the interpretation of the Multilateral Convention. Article 31(1) of the Vienna Convention presents the general rule of interpretation of treaties as follows: 'a treaty shall be interpreted in good faith in accordance with the ordinary meaning to be given to the terms of the treaty in their context and in the light of its object and purpose'. Therefore, under the general rule of interpretation, one must simultaneously consider different elements (i.e., good faith, ordinary meaning, context and object and purpose); these different elements together form a 'single closely integrated rule of interpretation'.[100] This means that the text of the Multilateral Convention must be examined in good faith, together with its context and in the light of its object and purpose. Furthermore, according to Article 31(3) of the Vienna Convention, other elements must be also taken into account with the context

95. *See supra* n. 14, Nathalie Bravo, s. 3.3.3.
96. *Ibid.*
97. *See supra* n. 14, Nathalie Bravo, s. 3.6.
98. *See supra* n. 38, p. 153.
99. Michael Lang, *Introduction to the Law of Double Taxation Conventions* (IBFD Linde, 2013), 41; 'Therefore, the rules of the Vienna Convention are used in case law on the interpretation of double taxation treaties today as a basis even with regard to states which have not yet ratified the Vienna Convention' (Klaus Vogel et al., *Klaus Vogel on Double Taxation Conventions* (Kluwer Law International 1997), 35); 'International tax scholars commonly accept that tax treaties are to be interpreted according to the rules of interpretation found in Arts 31 et seq. of the VCLT (...)' (Guglielmo Maisto, *Domestic Anti-abuse Rules and Bilateral Tax Conventions in the Light of Public International Law* in Essays on Tax Treaties: A Tribute to David A. Ward (Guglielmo Maisto, Angelo Nikolakakis & John Michael Ulmer eds., IBFD 2012), 325-334, at pp. 332-333).
100. 'Thus, article 27 [now article 31] is entitled "General rule of interpretation" in the singular, not "General rules" in the plural, because the Commission desired to emphasize that the process of interpretation is a unity and that the provisions of the article form a single, closely integrated rule' (*see supra* n. 10, commentary on Article 27 (current Article 31), para. 8).

(i.e., any subsequent agreement between the parties regarding the interpretation of the treaty or the application of its provisions; any subsequent practice in the application of the treaty that establishes the agreement of the parties regarding its interpretation; and any relevant rules of international law applicable in the relations between the parties). These extra elements are referred to as 'further authentic elements of interpretation'[101] by the Commentaries of the Vienna Convention and are considered primary materials in the general rule of interpretation.

The interpretation of treaties must then first be established on the basis of the general rule of interpretation according to Article 31 of the Vienna Convention, but the interpreter can make use of the supplementary means of interpretation in Article 32 of the Vienna Convention to either confirm the meaning resulting from the general rule of interpretation or determine the meaning in case the interpretation according to the general rule leaves it ambiguous or obscure, or leads to a manifestly absurd or unreasonable result. Article 33 of the Vienna Convention brings the rules on interpretation of treaties authenticated in two or more languages.

It is not the purpose of this section to explain the general rule of interpretation in the Vienna Convention. Instead, specific issues arising in the interpretation of the Multilateral Convention will be addressed based on the rules of interpretation in public international law.

3.3.1 *The Role of Selected Related Documents in the Interpretation of the Multilateral Convention*

One important step in the interpretation of treaties is to assess which documents are relevant and can be used in this process and which status they have under public international law. In this respect, assessing whether these documents can qualify as part of the general rule of interpretation in Article 31 of the Vienna Convention or as part of the supplementary means of interpretation in Article 32 of the Vienna Convention has an important impact on the influence that the relevant material has in the interpretation of the treaty. This is because the interpretation of treaties must first be established on the basis of the general rule of interpretation, while the supplementary means of interpretation serve only to either confirm that interpretation or to determine the meaning in case that interpretation leaves it ambiguous or obscure, or leads to a manifestly absurd or unreasonable result. In the general rule of interpretation, interpretative materials thus have a higher degree of importance in the interpretative process than those qualified as supplementary means of interpretation. In this sense, scholars have been debating the relevance of specific materials linked to the Multilateral Convention and their role in its interpretation under public international law.

101. *See supra* n. 10, commentary on Article 27 (current Article 31), para. 14.

One of the most discussed documents in this respect is the Explanatory Statement prepared by the participants in the ad hoc Group[102] and in the Sub-Group on Arbitration[103] to provide clarification on the approach taken in the Multilateral Convention and on how each provision is intended to affect covered bilateral tax treaties.[104] According to the Explanatory Statement itself, it 'reflects the agreed understanding of the negotiators with respect to the [Multilateral] Convention'.[105] Because of this purpose and because the ad hoc Group adopted the Explanatory Statement and the text of the Multilateral Convention at the same time,[106] the question raised is whether this document could fall within Article 31(2)(a) of the Vienna Convention; that is, if it could be qualified as 'context' in the general rule of interpretation for being an 'agreement relating to the treaty which was made between all the parties in connection with the conclusion of the treaty'.[107]

The Explanatory Statement tries to confirm this interpretation by indicating in its own text that it is qualified as an 'agreement relating to the treaty which was made between all the parties in connection with the conclusion of a treaty'. The Explanatory Statement may be easily qualified as an agreement 'relating to' and made 'in connection with the conclusion of' the Multilateral Convention, as required by Article 31(2)(a) of the Vienna Convention, due to the fact that not only it intends to clarify the approach of the Multilateral Convention, but also because they were both adopted at the same time.[108][109] However, the requirement 'made between all the parties' may raise doubts in respect of this qualification for some states. In what concerns the state members of the ad hoc Group involved in the preparation of the Explanatory Statement, some take the position that this requirement is certainly met and, therefore, the Explanatory Statement may be considered 'context' in the interpretation of the MLI as an 'agreement relating to the treaty which was made between all the parties in connection with

102. The ad hoc Group was open to all interested countries participating on an equal footing. 99 countries participated in the ad hoc Group as members. Four non-State jurisdictions and seven international or regional organizations participated as observers (*see supra* n. 7, para. 7).
103. The ad hoc Group established a Sub-Group on Arbitration for this purpose in which 27 countries participated as members (*See supra* n. 7, para. 9).
104. *See supra* n. 7, para. 11.
105. *Ibid.*
106. The Explanatory Statement indicates that 'The members of the *ad hoc* Group adopted this Explanatory Statement on 24 November 2016 at the same time as adopting the text of the Convention' (*see supra* n. 7, para. 11) and the website of the OECD confirms that 'the text of the Multilateral Instrument (MLI) and its Explanatory Statement were developed through a negotiation involving more than 100 countries and jurisdictions and adopted on 24 November 2016, under a mandate delivered by G20 Finance Ministers and Central Bank Governors at their February 2015 meeting' (https://www.oecd.org/tax/treaties/multilateral-convention-to-implement-tax-treaty-related-measures-to-prevent-beps.htm).
107. *See supra* n. 5, Article 31(2)(a).
108. '(...) the fact that the Explanatory Statement was formally "adopted" at the same time as the text of the MLI provides an indication that the intention was to make it part of the "context" for purposes of the rule for treaty interpretation set out in article 31 of the Vienna Convention (1969). It is "an agreement" "made in connection with the conclusion" (in the future) of the MLI by signatory states who were members of the ad hoc group' (Johann Hattingh, *The Multilateral Instrument from a Legal Perspective: What May Be the Challenges?*, 71 Bulletin for International Taxation 3/4 (IBFD 2017), s. 6.3).
109. The Explanatory Statement itself seems to support this view (*see supra* n. 7, para. 11).

the conclusion of the treaty'.[110] However, some still question if the ad hoc member countries are formally 'parties' for this purpose, since it was the negotiating states, who were not at the time signatory states of the Multilateral Convention, who agreed to the Explanatory Statement.[111]

For the other states that signed the Multilateral Convention without having previously been involved in the ad hoc Group, there can be a discussion on whether the Explanatory Statement could still be 'context' by virtue of Article 31(2)(b) of the Vienna Convention as an 'instrument which was made by one or more parties in connection with the conclusion of the treaty and accepted by the other parties as an instrument related to the treaty'. This is considered a possibility provided that the state accepted it as an instrument related to the Multilateral Convention, which for some could be considered done through the signing of this multilateral treaty and adoption of the Explanatory Statement.[112] Others may however consider that there is no evidence that 'other parties' accepted the Explanatory Statement as an instrument related to a treaty.[113]

There are also doubts on whether the Explanatory Statement could qualify as any of the other elements to be taken into account with the context as per Article 31(3) of the Vienna Convention (i.e., any subsequent agreement between the parties regarding the interpretation of the treaty or the application of its provisions; any subsequent practice in the application of the treaty which establishes the agreement of the parties regarding its interpretation; any relevant rules of international law applicable in the relations between the parties), since 'the Explanatory Statement is not an agreement *per se* and it cannot be viewed as a subsequent practice or relevant rule of international law', and 'it is not possible to assess whether the parties wanted to give a term a special meaning by means of the Explanatory Statement.'[114]

Most scholars, however, agree that there is not much discussion on whether it could be seen as a supplementary means of interpretation.[115] Indeed, supplementary means of interpretation in the sense of Article 32 of the Vienna Convention include the preparatory work of the treaty or *travaux preparatoires* (negotiating history) and the circumstances of a treaty's conclusion (the historical background), which could easily

110. For example, *see supra* n. 18, Werner C. Haslehner, s. 3.2; John F. Avery Jones, *Treaty Interpretation – Global Tax Treaty Commentaries* (IBFD, accessed on 4 April 2021), s. 5.3.3.
111. *See supra* n. 108, s. 6.3. In the same direction, 'the negotiators of the ad hoc group were not formally concluding a treaty; they were laying the groundwork for the eventual future conclusion of the treaty, which may not occur after all. It is also worth noting that there were members of the ad hoc group who decided not to adopt the MLI, thus it cannot be said that they were parties to the treaty as defined in article 2(1)(g) of the VCLT, as they were not bound by the MLI' (Rainer Prokisch & Fernando Souza de Man, *Chapter 7: Multilateralism and International Tax Law: The Interpretation of Tax Treaties in Light of the Multilateral Instrument* in International and EU Tax Multilateralism: Challenges Raised by the MLI (Ana Paula Dourado ed., IBFD 2020), s. 7.8).
112. Supporters of this view are, for example, John F. Avery Jones (*see supra* n. 110, s. 5.3.3); Werner C. Haslehner (*see supra* n. 18, s. 3.2).
113. *See supra* n. 111, s. 7.8.
114. *Ibid.*
115. 'The Explanatory Statement is otherwise clearly a supplementary means of interpretation under article 32 of the Vienna Convention (1969)' (*see supra* n. 108, s. 6.3).

comprise the Explanatory Statement. While there is less doubt in this regard, this conclusion has the downside of reducing the importance of the Explanatory Statement in the process of interpretation of the Multilateral Convention, as it could only be invoked to confirm the meaning obtained by reference to Article 31 or to deny it when this meaning is ambiguous or obscure or leads to a result that is manifestly absurd or unreasonable. However, this consequence alone cannot be a reason to dismiss the qualification itself.

Another issue in the interpretation of the Multilateral Convention is the one of identifying the role of the BEPS Reports on the tax treaty-related measures in BEPS Actions 2, 6, 7 and 14 (BEPS Reports) and that of the Commentaries on the OECD Model that was developed during the course of the BEPS Project (OECD Commentaries). According to John Avery Jones, because the Explanatory Statement indicates that the object and purpose of the Multilateral Convention is to implement the tax treaty-related BEPS measures,[116] it is 'clear that BEPS reports should be considered for interpretation purposes as object and purpose rather than context'.[117] However, some may question whether this statement by itself would make this conclusion true.[118] It has been raised that the BEPS Reports could alternatively be seen as establishing a special meaning for terms that the parties wanted to adopt in accordance with Article 31(4) of the Vienna Convention, or, at the very least, be regarded as supplementary means of interpretation under Article 32 of the Vienna Convention.[119]

Similar to what is stated in respect of the BEPS Report, the Explanatory Statement also refers to the importance of the OECD Commentaries in the interpretation of the Multilateral Convention by indicating that 'the commentary that was developed during the course of the BEPS Project and reflected in the Final BEPS Package has particular relevance in this regard'.[120] Some scholars support the OECD Commentaries as background to the conclusion to the Multilateral Convention, and therefore as supplementary means of interpretation as per Article 32 of the Vienna Convention.[121] This goes in line with the view (finding strong support in literature and courts) that the OECD Commentaries are supplementary means of interpretation for the purpose of

116. *See supra* n. 7, para. 12.
117. *See supra* n. 110, s. 5.3.3.
118. *See supra* n. 18, Werner C. Haslehner, s. 3.2; *See supra* n. 18.
119. *See supra* n. 18, Werner C. Haslehner, s. 3.2.
120. *See supra* n. 7, para. 12.
121. 'Third, with regard to the relevance of the OECD Model and the Commentaries on the OECD Model for purposes of interpreting the MLI, they surely form the background to its conclusion, but that does not amount to them qualifying as "context" as defined in the Vienna Convention (1969). The same is true also for bilateral tax treaties that were concluded prior to the adoption of the MLI. Under the hierarchy of materials used for interpretation set up by the Vienna Convention (1969), these can – at most – be considered to be "supplementary material" having relevance in specific circumstances according to Article 32 of the Vienna Convention (1969). That provision refers to "preparatory work and circumstances" of the conclusion of a treaty. The OECD Model and the OECD Commentaries at the time of adoption of the MLI certainly fall under these, at least as relevant (factual) circumstances that provide background understanding and inform the understanding of the agreement' (*See supra* n. 18, Werner C. Haslehner, s. 3.2).

interpretation of tax treaties in general.[122] Indeed, as indicated by John Avery Jones, 'as far as the substantive provisions of the MLI modifying the CTAs are concerned, the Commentary on the relevant BEPS provision will apply in a similar way as the Commentary on the OECD Model and would seem to have similar status'.[123]

Most scholars suggest that later versions of the OECD Commentaries should have little or no relevance in the interpretation of the Multilateral Convention,[124] therefore favouring the static approach as opposed to the ambulatory approach in the use of the OECD Commentaries.[125] This view opposes the official position of the OECD favouring the ambulatory approach in the use of the OECD Commentaries for interpretation of tax treaties in general,[126] but goes in line with the prevailing view in favour of the static approach as a general rule and to refer to the later version of the OECD Commentaries only where changes were incorporated as a matter of clarification or to reflect practice previously common (to the extent that the changes are genuinely interpretative).[127]

3.3.2 The Interpretation of Terms Not Defined in the Multilateral Convention

Article 2(2) of the Multilateral Convention brings an additional rule of interpretation for terms not therein defined. Accordingly, any term not defined in the Multilateral Convention shall, unless the context otherwise requires, have the meaning that it has at that time under the relevant covered bilateral tax treaty.[128] Although this is not a provision commonly found in non-tax treaties and therefore not much discussed in

122. Although the OECD Commentaries do not strictly qualify as 'preparatory works of the treaty' or 'circumstances of its conclusion', they may still be considered supplementary means of interpretation, since Article 32 refers to these two materials only as examples.
123. *See supra* n. 110, s. 5.3.3. Of course, if one considers the OECD Commentaries not as a supplementary means of interpretation for treaties in general, but as 'context' for example, this same status would be retained for the purpose of interpretation of the Multilateral Convention under this rationale.
124. '(...) any later versions of the OECD Model and the OECD Commentaries cannot have any relevance to the interpretation of the MLI itself' (*See supra* n. 18, Werner C. Haslehner, s. 3.2); 'Thus, the Commentaries can help with the interpretation of the MLI, but only those in existence when the CTA was signed. This will clearly reduce any role the Commentaries might have in the interpretation process, but it is, in our opinion, the soundest approach, as it does not employ posterior amendments, unknown to the parties at the time of signing the CTA, in interpreting this legal instrument' (*See supra* n. 108, s. 7.9).
125. 'One of the relevant questions frequently asked in respect of the use of the OECD Commentaries in the process of interpretation is which version the interpreter should rely on: the version of the OECD Commentaries in force at the time of the conclusion of the treaty (the static approach) or the latest version of the OECD Commentaries, which may include changes to the version in force at the time of the conclusion of the treaty (the ambulatory approach)' (Vanessa Arruda Ferreira, *Chapter 22: Role of the OECD Commentaries* in Roy Rohatgi on International Taxation: Volume 1 Principles (Ola Ostaszewska & Belema Obuoforibo eds., IBFD 2018), s. 22.3).
126. The OECD advocates the use of the later version of the OECD Commentaries (ambulatory approach) as a general rule, with an exception in regard to changes in the OECD Commentaries that are incorporated as a consequence of changes to the text of the related article in the OECD Model (which would then no longer match the provision in a treaty that was based on previous versions).
127. *See* more on this in *supra* n. 125, s. 22.3.
128. *See supra* n. 1, Article 2(2).

public international law doctrine, this special rule of interpretation for undefined terms is easily recognized by international tax practitioners in view of the similar rule in Article 3(2) of the OECD Model; while Article 3(2) of the OECD Model retains the domestic law meaning for undefined terms, Article 2(2) of the Multilateral Convention resort to the meaning in the covered tax treaties. This means that, if the term is not defined in the Multilateral Convention, one must ascertain the term's meaning in the relevant covered tax treaty and retain that meaning for the Multilateral Convention, unless the context otherwise requires. However, if the covered tax treaty does not contain a definition, but nevertheless contains the term, the meaning that is to be used is the one from the relevant domestic law as a result of Article 3(2) of the covered tax treaty, unless the context requires otherwise. If the term in question is not used in the covered tax treaty, no reference can be made to domestic law and, instead, the meaning is to be determined by reference to the general rules of interpretation in the Vienna Convention.[129]

Resorting to the covered tax treaties seems to be a rule that is consistent with the idea of linking the Multilateral Convention to the related covered agreements.[130] However, the use of the meaning in the relevant covered bilateral tax treaty is allowed, as long as the context does not require otherwise. The term 'context' referred to in Article 2(2) of the Multilateral Convention has a different meaning from the 'context' in Article 31 of the Vienna Convention and from that used in Article 3(2) of the OECD Model. Some scholars understand that the 'context' in 2(2) of the Multilateral Convention should include the object and purpose of the Multilateral Convention, the Explanatory Statement, and, indirectly, the related bilateral tax treaty if it follows the OECD Model.[131,132] Some scholars defend an interpretation of the term 'context' in Article 2(2) of the Multilateral Convention in a way narrower than the 'context' in Article 3(2) of the OECD Model.[133]

---

129. *See supra* n. 18, Werner C. Haslehner, s. 3.1.
130. 'From a bilateral standpoint it thus seems perfectly reasonable to seek recourse in the CTA, since it is the CTA that forms the substantive basis of the legal relationship between the two contracting states. The MLI has no independent legal meaning without its application alongside the CTA. Seeking recourse in the CTA in the event of undefined terms therefore seems consistent with the idea of linking both instruments as closely as possible' (*See supra* n. 22, Rita Szudoczky & Daniel Blum, s. 5.3.4).
131. 'Of course, the CTA can only be understood to indirectly form part of the context because it is not the specific CTA that is part of the MLI's context but certain concepts enshrined in the OECD Model which are implicitly presupposed by the MLI's drafters. If the term context is understood in this way, direct recourse to the CTA becomes redundant. (...) Admittedly, this interpretation of the term "context" only yields defensible results if the CTA's rule in question is actually based on the OECD Model. This approach does not work in cases where there are discrepancies between the CTA and the OECD Model, since it can hardly be assumed that all individual CTAs form part of the MLI's overall context. However, this is not necessarily the end of the inquiry. As is the case under Article 3(2) of the OECD Model in relation to domestic law, the MLI's context can in and of itself require seeking recourse in the respective CTA. After all, it is the CTA that should be amended by the MLI' (*see supra* n. 22, Rita Szudoczky & Daniel Blum, s. 5.3.4).
132. *See supra* n. 22, Rita Szudoczky & Daniel Blum, s. 5.3.4.
133. 'There [in article 3(2)], the reference is understood broadly to give a largely "contextual" or "teleological" bend to tax treaty interpretation. This is sensible insofar as tax treaties are characterized by clear and unconditional rules working towards a certain purpose. In contrast,

As indicated, from the wording of Article 2(2) of the Multilateral Convention, one may conclude that where the term in question is used in the Multilateral Convention but not in the covered tax treaties, reference to domestic law meaning is not allowed.[134] Indeed, it seems that the use of domestic law meaning is only permitted through the use of Article 3(2) of the OECD Model, which only plays a role for terms existing in the relevant tax treaty. In such case, the interpretation of terms not defined in the Multilateral Convention must be carried on the basis of the rules of interpretation in Articles 31-33 of the Vienna Convention (*see* 3.3.1. and 3.3.3.).

3.3.3 The Multilateral Convention and the Language Issue

Tax treaties are often drafted in the languages of the contracting states and are thus often signed in two or more language versions. But the conclusion of treaties in different languages may raise the question of which language version to use or how to proceed when facing a language inconsistency. For this reason, Article 33 of the Vienna Convention rules on the interpretation of treaties authenticated[135] in two or more languages. The first rule states that when a treaty has been authenticated in two or more languages, the text is equally authoritative in each language, unless the treaty provides or the parties agree that, in case of divergence, a particular text shall prevail.[136] The general rule is therefore of the equality of the languages and the equal authenticity of the texts in the absence of any provision to the contrary,[137] which suggests that the interpreter may rely on any of the authenticated language versions. However, treaties often contain an express provision determining the status of the different language versions. Despite the presumption that the terms of the treaty have the same meaning in each authentic text,[138] Article 33(4) of the Vienna Convention determines that, when a comparison of the authentic texts discloses a difference of meaning that the application of Articles 31 and 32 of the Vienna Convention does not remove, the meaning that best reconciles the texts, having regard to the object and purpose of the treaty, is to be adopted - except where a particular text prevails according to the treaty.

Because the Vienna Convention refers to the act of comparing authentic texts, the question arises as to whether a legal obligation to compare the authentic versions of the treaty exists in the process of interpretation. This legal obligation would, however,

---

the MLI is characterized by flexibility rather than clarity and strictness, which should be considered an argument to understand the "context" more narrowly for purposes of article 2(2) of the MLI, thereby aiming to protect the bilateral nature of the MLI over its multilateral one. Even so, the term is likely to be taken to have a broader meaning than under article 31 of the Vienna Convention (1969). It, therefore, must be read to include the Explanatory Statement' (*see supra* n. 18, Werner C. Haslehner, s. 3.1).

134. *See supra* n. 18, Werner C. Haslehner, s. 3.1.
135. 'Authentication is the process by which this definitive text is established, and it consists in some act or procedure which certifies the text as the correct and authentic text' (*see supra* n. 10, commentary on Article 9 (current Article 10), para. 1).
136. *See supra* n. 5, Article 33(1).
137. *See supra* n. 10, commentary on Article 29 (current Article 33), para. 2.
138. *See supra* n. 5, Article 33(3).

conflict with both the principle that each authentic text is equally authoritative and with the statement that the terms in each version are presumed to have the same meaning – what would support the conclusion that one could rely on any single authentic text for the purpose of interpretation.[139] In addition, this legal obligation would encounter practical obstacles, in the sense that most interpreters do not hold the required proficiency in the many languages currently used in treaties. As a result, the prevailing view is that there is no such obligation,[140] but because the absence of such a legal obligation could result in textual divergences being overlooked and treaties being incorrectly interpreted, scholars understand that the right to rely on a single text should be exercised in good faith.

The Multilateral Convention has two equally authoritative texts, in English and French, neither of which is a prevailing text.[141] Members of the ad hoc Group established to develop the Multilateral Convention have so far prepared translations into Arabic, Chinese, Dutch, German, Greek, Italian, Japanese, Portuguese, Serbian, Spanish and Swedish.[142] These translations are however for information purposes only, as the signed English and French versions of the Multilateral Convention are the sole applicable authentic texts.

The OECD decision of keeping the Multilateral Convention as a bilingual text was based on the fact that 'drafting a multilateral instrument in a number of languages would increase its cost, the risk of conflict between versions in different languages and practical challenges in its administration.'[143] However, this policy choice has adverse consequences in the practical application of the Multilateral Convention, not only because of the difficulties in case of divergences between the two versions but also because the Multilateral Convention aims at modifying covered bilateral tax treaties that are written in different languages.

In respect to the first problem, one may think that eventual discrepancies between French and English versions of the Multilateral Convention would not frequently arise, as most interpreters can simply rely on one language text of their choice (English or French) and ignore the other, as long as the text interpreted is clear and a divergence between the two versions is not raised. However, the author agrees with Richard Resch that the prevailing view among scholars for routine interpretation (i.e., lack of obligation to compare the versions) is in violation of the Vienna Convention principles of interpretation because of the specific properties of tax treaties and the resulting indeterminacy of a single text interpreted in isolation.[144] In this

139. *See supra* n. 4, s. 21.2.4.
140. Contra: Richard Xenophon Resch, *The OECD BEPS Multilateral Instrument and the Issue of Language*, 47 Intertax 6/7 (Alphen aan den Rijn 2019), 563-572, and the present author, as explained further in this s..
141. 'In witness whereof the undersigned, being duly authorised thereto, have signed this Convention. Done at Paris, the 24th day of November 2016, in English and French, both texts being equally authentic, in a single copy which shall be deposited in the archives of the Organisation for Economic Co-operation and Development' (*see supra* n. 1, Article 39).
142. The translations are available here: https://www.oecd.org/tax/treaties/multilateral-convention-to-implement-tax-treaty-related-measures-to-prevent-beps.htm.
143. *See supra* n. 82, p. 22.
144. *See supra* n. 140, p. 566.

respect, Articles 31-33 in combination with Article 26 of the Vienna Convention require the interpreter to give effect to the common intentions of the parties and, therefore:

> [W]hat matters is that the common intention of the contracting states as expressed by the treaty is observed, not whatever may be expressed by any single text considered in isolation, which may be at variance. Consequently, what matters is not that divergences remain undetected but that they are excluded, that is, that they are either ascertained not to exist or resolved by way of interpretation to arrive at the one true meaning of the treaty implementing the common intention of the contracting states.[145]

For this reason, contrary to the prevailing view, the author subscribes to the view that courts are obliged to compare all texts of a plurilingual tax treaty under the principles of treaty interpretation in the Vienna Convention if the treaty designates none of the texts as prevailing. Regardless of whether one understands the comparison between the language versions as obligatory or not, the choice of having only two language versions creates problems that would not arise if only one version existed (or a prevailing text) or even three or more versions - since a third version, for example, could give additional context and help with elucidating the correct interpretation in case of discrepancies between the other two.[146]

Concerning the second problem, according to Richard Resch, the choice of having the English and French versions of the Multilateral Convention as equally authoritative texts implements a political anachronism on a global scale that ignores the reality that the vast majority of tax treaties (92.32%) do not feature French texts and that the world at large prefers and implements English as treaty *lingua franca.*[147] Also, under the view that both versions must be compared, even if the modified treaty originally designates its English text as prevailing, the court must still compare the French text of the Multilateral Convention concerning the introduced modifications.

---

145. *Ibid.*
146. 'Unfortunately, although the OECD realized that "Drafting a multilateral instrument in a number of languages would increase its cost, the risk of conflict between versions in different languages and practical challenges in its administration", it chose the worst option available in this respect, namely, two equally authoritative texts in equally authentic languages, which increases the interpretative burden in case of divergences to the comparably largest extent' (*See supra* n. 140, p. 570). He rightly adds: 'Like many authors on the subject (...), the OECD fails to appreciate that the correlation between additional interpretational complexity and the number of equally authoritative language texts is not linear. While lowest for unilingual treaties, it is highest for two texts and decreases with the number of languages added because of the additional context. In consequence, although the drafting and administration costs may be slightly lower for treaties concluded in two languages rather than three or more, the costs incurred by the international community as a whole with respect to the interpretation and application of tax treaties in practice are incomparably higher for two texts versus any other number and, of course, most versus a unilingual MLI or one with a prevailing text' (*See supra* n. 140, p. 570, footnote 59).
147. 'Almost two-thirds of all treaties in the global tax treaty network are either unilingual in English or have an English prevailing text. The equivalent share of French in second place is already very low (roughly 3%), and its use as a (true) diplomatic language is even more marginal. All other languages are used as unilingual treaty or prevailing text language only to a very limited extent (combined, roughly 5% of the global tax treaty network), confined to certain linguistic, geographical, or political regions, merely exhausting the potential for unilingual treaties attributable to a shared native Intertax o/r official language' (*see supra* n. 140, p. 566).

According to Stéphane Austry et al., one solution would be that:

> [S]tates could adopt the modifications to existing tax treaties and the Explanatory Statements either in English only, or French only, or both (which Canada would adopt for constitutional reasons), in which case both versions would have equal authority. Regardless of which version a state adopted, the English version would apply to modify a treaty solely in English or with a prevailing English text (and similarly with French). If the tax treaty being modified is between two states that have adopted the English version, that version of the modifications and Explanatory Statements would apply. If the tax treaty being modified is between two states that have adopted different versions, both versions would apply and be equally authoritative. However, states could, when signing the MLI, agree to use a different one of those languages in relation to a particular tax treaty, so that two countries both adopting the English version could modify a treaty in two Romance languages in French.[148]

However, the current wording of the final clause[149] of the Multilateral Convention and of the Explanatory Statement does not seem to allow this possibility for states.[150] Other ways of circumventing this obstacle and implementing the solution proposed by Stéphane Austry et al. were proposed by Richard Resch, including the option for states to amend the Multilateral Convention accordingly (i.e., to include the possibility for states to adopt the modifications to existing tax treaties and the Explanatory Statements either in English only, or French only, or both) or to expand the context concerning the interpretation and application of the final clause of the Multilateral Convention by a subsequent agreement of the parties under Article 31(3)(a) of the Vienna Convention (which could be done by any two parties concerning their tax treaties on the basis of Article 32(1) of the Multilateral Convention in combination with the treaty MAP).[151]

4 CONCLUDING REMARKS

The fast evolution of international relations and increasing coordination between states have brought new challenges to the international tax community. The conclusion of special types of international agreements, such as multilateral treaties, and the increased complexity in the interaction between successive treaties on the same subject matter are examples of the unusual areas tax practitioners must still cross, despite decades of experience in tax treaty application. No matter how inspiring the tax

148. Stéphane Austry et al., *The Proposed OECD Multilateral Instrument Amending Tax Treaties*, 70(12) Bulletin for International Taxation (IBFD 2016), s. 3.
149. *See supra* n. 141.
150. '(...) in view of the MLI final clause wording and the overall content and composition of the VCLT with respect to Arts 10 and 31-33, the Explanatory Statement formulation as it stands is too indistinct to provide enough traction for an application along the lines suggested here; the final clause wording itself should be different in order to explicitly implement such application' (*see supra* n. 140, p. 571).
151. *See supra* n. 140, pp. 571-572.

technical debate may be, the law of treaties codified in the Vienna Convention still dictates the ground rules to be observed by all interpreters, be it public international lawyers or international tax practitioners. Knowing the rules of the game is essential for the relevant players and, in this respect, public international law rules and principles are, now more than ever, the key to a successful path in the field of tax treaties.

CHAPTER 3

Is the Multilateral Instrument Really Multilateral?

Nathalie Bravo[*]

Nathalie Bravo uses historical and comparative analysis to further examine the nature of the Multilateral Instrument (MLI). The chapter examines a number of public international law precedents for the structure and application of the MLI and analyzes the ways in which the MLI adheres to and departs from these examples. The chapter explains that the nature of the MLI as a MLI derives from the common interests of the parties that signed it, and that this nature is distinct from its scope and application in any particular case. It argues that while multilateralism does not necessarily imply complete uniformity, the MLI promotes uniform interpretation in structure and purpose.

1 INTRODUCTION

The Multilateral Convention to Implement Tax Treaty Related Measures to Prevent base erosion and profit shifting (BEPS) (commonly referred to as the MLI)[1] concluded on November 24, 2016 was negotiated by over a hundred states and non-state jurisdictions. As of April 2021, the MLI has been signed and ratified by 95 states and non-state jurisdictions. Before the MLI, no other worldwide treaty dealing with income taxation had ever been concluded.

* The author would like to thank Priv.-Doz. Dr. Kasper Dziurdź for his very valuable input. The views expressed in this article are the author's own.

1. OECD, *Multilateral Convention to Implement Tax Treaty Related Measures to Prevent Base Erosion And Profit Shifting* (2016).

Despite the number of negotiating jurisdictions and parties to the MLI, some of the features of the instrument have caused tax experts to question its multilateral nature. These experts have rejected the idea that a shift into multilateralism has taken place in international tax law. Some of the arguments posited by tax experts rejecting the multilateral nature of the MLI will be summarized in section 1. This chapter provides a discussion about the multilateral nature of the MLI by analyzing the concept of bilateral and multilateral treaties from the perspective of public international law in section 2. Subsequently, section 3 discusses the nature of obligations that can be set out in multilateral treaties. Finally, section 4 tests the concepts presented in sections 2 and 3 against the MLI.

Determining whether the MLI is a bilateral or a multilateral treaty is not a theoretical matter, but rather a practical one. The nature of the MLI determines the importance of its preamble and its context for the interpretation of the tax treaties it modifies,[2] which are defined in the MLI as Covered Tax Agreements (CTAs).[3] The nature of the MLI also determines the relevance that a decision of the conference of the parties might have for the common and uniform interpretation of the provisions of the instrument.[4] It also determines the role of the conference of the parties for further modifying tax treaty rules.[5] Moreover, it determines whether the state responsibility of one of the parties to the MLI may be invoked not only by a party to a CTA directly affected by an infringement but also by the rest of the parties to the MLI that have an interest in the application, interpretation and faithful discharge of the instrument's provisions.[6]

2 REVIEW OF TAX LITERATURE ON THE NATURE OF THE MLI

The MLI modifies CTAs without replacing them.[7] Thus, the MLI can be categorized as a modifying or amending treaty; that is, a successive treaty in which parties deliberately embark on altering an earlier treaty[8] without terminating or replacing it.

Modifying treaties are not intended to be read as an autonomous text. They are intended to be read together with the treaty they modify unless the parties to the

2. *See* Preamble and Article 2(2) of the MLI.
3. Covered Tax Agreements are defined in Article 2(1)(a) of the MLI. For a tax treaty to be considered a Covered Tax Agreement two conditions must be fulfilled: (i) the tax treaty must have been concluded between two or more parties to the MLI in order to avoid double taxation with respect to taxes on income; and, (ii) all the parties to the tax treaty must have sent a notification to the depositary listing it as a Covered Tax Agreement.
4. *See* Articles 31 and 32 of the MLI.
5. *See* Articles 31 and 33 of the MLI.
6. *See* s. 4 below.
7. Article 1 of the MLI. Also, OECD, *Explanatory Statement to the MLI*, para. 13 (2016); and, OECD, *Developing a Multilateral Instrument to Modify Bilateral Tax Treaties, Action 15—2015 Final Report*, OECD/G20 Base Erosion and Profit Shifting Project, at 24-25 (2015). For a detailed analysis, *see* N. Bravo, *A Multilateral Instrument for Updating the Tax Treaty Network*, at 56-65 (IBFD 2020).
8. On a similar note, *see* the comment of Mr. Jiménez de Aréchaga, in International Law Commission (ILC), Summary records of the eighteenth session 859th Meeting p. 113, UN Doc. A/CN.4/186 and Addenda; A/CN.4/L.107, L.115, Yearbook of the ILC Vol. I, Part II (1966).

modifying treaty agree otherwise. Therefore, the MLI and the CTAs, which in their majority are of a bilateral nature, coexist. As such, the MLI and the CTAs must be interpreted side-by-side.[9]

Within tax scholarship, some suggest that the MLI is not truly a multilateral treaty, but rather a hybrid between a multilateral and a bilateral one. Daniel Blum has reached this conclusion by arguing that "(...) the MLI does not constitute a single body of coherent and identical rules to which all or, at least, to which the great majority of the parties involved have comprehensively subscribed. Instead, the MLI facilitates the amendment of bilateral tax treaties by providing a centralized legal framework for realizing this."[10] As the MLI is not a "self-sustaining international agreement and its scope and application depends on the existence of a [CTA],"[11] it is not possible to speak of multilateralism when referring to it.[12]

Likewise, Werner Haslehner has indicated that the purpose of the MLI "is not to harmonize international tax law, but merely to close gaps existing in bilateral relationships."[13] Thus, in his view, when applying Article 2(2) of the MLI concerning the interpretation of undefined terms, the context of the MLI must be understood narrowly "to protect [its] bilateral nature ... over its multilateral one."

Similarly, Ricardo Garcia Anton has argued that the MLI is a Janus-faced instrument because it presents "on one side the multilateral layer representing a high degree of consensus in the long march towards customary international law, and on the other side, the bilateral layer introducing a high degree of flexibility,"[14] which leads to a non-coherent legal instrument.[15] According to Professor Garcia Anton, the bilateral nature of the MLI is evidenced from: (i) the "sui generis" system of reservations provided in the MLI, which in some cases grants asymmetrical effects to reservations;[16] and (ii) the power of the parties to conclude subsequent modifications contracting out from the terms of the MLI including the provisions that provide for the minimum standards.[17]

9. *See also* J.F. Avery Jones, *Treaty Interpretation* (updated 2017), sec. 5.3.1., in *Global Tax Treaty Commentaries* (R. Vann ed., IBFD 2014).
10. *See* D. Blum, *The Relationship Between the OECD Multilateral Instrument and Covered Tax Agreements: Multilateralism and the Interpretation of the MLI*, 72 Bull. Intl. Taxn. 3, at 135 (2018).
11. *See* D. Blum, *The Relationship Between the OECD Multilateral Instrument and Covered Tax Agreements: Multilateralism and the Interpretation of the MLI*, 72 Bull. Intl. Taxn. 3, at 133 (2018).
12. *See* D. Blum, *The Relationship Between the OECD Multilateral Instrument and Covered Tax Agreements: Multilateralism and the Interpretation of the MLI*, 72 Bull. Intl. Taxn. 3, at 135 (2018).
13. W. Haslehner, *A Multilateral Interpretation of the MLI (and Covered Tax Agreements)?*, 74 Bull. Intl. Taxn. 4/5, at 228 (2020).
14. R. García Antón, *Multilateral Dynamics in Bilateral Settings: Back to Realpolitik*, BTR 4, at 499 (2019).
15. R. García Antón, *Multilateral Dynamics in Bilateral Settings: Back to Realpolitik*, BTR 4, at 498 (2019).
16. R. García Antón, *Multilateral Dynamics in Bilateral Settings: Back to Realpolitik*, BTR 4, at 500-502 (2019).
17. R. García Antón, *Multilateral Dynamics in Bilateral Settings: Back to Realpolitik*, BTR 4, at 502-503 (2019).

In a more recent contribution of Dr. Blum and Rita Szudoczky, the authors conclude that the MLI does not represent a shift into multilateralism because it is "merely the means through which some of the substantive provisions developed in the course of the BEPS Project are transformed into a legal act that carries out the modification of existing bilateral tax treaties, [thus] it is hard to claim any sort of value-based normative quality of the MLI."[18] They also indicate that "[a]s a result of excluding from the MLI's drafting process substantive issues that could override or go further than the measures decided upon in the framework of BEPS, the MLI was doomed to fall short of a multilateralism that goes beyond the technical aspect of the term and implies an inclusive multilateral process leading to a higher level of international tax coordination governed by value-based policy goals."[19] These authors have adhered to the idea that multilateralism exists in international tax law only if inclusiveness and participation in the decision-making process by all states on equal footing is attained;[20] or alternatively, if an agenda aimed at the elimination of global inequalities and the implementation of distributive justice is pursued.[21]

To summarize, the arguments used by the quoted authors to show that the MLI is not a multilateral treaty and thus that it does not represent a shift into multilateralism in international tax law include: (i) the application of the MLI depends on the existence of CTAs; (ii) the MLI does not reflect any value-based normative quality; (iii) not all the signatories and parties to the MLI, particularly developing countries, participated in the negotiation process of the Treaty-related BEPS measures implemented through the MLI; and (iv) the MLI does not harmonize tax treaty rules, it only modifies CTA for which purpose it provides too much flexibility to its parties.

In the following section, the concept of bilateral treaty and multilateral treaty as understood under public international law will be analyzed.

3 BILATERAL TREATY VERSUS MULTILATERAL TREATY UNDER PUBLIC INTERNATIONAL LAW

Under the Vienna Convention on the Law of Treaties (the Vienna Convention), the concept of treaties focuses on the instrument itself instead of the obligations agreed by

18. R. Szudoczky & D. Blum, *Chapter 5: Unveiling the MLI: An Analysis of Its Nature, Relationship to Covered Tax Agreements and Interpretation in Light of the Obligations of Its Parties, sec. 5.2.2.1.*, in *International and EU Tax Multilateralism: Challenges Raised by the MLI* (A.P. Dourado ed., IBFD 2020).
19. *Id.*
20. R. Szudoczky & D. Blum, *Chapter 5: Unveiling the MLI: An Analysis of Its Nature, Relationship to Covered Tax Agreements and Interpretation in Light of the Obligations of Its Parties, sec. 5.2.1.*, in *International and EU Tax Multilateralism: Challenges Raised by the MLI* (A.P. Dourado ed., IBFD 2020). This idea is based on the arguments presented in I. Mosquera Valderrama, *Legitimacy and the Making of International Tax Law: The Challenges of Multilateralism*, 7 World Tax J. 3, at 344-366 (2015).
21. R. Szudoczky & D. Blum, *Chapter 5: Unveiling the MLI: An Analysis of Its Nature, Relationship to Covered Tax Agreements and Interpretation in Light of the Obligations of Its Parties, sec. 5.2.1.*, in *International and EU Tax Multilateralism: Challenges Raised by the MLI* (A.P. Dourado ed., IBFD 2020). This idea was originally posted in R. García Antón, *The 21st Century Multilateralism in International Taxation: The Emperor's New Clothes?*, 8 World Tax J. 2, at 147-192 (2016).

the parties.[22] Article 2(1) of the Vienna Convention defines a treaty as "an international agreement concluded between States in written form and governed by international law, whether embodied in a single instrument or in two or more related instruments, whatever its particular designation" might be.

The Vienna Convention does not distinguish between bilateral or multilateral treaties,[23] neither does it establish a hierarchy between bilateral and multilateral treaties or differentiate between contractual treaties (generally associated with bilateral treaties) and law-making treaties (generally associated with multilateral treaties).[24] For this reason, bilateral treaties are simply defined as agreements between two states governed by international law,[25] and multilateral treaties are defined as agreements concluded between three or more states governed by international law.[26] Bilateral treaties and multilateral treaties do not exclude each other; in fact, they often coexist within a single regime. Among others, more advantageous bilateral treaties coexist with the World Trade Organization (WTO) agreements and more advantageous bilateral treaties coexist with the UN Framework Convention on Climate Change[27] and its Kyoto Protocol.[28,29] Thus, in some cases, the provisions of a bilateral treaty may modify the provisions of a multilateral treaty. In other cases, provisions of a multilateral treaty may modify the provisions of bilateral treaties. For example, the following multilateral treaties have all modified several bilateral treaties: the European Convention on Extradition,[30] the Agreement on Extradition between the European Union and the United States of America,[31] the Agreement on Mutual Legal Assistance between the European Union and the United States of America,[32] the European Convention on the Repatriation of Minors,[33] the International Convention for the Suppression of the Financing of Terrorism[34] and the United Nations Convention on Transparency in Treaty-based Investor-State Arbitration.[35]

22. S. Rosenne, *Bilateralism and Community Interest in the Codified Law of Treaties*, at 205, in *Transnational Law in a Changing Society—Essays in Honor of Philip C. Jessup* (W. Friedmann et al. ed., Columbia University Press 1972).
23. A. Aust, *Modern Treaty Law and Practice*, at 10 (2nd ed., Cambridge University Press 2007).
24. G. Blum, *Bilateralism, Multilateralism, and the Architecture of International Law*, at 329, 49 Harvard Int'l L. J. 2, at 329 (2008).
25. ILC, *First Report on the Law of Treaties by the Special Rapporteur G. Fitzmaurice, UN Doc. A/CN.4/101, Yearbook of the ILC Vol. II*, at 90 (1956).
26. A. Aust, *Modern Treaty Law and Practice*, at 10 (2nd ed., Cambridge University Press 2007).
27. *UN Framework Convention on Climate Change* (May 9, 1992).
28. *Kyoto Protocol* (December 11, 1997).
29. A. Thompson & D. Verdier, *Multilateralism, Bilateralism and Regime Design*, 58 Int'l Stud. Q. 1, at 24-25 (2014).
30. *European Convention on Extradition*, Article 28 (December 13, 1957).
31. *Agreement on Extradition Between the European Union and the United States of America*, Article 3 (June 25, 2003).
32. *Agreement on Mutual Legal Assistance between the European Union and the United States of America*, Article 3 (June 25, 2003).
33. *European Convention on the Repatriation of Minors*, Article 27 (May 2, 1970).
34. *International Convention for the Suppression of the Financing of Terrorism*, Article 11 (December 9, 1999).
35. *United Nations Convention on Transparency in Treaty-based Investor-State Arbitration*, Articles 1 and 2 (December 10, 2014).

Bilateral treaties allow parties to tailor their commitments to the specific needs and circumstances of their relationship, which is preferred in many cases because "[t]he legal relationship between states varies enormously depending on the states concerned."[36] The preference for bilateral treaties can be found in diverse areas such as extradition, investment, and taxation since the uniformity of obligations and rights for all states of the international community in these particular areas is ostensibly undesirable and/or inefficient.[37]

Conversely, many multilateral treaties invite the international community at large to join them. Therefore, they tend to deal with areas of interest for the international community as a whole, where, in principle, conflicts do not arise among states. In this sense, Gabriella Blum has indicated that multilateral treaties "are instinctively, though often wrongly, associated with 'higher politics'—security, human rights, environment, and trade."[38] Nonetheless, multilateral treaties do not always deal with "higher politics" such as the elimination of global inequalities and the implementation of distributive justice.[39] Many multilateral treaties in fact deal with technical matters;[40] examples of which include the Convention on Road Traffic,[41] the Agreement for Facilitating the International Circulation of Visual and Auditory Materials of an Educational, Scientific and Cultural Character,[42] and the International Agreement on Olive Oil and Table Olives.[43]

As section 3 will further explain, multilateral treaties do not always provide for obligations that are of general or community interest—i.e., *erga omnes* obligations. Multilateral treaties may—and often do—establish mutually reciprocal rights and obligations—i.e., bilateral provisions that concern only pairs of states. In this case, standardization and coordination call for the adoption of multilateral treaties over bilateral treaties.

It is up to the negotiating states of multilateral treaties to decide on the scope and content of the treaty provisions and whether the parties may commit at different levels. Some multilateral treaties provide for the possibility for the parties to commit at different levels in the text itself, for which opt-ins, alternative provisions, and opt-outs

36. J. Pauwelyn, *The Role of Public International Law in the WTO: How Far Can We Go?*, 95 The American J. Int'l L. 3, at 536 (2001).
37. G. Blum, *Bilateralism, Multilateralism, and the Architecture of International Law*, 49 Harv. Int'l L. J. 2, at 360 (2008).
38. G. Blum, *Bilateralism, Multilateralism, and the Architecture of International Law*, 49 Harv. Int'l L. J. 2, at 327 (2008).
39. For a different view, *see* R. García Antón, *The 21st Century Multilateralism in International Taxation: The Emperor's New Clothes?*, 8 World Tax J. 2, at 147-192 (2016); and R. Szudoczky & D. Blum, *Chapter 5: Unveiling the MLI: An Analysis of Its Nature, Relationship to Covered Tax Agreements and Interpretation in Light of the Obligations of Its Parties, sec. 5.2.1.*, in *International and EU Tax Multilateralism: Challenges Raised by the MLI* (A.P. Dourado ed., IBFD 2020).
40. G. Blum, *Bilateralism, Multilateralism, and the Architecture of International Law*, 49 Har. Int'l L. J. 2, at 345 (2008).
41. *Convention on Road Traffic* (November 8, 1968).
42. *Agreement For Facilitating the International Circulation of Visual and Auditory Materials of an Educational, Scientific and Cultural character with Protocol of Signature and model form of certificate provided for in Article IV of the above-mentioned Agreement 1948* (December 10, 1948).
43. *International Agreement on Olive Oil and Table Olives* (October 9, 2015).

in the form of reservations are used.[44] In any case, few multilateral treaties establish limitations to the power of the parties to make reservations and declarations regarding the interpretation and application of their provisions. Therefore, multilateral treaties do not always require that parties adopt uniform obligations.[45] It has been acknowledged in this regard that "the ability of states to pick and choose their obligations, even when ideals are multilaterally established"[46] makes the creation of a uniform body of international law a chimera.[47] On the other hand, flexibility in multilateral treaties promotes not only the participation of states with different interests and policies but also the depth of their participation.[48] If parties are not allowed to exclude the effect of certain treaty provisions, the provisions must be watered down so that all the parties accept them.[49]

Hence, what seems to characterize multilateral treaties is the existence of a conventional community interested in the application, interpretation, and faithful discharge of the treaty provisions.[50] Nonetheless, the conventional community must not include all states of the world. It is up to the negotiating states to determine which states and/or other subjects of international law may participate in the multilateral treaty.[51] Moreover, in practice, certain treaties are designed with the purpose of attaining universal participation but end up being ratified by only a few states,[52] while others are designed to regulate relations between few countries but end up attracting broader participation.[53] Consequently, at least from a public international perspective, not all multilateral treaties aspire to reach global consensus and set customary law.[54]

44. For a more detailed analysis, *see* N. Bravo, *A Multilateral Instrument for Updating the Tax Treaty Network*, at 169-244 (IBFD 2020).
45. For a different view, *see* R. García Antón, *Multilateral Dynamics in Bilateral Settings: Back to Realpolitik*, 490-491 BTR 4, at 490 (2019); D. Blum, *The Relationship Between the OECD Multilateral Instrument and Covered Tax Agreements: Multilateralism and the Interpretation of the MLI*, 72 Bull. Intl. Taxn. 3, at 135 (2018); and, W. Haslehner, *A Multilateral Interpretation of the MLI (and Covered Tax Agreements)?*, 74 Bull. Intl. Taxn. 4/5, at 228 (2020).
46. G. Blum, *Bilateralism, Multilateralism, and the Architecture of International Law*, 49 Harv. Int'l L. J. 2, at 339 (2008).
47. *Id.*, at 339.
48. E. Swaine, *Reserving*, 31 The Yale J. Int'l L. 2, at 331 (2006).
49. C. Walter, *Formulation of Reservations*, at 240, in *Vienna Convention on the Law of Treaties: A Commentary* (O. Dörr & K. Schmalenbach ed., Springer Verlag 2012).
50. *See* S. Rosenne, *Bilateralism and Community Interest in the Codified Law of Treaties*, at 222, in *Transnational Law in a Changing Society—Essays in Honor of Philip C. Jessup* (W. Friedmann et al. ed., Columbia University Press 1972).
51. A. Aust, *Modern Treaty Law and Practice*, at 94 (2nd ed., Cambridge University Press 2007). In this regard, the MLI expressly accepts in its Article 27 the participation of non-state jurisdictions, such as Guernsey, Hong Kong, the Isle of Man and Jersey.
52. G. Blum reports as examples of multilateral treaties of interest of the international community as a whole that have been ratified by relative few countries the following ones: the International Convention on the Protection of the Rights of All Migrant Workers and Members of their Families which only has 37 parties; the Convention on the Reduction of Statelessness which only has 34 parties and the Convention for the Suppression of the Traffic in Persons and of the Exploitation of the Prostitution of Others which only has 79 parties. G. Blum, *Bilateralism, Multilateralism, and the Architecture of International Law*, 49 Harv. Int'l L. J. 2, at 345-356 (2008).
53. *See* the reference to the GATT/ WTO Agreements below in this section.
54. For a different view, *see* R. García Antón, *Multilateral Dynamics in Bilateral Settings: Back to Realpolitik*, at 484 and 490-495, BTR 4 (2019).

In the same spirit, all states are not obligated to participate in the negotiations of multilateral treaties[55] nor are all states that participated in the negotiations required to ratify them.[56] Moreover, negotiations of multilateral treaties are generally led by a small group of states moved by their resources or greater interests, who enlist the cooperation of other states.[57] The WTO/General Agreement on Tariffs and Trade (GATT) agreements are examples of this. This regime started with a membership of only 23 states[58] and its application was limited in time, i.e. only until the entrance into force of the International Trade Organization (ITO), a UN specialized agency. Nonetheless, as the ITO never entered into force, GATT turned into a de facto international organization. As of 2016, the WTO has 164 members.[59] Many of the issues contained in the WTO agreements were negotiated in previous trade negotiations under GATT, which means that not all the current members of the WTO negotiated each of the treaty provisions of the WTO agreements.

It is common for states to participate in the negotiations of multilateral treaties to protect their interests and decide at a later stage whether to ratify it or not. For example, the United States has taken recourse to this practice in different areas of international law and human rights, with the negotiations of the American Convention on Human Rights,[60] the Convention on the Elimination of All Forms of Discrimination Against Women,[61] and the Convention on the Rights of the Child;[62] in environmental law, with the negotiations of the Kyoto Protocol and the Rio Convention on Biological Diversity;[63] and, in international tax law, with the MLI.[64] This practice has been established not only by developed countries but also by less developed economies. For example,

55. Accession to multilateral treaties is common and is regulated in Article 15 of the Vienna Convention. Through accession, a state agrees to be bound by a treaty even if it did not participate in its negotiations. As A. Aust reports the Council of Europe National Minorities Protection Framework Convention is an example of a multilateral treaty in which non-members of the referred Council may be invited to accede, i.e., non-members of the Council of Europe may become parties to the Convention only after it had entered into force. *See* A. Aust, *Modern Treaty Law and Practice*, at 112 (2nd ed., Cambridge University Press 2007).
56. For a different view, *see* R. Szudoczky & D. Blum, *Chapter 5: Unveiling the MLI: An Analysis of Its Nature, Relationship to Covered Tax Agreements and Interpretation in Light of the Obligations of Its Parties, sec. 5.2.1.*, in *International and EU Tax Multilateralism: Challenges Raised by the MLI* (A.P. Dourado eds., IBFD 2020).
57. A. Thompson and D. Verdier, *Multilateralism, Bilateralism and Regime Design*, 58 Int'l Stud. Q. 1 (2014), p. 15.
58. *See Press Brief of the Fiftieth Anniversary of the Multilateral Trading System*, available at https://www.wto.org/english/thewto_e/minist_e/min96_e/chrono.htm (accessed on April 1, 2021).
59. https://www.wto.org/english/thewto_e/whatis_e/tif_e/org6_e.htm (accessed on April 1, 2021).
60. American Convention on Human Rights (November 22, 1969).
61. Convention on the Elimination of All Forms of Discrimination Against Women (December 18, 1979).
62. Convention on the Rights of the Child (November 20, 1989).
63. Rio Convention on Biological Diversity (June 5, 1992).
64. The United States participated in the ad hoc Group but abandoned the negotiations before the MLI was concluded. Afterwards, officials formally reported that the United States does not intend to ratify the MLI.

Venezuela actively participated in the negotiations of the Vienna Convention[65] but decided not to ratify it since the doctrine of estoppel enshrined in Article 45 of this Convention goes against Venezuela's interests in the territorial dispute with Guyana over the Essequibo Region. Before that, however, the Delegation of Venezuela proposed a modification to Article 45 of the Vienna Convention to safeguard the country's interests. Most Latin American countries aligned with Venezuela. Nonetheless, the Venezuelan proposal was finally rejected.[66]

Summarizing the arguments provided in this section, multilateral treaties do not always require parties to adopt uniform obligations. In fact, flexibility is allowed in most multilateral treaties to promote participation and the depth of the parties' participation. Many multilateral treaties deal with technical matters rather than "higher politics" such as the elimination of global inequalities and the implementation of distributive justice. The negotiations of multilateral treaties do not need to involve the participation of all the parties and signatories, nor do all states participating in the negotiations of multilateral treaties need to ratify them. Moreover, bilateral and multilateral treaties often coexist within a single regime.

To further understand the concept of multilateral treaties, an in-depth analysis of the types of obligations that may be provided from them is valuable. This analysis will be provided in the following section from the perspectives of the law of treaties and the law of state responsibility, as in both subfields of public international law this matter has been subjected to year-long discussions. This analysis will show that the nature of the treaty itself must not be confused with the nature of the provisions it provides.

4 MULTILATERAL TREATY OBLIGATIONS

4.1 The Law of Treaties

The typology of obligations that can be found in multilateral treaties was likely discussed for the first time in the postwar era when the International Court of Justice (ICJ) examined the possibility to formulate reservations to the provisions of the Genocide Convention.[67] Based on the object and purpose of the mentioned Convention, which is humanitarian—i.e., to condemn and punish genocide as a crime –the ICJ stated in its Advisory Opinion:

> [t]he contracting states do not have any interest of their own; they merely have, one and all, a common interest, namely, the accomplishment of those high purposes which are the *raison d'etre of the convention.* Consequently, in a convention of this type one cannot speak of individual advantages to states, or of

65. The representative of Venezuela was elected as one of the Vice-President of the United Nations Conference on the Law of Treaties. *See* Final Act of the United Nations Conference on the Law of Treaties and Annexes thereto, available at https://link.springer.com/content/pdf/bbm%3A978-3-662-55160-8%2F1.pdf (accessed on June 23, 2021).
66. The Venezuelan proposal was rejected by 47 votes, approved by only 20 and 37 abstentions. For more details, *see* https://codeiv.org/el-stoppel/ (accessed on March 30, 2021).
67. *Convention on the Prevention and Punishment of the Crime of Genocide* (December 9, 1958).

> the maintenance of a perfect contractual balance between rights and duties. The high ideals which inspired the convention provide, by virtue of the common will of the parties, the foundation and measure of all its provisions.[68]

This way, the ICJ recognized that some multilateral treaties might contain obligations of general or community interest; that is, obligations with an *erga omnes* nature. Yet, other multilateral treaties provide for mutually reciprocal rights and obligations between the parties, and, therefore, their provisions have a bilateral nature.

The need to distinguish between different types of multilateral treaty obligations was restated by Sir Gerald Fitzmaurice in his Second[69] and Third Reports on the Law of Treaties.[70] He classified multilateral treaty obligations into three types. First, he referred to obligations that are "synallagmatic"; that is, mutual and reciprocal between two parties to a multilateral treaty. He called them reciprocal obligations and gave as an example the obligations provided in the Vienna Convention on Diplomatic Relations.[71] A vast number of multilateral treaties are composed of "bundles of bilateral rights and obligations merely tied together,"[72] which seems to be a consequence of the bilateralist features of international law. Indeed, due to the principle of sovereign equality of states[73] and the impossibility to create rights and obligations for third states without their consent,[74] a state usually engages to undertake certain conducts vis-à-vis another state that is ready to accept the same rights and obligations.

Second, he referred to obligations that performance does not depend on the corresponding performance of the rest of the parties, but rather are a duty towards the whole world. The Special Rapporteur named these obligations "integral" and gave as an example the obligations contained in a treaty on human rights, a treaty providing for standard working conditions or for standards of safety at sea. Some scholars criticized that Sir Fitzmaurice had defined integral obligations as duties towards the "whole world" because not all integral obligations are relevant to the international community as a whole. Integral obligations are relevant only to the parties to the treaty; for example, solely the parties to a regional treaty regarding human rights would, in principle, be interested in the fulfillment of the multilateral obligations provided therein.[75] Consequently, according to these scholars, a more suitable description of integral obligations would be those obligations which performance does not depend on

68. *Reservations to the Convention on Genocide* (Advisory Opinion), at 23, ICJ Report 15 (1951).
69. *Second Report on the Law of Treaties by the Special Rapporteur G. Fitzmaurice, UN doc. A/CN.4/107*, YILC Vol. II (1957), at 53-54.
70. *Third Report on the Law of Treaties by the Special Rapporteur G. Fitzmaurice, UN doc. A/CN.4/115*, YILC Vol. II (1958), at 27-28.
71. *Vienna Convention on Diplomatic Relations* (April 18, 1961).
72. B. Simma, *Bilateralism and Community Interest in the Law of state Responsibility*, at 822, in *International Law at a Time of Perplexity: Essays in Honour of Shabtai Rosenne* (Y. Dinstein & M. Tabory eds., Martinus Nijhoff Publishers 1989).
73. This principle is enshrined in Article 2(1) of the *Charter of the United Nations* (June 26, 1945).
74. This principle is known as the "*pacta tertiis nec nocent nec prosunt*" and is enshrined in Article 34 of the Vienna Convention.
75. *See* L.A. Sicilianos, *The Classification of Obligations and the Multilateral Dimension of the Relations of International Responsibility*, at 1136, 13 EJIL 5 (2002); and, P. Dupuy, *A General Stocktaking of the Connections Between the Multilateral Dimension of Obligations and Codification of the Law of Responsibility*, at 1072, 13 EJIL 5 (2002).

the corresponding performance of the rest of the parties, but rather constitutes a duty towards the conventional community.[76]

Finally, Sir Fitzmaurice referred to obligations which performance depends on the corresponding performance of the same obligation by the rest of the parties. He called these obligations "interdependent" and gave as an example a treaty on disarmament, as the obligation of a party to disarm dependents in turn on the disarmament of all the other parties to the multilateral treaty. Thus, the failure of a party to perform its interdependent obligations would threaten the regime created by the treaty in respect of all the other parties.[77] In interdependent obligations, reciprocity is not owed to one treaty partner only, but to all parties to the multilateral treaty. It can be considered that Sir Fitzmaurice was the creator of the interdependent obligations concept since the ICJ in its Advisory Opinion in the Genocide Convention case apparently only referred to collective obligations; that is integral obligations in the Special Rapporteur's typology of multilateral treaty obligations, and bilateral obligations, or reciprocal obligations in the Special Rapporteur's typology of multilateral treaty obligations.

According to Sir Fitzmaurice, the distinction between multilateral treaty obligations was relevant for the termination or suspension of treaties as a consequence of a "fundamental breach" by one of the parties. In his opinion, not all types of multilateral treaties could be terminated or suspended as a consequence of a "fundamental breach." In some cases, the injured party together with the rest of the parties—whether also affected or not—should continue to fulfill their treaty obligations. These cases involved multilateral treaties that provide for integral obligations. As already mentioned, the duty to fulfill integral obligations does not depend on the performance of the rest of the parties to the treaty, but it is rather a duty towards the whole world—or at least towards the conventional community. Therefore, a "fundamental breach" of integral obligations provided for in multilateral treaties could not give the right to the parties to terminate or suspend the whole treaty.[78] Conversely, the injured party and the rest of the parties should still fulfill their treaty obligations not only among themselves but also in connection with the citizens of the defaulting party, because in integral obligations "the beneficiary of the right is an individual, independent of ties of

76. However, if integral obligations provided in multilateral treaties enshrined peremptory norms of general international law or *jus cogens*, as it is the example of human rights obligations contained in a regional treaty, not only the conventional community but actually the international community as a whole will be interested in the fulfilment of the parties' obligations. In this case, the conventional community would be interested in the performance of the treaty obligations while other countries would be interested in the performance of *jus cogens* obligations. The difference lies in the source of the obligation, i.e., a treaty or a peremptory norm of general international law; however, the duty will be the same for the obliged state.
77. *Second Report on the Law of Treaties by the Special Rapporteur G. Fitzmaurice, UN doc. A/CN.4/107,* YILC Vol. II (1957), at 54.
78. *Second Report on the Law of Treaties by the Special Rapporteur G. Fitzmaurice, UN doc. A/CN.4/107,* YILC Vol. II (1957), at 53.

nationality."[79] That is, if a state breaches its obligations under the Genocide Convention, the rest of the parties should continue to apply the terms of this Convention to their own citizens and to the citizens of that state.[80]

Sir Fitzmaurice also found that the distinction between multilateral treaty obligations was relevant for resolving conflicts of treaties. For him, if a multilateral treaty provided for interdependent or integral obligations, any subsequent treaties concluded by two or more of the parties that conflict directly with the earlier treaty should be regarded null and void.[81] In contrast, if a multilateral treaty provided for reciprocal obligations, any subsequent treaties concluded by identical parties should prevail, since the later treaty should be regarded as modifying or abrogating the earlier one.[82]

4.2 The Law of State Responsibility

In the Barcelona Traction case, the ICJ came back to the study of the different types of obligations in international law. The Court indicated that: "an essential distinction should be drawn between the obligations of a state towards the international community as a whole, and those arising vis-à-vis another state in the field of diplomatic protection. By their very nature the former are the concern of all states. In view of the importance of the rights involved, all states can be held to have a legal interest in their protection; they are obligations erga omnes."[83] As examples of obligations *erga omnes*, the ICJ listed those banning acts of aggression and genocide and those recognizing human rights, as the prohibition of slavery and discrimination.[84]

In the mentioned case, the ICJ confirmed the importance of distinguishing between types of obligations in international law, as they lead to different legal consequences. The ICJ analysis focused on who can invoke the responsibility of a state that has infringed its international obligations. Based on the nature of the obligations breached, the responsibility of the defaulting state "is engaged not only in regard to the state which was the direct victim of the breach: [but] it is also engaged in regard to all the other members of the international community ...,"[85] each of which can invoke the responsibility of the defaulting state. With the notion of obligations *erga omnes* contained in the Barcelona Traction dictum, the ICJ gave legal expression to the right of each and every state to defend the interests of the international community.

79. P. Dupuy, *A General Stocktaking of the Connections between the Multilateral Dimension of Obligations and Codification of the Law of Responsibility,* at 1070, 13 EJIL 5 (2002).
80. *Second Report on the Law of Treaties by the Special Rapporteur G. Fitzmaurice, UN doc. A/CN.4/107,* YILC Vol. II (1957), at 54.
81. *Third Report on the Law of Treaties by the Special Rapporteur G. Fitzmaurice, UN doc. A/CN.4/115,* YILC Vol. II (1958), at 27-28.
82. *Third Report on the Law of Treaties by the Special Rapporteur G. Fitzmaurice, UN doc. A/CN.4/115,* YILC Vol. II (1958), at 27.
83. *Case concerning Barcelona Traction, Light and Power Company, Limited (Belgium v. Spain)* at paras 33-35 ICJ Report (1970).
84. *Id.*, at para. 34.
85. *Fifth Report on State Responsibility by the Special Rapporteur R. Ago, UN doc. A/CN.4/SER.A/1976Add 1 part 1,* YILC Vol. II (1976), at 99.

The distinction between bilateral reciprocal obligations, integral obligations, and interdependent obligations in multilateral treaties also influenced the drafting of the ILC Articles on State Responsibility for Internationally Wrongful Acts.[86] Numerous scholars in public international law have written about the classification of obligations in multilateral treaties and its relevance for the ILC Articles on State Responsibility, even before the ILC Articles gained their current shape. Among them, Bruno Simma with his article "Bilateralism and Community Interest in the Law of State Responsibility"[87] has received special attention.

In his famous article, Professor Simma recognized that international law obligations traditionally compel a state to undertake certain conducts vis-à-vis other states. Inasmuch as that international law obligations engage the performance of pairs of states, only the injured state would be interested in: (i) invoking the responsibility of the defaulting state due to the damages caused by the breach of its obligations; and (ii) forcing a return to legality.[88] Multilateral treaties often maintain this bilateral feature, as they establish "bundles of bilateral rights and obligations" characterized by reciprocity between pairs of parties. Consequently, although they derived from a multilateral treaty, many relations of responsibility are bilateral or bilateralizable and therefore also exclusively exist between a defaulting party and an injured party. However, as not all the obligations contained in multilateral treaties can be split into bundles of bilateral relations, other solutions are needed. Because the performance of integral and interdependent obligations is due to all parties to a multilateral treaty, all of them should be allowed to invoke the state responsibility of a party that has infringed an integral or interdependent obligation.[89]

The ILC Articles on State Responsibility adopted in 2001, which have become almost as authoritative as the Vienna Convention,[90] have adopted Professor Simma's approach referred above. In contrast to the Vienna Convention where only traces can be found, the ILC Articles on State Responsibility provide for the distinction between types of obligations in multilateral treaties in express terms.[91] The reason why the ILC Articles on State Responsibility clearly set the distinction between obligations in

86. *See* M. Spinedi, *From One Codification to Another: Bilateralism and Multilateralism in the Genesis of the Codification of the Law of Treaties and the Law of States Responsibility*, at 1123-1123, 13 EJIL 5 (2002), C. Dominicé, *The International Responsibility of States for Breach of Multilateral Obligations*, at 359, 10 EJIL 2 (1999), P. Dupuy, *A General Stocktaking of the Connections Between the Multilateral Dimension of Obligations and Codification of the Law of Responsibility*, at 1059 and 1071-1072, 13 EJIL 5 (2002); and, L.A. Sicilianos, *The Classification of Obligations and the Multilateral Dimension of the Relations of International Responsibility*, at 1133, 13 EJIL 5 (2002).
87. B. Simma, *Bilateralism and Community Interest in the Law of State Responsibility*, at 821-844, in *International Law at a Time of Perplexity: Essays in Honour of Shabtai Rosenne* (Y. Dinstein & M. Tabory eds., Martinus Nijhoff Publishers 1989).
88. *Id.*, at 821.
89. *Id.*, at 830-831.
90. A. Paulus, *Reciprocity Revisited*, at 119, in *From Bilateralism to Community Interest –Essays in Honour of Judge Bruno Simma* (U. Fastenrath et al. eds., Oxford University Press 2011).
91. J. Pauwelyn, *A Typology of Multilateral Treaty Obligations: Are WTO Obligations Bilateral or Collective in Nature?*, at 916, 14 EJIL 5 (2003).

multilateral treaties is because it serves as a "functional scheme"[92] to determine which parties may have the right to invoke the responsibility of a defaulting party.

The classification set in the ILC Articles on State Responsibility includes bilateral or bilateralizable obligations, which corresponds to the reciprocal obligations proposed by Sir Fitzmaurice. They are defined as obligations individually owed to one particular party to the multilateral treaty.[93] As the infringement of a bilateral or bilateralizable obligation can only injure the interest of one of the parties involved in the bilateral relation, this party is the only one entitled to invoke the state responsibility of the defaulting party.[94] Then, the ILC Articles on State Responsibility refer to collective obligations, which encompass both the integral obligations and the interdependent obligations identified by Sir Fitzmaurice. The description of collective obligations given by the ILC[95] is that of obligations "that apply between more than two states and whose performance in the given case is not owed to one state individually, but to a group of states or even the international community as a whole."[96] Thus, depending on the case, any of the parties to the multilateral treaty or any state of the international community (even if not a party to the applicable multilateral treaty) may be entitled to invoke the state responsibility of the defaulting party in such a case.

To summarize, multilateral treaties can provide for different types of obligations. The distinction is widely accepted. Particularly relevant is the fact that multilateral treaties can provide for bilateral obligations that create mutual reciprocal benefits and concessions between two parties to the treaty. It is commonly said that this type of multilateral treaties provides for bundles or dyads of bilateral obligations.[97] In this type of multilateral treaties, the "*particular interest of each party in seeing that its own rights under the treaty were respected*"[98] emerges as the main characteristic.

Based on the analysis contained in sections 2 and 3, the nature of the MLI and its substantive provisions will be discussed in the following section. The purpose of section 4 is to evaluate whether the MLI is a multilateral treaty or not. If the MLI is not a multilateral treaty, but rather a bilateral or hybrid instrument as argued by the scholars quoted in section 1, it may be concluded that a shift into multilateralism has not taken place in international tax law.

92. L.A. Sicilianos, *The Classification of Obligations and the Multilateral Dimension of the Relations of International Responsibility*, at 1133, 13 EJIL 5 (2002).
93. *Report of the ILC of Its 53rd Session, General Assembly, Official Records, 56th Session, Supplement No. 10 (A/56/10)*, Chapter IV, at 297.
94. *See Articles on Responsibility of states for Internationally Wrongful Acts*, YILC Vol. II (2001), Article 42(a).
95. *See Id*, Articles 42(b) and 48.
96. *Report of the ILC of Its 53rd Session, General Assembly, Official Records, 56th Session, Supplement No. 10 (A/56/10)*, Chapter IV, at 299.
97. *See, e.g.*, C. Dominicé, *The International Responsibility of States for Breach of Multilateral Obligations*, at 354, 10 EJIL 2 (1999); and, L.A. Sicilianos, *The Classification of Obligations and the Multilateral Dimension of the Relations of International Responsibility*, at 1133, 13 EJIL 5 (2002).
98. Summary records of the ILC on the second part of its seventeenth session, UN doc. A/CN.4/183 and Add.1-4, A/CN.4/L.107, YILC Vol. I, Part I (1966), at 62.

5 THE NATURE OF THE MLI AND ITS SUBSTANTIVE PROVISIONS[99]

5.1 The Nature of the MLI

The MLI builds on the current tax treaty network. The scope of the MLI is established in Article 1 "*This Convention modifies all Covered Tax Agreements as defined in subparagraph a) of paragraph 1 of Article 2 (Interpretation of Terms).*" The MLI and the CTAs need to be applied and interpreted side-by-side. Thus, the application of the MLI does depend on the existence of CTAs. Nevertheless, this feature of the MLI does not influence its nature. As demonstrated in section 2, bilateral treaties and multilateral treaties do not exclude each other, but often coexist within a single regime.

The modifying nature of the MLI explains why it builds on the current tax treaty network. In addition, the MLI is a partial convention. It exclusively implements measures to eliminate BEPS as agreed in the course of the BEPS Project. More controversial issues in international tax law, such as provisions with major distributive impact on the economies of states—i.e., allocation of income to the state of source or the state of residence—withholding rates on passive income and the exemption of income subject to exclusive taxation by the state of source are not addressed in the MLI.[100] This characteristic of the MLI has made it possible for developed and less developed countries to conclude the MLI and agree to implement uniform tax treaty-related BEPS rules across the tax treaty network.

Indeed, this feature of the MLI allows its parties to continue taking into account their investment flows with different treaty partners to establish appropriate reciprocal rules in their bilateral tax treaties. In this form, the MLI avoids threatening the principle of reciprocity and preserves the tax sovereignty of its parties, overcoming the two main barriers to the conclusion of a worldwide multilateral tax treaty in the past.

As indicated by some of the authors referred to in section 1, the MLI does not aim to eliminate global inequalities and implement distributive justice. Thus, the MLI does not reflect a value-based normative quality. However, as shown in section 3, a treaty does not need to deal with "higher politics" for qualifying as a multilateral treaty. It is enough that the parties to the multilateral treaty share a common interest that encourages them to agree on standard and/or coordinated rules.

The parties to the MLI share a common interest: the elimination of BEPS practices through the implementation of the treaty-related BEPS measures. This common

99. This section includes extracts previously published in N. Bravo, *A Multilateral Instrument for Updating the Tax Treaty Network* (IBFD 2020); and, N. Bravo, *Future Changes to Covered Tax Agreements and of the Multilateral Convention to Implement Tax Treaty Related Measures to Prevent BEPS*, at 237-264, in *The OECD Multilateral Instrument for Tax Treaties—Analysis and Effects* (M. Lang et al. eds., Kluwer Law International 2018).

100. D. Broekhuijsen has previously argued that multilateral initiatives may be widespread accepted if provisions dealing with distributional effects are avoided. *See* D. Broekhuijsen, *A Multilateral Tax Treaty, Designing an Instrument to Modernise International Tax Law*, at 82-83 (Proefschrift, Universiteit Leiden 2017); and, D. Broekhuijsen & H. Vording, *The Multilateral Tax Instrument: How to Avoid a Stalemate On Distributional Issues?*, at 39-61, BTR 1 (2016).

interest is recognized in the preamble of the instrument, which includes the following statements:

> Conscious of the need to ensure swift, co-ordinated and consistent implementation of the treaty-related BEPS measures in a multilateral context; ...
>
> Recognising the need for an effective mechanism to implement agreed changes in a synchronised and efficient manner across the network of existing agreements for the avoidance of double taxation on income without the need to bilaterally renegotiate each such agreement; ... .

Hence, the MLI creates a multilateral context for implementing uniform international tax rules across the tax treaty network. Moreover, the parties to the MLI are interested in the application, interpretation and faithful discharge of the instrument's provisions.

As posited in some of the summarized literature in section 1, it is true that all the provisions of the MLI, including the ones that establish minimum standards, allow parties to make reservations to exclude part of or an entire article. It is also true that reservations limit the harmonization and/or coordination that may be achieved with the MLI. Reservations change the scope of application of the treaty provisions for the reserving state and the party that accepts the reservation—the accepting state—and for the reserving state and the party that opposes the reservation—the objecting state. Nonetheless, as discussed in section 2, reservations are a common feature of multilateral treaties. Moreover, in theory, all of the provisions of a multilateral treaty may be subject to reservations without affecting the nature of the treaty. In this sense, Christian Tomuschat indicated in 1967:

> [I]t is imaginable, at least in theory, that all provisions of a treaty, without exception, are declared subject to reservations. This second hypothesis, however, is most improbable, and as far as can be seen, there is not a single example for such a reservation clause admitting all possible unilateral modifications of a treaty ....[101]

The MLI is one of those improbable examples mentioned by Professor Tomuschat, as all of its substantive provisions are subject to reservations. Nonetheless, reservations are not an unlimited exercise in the MLI. The MLI lists the only reservations that parties and signatories can make and precludes them from making any other reservations not listed therein.[102] Although parties to the MLI can commit to differing extents by making reservations, they can only make the reservations that were acceptable to the treaty makers from an international tax policy perspective in the fight against BEPS. If parties avail themselves of the flexibility provided by the treaty makers and reserve the application of some of the rules of the MLI, then uniform rules will still be implemented across the tax treaty network, even though not all of the parties will adopt all of the rules of the instrument. This already results in uniformity.

101. C. Tomuschat, *Admissibility and Legal Effects of Reservation to Multilateral Treaties: Comments on Arts. 16 and 17 of the ILC's 1966 Draft Articles on the Law of Treaties*, at 473, 27 ZaöRV (1967).
102. Article 28(1) of the MLI.

Moreover, despite the different levels of commitment that parties may adhere to through the MLI, coordination in applying the treaty-related BEPS measures can be attained. The clearest example of the coordinating effect that may be achieved with the MLI is found in the provisions that set out the minimum standards, as parties can reserve their application only when their CTAs already meet these standards or if they commit to meeting them in an alternative manner. By April 2021, all the 95 signatories and parties to the MLI have accepted the application of the PPT rule in order to fulfill the minimum standard on treaty abuse.[103] Therefore, even though flexibility is provided in the text of the MLI, in practice its parties have accepted the application of the PPT rule creating a high degree of uniformity across the tax treaty network. Furthermore, even though not all signatories and parties to the MLI participated in the negotiation process of the treaty-related BEPS measures, some of this output has been accepted by both developed and less developed economies alike. The wide acceptance of the PPT rule of the MLI has made some authors recently claim that the PPT rule may be seen as a rule of customary international tax law.[104]

The coordinating effect of the MLI is even more obvious if it is acknowledged that the reservations apply to all the CTAs of a reserving state.[105] Thus, when parties decide on their reservations, they must make decisions based on tax policy rather than their economic interests vis-à-vis other parties to a CTA. This feature of the reservations contributes to the creation of an international tax playing field and avoids the creation of inadmissible disparities, which could be used for BEPS practices. Opt-ins and alternative provisions established in the MLI, in general, also apply to all of the CTAs of the party that declares to opt into those provisions. The coordinated implementation of the treaty-related BEPS measures can diminish the competitive advantages and disadvantages derived from the use of certain tax treaties and, consequently, diminish treaty-shopping and tax arbitrage opportunities[106] as well as unintended cases of double non-taxation.

The design of the opt-ins, alternative provisions, and opt-outs in the form of reservations in the MLI shows that the common interest of its parties in eliminating BEPS is protected. The common interest of its parties is also protected by other features of the MLI, such as limitations on producing late reservations, which are expressly prohibited in Article 28(5) of the MLI. The only situations in which making late reservations is allowed under the MLI is when a new CTA is included under the scope of the MLI and that CTA is the first one to fall under a reservation and when a party chooses to apply the mandatory binding arbitration after it has become a party to the MLI. Except for these particular cases, reservations may be made only at the time of the signature of the instrument or at the time of the deposit of the instrument of ratification,

103. *See MLI Database—Matrix of Options and Reservations*, available at https://www.oecd.org/tax/treaties/mli-database-matrix-options-and-reservations.htm (accessed on April 1, 2021).
104. D. Broekhuijsen & I. Mosquera Valderrama, *Revisiting the Case of Customary International Tax Law*, at 98-102, Int'l Community L. Rev. 23 (2021).
105. OECD, *Explanatory Statement to the MLI*, para. 14 (2016).
106. M. Helminen, *The Nordic Multilateral Tax Treaty as a Model for a Multilateral EU Tax Treaty*, at 6 (IBFD 2014).

acceptance, or approval.[107] Making late reservations seems to be expressly prohibited in the MLI to eliminate the possibility for parties to restrict their commitment to avoiding BEPS practices after the ratification and entry of the instrument into force.

Additionally, the common interest of the parties is protected by the possibility of withdrawing or replacing reservations at any time, which ensures that parties may implement more of the treaty-related BEPS measures provided in the MLI in the future. As the purpose of a reservation is the exclusion or modification of the legal effects of the provision of a multilateral treaty in its application to the party that makes it, when a party withdraws a reservation, it accepts the entire application of the treaty provision to which the reservation relates.[108] Moreover, when a party replaces a reservation, it limits the legal effects of the reservation and accepts the partial application of the treaty provision.

In the context of the MLI, when Article 28(9) permits the withdrawal and replacement of reservations at any time,[109] it aims that the party that withdraws or replaces the reservation expands its commitment to prevent BEPS practices. This explains why Article 28(9) establishes a condition that for the replacement of a reservation, the new reservation must have a more limited scope. If the new reservation were to have a broader scope, i.e., encourages BEPS, the new reservation would not be permitted. Once a party has committed to combat BEPS, whether through the implementation of provisions that are minimum standards or through the implementation of provisions that are optional, the MLI does not allow this party to diminish the scope of its commitments by replacing its reservations.[110]

The limited effects assigned to a withdrawal from the MLI is another measure implemented in the instrument to protect the common interest of its parties. Under Article 37 of the MLI, parties may withdraw from the MLI at any time by means of a notification addressed to the depositary. However, the provisions of the CTAs as modified through the MLI will remain modified after the withdrawal becomes effective.[111] Article 37 of the MLI establishes a different result than the residual rules of the

107. Article 28(5) of the MLI establishes that "*Reservations shall be made at the time of signature or when depositing the instrument of ratification, acceptance or approval, subject to the provisions of paragraphs 2, 6 and 9 of this Article, and paragraph 5 of Article 29 (Notifications). However, for a Party which chooses under Article 18 (Choice to Apply Part VI) to apply Part VI (Arbitration) after it has become a Party to this Convention, reservations described in subparagraphs p), q), r) and s) of paragraph 1 of this Article shall be made at the same time as that Party's notification to the Depositary pursuant to Article 18 (Choice to Apply Part VI).*"

108. ILC, *Guide to Practice on Reservations to Treaties*, at 11, Yearbook of the International Law Commission, 2011 Vol. II, Part Two, Guideline 2.5.7.

109. Article 28(9) of the MLI provides that "*Any Party which has made a reservation in accordance with paragraph 1 or 2 may at any time withdraw it or replace it with a more limited reservation by means of a notification addressed to the Depositary. Such Party shall make any additional notifications pursuant to paragraph 6 of Article 29 (Notifications) which may be required as a result of the withdrawal or replacement of the reservation … .*"

110. ILC, *Guide to Practice on Reservations to Treaties*, at 11, Yearbook of the International Law Commission, 2011 Vol. II, Part Two, Guideline 2.5.10.

111. Under Article 37 of the MLI: "*1. Any Party may, at any time, withdraw from this Convention by means of a notification addressed to the Depositary. 2. Withdrawal pursuant to paragraph 1 shall become effective on the date of receipt of the notification by the Depositary. In cases where this Convention has entered into force with respect to all Contracting Jurisdictions to a Covered*

Vienna Convention dealing with the withdrawal from a treaty.[112] Under the residual rules of the Vienna Convention,[113] when a party withdraws from a treaty, it is liberated from its obligation to execute the treaty towards the rest of the parties, while the rest of the parties remain bound by the treaty in their mutual relations.[114] As the MLI provides for a special rule dealing with the withdrawal from this instrument, the effects derived from the rules of the Vienna Convention cannot apply.

According to the Explanatory Statement, the purpose of Article 37 of the MLI is to prevent a party to the MLI from unilaterally reversing its effects and thereby producing unilateral changes to a CTA already modified through the MLI.[115] Nonetheless, Article 37 of the MLI also contributes to preserving the multilateral context created with the purpose of combating BEPS practices. Once the tax treaty-related BEPS project output is implemented in the CTAs of a party, the treaty provisions as modified through the MLI remain in place, even if that party decides to detach from the MLI. For the parties, it is not possible to contract out from the commitment to combat BEPS practices solely by withdrawing from the instrument. They would also need to renegotiate all the modified treaties. This might prove difficult if their treaty partners would still be parties to the MLI and the BEPS Inclusive Framework and as such politically committed to tackling BEPS.

Additionally, common and uniform interpretation of the MLI provisions can be achieved in practice because the MLI establishes the possibility of convening a conference of the parties in Article 31. According to the article, the conference of the parties has the purpose of making decisions or exercising the functions that may be required under the provisions of the instrument. In particular, Article 32(2) of the MLI

Tax Agreement before the date on which a Party's withdrawal becomes effective, that Covered Tax Agreement shall remain as modified by this Convention."

112. Scholars acknowledge that multilateral treaties may provide that the withdrawal of a party does not release it from its treaty obligations. *See, e.g.*, M. Villiger, *Commentary on the 1969 Vienna Convention on the Law of Treaties*, at 874 (Martinus Nijhoff Publishers 2009) ("In the case of multilateral treaties, the treaty itself may regulate the consequences of termination, i.e., if one party denounces or withdraws from the treaty, it will not be released from its obligations.")

    Also, Ascensio deals with this matter ("Certain treaties furthermore foresee the extension of certain effects of the treaty beyond the date at which it ends for the denouncing party. The ILC travaux cite the example of Article XIX of the Convention on the Liability of Operators of Nuclear Ships of May 25, 1962, under which responsibility for a nuclear incident will continue for a certain time after the termination of the Convention for ships the operation of which was licensed while the Convention was in force. The denunciation provision of the Geneva Conventions (Article 63/62/142/158) also illustrates this case; it specifies that if the denouncing party is a state involved in a conflict, the denunciation 'shall not take effect until peace has been concluded, and until after the operations connected with release and repatriation of the persons protected by the presentation have been terminated.'."). H. Ascensio, *Article 70 Consequences of the Termination of a Treaty*, at 1589, in *The Vienna Conventions on the Law of Treaties: A Commentary* (O. Corten & P. Klein eds., Oxford University Press 2011).
113. Articles 54, 56 and 70 of the Vienna Convention.
114. V. Chapaux, *Article 54 Termination of or Withdrawal from a Treaty under Its Provisions or by Consent of the Parties*, at 1242, *The Vienna Conventions on the Law of Treaties: A Commentary* (O. Corten & P. Klein eds., Oxford University Press 2011); and, M. Villiger, *Commentary on the 1969 Vienna Convention on the Law of Treaties*, at 68 and 874 (Martinus Nijhoff Publishers 2009).
115. OECD, *Explanatory Statement to the MLI*, para. 353 (2016).

establishes that the conference of the parties may be convened to resolve any questions that arise as to the interpretation or implementation of the instrument. The possibility of convening a conference of the parties for interpretative purposes is evidence that the parties to the MLI have an interest in producing common and uniform interpretations of the provisions of the instrument. In other words, the parties to the MLI are interested in the application, interpretation, and faithful discharge of the instrument's provisions. As analyzed in section 2, this is what defines multilateral treaties under public international law.

Likewise, the conference of the parties may amend the provisions of the MLI to further modify their tax treaty relations. According to Article 33 of the MLI, any of the parties may suggest amendments to the text of the instrument. Once a party to the MLI has proposed an amendment, a conference of the parties may be convened with the aim of studying the merits of the amendment. Thus, parties of the MLI can decide on modifications to the current provisions of the MLI and/or on extending the scope of application of the instrument;[116] for example, to implement the tax treaty changes that may result from the current discussions of the BEPS Inclusive Framework on the tax challenges arising from the digitalization of the economy.[117]

Finally, the Explanatory Statement to the MLI can also be seen as a tool for attaining uniform interpretation and application of the provisions of the instrument.[118] The Explanatory Statement was prepared by the ad hoc Group and was adopted together with the final text of the MLI.[119] The Explanatory Statement clarifies the approach taken in the MLI. Although not intended to address the interpretation of the treaty-related BEPS measures, it nevertheless promotes a uniform interpretation of the functioning of the MLI and the mandatory binding arbitration procedure.[120]

The Explanatory Statement clarifies the types of provisions found in CTAs targeted by each provision of the MLI. It explains how the interpreter should apply the provisions of the MLI in relation to the relevant provisions of the CTAs, i.e. how the MLI modifies them. It also clarifies the effects of the provisions of the MLI in cases where the parties have notified that a similar provision exists or does not exist in their CTAs. In addition, the Explanatory Statement deals with the procedural rules of the

116. *See* also, T. Magalhaes, *Chapter 6: The OECD Multilateral Instrument: Challenge or Opportunity of Multilateralism in International Tax?*, at sec. 6.3.2., in *The Aftermath of BEPS* (J. Wheeler eds., IBFD 2020).
117. OECD, *Explanatory Statement to the MLI*, paras. 215-259 (2016).
118. Scholars have started to discuss the legal status that should be attributed to the Explanatory Statement. Some scholars have posited that the Explanatory Statement should be considered context within the meaning of Article 31(2)(a) Vienna Convention (1969): *see, e.g.*, J.F. Avery Jones, *Treaty Interpretation* (updated 2017), sec. 5.3.3., in *Global Tax Treaty Commentaries*, (R. Vann eds., IBFD 2014); and A. Bosman, *General Aspects of the Multilateral Instrument*, 45 Intertax 10, p. 647 (2017). Others have posited that the Explanatory Statement should, at most, be considered a supplementary means of interpretation within the meaning of Article 32 Vienna Convention (1969): *see* Y. Brauner, *McBEPS: The MLI—The First Multilateral Tax Treaty that Has Never Been*, at 16, 46 Intertax 1, p. 12 (2018); and S. Wakounig, *Interpretation of Terms Used in the Multilateral Instrument*, at 24-25, in *The OECD Multilateral Instrument for Tax Treaties—Analysis and Effects* (M. Lang et al. eds., Kluwer Law International 2018).
119. OECD, *Explanatory Statement to the MLI*, para. 11 (2016).
120. OECD, *Explanatory Statement to the MLI*, para. 12 (2016).

MLI, such as signature and ratification processes of the instrument, reservations, notifications, amendment, entry into force, entry into effect, and withdrawal. This systematic approach is helpful for obtaining a uniform interpretation and application of the MLI's provisions.

Furthermore, the Explanatory Statement clarifies how a mandatory binding arbitration procedure should be conducted.[121] As the subgroup on arbitration not only designed the provisions of the mandatory binding arbitration procedure but also drafted their substance, the Explanatory Statement is a useful tool for the interpretation of these provisions established in Articles 18-26 of the MLI.

The MLI has been the object of study within the investment law community. Just as the tax treaty network, the investment treaty network comprises more than 3,000 treaties.[122] Many of them require modification. However, the conclusion of a multilateral investment treaty that would replace all of them has also shown to be unfeasible.[123] Thus, experts in international investment law have found a model for the modification of bilateral investment treaties in the MLI.[124] Interestingly, these experts have not only recognized the multilateral nature of the MLI, but also praise its design. Wolfgang Alschner, for example, has indicated:

> The MLI takes the form of a multilateral opt-in convention, which modifies DTTs under its scope. The MLI thereby leaves the bilateral governance structure of the tax regime intact, but adds a lightweight multilateral superstructure.[125]
>
> (...)
>
> This ability to deliver global standards where needed while preserving national preferences where possible is an attractive model for investment law because its multilateral reform will need to strike a similar balance to be successful.[126]

The discussion above demonstrates that based on the concepts accepted under public international law, the MLI is a multilateral treaty. All the parties to the MLI have interest in the implementation of uniform international tax rules across the tax treaty network. Moreover, the parties to the MLI are interested in the application, interpretation, and faithful discharge of the instrument's provisions. As the multilateral nature

121. OECD, *Explanatory Statement to the MLI*, paras. 215-219 (2016).
122. For more details, *see* N. Bravo, *The Mauritius Convention on Transparency and the Multilateral Tax Instrument: Models for the Modification of Treaties?*, at 85-109, 25 Transnat'l Corp. 3 (2018).
123. As it is the case of the never adopted Multilateral Agreement on Investment (MAI), which negotiations were launched by the OECD in May 1995 and definitely discontinued in April 1998. For more details, *see* https://www.oecd.org/investment/internationalinvestmentagreements/multilateralagreementoninvestment.htm (accessed on March 29, 2021).
124. *See, e.g.*, C. Titi, *Procedural Multilateralism and Multilateral Investment Court: Procedural Multilateralism and Multilateral Investment Court*, at 141-144, in *Institutionalisation Beyond the Nation State* (Elaine Fahey ed., Springer 2018); and, W. Alschner, *The OECD Multilateral Tax Instrument: A Model for Reforming The International Investment Regime?*, at 2-72, 45 Brook. J. Int'l L. 1 (2019).
125. W. Alschner, *The OECD Multilateral Tax Instrument: A Model for Reforming The International Investment Regime?*, at 474, 5 Broo. J. Int'l L. 1 (2019).
126. *Id.*, at 63.

of the MLI has been proved, the nature of the obligations therein provided will be reviewed below.

5.2 The Nature of the Substantive Provisions of the MLI

As discussed in section 3, the provisions of multilateral treaties may be bilateral, interdependent, or integral. Despite the common interest shared by parties to the MLI, its provisions are not the concern of all states. Neither are they reciprocally owned to a group of states, nor are they owned to the international community as a whole. Conversely, as they modify the provisions of CTAs, the provisions of the MLI only concern the parties sitting at the two ends of a tax treaty relation. This is evident if one takes into account that parties to the MLI are not obliged to modify all their tax treaties through the MLI.

According to Article 2(1)(ii) of the MLI, each party must submit to the Depositary a list with the tax treaties they wish to modify through the MLI. Therefore, parties may exclude some of their tax treaties from the scope of the MLI. Parties that have excluded some of their tax treaties from the scope of application of the MLI can, of course, still amend their tax treaties in a bilateral fashion to implement the treaty-related BEPS measures. Although it is expected that parties do not include their tax treaties under the scope of the MLI in limited circumstances, i.e. when the tax treaty has already been amended to implement the treaty-related BEPS measures,[127] the truth is that parties may decide to exclude some of their tax treaties if they have the valid expectation that their interests will be more favored if the treaties are renegotiated on a bilateral basis.

Furthermore, in its Advisory Opinion on the Genocide Convention, the ICJ rejected the possibility to formulate reservations if they frustrate the object and purpose of a multilateral treaty that establishes collective obligations.[128] Nonetheless, as discussed above, parties to the MLI are allowed to make multiple reservations and to opt into different opt-ins and alternative provisions. Under the MLI, parties may reserve the application of entire articles. They may even end up accepting only the application of the provisions that set out minimum standards if they make reservations to the totality of the rest of the articles of the instrument. Although in limited circumstances,[129] provisions that set out minimum standards are subject to reservations too.[130] All this flexibility provided in the MLI to ensure universal participation and the protection of the parties' tax sovereignty[131] shows that the MLI does not provide collective obligations. The notification of reservations under the MLI does not frustrate its object and purpose. As argued before, the flexibility provided in the MLI does not hinder the parties' interest in the application, interpretation, and faithful discharge of the instrument's provisions.

127. OECD, *Explanatory Statement to the MLI*, para. 26 (2016).
128. *Reservations to the Convention on Genocide* (Advisory Opinion), at 24, ICJ Report 15 (1951).
129. OECD, *Explanatory Statement to the MLI*, para. 14 (2016).
130. Articles 7(15) and 16(5) of the MLI.
131. OECD, *Developing a Multilateral Instrument to Modify Bilateral Tax Treaties, Action 15—2015 Final Report*, OECD/G20 Base Erosion and Profit Shifting Project, at 13 (2015).

Finally, the fact that the substantive provisions of the MLI only bind parties that have previously concluded a CTA also shows that the substantive provisions of the MLI are bilateral; that is, between a state of residence and a state of source. Some expressions used in the MLI evidence the bilateral nature of the obligations therein provided. These expressions include: (i) "in the other Contracting Jurisdiction";[132] (ii) "under the law of either Contracting Jurisdiction";[133] (iii) "shall not apply where the other Contracting Jurisdiction applies the provisions of the Covered Tax Agreement";[134] (iv) "may be taxed in the other Contracting Jurisdiction";[135] (v) "shall consult with the competent authority of that other Contracting Jurisdiction";[136] (vi) "income derived from the other Contracting Jurisdiction";[137] (vii) "under the laws of either Contracting Jurisdiction";[138] (viii) "according to the domestic law of the other Contracting Jurisdiction";[139] (ix) "following an initial adjustment made by the other Contracting Jurisdiction";[140] and (x) "the income that the other Contracting Jurisdiction may tax in accordance with the Covered Tax Agreement."[141,142]

However, as indicated above, the bilateral nature of the substantive provisions of the MLI does not mean that the MLI is not a multilateral treaty. Multilateral treaties often provide for bundles of bilateral obligations. The nature of the obligations provided in a multilateral treaty cannot be confused with the nature of the instrument itself.

As the obligations of the MLI are divisible between parties that have concluded a CTA, material breaches of an MLI provision will only change the position of the party directly affected by it. Material breaches of the provisions of the MLI will neither dramatically change the position of all the other parties, nor will they affect the international community as a whole. Consequently, following the principles set out in the Vienna Convention and the ILC Articles on State Responsibility, only the party or parties directly affected by the infringement will be entitled to invoke the responsibility of the defaulting party. The rest of the parties to the MLI will not be entitled to request the suspension or termination of the instrument due to the infringement.[143] Nor will they be entitled to invoke the state responsibility of the defaulting state.

Additionally, since the obligations of the MLI are divisible between parties that have concluded a CTA, two or more parties to a CTA may further change their tax treaty relations through *inter se* agreements without affecting the enjoyment of the rights or

132. Articles 3(2), 7(10)(b) and 9(1) and (2) of the MLI.
133. Article 3(4) of the MLI.
134. Article 5(2) of the MLI.
135. Articles 5(6) and 9(2) of the MLI.
136. Article 7(4) of the MLI.
137. Articles 7(13)(a)(i) and 10(1)(a) and (2) of the MLI.
138. Article 7(4) of the MLI.
139. Article 10(1) of the MLI.
140. Article 11(1)(a) of the MLI.
141. Article 11(1)(d) of the MLI.
142. It must be mentioned that the term "Contracting Jurisdiction" is defined in Article 2(1)(c) of the MLI as a party to a Covered Tax Agreement. It is used in the instrument to refer not only to states but also to non-state jurisdictions that are authorized to become a party to the MLI. *See* also, *supra* n. 51.
143. Article 60(2) of the Vienna Convention.

the performance of the obligations of the rest of the parties to the MLI.[144] The nature of the obligations established in the MLI was probably taken into account by its treaty makers, who in Article 30 established that "*the provisions in this Convention are without prejudice to subsequent modifications to a Covered Tax Agreement which may be agreed between the Contracting Jurisdictions of the Covered Tax Agreement.*" That is, parties are expressively allowed to modify the provisions of the MLI through *inter se* agreements that will have effect among themselves alone.

This author has previously argued that a different outcome would have been desirable to avoid BEPS over time.[145] Nonetheless, according to Article 30 of the MLI, its parties remain free to contract out from the provisions of this instrument, even if the agreed changes reverse their commitments to avoid creating opportunities for BEPS. Based on state sovereignty, which is protected through the MLI, parties to the instrument are free to update their tax treaty relations among themselves alone as required by their common economic interests and tax policies.[146]

The possibilities to exclude tax treaties from the scope of the MLI make multiple reservations, and conclude *inter se* modifications, as well as the consequences of potential infringements of the MLI provisions, demonstrate that the performance of the obligations established in the MLI does not transcend the sphere of the bilateral relations of its parties. In fact, the listed features of the MLI confirm that its provisions only create obligations between a party vis-à-vis the party sitting at the other end of a tax treaty relation.

6 CONCLUSIONS

It is possible to conclude that the nature of the MLI is multilateral, although its obligations are of a bilateral nature because they provide for mutually reciprocal obligations between the parties. The nature of the instrument, however, cannot be confused with the nature of the obligations it provides.

International tax law continues to be dominated by bilateral structures. Bilateral tax treaties continue to apply and will continue to be negotiated and concluded on a bilateral basis because through bilateral tax treaties, states can adapt the tax treaty rules to their reciprocal economic interests and tax policies. Nonetheless, in those areas where agreement is reached among an important number of countries, modifications to tax treaties rules may continue to be implemented on a multilateral basis, whether through the MLI or a different multilateral treaty. Again, the fact that bilateral tax treaties will continue to exist in international tax law does not imply that the nature of the MLI or other treaties implementing tax treaty changes multilaterally agreed is bilateral.

144. Article 41 of the Vienna Convention.
145. *See, e.g.*, N. Bravo, *Future Changes to Covered Tax Agreements and of the Multilateral Convention to Implement Tax Treaty- Related Measures to Prevent BEPS*, at 243-248, in *The OECD Multilateral Instrument for Tax Treaties—Analysis and Effects* (M. Lang et al. eds., Kluwer Law International 2018).
146. N. Bravo, *A Multilateral Instrument for Updating the Tax Treaty Network*, at 268 (IBFD 2020).

The MLI is the first attempt in international tax law to shift from bilateralism. Although the Instrument preserves and builds on the tax treaty network, an in-depth analysis shows its intrinsic multilateral features. The fact that the MLI builds on the tax treaty network is not necessarily negative. The prospects for concluding a comprehensive worldwide multilateral tax treaty have been regarded as non-existent multiple times. Due to the low probability of concluding a comprehensive worldwide multilateral tax treaty, previous recommendations proposed the adoption of partial multilateral conventions on certain types of income or on concepts on which uniform international tax treatment had achieved some level of acceptance. The MLI has precisely adopted such an approach by exclusively implementing provisions relating to BEPS, on which a certain level of acceptance has already been reached. The coordination of the international tax rules of a vast number of the tax treaties and the creation of tools that work towards the uniform interpretation of those rules is already a major achievement. Of course, only time will tell whether multilateralism is the way forward in international tax law, or whether one should stick to bilateralism.

CHAPTER 4

Risk Society and International Tax Multilateralism

Sergio André Rocha

1 INTRODUCTION

In 2017, Allison Christians and I edited a book on tax sovereignty in post-BEPS (base erosion and profit shifting) times.[1] There are many connections between that publication and this article. Indeed, it is multilateralism that puts in check the traditional notion of tax sovereignty. As noted by Luís Eduardo Schoueri and Ricardo André Galendi Júnior, "Sovereignty implies independence: every Nation is free to manage its domestic and external affairs solely guided by its will, to enact the legislation it wishes and to choose its own system of administration, as well as the size of its public sector and the benefits it grants to its citizens."[2]

However, as stated by Yariv Brauner, "Given the scope of the sovereignty doctrine, appears the argument that sovereignty does not give countries carte blanche to tax as they wish, without international intervention (even if we assume that such taxation is domestically legitimate—let's say democratically decided—and appropriate in terms of basic human rights) seems, on the face of it, to contradict the very heart of the sovereignty notion. However, if there truly was a dichotomy, we would probably be

1. Sergio André Rocha & Allison Christians, *Tax Sovereignty in the BEPS Era* (The Netherlands: Kluwer, 2017).
2. Luís Eduardo Schoueri & Ricardo André Galendi Júnior, "Justification and Implementation of the International Allocation of Taxing Rights: Can We Take One Thing at a Time?," Sergio André Rocha & Allison Christians, *Tax Sovereignty in the BEPS Era* (The Netherlands: Kluwer, 2017) p. 64.

living in a world that most of us would not like. The majority of us would be poor or oppressed (or, more likely both)."[3]

Considering this approach to tax sovereignty, in the 2017 book it was argued that multilateralism was an inevitable feature of 21st-century international taxation.

According to my co-editor Allison Christians, "Multilateralism in taxation is difficult because countries are in different economic positions, but this is precisely why getting to a principled solution requires a laborious process involving broad participation and enduring contestation. Unilateralism and bilateralism have tried and failed for a century to facilitate national taxing powers in a manner that is equitable, or efficient, or administrable. The contemporary result is growing distrust in tax governance and skepticism about the underlying motivations of tax policymakers. Avoiding multilateralism by continuing to constrain debate and control consensus prolongs this status quo and puts the power to tax with autonomy at risk throughout the world."[4]

Likewise, Reuven S. Avi-Yonah and Haiyan Xu argued that "Global Challenges need global solution. BEPS, as a global concern, is made possible by uncoordinated tax rules at domestic and international levels. Therefore, the global solutions need to be on inclusive and multilateral global governance. This means each and every country should be offered equal opportunity and equal weight to shape the outcome of the global solutions."[5]

In this article, I resume the debate from where I left off in my article in the 2017 book,[6] to raise the following question: Is multilateralism actually inevitable as a general assumption? Or is multilateralism required for the achievement of certain objectives, but is not an overall requirement that applies to the circumstances of all countries?

I start my comments departing from some remarks that I presented briefly in the 2017 article: the analysis of risk society and its implications on the design of international taxation.

2 REFLEXIVE MODERNIZATION AND RISK SOCIETY

The past half-century has brought remarkable changes to the dynamics of people's lives. In fact, for the first time in our history, technical-scientific development, as well as the vicissitudes of the prevailing socioeconomic model, put the perpetuation of our way of life at risk.

On the other hand, as noted by the Spanish scholar Manuel Atienza, there is a paradox, since also for the first time in history, humanity has knowledge and resources so that everyone has access to basic levels of education, health, housing, and food, but

3. Yariv Brauner, "An Essay on BEPS, Sovereignty, and Taxation," Sergio André Rocha & Allison Christians, *Tax Sovereignty in the BEPS Era* (The Netherlands: Kluwer, 2017) p. 75.
4. Allison Christians, "BEPS and the Power to Tax," Sergio André Rocha & Allison Christians, *Tax Sovereignty in the BEPS Era* (The Netherlands: Kluwer, 2017) p. 27.
5. Reuven S. Avi-Yonah & Haiyan Xu, "Evaluating BEPS," Sergio André Rocha & Allison Christians, *Tax Sovereignty in the BEPS Era* (The Netherlands: Kluwer, 2017) p. 105.
6. Sergio André Rocha, "The Other Side of BEPS: 'Imperial Taxation' and 'International Tax Imperialism'," Sergio André Rocha & Allison Christians, *Tax Sovereignty in the BEPS Era* (The Netherlands: Kluwer, 2017) pp. 179-200.

without having reached a rudimentary stage of global social justice.[7] As Anthony Giddens points out:

> In pursuing my enquiry into the character of modernity, I want to concentrate a substantial portion of the discussion upon themes of *security versus danger* and *trust versus risk. Modernity, as everyone living in the closing years of the twentieth century can see, is a double-edged phenomenon. The development of modern social institutions and their worldwide spread have created vastly greater opportunities for human beings to enjoy a secure and rewarding existence than any type of pre-modern system. But modernity also has a somber side, which has become very apparent in the present century.*[8] (Emphasis added)

The transformations that started in the last century and that continue now have brought with them the phenomenon referred to as *reflexive modernization*,[9] which, in the words of Ulrich Beck, represents the "possibility of a creative (self-) destruction for an entire epoch: that of industrial society." As the German sociologist adds, "The 'subject' of this creative destruction is not the revolution, not the crisis, but the victory of Western modernization."[10]

With the overcoming of industrial society paradigms through reflexive modernization, the concept of *risk society* emerges. Quoting Ulrich Beck again, it "designates a stage of modernity in which the threats produced so far on the path of industrial society begin to predominate."[11]

Naturally, risks have always been present throughout history. However, risk society implies something more than the recognition that human beings expose themselves to natural and social risks that threaten the continuity of their individual existence. Risk society brings with it risks that go far beyond the individuality of people, local communities, and even countries, due to the global scale of risks.

On the other hand, the risks present in risk society are not natural, which means they are a result of the technical, political, economic, etc. development of humanity itself and the way in which human beings play the role of the predominant species on Earth.

Quoting Anthony Giddens again, "a skeptic might ask, is there anything new here? Hasn't human life always been marked by contingency? Hasn't the future always been open and problematic? The answer is 'yes' to each of these questions. It is not that our life-circumstances today have become less predictable than they used to be; rather

7. Manuel Atienza, *El Sentido del Derecho* (Barcelona: Ariel, 2003) p. 20.
8. Antony Giddens, *The Consequences of Modernity* (California: Stanford University Press, 1990) p. 7.
9. As highlighted by Eduardo C.B. Bittar, the name of this historical moment varies from author to author, being referred to as reflexive modernity, post-modernity, super-modernity, etc. *See*: Eduardo C.B. Bittar, *O Direito na Pós-Modernindade* (Rio de Janeiro: Forense, 2005) pp. 96-97.
10. Ulrich Beck, "The Reinvention of Politics," Ulrich Beck, Antony Giddens & Scott Lash (eds.), *Reflexive Modernization* (California: Stanford University Press, 1990) p. 2. *See also*: Antony Giddens, *The Consequences of Modernity* (California: Stanford University Press, 1990) pp. 36-45.
11. Ulrich Beck, "The Reinvention of Politics," Ulrich Beck, Antony Giddens & Scott Lash (eds.), *Reflexive Modernization* (California: Stanford University Press, 1990) p. 6.

the origins of unpredictability have changed. Many of the uncertainties which face us today have been created by the very growth of human knowledge."[12]

Industrial society, developed under the political-economic framework of proto-liberalism, lived with social risks that were controllable through the action of legislators. Hence, industrial society encouraged the belief in the infallibility of legislators in regulating life's vicissitudes.

Post-modern society challenged the belief in such a model. At first, the emergence of financial risks that could not be assumed by individuals and had to be disseminated throughout the community led to the development of the insurance contract, which has as one of its main scopes the collective assumption of individual losses that cannot be supported by individuals and companies themselves.

In risk society, however, collective risks transcend the controlling powers of legislators, at the same time as they make it impossible for all individuals to cover their costs through insurance contracts. As noted by Willis Santiago Guerra Filho:

> Law, like ethics, can be conceived as a repository of socially consecrated norms to guide human conduct. Such guidance, however, presupposes knowledge about the conditions under which human action takes place, knowledge that, in our society, is expected to be provided basically by science. The growing complexity of this society, at a dizzying pace, makes those repositories, as well as the knowledge accumulated in the past, largely obsolete, or at the very least insufficient, as they do not offer solutions to radically new and complex problems that we have to deal with. Problems of this type are those arising from the intervention of man in his natural environment, including the genetic material that constitutes it, giving rise to the emergence of new branches of science, law and ethics, namely, ecology, environmental law and bioethics.[13]

In risk society, we are facing nuclear risks, the risk of an irreversible depredation of the environment, the risk of economic crises of global proportions, such as we experienced in 2008, which leads to global impoverishment and the bankruptcy of states, the risk of drugs, terrorism, and sadly, the risk of global pandemics.

The subject of risk society and its effects is very rich and has several points of intersection with law and regulation, intertwining with various legal areas, including tax law—domestic and international. As Professor Ricardo Lobo points out, "Risk society is characterized by some relevant notes: ambivalence, insecurity, the search for new principles and the redesign of the relationship between the attributions of State institutions and society itself."[14]

In my view, the recognition of the ambivalent nature of taxation is of the utmost importance.

---

12. Anthony Giddens, "Risk, Trust, Reflexivity," Ulrich Beck, Antony Giddens & Scott Lash (eds.), *Reflexive Modernization* (California: Stanford University Press, 1990) p. 185.
13. Willis Santiago Guerra Filho, "Epistemologia Sistêmica para Fundamentação de um Direito Tributário da Cidadania Democrática e Global," Heleno Taveira Torres (ed.), *Direito Tributário Ambiental* (São Paulo: Malheiros, 2005) p. 586.
14. Ricardo Lobo Torres, *Tratado de Direito Constitucional, Financeiro e Tributário* (Rio de Janeiro: Renovar, 2005) v. II, p. 177.

According to Zygmunt Bauman, "Ambivalence, the possibility of assigning an object or an event to more than one category, is a language-specific disorder: a failure of the naming (segregating) function that language is meant to perform. The main symptom of disorder is the acute discomfort we feel when we are unable to read the situation properly and to choose between alternative actions."[15]

As stated above, this is a key concept to understand current issues that challenge experts in several different areas, including taxation, as I explore in the next section.

3 RISK SOCIETY AND TAXATION

There are relevant connections between risk society and taxation.

First, there is a close link between post-modern risk society and public financing. Even though Western countries have different levels of social protection networks, it is certain at this stage that the functioning of any of these countries requires funding through the collection of taxes.[16] As noted by Stephen Holmes and Cass R. Sunstein—who analyzed this matter from an American perspective:

> "The rights of Americans are neither divine rights nor fruits of nature; they are not self-enforcing and cannot be reliably protected when government is insolvent or incapacitated; they need not be a recipe for irresponsible egoism; they do not imply that individuals can secure personal freedom without social cooperation; and they are not uncompromisable claims."
>
> "A more adequate approach to rights has a disarmingly simple premise: private liberties have public costs. This is true not only of rights to Social Security, Medicare, and food stamps, but also of rights to private property, freedom of speech, immunity from police abuse, contractual liberty, free exercise of religion, and indeed the full panoply of rights characteristic of the American tradition. From the perspective of public finance, all rights are licenses for individuals to pursue their joint and separate purposes by taking advantage of collective assets, which include a share of those private assets accumulated under community's protection."[17]

Risk society requires a new approach to the role of taxation, which is still perceived as a form of illegitimate private property expropriation by some authors as if there were a sort of pre-tax income that is earned in a stateless parallel reality. Nevertheless, as noted by Liam Murphy and Tomas Nagel:

> "If there is a dominant theme that runs through our discussion, it is this: Private property is a legal convention, defined in part by the tax system; therefore, the tax system cannot be evaluated by looking at its impact on private property, conceived as something that has independent existence and validity. Taxes must be evaluated as part of the overall system of property rights that they help create. Justice or

---

15. Zygmunt Bauman, *Modernity and Ambivalence* (Cambridge: Polity Press, 2007) p. 1.
16. Tisilly Dagan, *International Tax Policy: Between Competition and Cooperation* (Cambridge: Cambridge University Press, 2018) pp. 17-19.
17. Stephen Holmes & Cass R. Sunstein, *The Cost of Rights: Why Liberty Depends on Taxes* (New York: W.W. Norton & Company, 1999) p. 221. *See* Sergio André Rocha, *Fundamentos do Direito Tributário Brasileiro* (Belo Horizonte: Letramentos, 2020) pp. 11-27.

> injustice in taxation can only mean justice or injustice in the system of property rights and entitlements that result from a particular tax regime."
>
> [...]
>
> "In the case of taxes and property, the situation is more complicated, and it can even be more absurd. The feeling of natural entitlement produced by an unreflective sense of what are in fact conventionally defined property rights can encourage complacency about the status quo, as something more or less self-justifying. But it can also give rise to an even more confused criticism of the existing system on the ground that it violates natural property rights, when, in fact, these 'natural' rights are namely misperceptions of the legal consequences of the system itself. *It is illegitimate to appeal to a baseline of property rights in, say, 'pretax income', for the purpose of evaluating tax policies, when all such figures are the product of a system of which taxes are an inextricable part.* One can neither justify nor criticize an economic regime by taking as an independent norm something that is, in fact, one of its consequences."[18] (emphasis added)

These comments by Stephen Holmes and Cass R. Sunstein, and Liam Murphy, and Tomas Nagel highlight the ambivalence of taxation. On the one hand, taxes are instrumental to the financing of any democratic state. As highlighted by Ricardo Lobo Torres, taxes are the price of liberty, in the sense that citizens pay taxes to be free to make their life choices without government intervention. However, on the other hand, taxes can also destroy the same liberty they are meant to guarantee.[19]

This means that fiscal crises are not just an economic problem; they jeopardize the very fabric of society. The risk of state bankruptcy undermines people's healthcare, education, culture, social security, etc. In addition, it impairs states' capacity to protect the environment, regulate the economy, create jobs, etc. In recent times, no period other than the present has proven how states are people's last line of defense in the face of unexpected dire situations—and how their actions are funded mainly by taxes.

The ambivalence and uncertainty of risk society have an impact on the relationship between the tax authorities and taxpayers. The traditional formulation of fundamental tax principles, most related to legal certainty, falls short.

4 NEW TAX PRINCIPLES

The complexity, ambivalence, and uncertainty of risk society require a new set of tax principles that shed some light on the otherwise opaque transactions and operations carried out by taxpayers and states.

The *principle of transparency*[20] is typical of risk society, guiding domestic tax systems as well as international taxation. The fight against tax havens and aggressive tax planning, the enactment of anti-abuse rules, the exchange of information for tax

18. Liam Murphy & Thomas Nagel, *The Myth of Ownership* (Oxford: Oxford University Press, 2002) pp. 8-9.
19. *See*: Ricardo Lobo Torres, *Tratado de Direito Constitucional Financeiro e Tributário: Os Direitos Humanos e a Tributação, Imunidades e Isonomia* (Rio de Janeiro: Renovar, 1999) v. III, pp. 1-6.
20. *See*: Sergio André Rocha, "The Other Side of BEPS: 'Imperial Taxation' and 'International Tax Imperialism'," Sergio André Rocha & Allison Christians, *Tax Sovereignty in the BEPS Era* (The Netherlands: Kluwer, 2017) pp. 185-186.

purposes, as well as budgetary transparency, are all instruments to materialize transparency in the relations between taxpayers and tax authorities.

Another relevant principle in risk society is the *principle of cooperation*. It points to a horizon of economic interdependence and mutual assistance among countries.

The principle of cooperation shows the ambivalent face of post-modernity, characteristic of risk society. In the contemporary international economic scenario, this is present insofar as competition and cooperation are forced to coexist. There is a significant mobilization to fight harmful tax competition. However, countries that compete for tax revenues also cooperate with a view to making their domestic tax rules effective. As Italian scholar Claudio Sacchetto points out, international cooperation "Is one of the paradoxes of the arrival of globalization: on the one hand, states confront each other in terms of tax competition, while on the other they must cooperate to safeguard their own internal tax systems."[21]

Given the features of risk society and the consequent impossibility of anticipating the results of the measures adopted to face social and natural risks, the *principle of tolerance* plays a prominent role in post-modernity. Indeed, as Arthur Kaufmann points out, intolerance can be quite harmful, since it can encourage decision-makers in risky situations to remain idle. In the words of the German legal philosopher, "behaving too cautiously is by no means the correct answer to all supposedly risky situations."[22]

Thus, faced with a complex society, in which there is no way to ensure that, among the various possible lines of action, the one adopted is the best, tolerance emerges as an instrument to enable the assumption of responsibilities by mankind.

However, the principle of tolerance must be balanced with the *principle of responsibility*, in order to prevent tolerance from becoming an incentive to neglect and lack of commitment to decisions and actions undertaken by different actors. Once again as argued by Arthur Kaufmann:

> Tolerance makes it possible to act responsibly. It also makes irresponsible conduct possible. Consequently, the principle of tolerance has to be completed with the principle of responsibility. In biotechnology, above all in genetic technology, this is of particular importance, since harmful effects, including severe ones, are often unpredictable and uncontrollable.[23]

These principles have application in the tax field. Indeed, it must be understood that measures adopted by governments will not always achieve the intended purpose, and on the other hand there is room for rethinking the reaction to taxpayers' faults.

21. Claudio Sacchetto, "A Cooperação Fiscal Internacional: a Troca de Informações como Instrumento de Combate à Evasão" (2008) 22 *Revista Direito Tributário Atual*, p. 81.
22. Arthur Kaufmann, *Filosofía del Derecho* (Bogotá: Universidad Externado de Colombia, 1999) p. 530.
23. Arthur Kaufmann, *Filosofía del Derecho* (Bogotá: Universidad Externado de Colombia, 1999) p. 542.

5 RISK-SOCIETY PROBLEMS CAN BE MANAGED, BUT NOT SOLVED

One of the illusions we have inherited from past generations is the notion that problems that emerge in society can be dealt with and solved by enacting laws. However, post-modern risk society's problems cannot be solved, they can only be managed.

In other words, it is vain to imagine that complex 21st century problems will disappear. This is as true for problems such as terrorism, environmental depletion, and pandemics as it is for issues like tax evasion and aggressive tax planning.

One cannot hope for a terrorism-free world, just like a tax planning-free world is unimaginable. On the other hand, the ambivalence of risk society puts in check certain objectives. For example, Chinese industrial production is harmful to the environment while at the same time it is a key for maintaining current levels of social and economic development in many nations, if not in the whole world. There are hardly any one-sided hard topics in the post-modern world.

As noted above, the same thing can be stated about issues such as tax evasion and aggressive tax planning.

However, aggressive tax planning, for instance, is an ambiguous and ambivalent phenomenon in itself, as part of it is certainly a consequence of harmful tax competition, which is paradoxical in nature.

Indeed, as pointed out by Hugh Ault, Wolfgang Schön, and Stephen Shay, "MNE behavior is only one side of the coin. International profit shifting and base erosion envisaged by large business enterprises would be ineffective without countries offering preferential tax rules, including low/no tax regimes for particular taxpayers or income categories and benign provisions on profit measurement."[24]

Luís Eduardo Schoueri holds the same position, stating that: "The responsibility of the states themselves cannot be denied, because in many cases the taxpayers do nothing but use alternatives that the tax regulations allow, either explicitly (via tax incentives), or because of flaws and loopholes paradoxically created by the excessive details of legislation."[25]

This connection between tax planning and state induction was already noted by Heleno Taveira Tôrres over a decade ago, when he stated that, "If there is tax planning, as an activity par excellence of taxpayers, who are bound to run a business organization with the least tax repercussion, such a plan can only be elaborated, in many cases, because there are 'tax options' freely granted by States."[26]

---

24. Hugh J. Ault, Wolfgang Schön & Stephen E. Shay, "Base Erosion and Profit Shifting: A Roadmap for Reform" (2014) 68(8) *Bulletin for International Taxation*, p. 276. Also *see*: Gemma Patón Garcia, "Análisis de las Medidas Españolas Alineadas con el Plan de Acción BEPS: Desafíos en la Implementación e Incidencia en Latinoamérica," ILADT, *Memorias de las XXVII Jornadas Latinoamericanas de Derecho Tributario* (ILADT: Mexico, 2015) p. 186.
25. Luís Eduardo Schoueri, "O Projeto BEPS: Ainda uma Estratégia Militar," Marcus Livio Gomes & Luís Eduardo Schoueri (eds.), *A Tributação Internacional na Era Pós-BERS* (Rio de Janeiro: Lumen Juris, 2016) v. I, p. 30.
26. Heleno Taveira Tôrres, *Direito Tributário Internacional: Planejamento Tributário e Operações Transnacionais* (São Paulo: Revista dos Tribunais, 2001) p. 68.

The ambiguous nature of risk-society problems reinforces the assumption that one can only pretend to manage them and aim to reduce their negative externalities. However, it seems naïve at best to imagine that these problems will simply disappear.

6 RISK-SOCIETY PROBLEMS CANNOT BE ENTIRELY MANAGED UNILATERALLY

One of the features of risk-society problems is that they cannot be entirely managed unilaterally.

On October 26, 2001, the United States, the most powerful nation in the world, enacted the "Uniting and Strengthening America by Providing Appropriate Tools Required to Intercept and Obstruct Terrorism (USA Patriot Act) Act of 2001." It is a 132-page law drafted in reaction to the September 11 terrorist attacks.

The USA Patriot Act raised several questions and controversies regarding the violation of civil liberties, international and domestic. It is certainly not my focus to discuss the pros and cons of this law. Nevertheless, one thing is certain: it did not put an end to terrorism.

My point here is that no nation, even the world's most powerful one, has the muscle to entirely manage complex risk society problems alone.

We probably are living through one of the saddest periods in recent history, witnessing hundreds of thousands of lives lost. However, there is no country that can enact a law to end a pandemic—the current and future ones.

Likewise, the taxation of big-tech companies has been challenging some of the most developed countries in the world for almost a decade now. The only thing unilateral action has been able to achieve is to increase uncertainty and disputes.

These brief comments lead to a simple truth: ultra-complex risk society problems *cannot be entirely managed unilaterally.*

This fact adds complexity to already complex problems since their management requires a great deal of *transparency, cooperation, and coordination.*

However, there is an important aspect that must be highlighted: not all countries have the same level of exposure to risk-society problems. I explore this assumption a bit more in the next section.

7 RISK-SOCIETY PROBLEMS ARE NOT THE SAME FOR EVERY COUNTRY

Risk-society problems do not impact all countries the same. Of course, there are problems that might affect everyone on earth eventually, like the depletion of the environment and global warming. The same goes for the consequences of a global pandemic. However, even in these cases, the current impacts of these problems are not felt the same everywhere.

There are areas in which the uneven impact of risk-society problems is even clearer. For instance, even though all human beings should be morally affected by terrorism, it is hard to say that all countries have the same problem with it. A country like Brazil, for example, has hardly any problems involving international or domestic terrorism.

This is a very relevant topic. One can agree that some level of multilateralism and coordination is necessary for the war against terror. Nevertheless, there is also likely agreement that the concerns of the United States, Europe and Israel with this issue are much more important than Brazil's.

Considering these brief comments, assume for a moment that as a consequence of a "multilateral initiative," the United States led a global reaction to terrorism that would require all countries to invest in the same infrastructure to fight terror, even those countries where terrorism is not even an issue. Would this make any sense?

The fact that terrorism is a typical risk-society problem does not make it universal or evenly distributed.

It seems that the same happens with BEPS issues. It is likely that most countries have BEPS problems. However, it is very unlikely that all countries have the same level of BEPS issues. Likewise, it is also unlikely that developed countries and emerging countries have the same extent of BEPS problems.

Just like with the war on terror example, it would be unreasonable to imagine a single solution to combat BEPS that would be applicable to all countries.

The same argument can be made about the tax implications of the digitalization of the economy or the creation of minimum tax levels. There is no indication that all countries have the same type of tax issues due to the digitalization of the economy, or that they all need to implement pillar-2-type of legislation.

Therefore, a one-size-fits-all multilateralism cannot be expected to equally benefit all countries. In addition, it seems flatly false to argue that all countries need to put the same level of effort to find global solutions to problems that they might not even have.

8 RISK SOCIETY, AGGRESSIVE TAX PLANNING, BEPS, AND MULTILATERALISM

Typical risk-society problems require a combined effort from countries and international—and national—institutions to pursue solutions. In other words, such a solution more often than not will be a multilateral endeavor, rather than an isolated effort. As Yariv Brauner points out, "Countries, even those with the strongest economies, are not powerful enough to satisfactorily enforce their tax laws pursuant to the current tax regime."[27]

Globalization,[28] the emergence of the digital economy,[29] the mobility of income,[30] harmful tax competition among countries,[31] and the new role of services and

27. Yariv Brauner, "What the BEPS?" (2014) 16(2) *Florida Tax Review*, p. 59.
28. Frederico Silva Bastos, *O Intercâmbio Internacional de Informações Tributárias no Brasil* (Porto Alegre: BUQUI, 2015), pp. 25-40.
29. César García Novoa, "Reflexiones sobre la Influencia de la Globalización em los Princípios Tributarios," Heleno Taveira Tôrres (ed.), *Direito Tributário Internacional Aplicado* (São Paulo: Quartier Latin, 2003), pp. 34-44.
30. *See*: Marco Aurélio Greco, "Crise do Imposto sobre a Renda na sua Feição Tradicional," Condorcet Rezende (ed.), *Estudos Tributários* (Rio de Janeiro: Renovar, 1999) pp. 422-423.

intangibles all have created a potential environment for tax evasion and aggressive tax planning.[32]

These are not new topics. However, the series of global financial crises that began in 2008 has forced the world to deal with the consequences of the improper allocation of tax revenues.

It was in this context that the work of Thomas Piketty gained special attention. One of the pillars of the French economist's research is the finding that harmful tax competition has led to the more favorable treatment of capital income[33] to the detriment of labor income, thereby beginning a crisis of income tax progressivity and inability to fairly distribute the tax burden.[34] In his words:

> At the same time, the recent rise of tax competition in a world of free-flowing capital has led many governments to exempt income from the progressive income tax. This is particularly true in Europe, whose relatively small states have thus far proved incapable of achieving a coordinated tax policy. The result is an endless race to the bottom, leading, for example, to cuts in corporate tax rates and to the exemption of interest, dividends, and other financial revenues from the taxes to which labor income is subject.[35]

Claims for the protection of the so-called fair share of tax of each country have become ever more strident. First, there was a decisive movement towards tax transparency—mostly through the Global Forum on Transparency and Exchange of Information—and later the creation and development of the Organisation for Economic Co-operation and Development (OECD)/G-20 BEPS Project.

Regarding the relation between income mobility and harmful tax competition, *see*: Bem J. Kiekebled, *Harmful Tax Competition in the European Union* (The Netherlands: Kluwer, 2004), pp. 1-2.

31. It is worth transcribing the words of Michael Rodi, for whom "A tax system is ultimately characterized as 'harmful' when it causes investors to be drawn into doing business in a particular country mainly for tax reasons, so that there is no true decision on the place of business." Michael Rodi, "Concorrência Tributária Internacional por Investimentos" (2007) 21 *Revista Direito Tributário Atual*, p. 32. Also *see*: Hugh J. Ault, "Tax Competition: What (If Anything) To Do About It," Paul Kirchhof et al. (ed.), *International and Comparative Taxation: Essays in Honor of Klaus Vogel* (The Netherlands: Kluwer, 2002) pp. 2-4; Joachim Lang, "Justiça Fiscal e Globalização" (2010) 24 *Revista Direito Tributário Atual*, p. 76; Clara Gomes Moreira, "Combate às Práticas Fiscais Danosas e a Soberania dos Estados," Marcus Lívio Gomes & Luís Eduardo Schoueri (eds.), *A Tributação Internacional na Era Pós-BEPS* (Rio de Janeiro: Lumen Juris, 2016) v. I, pp. 265-283.
32. *See* Victor Uckmar et al., *Diritto Tributario Internazionale* (Milani: CEDAM, 2012) pp. XXVI-XXXII.
33. It is interesting to note Philip Baker's view that "much of the role of international tax planners obviously involves the use of favored tax regimes or, if you prefer, tax havens or offshore financial centers. I believe that this is something that must remain in the 21st century, that there will continue to be favored tax regimes. This is one aspect of tax competition between states. I suspect this will continue although possibly with the most harmful aspects being gradually identified and removed." Philip Baker, "A Tributação Internacional no Século XXI" (2005) 19 *Revista Direito Tributário Atual*, p. 45.
34. *See*: Reuven Avi-Yonah, "Globalization, Tax Competition and the Fiscal Crisis of the Welfare State" (2000) 113 (7) *Harvard Law Review*, pp. 1579-1603.
35. Thomas Piketty, *Capital in the Twenty-First Century* (Cambridge: The Belknap Press of Harvard University Press, 2014), p. 496.

Since this is a typical risk-society problem, marked by features such as ambivalence and complexity,[36] it is natural that the search for a broad global solution can only be multilateral, which demands a change in the perspective of international taxation.

Indeed, although the first international treaty to avoid double taxation was concluded in 1899 between Prussia and the Austro-Hungarian Empire,[37] it was only after the end of World War I that more decisive efforts towards the development of international taxation were conceived within the scope of the League of Nations. This resulted in the first model of an international convention to avoid double taxation of income, which was published in 1928.[38]

The "International Tax Regime"[39] inaugurated in 1928 had as fundamental characteristics bilateralism and competition between several countries. Such a regime prevailed basically unchanged and unchallenged until the 21st century when harmful tax competition and especially the digital economy made it obsolete.

The multilateral approach in the field of international tax law has always been considered secondary to bilateralism. Nevertheless, the scenario has recently changed, with the perception that some problems of contemporary international taxation can only be satisfactorily addressed from a multilateral perspective. Note that this does not mean that the bilateral approach is outmoded. What it does mean is that some of the current problems in international taxation require a more collaborative/multilateral approach.

The first major multilateral initiative in the field of international taxation is in the context of transparency and the exchange of information for tax purposes: The Multilateral Convention on Mutual Administrative Assistance in Tax Matters. It became the cornerstone of the international transparency system and some actions of the BEPS Project.[40] This trend was not overlooked by Pasquale Pistone. According to him:

> From a legal perspective, formal bilateralism on mutual assistance in tax matters, as preserved by articles 26 and 27 of tax treaties, is gradually becoming obsolete. Since 2009, any inconsistency with internationally agreed standards of fiscal transparency exposes the State to the opposition of a significantly larger share of the global community in the context of the forum for fiscal transparency. Indeed, States have lost their power to negotiate the content of this part of their bilateral

36. *See*: Sergio André Rocha, *Tributação Internacional* (São Paulo: Quartier Latin, 2013), pp. 16-21.
37. *See*: Sunita Jogarajan, "Prelude to the International Tax Treaty Network: 1815-1914 Early Tax Treaties and the Conditions for Action" (2011) *Oxford Journal of Legal Studies*, p. 12; Christian Freiherr von Roenne, "The Very Beginning — The First Tax Treaties," Thomas Ecker & Gernot Ressler (eds.), *History of Tax Treaties* (Wien: Linde, 2011), pp. 24-26.
38. Regarding this topic, *see*: Sergio André Rocha, *Interpretation of Double Taxation Conventions: General Theory and Brazilian Perspective* (The Netherlands: Kluwer, 2009), pp. 1-4.
39. Reuven Avi-Yonah argues that there is an "International Tax Regime" which, according to the author, would have as a practical consequence the fact, "that countries are not free to adopt any international tax rules they please, but rather operate in the context of the regime, which changes in the same ways international law changes over time." Reuven Avi-Yonah, *International Tax as International Law: An Analysis of the International Tax Regime* (Cambridge: Cambridge University Press, 2007), p. 1.
40. *See*: Sergio André Rocha, *Troca Internacional de Informações para Fins Fiscais* (São Paulo: Quartier Latin, 2015) pp. 113-115.

> treaties. In these circumstances, it no longer makes sense to maintain mutual assistance regulated on a bilateral level through treaties whose clauses are becoming homogeneous as to their wording and scope. This explains why more States adhere to multilateral legal instruments on mutual assistance [...].[41]

The OECD/G-20's BEPS Project further accentuated the multilateral nature of current international taxation. As already pointed out, no state can unilaterally overcome the challenges related to preventing international tax evasion and aggressive tax planning. This reinforces the multilateral approach to international tax law—not in substitution of bilateralism but in addition to it. Yariv Brauner supports this approach by stating that, "The heart of this insight is the understanding that uncoordinated domestic law actions can never succeed (other than by chance), regardless of their content. The interdependence of the players on the global market therefore requires collaboration."[42]

At this point, my position is starting to take shape. The question is not whether or not all countries will engage in some type of multilateral international tax initiative, but the extent of such engagement. Therefore, this is a matter of degree.

9 BEPS, MULTILATERALISM, AND EPISTEMOLOGIES OF THE SOUTH

For a long time now, I have been claiming that international taxation is driven by the interests of developed countries, which have been successful in turning international tax principles and standards that favor their positions into universal and general principles of international taxation. This state of affairs results in what I have named "international tax imperialism," which means "the transformation of certain tax criteria that favor the interests of developed economies in international tax standards that become considered as basic principles of international taxation."[43] My position was later supported by Tarcisio Magalhaes.[44]

A similar view was advocated by Tsilly Dagan, in her book *International Policy and Cooperation*. This book is a must-read for all those who feel there has been something out of place with the dogmas surrounding international taxation for almost a century. It is worth quoting the following paragraphs from her study:

> For almost a century, the impressive multinational cooperative campaigns in the international tax arena have been led primarily by OECD countries, some more successfully than others. In this period, OECD countries have relentlessly advanced cooperative initiatives, in line with the premise (or at least rhetoric) that

41. Pasquale Pistone, "Coordinating the Action of Regional and Global Players During the Shift from Bilateralism to Multilateralism in International Tax Law" (2014) 6 *World Tax Journal*, pp. 3-4.
42. Yariv Brauner, "BEPS: An Interim Evaluation" (2014) 6 *World Tax Journal*, p. 13.
43. Sergio André Rocha, "The Other Side of BEPS: 'Imperial Taxation' and 'International Tax Imperialism'," Sergio André Rocha & Allison Christians, *Tax Sovereignty in the BEPS Era* (The Netherlands: Kluwer, 2017) p. 188.
44. Tarcísio Magalhães, "International Taxation Without International Representation? Legality and Legitimacy in Global Tax Governance," Bruno Peeters, Hans Gibnau & Jo Badisco (eds.), *Building Trust in Taxation*, (Cambridge: Intersentia, 2017), p. 273.

> cooperation is beneficial for all of its participants. This assertion is consistent with the classic collective-action rationale that everyone stands to lose if every state-actor promotes its own self-interests and rejects cooperation. We see here the problematic strategic dynamics of the game that cause some state-actors to choose an action (defection) that conflicts with their best interests. However, the pro-cooperation narrative misses the converse alternative: that for some states the fact that cooperate does not necessarily mean that this is their best option. As I have sought to show in this chapter, sometimes states cooperate *despite* this not being in their best interests. That is not to say, of course, that *any* cooperation is bad but, rather, that instead of assuming that a country's cooperation is proof per se that the initiative is beneficial to it, we must look more closely at the interests at stake.
>
> [...]
>
> The chapter illuminated the mechanisms in which international tax game can be constructed to benefit some (that is, developed) countries at the expense of other (that is, developing) states. I would not go so far as to suggest that developed countries cooperated in a premeditated manner so as to deliberately create negative externalities on developing countries. But even assuming the current international tax system was not intentionally designed to impose these externalities on developing countries, by pursuing the interests of OECD countries in limiting tax competition and increasing their tax revenues while disregarding the interests of developing countries, it has de facto led to a reality in which the latter face a very narrow range of choices.[45]

This situation leads to the tax colonization of minds from developing and emerging economies, who are likely to think of their own countries' international tax policies from the perspective of the "international" framework.[46]

The line of thought I have been developing in the field of international taxation overlaps the arguments presented by the Portuguese sociologist Boaventura Souza Santos, who has been criticizing how the "social theory of the global North" presents itself as a universal theory, ignoring the contributions of the global South. In his words:

> The global north is getting smaller and smaller in economic as well as political and cultural terms, and yet it cannot make sense of the world at large other than through general theories and universal ideas. Observed from the outside, such a *habitus* is less and less convincing and can be viewed as the expression of a somewhat anachronistic manifestation of the Western exceptionalism, even if it remains very destructive when translated into imperial politics. In sum, from this perspective, the global North seems to have little to teach the world. Is this all that important? Would not the historical opportunity for the global North to learn from the experiences of the global South lie precisely here? *The truth of the matter is that, after five centuries of 'teaching' the world, the global North seems to have lost the capacity to learn from the experiences of the world. In other words, it looks as if colonialism has disabled the global North from learning in noncolonial terms, that is, in terms that allow for the existence of histories other than the universal history of the West.*

45. Tisilly Dagan, *International Tax Policy: Between Competition and Cooperation* (Cambridge: Cambridge University Press, 2018) pp. 183-184.
46. Sergio André Rocha, "The Other Side of BEPS: 'Imperial Taxation' and 'International Tax Imperialism'," Sergio André Rocha & Allison Christians, *Tax Sovereignty in the BEPS Era* (The Netherlands: Kluwer, 2017) p. 190.

> This condition is reflected in all the intellectual work produced in the global North and, most specifically, in Western, Eurocentric critical theory. A sense of exhaustion haunts the Western, Eurocentric critical tradition. It manifests itself in a peculiar and diffuse uneasiness expressed in multiple ways: irrelevance, inadequacy, impotence, stagnation, paralysis. Such uneasiness is all the more disquieting because we are living in a world in which there is so much to be criticized, in a world, moreover, in which an ever-growing number of people live in critical conditions that imply both crisis and critique. If there is so much to criticize, which has it become so difficult to build convincing, widely shared, powerful, critical theories, theories that give rise to effective and profound transformative practices.[47] (Emphasis added)

Among the difficulties of "confronting Eurocentric emancipatory imagination," Boaventura Souza Santos mentions colonialism. According to him, "It is as difficult to imagine the end of colonialism as it is to imagine that colonialism has no end. Postcolonial or decolonial studies and struggles in the past three decades have shown how entrenched colonialism is in both private and public life, even many decades after the end of historical colonialism. On the other hand, as in the case of capitalism without end, it is hard to believe that colonialism will escape the fate of other social phenomena and have no end. In this case as well, Eurocentric emancipatory imagination and politics have been split into two main responses. A first strand is blocked by the first difficulty; incapable of imagining the end of colonialism, it denies the existence of colonialism itself. According to this strand, the political independence of the colonies meant the end of colonialism; since then, anticapitalism has been the only political objective of emancipatory politics. This line of Eurocentric critical thinking focuses on class struggle and hence does not acknowledge the validity of the ethnocultural-racial struggles. On the contrary, it valorizes hybridity (*mestizaje*)—which, for instance, it identifies as a key failure of Iberian colonialism—as extra proof that colonialism has been overcome. *Accordingly, the idea of racial democracy, rather than being defended as a legitimate aspiration, is celebrated as being already fully accomplished.*"[48] (Emphasis added)

This final part of Souza Santos's comments seems entirely applicable to the debates in the area of international taxation. Whenever one argues there are legitimacy deficits in this field, there is always support of the opposite view. In other words, that inclusion has already been achieved, or all countries are on the same side or have the same voice. Positions in this sense are reinforced by initiatives such as the Global Forum on Transparency and Exchange of Information for Tax Purposes and the inclusive framework in the BEPS Project.[49]

This same view of how social sciences have developed over time is also supported by Raewyn Connell. In his opinion, "Social science is, at best, ambiguously democratic. *Its dominant genres picture the world as it is seen by men, by capitalists, by*

47. Boaventura de Souza Santos, *Epistemologies of the South: Justice Against Epistemicide* (London: Routledge, 2016), pp. 19-20.
48. Boaventura de Souza Santos, *Epistemologies of the South: Justice Against Epistemicide* (London: Routledge, 2016) p. 26.
49. Sergio André Rocha, *Brazil's International Tax Policy* (Rio de Janeiro: Lumen Juris, 2017) pp. 204-205.

the educated and affluent. Most important, they picture the world as seen from the rich capital-exporting countries of Europe and North America—the global metropole. To ground knowledge of society in other experiences remains a fragile project."[50] (emphasis added)

This author also highlighted the attempt to present the views of the dominant countries of the world as universal. According to her, "Modern social science embeds the viewpoints, perspectives and problems of metropolitan society, while presenting itself as universal knowledge."[51]

The resemblance between these positions regarding social sciences and the OECD-centric international taxation approach is evident.

In fields like transfer pricing, attribution of profits to permanent establishments, BEPS, etc., the OECD's view is presented as universally valid and applicable, regardless of the characteristics of each country—economic profile, legal system, and, most importantly, institutional capacities.

10 MULTILATERALISM AND THE IMPORTANCE OF INSTITUTIONAL CAPACITIES

It is not unusual for theories and models to be created and defended disconnected from the actual institutional capacities of countries, entities, etc. This topic is analyzed by Cass R. Sunstein and Adrian Vermeule in a study focused on the theory of interpretation. Their starting point is that legal interpretation theories often focus on "how, in principle, should a text be interpreted" while the real question should be "how should certain institutions, with their distinctive abilities and limitations, interpret certain texts."[52] Their conclusion is clear:

> We have argued that issues of legal interpretation cannot be adequately resolved without attention to institutional issues. An extraordinary variety of distinguished people have explored interpretive strategies without attending to the fact that such strategies will inevitably be used by fallible people and with likely dynamic effects extending far beyond the case at hand. Two mechanisms seem principally responsible for this institutional blindness. One is a role-related trap: interpretive theorists ask themselves "how would I decide the case, if I were a judge?"—a question whose very form suppresses the key consideration that the relevant interpretive rules are to be used by judges rather than theorists. Another is a cognitive trap: specialists, such as legal academics, criticize the insufficiently nuanced opinions issued by generalist judges in particular cases, overlooking that the same judges might well have done far worse, over a series of cases, by attempting to emulate the specialists' approach. Overall, the key question seems to be, "how would perfect judges decide cases?" rather than "how should fallible judges proceed, in light of their fallibility and their place in a complex system of private and public ordering?"

50. Raewyn Connell, *Southern Theory* (Cambridge: Polity Press, 2009) p. vii.
51. Raewyn Connell, *Southern Theory* (Cambridge: Polity Press, 2009) pp. vii-viii.
52. Cass R. Sunstein & Adrian Vermeule, "Interpretation and Institutions," *Coase-Sandor Working Paper Series in Law and Economics*, p. 2 (2002).

> "Our minimal submission has been that answers to the former question are hopelessly inadequate. We have argued as well that in some cases, an appreciation of judicial fallibility and of dynamic effects will enable people to converge on an appropriate approach despite their disagreements about the right path for perfect judges to follow. At the very least, an appreciation of institutional questions should make it possible for people to have a better appreciation of what they are disagreeing about, and also of strategies for making some progress in the future. We have emphasized the importance of asking about the likelihood of legislative oversight and correction; the values of planning and predictability, and the effects, on these values, of one or another interpretive choice in the particular context; and the actual performance of courts that follow textualism, purposivism, or some other approach. Here there is much room for empirical work, involving, for example, the nature and effects of different interpretive approaches within different states, the responsiveness of state legislatures to those different approaches, and the possible connection between formality in interpretation and legislative attentiveness in various domains of law."[53]

Sunstein and Vermeule's point is quite convincing: legal interpretation theorists argue their positions *disregarding the actual institutions that will interpret and apply the law in concrete cases.* A theory that does not take institutional capacities into account is likely to fail in the real world.

These authors' comments can be expanded to several areas and fit perfectly in the field of international taxation.

Indeed, the OECD-centric approach to international taxation and the view that it can be universally applied fails to consider the institutional capacities of each country.

Tsilly Dagan's comment quoted previously applies in this context. There is an awkward tendency of some developing and emerging countries to act against their own domestic tax interests under the banner of cooperation. It is as if the interest in belonging, the chance of joining the club, is stronger than a country's own interests.

11 ARE UNILATERAL APPROACHES STILL POSSIBLE?

Based on countries' objectives in the field of international taxation, there is no evidence that unilateral measures are no longer possible, at least in part and in relation to certain topics.

Indeed, the perception that adhering to a sort of one-size-fits-all multilateralism is the only way for a country to defend its economic and political interests seems biased. It is probably another example of exportation of problems of the global North, which are automatically considered to be equally present all over the globe.

It is important to stress that *unilateral does not equal isolated.* What I am advocating is that countries should have the leeway to adopt a type of ad hoc multilateralism whenever possible.

53. Cass R. Sunstein & Adrian Vermeule, "Interpretation and Institutions," *Coase-Sandor Working Paper Series in Law and Economics*, pp. 46-47 (2002).

For instance, is it possible to reduce BEPS to tolerable levels using domestic regulations? That will depend on the answer to the following question: What is aggressive tax planning?

11.1 What Is Aggressive Tax Planning?

One of the most used expressions of the BEPS Project Reports is "aggressive tax planning." However, it is not easy to define what this means. This is definitely one of the biggest challenges of the BEPS Project: to draw the line between legitimate tax planning and so-called aggressive tax planning.

Various BEPS Actions deal with the concept of aggressive tax planning. However, none of them is closer to the subject than Action 12, which involves the "Disclosure of Aggressive Tax Planning."[54] According to the OECD BEPS Action Plan, the major goal of Action 12 is to "develop recommendations regarding the design of mandatory disclosure rules for aggressive or abusive transactions, arrangements, or structures, taking into consideration the administrative costs for tax administrations and businesses and drawing on experiences of the increasing number of countries that have such rules."[55]

However, even though the concept of aggressive tax planning is central to the BEPS Project, neither the BEPS Action Plan nor any of the BEPS Actions' deliverables and discussion drafts—including that of Action 12—hazard to define aggressive tax planning.

In the glossary included in its 2008 "Study on the Role of Tax Intermediaries," the OECD presented a somewhat clear definition of aggressive tax planning:

> "*Aggressive tax planning.* This refers to two areas of concern for revenue bodies:
>
> "*Planning involving a tax position that is tenable but has unintended and unexpected tax revenue consequences.* Revenue bodies' concerns relate to the risk that tax legislation can be misused to achieve results which were not foreseen by the legislators. This is exacerbated by the often lengthy period between the time schemes are created and sold and the time revenue bodies discover them and remedial legislation is enacted."
>
> "*Taking a tax position that is favourable to the taxpayer without openly disclosing that there is uncertainty whether significant matters in the tax return accord with the law.* Revenue bodies' concerns relate to the risk that taxpayers will not disclose their view on the uncertainty or risk taken in relation to grey areas of law (sometimes, revenue bodies would not even agree that the law is in doubt)."[56] (emphasis added)

---

54. For an analysis of the development of the OECD's concept of aggressive tax planning, *see*: Marta Caldas, *O Conceito de Planejamento Fiscal Agressivo: Novos Limites ao Planejamento Fiscal?* (Lisboa: Almedina, 2015) pp. 67-76. For a study analyzing the distinction between "aggressive" and "abusive" tax planning, *see*: Paolo Piantavigna, "Tax Abuse and Aggressive Tax Planning in the BEPS Era: How EU Law and the OECD Are Establishing a Unifying Conceptual Framework in International Tax Law, despite Linguistic Discrepancies" (2017) 9(1) *World Tax Journal*, pp. 47-98.
55. OECD, *Action Plan on Base Erosion and Profit Shifting* (Paris: OECD, 2013) p. 22.
56. OECD, *Study into the Role of Tax Intermediaries* (Paris: OECD, 2008) p. 87.

In reviewing this OECD report, the Portuguese author Marta Caldas characterized the scope of the "aggressive" tax planning concept as including situations in which no traces of artificiality or abuse are identified. In her words, "At the OECD level, in the Study on the Role of Tax Intermediaries, an OECD Report from 2008, for example, aggressive fiscal planning is precisely delimited, by one of its lines of research, as planning that involves a legitimate fiscal situation, but with *unexpected consequences* in terms of tax revenues, and in which access to information is assumed to be a key instrument for good tax governance, which will not only enable tax administrations to reduce administrative costs with assessments, but *also enable the tax lawmakers to correct inconsistencies in unintentionally generated tax rules.*"[57] (highlights in original)

This OECD "definition" was criticized by Philip Baker, who argued that it "Suggests that the focus of the OECD's concern with regards to aggressive tax planning relates either to schemes or arrangements that achieve a result not foreseen by the legislators, or that rely upon an uncertain tax position. Frankly, this is not a particularly helpful approach to identifying aggressive tax planning. The first leg relies upon an understanding of what was and was not foreseen by legislators: in all too many cases, the legislature has neither any clear idea or what it wishes to achieve by tax legislation, nor makes its intentions clear in any form that could give helpful guidance to taxpayers. The second leg of the definition gives no clear indication of the degree of uncertainty in the tax position."[58]

Philip Baker's criticism of the definition previously transcribed goes directly to the point. It seems reasonable to state that the OECD does not have a clear definition of aggressive tax planning. However, it is fair to say that it includes at least two situations: (i) the so-called abusive tax planning, in which the taxpayer uses an artificial structure or transaction to achieve a more advantageous tax effect; and (ii) situations where artificiality is not identified, but it is understood that the taxpayer receives an unintended tax advantage—in the sense of a fiscal effect that was not intentionally provided for by law.[59]

One of the features that makes it harder to counteract aggressive tax planning is that sometimes it is a consequence of gaps and mismatches of domestic tax systems, which can have unintended consequences. As noted by Ana Paula Dourado, "In contrast to the principle of abuse, aggressive tax planning also covers the existence of legal gaps or mismatches exploited in transnational situations."[60]

57. Marta Caldas, *O Conceito de Planejamento Fiscal Agressivo* (Lisboa: Almedina, 2015) p. 119.
58. Philip Baker, "The BEPS Project: Disclosure of Aggressive Tax Planning Schemes" (2015) 43 (1) *Intertax*, p. 86.
59. Therefore, the definition of James Alm seems to be incomplete—at least from the BEPS Project's perspective—when he states: "The ATP is often seen as a tax avoidance transaction that complies with literality but abuses the spirit of the law." *See*: James Alm, "Um Sistema Tributário Transparente Desencorajaria o 'Planejamento Tributário Agressivo'?," Eurico Marcos Diniz de Santi (ed.), *Transparência Fiscal e Desenvolvimento: Homenagem ao Professor Isaias Coelho* (São Paulo: Editora FISCOsoft, 2013), p. 276.
60. Ana Paula Dourado, "Aggressive Tax Planning in EU Law and in the Light of BEPS: The EC Recommendation on Aggressive Tax Planning and BEPS Actions 2 and 6" (2015) 43 (1) *Intertax*, p. 48. Also *see*: José Manuel Calderón Carrero & Alberto Quintas Serra, *Cumplimiento Tributario Cooperativo y Buena Governanza Fiscal en la Era BEPS* (Navarra: Civitas, 2015), pp. 45-50.

With these comments in mind, I now return to the initial question of this section: Are unilateral approaches still possible? It clearly depends on whether this fight against hybrid mismatches is relevant for the country.

Indeed, a lot can be done to counteract abusive tax planning using domestic legislation. It does not seem that global coordination is required for these purposes. However, if the idea is to harmonize domestic legislation aiming at avoiding gaps and loopholes that result in more favorable tax treatments, a greater level of coordination is required. Likewise, if the focus is to control harmful tax competition—notably that type of competition from countries that are not low-tax jurisdictions—coordination and multilateralism are keys. However, there is no indication that BEPS cannot be successfully managed unilaterally—up to a certain level that might be enough for some countries.

12 THE BRAZILIAN CASE

Brazil is an interesting case to prove the point I made in the previous section. This country has what is probably one of the most extensive anti-BEPS regulations. Some of its provisions include the following.

- Payments to low-tax jurisdictions are subject to a 25% withholding tax—the only exception (which might be short-lived) being dividend payments.
- In some cases, payments to entities under privileged tax regimes are also subject to a 25% withholding tax.
- Payments to regular taxing countries are generally subject to a 15% withholding tax.
- Payments for services are subject to additional levies of social contributions (10% for CIDE- "Contribution for Economic Intervention" - and 9.25% for PIS/Cofins-Importação - Social Contribution on Imports), and 5% service tax.
- Royalty payments are subject to an additional 10% CIDE.
- All payments to low-tax jurisdictions or to beneficiaries under privileged tax regimes are subject to transfer pricing control.
- Transactions with related parties are generally subject to transfer pricing control.
- All payments to low-tax jurisdictions or to beneficiaries under privileged tax regimes are not deductible for income tax purposes unless some requirements are met—including proof that the recipient of the payments is the beneficial owner.
- Brazil has probably the most extensive CFC (Controlled Foreign Companies) regulations in the world, with a full-inclusion system that taxes at year-end all profits earned by CFCs.
- Thin capitalization rules apply not only to financial transactions with related parties but also to any transaction with an entity located in a low-tax jurisdiction or subject to a privileged tax regime.

- Anti-abuse practices allow tax authorities to disregard and reclassify transactions that are deemed artificially structured to avoid tax payments or to reduce or postpone the tax liability.
- Some tax incentives that benefit non-residents do not apply if the entity or the individual is resident in a low-tax jurisdiction.

These are just some of the features of Brazil's anti-BEPS system. Anyone familiar with Brazilian tax regulations knows that this is not a BEPS friendly jurisdiction. I am certainly not saying that Brazil's system is perfect or that it prevents BEPS in one hundred percent of the cases. After all, perfection is not a typical attribute of the works of people. Nevertheless, it is hard to imagine that anyone confronted with the question "What are Brazil's worst tax problems?" would reply by saying "BEPS."

In addition to not being BEPS friendly, Brazil's system has other relevant features.

First, Brazil has a special treaty policy that basically dehydrates Article 7 of the country's conventions based on the OECD model.[61] Therefore, Brazil has little trouble taxing publicity services and other digital economy activities at the source as technical services—as long as there is a source of payment in the country.

In addition, Brazil has no tradition of applying permanent establishment rules.[62] Therefore, it never relied on the physical presence of the non-resident person as a triggering event for it to exercise taxing rights.

Anyone closely following Brazil's participation in the inclusive framework of the BEPS Project would most likely acknowledge that the country's work with the OECD has had positive impacts on its tax administration. The same can be said about the joint work developed by Brazilian and OECD authorities towards development of new transfer pricing rules for the country.

However, the hard truth is that there is no indication, for instance, that if pillars 1 and 2 of Action 1 of the BEPS Project are ever approved, they will have a significant impact on the country's tax practices.

As previously stated, rejecting the assumption that multilateralism is the only way for a country to operate in the current international environment is not the same as saying that countries should isolate themselves. What I am saying is just that there is no indication that countries will always benefit from multilateral approaches.

13 WILL THE WORLD'S TAXING POWERS LET YOU FOLLOW YOUR PATH?

If there are good arguments to support the position that some countries might be better off following their own tax agendas, there is of course the subsequent question of whether the global tax leaders will let them act this way.

61. *See*: Sergio André Rocha, *Brazil's International Tax Policy* (Rio de Janeiro: Lumen Juris, 2017), pp. 50-55.
62. *See*: Sergio André Rocha, "Agency Permanent Establishment 'Brazilian Style': Taxation of Profits Earned Through Commission Merchants, Agents and Representatives" (2013) 42 (8 & 9) *Intertax*.

This question raises relevant concerns about multilateral approaches, which can be used to foster tax practices that benefit some countries to the detriment of others. In fact, even though much is said about inter-nation equity, I agree with Luís Eduardo Schoueri and Ricardo Galendi Júnior, who state the following:

> Indeed, inter-nations equity has never played a significant role in the international allocation of taxing rights, despite the significant contributions of scholars in this field. As a consequence of the democratic principle, States are incentivized to prioritize the interests of their citizens, instead of seeking global justice, and there are generally no deviations from this expected behavior. The centrality of the Nation State is still an undeniable fact and has led to rather skeptic statements on the impossibility of determining what would be a fair outcome under the perspective of inter-nations equity. After all, "we regard our obligation for the well-being of our fellow citizens as more pressing than for people in need elsewhere in the world.
>
> The assumption that States behave like egoistic value maximizers is common to most theories on international relations. Value maximization is inherent to States' negotiations and the current international tax scenario has already been described as 'polluted by power play and deception,' which are the 'two striking elements that can be detected in the actual struggle for international tax justice.' In this context, it is difficult to believe in any other positive duty arising from sovereignty than of non-interference in the execution of the external policies of other Nations. Absent a treaty provision, no State has the right to tell another one which legislation it should approve and follow."[63]

It is certainly true that countries are not entirely free to decide what their international tax policies will be. On the other hand, it seems hard to dispute the assumption that countries are mostly guided by their own self-interests when defending certain positions internationally.

Hence, it is reasonable to conclude that even though it might not be in their best interests to join international multilateral tax efforts, countries will not always be in a position to stand their ground and follow their own paths.

14 ARE UNILATERAL APPROACHES EFFICIENT IN THE CURRENT SCENARIO?

One thing is to question whether multilateralism is mandatory in the current international tax scenario; it is another thing is to wonder whether it is more efficient. Just like I argued in the previous section, there does not seem to be evidence that multilateralism will always be equally efficient for all countries.

Multilateralism is a very recent trend in international taxation. In my view, there is simply no global experience with a multilateral approach applied to distributive international tax rules. Therefore, it is impossible to predict how they would look in

63. Luís Eduardo Schoueri & Ricardo André Galendi Júnior, "Justification and Implementation of the International Allocation of Taxing Rights: Can We Take One Thing at a Time?," Sergio André Rocha & Allison Christians, *Tax Sovereignty in the BEPS Era* (The Netherlands: Kluwer, 2017) pp. 64-65.

real life, how complex their implementation would be, and how intricate their application would become.

For instance, in this case, a multilateral agreement will not be enough, since changes in domestic tax legislation will require laws passed by countries' legislative bodies. Is this feasible? How long will it take?

So far, successful multilateral approaches have been applied to procedural fields, such as exchange of information and control of the improper use of tax conventions—even though it is unclear how the latter will work, since there are few cases of application of the principal purpose test clause, for instance.[64]

The point is, even though evidence shows that unilateral approaches will not always be more efficient, one can also make a valid point that there is no evidence that multilateralism will always be more efficient, regardless of each country's situation.

15 WHAT HAPPENS IF A COUNTRY WANTS TO PARTAKE IN MULTILATERAL ENDEAVORS?

An important aspect of the position I am expressing is that there is no one-size-fits-all solution to international tax problems. A country might believe that a multilateral approach is more adequate in one situation—for instance, international tax transparency—and inadequate in another—say, taxation of digital companies.

The problem—and this might be one of the greatest problems seeking solution in international taxation—is that the current international tax governance is completely biased to favor the positions of a handful of developed countries.

As well noticed by Allison Christians, one of the greatest tricks of those pulling the strings in this field is to convince people—and countries—that international taxation issues are technical in nature. Therefore, each choice is not a mere exercise of power, but a technical decision that must be accepted and followed. In her words:

> In 1963, economist Nicholas Kaldor famously asked whether poor countries would ever "learn to tax." He might have done better to direct his inquiry toward the wealthy nations of the world. Learning to tax is not about acquiring knowledge. Making a claim of right over the global income tax base is, very simply, a matter of power rather than principle. We may wish that nations were guided by normative principles, and we may try to find evidence that normative principles have guided behavior in the past, but this is a challenging task. Dividing the global tax base has always been a power struggle amongst nations. To be sure, powerful nations have chosen to exercise their power to control taxation through economic, rather than military force. In practice this has meant that richer countries have set up systems and rules to benefit themselves. This is a constraint on policy-making that we must expect will continue.
>
> Accordingly, some countries have learned that they have the power to effect immediate change in the international tax status quo. Others do not have that power, no matter what they may learn about international taxation. In reviewing the 1923 Report for purposes of explaining the US position on international tax

64. On this topic, *see*: Marcus Lívio Gomes, *The Principal Purpose Test in the Multilateral Instrument* (Rio de Janeiro: Lumen Juris, 2021).

> treaties in the early 1980s, Professors David Rosenbloom and Stanley Langbein rejected unilateral measures as "almost inevitably ineffectual." The events of the past several years suggest that unilateralism can be a highly effective strategy for powerful nations. But the outcome of these events makes a strong case for working ever harder toward multilateralism.
>
> Unilateralism in taxation is not always or necessarily ineffective; rather, it can be asymmetrically effective, which results in a transfer among nations of the burdens and benefits of the power to tax. The ongoing global effort by the United States to achieve its goals with respect to tax evasion by US persons is illustrative in this regard, especially when juxtaposed against its approach to the problem of tax avoidance by multinational companies.[65]

Indeed, there is just no institutional design for international tax multilateralism that can overcome the asymmetries of power among nations. One might argue that the United Nations is more suited to be the arena where global tax policy is debated. However, it has clearly lost this role to the OECD. The latter has been trying to overcome its legitimacy deficits by adopting more inclusive structures, such as the Global Forum on Transparency and Exchange of Information for Tax Purposes and the BEPS Project's inclusive framework. However, there is no indication that the so-called equal footing has become—or will ever become—reality.

16 EXPLAINING THE APPARENT PARADOX

Readers who have reached this point of this text might be a little confused. Is multilateralism an inevitable requirement of international taxation in the context of risk society or is it accidental and secondary?

My point is that it is incontestable that risk-society problems require multilateral action. However, that does not necessarily mean that all countries are equally interested in multilateral initiatives. The assumption that some problems are universal seems to be just plain wrong.

Hence, I am not disputing the assumption that risk-society problems are better managed multilaterally. However, I am challenging the notion that such problems are equally important to all countries and therefore all of them should take part in related multilateral initiatives.

As contradictory as it might seem, I am arguing in favor of a "unilateral multilateralism," which safeguards the right of countries not to engage in multilateral initiatives that either are not to their advantage or do not provide the necessary governance structure for them to participate on equal footing.

17 CONCLUSION

Multilateralism has become one of the mantras of the 21st century's international tax debate. It is as if suddenly all countries have been forced to follow the lead of the

65. Allison Christians, "BEPS and the Power to Tax," Sergio André Rocha & Allison Christians, *Tax Sovereignty in the BEPS Era* (The Netherlands: Kluwer, 2017), pp. 19-20.

handful of countries that are trying to reshape international tax rules that are no longer suitable for some of them.

It is usually forgotten in this debate that the same rules have always been unfavorable to developing and emerging countries. It is as if all of a sudden, developed countries realized what has been common knowledge of poorer countries for almost a century: the permanent establishment is a flawed criterion for the allocation of taxing rights. This is not a consequence of the digitalization of the economy. It has been so since the first League of Nations Models decided to use the permanent establishment as the nexus for the allocation of taxing rights over active income.

Now that some developed countries realize the unfairness of this criterion, they have decided that this is a global problem that requires the engagement of all countries. Simpler measures such as the taxation of digital services at the source—in line with the United Nations' Article 12-B—have been quickly discarded.

In this context, my main conclusion is that even though risk-society problems are better managed multilaterally, countries should consider first whether they have the problem; second, if the multilateral solution is more efficient in its particular case; and third, whether a multilateral body exists in which it can actually participate. However, the idea that international tax multilateralism is some sort of tax Woodstock and that all countries should participate seems to be flatly wrong.

Part II Structure and Adoption

CHAPTER 5
The Framework of the Multilateral Instrument

Ramon Tomazela Santos

Ramon Tomazela Santos provides a detailed examination of the structure and components of the Multilateral Instrument (MLI). The chapter serves as a comprehensive explanation of the four main parts of the MLI, namely the minimum standards and optional additional coordinative enhancements aimed at hybrid mismatches, treaty abuse, permanent establishments (Pes), and dispute resolution. In addition to providing a thorough overview of the MLI, Tomazela Santos provides a brief critical analysis of the main provisions.

1 INTRODUCTION

On June 7, 2017, the signing ceremony of the Multilateral Convention to Implement Tax Treaty Related Measures to Prevent Base Erosion and Profit Shifting (MLI) took place in Paris, with the aim of updating the international tax treaty network in relation to tax measures proposed in the BEPS Project (Base Erosion and Profit Shifting). As bilateral negotiations between Contracting States would be burdensome and time-consuming, the MLI was designed to implement tax treaty-related BEPS measures in a swift and efficient manner.

The MLI represents a remarkable achievement in tax treaty history, not only because of its innovative character but also because of its conception in a relatively short period.[1]

1. P.J. Hattingh, The Multilateral Instrument from a Legal Perspective: What May Be the Challenges?, 71 Bull. Intl. Taxn. 3/4 (2017), Journal Articles & Opinion Pieces IBFD (accessed April 23, 2021).

In this context, the objective of this paper is to examine the general framework of the MLI and provide a brief critical analysis of its main provisions. To that end, this article addresses issues that the Organisation for Economic Co-operation and Development (OECD) intended to solve with the proposed amendments to the current tax treaty network and the potential shortcomings of such solutions. The article follows the basic structure of the MLI and is composed of four main sections: hybrid mismatches, prevention of treaty abuse, PE, and dispute resolution.

This article, which is certainly not meant to be exhaustive, does not address every controversy that may arise upon the application of treaty provisions amended by the MLI. It only intends to contribute to the academic debate by offering a critical assessment of such issues.

2 HYBRID MISMATCHES

The hybrid mismatches chapter (Part II) of the MLI consists of three provisions: Article 3 (transparent Entities), Article 4 (dual resident entities), and Article 5 (methods for elimination of double taxation). All these MLI provisions related to hybrid mismatch arrangements, recommended under Action 2 of the BEPS Project,[2] do not constitute minimum standards.

2.1 Article 3: Treaty Entitlement for Hybrid Entities

Article 3 of the MLI, currently reproduced in Article 1(2) of the OECD MC,[3] deals with income obtained by or through hybrid entities. In general, it states that when one of the Contracting States considers an entity or arrangement to be fiscally transparent, the income derived by or through such entity or arrangement shall be qualified as income of a resident, but only to the extent that the income is treated as the income of a resident of that Contracting State.

The aim of Article 3 of the MLI is to insert in the tax treaty network the general approach established in the Partnership Report in 1999,[4] where the OECD sought to address several issues experienced by OECD member countries regarding the peculiar nature of partnerships and conflicts of income allocation derived therefrom.[5] In brief, the Partnership Report stated that in cases where partnerships are concerned, the source State should consider, as a part of the factual context in which the tax treaty is to be applied, the way in which an item of income is treated in the jurisdiction where

2. OECD/G20 Base Erosion and Profit Shifting Project, Neutralizing the Effects of Hybrid Mismatch Arrangements, BEPS Action 2: 2015 Final Report.
3. OECD Model Tax Convention on Income and on Capital (November 21, 2017).
4. OECD, The Application of the OECD Model Tax Convention to Partnerships (OECD 1999) [hereinafter: the Partnership Report].
5. C. Bergedahl, Hybrid Entities and the OECD Model (2017): The End of the Road? 72 Bull. Intl. Taxn. 7 (2018), Journal Articles & Opinion Pieces IBFD (accessed March 6, 2021); L. Parada, Chapter 1: Tax Treaty Entitlement and Fiscally Transparent Entities: Improvements or Unnecessary Complications? in The Aftermath of BEPS (J.C. Wheeler ed., IBFD 2020), Books IBFD (accessed March 12, 2021).

the taxpayer is resident.[6] On this basis, the Partnership Report has concluded that treaty entitlement for partnerships should follow the attribution of income in the resident State.[7] The main difference is that the Partnership Report exclusively dealt with partnerships and other noncorporate entities, whereas Article 3 of the MLI also reaches other (wholly or partially) transparent arrangements, such as trusts.[8]

It should be mentioned that there is an optional *saving clause* in Article 3(3) of the MLI, according to which, if a State reserves its right not to opt for the saving clause, it should add the following sentence at the end of the anti-hybrid provision: "In no case shall the provisions of this paragraph be construed to affect a Contracting Jurisdiction's right to tax the residents of that Contracting Jurisdiction." The scope of the limited *saving clause* is considerably more restrictive than the one found in Article 11 of the MLI because it is only an exception to the new Article 1(2). While the broad saving clause (Article 11 of the MLI) states that this Convention does not prevent a State from taxing its own residents, the limited saving clause only provides that the anti-hybrid rule does not prevent a jurisdiction from taxing its own residents. In the way it is drafted, it implies that not only do tax treaties not prevent a resident State from applying its own attribution rules to hybrid entities[9] but also that all treaty provisions other than Article 1(2) of the OECD MC restrict a State's right to tax its own residents. A quick comparison between both provisions will highlight the differences in scope:

Broad Saving Clause	*Limited Saving Clause*
This Convention shall not affect the taxation, by a Contracting State, of its residents except with respect to the benefits granted under paragraph 3 of Article 7, paragraph 2 of Article 9 and Articles 19, 20, 23 [A] [B], 24, 25 and 28.	"In no case shall the provisions of *this paragraph* be construed to affect a Contracting Jurisdiction's right to tax the residents of that Contracting Jurisdiction."

The limited saving clause is inspired by the position held by the OECD in paragraph 15 of the Commentaries on Article 1 of the OECD MC, which states that the new Article 1(2) does not restrict in any way a State's right to tax its own residents.[10] This approach may be relevant, for example, when the jurisdiction where the partnership is established treats it as a taxable entity, but one of its members is a resident of the other Contracting State, which treats the partnership as a transparent entity. This can be illustrated by Example 16 of the Partnership Report, in which P, a partnership

6. OECD, The Application of the OECD Model Tax Convention to Partnerships (OECD 1999), para. 53.
7. M.L. Brabazon, Are We There Yet? International Implementation of Hybrid Mismatch Rules, 73 Bull. Intl. Taxn. 6/7 (2019), Journal Articles & Opinion Pieces IBFD (accessed March 26, 2021).
8. C. Garbarino, A Multi-Level Approach to "Treaty Entitlement" under the BEPS Project, 58 Eur. Taxn. 12 (2018), Journal Articles & Opinion Pieces IBFD (accessed March 26, 2021).
9. V. Chand, Should States opt for the Saving Clause in the Multilateral Instrument? 86 Tax Notes Int'l 689 (May 22, 2017).
10. OECD Model Tax Convention on Income and on Capital: Commentary on Article 1 para. 15 (2017).

established and treated as a taxable entity in State P, derives royalty income from State R, which treats it as a transparent entity.[11] If State R were to follow the attribution of income made by State P, the royalties would be attributable to the partnership, and State R would be prevented from taxing it. Nevertheless, in the Partnership Report, most countries believed that State R should be able to tax partner B because, from State R's perspective, this is a domestic situation. For this reason, the OECD concluded that in such a situation, State R should have the right to tax its own resident. This approach adopted by the OECD is a deviation from the general principle of the Partnership Report, under which the source State must follow the income attribution of the resident State to determine the treaty entitlement of transparent entities.

In summary, the *limited saving clause* seems to be an adequate alternative to the saving clause of Article 11 of the MLI, given the high risk of double taxation generated by such a broad and complex provision,[12] which undermines legal certainty and defeats the object and purpose of tax treaties.

Finally, it is interesting to mention that almost 68% of signatory countries chose not to include Article 3 of the MLI in their tax treaties.[13] In any case, this does not necessarily mean that treaty entitlement for hybrid entities will automatically be denied. A jurisdiction may treat all partnerships as fiscally opaque entities (liable to tax) and therefore entitled to treaty benefit or may apply the general guidelines of the Partnership Report, under which the Source state must follow the attribution of income of the resident State to determine the treaty entitlement of partnerships.

2.2 Article 4: Dual Resident Entities (Nonindividual Persons)

Article 4 of the MLI modifies the tiebreaker rule for dual resident entities by stating that competent authorities shall endeavor to determine tax residence by mutual agreement procedure (MAP). Thus, in the case of dual resident entities, the tiebreaker criterion will no longer be the place of effective management (POEM), in such a way that the Contracting States will have to define the tax residence that will prevail based on the facts and circumstances surrounding each specific case, having regard to its POEM, the place where it is incorporated and any other relevant factors. In practice, this means that dual resident entities cannot access treaty benefits and shall not be entitled to any relief or exemption unless the competent authorities reach an agreement.

Essentially, Article 4 of the MLI seeks to prohibit dual resident companies from obtaining tax advantages by exploiting the interaction of tax treaties and domestic law provisions. Due to their dual residence status, dual tax resident entities would have both income and expenses recognized in each of these jurisdictions (i.e., dual inclusion

11. OECD, The Application of the OECD Model Tax Convention to Partnerships (1999), para. 139.
12. V. Chand, Should States Opt for the Saving Clause in the Multilateral Instrument? 86 Tax Notes Int'l 689 (May 22, 2017).
13. Out of 95 signatory jurisdictions, 65 reserved their right not to include Article 3 in their covered tax agreements. On the matter, *see* L.E. Schoueri & G. Galdino, Action 2 and the Multilateral Instrument: Is the Reservation Power Putting Coordination at Stake? 46(2) Intertax (2018) (accessed March 12, 2021).

of income and expenses). However, as tax treaties may prevent the taxation of certain types of income by the losing Contracting State, double deduction of certain expenses might be obtained in certain circumstances, especially when the relevant domestic law does not have any rule requiring a correlation between the deduction of expenses and the recognition of income. This type of tax planning strategy tends to be mitigated after the adoption of Article 4 of the MLI since dual resident companies will not be able to self-determine their tax residence for the purpose of tax treaty entitlement. As a result, Article 4 of the MLI is expected to prevent taxpayers from exploiting tiebreaker rules in hybrid mismatches arrangements.

Despite the underlying rationale of Article 4 of the MLI, it is possible to address the concerns surrounding the application of the MAP-tiebreaker for dual resident entities.

First, as most non-signatory jurisdictions examined are developing countries, the determination of a taxpayer's tax residence status through MAP would probably give rise to costs that could be avoided with a tiebreaker rule based on predetermined criteria, such as the POEM. In addition to increased costs, the approach of Article 4 of the MLI may exacerbate the problem of an ever-increasing caseload of pending MAP. One should note, however, that even States that have signed the MLI (including developed countries) also do not seem eager to follow the Article 4 solution, upholding a predetermined tiebreaker criterion which presumably reflects the jurisdiction with which the taxpayer has stronger ties.

Second, as the functioning of tax treaties depends on the identification of state of residence, the absence of a predetermined tiebreaker criterion may put the very application of tax treaties at risk because it will depend on a MAP decision which may never be achieved. As Contracting States shall only endeavor to determine the residence of taxpayer by MAP without being bound to reach an agreement, double taxation cases that would be addressed under the previous wording of Article 4(3) of CM OCDE may no longer be solved. In theory, if Contracting States do not settle the dispute, the taxpayer could demand a mandatory arbitration procedure pursuant to Article 25(5) of the OECD MC.[14] However, it is well-known that the arbitration provision has not been widely implemented in treaty practice, which renders this theoretical possibility improbable and ineffective.

Third, the use of the MAP as a tiebreaker rule may also give too much discretion to the tax authorities in resolving dual residence cases, thus leading to a scenario of extreme legal uncertainty for taxpayers. This uncertainty is further exacerbated because the taxpayer has no influence on the outcome of a MAP under Article 25 of the OECD MC.[15]

Fourth, denying treaty entitlement for dual resident companies based on the argument that this strategy is commonly used for tax planning purposes is an

14. C. Gerlach & N. Niemeyer, The New Tie-Breaker-Rule for Companies According BEPS Action Point 6: A (Too) Radical Change? 46 Intertax, 10 (2018) (accessed March 7, 2021).
15. C. Gerlach & N. Niemeyer, The New Tie-Breaker-Rule for Companies According BEPS Action Point 6: A (Too) Radical Change? 46 Intertax, 10 (accessed March 7, 2021).

overreaction and a disproportional tax measure, especially in tax treaties with the Principal Purposes Test (PPT) clause.[16]

In conclusion, despite the flaws involved in the use of the POEM test as the sole tie-breaking criterion for dual resident entities, which are mainly caused by modern business models and management structures (e.g., changing meeting locations, digital conferences, decentralized executive functions), the solution of conditioning all cases of dual residency to a MAP without a self-executing rule does not seem to be adequate, not only because countries may fail to reach an agreement, but also because dual residence cases are not necessarily abusive.

Case-by-case solutions may be used by countries to deal with "hard cases," which cannot be properly resolved by the tiebreaker rule. However, exclusively using a case-by-case analysis for all issues that arise in practice is likely to create more problems than solutions. Rules exist precisely to avoid problems of coordination, deliberation, costs, and knowledge, thereby promoting efficiency, legal certainty, and predictability, and, concomitantly, avoiding errors and arbitrariness in the application of the law.[17]

2.3 Article 5: Methods for the Elimination of Double Taxation

Article 5 of the MLI intends to modify the method for the elimination of double taxation of existing tax treaties, either through: (i) a provision precluding the exemption method where the other Contracting State applies provisions of a tax treaty to exempt or limit tax rates levied on an item of income or capital; (ii) a switchover clause allowing Contracting States to apply the credit method, instead of the exemption method, for payments that are deductible in the payer State; or (iii) the replacement of the exemption method with the credit method.

Under the OECD Model Convention, both the exemption method (Article 23-A) and credit method (Article 23-B) can be used by countries to relieve international double taxation. Thus, each jurisdiction is free to make its own choice according to its tax policy. However, even for countries that have opted for the exemption method, Article 23-A(2) of the OECD suggests the adoption of the credit methods for dividends and interest due to the cumulative allocation of taxing rights for both contracting States. Moreover, in order to avoid double non-taxation resulting from disagreements between the resident State and the source State on the facts of the case or on the interpretation of the provisions of the Convention, Article 23-A(4) states that the resident State is not obliged to exempt an item of income where the other contracting state applies the provisions of the convention to exempt such income or applies such income to the reduced tax rate provided for in Articles 10 and 11.

16. G. Maisto et al., Dual Residence of Companies under Tax Treaties, Intl. Tax Stud. 1 (2018), Journal Articles & Opinion Pieces IBFD (accessed March 7, 2021).
17. F. Schauer, Playing by the Rules—A Philosophical Examination of Rule-Based Decision-Making in Law and in Life (Oxford University Press, 1991), pp. 141-142; Á. Humberto Ávila, Teoria da Igualdade Tributária, 2nd Edition (Malheiros, 2009), p. 82; J. Brand-Ballard, Limits of Legality: The Ethics of Lawless Judging (Oxford University Press, 2010), pp. 181-201.

Option A of the MLI basically intends to modify tax treaties that do not have Article 23(A)(4) of the OECD Model Convention to avoid double non-taxation. Thus, it provides for the non-application of the exemption method when another Contracting State applies treaty provisions that exempt or limit the tax rate levied on the relevant income or capital.

Option B provided for in the MLI is a switchover clause. In essence, countries that adopt the exemption method should refrain from doing so when the relevant income gives rise to a deduction in the other Contracting State. In such a case, the income will be taxed and the double taxation derived therefrom eliminated by the credit method. Up to this point, the OECD has failed to give convincing reasons for the introduction of switchover clauses in tax treaties. The adoption of switchover clauses is even more questionable when there is no artificiality or hybrid element in the transaction carried out by the taxpayer because it widens the taxing rights of the resident State, which will no longer be required to exempt such income without any reasonable justification. The mere deduction of a payment, deprived of any other element (e.g., a conflict of qualification or a hybrid element in the transaction), should not be enough to justify the application of switchover clauses, as tax treaties generally do not regulate how expenses will be treated for the purpose of determining the taxable profits of a resident (except for the nondiscrimination clause and the attribution of profits to PEs).

More broadly, the switchover may even distort or undermine the tax policy followed by a jurisdiction in relation to international capital allocation, since it entails a change from capital import neutrality (CIN) to capital export neutrality (CEN). Consequently, companies from such jurisdictions may be placed at a competitive disadvantage vis-à-vis local businesses if their residence jurisdiction starts to tax their income due to switchover clauses.[18] While the credit method better serves the purpose of CEN, it follows that the exemption method implies less restrictions on cross-border activities, thereby preserving the competitiveness of domestic industries and the objectives of a given tax system.[19]

With respect to developing countries, the lack of switchover clauses may also be related to the fact that only a few of these countries would find themselves in a relevant position as a resident State under the current configuration of cross-border income flows. In general, developing countries will probably be more significantly impacted by switchover clauses than source countries.[20] As a result, these countries may be unwilling to include a broad switchover clause in their tax treaties, despite the trend in the Pillar Two Blueprint[21] of the introduction of activity clauses, switchover provisions,

18. J. Englisch & J. (Johannes) Becker, International Effective Minimum Taxation—The GloBE Proposal, 11 World Tax J. (2019), Journal Articles & Opinion Pieces IBFD (accessed March 27, 2021).
19. L. Gerzova & B. (Benjamin) Rodriguez, Chapter 4: The Switch-Over Rule in Global Minimum Taxation? An Analysis of the Global Anti-Base Erosion Initiative (A. Perdelwitz & A. Turina eds., IBFD 2020), Books IBFD (accessed March 27, 2021).
20. S. Marsit, Chapter 12: The Pillar Two Initiative and Developing Countries in Global Minimum Taxation? An Analysis of the Global Anti-Base Erosion Initiative (A. Perdelwitz & A. Turina eds., IBFD 2020), Books IBFD (accessed March 27, 2021).
21. OECD, Tax Challenges Arising from Digitalisation—Report on Pillar Two Blueprint (OECD, 2020).

and subject-to-tax rules to impose a minimum taxation threshold in cross-border structures.[22]

It is interesting to note that the MLI does not deal with the existence of tax sparing clauses in a covered tax treaty. Theoretically, the application of the credit method, instead of the exemption method, could oblige the resident State to grant tax sparing credits that have been included in covered tax treaties, unless an exception is expressly set forth by the Contracting States. As tax sparing credits may be more favorable than the exemption method in certain circumstances, this aspect may have led countries not to opt for the switchover clause.

Finally, Option C of the MLI is a more general solution against double non-taxation of income, under which the exemption method is completely replaced by the credit method. This solution is not immune from criticism, because countries may have different preferences in relation to the method of relief from double taxation, depending on their general tax policy, the structure of their tax system, and historical factors, among others. This is especially relevant for countries that seek to maintain consistency of tax treaty policy with domestic law.[23]

3 PREVENTION OF TREATY ABUSE

The compliance with the Action 6 minimum standard requires countries integrating the BEPS Inclusive Framework to include in their tax treaties (i) a new preamble stating that their common intention is to eliminate double taxation without creating opportunities for non-taxation or reduced taxation through tax evasion or avoidance, including through treaty shopping arrangements; and (ii) anti-abuse treaty provisions, comprising one of the following alternatives: (a) the PPT; (b) the PPT along with a Simplified Limitation on Benefits (LoB) provision; or (c) a stand-alone detailed LoB provision supplemented by an anti-conduit rule.[24]

In addition to the minimum standard on treaty abuse, the MLI also proposes the following modifications to existing tax treaties:

- A minimum shareholding period to qualify for the reduced tax rates applicable on dividends derived from substantial shareholdings.

22. On the topic, *see* J. Englisch & J. (Johannes) Becker, International Effective Minimum Taxation—The GloBE Proposal, 11 World Tax J. (2019), Journal Articles & Opinion Pieces IBFD (accessed March 27, 2021); P. Pistone et al., The OECD Public Consultation Document "Global Anti-Base Erosion (GloBE) Proposal—Pillar Two:" An Assessment, 74 Bull. Intl. Taxn. 2 (2020), Journal Articles & Opinion Pieces IBFD (accessed March 27, 2021); F. De Lillo, Chapter 1: Introducing Pillar Two: Towards a Global Minimum Effective Tax Rate in Global Minimum Taxation? An Analysis of the Global Anti-Base Erosion Initiative (A. Perdelwitz & A. Turina eds., IBFD 2020), Books IBFD (accessed March 27, 2021).
23. G. Maisto, Credit Versus Exemption under Domestic Tax Law and Treaties in Tax Treaties: Building Bridges Between Law and Economics (M. Lang et al. eds., IBFD 2010), Books IBFD (accessed April 23, 2021).
24. OECD/G20 Inclusive Framework on BEPS—Progress report July 2017-June 2018 (Paris: OCDE), p. 19 http://www.oecd.org/tax/beps/inclusive-framework-on-beps-progress-report-july-2017-june-2018.pdf.

- 365-day lookback test for capital gains derived from immovable properties.
- An anti-abuse rule for PEs located in third countries and which are subject to a relatively low tax rate in the third jurisdiction.
- A "saving clause" confirming the right of a State to tax its own residents.

3.1 Article 6: Preamble

As mentioned, Article 6 of the MLI intends to include in the preamble of tax treaties an express statement that the common intention of the Contracting States is to eliminate double taxation without creating opportunities for non-taxation or reduced taxation through tax evasion or avoidance, including through treaty-shopping arrangements aimed at obtaining reliefs provided in this agreement for the indirect benefit of residents of third jurisdictions. Thus, the purpose of the new preamble is to declare that tax treaties are not intended to be used to generate double non-taxation.[25]

Countries may also opt for the inclusion of an additional phrase stating their desire to develop economic relationships and to enhance tax cooperation, in the following terms: "Desiring to further develop their economic relationship and to enhance their co-operation in tax matters." In contrast to the preamble,[26] this additional phrase is not a minimum standard.

Indeed, the OECD clearly states that the new preamble constitutes a minimum standard. Under the MLI, a reservation is provided for in Article 6(4) of the MLI if the preamble language of the covered tax treaty already mentions the intent of eliminating double taxation without creating opportunities for non-taxation or reduced taxation, regardless of whether the language is limited to cases of tax evasion or avoidance or applies more broadly:

> A Party may reserve the right for paragraph 1 not to apply to its Covered Tax Agreements that already contain preamble language describing the intent of the Contracting Jurisdictions to eliminate double taxation without creating opportunities for non-taxation or reduced taxation, whether that language is limited to cases of *tax evasion or avoidance* (including through treaty-shopping arrangements aimed at obtaining reliefs provided in the Covered Tax Agreement for the indirect benefit of residents of third jurisdictions) or applies more broadly.

The wording of this provision is not perfectly clear, as it mentions "tax evasion or avoidance." One would argue that the conjunction "or" suggests that a preamble that only states an aim to prevent tax evasion complies with the minimum standard, especially when the tax systems of both Contracting States do not draw a clear

25. OECD, Action 6 Final Report 2015—Preventing the Granting of Treaty Benefits in Inappropriate Circumstances (OECD 2015), paras. 3 and 68; L. De Broe, Role of the Preamble for the Interpretation of Old and New Tax Treaties and on the Policy of the Prevention of Treaty Abuse, 74 Bull. Intl. Taxn. 4/5 (2020), Journal Articles & Opinion Pieces IBFD (accessed March 26, 2021).
26. OECD/G20 Inclusive Framework on BEPS—Progress report July 2017-June 2018 (Paris: OCDE), p. 19 http://www.oecd.org/tax/beps/inclusive-framework-on-beps-progress-report-july-2017-june-2018.pdf.

distinction between tax evasion and tax avoidance.[27] However, this argument does not find support in paragraph 85 of the Explanatory Statement of the MLI, according to which countries can only opt out of the new preamble in relation to tax treaties "that already satisfy the minimum standard."

In any case, it should be mentioned that the general intentions declared by Contracting States must find their expression in the wording of treaty provisions.[28] The inclusion of prevention of tax avoidance in the preamble does not mean that a tax treaty must be construed so as to achieve such objective at any cost, without clear support in its substantive provisions.[29] Therefore, even when the new preamble has been inserted in the relevant tax treaty, it cannot be used to deny treaty benefits beyond the text of the potentially applicable treaty anti-avoidance provisions.[30]

A potential effect of the new preamble, besides shedding light on the interpretation of all other treaty provisions,[31] is to give more freedom to tax authorities to apply domestic anti-abuse provisions in a tax treaty context. According to the OECD, the application of domestic general anti-avoidance rules (GAARs) is generally consistent with tax treaties,[32] and "domestic anti-abuse rules and judicial doctrines play an important role in preventing treaty benefits from being granted in appropriate circumstances."[33] Nevertheless, in the absence of the new preamble, judicial courts may understand that States can only rely on anti-abuse rules set out in the tax treaty itself to tackle treaty-shopping arrangements and other tax planning structures.[34]

27. According to Philip Baker: "Many national tax systems make a distinction between tax evasion, which involves a taxpayer escaping from a tax liability that has already arisen (...), and the avoidance of tax liabilities that have not otherwise arisen (...). Not all tax systems make this distinction so clearly (...)." (P. Baker, Improper Use of Tax Treaties, Tax Avoidance and Tax Evasion, 9-A Papers on Tax Treaties 1-17 (May 2013).
28. Rainer Prokisch & Fernando Souza de Man, Chapter 7: Multilateralism and International Tax Law: The Interpretation of Tax Treaties in Light of the Multilateral Instrument in International and EU Tax Multilateralism: Challenges Raised by the MLI (A.P. Dourado ed., IBFD 2020), Books IBFD (accessed February 27, 2021); B. Kuźniacki, The Principal Purpose Test (PPT) in BEPS Action 6 and the MLI: Exploring Challenges Arising from Its Legal Implementation and Practical Application, 10 World Tax J. (2018), Journal Articles & Opinion Pieces IBFD (accessed March 25, 2021).
29. R.J. Danon, Treaty Abuse in the Post-BEPS World: Analysis of the Policy Shift and Impact of the Principal Purpose Test for MNE Groups, 72 Bull. Intl. Taxn. 1 (2018), Journal Articles & Opinion Pieces IBFD (accessed March 25, 2021).
30. R.J. Danon, Treaty Abuse in the Post-BEPS World: Analysis of the Policy Shift and Impact of the Principal Purpose Test for MNE Groups, 72 Bull. Intl. Taxn. 1 (2018), Journal Articles & Opinion Pieces IBFD (accessed March 12, 2021).
31. Article 31(1) of the Vienna Convention on the Law of Treaties states that a treaty must be interpreted in good faith in accordance with the ordinary meaning to be given to the terms of the treaty in their context and in the light of its object and purpose. *See* L. De Broe, Role of the Preamble for the Interpretation of Old and New Tax Treaties and on the Policy of the Prevention of Treaty Abuse, 74 Bull. Intl. Taxn. 4/5 (2020), Journal Articles & Opinion Pieces IBFD (accessed March 26, 2021).
32. OECD Model Tax Convention on Income and on Capital: Commentary on Article 1 (2017), para. 77.
33. OECD Model Tax Convention on Income and on Capital: Commentary on Article 1 (2017), para. 67.
34. On the topic, *see* J.S. Schwarz, The Impact of the New Preamble on the Interpretation of Old and New Treaties and on the Policy of Abuse Prevention, 74 Bull. Intl. Taxn. 4/5 (2020), Journal Articles & Opinion Pieces IBFD (accessed March 26, 2021).

The OECD's position in relation to the use of domestic anti-abuse rules to deny tax treaty benefits is open to criticism, as domestic law cannot limit the scope of tax treaties. To comply with international commitments, States should include a provision in the tax treaty itself expressly authorizing the application of domestic anti-abuse rules. Therefore, in the absence of an inherent anti-abuse provision in international law, domestic anti-abuse provisions can only be used to withdraw treaty benefits if the tax treaty in question explicitly authorizes it.[35]

3.2 Article 7: Prevention of Treaty Abuse

According to Article 7(1) of the MLI, a tax treat benefit shall not be granted in respect of an item of income or capital if it is reasonable to conclude, having regard to all relevant facts and circumstances, that obtaining that benefit was one of the principal purposes of any arrangement or transaction unless it is established that granting that benefit in these circumstances would be in accordance with the object and purpose of the relevant provisions of the tax treaty.

The aim of the PPT clause is to ensure that tax treaty benefits will only be granted to bona fide exchanges of goods and services, and movements of capital and persons, as opposed to arrangements driven by tax avoidance motives and lacking valid commercial reasons.[36] Thus, the PPT clause has far-reaching implications for tax treaty benefits and it is probably the most important provision of the MLI to counter treaty abuse.

In general, it is not surprising that most signatory countries opted for the PPT provision since it is a more open, flexible, and easily enforceable rule. These features make the PPT the easiest way to satisfy the minimum standard on treaty abuse and a more effective alternative to counteract unforeseen types of tax treaty abuse in comparison with mechanical tests provided for in the LoB provision,[37] mainly because it has been designed not only to target treaty shopping but also to cover other forms of tax treaty abuse (e.g., rule shopping).[38] Thus, it is not by chance that the Explanatory Statement of the MLI states that the PPT is the "only approach that can satisfy the minimum standard on its own."[39]

Moreover, tax authorities of different countries usually have experience in applying domestic GAARs to counter tax avoidance transactions, which may be useful

35. L.E. Schoueri, Planejamento Fiscal através de Acordos de Bitributação: Treaty Shopping, São Paulo: Revista dos Tribunais (1995), pp. 178-179; *See* also V. Chand & C. Elliffe, The Interaction of Domestic Anti-Avoidance Rules with Tax Treaties in the Post-BEPS and Digitalized World, 74 Bull. Intl. Taxn. 4/5 (2020), Journal Articles & Opinion Pieces IBFD (accessed March 26, 2021).
36. M. Stewart, Abuse and Economic Substance in a Digital BEPS World, 69 Bull. Intl. Taxn. 6/7 (2015), Journal Articles & Opinion Pieces IBFD (accessed March 3, 2021).
37. D.G. Duff & D. Gutmann, General Report, IFA Cahiers 2020—Volume 105A: Reconstructing the Treaty Network (2020), p. 31.
38. B. Kuźniacki, Chapter 10: Implementation and Application of the LOB Clause in BEPS Action 6/MLI: Legal and Pragmatic Challenges in International and EU Tax Multilateralism: Challenges Raised by the MLI (A.P. Dourado ed., IBFD 2020), Books IBFD (accessed March 12, 2021).
39. Explanatory Statement to the Multilateral Convention to Implement Tax Treaty Related Measures to Prevent Base Erosion and Profit Shifting, para. 90.

in the application of the PPT. That is because the concept underpinning the PPT clause has been largely influenced by domestic GAARs, mainly the United Kingdom's GAAR.[40]

Nonetheless, it must be acknowledged that the PPT clause has a low threshold for abuse and gives a wide-ranging discretion to tax authorities, thus affecting the balance between tax authorities' enforcement powers and taxpayers' rights. Legal certainty is a valuable element for the attraction of investments, given the fact that investors seek clear rules before deciding on where to invest their funds.[41] Consequently, the arbitrary nature of the PPT clause may inhibit investments, mainly in developing countries with more aggressive tax authorities, since its large scope opens room for selective enforcement, costly litigation, and uncoordinated application in different jurisdictions.[42]

3.3 Article 8: Dividend Transfer Transactions

According to Article 8(1) of the MLI, treaty provisions that exempt dividends or limit the rate at which such dividends may be taxed shall apply only if the ownership conditions described in those provisions are met throughout a 365-day period. Thus, a minimum shareholding period of 365 days is required for a beneficiary to be entitled to the special tax treatment granted (reduced tax rate or exemption) to substantial shareholdings.

Given that this provision is not part of the minimum standard, countries may decide not to include the minimum holding period in their tax treaties.

A potential issue related to the 365-day holding period provided for in Article 8 of the MLI includes the fact that this rule could deny treaty benefits in circumstances that are not abusive. Moreover, the addition of this holding period in some tax treaties and not in others could lead to unintended tax planning strategies, because investors may channel their short-term investments via countries without the holding period.[43] Finally, the PPT clause may properly counter such abusive transactions, which would make this provision unnecessary.

3.4 Article 9: Capital Gains Derived from Immovable Properties

Article 9(1) of the MLI deals with the taxation of capital gains earned on the sale of shares or other participation interests (e.g., partnership or trust) that, at any time during the 365 days preceding the alienation, derive over 50% of their value directly or indirectly from immovable property situated in that other State. It intends to provide two amendments in Article 13(4) of tax treaties: (i) the introduction of a testing period

40. J. Freedman, The UK General Anti-Avoidance Rule: Transplants and Lessons, 73 Bull. Intl. Taxn. 6/7 (2019), Journal Articles & Opinion Pieces IBFD (accessed March 27, 2021).
41. L.E. Schoueri & G. Galdino, Implementing the Multilateral Instrument in Brazil (in press).
42. C. Elliffe, The Meaning of the Principal Purpose Test: One Ring to Bind Them All? 11 World Tax J. (2019), Journal Articles & Opinion Pieces IBFD (accessed March 26, 2021).
43. Li Na, The Impact of the Multilateral Instrument on China, 24 Asia-Pac. Tax Bull. 6 (2018), Journal Articles & Opinion Pieces IBFD (accessed March 6, 2021).

for determining whether the condition on the value threshold is met; and (ii) the expansion of the scope to include interests comparable to shares, such as interests in a partnership or trust.

Upon the introduction of the 365-day lookback test, the source State's right to tax will not be exclusively determined at the moment of the alienation of shares (or other participation interests) by the taxpayer, but rather consider whether the relevant value threshold has been met at any time during the 365 days before the disposition.[44] According to paragraph 128 of the Explanatory Statement to the MLI, this provision addresses situations in which assets are contributed to an entity shortly before the sale of shares to dilute the proportion of its value that is derived from immovable properties.[45]

As Article 9(1) of the MLI is not required to meet the minimum standard, countries may decide not to include this provision in their bilateral tax treaties. One could argue that the lookback provision is not part of the minimum standard because it is unnecessary, since the PPT clause is broad enough to deal with tax planning structures targeted by Article 9(1) of the MLI. However, even if that is the case, the introduction of the lookback provision could avoid further discussion, given that in the presence of a specific anti-avoidance rule (SAAR) such as Article 13(4) of the OECD MC, one could argue that the application of the PPT clause might be against the traditional canon of "*generalia specialibus non derogant*" (a general statute must yield to a specific statute).[46]

Finally, it is worth mentioning that the 365-day lookback test has been included in the current versions of the OECD Model Convention and United Nation Model Convention.[47]

3.5 Article 10: Anti-abuse Rule for PEs Situated in Third States

Article 10(1) of the MLI includes a specific anti-abuse rule in tax treaties targeting triangular tax planning structures with PEs located in third States, whose profits are low-taxed. This provision, recently inserted in Article 29(8) of the OECD MC within the framework of BEPS Action 6, was inspired by the "triangular PE provision" included in the 1993 protocol to the tax treaty signed between the United States and the Netherlands.[48]

44. S. Suarez, How the MLI Will Change Capital Gains Taxation in Canada, 98 Tax Notes Int'l 657 (May 11, 2020) (accessed March 3, 2021); S. Doobay, The MLI Enters into Force for Canada on 1 December 2019, 21 Fin. & Cap. Mkts 6 (2019), Journal Articles & Opinion Pieces IBFD (accessed March 25, 2021).
45. Explanatory Statement to the Multilateral Convention to Implement Tax Treaty Related Measures to Prevent Base Erosion and Profit Shifting, para. 128.
46. S. Sanghvi & J. Bhatt, MLI—Intensifying the Need for "Substance" in Cross-Border Taxation, 99 Tax Notes Int'l 245 (July 13, 2020). (accessed March 3, 2021).
47. L. Kurth Marques Carvalho, Taxation of Offshore Indirect Transfers in Brazil in Need of Reform, 74 Bull. Intl. Taxn. 3 (2020), Journal Articles & Opinion Pieces IBFD (accessed March 27, 2021).
48. J-P. Van West, Chapter 3: The Origins of Article 29(8) of the OECD Model in The Anti-Abuse Rule for Permanent Establishments Situated in Third States: A Legal Analysis of Article 29(8) OECD Model (IBFD 2020), Books IBFD (accessed Mach 4, 2021).

Triangular PE provisions have gained momentum after the state aid investigation initiated by the European Commission against McDonald's,[49] which had a U.S. branch with franchise rights. Royalties and franchise fees allocated to the U.S. branch were tax-exempt in Luxembourg, while in the United States such amounts were not considered as "U.S. trade or business," which is the domestic law threshold required to trigger U.S. taxation. Therefore, a significant part of such income has not been taxed anywhere.[50]

Essentially, Article 10(1) of the MLI provides that in triangular situations, if the taxpayer in the resident State derives income from the other Contracting State, but such income is attributed to a PE located in a third State whose tax treaty with the resident State adopts the exemption method, the granting of treaty benefits to such income will be denied if taxation in the jurisdiction where the PE is located represents less than 60% of the tax burden that would be charged by the resident State if the PE was located in its jurisdiction.

Generally, triangular PE arrangements allow companies to achieve double non-taxation or reduced taxation in cross-border transactions, mostly in cases involving dividend, interest, or royalty income[51] because the source State will typically reduce the withholding income tax levied on the payment made to the nonresident, while the resident State will exempt the items of income attributable to a PE located in a third-country jurisdiction. For example, in the United States, triangular PE arrangements have often been used to finance the operations of U.S. affiliates through Luxembourg.[52]

To prevent this from occurring, the triangular PE provision included in the MLI intends to deny treaty benefits if the income derived by the resident taxpayer is attributable to a PE in a third jurisdiction and is exempted under the resident State. In any case, as this provision is not part of the minimum standard, countries are free to include it in their treaties.

Several signatory countries made a reservation to the triangular PE provision in the MLI, which suggests that many States do not perceive PE triangular cases as abusive.[53]

In addition, the triangular PE provision is complex and overinclusive, as its scope might reach genuine business transactions. Ideally, it should target cases where a taxpayer transfers shares, debt claims, rights, or property to PEs set up solely for tax

49. EU: Commission letter to Luxembourg, State aid SA. 38945 (2015/C) (ex 2015/NN)—Luxembourg Alleged aid to McDonald's, *C (2015) 8343 final*, December 3, 2015.
50. C. Turley, D.G. Chamberlain & M. Petriccione, A New Dawn for the International Tax System: Evolution from Past to Future and What Role Will China Play? (IBFD 2017), Books IBFD (accessed March 27, 2021).
51. J-P. Van West, Chapter 1: Introduction to PE Triangular Cases and Article 29(8) of the OECD Model in The Anti-Abuse Rule for Permanent Establishments Situated in Third States: A Legal Analysis of Article 29(8) OECD Model (IBFD 2020), Books IBFD (accessed March 4, 2021).
52. E. Brandt, BEPS Aftermath: Mechanisms to Curtail Treaty Shopping and Abuse, 93 Tax Notes Int'l 1265 (March 25, 2019) (accessed March 3, 2021).
53. J-P. Van West, Chapter 6: Conclusions in The Anti-Abuse Rule for Permanent Establishments Situated in Third States: A Legal Analysis of Article 29(8) OECD Model (IBFD 2020), Books IBFD (accessed March 4, 2021).

planning purposes in countries where income derived from such assets are low-taxed. Obviously, the competent authority relief clause attenuates its over-inclusiveness, but countries may be reluctant to rely on that, since the lack of legal certainty may inhibit investments.

3.6 Article 11: Saving Clause

According to Article 11(1) of the MLI, with a few exceptions, tax treaties shall not affect the taxation, by a Contracting State, of its own residents. This saving clause is grounded by the debatable premise that tax treaty provisions operate to restrict the taxing rights of the source State, as opposed to the taxing rights of the state of the taxpayer's residence.[54]

The saving clause has been a key feature of U.S. treaty policy to ensure that treaty benefits do not accrue to U.S. citizens who are tax residents in other countries. It provides that the U.S. may tax its residents and citizens as if the treaty had not come into effect.[55] In such a case, the tax treaty would restrict taxing rights on income derived by nonresidents, but it would have no effect on resident taxpayers.[56]

The underlying premise of the saving clause is debatable not only because of several exceptions that restrict its scope but also because tax treaties have distributive rules with an objective scope, focusing on specific items of income, regardless of the relative position of each Contracting State. In addition, some distributive rules that restrict the taxing rights of the resident State were not expressly excluded from its scope, such as Article 9(1) of the OECD MC on transfer pricing adjustments,[57] as well as Article 8(1) of the OECD MC, in cases of divergence between the place of incorporation and the POEM of enterprises operating ships or aircraft in international traffic, as read in the 2014 version of OECD MC. Thus, if the aim of the saving clause is to allow the application of domestic anti-avoidance rules by a State to its own residents, such as Controlled Foreign Company ("CFC") rules and exit taxes, it would be better to restrict its scope to tax avoidance cases.

In any case, as the saving clause is not part of the minimum standard, countries may decide not to include this provision in their tax treaties. After all, it is widely accepted that a tax treaty can limit, but never amplify a country's tax jurisdiction.[58] In doing so, it can restrict a country's right to tax its own citizens, as no general principles of law recognized by civilized nations or customary international laws state otherwise.

54. OECD, "Preventing the Granting of Treaty Benefits in Inappropriate Circumstances, Action 6 — 2015 Final Report" (October 5, 2015), at para. 60.
55. R. Stack, D. Shah & D. Lenter, United States Branch Report, IFA Cahiers 2020—Volume 105A: Reconstructing the Treaty Network (2020), p. 876.
56. R.L. Doernberg & K. Ran Raad, Commentary: The Forthcoming U.S. Model Income Tax Treaty and the Saving Clause, 5 Tax Notes Int'l 775 (October 12, 1992).
57. G.W. Kofler & I. Verlinden, Unlimited Adjustments: Some Reflections on Transfer Pricing, General Anti-avoidance and Controlled Foreign Company Rules, and the "Saving Clause," 74 Bull. Intl. Taxn. 4/5 (2020), Journal Articles & Opinion Pieces IBFD (accessed March 26, 2021).
58. K. Vogel, Klaus Vogel on Double Taxation Conventions: A Commentary to the OECD, UN, and US Model Conventions for the Avoidance of Double Taxation on Income and Capital, with Particular Reference to German Treaty Practice 3rd edn. (Kluwer Law International 1997) at

In the author's opinion, in addition to being complex and excessively broad, the saving clause can easily lead to cases of double taxation, mainly in cases of residence-residence conflicts.[59] Legal certainty and clarity are relevant both for tax administrations and taxpayers in international tax matters[60] and these tax policy goals may be significantly undermined by the saving clause, which can significantly reduce the scope of tax treaties.

4 PERMANENT ESTABLISHMENT

Part IV of the MLI introduces tax measures resulting from Action 7 of the BEPS Project,[61] which were designed to counter the artificial avoidance of PE status through commissionaire arrangements and similar strategies (Article 12 of the MLI), specific activity exemptions (Article 13 of the MLI) and splitting-up of contracts (Article 14 of the MLI). These provisions do not constitute minimum standards.

4.1 Article 12: Commissionaire Arrangements and Similar Strategies

To prevent the artificial avoidance of PE status, Article 12 of the MLI extends the scope of the dependent agent PE rule found in Article 5(5) of the OECD MC to include an agent that habitually concludes contracts on behalf of another person or plays the principal role in negotiating contracts routinely concluded, without modifications by the principal.

This provision was designed to reach commissionaire arrangements and similar strategies in which the commissionaire acts in its own name but on the account of its principal.[62] Before this amendment, enterprises could easily exploit commissionaire arrangements to avoid the creation of a PE, thereby reducing their tax burden in the host jurisdiction, whilst reaching a nearly identical economic result compared to conventional distribution arrangements. These tax planning strategies were possible because, by not fulfilling the "authority to conclude contracts" condition, cases of indirect representation under a commissionaire arrangement fell outside the scope of PE concept.[63] Thus, Article 12 of the MLI extends the scope of the agency PE provision

para. 56; L.E. Schoueri, Arm's Length: Beyond the Guidelines of the OECD: "It Is Better to Be Roughly Right than Precisely Wrong." (John Maynard Keynes), 69 Bull. Intl. Taxn. 12 (2015), Journal Articles & Papers IBFD.

59. V. Chand, Should States Opt for the Saving Clause in the Multilateral Instrument? 86 Tax Notes Int'l 689 (May 22, 2017).
60. A. Chan, Applying the Multilateral Instrument's Specific Activity Exemption, 96 Tax Notes Int'l 991 (December 16, 2019).
61. OECD, Action 7 Final Report 2015—Preventing the Artificial Avoidance of Permanent Establishment Status (OECD 2015).
62. F.A. García Prats, OECD—Commentary on Article 5 of the OECD Model, Country Tax Guides IBFD (accessed March 26, 2021).
63. K. Prakash, Permanent Establishments under the OECD Model (2017) Based on the Principal Role Leading to the Conclusion of Contracts—A Doctrinal and Policy Analysis, 74 Bull. Intl. Taxn. 11 (2020), Journal Articles & Opinion Pieces IBFD (accessed March 26, 2021).

to reach business models currently used by multinational enterprises.[64] In any case, as the strengthening of such rules regarding PE status focuses on tax planning strategies used to circumvent the current concept of a PE, an agent of an independent status acting in the ordinary course of business will not be treated as a dependent agent.[65]

The general effect of Article 12 of the MLI is to lower the dependent agent PE threshold and, consequently, the point at which a source State has taxation rights on a nonresident through the PE rules. Therefore, this amendment tends to benefit countries that are net capital importers, strengthening their taxing rights from a source State perspective.

As previously mentioned, Article 12 of the MLI is not part of the minimum standard. A possible reason for this includes the fact that this provision departs from the pure legal interpretation of the dependent agent PE concept, which can lead to controversies in civil law countries that follow a more formal approach in the analysis of legal transactions.[66] This strict and formalistic interpretation has been adopted, for instance, in Zimmer[67] and Dell Norway[68] cases. Historically, the characterization of dependent agents was conditional upon the "authority to conclude contracts." A legalistic approach interpreted this requirement as a legal test which investigated whether the agent had power to conclude legally binding contracts for its principal. This legalistic interpretation has had greater weight in different countries such as the United Kingdom,[69] given that tax disputes were ultimately decided by judicial courts. Consequently, a fact-oriented approach to the definition of the agent PE, which ignores formal aspects of the agreement (such as in whose name the contract is concluded), may not be well accepted in all jurisdictions.

Finally, it is important to bear in mind that countries would have to change the concept of PE in their domestic laws to make this new provision effective for tax purposes, given the fact that tax treaties do not give rise to tax liabilities. Thus, if a review of the domestic legislation is not intended from a tax policy perspective, it would make no sense to adhere to the normative solutions proposed by the MLI for the avoidance of PE status.

64. A. Storck & A. Zeiler, "Beyond the OECD Update 2014: Changes to the Concepts of Permanent Establishments in the Light of the BEPS Discussion," The OECD-Model-Convention and its Update 2014, (Michael Lang ed.), Linde, 2014, p. 262.
65. B. Hassan, Implementation of the OECD BEPS Action Plan, 25 Asia-Pac. Tax Bull. 5 (2019), Journal Articles & Opinion Pieces IBFD (accessed March 3, 2021).
66. K. Prakash, Permanent Establishments under the OECD Model (2017) Based on the Principal Role Leading to the Conclusion of Contracts—A Doctrinal and Policy Analysis, 74 Bull. Intl. Taxn. 11 (2020), Journal Articles & Opinion Pieces IBFD (accessed March 26, 2021); S. Roberts, "The Agency Element of Permanent Establishment: The OECD Commentaries from the Civil Law View," 48 Eur. Taxn 3 (2008) (accessed March 26, 2021).
67. French Conseil d'État (Supreme Administrative Court, CE) in FR: CE, March 31, 2010, Cases Nos. 304715 and 308525 (Zimmer), Case Law IBFD.
68. Norwegian Høyesterett (Supreme Court, Ht) in NO: Ht, December 2, 2011, HR-2011-02245-A (sak nr. 2011/755), (Dell Norway), Case Law IBFD.
69. S. Watson, N. Palazzo-Corner & S. Haemmerle, UK View on Revised PE Standards in the Multilateral Instrument, 24 Int'l. Transfer Pricing J. 3 (2017), Journal Articles & Opinion Pieces IBFD (accessed March 3, 2021); A. Storck & A. Zeiler, "Beyond the OECD Update 2014: Changes to the Concepts of Permanent Establishments in the Light of the BEPS Discussion," The OECD-Model-Convention and its Update 2014, (Michael Lang ed.), Linde, 2014, p. 259.

4.2 Article 13: Specific Activity Exemptions

Article 13 of the MLI deals with the list of auxiliary or preparatory activities, which are treated as exemptions to the general definition of PE (i.e., a PE is deemed not to exist where a place of business is used solely for the exempted activities). The objective of the MLI is to restrict the scope of the PE exemptions found in Article 5(4) of tax treaties patterned on the OECD MC, which opened up room for tax planning structures carried out by companies that sell products on the Internet but need to maintain the physical inventory of products in strategic jurisdictions to deliver goods quickly and cheaply. The same goes for companies that have a fixed place of business and ostensibly act in collecting information.

To that end, based on the conclusions of Action 7 of the BEPS Project, Article 13 of the MLI allows signatories countries to either: (i) explicitly state that the PE exemptions are restricted to activities that are of a preparatory or auxiliary nature (Option A); or (ii) retain the current wording of Article 5(4) of tax treaties patterned on the OECD MC, assuming that such exempted activities are intrinsically preparatory or auxiliary (Option B), in line with the second-best solution proposed as an alternative text in the 2017 Commentary.[70]

Under both alternatives, the PE exemptions should only apply if the overall activity of a PE is of a preparatory or auxiliary nature. Consequently, it prevents the automatic application of the specific activity exemptions to avoid the PE status, thus emphasizing the importance of considering the particularities of the business conducted in the source state and the overall activities of the enterprises.[71] For instance, under Article 13 of the MLI, warehouses and delivery centers of large e-commerce companies, which play a crucial role in their business models, may lead to the characterization of a PE in the host State.[72]

In this respect, it should be noted that the MLI's alternatives do not solve the vagueness of the terms "preparatory" and "auxiliary," whose meanings depend on the analysis of the facts and circumstances of each case. It can be difficult to distinguish between mainstream business activities and ancillary activities, which may require additional guidance on qualitative and quantitative factors to be considered in this respect.

---

70. Paragraph 78 OECD Model: Commentary on Article 5 (2017). *See* P. Arginelli, Chapter 5: PE Negative List and Fragmentation of Activities Within Groups of Companies in New Trends in the Definition of Permanent Establishment (G. Maisto ed., IBFD 2019), Books IBFD (accessed March 7, 2021).
71. Y. Uslu, An Analysis of "Google Taxes" in the Context of Action 7 of the OECD/G20 Base Erosion and Profit Shifting Initiative, 72 Bull. Intl. Taxn. 4a/Special Issue (2018), Journal Articles & Opinion Pieces IBFD (accessed March 3, 2021).
72. K. Spies, Permanent Establishment versus Fixed Establishment: The Same or Different? 71 Bull. Intl. Taxn. 12 (2017), Journal Articles & Opinion Pieces IBFD (accessed March 1, 2021).

4.3 Article 14: Splitting-Up of Contracts

Article 14 of the MLI introduces an anti-abuse rule to tackle the avoidance of PE status in the host jurisdiction by the splitting-up of contracts to circumvent the 12-month threshold or similar time tests provided for in tax treaties.

To this end, Article 14 of the MLI introduces a special rule for counting the stipulated time period in tax treaties for the characterization of a PE, with the intention of countering the artificial splitting-up of longer-term contracts.[73] According to this provision, in the case of activities carried out on a building site, construction project, installation project, or other specific projects, the execution period by closely related companies, when exceeding 30 days, shall be added up for the purpose of verifying the time threshold required for the characterization of the PE. With this new provision, the overall period of split contracts would be considered in determining the 12-month threshold.[74] As a result, enterprises will no longer be able to split up their contracts into several parts attributed to different closely related companies, with each of them covering a period of less than 12 months in the host State (e.g., contractors or subcontractors working on the continental shelf).

As previously mentioned, Article 14 of the MLI is not part of the minimum standard. Despite this, much artificial avoidance of the PE status could be captured through a proper interpretation of the current PE definition, without significant amendments in its wording.[75] In other countries, the artificial splitting-up of contracts may be countered based on a proper interpretation of the PE definition in the light of the concept of sham, which demands an examination of real facts underlying the legal arrangements.[76] Other countries may challenge such transactions through domestic anti-avoidance rules or judicial doctrines.[77]

Furthermore, Action 7 of the BEPS Project suggests that the PPT can be used to counter the splitting-up of contracts to circumvent the 12-month threshold.[78] This statement may justify the absence of Article 14 of the MLI in part of the covered tax treaties.

73. S. Watson, N. Palazzo-Corner & S. Haemmerle, UK View on Revised PE Standards in the Multilateral Instrument, 24 Intl. Transfer Pricing J. 3 (2017), Journal Articles & Opinion Pieces IBFD (accessed March 3, 2021).
74. Y. Uslu, An Analysis of "Google Taxes" in the Context of Action 7 of the OECD/G20 Base Erosion and Profit Shifting Initiative, 72 Bull. Intl. Taxn. 4a/Special Issue (2018), Journal Articles & Opinion Pieces IBFD (accessed March 3, 2021).
75. S. Watson, N. Palazzo-Corner & S. Haemmerle, UK View on Revised PE Standards in the Multilateral Instrument, 24 Intl. Transfer Pricing J. 3 (2017), Journal Articles & Opinion Pieces IBFD (accessed March 3, 2021).
76. M. Stewart, Abuse and Economic Substance in a Digital BEPS World, 69 Bull. Intl. Taxn. 6/7 (2015), Journal Articles & Opinion Pieces IBFD (accessed March 3, 2021).
77. D. G. Duff, D. Gutmann, General Report, IFA Cahiers 2020—Volume 105A: Reconstructing the Treaty Network (2020), p. 27.
78. OECD, Action 7 Final Report 2015—Preventing the Artificial Avoidance of Permanent Establishment Status (OECD 2015), at pp. 42-44.

5 IMPROVING DISPUTE RESOLUTION

5.1 Article 16: Mutual Agreement Procedure

Article 16 of the MLI seeks to establish a minimum standard for the MAP to make dispute resolution mechanisms of tax treaties more effective, thereby promoting legal certainty and reducing risks of double taxation. After all, cross-border tax disputes are a common impediment to fulfilling the objective and purpose of tax treaties.

According to Article 16 of the MLI, where a person considers that the actions of one or both Contracting States result or will result in taxation not in accordance with the provisions of the relevant tax treaty, that person may, irrespective of the remedies provided by the domestic law of those Contracting States, submit the case to the competent authority of either Contracting Jurisdiction within three years from the first notification of the action resulting in taxation, not in accordance with the treaty provisions. Article 16 of the MLI essentially reflects the current wording of Article 25 of the 2017 OECD MC.

The substantial change resulting from Article 16 of the MLI is that the taxpayer may now present the case to the competent authority of either of the Contracting States, within three years from the first notification of the action resulting in taxation, not in accordance with the relevant tax treaty.[79] The competent authority to which the case is presented shall then endeavor to resolve the MAP case with the competent authority of the other Contracting State if it cannot arrive at a satisfactory solution by itself. The agreement reached under the MAP must be implemented by the Contracting States, irrespective of domestic time limits.

The possibility of submitting the MAP case to the competent authority of either Contracting State is welcomed not only because taxpayers in certain countries may face difficulties with accessing competent authorities in their state of residence, but also because some tax treaty provisions are not necessarily dependent on the concept of residence.[80]

Alternatively, Article 13(5)(a) of the MLI provides that countries may reserve their right to meet the minimum standard maintaining the submission of the MAP to the competent authority of the jurisdiction of which the person is a resident or national, the latter in cases of nondiscrimination based on nationality. In such a scenario, the competent authority must implement a bilateral consultation process with the competent authority of the other Contracting State if it considers that the taxpayer's objection is not justified. This bilateral consultation process is the innovation in relation to Article 25 of the 2010 OECD MC.

79. J.A. Becerra, The Influence of the OECD Multilateral Convention on Mexico's Tax Treaties, 71 Bull. Intl. Taxn. 10 (2017), Journal Articles & Opinion Pieces IBFD (accessed March 1, 2021).
80. S.P. Govind & J. (Jérôme) Monsenego, Chapter 11: Multilateralism in Dispute Resolution: Some Thoughts on the OECD Multilateral Instrument and the EU Dispute Resolution Directive in International and EU Tax Multilateralism: Challenges Raised by the MLI (A.P. Dourado ed., IBFD 2020), Books IBFD (accessed March 11, 2021).

In general, initiatives to make the MAP more efficient are praiseworthy, since its adoption to solve cross-border tax disputes may avoid costly litigation and provide legal certainty for foreign investors.[81] Unfortunately, criticisms often directed at the shortcomings and limitations of the MAP process (such as the lack of taxpayer active involvement and non-assurance that a solution will be reached by the Contracting States) were not significantly addressed by the MLI.[82]

5.2 Article 17: Corresponding Transfer Pricing Adjustments

Article 17 of the MLI intends to include corresponding transfer pricing adjustments in tax treaties, following the wording typically found in Article 9(2) of the OECD MC. According to this provision, in order to mitigate the economic double taxation caused by the primary transfer pricing adjustment made by one Contracting State, a corresponding adjustment must be made by the other Contracting State through a downward adjustment in the tax liability of the associated enterprise, so that the allocation of profits between two jurisdictions becomes consistent and no economic double taxation occurs.[83]

Prior to the MLI, the noninclusion of Article 9(2) of the OECD MC in certain tax treaties was usually related to the fact that some countries, such as the Czech Republic and Hungary, were of the opinion that, if associated enterprises entered into profit-shifting strategies and priced their transactions without complying with the arm's-length standard, they must bear the consequences of their actions, including potential economic double taxation.[84]

In the author's opinion, despite the absence of Article 9(2) of the OECD MC in certain tax treaties, the MAP can be used to solve cases of economic double taxation arising from the application of transfer pricing rules. Unfortunately, this is not a

81. L.E. Schoueri & M. Calicchio Barbosa, Chapter 5: Brazil in Tax Treaty Arbitration (M. Lang et al. eds., IBFD 2020), Books IBFD (accessed March 3, 2021); L.E. Schoueri, Chapter 8: Arbitration and Constitutional Issues in International Arbitration in Tax Matters (M. Lang et al. eds., IBFD 2016), Books IBFD (accessed March 13, 2021).
82. S.P. Govind & J. (Jérôme) Monsenego, Chapter 11: Multilateralism in Dispute Resolution: Some Thoughts on the OECD Multilateral Instrument and the EU Dispute Resolution Directive in International and EU Tax Multilateralism: Challenges Raised by the MLI (A.P. Dourado ed., IBFD 2020), Books IBFD (accessed March 11, 2021); G. Groen, The Nature and Scope of the Mandatory Arbitration Provision in the OECD Multilateral Convention (2016), 71 Bull. Intl. Taxn. 11 (2017), Journal Articles & Opinion Pieces IBFD (accessed March 26, 2021); E. Snodgrass, Tax Controversies and Dispute Resolution under Tax Treaties: Insights from the Arbitration Sphere, 19 Fin. & Cap. Mkts 5 (2017), Journal Articles & Opinion Pieces IBFD (accessed March 26, 2021); G.M. Luchena Mozo, A Collaborative Relationship in the Resolution of International Tax Disputes and Alternative Measures for Dispute Resolution in a Post-BEPS Era, 58 Eur. Taxn. 1 (2018), Journal Articles & Opinion Pieces IBFD (accessed March 26, 2021).
83. P. Das, Corresponding Adjustment and Its Interaction with the Mutual Agreement Procedure under Article 25 of the OECD Model, 26 Intl. Transfer Pricing J. 1 (2019), Journal Articles & Opinion Pieces IBFD (accessed March 6, 2021); B. Timbadia, Multilateral Instrument Opens Window for Alternate Dispute Resolution for Indian Companies, 23 Asia-Pac. Tax Bull. 4 (2017), Journal Articles & Opinion Pieces IBFD (accessed March 26, 2021).
84. V. Solilová & M. Steindl, Tax Treaty Policy on Article 9 of the OECD Model Scrutinized, 67 Bull. Intl. Taxn. 3 (2013), Journal Articles & Opinion Pieces IBFD (accessed March 6, 2021).

unanimous position in international tax treaty practice. For example, India has taken the position that, in the absence of Article 9(2) in a bilateral tax treaty, tax authorities will not enter into MAP negotiations to grant the corresponding adjustment.[85]

5.3 Article 19: Mandatory Binding Arbitration

Article 19 of the MLI essentially reproduces the arbitration clause found in Article 25(5) of the OECD MC with the aim of updating the international tax treaty network, in which few countries effectively use this mechanism of dispute resolution.

There are two alternatives for countries opting for the binding arbitration procedure. Under the independent opinion approach, the arbitration panel hands down an independent decision on the case based on its own analysis and underlying rationale. Under the final offer arbitration, the arbitration panel can only choose one of the proposals presented by the competent authorities concerned as to how the case should be resolved.[86]

As known, most signatory jurisdictions have not adopted mandatory arbitration in the MLI. The resistance to arbitration was somehow expected since there was no consensus among countries participating in Action 14 of the BEPS Project on the use of binding arbitration as a final stage in the MAP for settling tax treaty disputes. Indeed, few countries involved in the BEPS Project believed that mandatory binding arbitration was the best alternative to resolve tax treaty disputes, such as Australia, France, Germany, Japan, the United Kingdom, and the United States.[87] These countries developed a binding MAP arbitration provision as a part of the MLI, but it does not constitute a minimum standard.

In general, countries are still reluctant to adopt mandatory arbitration in their tax treaties, based on the idea that it may impinge their sovereignty in tax matters and undermine available domestic legal remedies. Other arguments generally raised against the inclusion of arbitration clauses in tax treaties involve the principle of legality and the prohibition of waiver of tax revenues.[88] Moreover, with respect to developing countries, potential costs of arbitration procedures should not be underestimated, given the fact that Contracting States must mutually agree on sharing arbitrator fees and the expenses incurred during the arbitration procedure. Developing

85. B. Timbadia, Multilateral Instrument Opens Window for Alternate Dispute Resolution for Indian Companies, 23 Asia-Pac. Tax Bull. 4 (2017), Journal Articles & Opinion Pieces IBFD (accessed March 26, 2021).
86. H. M. Pit, Arbitration under the OECD Multilateral Instrument: Reservations, Options and Choices, 71 Bull. Intl. Taxn. 10 (2017), Journal Articles & Opinion Pieces IBFD (accessed March 2, 2021); E. Snodgrass, Tax Controversies and Dispute Resolution under Tax Treaties: Insights from the Arbitration Sphere, 19 Fin. & Cap. Mkts 5 (2017), Journal Articles & Opinion Pieces IBFD (accessed March 26, 2021).
87. J.M. Kadet, BEPS Primer: Past, Present, and Future, 99 Tax Notes Int'l 51 (July 6, 2020).
88. L.E. Schoueri, Chapter 8: Arbitration and Constitutional Issues in International Arbitration in Tax Matters (M. Lang et al. eds., IBFD 2016), Books IBFD (accessed March 13, 2021).

countries also resist mandatory arbitration for fear of losing control over the source taxation of nonresidents, which may constitute a large part of their total tax revenues.[89]

Even if one accepts that binding arbitration is mainly a mechanism to encourage countries to settle their tax disputes before becoming subject to mandatory arbitration (which may be debatable in light of OECD MAP statistics[90] and in the absence of sanctions on authorities forsaking their obligation to submit the case to arbitration),[91] most countries are not willing to accept the mere possibility of having their highly sensitive cross-border tax disputes arbitrated by an ad hoc panel outside of their judicial system. The final of offer arbitration may alleviate part of that concern, as it allows countries to anticipate and control the ultimate decision.[92] All other obstacles may also be surpassed if one considers that resorting to arbitration involves the correct delimitation of the jurisdiction of the Contracting States and that no violation of individual rights will occur if the taxpayer agrees to submit his case to arbitration.[93] Nonetheless, progress in the field of tax treaty arbitration is still modest and highly controversial in many countries.

Therefore, if the OECD considers mandatory arbitration as the best alternative to make dispute resolution mechanisms more effective, then it should also discuss the possibility of establishing an international arbitration court to solve cross-border tax disputes, where it would be possible to reach consistent and coherent case law at a worldwide level.[94] Until then, countries will probably avoid arbitration procedures whose decisions may vary according to the countries involved and the will of the members of the arbitration panel.

6 FINAL REMARKS

In summary, this article sought to present the general framework of the MLI, providing a brief critical analysis of its main provisions.

In general, several provisions of the MLI suffer from over-inclusiveness and lack of due consideration of their potential negative impacts. The relatively short deadline for the completion of the BEPS Project made the OECD opt for "quick fix" solutions,

89. G. Groen, The Nature and Scope of the Mandatory Arbitration Provision in the OECD Multilateral Convention (2016), 71 Bull. Intl. Taxn. 11 (2017), Journal Articles & Opinion Pieces IBFD (accessed March 26, 2021); M. Lennard, International Tax Arbitration and Developing Countries, in International Arbitration in Tax Matters ch. 19 (M. Lang & J. Owens eds., IBFD 2016) Online Books IBFD (accessed March 26, 2021).
90. *See* OECD, Mutual Agreement Procedure Statistics for 2017, 2018, and 2019, in which the average cycle time of MAP has not improved due to the introduction of arbitration.
91. H. Mooij, Chapter 14: MAP Arbitration in Tax Treaty Disputes in Flexible Multi-Tier Dispute Resolution in International Tax Disputes (P. Pistone & J.J.P. de Goede eds., IBFD 2021), Books IBFD (accessed March 3, 2021).
92. The United States uses the final offer arbitration in its tax treaties with arbitration provision.
93. L.E. Schoueri, Chapter 8: Arbitration and Constitutional Issues in International Arbitration in Tax Matters (M. Lang et al. eds., IBFD 2016), Books IBFD (accessed March 13, 2021).
94. A.P. Dourado & P. Pistone, Arbitrating Cross-Border Tax Disputes in Line with European Union Law: Issues and Solutions, International Taxation in a Changing Landscape: Liber Amicorum in Honour of Bertil Wiman (Kluwer Law International B.V 2019), p. 67.

which are not necessarily in line with the juridical principles and tax policy goals that shape the international tax regime.

Moreover, the limited level of flexibility allowed in the MLI, whose reservations (opt-outs) and optional provisions (opt-ins) are predetermined in its text, restricts the abilities of the parties to shape their international commitments. For countries that have struggled over decades to formulate an independent tax treaty policy, the adoption of the standardized solutions of the MLI may jeopardize the equilibrium of their bilateral tax treaties.[95]

Therefore, countries should bear in mind that, with respect to tax treaties, the advantages brought by multilateral instruments (MLI) come at a cost. On the one hand, the limited level of flexibility existing in a MLI restricts the power of a state to shape its international commitments thereby undermining its tax treaty policy. On the other hand, the reserves and options placed in a MLI, even if limited and predetermined, may jeopardize the very objective of achieving coordination in the international tax arena, due to their intricate and complex interaction with other provisions of existing tax treaties.

95. L. E. Schoueri & G. Galdino, Implementing the Multilateral Instrument in Brazil (in press).

CHAPTER 6

MLI Implementation and Impact from the Latin American Perspective

Andrea Laura Riccardi Sacchi[*]

Andrea Laura Riccardi Sacchi surveys the use of the "Multilateral Convention to Implement Tax Treaty Related Measures to Prevent Base Erosion and Profit Shifting" (hereinafter "MLI") to implement the BEPS minimum standards by thirty-three Latin American and Caribbean countries. She notes that most of these countries had little or no role in the formulation of the Organisation for Economic Co-operation and Development (OECD's) BEPS (Base Erosion and Profit Shifting) initiative. Nine of the studied countries are nonmembers of the Inclusive Framework, none of which has signed on to the MLI, but even among the twenty-four countries that are Inclusive Framework Members, only eleven have signed the MLI to date. She analyzes the breadth of coverage of the MLI signatories and the rationales for the different choices made by Latin American and Caribbean countries with respect to the MLI.

1 INTRODUCTION

Action 15 of the OECD/G20 (anti-)BEPS Project was set forth as an instrumental action, aimed at transposing the results derived from other actions of the 15-point Action Plan into existing bilateral tax treaties.[1] In particular, the Action targeted BEPS measures for

* The opinions expressed herein are the sole responsibility of the author and do not necessarily reflect the position of any of the organizations with which she is affiliated.
1. The estimate is that the number of existing bilateral tax treaties, "largely fashioned after" the OECD Model Tax Convention (OECD MC), is over 3,000 worldwide. BRAUNER, YARIV, *Tax Treaty Negotiations: Myth and Reality*, 2020, p. 2.

fighting treaty abuse and enhancing dispute resolution contained in the so-called BEPS minimum standards,[2] to which all members of the Inclusive Framework on BEPS of the OECD/G20 commit when joining the initiative.

For this purpose, an Ad Hoc Group gathering members from over 100 jurisdictions developed the "Multilateral Convention to Implement Tax Treaty Related Measures to Prevent Base Erosion and Profit Shifting" (hereinafter "MLI"), which was adopted by said group on November 24, 2016, and signed by 68 jurisdictions on June 7, 2017. As of February 18, 2021, the number of Signatories and Parties[3] to this novel instrument[4]—which is open for signature—arose to 95.

At the MLI signing ceremony on June 7, 2017, the OECD Secretary-General, José Ángel Gurría,[5] made the following opening remarks:

> [t]he conclusion of this multilateral instrument marks *a new turning point in tax treaty history*. We are moving towards *rapid implementation of the far-reaching reforms agreed under the BEPS Project* in more than 1,650 treaties worldwide. In addition to *saving jurisdictions from the burden of bilaterally re-negotiating* these treaties, the "MLI" results in *more certainty and predictability for businesses*, and *a better functioning international tax system* for the benefit of our citizens[6] [emphasis added].

As per the adherence to the MLI, and Secretary-General Gurria's words, the instrument seems promising and quite a success. However, its ultimate success may be relative, depending on the eye of the beholder. In this regard, the author, coming from the Latin American and the Caribbean (hereinafter "LAC") region, poses the following research question: do the words quoted above hold true from a LAC perspective?

For the purposes of this discussion, "Latin America and the Caribbean" (LAC) refers to the geographic region comprising the Caribbean, Central America, and South America, including:

(i) in the Caribbean: Antigua and Barbuda, Bahamas, Barbados, Cuba, Dominica, Dominican Republic, Grenada, Haiti, Jamaica, Saint Kitts and Nevis, Saint Lucia, Saint Vincent and the Grenadines, Trinidad and Tobago;

---

2. Actions were grouped under "minimum standards," "reinforced international standards," "common approaches and best practices," which imply different levels of commitment to each BEPS measure.
3. The term "Signatory" refers to any State or jurisdiction which has signed the MLI but for which this is not yet in force, while the term "Party" refers to any State or jurisdiction for which the MLI has entered into force (Article 2 of the MLI).
4. As pointed out by Bravo, "[a]ltough in other fields multilateral treaties have been used before to modify existing bilateral treaties, this has not been the case in international tax law"; indeed, she points out that previous multilateral experiences in international tax law cannot be compared with the MLI: those previous conventions "did not intend to modify existing tax treaties. Once adopted, they completely replaced all tax treaties that were in place between the contracting states" (BRAVO, NATHALIE, The Multilateral Tax Instrument and Its Relationship with Tax Treaties, World Tax Journal, Vol. 8, Issue 3, 2016, pp. 280-281).
5. OECD Secretary-General from June 1, 2006 to May 31, 2021.
6. OECD, Multilateral Instrument, Information Brochure, May 2020 (accessible at http://www.oecd.org/tax/beps/multilateral-instrument-BEPS-tax-treaty-information-brochure.pdf, February 27, 2021).

(ii) in Central America: Belize, Costa Rica, El Salvador, Guatemala, Honduras, Mexico, Nicaragua, Panama; and
(iii) in South America: Argentina, Bolivia, Brazil, Chile, Colombia, Ecuador, Guyana, Paraguay, Peru, Suriname, Uruguay, Venezuela.[7]

In the author's opinion, "the Latin American and the Caribbean (LAC) perspective" cannot oversee the two following elements: LAC is a developing region; and, in the tax field, LAC has historically been a "source" defender. Therefore, this contribution adopts a broader perspective and focuses on assessing the MLI, taking into consideration these two parameters. *A priori*, the author believes that such assessment will show that Gurria's words do not completely hold true for the countries of the LAC region. Indeed, LAC countries may have rushed into committing to the BEPS Project and the MLI, without careful consideration of the broader effects and missing, in particular, the opportunity to revisit their tax treaty policy. For verifying whether this intuitive answer to the research question previously formulated is valid, the author structured section 2 of this contribution as follows: after briefly referring to the "BEPS phenomenon" (2.1.1.) and the main characteristics and role of the MLI within the BEPS Project (2.1.2.), the author focuses on the LAC region (2.2.). She first refers to the region's traditional claim for source taxation and a more balanced international distribution of taxing rights (2.2.1.1) and explores the tax treaty network that exists in the region (2.2.1.2.). Afterward, she examines the region's degree of involvement in the BEPS Project; she identifies LAC countries' participation either as an OECD, G20, and/or Inclusive Framework Member (2.2.2.1.), the reasons that may have motivated such participation (2.2.2.2.), and, particularly, their adherence to the MLI. Focusing on those countries that have signed and deposited the MLI, she then comments on some of the most imminent challenges these countries face (2.2.2.3.). Finally, in section III, the author draws her conclusions on the effects of the MLI for the LAC region by answering the research question and sharing some final remarks for further consideration.

2 ASSESSING THE MLI FROM THE LAC PERSPECTIVE

2.1 The Role of the MLI Within the BEPS Project

To identify the precise role played by the MLI as part of the so-called BEPS package, the author first presents the basics of the OECD/G20 BEPS Project, briefly describing the

7. The author followed the "UN Standard country or area codes for statistical use (M49)" (accessible at https://unstats.un.org/unsd/methodology/m49/, February 27, 2021), leaving out of this contribution's scope—because of their particular status—the following jurisdictions: (i) Aruba, Curacao and Saint Maarten—autonomous countries part of the Kingdom of the Netherlands, and Bonaire, Sint Eustatius and Saba—special municipalities/public bodies of the Netherlands, the forth country of the Kingdom; (ii) British Overseas Territories, i.e., Anguilla, British Virgin Islands, Cayman Islands, Falklands Islands (Malvinas), Montserrat, South Georgia and the South Sandwich Islands, and Turks and Caicos Islands; (iii) French Overseas departments-regions and Overseas communities, i.e., Guadeloupe, Martinique, French Guiana, and Saint Barthélemy and Saint Martin, respectively; (iv) Puerto Rico, an unincorporated territory of the United States; United States Virgin Islands, an unincorporated and organized territory of the United States; and the Bouvet Island, a dependency of Norway.

phenomenon it intends to resolve with its 15-point Action Plan. The second subsection focuses on the objective of Action 15 as part of the said package while providing some insights on the MLI "negotiation."

2.1.1 The (Old Acquaintance) "BEPS Phenomenon"

The BEPS project was launched by the OECD in 2013, with political support from the G20. Its objective was to close the gaps and mismatches in international tax rules, as these were said to be exploited by multinational enterprises (MNEs) that artificially shifted their profits to low or no-tax jurisdictions, eliminating or significantly reducing their global tax burden. The erosion of tax bases was threatening the integrity of the corporate income tax (CIT), and most importantly, damaging voluntary tax compliance systems for all taxpayers, including individuals.[8] This phenomenon—which *was no novelty*—gained increasing attention from the G20 and the OECD.[9] Indeed, the phenomenon *did become an issue for the developed world* once this experienced the economic, social, and political consequences of the 2008 financial crisis.

Unfortunately, the BEPS project did not adopt a critical and open-minded approach and was not intended[10] to revisit international standards on nexus and profit allocation rules promoted through the OECD Model Tax Convention (OECD MC).[11] Contrarily, the project while also referring to new unprecise terminology, such as "value creation,"[12] pushed for the existing *status quo* and the international strengthening and harmonization of anti-abuse measures in national legislation and tax treaties.[13] Indeed, in a two-year period[14] after diagnosing the *old acquaintance* BEPS

---

8. OECD, *Addressing Base Erosion and Profit Shifting*, OECD Publishing, Paris, 2013.
9. *OECD members*: Australia, Austria, Belgium, Canada, Chile, Colombia, Czech Republic, Denmark, Estonia, Finland, France, Germany, Greece, Hungary, Iceland, Ireland, Israel, Italy, Japan, Korea, Latvia, Lithuania, Luxembourg, Mexico, the Netherlands, New Zealand, Norway, Poland, Portugal, Slovak Republic, Slovenia, Spain, Sweden, Switzerland, Turkey, the United Kingdom, the United Sates. *G20 members*: Argentina, Australia, Brazil, Canada, China, France, Germany, India, Indonesia, Italia, Japan, Mexico, Russia, Saudi Arabia, South Africa, South Korea, Turkey, the United Kingdom, the United States, and the European Union.
10. "In the changing international tax environment, a number of countries have expressed a concern about how international standards on which bilateral tax treaties are based allocate taxing rights between source and residence States. This Action Plan is focused on addressing BEPS. While actions to address BEPS will restore both source and residence taxation in a number of cases where cross-border income would otherwise go untaxed or would be taxed at very low rates, these actions are not directly aimed at changing the existing international standards on the allocation of taxing rights on cross-border income"; OECD, *Addressing Base Erosion and Profit Shifting ..., supra*.
11. OECD, *Model Tax Convention on Income and on Capital: Condensed Version 2017*, OECD Publishing, Paris, 2017, p. 654.
12. In the author's opinion the notion of "aligning taxation and value creation" is a remake of the "source principle" and the use of the new terminology, a way to avoid recognizing, in black and white, source jurisdictions' legitimate and primary right to tax. *See* RICCARDI SACCHI, ANDREA LAURA, *Una solución global a la imposición sobre la renta societaria: La revitalización de la fuente*, Tirant lo Blanch, Valencia, 2021 (in press).
13. In the author's opinion such path to "harmonization" only added complexity and lack of clarity. Meanwhile solving the "true problem," i.e., the lack of consensus on key concepts in the international tax arena, such as source and residence, was left behind. *Ibid.*

phenomenon, the OECD working together with non-OECD G20 Members,[15] designed and agreed on a plan comprised of 15 actions[16] that mainly proposed a set of *déjà vu* measures.[17]

Based on the trilogy of coherence,[18] substance,[19] and transparency,[20] the BEPS Action Plan implied introducing changes not only at the domestic level but also within the existing bilateral tax treaty network. "Surprisingly," tax treaties—3,000 worldwide[21]—structured around the concept of tax residence[22] were in the spotlight by recurrently being part of taxpayers' BEPS strategies. Tax treaties, which provide tax advantages[23] to eliminate the possible negative effects derived from double taxation on cross-border trade, investment, movement of persons, etc., were being *improperly* used. The use of conduit companies to indirectly access such benefits (so-called treaty

---

14. Except for the so-called Action 1, on addressing tax challenges derived from the digitalization of the economy, final reports with specific conclusions were issued for the other 14 actions.
15. Strictly speaking, the diagnosis and definitions of the items of the BEPS Action Plan were developed by the "select group of jurisdictions comprising the bureau of the OECD CFA," which worked closely with the OECD Secretariat; IFA, *Assessing BEPS: origins, standards, and responses*, Cahiers de droit fiscal international, Vol 102A, Rotterdam, 2017, p. 26 (General report by CHRISTIANS AND SHAY). The current composition of the Committee on Fiscal Affairs (CFA) can be found at https://oecdgroups.oecd.org/Bodies/ShowBodyView.aspx?BodyID = 963&Lang = en, March 30, 2021.
16. OECD, *Action Plan on Base Erosion and Profit Shifting*, OECD Publishing, Paris, 2013.
17. Escribano notes that BEPS actions "reawaken in us some sort of *déjà vu*" (the author´s translation). Indeed, many past discussions, and some already part of the Commentaries to the OECD MC, where readdressed; just to mention some of those previous studies: "Hybrid Mismatch Arrangements: Tax Policy and Compliance issues" (2012), "Restricting the Entitlement to Treaty Benefits" (2003), "The application of the OECD Model Tax Convention to Partnerships" (1999), "Harmful Tax Competition: An Emerging Global Issue" (1998), "Double Taxation Conventions and the Use of Conduit Companies" (1986). *See* ESCRIBANO, EVA, "¿Se ha equivocado el Proyecto BEPS en el planteamiento? Los paradigmas de la fiscalidad internacional que no han sido cuestionados," in ALMUDÍ CID, JOSÉ M. et al. (Dir.): El plan de acción sobre erosión de bases imponibles y traslado de beneficios (BEPS): G20, OCDE y UE, Aranzadi, Navarra, 2017, pp. 513-516.
18. Action 2: Neutralize the effects of hybrid mismatch arrangements; Action 3: Strengthen controlled foreign company rules; Action 4: Limit base erosion via interest deductions and other financial payments; Action 5: Counter harmful tax practices more effectively taking into account transparency and substance.
19. Action 6: Prevent treaty abuse; Action 7: Prevent the artificial avoidance of permanent establishment status; Actions 8, 9, 10: Assure that transfer pricing outcomes are in line with value creation.
20. Action 11: Establish methodologies to collect and analyze data on BEPS and the actions to address it; Action 12: Require taxpayers to disclose their aggressive tax planning arrangements; Action 13: Re-examine transfer pricing documentation; Action 14: Make dispute resolution mechanisms more effective.
21. *Supra* n. 1.
22. Since tax treaties are applicable to persons who are resident in one or both Contracting States (subjective scope), the concept of tax residence is central to the functioning of tax treaties and the distribution of taxing rights.
23. No or limited taxation in one or other of the Contracting states (generally the "source" jurisdiction) and the elimination of double taxation by the residence jurisdiction via the tax credit or the exemption methods. Distributive rules contained in tax treaties are based on a general premise: the State of residence can always tax. However, when tax jurisdiction is shared by the State of residence and the other Contracting State ("State of source"), the former has to provide relief to avoid double taxation; this may explain why taxing rights in the State of source are normally limited or denied.

shopping) or the circumvention of treaty thresholds requirements,[24] were among those recurrent practices.

2.1.2 *What Role for the MLI?*

Within this context, while updating the text of the OECD MC and its Commentaries,[25] for future reference in the negotiation, application, and interpretation of bilateral tax treaties, the existing network needed to be amended to rapidly counter BEPS practices. This is why as part of the BEPS Action Plan Action 15 was conceived to fulfill an instrumental purpose and:

> [a]nalyse the tax and public international law issues related to the development of a multilateral instrument to enable jurisdictions that wish to do so to implement measures developed in the course of the work on BEPS and amend bilateral tax treaties. On the basis of this analysis, interested Parties will develop a multilateral instrument designed to provide an innovative approach to international tax matters, reflecting the rapidly evolving nature of the global economy and the need to adapt quickly to this evolution.[26]

An interim report on Action 15 (the "2014 Deliverable"),[27] which received input from an informal group of experts in tax and public international law was approved by the OECD Committee on Fiscal Affairs (CFA) and delivered to the G20. The interim report concluded that a multilateral instrument was "desirable and feasible" and recommended its *negotiation* "through an International Conference, open to G20 countries, OECD members and other interested countries and convened under the aegis of the OECD and the G20."[28] It is relevant to highlight that the report suggested that the mandate of this Conference "should be limited in scope (implementation of the BEPS package) and in time (up to a two-year period)."[29] On this basis, the CFA elaborated a document[30] presenting a mandate to form an Ad Hoc Group, expressively stating that "the development of the instrument would not involve reopening issues *that have already been decided at the level of the CFA and G20*"[31] [emphasis added]. The mandate was endorsed by the G20 in February 2015 and the Ad Hoc Group started working in May.[32] By November 2016, a multilateral instrument to provide a "swift,

24. BAKER, PHILIP, *Improper Use of Tax Treaties, Tax Avoidance and Tax Evasion*, Papers on Selected Topics in Administration of Tax Treaties for Developing Countries, No. 9-A, May 2013.
25. In 2017, a new version of the OECD MC was published, including such updates.
26. OECD, *Action Plan on Base Erosion and Profit Shifting ..., supra*, p. 24.
27. OECD, *Action 15: 2014 Deliverable— - Developing a Multilateral Instrument to Modify Bilateral Tax Treaties, OECD/G20 Base Erosion and Profit Shifting*, OECD Publishing, Paris, 2014.
28. *Ibid.*, p. 14.
29. *Ibid.*
30. OECD, *Action 15: A Mandate for the Development of a Multilateral Instrument on Tax Treaty Measures to Tackle BEPS, OECD/G20 Base Erosion and Profit Shifting Project*, 2015 (accessible at http://www.oecd.org/ctp/beps-action-15-mandate-for-development-of-multilateral-instrument.pdf, February 27, 2021).
31. *Ibid.*, p. 5.
32. A request for input on the development of the multilateral instrument took place between May 13 to June 13, 2016; however, the scope of said request was limited to specific technical

synchronized, and consistent" implementation of BEPS tax treaty-related measures had been developed.[33]

Over 100 jurisdictions participated in the Ad Hoc Group;[34] however, such participation did not oblige jurisdictions to later sign on the instrument. The instrument, designed in a flexible manner[35] to coexist with existing bilateral tax treaties[36] foresees substantive provisions[37] that capture the treaty-related output resulting from Action 2 on the neutralization of the effects of hybrid mismatch arrangements,[38] Action 6 on preventing tax treaty abuse,[39] Action 7 on preventing the avoidance of the permanent establishment (PE) status,[40] and Action 14 on improving dispute resolution,[41] including promoting tax treaty arbitration.[42] Furthermore, measures resulting from two of these actions—Actions 6 and 14—constitute, along with those resulting

---

implementation issues (and the MAP arbitration provisions), and no draft of the instrument was shared. It was argued that "[a]s with other bilateral and multilateral treaty negotiations, the draft text of the multilateral instrument is the subject of intergovernmental discussions in a confidential setting"; OECD, *Public Discussion Draft, BEPS Action 15—Development of a Multilateral Instrument to Implement the Tax Treaty related BEPS Measures*, May 31—June 30, 2016.

33. On November 24, 2016, the Ad hoc Group concluded the negotiations and adopted the Text of the MLI as well as its accompanying Explanatory Statement. This "Explanatory Statement" intends to clarify the mechanics of the MLI, i.e., how it applies alongside bilateral tax agreements, and except with respect to Part VI of the MLI, does not address the interpretation of the underlying substantive (BEPS) measures.
34. Ninety-nine countries have participated as *Members of the Ad Hoc Group*: Andorra, Argentina, Australia, Austria, Azerbaijan, Bangladesh, Barbados, Belgium, Benin, Bhutan, Brazil, Bulgaria, Burkina Faso, Cameroon, Canada, Chile, China (People's Rep.), Colombia, Costa Rica, Croatia, Cyprus, Czech Republic, Denmark, Dominican Republic, Egypt, Estonia, Fiji, Finland, France, Gabon, Georgia, Germany, Greece, Guatemala, Haiti, Hungary, Iceland, India, Indonesia, Ireland, Israel, Italy, Ivory Coast, Jamaica, Japan, Jordan, Kazakhstan, Kenya, Korea, Latvia, Lebanon, Liberia, Liechtenstein, Lithuania, Luxembourg, Malaysia, Malta, Marshall Islands, Mauritania, Mauritius, Mexico, Moldova, Mongolia, Morocco, Netherlands, New Zealand, Nigeria, Norway, Pakistan, Philippines, Poland, Portugal, Qatar, Romania, Russia, San Marino, Saudi Arabia, Senegal, Serbia, Singapore, Slovak Republic, Slovenia, South Africa, Spain, Sri Lanka, Swaziland, Sweden, Switzerland, Tanzania, Thailand, Tunisia, Turkey, Ukraine, United Kingdom, United States, Uruguay, Vietnam, Zambia and Zimbabwe. Four non-State jurisdictions (Guernsey, Hong Kong, Isle of Man, Jersey) and seven regional/international organizations participated as *Observers* (African Tax Administration Forum, Association of Tax Authorities of Islamic Countries, *Centre de rencontres et d'études des dirigeants des administrations fiscales*, Commonwealth Associations of Tax Administrators, Inter-American Centre of Tax Administrations, International Monetary Fund, Intra-European Organisation of Tax Administrations).
35. Elements of flexibility include specifying bilateral tax treaties to be covered, opting-out of non-minimum standard provisions, and choosing to apply optional and alternative provisions.
36. The relationship between the MLI and covered bilateral tax treaties is defined through the inclusion of the so-called compatibility clauses: "in place of," "apply to" or "modify," "in the absence of," "in place of or in the absence of."
37. Articles 3-26 of the MLI. An analysis of these articles exceeds the objective of this contribution. Except for Part VI (Arts 18-26), each MLI "substantive article" (i.e., those that are intended to implement tax treaty-related measures to counter BEPS) are structured as follows: a tax treaty-related measure, a compatibility clause, possible reservations, and required notifications.
38. Articles 3 (Transparent Entities) and 5 (Application of Methods for Elimination of Double Taxation) of the MLI.
39. Article 4 (Dual Resident Entities) and Part III of the MLI (Treaty Abuse), Arts. 6-11.
40. Part IV of the MLI (Avoidance of Permanent Establishment Status), Arts. 12-15.
41. Part V of the MLI (Improving Dispute Resolution), Arts 16 and 17.
42. Part VI of the MLI (Arbitration), Arts 18-26.

from Actions 5 on countering harmful tax practices and Action 13 on transfer pricing (hereinafter "TP") documentation, the so-called BEPS minimum standards, i.e., the measures that need no matter what to be implemented by Inclusive Framework Members.[43]

The MLI itself began its legal existence on July 1, 2018, once the fifth instrument of ratification, acceptance, or approval[44] was deposited. However, for the MLI to modify the application of a specific bilateral tax treaty, certain conditions must be met. First, both Contracting States must have signed, ratified, and deposited the MLI which must have entered into force,[45] and the specific tax treaty must be a "Covered Tax Agreement."[46] Furthermore, for a specific MLI provision to apply to a Covered Tax Agreement, it is necessary that none of the Contracting States have made a reservation[47] on the application of such provision and both Contracting States have chosen to apply the same optional provision. Additionally, and depending on the type of the "compatibility clause,"[48] it is necessary that no "notification mismatch" arises.[49] The OECD Secretariat developed relevant tools[50] to facilitate the application of the MLI, among which the so-called MLI Matching Database has been, in the author's opinion, of utmost importance. The author refers to this database later in this contribution.

On the development of the MLI, there has been an emphasis on presenting the elaboration process as an "inter-state process," governed by participating States: these States contributed to the financing and chose the leadership (a president and three vice-presidents) of the group, the decisions of which were taken in the Plenary.[51] However, the scope of this "inclusive negotiation" was limited. As mentioned, discussions on which measures should be incorporated into the text of the

43. The minimum standards comprise: the introduction of specific treaty measures and a new treaty preamble to prevent treaty abuse (Action 6); the adoption of the so-called Country-by-Country (CbC) Reporting (Action 13); the elimination/amendment and monitoring of harmful tax regimes as well as the mandatory spontaneous exchange of tax rulings (Action 5); and the commitment to the effective and timely resolution of disputes via the mutual agreement procedure or MAP (Action 14).
44. Slovenia's on March 22, 2018. The first five jurisdictions that made the deposit were: Austria, Isle of Man, Jersey, Polonia and Slovenia.
45. The MLI enters into force with respect to each of its Parties on the first day of the month following three calendar months after the deposit of their instrument of ratification, acceptance or approval (Article 34 of the MLI).
46. This means that both Contracting States have listed in their MLI Positions the bilateral tax treaty as an agreement they wish to be covered by the MLI.
47. Contracting States can make a reservation on the application of a provision of the MLI as long as this provision is not a minimum standard.
48. *Supra* n. 36.
49. A notification mismatch arises when one of the Contracting States has notified an existing provision to be modified by the MLI but the other has not, or when both States have made a different notification.
50. *See* the *Toolkit for Application of the Multilateral Instrument for BEPS Tax Treaty Related Measures* at http://www.oecd.org/tax/treaties/application-toolkit-multilateral-instrument-for-beps-tax-treaty-measures.htm, March 22, 2021.
51. Zornoza Pérez, Juan, "Acción 15. El instrumento multilateral y el plan de acción BEPS" in Ramos Prieto, Jesús (Coord.): *Erosión de la base imponible y traslado de beneficios: estudios sobre el plan de acción de la OCDE. Comentarios a las Acciones 1, 2, 5, 6, 8, 13 y 15*, Thomson Reuters Aranzadi, Navarra, 2016, p. 457.

MLI—"curiously," except for Part VI of the MLI on Arbitration—and the level of commitment to each one, were not part of said process. Indeed, BEPS measures—contained in the 2015 BEPS reports—and the level of commitment to each one were agreed on by OECD/G20 countries, before the Inclusive Framework even existed.[52] The only new substantive content elaborated during the "negotiations" was the introduction of mandatory binding arbitration of mutual agreement procedure (MAP) cases, which is a proposal supported by many developed economies.[53]

Indeed, it is significant that the BEPS Project's doors were opened to non-OECD/G20 jurisdictions only after the BEPS package had been designed. The Inclusive Framework was set up in June 2016 and opened to interested jurisdictions to work "on an equal footing," but to do so *on the implementation of the BEPS package*.[54] There may be a reason for this timely "openness:" the implementation of the package by as many countries as possible in order to grant the BEPS Action Plan (particularly, its minimum standards) true effectiveness.

As of February 2021, the Inclusive Framework gathers 139 members, including all OECD Members, CFA Associates, and Associates in the BEPS Project. When joining the BEPS Project, each jurisdiction agrees to implement at least the BEPS minimum standards and to be monitored on the fulfillment of said implementation under a peer review mechanism.[55] The components of said minimum standards were also agreed upon during the exclusive OECD/G20 working process, "to tackle issues in cases where no action by some countries or jurisdictions would have created negative spillovers (including adverse impacts of competitiveness) on others."[56]

Regarding treaty abuse, the minimum standard requires the inclusion in tax treaties of an express statement that the common intention is to eliminate double taxation without creating opportunities for non-taxation or reduced taxation through tax evasion or avoidance, including through treaty shopping arrangements, and the

52. As expressively state in the Note on the functioning of the MLI under public international law issued by the OECD Directorate for Legal Affairs: "10. Since the substance of the tax treaty related BEPS measures had already been agreed, the role of the ad hoc Group that negotiated the MLI was to determine the way in which the MLI would modify the provisions of the bilateral tax treaties in order to implement those measures. The one exception was Part VI of the MLI which contains a set of provisions on mandatory binding mutual agreement procedure (MAP) arbitration. The substance of these provisions was developed as part of the negotiation of the MLI by a Sub-Group on Arbitration" (OECD, *Multilateral Convention to Implement Tax Treaty Related Measures to Prevent Base Erosion and Profit Shifting: Functioning under Public International Law, Note by the OECD Directorate for Legal Affairs* (accessed at http://www.oecd.org/tax/treaties/legal-note-on-the-functioning-of-the-MLI-under-public-international-law.pdf, March 21, 2021)).
53. For this development, a Sub-Group on Arbitration was established.
54. "We, therefore, strongly urge the timely implementation of the project and encourage all countries and jurisdictions, including developing ones, to participate. To monitor the implementation of the BEPS project globally, we call on the OECD to develop an inclusive framework by early 2016 with the involvement of interested non-G20 countries and jurisdictions which commit to implement the BEPS project, including developing economies, on an equal footing"; G20, G20 Leaders' Communiqué Antalya Summit, November, 15-16 2015 (accessible at http://g20.org.tr/g20-leaders-commenced-the-antalya-summit/, February 22, 2021).
55. Members must also pay a fee.
56. OECD, *Background Brief, Inclusive Framework on BEPS*, January 2017, p. 6.

implementation of this common intention by the inclusion of: (i) the principal purpose test (PPT) rule, (ii) a detailed limitation on benefits (LoB) rule supplemented by a mechanism that would deal with conduit arrangement, or (iii) both the PPT rule and a (detailed or simplified) LoB rule.[57] In respect to tax treaty dispute resolution, the minimum standard implies: (i) ensuring that treaty obligations related to the "MAP" are fully implemented in good faith and MAP cases are resolved in a timely manner, (ii) ensuring the implementation of administrative processes that promote the prevention and timely resolution of treaty-related disputes, and (iii) ensuring taxpayers can access the MAP when eligible.[58]

2.2 The MLI in Latin America and the Caribbean

Subsection 2.2.1. explores business income taxation in LAC, focusing first on the commonalities of national tax systems and, second, on tax treaties adopted in the region. Subsection 2.2.2. analyzes LAC countries' participation in the BEPS Project, the reasons for joining the initiative as well as their adherence to the MLI, and the most imminent challenges faced.

2.2.1 Business Income Taxation in LAC

2.2.1.1 The Traditional Defense of Source Taxation

LAC countries are characterized as "developing economies" according to the United Nations Conference on Trade and Development (UNCTAD) classification.[59] However, the region is widely diverse, not only in respect to the precise stage of economic development but also in respect to many other factors, such as the volume of population and market size, existence of non-renewable natural resources, the political ideology of the government in office, etc. Therefore, different priorities may arise, conditioning public policies, including tax policy.

Despite such economic, political, and social heterogeneity, conditioning tax measures, LAC countries have historically defended source taxation. Indeed, being, in general, net capital importing countries and not the seat of the headquarters of the biggest multinational groups[60] means, from an international tax perspective, acting

57. OECD, *Action 6: 2015 Final Report, Preventing the Granting of Treaty Benefits in Inappropriate Circumstances, OECD/G20 Base Erosion and Profit Shifting Project*, OECD Publishing, Paris, 2015.
58. OECD, *Action 14: 2015 Final Report, Making Dispute Resolution Mechanisms More Effective, OECD/G20 Base Erosion and Profit Shifting Project*, OECD Publishing, Paris, 2015.
59. UNCTAD, *Development Status Groups and Composition* (accessible at https://unctadstat.unctad.org/EN/Classifications.html, f.c. March 15, 2021).
60. A study examining headquarters location of top companies showed that the United States, China, Japan and the United Kingdom were in the year 2017 the four countries with the largest share of big companies (Clausing, Kimberly A., Does Tax Drive the Headquarters Locations of the World's Biggest Companies?, Transnational Corporations, Vol. 25, Issue 2, 2018, pp. 37-65).

mainly as "source jurisdictions." The intensity of this defense of course varies for each country, for each activity sector, etc.

The net capital importing status has explained not only LAC countries' long-standing tradition of defending the source principle (i.e., taxing income where it is sourced) but, most importantly—and consequently—their national income tax systems, structured around the concept and definition of "source of income." Moreover, some countries still exclusively apply the source principle for "CIT" purposes, i.e., they tax both their resident and non-resident businesses based on this principle.[61]

Following the "source of production" concept, LAC national tax systems generally define "domestic sourced income" as income derived from goods—tangible or intangible—situated or exploited in the country, as well as from activities developed in the country.[62] However, within LAC countries, it is possible to increasingly identify source rules that, based on "anti-abusive" or "protectionist" arguments, go far beyond the abovementioned source of production concept; most notably, in relation to income obtained for the provision of technical services.[63] As per the digitalized economy, source rules started being extended even more for income derived from the provision of digital services, sometimes bordering on the destination criterion.[64] The tendency to define source of income beyond the source of production concept has been, to some extent, reflected in the work of the UN Committee of Experts on International Cooperation in Tax Matters on Article 12A of the UN MC (Fees for technical services) and the proposal of a new Article 12B (Income from automated digital services), which

61. For example, Bolivia, Costa Rica, El Salvador, Guatemala, Honduras, Nicaragua, Panamá and Uruguay. Furthermore, Ecuador taxes worldwide income obtained by residents but applying an exemption regime for foreign-sourced income (provided such income has not been obtained in "tax havens"), and the Domenica Republic, applies worldwide taxation but only on financial income. Meanwhile Paraguay has recently passed a law (Law No. 6380/2019) qualifying income obtained from the development of activities outsaid Paraguay as "Paraguayan sourced income" unless such income has already been taxed at a tax rate equal or higher than 10%, which is the Paraguayan tax rate.
62. The definition of "domestic sourced income" contained in several LAC countries' domestic legislation has been analyzed by the author in Riccardi Sacchi, Andrea Laura, *Una solución global a la imposición sobre la renta societaria ..., supra.*
63. The author has been critical of the arguments behind (in her view, excessive) practices of extending the source definition beyond the source of production concept, which in the end leads to a conceptual bipolarity around the source of income, referred by the author as the "Hispano-American chaos" (Hispano-American due to the scope of the specific analysis). As this situation may be (or is being) globally replicated ("risk of replica"), the author claims the need to build a global consensus around a unique conceptual framework; specifically, she claims for the revitalization of source, i.e., source conceived as "source of production" but revisited, proposing an alternative to be implemented globally. *Ibid.*
64. For example, in Paraguay, Article 73 of Law No. 6380 (Non-Residents Income Tax) established that Paraguayan sourced income includes income from digital services when these are "used" in the country ("cuando sean utilizados o aprovechados efectivamente en el país"), covering B2B and B2C transactions. *See also* the case of Uruguay in Riccardi Sacchi, Andrea Laura, *While in the Quest of the Holy Grail ... Uruguay Is Already Taxing Income from Uber and Netflix*, Blog GLOBTAXGOV, Leiden University, March 8, 2019 (accessible at https://globtaxgov.weblog.leidenuniv.nl/2019/03/08/while-in-the-quest-for-the-holy-grail-uruguay-is-already-taxing-income-from-uber-and-netflix/).

the committee has already agreed to introduce.[65] The Committee of Experts, which has historically been criticized[66] for largely following the OECD by structuring the UN MC[67] around "the essence" of the OECD MC,[68] may have in part reacted to such criticism, by notwithstanding accompanying the implementation of the BEPS package with the introduction to the UN MC of Article 12A[69] and, in a near future, of Article 12B.

2.2.1.2 The Tax Treaty Network

Having referred to the OECD/UN MC, it now seems relevant to analyze if LAC countries have indeed adopted bilateral tax treaties and, if so, whether these treaties follow any specific model convention. As mentioned, the MLI has been developed to rapidly and consistently implement tax treaty-related BEPS measures into bilateral tax treaties and is applied alongside them, modifying their application. Therefore, the discussion below first focuses on the existing tax treaty network in LAC, whether countries have adopted treaties following the standards promoted by the OECD MC, and if so, how many tax treaties have been adopted by each jurisdiction. This information may explain in part the attention given in the region to the fight against treaty abuse and, in particular, to Action 15 and the signature of the MLI.

65. *See* UN, *Update Message from Co-Coordinators of the Subcommittee on Tax Challenges Related to the Digitalization of the Economy—William Babatunde Fowler and Aart Roelofsen*, 2020 (accessible at https://www.un.org/development/desa/financing/sites/www.un.org.development.desa.financing/files/2020-11/Update%20message%20for%20Digitalization_0.pdf, March 25, 2021).
66. For instance, *see* FIGUEROA, ANTONIO H., "La historia de los convenios de doble imposición internacional," in MAZZ, ADDY Y PISTONE, PASQUALE (Coord.): Reflexiones en torno a un Modelo Latinoamericano de Convenio de Doble Imposición, 1ª Ed., FCU, Montevideo, 2010, p. 26 ("Hoy, el Comité de Expertos de la ONU .... ha sido cooptado, absorbido, por la OCDE y el FMI, funcionales a las estrategias de ciertos países y de organizaciones empresarias mundiales (ICC), para consagrar *urbi et orbe* tales estrategias"). This long-standing criticism have existed since the origins of the committee. According to the Resolution of the VI Congress (Punta del Este, 1970) of the Latin American Institute of Tax Law (ILADT, as per the Spanish abbreviation) the work of the committee "no cumple ni con la letra ni con el espíritu que motivó su creación" (ILADT, *Estatutos Resoluciones de las Jornadas*, Montevideo, 1987).
67. UN, *Model Double Taxation Convention between developed and Developing Countries 2017*, New York, 2018, p. 813.
68. While the UN Economic and Social Council Resolution 486-B (XVI) of July 9, 1953 recommended that the source principle shall constitute the primary base of tax treaties between developed and developing countries, position further supported by Resolutions 1273 (XLIII) of August 4, 1967 and 1430 (XLVI) of June 6, 1969, since the beginning (1980) the UN MC has been following the general scheme of distribution of taxing rights and reduction of source taxation, though with some deviations (e.g. services PE, source taxation for royalties), and, as Valdés Costa has pointed out, adopting concepts such as the PE which ignores the source principle in respect to business income ("conceptos contrarios en aspectos tan importantes como el desconocimiento del principio de la fuente en lo que respecta a los beneficios de las empresas, sosteniendo el del domicilio, que se manifiesta en la exigencia de que exista un establecimiento permanente como requisito para reconocer el derecho del país donde la ganancia se materializa"; VALDÉS COSTA, RAMÓN, "Las empresas multinacionales ante el Derecho Tributario," Revista Tributaria (IUET), Tomo XXIII, No 131, 1996, p. 157).
69. For a deep analysis on the UN MC *see* BINDER, ANNA AND WOHRER, VIKTORIA (Ed.), *Special Features of the UN Model Convention*, Linde, Wien, 2019.

To start with (and closely linked to the previous subsection on the defense of the source principle), two multilateral tax treaties exist in the LAC region:

(i) the Andean Community Decision 578 on a "Regime to avoid Double Taxation and prevent Fiscal Evasion"[70] (hereinafter the "Andean tax treaty") of May 4, 2004, between Bolivia, Colombia, Ecuador, and Peru;[71]

(ii) the "Agreement among the Governments of the Member States of the Caribbean Community for the Avoidance of Double Taxation and the Prevention of Fiscal Evasion with Respect to Taxes on Income, Profits, or Gains and Capital Gains and for the Encouragement of Regional Trade and Investment" (hereinafter the "Caribbean tax treaty") of July 6, 1994, between Antigua and Barbuda, Barbados, Belize, Dominica, Grenada, Guyana, Jamaica, Saint Kitts and Nevis, Saint Lucia, Saint Vincent and the Grenadines, and Trinidad and Tobago, all former British colonies, currently part of the Commonwealth.[72]

Both conventions are examples of regional multilateral treaties concluded among countries that share similar tax policies concerns and systems. They enshrine the source principle[73] by stating that income shall only be taxable where it is sourced, i.e., where "the income has its source of production"[74] as stated in the Andean treaty, or where "the income arises" as stated in the Caribbean treaty. For business income, this means that *the existence of a PE*—which is the premise in the OECD and, to a lesser degree, the UN MC for assigning taxing rights on business profits to a State that is not

70. The author's translation of *Régimen para evitar la Doble Tributación y Prevenir la Evasión Fiscal.*
71. The Andean Pact was created on May 26, 1969, when the Cartagena Agreement was signed, as a subregional group within the Latin American Free Trade Association (ALALC, as per the Spanish abbreviation). Chile dropped out in 1976 and Venezuela, that had joined the Pact in 1973, resigned in 2006 (effective as of 2011). On November 16, 1971, the Decision 40 of the Cartagena Agreement Commission was approved, enacting a tax convention between signatory countries (*Convenio para Evitar la doble tributación entre los países Miembros*) as well as a Model Convention for subscribing tax treaties with third countries (*Convenio Tipo para evitar la doble tributación entre los Países Miembros y otros Estados ajenos a la Subregión*); accessible at http://www.sice.oas.org/trade/junac/decisiones/Dec040s.asp, March 25, 2020. Decision 578 of the Andean Community Commission (*Régimen para evitar la Doble Tributación y Prevenir la Evasión Fiscal*) of 4 May 2004, updated the text of the convention between Andean countries (accessible at http://www.sice.oas.org/trade/junac/Decisiones/DEC578s.asp, March 25, 2021).
72. The Caribbean Community (CARICOM) gathers, as Member States, Antigua and Barbuda, Bahamas, Barbados, Belize, Dominica, Grenada, Guyana, Haiti, Jamaica, Montserrat, Saint Lucia, Saint Kitts and Nevis, Saint Vincent and the Grenadines, Surinam, Trinidad and Tobago, and, as Associate Members, Anguilla, Bermuda, British Virgin Islands, Cayman Islands and Turks and Caicos. The community was established by the subscription of the Chaguaramas Treaty of July 4, 1973, functioning as from 2001 under the Revised Chaguaramas Treaty. The 1994 treaty substituted that signed in 1973 which divided signatories into two groups, more developed and less developed countries, allocating greater taxing rights to the less developed ones (*see* Brooks, Kim, "The Potential of Multilateral Tax Treaties," in Lang, Michael et al. (Ed.): *Tax Treaties: Building Bridges Between Law and Economics*, IBFD, 2010).
73. Except for income, basically, derived from transport businesses, which shall be taxable in the State of domicile/residence.
74. Which refers to "the activity, right or good that generates or can generate the income."

the State of residence—is not, within these treaties, a precondition for taxing non-resident businesses. This matter is addressed further in Subsection 2.2.2.2.

Furthermore, regional organizations have developed certain criteria and model conventions in the tax field. In the 1970s, the Andean Community also agreed on a "Model Convention for adopting [bilateral] tax treaties with third countries."[75] Meanwhile, the Latin American Integration Association (ALADI, as per the Spanish abbreviation), by that time, the ALALC or Latin American Free Trade Association, formulated technical criteria,[76] including a bilateral MC, which also enshrines the taxation of income where the source of production[77] is located. Valdés Costa referred to both models as "the most genuine and systematic expression of the Latin American traditional position."[78] Consequently, he suggested they should be considered as a point of departure for treaty negotiation purposes.[79] Nevertheless, as shown by the analysis of the LAC tax treaty network shared below, these MC have had scarce (not to say, null) influence in LAC tax treaty practice. During those years, another MC[80] was also developed by a technical group convened under the auspices of the "Cuenca del Plata",[81] an initiative that aims to foster the development and integration of this geographic area. The Cuenca del Plata model convention also enshrined the source principle.

More recently, the Latin American Institute of Tax Law, which gathers not only scholarship from Latin America but also from Spain, Portugal, and Italy, approved the *Modelo ILADT de Convenio Multilateral de Doble Imposición para América Latina* (ILADT MC)[82] as an alternative to be considered by Latin American countries when negotiating either bilateral or multilateral tax treaties.[83] In respect to business profits, and in contrast to the abovementioned MCs, the ILADT MC adopts the PE concept with an intent to enforce source taxation through a broader PE definition and taxing rights exclusively assigned to the State of the PE.[84] Indeed, it foresees taxation only in the residence jurisdiction unless the activity is carried out through a PE in one or more

75. *See supra* n. 71.
76. *See* ALALC, *Criterios de armonización aplicables a tratados tributarios celebrados entre países de la ALALC,* Montevideo, July 1979, p. 57.
77. Defined as "material or immaterial capital, labor or a combination of both factors."
78. The author's translation; Valdés Costa, Ramón, *Estudios de Derecho Tributario Internacional,* Rosgal, Montevideo, 1978, pp. 175 and 176.
79. Valdés Costa, Ramón, *Estudios de Derecho Tributario Internacional ..., supra.,* p. 129.
80. Cuenca del Plata, *Modelo de Convenio sobre doble Imposición, recomendado por los Cancilleres de los países integrantes de la Cuenca del Plata,* Revista Tributaria (IUET), Tomo V, No. 27, 1978, pp. 513-534.
81. *See* https://cicplata.org/es/.
82. ILADT, *Modelo ILADT de Convenio Multilateral de Doble Imposición para América Latina, Cuaderno Tributario ICDT,* Bogotá, 2012, p. 39.
83. The development of this MC was commended to a working group integrated by Addz Mazz (Uruguay), Antonio H. Figueroa (Argentina), Heleno Taveira-Torres (Brasil), Jaques Malherbe (Belgium), Natalia Quiñones (Colombia) and Pasquale Pistone (Italy). Their work can be found in Mazz, Addy & Pistone, Pasquale (Coord.), *Reflexiones en torno a un Modelo Latinoamericano de Convenio de doble imposición,* 1ª Ed. FCU, Montevideo, 2010, p. 311.
84. *Ibid.,* p. 124. The ILADT MC foresees a definition of the PE in Article 4 under the subheading "Definitions and interpretation."

States, in which case, income attributable to the PE shall be taxable only in the State of the PE. The author is not aware of any LAC tax treaty following this criterion.

On the bilateral tax treaty network in LAC (*see* Table 6.1[85]), the author identified the number of tax treaties adopted by each jurisdiction and whether or not these treaties follow the residence-PE standard. Once a country has joined the BEPS initiative and committed to the minimum standards, the number of existing bilateral tax treaties may represent a relevant factor for deciding whether to embrace the MLI. Depending on the size of each countries' network, the alternative (i.e., the renegotiation or negotiation of an amending protocol with each counterpart) may or may not be cost-efficient. Such an alternative may, however, provide jurisdictions with the opportunity to discuss items beyond the BEPS Project agenda and design; bilateral channels are more flexible and can result in adaptations to specific country conditions. Though countries are not obliged to become signatories to the MLI (i.e., the signature of the MLI is not a minimum standard), and jurisdictions can resort to bilateral channels to comply, the BEPS Project clearly pushed for the signature of the instrument; bilateral channels' flexibility may certainly threaten the objective of "swift, synchronized and consistent" implementation of the BEPS measures.

Table 6.1 Number of Bilateral Tax Treaties Subscribed, Per Decade, by LAC Countries

Country	*1940-1949*	*1950-1959*	*1960-1969*	*1970-1979*	*1980-1989*	*1990-1999*	*2000-2009*	*2010-2019*	*2020-2021*	*Total*
Antigua y Barbuda	1	–	1	–	–	–	–	–	–	2
Argentina	–	–	–	4	1	9	1	11	–	26
Bahamas	–	–	–	–	–	–	–	–	–	–
Barbados	–	–	1	–	3	4	10	15	–	33
Belize	1	–	1	–	–	–	1	–	–	3
Bolivia	–	–	–	1	–	5	–	–	–	6
Brazil	–	–	1	7	10	4	10	5	–	37
Chile	–	–	–	–	–	3	21	11	2	37
Colombia	–	–	–	–	–	–	5	9	–	14
Costa Rica	–	–	–	–	–	–	1	3	–	4
Cuba	–	–	–	–	–	2	7	–	–	9
Dominica	–	–	1	–	–	–	–	–	–	1

85. *See* Table 6.1— Number of bilateral tax treaties subscribed, per decade, by LAC countries. The information was collected from the tax authorities' webpages (either the Tax Administration or the Ministry of Economic and Finance/Foreign Affairs webpage), complemented with PWC Worldwide Tax Summaries (https://taxsummaries.pwc.com/) and the IBFD database (https://www.ibfd.org/).

Country	*1940-1949*	*1950-1959*	*1960-1969*	*1970-1979*	*1980-1989*	*1990-1999*	*2000-2009*	*2010-2019*	*2020-2021*	*Total*
Dominican Republic	–	–	–	1	–	–	–	1	–	2
Ecuador	–	–	–	–	4	6	1	8	–	19
El Salvador	–	–	–	–	–	–	1	–	–	1
Grenada	1	–	2	–	–	–	–	–	–	3
Guatemala	–	–	–	–	–	–	–	1	–	1
Guyana	–	–	–	–	1	1	–	–	–	2
Haiti	–	–	–	–	–	–	–	–	–	–
Honduras	–	–	–	–	–	–	–	–	–	–
Jamaica	–	–	–	3	3	5	1	2	–	14
Mexico	–	–	–	–	–	22	21	19	–	62
Nicaragua	–	–	–	–	–	–	–	–	–	–
Panama	–	–	–	–	–	–	–	17	–	17
Paraguay	–	–	–	–	–	1	1	3	–	5
Peru	–	–	–	–	–	–	3	5	–	8
Saint Kitts and Nevis	1	–	1	–	–	–	1	2	–	5
Saint Lucia	–	–	1	–	–	–	–	–	–	1
Saint Vincent and the Grenadines	–	–	1	–	–	–	–	–	–	1
Suriname	–	–	–	1	–	–	1	–	–	2
Trinidad and Tobago	–	–	2	4	3	3	4	–	–	16
Uruguay	–	–	–	–	1	–	3	20	–	24
Venezuela	–	–	–	–	–	17	14	4	–	35

Source: Table elaborated by the author in April 2021 based on the data available at the Tax Authorities' webpage, the PWC Summaries, and the IBFD Database.

Having identified the exact number of tax treaties subscribed per jurisdiction, it is possible to say that, except for the Mexican case, this number is quite small (smaller if we exclude tax treaties signed after the 2015 BEPS reports[86]) in comparison to the one evidenced in countries from the developed world, which can be over a hundred.[87] In this regard—and the reader will understand from the data shared below—why the author was quite surprised when at the 2020 International Fiscal Association (virtual) Congress, the panel on Subject 1, "Reconstructing the Tax Treaty Network," gave the example of New Zealand—that has about 40[88] tax treaties—as one country with a "small treaty network."[89]

Starting with the members of the Andean Community, Bolivia's tax treaty network includes just six[90] bilateral tax treaties, the last of which was signed in 1997. Of these, just one (with Argentina, subscribed in 1976) follows the Andean Community MC. Meanwhile, Ecuador reports 19[91] bilateral tax treaties based on the OECD/UN MC, 10 of which were subscribed during the 1980s and 1990s. Colombia's and Peru's bilateral tax treaty network, fully based on the OECD/UN MC, is "newer" and includes 14[92] and 8[93] treaties, respectively.

Regarding signatories to the Caribbean tax treaty, Barbados stands out with 33[94] bilateral tax treaties, all based on the OECD/UN MC. Barbados is followed by Trinidad and Tobago and Jamaica, with 16[95] and 14[96] tax treaties, respectively. The rest reports less than five tax treaties: Antigua y Barbuda (2[97]), Belize (3[98]), Dominica (1[99]),

86. If the country is a "BEPS supporter," these treaties probably already include BEPS measures.
87. *See* the size of European countries' tax treaty network in Zvinys, A. Kristina, Tax Treaty Network of European Countries, September 3, 2020, Tax Foundation (accessible at https://taxfoundation.org/tax-treaties-european-tax-treaty-network-2020/).
88. *See* https://taxpolicy.ird.govt.nz/tax-treaties, March 29, 2021.
89. *See* the recorded version of IFA Conference of 16 November 2020 (accessible at https://www.youtube.com/watch?v=3F5DJE26j7g, March 29, 2021).
90. Argentina (1976), France (1994), Germany (1992), Spain (1997), Sweden (1994), United Kingdom (1994).
91. Belarus (2016), Belgium (1996), Brazil (1983), Canada (2001), Chile (1999), China (2013), France (1989), Germany (1982), Italy (1984), Japan (2019), Korea (2012), Mexico (1992), Qatar (2014), Romania (1992), Russia (2016), Singapore (2013), Spain (1991), Switzerland (1994), Uruguay (2011).
92. Canada (2008), Chile (2007), Czech Republic (2012), France (2015), India (2011), Italy (2018), Japan (2018), Korea (2010), Mexico (2009), Spain (2005), Portugal (2010), Switzerland (2007), United Arab Emirates (2017), United Kingdom (2016).
93. Chile (2001), Canada (2001), Brazil (2006), Mexico (2011), Korea (2012), Suiza (2012), Portugal (2012), Japón (2019).
94. Austria (2006), Bahrain (2012), Botswana (2005), Canada (1980), China (2000), Cuba (1999), Cyprus (2017), Czech Republic (2010), Finland (1989), Ghana (2008), Iceland (2011), Italy (2015), Luxembourg (2009), Malta (2001), Mauritius (2004), Mexico (2008), Netherlands (2006), Norway (1990), Panama (2010), Portugal (2010), Qatar (2012), Rwanda (2014), San Marino (2012), Seychelles (2007), Singapore (2013), Slovak Republic (2015), Spain (2010), Sweden (1991), Switzerland (1963), United Arab Emirates (2014), United Kingdom (2012), United States (1984), Venezuela (1998).
95. Brazil (2008), Canada (1995), China (2003), Denmark (1969), France (1987), Germany (1976), India (1999), Italy (1971), Luxembourg (2001), Norway (1969), Spain (2009), Sweden (1984), Switzerland (1973), United Kingdom (1982), United States (1970), Venezuela (1996).
96. Canada (1978), China (1996), Denmark (1990), France (1995), Germany (1974), Israel (1984), Italy (2018), Mexico (2016), Norway (1991), Spain (2008), Sweden (1985), Switzerland (1994), United Kingdom (1973), United Sates (1980).
97. Switzerland (1963), United Kingdom (1947).
98. Austria (2002), Switzerland (1963), United Kingdom (1947).

Grenada (3[100]), Guyana (2[101]), Saint Kitts and Nevis (5[102]), Saint Lucia (1[103]), Saint Vincent and the Grenadines (1[104]). Errors excepted, all of these treaties adopt a distributive rule for business profits based on the residence and PE concepts. The tax treaty between Trinidad and Tobago and the United States signed in 1970 caught the attention of the author, as it includes an Article under the subhead "Source of income" which grants exclusive taxing rights to the State of the PE.

Mexico, which has been an OECD Member since 1994 and subscribed to 62[105] tax treaties, reports the largest network in the region. Mexico is followed by Brazil[106] and Chile[107] with 37 tax treaties each, Venezuela (35[108]), Argentina (26[109]), and Uruguay

99. Switzerland (1963).
100. United Kingdom (1949), South Africa (1960), Switzerland (1963).
101. Canada (1985), United Kingdom (1992).
102. Monaco (2009), San Marino (2010), Switzerland (1963), United Arab Emirates (2016), United Kingdom (1947).
103. Switzerland (1963).
104. *Ibid.*
105. Argentina (2015), Australia (2002), Austria (2004), Bahrain (2010), Barbados (2008), Belgium (1992), Brazil (2003), Canada (2006), Chile (1998), China (2005), Colombia (2009), Costa Rica (2014), Czech Republic (2002), Denmark (1997), Ecuador (1992), Estonia (2012), Finland (1997), France (1991), Germany (2008), Greece (2004), Guatemala (2015), Hong Kong (2012), Hungary (2011), Iceland (2008), India (2007), Indonesia (2002), Ireland (1998), Israel (1999), Italy (1991), Jamaica (2016), Japan (1996), Korea (1994), Kuwait (2009), Latvia (2012), Lithuania (2012), Luxembourg (2001), Malta (2012), Netherlands (1993), New Zealand (2006), Norway (1995), Panama (2010), Peru (2011), Philippines (2015), Poland (1998), Portugal (1999), Qatar (2012), Romania (2000), Russia (2004), Saudi Arabia (2016), Singapore (1994), Slovak Republic (2006), South Africa (2009), Spain (1992), Sweden (1992), Switzerland (1993), Turkey (2013), Ukraine (2012), United Arab Emirates (2012), United Kingdom (1994), United Sates (1992), Uruguay (2009).
106. Argentina (1980), Austria (1975), Belgium (1972), Canada (1984), Chile (2001), China (1991), Czech Republic (1986), Denmark (1974), Ecuador (1983), Finland (1996), France (1971), Hungary (1986), India (1988), Israel (2002), Italy (1978), Japan (1967), Korea (1989), Luxembourg (1978), Mexico (2003), Netherlands (1990), Norway (1980), Peru (2006), Philippines (1983), Portugal (2000), Russia (2004), Singapore (2018), Slovak Republic (1986), South Africa (2003), Spain (1974), Sweden (1975), Switzerland (2018), Trinidad and Tobago (2008), Turkey (2010), United Arab Emirates (2018), Ukraine (2002), Uruguay (2019), Venezuela (2005).
107. Argentina (2015), Australia (2010), Austria (2012), Belgium (2007), Brazil (2001), Canada (1998), China (2015), Colombia (2007), Croatia (2003), Czech Republic (2015), Denmark (2002), Ecuador (1999), France (2004), India (2020), Ireland (2005), Italy (2015), Japan (2016), Korea (2002), Malaysia (2004), Mexico (1998), New Zealand (2003), Netherlands (2021), Norway (2001), Paraguay (2005), Peru (2001), Polonia (2000), Portugal (2005), Russia (2004), South Africa (2012), Spain (2003), Sweden (2004), Switzerland (2008), Thailand (2006), United Arab Emirates (2019), United Kingdom (2003), United States (2010), Uruguay (2016).
108. Austria (2006), Barbados (1998), Belarus (2007), Belgium (1993), Brazil (2005), Canada (2001), China (2001), Cuba (2003), Czech Republic (1996), Denmark (1998), France (1992), Germany (1995), Indonesia (1997), Iran (2005), Italy (1990), Korea (2006), Kuwait (2004), Malaysia (2006), Mexico (1997), Netherlands (1991), Norway (1997), Palestine (2014), Portugal (1996), Qatar (2006), Russia (2003), Saudi Arabia (2015), Spain (2003), Sweden (1993), Switzerland (1996), Trinidad and Tobago (1996), Turkey (2018), United Arab Emirates (2010), United Kingdom (1996), United States (1999), Vietnam (2008).
109. Australia (1999), Austria (2019), Belgium (1996), Bolivia (1976), Brazil (1980), Canada (1993), Chile (2015), China (2018), Denmark (1995), Finland (1994), France (1979), Germany (1978), Italy (1979), Japan (2019), Luxembourg (2019), Mexico (2015), Netherlands (1996), Norway

(24[110]).[111] Panama[112] reports 17 tax treaties, the vast majority signed within a period of just three years. All these treaties are based on the OECD/UN MC except for, as mentioned, the tax treaty between Argentina and Bolivia, based on the Andean Community MC. The 1976 tax treaty subscribed by Argentina and Chile, which was also based on said MC, was denounced by Argentina in 2012, and substituted by a new treaty based on the OECD/UN MC signed in 2015.

Some LAC countries have very few tax treaties: Costa Rica (4[113]), Cuba (9[114]), Dominican Republic (2[115]), El Salvador (1[116]), Guatemala (1[117]), Paraguay (5[118]), Suriname (2[119]). Others have not signed any tax treaties (Haiti, Honduras, Nicaragua), or even have no income tax at all, either on corporations or on individuals (Bahamas). The tax treaty between Paraguay and Uruguay, signed in 2017 and BEPS compliant (beyond the minimum standards) is quite interesting since its Protocol foresees that the "source" jurisdiction can tax business income according to its domestic legislation when such income has not been effectively taxed in the residence jurisdiction, even in the absence of a PE.[120] It may be relevant to say that both countries adhere to the source principle for taxing resident companies.[121]

To end this section, and as per the international discussion that currently takes place in respect to the introduction of a global minimum tax under the so-called Global

(1997), Qatar (2018), Russia (2001), Spain (2013), Sweden (1995), Switzerland (2014), Turkey (2018), United Arab Emirates (2016), United Kingdom (1996).

110. Belgium (2013), Brazil (2019), Chile (2016), Ecuador (2011), Finland (2011), Germany (2010), Hungary (1988), India (2011), Italy (2019), Japan (2019), Korea (2011), Liechtenstein (2010), Luxembourg (2015), Malta (2011), Mexico (2009), Paraguay (2017), Portugal (2009), Romania (2012), Singapore (2015), Spain (2009), Switzerland (2010), United Arab Emirates (2014), United Kingdom (2016), Vietnam (2013).

111. In the case of Uruguay, it is notorious how the tax treaty network increased after "the 2009 naming and shaming of countries" that were not complying with the internationally agreed standards on exchange of information. Indeed, the country, with no experience at all in this matter, signed almost 10 tax treaties in 3 years, some including very unfavorable provisions. From a technical perspective, it is clear that to comply with the exchange of information standard it could have been sufficient to adopt tax information exchange agreements and to subscribe to the Convention on Mutual Administrative Assistance in Tax Matters, which, by the way, was opened to all countries in 2010.

112. Barbados (2010), Czech Republic (2012), France (2011), Ireland (2011), Israel (2012), Italy (2010), Korea (2010), Luxembourg (2010), Mexico (2010), Netherlands (2010), Portugal (2010), Qatar (2010), Singapore (2010), Spain (2010), United Arab Emirates (2012), United Kingdom (2013), Vietnam (2016).

113. Germany (2016), Mexico (2014), Spain (2004), United Arab Emirates (2017).

114. Austria (2003), Barbados (1999), China (2001), Lebanon (2001), Portugal (2000), Russia (2000), Spain (1999), Venezuela (2003), Vietnam (2002).

115. Canada (1976), Spain (2011).

116. Spain (2008).

117. Mexico (2015).

118. Chile (2005), China (1994), Qatar (2018), United Arab Emirates (2018), Uruguay (2017).

119. Indonesia (2003), Netherlands (1975).

120. "Cuando de conformidad con el Artículo 7 de este Convenio, las utilidades de una empresa de un Estado Contratante no puedan someterse a imposición en el otro Estado, pero el Estado mencionado en primer lugar no someta efectivamente a imposición dichas utilidades, el último Estado mencionado podrá someter a imposición dichas utilidades, de acuerdo con su legislación interna."

121. See *supra* n. 61.

anti-Base Erosion (GloBE) proposal,[122] it may be appropriate to make a brief comment on the future of granting tax incentives, a tax policy decision of many LAC countries. which if correctly designed and monitored, may serve to attract foreign investment. Apparently, attracting foreign investment is also one of the motives of which a jurisdiction may justify signing a tax treaty. Under this context, and to strengthen that objective, many LAC countries have negotiated so-called tax sparing clauses in order to avoid the neutralization of tax incentives granted at source.[123] Brazil is well known for including this type of clause in its tax treaties.[124] However, not only has the OECD expressed some reluctance in relation to the adoption of tax sparing provisions,[125] but in the near future, the GloBE proposal may end neutralizing, at least in part, those LAC negotiation efforts.

From this Subsection 2.2.1. on business income taxation in LAC, it can be generally concluded that tax policies and standards promoted by the OECD via its MC diverge from those favored by the LAC region. This matter may in part explain the small size of the tax treaty network in the region.

2.2.2 Involvement in the BEPS Project and Adherence to the MLI

As mentioned, the MLI was developed with a clear objective: to transpose tax treaty-related measures resulting from the BEPS package into (as many as possible) existing tax treaties, including the BEPS minimum standards on treaty abuse and dispute resolution. Though all interested countries are able to subscribe to the MLI, irrespective of their membership to any of the "clubs" (G20, OECD, Inclusive Framework), one factor that may have influenced the adherence to the MLI is the degree of participation in the project.

The following Subsections examine whether the LAC region has participated in the BEPS project, and if so, what countries, how and for what reasons; then LAC signatories and parties to the MLI are identified along with the most imminent challenges derived from such adherence. "Participation"[126] in the BEPS Project could

---

122. *See* Riccardi Sacchi, Andrea Laura, Implementing a (Global?) Minimum Corporate Income Tax: An Assessment of the So-Called Pillar Two from the Perspective of Developing Countries, Nordic Journal on Law and Society, Vol. 4, Issue 1, 2021 (accessible at https://journals.ub.umu.se/index.php/njolas/article/view/188).
123. On this topic the author suggests reading Navarro, Aitor, Tax Sparing Clauses as a Policy Instrument of Developing Countries and Their Descent: Evidence from the Latin American Tax Treaty Network, CBS Law Research Paper Series No. 20-17, 2020.
124. On the Brazil policy, *see* Lang, Michael et al. (Ed.), *Trends and Player in Tax Policy*, IBFD, 2016, pp. 182-186 (Chapter 4—Brazil, Schoueri and Calicchio Barbosa).
125. The OECD has expressed some reluctance in relation to their adoption. *See* paras. 72-78.1 of the Commentaries to Article 23 A and 23 B of the OECD MC. In fact, tax sparing clauses that had been negotiated in the past, were later eliminated as part of a renegotiation process. This has been the case of the tax treaty concluded between Germany and Uruguay in 1987, and renegotiated in 2010.
126. Formal participation does not grant per se the actual involvement in the discussion and report elaboration processes as countries´ participation can be rather passive, for diverse reasons (e.g., constrains in resources, political decisions, economic pressures, etc.). The character of the participation (active or passive) however cannot be clearly inferred from the information

refer to the country's status as a Member of the OECD, the G20, and/or the Inclusive Framework, or to some other type of participation.

At this point, it seems relevant to share with the reader some general information on how non-OECD interested jurisdictions can participate in any of the OECD Committees, including the CFA, alongside the OECD Members. There are three types of participation:

(i) invitees, who are invited to one meeting at a time regarding non-confidential items;
(ii) participants, who are entitled to be invited to all of the Committee's non-confidential meetings; and
(iii) associates, who participate in a Committee, a project, or the development or discussion of a legal instrument with the same rights and obligations as OECD Members (but cannot attend discussions on the accession of new members).[127]

In particular, a jurisdiction can be an Associate in the CFA and all of its subsidiary bodies or an Associate in one or several of the CFA subsidiary bodies. Specifically, as per the BEPS Project, a jurisdiction can be an Associate in the BEPS Project *of the CFA* for the duration of the project. In this regard, non-OECD countries that are G20 members[128] became Associates in the BEPS Project in 2013. This was after the release of the OECD report diagnosing the BEPS phenomenon (February 2013), but more or less simultaneously with the BEPS Action Plan report (July 19, 2013).[129] OECD Members, CFA Associates, and Associates in the BEPS Project are the current 139 *Members of the BEPS Project*.

2.2.2.1 Participation in the BEPS Project

Participation in the BEPS Project of LAC countries is diverse, but the vast majority have participated neither in the setting of the BEPS agenda nor the elaboration of the 2015 final reports and definition of the minimum standards. Despite this fact, the BEPS Project has received considerable support from LAC via the Inclusive Framework membership.

Indeed, few LAC countries are G20 or OECD Members. Mexico is the only LAC country that belongs to both groups, and the first LAC country to have joined the OECD

publicly available. Some insights on this matter can be found in Christensen, Rasmus Colin, Hearson, Martin and Randriamanalina, Tovony, *At the Table, Off the Menu? Assessing the Participation of Lower-Income Countries in Global Tax Negotiations*, ICTD Working Paper 115, 2020.

127. This information is publicly available at http://www.oecd.org/global-relations/partnershipsinoecdbodies/, March 16, 2021.

128. Argentina, Brazil, China, India, Indonesia, Russia, Saudi Arabia, South Africa.

129. *See* OECD, *Participation Plan. Committee on Fiscal Affairs* (accessible at https://www.oecd.org/global-relations/partnershipsinoecdbodies/PP-CFA-PUBLIC-ENG.pdf).

(1994). Brazil and Argentina are G20 members but not OECD members.[130] Furthermore, Chile has been a member of the OECD since 2010 and Colombia became the OECD's 37th member country in April 2020. Costa Rica which was invited to join the OECD on May 15, 2020 as a candidate for accession became an Associate in the BEPS Project prior to the establishment of the Inclusive Framework but after the release of the 2015 final reports.

Since mid-2016, with the establishment of the Inclusive Framework, other LAC jurisdictions started becoming Associates in the BEPS Project:

(i) in the Caribbean: Antigua and Barbuda, Bahamas, Barbados, Dominica, Dominican Republic, Grenada, Haiti, Jamaica, Saint Kitts and Nevis, Saint Lucia, Saint Vincent and the Grenadines, Trinidad and Tobago;
(ii) in Central America: Belize, Honduras, Panama; and
(iii) in South America: Paraguay, Peru, Uruguay.[131]

To summarize (*see* Table 6.2[132]), 24 of the 33 LAC[133] countries currently have the status of Member of the BEPS Project, i.e., 72.7% of them have joined the initiative at some point in time. Of these 24 countries, 11 are former British colonies that are part of the Commonwealth and represent 91.6% of total LAC countries part of the Commonwealth.[134] Their colonial ties may explain the high percentage of adherence to the Inclusive Framework.[135] If we exclude them from the analysis, the percentage of LAC participation in the BEPS project drops to 59%.

Table 6.2 LAC Countries' Status as OECD/G20/Inclusive Framework Members

Country	*OECD*	*G20*	*Inclusive Framework*
Antigua y Barbuda	–	–	X
Argentina	– (1)	X	X
Bahamas	–	–	X
Barbados	–	–	X

130. Furthermore, Argentina has been an Associate in the CFA and all its subsidiary bodies since 2014.
131. Brazil, Costa Rica, Peru and Uruguay have been Participant in the CFA and its subsidiary bodies since 2016, 2014, 2019 and 2015, respectively.
132. Table 6.2—LAC countries' Status as OECD/G20/Inclusive Framework Members. The information was collected from the OECD's and G20's webpages.
133. According the scope defined for this contribution.
134. Of the 12 LAC countries that are part of the Commonwealth (Antigua and Barbuda, Bahamas, Barbados, Dominica, Grenada, Jamaica, Saint Kitts and Nevis, Saint Vincent and the Grenadines, Trinidad and Tobago, Belize and Guyana), just Guyana is not an Inclusive Framework Member.
135. However, as expressed in The Commonwealth´ webpage, this is "a voluntary association of 54 independent and equal countries. Its roots go back to the British Empire, but membership of the modern Commonwealth does not depend on formerly being part of the British Empire" (https://thecommonwealth.org/about-us/joining-the-commonwealth, March 30, 2021).

Country	*OECD*	*G20*	*Inclusive Framework*
Belize	–	–	X
Bolivia	–	–	–
Brazil	– (2)	X	X
Chile	X	–	X
Colombia	X (3)	–	X
Costa Rica	X (4)	–	X
Cuba	–	–	–
Dominica	–	–	X
Dominican Republic	–	–	X
Ecuador	–	–	–
El Salvador	–	–	–
Grenada	–	–	X
Guatemala	–	–	–
Guyana	–	–	–
Haiti	–	–	X
Honduras	–	–	X
Jamaica	–	–	X
Mexico	X	X	X
Nicaragua	–	–	–
Panama	–	–	X
Paraguay	–	–	X
Peru	– (2)	–	X
Saint Kitts and Nevis	–	–	X
Saint Lucia	–	–	X
Saint Vincent and the Grenadines	–	–	X
Suriname	–	–	–
Trinidad and Tobago	–	–	X
Uruguay	– (2)	–	X
Venezuela	–	–	–

(1) Argentina has been an Associate in the CFA and all its subsidiary bodies since 2014.

(2) Brazil, Costa Rica, Peru, and Uruguay have been Participants in the CFA and its subsidiaries' bodies since 2016, 2014, 2019, and 2015, respectively.
(3) Colombia became an OECD Member in April 2020.
(4) Costa Rica who was invited to join the OECD on May 15, 2020, became an Associate in the BEPS Project prior to the establishment of the Inclusive Framework.

Source: Table elaborated by the author in April 2021 based on the data available at the OECD's and G20 webpages.

Meanwhile, Cuba, El Salvador, Guatemala, Nicaragua, Bolivia, Ecuador, Guyana, Suriname, and Venezuela, which have also been invited to become Associates in the BEPS Project, have not accepted the invitation and remain part of a list of Invitees in the BEPS Project.[136]

2.2.2.2 *Why Did LAC Countries Join the BEPS Project?*

Despite poor participation in the elaboration of the BEPS package, the number of LAC countries joining the BEPS Project via the Inclusive Framework membership is quite significant. The question is, why did they join the initiative and committed to implement, at least, the minimum standard?

The Inclusive Framework Background Brief may provide some input to start answering this question by stating that developing economies—this is the case in LAC (2.2.1.1.)—could benefit from the BEPS Project:

> the OECD and G20 have ... recognised that *developing countries struggling to fight against tax avoidance* can benefit from the work that has already been done in the OECD/G20 BEPS Project as well as from joining the implementation of the BEPS package, with support from and assistance by international and regional organisations[137] [emphasis added].

But, first of all, are LAC countries "struggling to fight" or, at least, interested in fighting against tax avoidance? In this respect, the reasons argued in favor of fighting against tax avoidance and BEPS (the threat to the integrity of the CIT and the damage to the tax compliance system as a whole, mentioned in 2.1.1.), are valid arguments in the LAC region, where (i) in 2017, CIT revenues represented 15.5% of total tax revenues (against 9.3% in the OECD),[138] (ii) CIT revenues denote a higher relative weight in the total amount of income tax revenues[139] (and many countries actually

136. *See* footnote 7 in OECD, *Participation Plan. Committee on Fiscal Affairs* (accessible at https://www.oecd.org/global-relations/partnershipsinoecdbodies/PP-CFA-PUBLIC-ENG.pdf).
137. OECD, *Background Brief, Inclusive Framework on BEPS*, January 201, p. 7.
138. OECD, *Corporate Tax Statistics, Second Edition*, 2020, p. 4.
139. On average CIT revenues represent 72% of total income tax revenues (28% correspond to personal income tax revenues), while in the OECD, the numbers are inverted and 76% of income tax revenues derive from the personal income tax and 24% from the CIT (Pérez Zúñiga, José María, *Sistemas tributarios en España y América Latina*, Tirant lo Blanch, Valencia, 2016,

cannot rely on individual income taxation), and (ii) the "informal economy" reaches significant levels.[140]

However, and we insist, as mentioned above, the Inclusive Framework was established once the measures had been designed by OECD/G20 economies. Though it was stated that "developing countries and other neither OECD nor G20 economies have been extensively consulted through regional and global fora meetings and their input has been fed into the work,"[141] the action items and measures designed may have not addressed the specific BEPS issues that are experienced by developing countries and, in particular, LAC countries *as source jurisdictions*.

Indeed, Ault and Arnold have highlighted that developing countries require an independent BEPS analysis, based on the following specificity: (i) a primary concern with the reduction in source-based taxation, (ii) corporate tax on inward investment typically accounting for a greater share of total revenue, and (iii) limited administrative capacity. Were these elements considered during the setting of the BEPS agenda and the elaboration of the final reports?

The OECD answer to this question will be an absolute yes.[142] However, scholarship has been extensively written on this issue, denouncing an outcome biased towards the developed world. For instance, Mosquera[143] has identified "output legitimacy deficits," mentioning that relevant concerns of developing countries (particularly, the allocation of taxing rights between source and residence countries or the need to attract

p. 186 (quoting CEPAL, *Panorama Fiscal de América Latina y el Caribe 2015: dilemas y espacios de políticas*, Santiago de Chile, 2015, p. 87).

140. GONZÁLEZ, DARÍO, *La informalidad tributaria en ALC: ¿seguimos pescando dentro de la pecera?*, CIAT Blog, October 20, 2020 (accesible at https://www.ciat.org/ciatblog-la-informalidad-tributaria-en-alc-seguimos-pescando-dentro-de-la-pecera/, March 24, 3031), and GÓMEZ SABAÍNI, J.C. & MORÁN D., *Informalidad y tributación en América Latina: Explorando los nexo para mejorar la equidad*, CEPAL-AECID, Serie Macroeconomía del Desarrollo No. 124, 2012 (accesible at https://repositorio.cepal.org/bitstream/handle/11362/5356/1/S1200741_es.pdf).

141. *See* OECD, *Action 15: 2014 Deliverable—Developing a Multilateral Instrument to Modify Bilateral Tax Treaties ..., supra.*

142. *See* for instance, OECD, *Myth and Facts about BEPS*, https://www.oecd.org/ctp/myths-and-facts-about-beps.pdf, March 30, 2021) and the answer to the eight myth ("Developing countries have been kept out of the BEPS Project"): "[d]eveloping Country participation in the BEPS Project has been extensive. More than a dozen developing countries, representing a cross-section of regions and income levels, participate directly in the CFA meetings on BEPS, offering specific insight into the needs of developing countries. The United Nations, the International Monetary Fund and the World Bank Group, as well as the African Tax Administration Forum (ATAF) and the Inter-American Centre of Tax Administrations (CIAT) also participate. A series of regional meetings have been organised in Africa, Asia, Latin America and the Caucasus, to gather input from more than 40 developing countries that could not participate directly, in addition to Global Forum meetings organised in March and September of each year. Developing countries were asked to actively provide their perspective on the challenges they are facing, which resulted in the two-part report for the G20 Development Working Group. All the challenges identified by developing countries themselves are either being addressed through the BEPS Project directly, or through the parallel development of toolkits on items outside of the BEPS Project."

143. MOSQUERA VALDERRAMA, I.J., Legitimacy and the Making of International Tax Law, World Tax Journal, Vol. 7, Issue 3, 2015.

investment via tax incentives) were not dealt with by the initiative.[144] While highlighting that the original BEPS Project "was led by the OECD and G20 and focused on their priorities," Hearson has stated that "[w]ith a few small exceptions, it neither reallocated taxing rights nor simplified existing rules" which, in his opinion, are the two primary concerns that developing countries face with existing international tax rules. Particularly regarding LAC concerns, the conclusions of a regional meeting on international tax challenges, including the BEPS Project which took place in November 2016 and gathered participants from different LAC Tax Administrations,[145] captured "the need to take up the debate on the balance and distribution of taxing powers (source and residence) under the sphere of double tax treaties"[146] as one of the specific regional interests that have not been discussed or specifically developed in the BEPS Project.

This outcome may not have been deliberate, but the natural outcome of the composition of the "selected group" that first set the BEPS agenda, namely, the Bureau of the OECD CFA, and the larger "selected group" which later elaborated the reports; even references to the "OECD/G20 BEPS Project, Action Plan or Package" speak for themselves.

In 2014, the OECD made public a report entitled "Two-Part Report to G20 Developing Working Group on the Impact of BEPS in Low Income Countries,"[147] which recognized that BEPS risks and challenges to address those risks, may be different—both in nature and scale —for the developing and developed world. In particular, it mentioned that developing countries show lack of necessary legislative measures, information, and capacity to implement highly complex rules to address BEPS. Additionally, it showed which actions of the BEPS Action Plan were of most relevance to those countries, based on the findings derived from the "dialogue and consultations with developing countries, and the experiences of international organizations working with developing countries." In respect to BEPS actions that contain tax treaty-related measures, the report qualified Action 2 on hybrids arrangements as low relevance; Actions 6 and 7, on treaty abuse, as high relevance; Action 14 on dispute resolution as medium relevance; and Action 15—precisely, the development of a multilateral treaty—as low relevance.[148]

The qualification on Action 6 (Prevent treaty abuse) and Action 7 (Prevent the artificial avoidance of PE status) is understandable, as tax treaties based on the OECD

---

144. Hearson, Martin, *Corporate Tax Negotiations at the OECD: What's at Stake for Developing Countries in 2020?*, ICTD Summary Brief 20, 2020.

145. Organized by the International Cooperation Spanish Agency for Development (AECID, as per the Spanish abbreviation), the German Agency for Technical Cooperation (GIZ, as per the German abbreviation) and the Inter-American Center of Tax Administration (CIAT, as per the Spanish abbreviation). *See* https://www.ciat.org/conclusiones-del-reciente-encuentro-regional-sobre-desafios-en-el-ambito-de-la-tributacion-internacional-organizado-por-la-cooperacion-espanola-aecid-la-giz-de-alemania-la-aeat-d/, March 31, 2021.

146. The author's translation.

147. OECD, *Two-part Report to G20 Developing Working Group on the Impact of BEPS in Low Income Countries*, 2014, Paris, OECD Publishing. It must be said that the report uses, in the author´s opinion, incorrectly, "low income countries" and "developing countries" as synonyms.

148. For an insightful analysis of the contents of the report, the author suggests reading Báez Moreno, Andrés, *Los Países en Vías de Desarrollo (BEPS and Developing Countries)*, 2017.

MC (and to a lesser extent, the UN MC) clearly limit the exercise of taxing rights by so-called source jurisdictions. Indeed, as mentioned, the OECD/UN MC promotes taxation of business profits in the State of residence, limiting, in practice, source taxation to those cases where a PE arises. While Action 6 introduces measures to limit the benefits of tax treaties (including no or low source taxation), Action 7 intends to fight the avoidance of the PE status.

On Action 6, the aversion of developing economies to treaty shopping may be relative; some countries may even tolerate it as a means to attract capital and technology in the interest of long-term development.[149] Additionally, the Action 6 minimum standard, though flexible,[150] raises serious concerns globally, especially the PPT rule:[151] unpredictability on its application and interpretation by tax administrations and courts may translate into legal tax uncertainty. Those concerns, which are maximized in the LAC region, may negatively affect the investment environment and, therefore, the attraction of foreign capital. On the rules denying the benefits of a tax treaty, Baker warns:

> [t]reaties relieve from double taxation by reducing taxes or exempting from taxes or granting credits against taxes. If tax avoidance is too readily alleged, and treaty benefits denied, then the advantages of treaties in removing barriers to trade and investment may be nullified ... care has to be taken to distinguish between abusive arrangements and those that are consistent with the purpose for which the tax treaty was concluded.[152]

The measures proposed under Action 7,[153] may be perceived at first sight as granting more taxing rights to source jurisdictions. However, this statement does not seem accurate. Indeed, while in practice, the PE criterion allows in a limited number of cases for source taxation, conceptually speaking, it is not equivalent to the application or recognition of the source principle but rather the application of personal taxation based on the notional "PE" person.[154]

In line with the whole BEPS Project (not intended to modify the international distribution of taxing rights), Action 7 had a limited scope. Measures recommended under this action were targeted at preventing the abusive use of the PE status. The idea underlying the PE status (extending the residence criterion), as explained before, has not changed, and its definition is still based on the same pillars: the existence of physical presence of a stable nature, in time and space, in the host country. In other words, and as stated by Martín Jiménez, the aim of Action 7 was not to assign more

149. *See* Danon, Robert J., *The PPT in Post-BEPS Tax Treaty Law: It is a GAAR but Just a GAAR!* Bulletin for International Taxation, Vol. 74, Issue 4/5, 2020, pp. 245-246, quoting the Indian Supreme Court arguments on the *Azadi Bachao Andolan* case.
150. The flexibility of the minimum standard on Action 6 derives from the clash between Europe that prefers general anti-abuse rules, and the US, the father of LoB rules.
151. Danon, Robert J., The PPT in Post-BEPS Tax Treaty Law ..., *supra.*
152. Baker, Philip, *Improper Use of Tax Treaties ..., supra.*
153. Action 7 on PE abuse proposed changes to the PE definition in Article 5 of the OECD MC, targeting so-called commissioner arrangements, the scope of carve-outs and the splitting up of contracts.
154. Riccardi Sacchi, Andrea Laura, *Una solución global a la imposición sobre la renta societaria ..., supra.*

taxing rights to source States but simply to restore taxing rights that were already recognized by the international standards.[155] Indeed, as stated in the BEPS Action Plan report:

> [i]n the changing international tax environment, a number of countries have expressed a concern about how international standards on which bilateral tax treaties are based allocate taxing rights between source and residence States. This Action Plan is focused on addressing BEPS. While actions to address BEPS will restore both source and residence taxation in a number of cases where cross-border income would otherwise go untaxed or would be taxed at very low rates, these actions are not directly aimed at changing the existing international standards on the allocation of taxing rights on cross-border income.[156]

Additionally, Action 7 was criticized for being "incomplete";[157] profits attribution rules (how much of the profits should be attributed to the PE?) have not been properly addressed turning new provisions inefficient. The lack of updated PE profit attribution rules has prevented (or served as an excuse to) some countries from adopting MLI articles on the Avoidance of PE, i.e., provisions which, though indirectly, allows for source taxation.

To conclude, it seems that LAC's support of the BEPS initiative can barely be explained based mainly on tax reasons.

2.2.2.3 *Signatories and Parties to the MLI: The Most Imminent Challenges*

The MLI was developed to serve to a "swift and effective" implementation of the BEPS package and its underlying tax policies, which, as explained, may have not completely addressed LAC interests and concerns, especially those of small and medium economies.

During the XXX Congress of the ILADT,[158] arguments in favor of and against the MLI were posed. Different arguments in favor were mentioned: the fight against BEPS; staff constraints for treaty negotiations; international pressure and the need to maintain political allegiances; "club membership" necessary to stay in the OECD; and future potentiality of the instrument. On the other hand, the arguments against were: BEPS may not be at the top of the agenda but more relevance may be given to foreign direct

155. Martín Jiménez, Adolfo, "Preventing the Artificial Avoidance of PE Status," in Trepelkov, A. et al. (Ed.): Protecting the Tax Base of Developing Counties, 2° Ed., UN, New York, 2017, p. 375.
156. OECD, *Action Plan on Base Erosion and Profit Shifting ..., supra*, p. 11.
157. *See* Storck, Alfred & Mechtler, Lukas, "Permanent Establishments: Proposals Related to Article 5(3) and (4) of the OECD Model Convention," in Lang, M. et al. (Ed.): *Base Erosion and Profit Shifting (BEPS). The Proposals to Revise the OECD Model Convention*, Series on International Tax Law, Vol. 95, Linde, Wien, 2016, p. 79 y 80; y Storck, Alfred & Petruzzi, Raffaele, "Permanent Establishments: Proposals Related to Agency Permanent Establishments—Article 5(5) and (6) of the OECD Model Convention," in Lang, M. et al. (Ed.): *Base Erosion and Profit Shifting (BEPS). The Proposals to Revise the OECD Model Convention*, Series on International Tax Law, Vol. 95, Linde, Wien, 2016, p. 105.
158. ILADT, Seminario 7: "Aplicación del instrumento multilateral," XXX Jornadas Latinoamericas de Derecho Tributario (accesible at http://www.iladt.org/frontend/xxxjornadas.aspx, March 30, 2021).

investment; complexity; legal certainty; unskilled staff in respect to the application of the instrument and concerns on its application by courts; reinforcement of the OECD and the U.S. international tax policy; and benefits of bilateral negotiation (bargaining power).

Arguments in favor and against the MLI are numerous and depend on the specificities of each jurisdiction. As analyzed, the LAC region is very heterogeneous and its participation in the BEPS project, though significant, has also been different for each country. Furthermore, there has been no common or "regional" approach to the BEPS project.[159] This conclusion also holds in relation to the MLI signature.

The status of LAC countries in relation to the MLI has been summarized in Table 6.3.[160] Of the 9 LAC countries that are not Inclusive Framework Members,[161] none has so far signed the MLI. Of the 24 LAC countries that are Inclusive Framework Members, 11 have so far signed the MLI: Argentina, Barbados, Belize, Chile, Colombia, Costa Rica, Jamaica, Mexico, Panama, Peru, and Uruguay. This means that non-signatories that are members of the Inclusive Framework and therefore, have committed to implement at least the BEPS minimum standards, must do so via bilateral channels.

Table 6.3 LAC Countries' Status in Relation to the MLI

Country	*Inclusive Framework*	*Signature*	*Ratification*	*Deposit*
Antigua y Barbuda	X	–	–	–
Argentina	X	–	–	–
Bahamas	X	X	–	–
Barbados	X	X	X	X
Belize	X	X		
Bolivia	–	–	–	–
Brazil	X	–	–	–
Chile	X	X	X	X
Colombia	X	X	–	–
Costa Rica	X	X	X	X
Cuba	–	–	–	–
Dominica	X	–	–	–

159. The CIAT webpage has built a database on BEPS measures implemented by some of its members at https://www.ciat.org/base-de-datos-monitoreo-beps/, March 30, 2021.
160. Table 6.3— LAC countries' status in relation to the MLI. The information was collected from the tax authorities' webpage (either the Tax Administration or the Ministry of Economic and Finance/Foreign Affairs webpage) and the OECD´s webpage.
161. Any country can sign up for the MLI irrespective of their Membership of the Inclusive Framework on BEPS.

Country	*Inclusive Framework*	*Signature*	*Ratification*	*Deposit*
Dominican Republic	X	–	–	–
Ecuador	–	–	–	–
El Salvador	–	–	–	–
Grenada	X	–	–	–
Guatemala	–	–	–	–
Guyana	–	–	–	–
Haiti	X	–	–	–
Honduras	X	–	–	–
Jamaica	X	X	–	–
Mexico	X	X	–	–
Nicaragua	–	–	–	–
Panama	X	X	X	X
Paraguay	X	–	–	–
Peru	X	X	–	–
Saint Kitts and Nevis	X	–	–	–
Saint Lucia	X	–	–	–
Saint Vincent and the Grenadines	X	–	–	–
Suriname	–	–	–	–
Trinidad and Tobago	X	–	–	–
Uruguay	X	X	X	X
Venezuela	–	–	–	–

Source: Table elaborated by the author in April 2021 based on the data available at the Tax Authorities' and OECD's webpages.

Argentina, Brazil, Chile, Colombia, Costa Rica, Dominican Republic, Haiti, Jamaica, and Uruguay participated as Members in the Ad Hoc Group that developed the MLI.[162] As mentioned, their participation did not oblige them to sign the MLI. Brazil, the Dominican Republic, and Haiti are examples of countries that were Members of the Ad Hoc Group but have not yet signed the MLI. While Haiti has not signed any tax treaty so far, the Dominican Republic and Brazil do have existing tax treaties: 2 and 37, respectively. As Inclusive Framework members, these countries

162. CIAT participated as an Observer. *See supra* n. 34.

have committed to fulfilling the minimum standards. Since they are non-signatories to the MLI, they will have to do so through amendments to their existing bilateral agreements. In the case of the Dominican Republic, the two tax treaties in force signed in 1976 and 2011 with Canada and Spain, respectively, are not fully compliant with BEPS minimum standards. Amending two tax treaties may not justify signing up for the MLI due to the complexity derived from its implementation, application, and interpretation. In the case of Brazil, four treaties—not yet in force—of its 37 tax treaties, have been signed between 2018[163] and 2019[164] and are BEPS compliant, just two of the remaining 33 are BEPS compliant thanks to the signature of amending protocols. Indeed In July 2017, Brazil signed a protocol with Argentina to amend the tax treaty they have subscribed to in 1980, and, more recently, in March 2019, a protocol with Switzerland to update their 1975 tax treaty.

Following the signature of the MLI, each signatory must ratify the MLI in accordance with their domestic procedures and deposit its instrument of ratification with the Depositary (the Secretary-General of the OECD). Of the 11 LAC MLI Signatories, only 5 (Barbados,[165] Chile,[166] Costa Rica,[167] Panama,[168] Uruguay[169]) have already ratified and deposited[170] the instrument of ratification.

None of these jurisdictions—at least, so far as the author is aware—has published consolidated or, as recommended by the OECD,[171] synthesized texts of the tax treaties covered by the MLI. Despite the fact that those texts would be provided for information purposes only, they would certainly help both taxpayers and tax administration staff to understand the effects of the MLI and to apply it alongside bilateral tax treaties. In this respect, the OECD Matching Database[172] has been an invaluable contribution.[173] However, this base is solely in English and quite complex "to read" in comparison to a consolidated or synthesized text.

163. Singapore, Switzerland and United Arab Emirates.
164. Uruguay.
165. The author had no access to the national legislation ratifying the MLI.
166. *Oficio* No. 15.667 of July 9, 2020 (National Congress of Chile). Passed on December 10, 2020. Published on March 12, 2021.
167. Legislative Decree No. 9751 of September 29, 2019.
168. Law No. 170 of October 15, 2020. Official Gazette 29135-A of October 15, 2020.
169. Law No. 19.814 of September 18, 2019.
170. Barbados: December 21, 2020; Chile: November 26, 2020; Costa Rica: September 22, 2020; Panama: November 5, 2020; Uruguay: February 6, 2020.
171. OECD, *Guidance for the development of synthesised texts, Multilateral Convention to Implement Tax Treaty Measures to Prevent BEPS*, OECD, Paris, 2018.
172. The MLI Matching Database makes projections on how the MLI modifies specific tax treaties covered by matching information from MLI Positions. After ratification, Parties can change their MLI Positions by listing more treaties, adopting optional provisions, narrowing or withdrawing reservations.
173. It is appropriate to note that the MLI Matching Database has no legal value. *See* the Disclaimer at http://www.oecd.org/tax/treaties/MLI-database-disclaimer-and-manual.pdf, f.c. March 31, 2021.

Of the five countries that have already ratified the MLI, and based on the reasons explained below, it is worth mentioning the cases of Costa Rica and Panama.[174] Costa Rica, which became an OECD Member in 2021, signed the MLI on July 7, 2017 at the initial signing ceremony, being the first LAC country to deposit the instrument of ratification with the OECD Secretary-General. However, Costa Rica has adopted just four tax treaties, namely with Germany (2016), Mexico (2014) Spain (2014), and United Arab Emirates (2017). At the time of signature, Costa Rica listed the treaties with Germany, Mexico, and Spain. However, at the time of deposit, it withdrew the treaty with Germany, as this country had not listed the treaty in its respective MLI Position. Costa Rica indicated in the responses to the Action 6 Peer Review questionnaires[175] that bilateral negotiations would be used with Germany.[176] In the case of Costa Rica, the efficiency argument may have not been the reason to sign the MLI, but rather, political reasons and the OECD membership aspiration.

While Panama has listed all its tax treaties, it has made every possible reservation. All these treaties have been listed by the counterpart except for the treaty with the Czech Republic (a country that has already deposited its instrument of ratification but may in the future include the tax treaty with Panama within the MLI); Italy, Mexico, and Spain (that have not deposited the instrument yet[177]); Vietnam (an Inclusive Framework Member but not yet a signatory to the MLI). Meanwhile, the OECD MLI Matching Database reports a notification mismatch and requires extra checking for the tax treaty with Israel which additionally illustrates that the Database helps but is not a panacea.[178]

Finally, the commitment to implement the minimum standards also applies in respect to tax treaties subscribed with counterparts that are either non-Inclusive Framework Members or have not signed the MLI. This is how the "Inclusive Framework pressure" may work. Also, the commitment may apply in relation to the Andean tax treaty (Bolivia and Ecuador neither are Inclusive Framework members, nor have either signed the MLI), and for the treaty between Argentina and Bolivia. The Action 6 First and Second Peer Review documents note that "Colombia/Peru indicated in its

174. The Chilean and Uruguayan cases are exhaustively analyzed in IFA, *Reconstructing the Treaty Network*, Cahiers de droit fiscal international, Vol. 105A, Rotterdam, 2020 (Branch Reports by Suffiotti and Riccardi Sacchi, respectively).

175. OECD, *Prevention of Treaty Abuse—Peer Review Report on Treaty Shopping: Inclusive Framework on BEPS: Action 6*, OECD/G20 Base Erosion and Profit Shifting Project, OECD Publishing, Paris, 2019. OECD, *Prevention of Treaty Abuse—Second Peer Review Report on Treaty Shopping: Inclusive Framework on BEPS: Action 6*, OECD/G20 Base Erosion and Profit Shifting Project, OECD Publishing, Paris, 2020. OECD, *Prevention of Tax Treaty Abuse—Third Peer Review Report on Treaty Shopping: Inclusive Framework on BEPS: Action 6*, OECD/G20 Base Erosion and Profit Shifting Project, OECD Publishing, Paris, 2021.

176. Germany, which has already deposited the instrument of ratification, has not listed any of its tax treaties the counterpart of which is a LAC country.

177. Signatories to the MLI can *entirely change* their MLI Position until the deposit of the instrument of ratification.

178. The Database reports the following issue on Article 7 of the MLI (Prevention of Treaty Abuse): "Notification mismatch. Need to check whether both jurisdictions have identified the same provisions. Article 7(4) would not apply. The Simplified Limitation on Benefits Provision would not apply."

response to the Peer Review questionnaire that the Andean Community Agreement has not been listed under the MLI as it is a decision of the Andean Community Commission"; the Action 6 Second Peer Review document added that "Colombia indicated that it encountered difficulties in the renegotiation of the Andean Community Agreement." According to Action 6 Third Peer Review document:

> "Colombia indicated in its response to the Peer Review questionnaire that the Andean Community Agreement has not been listed under the MLI as it is a decision of the Andean Community Commission. However, in order to bring the Andean Community Agreement into compliance with the Action 6 minimum standard, Colombia has entered into negotiations with its treaty partners and reported that good process had been made."
>
> "Peru indicated in its response to the Peer Review questionnaire that the Andean Community Agreement has not been listed under the MLI as it is a decision of the Andean Community Commission and that it will renegotiate the agreement with its treaty partners."

The Caribbean tax treaty must also be BEPS compliant. Guyana is the only signatory to the Caribbean treaty that is neither an Inclusive Framework Member nor an MLI signatory. The Action 6 Second Peer Review document states for each of the Caribbean tax treaty signatories that each: "is encouraged to bring the CARICOM Agreement up to date by commencing talks among all the treaty partners." Furthermore, the document also refers to this matter under the heading "Difficulties in implementing the minimum standards," mentioning, *inter alia*, the "several unusual features not found in the OECD Model Tax Convention or the UN Model Double Taxation Convention," and stating "the impetus of the Inclusive Framework, and the commitment of its jurisdiction members to implement the BEPS minimum standards, now could provide an opportune time to modernise the CARICOM Agreement." Similar comments can be found in Action 6 Third Peer Review document. As mentioned above, all signatories to the Caribbean tax treaty are Inclusive Framework Members and therefore have committed to implement BEPS minimum standards. To what degree this agreement, based on the source principle, is "modernized" is still to be seen; in other words, may this modernization imply adopting the residence and PE concepts, reinforcing OECD tax policies?

3 CONCLUSIONS AND FINAL REMARKS

The adoption of the MLI (even the rapid implementation of BEPS measures) by LAC countries has been, in the author's view, a rushed approach to the whole "BEPS phenomenon," missing, in particular, the opportunity to *revisit their tax treaty policy*.

Returning to Secretary-General Gurría's words, the MLI is indeed "a new turning point in tax treaty history." That is why it is necessary to seriously reflect on its effects, that is, to analyze these effects from a broad perspective. Secondly, the references to "a rapid implementation" and "saving jurisdictions from the burden of bilaterally re-negotiating." may be debatable. The ratification process in LAC is taking some time, and multiple "mismatches" have arisen in MLI Positions. Third, on the apparently "far-reaching reforms agreed under the BEPS Project," these left unattended LAC historical claims in respect to the international distribution of taxing rights. On the contrary, the *status quo* was preserved, and the MLI served this purpose. Fourth, in respect to "more certainty and predictability for businesses" and a "better functioning international tax system," it may be too early to conclude, but the author dares to anticipate a very different scenario, a scenario that the Inclusive Framework may be trying to "fix" with the so-called Pillars One and Two.[179]

On this last point, the BEPS Project and MLI experiences should serve to provide food for thought for the current "international" discussion on addressing the challenges of the digitalized economy. The debate is so centered around what Europe and the United States are doing (between digital services taxes[180] and GILTI-type measures[181]) that it seems to the author that the whole discussion is again missing the existence of other regions, other policy preferences, and other tax systems and standards.[182] However, today, the discussion is taking place under the Inclusive Framework among the 139 members, and therefore there is no excuse. It is up to each one of the members, including the 24 LAC Members, to seriously analyze the alternatives and to ensure that their preferences are, first of all, *shared*, so they can be heard, and why not, implemented ... tomorrow may be too late.

BIBLIOGRAPHY

ALALC, *Criterios de armonización aplicables a tratados tributarios celebrados entre países de la ALALC*, Montevideo, July 1979, pp. 57.

Andrade Rodríguez, Betty, Implementation v. Adaptation: BEPS in Latin America Through the Lens of the ILADT Model, World Tax Journal, Vol. 9, No. 3, 2017.

André Rocha, Sergio and Christians, Allison, Tax Sovereignty in the BEPS Era, Wolters Kluwer, AH Alphen aan den Rijn, 2017, p. 303.

Ase, Elken, *What European OECD Countries Are Doing about Digital Services Taxes*, March 25, 2021, Tax Foundation (accessible at https://taxfoundation.org/digital

179. OECD, *Tax Challenges Arising from Digitalisation—Report on Pillar One Blueprint: Inclusive Framework on BEPS*, OECD/G20 Base Erosion and Profit Shifting Project, OECD Publishing, Paris, 2020; *Tax Challenges Arising from Digitalisation—Report on Pillar Two Blueprint: Inclusive Framework on BEPS*, OECD/G20 Base Erosion and Profit Shifting Project, OECD Publishing, Paris, 2020.
180. Digital services taxes have proliferated worldwide, but mostly in Europe. *See* Ase, Elken, *What European OECD Countries Are Doing about Digital Services Taxes*, March 25, 2021, Tax Foundation (accessible at https://taxfoundation.org/digital-tax-europe-2020/#: ~ :text = About %20half%20of%20all%20European%20OECD%20countries%20have,the%20United%20 States%20has%20responded%20with%20retaliatory%20threats).
181. The US Global Intangible Low-Taxed Income (GILTI) measure introduced a minimum level of US tax on outbound investment returns, inspiring the so-called GloBE proposal under Pillar Two. *See* Riccardi Sacchi,Andrea Laura, *Implementing a (Global?) Minimum Corporate Income Tax ..., supra.*
182. In respect to Pillar 1, *see* Riccardi Sacchi, Andrea Laura, El "eslabón perdido" en el diseño del Pilar 1 del Marco Inclusivo sobre BEPS de la OCDE/G20, May 12, 2021, Taxlatam; accesible at https://taxlatam.com/noticias/el-eslabon-perdido-en-el-diseno-del-pilar-1-del-marco-inclusivo-sobre-beps-de-la-ocde-g20/.

-tax-europe-2020/#: ~ :text = About%20half%20of%20all%20European%20OECD%20countries%20have,the%20United%20States%20has%20responded%20with%20retaliatory%20threats).

BAKER, PHILIP, *Improper Use of Tax Treaties, Tax Avoidance and Tax Evasion*, Papers on Selected Topics in Administration of Tax Treaties for Developing Countries, No. 9-A, May 2013.

BÁEZ MORENO, ANDRÉS, *Los Países en Vías de Desarrollo (BEPS and Developing Countries)*, 2017 (accesible at http://dx.doi.org/10.2139/ssrn.2956284, March 31, 2021).

BINDER, ANNA AND WOHRER, VIKTORIA (Ed.), *Special Features of the UN Model Convention*, Linde, Wien, 2019.

BRAVO, NATHALIE, "The Proposal for a Multilateral Tax Instrument for Updating Tax Treaties," in LANG, MICHAEL et al. (Eds.): Base Erosion and Profit Shifting (BEPS). The Proposals to Revise the OECD Model Convention, Linde, Wien, 2016, pp. 327-351.

BRAVO, NATHALIE, The Multilateral Tax Instrument and Its Relationship with Tax Treaties, World Tax Journal, Vol. 8, No. 3, 2016, pp. 279-304.

BRAVO, NATHALIE, A Multilateral Instrument for Updating the Tax Treaty *Network*, Amsterdam, IBFD, 2020, p. 339.

BRAUNER, YARIV, *Tax Treaty Negotiations: Myth and Reality*, 2020 (accessible at https://papers.ssrn.com/sol3/papers.cfm?abstract_id = 3722607, March 21, 2021).

BROOKS, KIM, "The Potential of Multilateral Tax Treaties," en LANG, MICHAEL et al. (ED.): *Tax Treaties: Building Bridges Between Law and Economics*, IBFD, 2010.

CABRERA, OMAR S., Análisis de las principales reservas en materia tributaria formuladas por Colombia en el acuerdo de adhesión a la OCDE, Revista Instituto Colombiano de Derecho Tributario, N° 81, enero de 2020, pp. 151-200.

CHRISTENSEN, RASMUS COLIN, HEARSON, MARTIN AND RANDRIAMANALINA, TOVONY, *At the Table, Off the Menu? Assessing the Participation of Lower-Income Countries in Global Tax Negotiations*, ICTD Working Paper 115, 2020.

CHRISTIANS, ALLISON, SCHÖN, WOLFGANG AND SHAY, STEPHEN E., Foreword: International Tax Policy in a Disruptive Environment. Bulletin for International Taxation, Vol. 72, Issue 4/5, 2018, pp. 191-195.

CHRISTIANS, ALLISON AND VAN APELDOORN, LAURENS, The OECD Inclusive Framework, Bulletin for International Taxation, Vol. 72, Issue 4/5, 2018, pp. 226-233.

CLAUSING, KIMBERLY A., Does Tax Drive the Headquarters Locations of the World's Biggest Companies?, Transnational Corporations, Vol. 25, No. 2, 2018, pp. 37-65.

CUENCA DEL PLATA, *Modelo de Convenio sobre doble Imposición, recomendado por los Cancilleres de los países integrantes de la Cuenca del Plata*, Revista Tributaria (IUET), Tomo V, No. 27, 1978, pp. 513-534.

DANON, ROBERT J., The PPT in Post-BEPS Tax Treaty Law: It is a GAAR but Just a GAAR! Bulletin for International Taxation, 2020 (Vol. 74), No. 4/5, pp. 242-263.

ESCRIBANO, EVA, "¿Se ha equivocado el Proyecto BEPS en el planteamiento? Los paradigmas de la fiscalidad internacional que no han sido cuestionados," in

Almudí Cid, José M. et al. (Dir.): El plan de acción sobre erosión de bases imponibles y traslado de beneficios (BEPS): G20, OCDE y UE, Aranzadi, Navarra, 2017, pp. 513-534.

Figueroa, Antonio H., "La historia de los convenios de doble imposición internacional," in Mazz, Addy y Pistone, Pasquale (Coord.): Reflexiones en torno a un Modelo Latinoamericano de Convenio de Doble Imposición, 1ª Ed., FCU, Montevideo, 2010, p. 26.

García Antón, Ricardo, *The 21st Century Multilateralism in International Taxation: the Emperor's New Clothes?*, World Tax Journal, Vol. 8, Issue 2, 2016, p. 147-192.

Gómez Sabaíni, J.C. & Morán D., *Informalidad y tributación en América Latina: Explorando los nexos para mejorar la equidad*, CEPAL-AECID, Serie Macroeconomía del Desarrollo No. 124, 2012 (accesible at https://repositorio.cepal.org/bitstream/handle/11362/5356/1/S1200741_es.pdf).

González, Darío, *La informalidad tributaria en ALC: ¿seguimos pescando dentro de la pecera?*, CIAT Blog, 20 October 2020 (accesible at https://www.ciat.org/ciatblog-la-informalidad-tributaria-en-alc-seguimos-pescando-dentro-de-la-pecera/, March 24, 3031).

González de Frutos, Ubaldo, La política fiscal en Perú en la encrucijada del acceso a la OCDE, Revista Análisis Tributario, No. 362, marzo de 2018, pp. 11-17.

G20, *G20 Leaders' Communiqué Antalya Summit*, 15-16 November 2015 (accessible at http://g20.org.tr/g20-leaders-commenced-the-antalya-summit/, March 22, 2021).

Hearson, Martin, *Corporate Tax Negotiations at the OECD: What's at Stake for Developing Countries in 2020?*, ICTD Summary Brief 20, 2020.

IFA, *Assessing BEPS: Origins, Standards, and Responses*, Cahiers de droit fiscal international, Vol. 102A, Rotterdam, 2017, p. 395.

IFA, *Reconstructing the Treaty Network*, Cahiers de droit fiscal international, Vol. 105A, Rotterdam, 2020, p. 385.

ILADT, *Estatutos Resoluciones de las Jornadas*, Montevideo, 1987.

ILADT, *Modelo ILADT de Convenio Multilateral de Doble Imposición para América Latina, Cuaderno Tributario ICDT*, Bogotá, 2012, p. 39.

ILADT, Seminario 7: "Aplicación del instrumento multilateral," XXX Jornadas Latinoamericas de Derecho Tributario (accesible at http://www.iladt.org/frontend/xxxjornadas.aspx, March 30, 2021).

Lang, Michael et al. (Ed.), *Tax Treaties: Building Bridges Between Law and Economics*, IBFD, 2010, p. 658.

Lang, Michael et al. (Ed.), *Trends and Player in Tax Policy*, IBFD, 2016, p. 820.

Kliest, David, A Multilateral Instrument for Implementing Changes to Double Tax Treaties: Problems and Prospects, Intertax, Vol. 44, Issue II, pp. 823-830.

Maldonado, Galo, Tendencias en los convenios para evitar la doble imposición suscritos por países de Latinoamérica, Documentos de Trabajo, CIAT, 2016 (accesible at https://biblioteca.ciat.org/opac/book/5482, f.c. February 31, 2021).

MARTÍN JIMÉNEZ, ADOLFO, "Preventing the Artificial Avoidance of PE Status," in TREPELKOV, A. et al. (Ed.): Protecting the Tax Base of Developing Counties, 2° Ed., UN, New York, 2017, pp. 365-477.

MAZZ, ADDY & PISTONE, PASQUALE (Coord.), *Reflexiones en torno a un Modelo Latinoamericano de Convenio de doble imposición*, 1ª Ed. FCU, Montevideo, 2010, p. 311.

MOSQUERA VALDERRAMA, I.J., Legitimacy and the Making of International Tax Law, World Tax Journal, Vol. 7, No. 3, 2015 (accessible at https://scholarlypublications.universiteitleiden.nl/handle/1887/62377, f.c.29/03/2021).

MOSQUERA VALDERRAMA, IRMA JOHANNA, Output Legitimacy Deficits and the Inclusive Framework of the OECD/G20 Base Erosion and Profit Shifting Initiative, Bulletin for International Taxation, Vol. 22, No. 3, 2018 (accessible at https://scholarlypublications.universiteitleiden.nl/handle/1887/59348, 29/03/2021).

NAVARRO, AITOR, Tax Sparing Clauses as a Policy Instrument of Developing Countries and Their Descent: Evidence from the Latin-American Tax Treaty Network, CBS Law Research Paper Series No. 20-17, 2020 (accessible at https://papers.ssrn.com/sol3/papers.cfm?abstract_id=3669121, 31/03/2021).

OECD, *Addressing Base Erosion and Profit Shifting*, OECD Publishing, Paris, 2013.

OECD, *Action Plan on Base Erosion and Profit Shifting*, OECD Publishing, Paris, 2013.

OECD, *Two-part Report to G20 Developing Working Group on the Impact of BEPS in Low Income Countries*, OECD Publishing, Paris, 2014.

OECD, *Action 15: 2014 Deliverable— - Developing a Multilateral Instrument to Modify Bilateral Tax Treaties, OECD/G20 Base Erosion and Profit Shifting*, OECD Publishing, Paris, 2014.

OECD, *Action 15: A Mandate for the Development of a Multilateral Instrument on Tax Treaty Measures to Tackle BEPS, OECD/G20 Base Erosion and Profit Shifting Project*, 2015 (accessible at http://www.oecd.org/ctp/beps-action-15-mandate-for-development-of-multilateral-instrument.pdf, February 27, 2021).

OECD, *Action 6: 2015 Final Report, Preventing the Granting of Treaty Benefits in Inappropriate Circumstances, OECD/G20 Base Erosion and Profit Shifting Project*, OECD Publishing, Paris, 2015.

OECD, *Action 14: 2015 Final Report, Making Dispute Resolution Mechanisms More Effective, OECD/G20 Base Erosion and Profit Shifting Project*, OECD Publishing, Paris, 2015.

OECD, *Action 15: 2015 Final Report—Developing a Multilateral Instrument to Modify Bilateral Tax Treaties, OECD/G20 Base Erosion and Profit Shifting Project*, 2015, Paris, OECD Publishing.

OECD, *Public Discussion Draft, BEPS Action 15—Development of a Multilateral Instrument to Implement the Tax Treaty related BEPS Measures*, May 31– June 30, 2016.

OECD, *Model Tax Convention on Income and on Capital: Condensed Version 2017*, OECD Publishing, Paris, 2017, p. 654.

OECD, *Background Brief, Inclusive Framework on BEPS*, January 2017 (accessible at http://www.oecd.org/tax/beps/background-brief-inclusive-framework-on-beps.pdf, March 24, 2021).

OECD, *Myth and Facts about BEPS*, https://www.oecd.org/ctp/myths-and-facts-about-beps.pdf, March 30, 2021).

OECD, *MLI Matching Database (beta)* (accessible at http://www.oecd.org/tax/treaties/mli-matching-database.htm, March 21, 2021).

OECD, *MLI Database—Matrix of options and reservations* (accessible at http://www.oecd.org/tax/treaties/mli-database-matrix-options-and-reservations.htm, March 21, 2021).

OECD, *Multilateral Convention to Implement Tax Treaty Related Measures to Prevent Base Erosion and Profit Shifting: Functioning under Public International Law, Note by the OECD Directorate for Legal Affairs* (accessible at http://www.oecd.org/tax/treaties/legal-note-on-the-functioning-of-the-MLI-under-public-international-law.pdf, March 21, 2021).

OECD, *Step-by-step overview on the application of the MLI* (accessible at http://www.oecd.org/tax/treaties/step-by-step-tool-on-the-application-of-the-MLI.pdf, March 21, 2021).

OECD, *Flowchart on the application of MLI provisions* (accessible at http://www.oecd.org/tax/treaties/application-toolkit-multilateral-instrument-for-beps-tax-treaty-measures.htm, March 21, 2021).

OECD, *Multilateral Convention to Implement Tax Treaty Related Measures to Prevent Base Erosion and Profit Shifting: Entry into effect under Article 35(1)(a), Note by the OECD Secretariat* (accessible at http://www.oecd.org/tax/treaties/beps-mli-secretariat-note-entry-into-effect-under-article-35-1-a.pdf, March 21, 2021).

OECD, *Guidance for the development of synthesised texts, Multilateral Convention to Implement Tax Treaty Measures to Prevent BEPS*, OECD, Paris, 2018.

OECD, *Prevention of Treaty Abuse—Peer Review Report on Treaty Shopping: Inclusive Framework on BEPS: Action 6*, OECD/G20 Base Erosion and Profit Shifting Project, OECD Publishing, Paris, 2019.

OECD, *Corporate Tax Statistics, Second Edition*, 2020, p. 51.

OECD, *Prevention of Treaty Abuse—Second Peer Review Report on Treaty Shopping: Inclusive Framework on BEPS: Action 6*, OECD/G20 Base Erosion and Profit Shifting Project, OECD Publishing, Paris, 2020.

OECD, *Multilateral Instrument, Information Brochure*, May 2020 (accessible at http://www.oecd.org/tax/beps/multilateral-instrument-BEPS-tax-treaty-information-brochure.pdf, February 27, 2021).

OECD, *Tax Challenges Arising from Digitalisation—Report on Pillar One Blueprint: Inclusive Framework on BEPS*, OECD/G20 Base Erosion and Profit Shifting Project, OECD Publishing, Paris, 2020.

OECD, *Tax Challenges Arising from Digitalisation—Report on Pillar Two Blueprint: Inclusive Framework on BEPS*, OECD/G20 Base Erosion and Profit Shifting Project, OECD Publishing, Paris, 2020.

OECD, *Prevention of Tax Treaty Abuse—Third Peer Review Report on Treaty Shopping: Inclusive Framework on BEPS: Action 6*, OECD/G20 Base Erosion and Profit Shifting Project, OECD Publishing, Paris, 2021.

OECD, *Members of the OECD/G20 Inclusive Framework on BEPS. Updated: February 2021* (accessible at: http://www.oecd.org/tax/beps/inclusive-framework-on-beps-composition.pdf, March 22, 2021).

OECD, *Signatories and Parties to the Multilateral Convention to Implement Tax Treaty Related Measures to Prevent Base Erosion and Profit. Status as of 18 February 2021* (accessible at: http://www.oecd.org/tax/treaties/beps-mli-signatories-and-parties.pdf, March 22, 2021).

PÉREZ ZÚÑIGA, JOSÉ MARÍA, *Sistemas tributarios en España y América Latina*, Tirant Lo Blanch, Valencia, 2016, p. 254.

RICCARDI SACCHI, ANDREA LAURA, *While in the Quest of the Holy Grail ... Uruguay is Already Taxing Income from Uber and Netflix*, Blog GLOBTAXGOV, Leiden University, March 8, 2019 (accessible at https://globtaxgov.weblog.leidenuniv.nl/2019/03/08/while-in-the-quest-for-the-holy-grail-uruguay-is-already-taxing-income-from-uber-and-netflix/).

RICCARDI SACCHI, ANDREA LAURA, Implementing a (Global?) Minimum Corporate Income Tax: An Assessment of the So-Called Pillar Two from the Perspective of Developing Countries, Nordic Journal on Law and Society, Vol. 4, No. 1, 2021 (accessible at https://journals.ub.umu.se/index.php/njolas/article/view/188).

RICCARDI SACCHI, ANDREA LAURA, *El "eslabón perdido" en el diseño del Pilar 1 del Marco Inclusivo sobre BEPS de la OCDE/G20*, May 12, 2021, Taxlatam; accesible at https://taxlatam.com/noticias/el-eslabon-perdido-en-el-diseno-del-pilar-1-del-marco-inclusivo-sobre-beps-de-la-ocde-g20/.

RICCARDI SACCHI, ANDREA LAURA, *Una solución global a la imposición sobre la renta societaria: La revitalización de la fuente*, Tirant lo Blanch, 2021, Valencia (in press).

SCHUCH, JOSEF & NEUBAUER, NIKOLAUS, "The Saving Clause: Article 1(3) of the OECD Model," in LANG, MICHAEL et al. (Eds.): Base Erosion and Profit Shifting (BEPS). The Proposals to Revise the OECD Model Convention, Linde, Wien, 2016, pp. 27-50.

SCHWARZ, JONATHAN, *Multilateral Tax Treaty: If We Build it, Will They Come?* Kluwer International Tax Blog, 5 September 2015 (accessible at http://kluwertaxblog.com/2015/09/05/multilateral-tax-treaty-if-we-build-it-will-they-come/, February 27, 2021).

SILBERZTEIN, CAROLINE & TRISTRAM, JEAN-BAPTISTE, *OECD: Multilateral Instrument to Implement BEPS*, International Transfer Pricing Journal, Vol. 23, No. 5, 2016, pp. 347-353.

STORCK, ALFRED & MECHTLER, LUKAS, "Permanent Establishments: Proposals Related to Article 5(3) and (4) of the OECD Model Convention," in LANG, M. et al. (Ed.): *Base Erosion and Profit Shifting (BEPS). The Proposals to Revise the OECD Model Convention*, Series on International Tax Law, Vol. 95, Linde, Wien, 2016, pp. 51-81.

STORCK, ALFRED & PETRUZZI, RAFFAELE, "Permanent Establishments: Proposals Related to Agency Permanent Establishments—Article 5(5) and (6) of the OECD Model Convention," in LANG, M. et al. (Ed.): *Base Erosion and Profit Shifting (BEPS). The*

Proposals to Revise the OECD Model Convention, Series on International Tax Law, Vol. 95, Linde, Wien, 2016, pp. 83-106.

UN, *Model Double Taxation Convention between Developed and Developing Countries 2017*, New York, 2018, p. 813.

UN, *Update Message from Co-Coordinators of the Subcommittee on Tax Challenges Related to the Digitalization of the Economy—William Babatunde Fowler and Aart Roelofsen*, 2020 (accessible at https://www.un.org/development/desa/financing/sites/www.un.org.development.desa.financing/files/2020-11/Update%20message%20for%20Digitalization_0.pdf, March 25, 2021).

UN, *Standard country or area codes for statistical use* (M49) (accessible at https://unstats.un.org/unsd/methodology/m49/, February 27, 2021).

UNCTAD, *Development status groups and composition* (accessible at https://unctadstat.unctad.org/EN/Classifications.html, March 15, 2021).

Valdés Costa, Ramón, *Estudios de Derecho Tributario Internacional*, Rosgal, Montevideo, 1978, p. 225.

Valdés Costa, Ramón, *Estudios de Derecho Tributario Latinoamericano*, Rosgal, Montevideo, 1982, p. 315.

Valdés Costa, Ramón, "Las empresas multinacionales ante el Derecho Tributario," Revista Tributaria (IUET), Tomo XXIII, No. 131, 1996, pp. 155-165.

Zvinys, A. Kristina, Tax Treaty Network of European Countries, September 3, 2020, Tax Foundation (accessible at https://taxfoundation.org/tax-treaties-european-tax-treaty-network-2020/).

Zornoza Pérez, Juan, "Acción 15. El instrumento multilateral y el plan de acción BEPS" in Ramos Prieto, Jesús (Coord.): *Erosión de la base imponible y traslado de beneficios: estudios sobre el plan de acción de la OCDE. Comentarios a las Acciones 1, 2, 5, 6, 8, 13 y 15*, Thomson Reuters Aranzadi, Navarra, 2016, pp. 435-471.

CHAPTER 7

A Cross-Jurisdictional Analysis of MLI Implementation to Date

Natalia Pushkareva

Natalia Pushkareva surveys the ninety-five covered tax agreements that had been registered as of March 2021 with an article-by-article comparison of the agreed terms. Focusing its analysis especially on the differences between developed and developing countries, the chapter provides detailed insights and analysis of the trends to date, showing that countries fall into distinct categories with respect to their embrace of the different articles and that these groupings shift from article to article. The chapter demonstrates that the MLI[1] signatories fall into demonstrably "more compliant" and "less compliant" groupings, with distinct policy stances revealed in the process.

1 INTRODUCTION

The Base Erosion and Profit Shifting (BEPS) project, including the MLI, was designed to assist jurisdictions in reaching consensus and coordinating their efforts to address complex issues that required a joint response from the international community.[2] After the rise of harmful tax competition and the race to the bottom that had been trending for years, if not decades, the completion of the MLI seemed to signal that a spirit of multilateralism and mutual responsibility had finally prevailed. Participating jurisdictions declared the enhancement of cooperation on tax matters as one of their main goals, and committed to coordination and finding common solutions. But did they

1. Multilateral Instrument.
2. More information about the project is available on the OECD website: https://www.oecd.org/tax/beps/.

achieve these goals with the MLI? This chapter seeks to answer this question by reflecting on the range of jurisdictional approaches to the MLI to date.

Such a study is needed because even though the MLI considerably simplifies the process of updating tax treaties, it remains complex, with a mix-and-match set of articles and options among which each jurisdiction must choose their preferred positions. Further, BEPS-related issues faced by "developed" and "developing"[3] countries differ, and these differences are reflected in national positions taken with respect to the issues covered by the MLI. Although the MLI was not aimed at solving the unique problems faced by developing countries in taxing international business activities, it definitely had the potential to benefit many of them by addressing the issues from which developing countries suffered disproportionately, such as treaty shopping and avoiding permanent establishment status (Oguttu, 2018). Yet developing countries were — and are — especially vulnerable in the face of uncertainty surrounding developed countries' policy choices. Professor Annet Wanyana Oguttu noted in her article "Should Developing Countries Sign the OECD Multilateral Instrument to Address Treaty-Related Base Erosion and Profit Shifting Measures?" (Oguttu, 2018) that almost all provisions of the MLI Convention have the potential to benefit developing countries. She further observed that "the value of the MLI to developing countries in large part depends on the options that treaty partners such as Switzerland, Netherlands, the UK, the US, and Ireland select" (Oguttu, 2018).

Given the implementation flexibility and the distinct circumstances faced by differently situated jurisdictions, the ultimate achievements of the MLI will not be fully clear until all participating territories have formulated all of their respective positions on the various terms, which is still an ongoing process. However, as of June 2021, 95 jurisdictions had implemented the MLI to some degree. This provides a starting point for comparative analysis. Accordingly, this chapter analyzes the patterns of MLI implementation from the data that were available to that date with respect to the seventeen most substantial articles (Articles 3-19) of the MLI. The first two articles of the MLI convention are "Scope of the Convention" and "Interpretation of Terms" and are not optional. Articles 3-17 form a basis of the Convention, and Articles 18 and 19 were included in the analysis to illustrate signatories' various attitudes towards mandatory binding arbitration. Starting with Article 20, countries made only a few reservations which would also be interesting to analyze, but the word limit prevented the author from doing so in this chapter.

The jurisdictional implementation of each Article is compared by first, analyzing the range of possible positions, and second, sorting each jurisdiction into its corresponding position for that article. Where relevant, the distinct positions of jurisdictions are analyzed, together with some of the motivating factors behind the distinct

3. Even though the World Bank moved away from using a term "developing country" some time ago (*see* https://blogs.worldbank.org/opendata/should-we-continue-use-term-developing-world for details), it is still widely used by development professionals. While the term is indeed incapable of reflecting the differences between lower-income countries and the variety of the challenges they are facing, for the purposes of this chapter, it refers to a group of countries that fare relatively and similarly poorly in social and economic measures.

jurisdictional positions. The chapter concludes that while a full analysis of MLI implementation is not yet possible, the sorting exercise undertaken here allows some observations about which articles appear to be broadly implemented and which less so, as well as the range of implementation by differently situated jurisdictions. These observations may provide important clues about the future of the MLI through the next phase of multilateral tax coordination.

2 COMPARATIVE ANALYSIS

2.1 Article 3: Transparent Entities

Article 3 is the first "substantial" article of the Multilateral Convention, and it is devoted to transparent entities. An entity is considered to be fiscally transparent if its legal structure allows entity's income to "flow through" its corporate identity directly to investors or owners, without being taxed at a corporate level. Some of the most common types of transparent legal entities include general partnerships, limited partnerships, and limited liability partnerships, and, in the United States, S corporations, income trusts, and limited liability companies.

In most jurisdictions, legislation obliges the members or shareholders of entities that are considered to be fiscally transparent to report the shares of income allocated to them in their annual tax returns. However, in some cases, using transparent entities can result in double non-taxation where both relevant jurisdictions fail to treat the income passing through such entities as income of their tax residents. Such income should be considered to be income of a resident of a Contracting Jurisdiction, but only to the extent that the income is treated, for purposes of taxation by that Contracting Jurisdiction, as the income of a resident of that Contracting Jurisdiction.

Article 3 aims to prevent double non-taxation of income that accrues to transparent entities, ensuring that for tax purposes such income is treated as income of a resident of a Contracting Jurisdiction and is taxed accordingly.

Jurisdictions appear to fall in one of three implementation preference groups: those rejecting to implement the article entirely, those agreeing to implement the article without any reservations, and territories accepting the article in principle but choosing not to apply paragraph 2. As evident from the table below, Article 3 is one of the least "popular" articles of the MLI Convention. Out of the 95 jurisdictions studied, 65 chose not to apply provisions of Article 3 at all, thereby leaving a risk of transparent legal entities being used for avoiding taxation. In addition, five jurisdictions including Japan, Ireland, Luxembourg, Malaysia, and the United Kingdom chose not to apply the provisions of paragraph 2 of Article 3, which states that "Provisions of a Covered Tax Agreement that require a Contracting Jurisdiction to exempt from income tax or provide a deduction or credit equal to the income tax paid with respect to income derived by a resident of that Contracting Jurisdiction which may be taxed in the other Contracting Jurisdiction according to the provisions of the Covered Tax Agreement shall not apply to the extent that such provisions allow taxation by that other Contracting Jurisdiction solely because the income is also income derived by a resident of that other Contracting Jurisdiction." Twenty-five territories, however, implemented the article fully and without making any reservations.

The jurisdictions that implemented the article in full include not only some "developed" economies, such as Belgium, Czech Republic, Denmark, Israel, the Netherlands, Norway, Poland, and Spain, but also developing countries supporting combating tax avoidance schemes using transparent legal entities, such as Kenya, Nigeria, Papua New Guinea, South Africa, Uruguay, and others.

Jurisdictions that decided not to apply the article include some jurisdictions topping the 2021 Corporate Tax Haven Index (Tax Justice Network, 2021), such as Hong Kong, Jersey, Singapore, Switzerland, and the UAE, all of which were listed in the Index's top 10 jurisdictions.

A jurisdiction chose not to apply the article entirely				
Albania	Austria	Bahrain	Barbados	Belize
Bosnia & Herzegovina	Bulgaria	Burkina Faso	Cameroon	Canada
China	Colombia	Costa Rica	Cote d'Ivoire	Curacao
Cyprus	Czech Republic	Egypt	Estonia	Finland
France	Gabon	Georgia	Germany	Greece
Guernsey	Hong Kong	Hungary	Iceland	India
Indonesia	Isle of Man	Italy	Jamaica	Jersey
Jordan	Kazakhstan	Korea	Kuwait	Latvia
Liechtenstein	Lithuania	Malta	Mauritius	Monaco
Morocco	North Macedonia	Oman	Pakistan	Panama
Peru	Portugal	Qatar	San Marino	Saudi Arabia
Senegal	Serbia	Seychelles	Singapore	Slovenia
Sweden	Switzerland	Tunisia	UAE	Ukraine
A jurisdiction chose not to apply paragraph 2 of the article				
Japan	Ireland	Luxembourg	Malaysia	UK
The article applies / no reservations / provisions already implemented				
Andorra	Argentina	Armenia	Australia	Belgium
Chile	Croatia	Denmark	Fiji	Israel
Kenya	Mexico	Netherlands	New Zealand	Nigeria
Norway	Papua New Guinea	Poland	Romania	Russia
Slovak Republic	South Africa	Spain	Turkey	Uruguay

2.2 Article 4: Dual Resident Entities

Article 4 of the Multilateral Convention is dedicated to dual resident entities (i.e., legal entities that are formally considered to be residents of two different jurisdictions). This article is intended to help the Contracting Parties prevent situations where such entities are able to enjoy double non-taxation owing to local tax legislation such as in the case of rules designed prior to the era of intensive globalization and digitalization of business that facilitated BEPS. Claiming tax benefits in both jurisdictions is one example of a situation that might lead to double not-taxation.

As shown in the table below, many jurisdictions traditionally seen as enablers of tax avoidance, including "developed" ones (including Belgium, France, Hong Kong, Jersey, Luxembourg, Switzerland, UAE, etc.) chose not to apply the provisions of Article 4 on Dual Resident Entities to their Double Tax Treaties, while more cooperative jurisdictions include Argentina, India, Kenya, Senegal, and South Africa among others, together with some developed economies supporting transparency and cooperation such as Canada, Denmark, and Israel.

In total, 58 jurisdictions chose not to apply Article 4 in its entirety, 24 countries accepted it without reservations, and 13 territories chose to implement the article with reservations of some kind.

Australia, Costa Rica, Fiji, Indonesia, Japan, and Papua New Guinea chose to replace the last sentence of Article 4(1) with the following text for the purposes of their Covered Tax Agreements: "In the absence of such agreement, such person shall not be entitled to any relief or exemption from tax provided by the Covered Tax Agreement."

Indonesia and Mexico reserved the right for the entirety of Article 4 not to apply to their Covered Tax Agreements that already address cases where a person other than an individual is a resident of more than one Contracting Jurisdiction by denying treaty benefits without requiring the competent authorities of the Contracting Jurisdictions to endeavor to reach mutual agreement on a single Contracting Jurisdiction of residence.

Ireland, Mexico, Norway, Oman, Peru, Romania, and Russia reserved the right for the entirety of Article 4 not to apply to their Covered Tax Agreements that already address cases where a person other than an individual is a resident of more than one Contracting Jurisdiction by requiring the competent authorities of the Contracting Jurisdictions to endeavor to reach mutual agreement on a single Contracting Jurisdiction of residence, and that set out the treatment of that person under the Covered Tax Agreement where such an agreement cannot be reached.

A jurisdiction chose not to apply the article entirely				
Albania	Andorra	Austria	Bahrain	Barbados
Belgium	Belize	Bosnia and Herzegovina	Bulgaria	Burkina Faso
Cameroon	Chile	Cote d'Ivoire	Croatia	Curacao
Cyprus	Czech Republic	Estonia	Finland	France

Gabon	Georgia	Germany	Greece	Guernsey
Hong Kong	Hungary	Iceland	Isle of Man	Italy
Jersey	Jordan	Korea	Kuwait	Latvia
Liechtenstein	Lithuania	Luxembourg	Malaysia	Malta
Mauritius	Monaco	Morocco	North Macedonia	Panama
Portugal	Qatar	San Marino	Saudi Arabia	Seychelles
Singapore	Spain	Sweden	Switzerland	Tunisia
Turkey	UAE			
Australia*	Costa Rica*	Fiji*	Japan*	Papua New Guinea*
Indonesia *,**	Mexico**,***	Norway***	Oman***	Peru*,***
Romania***	Russia***	Ireland ***,****		
The article applies / no reservations / provisions already implemented				
Argentina	Armenia	Canada	China	Colombia
Denmark	Egypt	India	Israel	Jamaica
Kazakhstan	Kenya	Netherlands	New Zealand	Nigeria
Pakistan	Poland	Senegal	Serbia	Slovak Republic
Slovenia	South Africa	UK	Uruguay	

* a jurisdiction chose to replace the last sentence of Article 4(1) with the following text for the purposes of its Covered Tax Agreements: "In the absence of such agreement, such person shall not be entitled to any relief or exemption from tax provided by the Covered Tax Agreement"

** pursuant to Article 4(3)(c) of the Convention, a jurisdiction reserves the right for the entirety of Article 4 not to apply to its Covered Tax Agreements that already address cases where a person other than an individual is a resident of more than one Contracting Jurisdiction by denying treaty benefits without requiring the competent authorities of the Contracting Jurisdictions to endeavour to reach mutual agreement on a single Contracting Jurisdiction of residence

*** pursuant to Article 4(3)(d) of the Convention, a jurisdiction reserves the right for the entirety of Article 4 not to apply to its Covered Tax Agreements that already address cases where a person other than an individual is a resident of more than one Contracting Jurisdiction by requiring the competent authorities of the Contracting Jurisdictions to endeavour to reach mutual agreement on a single Contracting Jurisdiction of residence, and that set out the treatment of that person under the Covered Tax Agreement where such an agreement cannot be reached

**** pursuant to Article 4(3)(f) of the Convention, a jurisdiction reserves the right for the entirety of Article 4 not to apply to its Covered Tax Agreements with Parties that have made the reservation described in Article 4(3)(e)

2.3 Article 5: Application of Methods for Elimination of Double Taxation

Article 5 of the Multilateral Convention aims to stop double non-taxation, where the tax legislation of two contracting jurisdictions interacts in a way that allows a taxpayer to avoid paying "fair" amounts of taxes on income or capital in both jurisdictions. The article provides the Contracting States with a choice between three options (A, B, and C), with different wording of amendments to jurisdiction's DTCs[4] to ensure that income or capital are taxed effectively in at least one jurisdiction. The mechanisms of each option are as follows.

Option A denies tax exemptions for income derived or capital owned by a jurisdiction's resident from tax in that jurisdiction if another Contracting Jurisdiction has already exempted such income or capital from taxation, or limited a tax rate applicable to the income or capital in question.

According to Option B, income in form of dividends should not be exempt by one Contracting Jurisdiction where such income gives rise to a deduction for the purpose of determining the taxable profits of a resident of the other Contracting Jurisdiction under the laws of that other Contracting Jurisdiction.

Finally, Option C states that if a resident of one jurisdiction derives income or owns capital which may be taxable in another jurisdiction in accordance with the provisions of a Covered Tax Agreement, the former jurisdiction shall allow a tax deduction of the amount equal to the income or capital tax paid in another jurisdiction. Such a deduction shall not, however, exceed that part of the income tax or capital tax, as computed before the deduction is given, which is attributable to the income or the capital which may be taxed in that other Contracting Jurisdiction.

Jurisdictions that did not choose to apply Option C themselves could reserve the right not to permit the use of Option C by other Contracting Jurisdictions, and any jurisdiction signing MLI could also decide not to choose any of the options offered.

Thirty-nine territories chose not to apply the article entirely, while 32 implemented it without any reservations or indication of the options chosen. Canada and Greece decided not to apply the article to majority of their Covered Tax Agreements. However, Canada agreed to implement provisions of Article 5 for agreements with Gabon, Cote d'Ivoire, Morocco, and Poland, and Greece accepted the article for Double Tax Treaties with Poland and the Slovak Republic. Estonia, Liechtenstein, Luxembourg, Switzerland, Austria, Cote d'Ivoire, Curacao, and the Netherlands chose to implement Option A, first four countries also forbidding other Contracting Jurisdictions from applying Option C. Option C was chosen by Argentina, Cameroon, Denmark, Gabon, India, Norway, Pakistan, Poland, Portugal, Romania, Senegal, Slovak Republic, Spain, and Uruguay. No jurisdiction chose to apply Option B so far.

Like with other Convention articles, many enabling tax avoidance jurisdictions chose not to apply provisions of Article 5. Interestingly, Estonia, Liechtenstein, Luxembourg, and Switzerland, all being European countries notorious for tax avoidance scandals, were the only four jurisdictions that chose the "no option C by other

4. Double Tax Conventions.

jurisdictions" option. Implementation strategies for Article 5 of the MLI Convention are summarized in the table below.

A jurisdiction chose not to apply the article entirely				
Albania	Bahrain	Bosnia & Herzegovina	Bulgaria	Costa Rica
Croatia	Cyprus	Czech Republic	France	Guernsey
Hong Kong	Hungary	Iceland	Indonesia	Isle of Man
Jamaica	Jersey	Kazakhstan	Kenya	Korea
Latvia	Malaysia	Malta	Mauritius	Morocco
North Macedonia	Oman	Panama	Qatar	Russia
Saudi Arabia	Saudi Arabia	Serbia	Seychelles	Singapore
South Africa	Sweden	Turkey	Ukraine	
A jurisdiction chose not to apply the article to majority of its DTCs				
Canada	Greece			
A jurisdiction chose to apply Option A and not to allow other Contracting Jurisdictions to apply Option C				
Estonia (Option A)	Liechtenstein (Option A)	Luxembourg (Option A)	Switzerland (Option A)	
A jurisdiction chose to apply Option A				
Austria (Option A)	Cote d'Ivoire (Option A)	Curacao (Option A)	Netherlands (Option A)	
A jurisdiction chose to apply Option C				
Argentina (Option C)	Cameroon (Option C)	Denmark (Option C) (w/ notes)	Gabon (Option C)	India (Option C)
Norway (Option C)	Pakistan (Option C)	Poland (Option C)	Portugal (Option C)	Romania (Option C)
Senegal (Option C)	Slovak Republic (Option C)	Spain (Option C)	Uruguay (Option C)	
The article applies / no reservations / provisions already implemented				
Andorra	Armenia	Australia	Barbados	Belgium
Belize	Burkina Faso	Chile	China	Colombia
Egypt	Fiji	Finland	Georgia	Germany
Ireland	Israel	Italy	Japan	Jordan

Kuwait	Lithuania	Mexico	Monaco	New Zealand
Nigeria	Papua New Guinea	Peru	Slovenia	Tunisia
UAE	UK			

2.4 Article 6: Purpose of a Covered Tax Agreement

Article 6 of the Multilateral Convention seeks to modify the DTCs of Contracting Parties by including a preamble text highlighting that the treaties to be modified serve not only a purpose of eliminating double taxation but also equally seek to eliminate loopholes allowing for double non-taxation (paragraph 6.1 of the article).

Paragraph 6(3) provides countries with an opportunity to also revise their DTC preambles with a clause proclaiming their desire to enhance cooperation in tax matters.

According to paragraph 6(4), "A Party may reserve the right for paragraph 1 not to apply to its Covered Tax Agreements that already contain preamble language describing the intent of the Contracting Jurisdictions to eliminate double taxation without creating opportunities for non-taxation or reduced taxation, whether that language is limited to cases of tax evasion or avoidance (including through treaty-shopping arrangements aimed at obtaining reliefs provided in the Covered Tax Agreement for the indirect benefit of residents of third jurisdictions) or applies more broadly." Implementation of the article is summarized below.

Signatories fall into three major categories when implementing Article 6. Thirty-one jurisdictions made no reservations and applied the article fully, while 61 signatories added paragraph 6(3) highlighting the importance of cooperative spirit. Eleven jurisdictions, namely Argentina, Bulgaria, Chile, Colombia, Germany, Hong Kong, Japan, Luxembourg, Mexico, Senegal, and Spain, reserved the right for Article 6(1) not to apply to their Covered Tax Agreements that already contain preamble language describing the intent of the Contracting Jurisdictions to eliminate double taxation without creating opportunities for non-taxation or reduced taxation.

The article applies / no reservations / provisions already implemented				
Albania	Armenia	Austria	Bosnia & Herzegovina	Burkina Faso
Canada	Cote d'Ivoire	Czech Republic	Denmark	Estonia
Finland	Gabon	Guernsey	Iceland	India
Indonesia	Isle of Man	Israel	Italy	Jersey
Kazakhstan	Korea	Latvia	Lithuania	Malaysia
Morocco	New Zealand	Oman	Poland	Portugal
Sweden				

A jurisdiction chose to apply paragraph 6.3 of the article				
Andorra	Argentina (6.1 NA if provisions are already in the DTC)	Australia	Bahrain	Barbados
Belgium	Belize	Cameroon	Chile (6.1 NA if already in the DTC)	China
Costa Rica	Croatia	Curacao	Cyprus	Egypt
Fiji	France	Georgia	Greece	Hong Kong (6.1 NA if already in the DTC)
Hungary	Ireland	Jamaica	Japan	(6.1 NA if already in the DTC)
Jordan	Kenya	Kuwait	Liechtenstein	Luxembourg (6.1 NA if provisions are already in the DTC)
Malta	Mauritius	Mexico (6.1 NA if already in the DTC)	Monaco	Netherlands
Nigeria	North Macedonia	Norway	Pakistan	Panama
Papua New Guinea	Peru	Qatar	Romania	Russia
San Marino	Saudi Arabia	Senegal (6.1 NA if already in the DTC)	Serbia	Seychelles
Singapore	Slovak Republic	Slovenia	South Africa	Spain (6.1 NA if already in the DTC)
Switzerland	Tunisia	Turkey	UAE	UK
Ukraine	Uruguay			
A jurisdiction reserves the right for Article 6(1) not to apply to its Covered Tax Agreements that already contain preamble language describing the intent of the Contracting Jurisdictions to eliminate double taxation without creating opportunities for non-taxation or reduced taxation				
Bulgaria	Colombia	Germany		

2.5 Article 7: Prevention of Treaty Abuse

Article 7 of the MLI is dedicated to a fundamental issue, namely treaty abuse prevention. This article provides jurisdictions with multiple options for amending their DTCs to address this problem. As a general rule, paragraph 1 of the article denies tax benefits for income as well as capital in cases where it is reasonable to conclude that obtaining that benefit was one of the main goals of the transaction.

Where a tax benefit is denied under Article 7(1), "the competent authority of the Contracting Jurisdiction that would otherwise have granted this benefit shall nevertheless treat that person as being entitled to this benefit, or to different benefits with respect to a specific item of income or capital, if such competent authority, upon request from that person and after consideration of the relevant facts and circumstances, determines that such benefits would have been granted to that person in the absence of the transaction or arrangement." (Article 7(4)).

The article provides the Contracting Jurisdictions with multiple options that they can implement, including a Simplified Limitation of Benefits Provision (SLB) that limits the provision of most benefits to "qualified persons." According to the MLI convention:

> "A resident of a Contracting Jurisdiction to a Covered Tax Agreement shall be a qualified person at a time when a benefit would otherwise be accorded by the Covered Tax Agreement if, at that time, the resident is:
>
> a) an individual;
> b) that Contracting Jurisdiction, or a political subdivision or local authority thereof, or an agency or instrumentality of any such Contracting Jurisdiction, political subdivision or local authority;
> c) a company or other entity, if the principal class of its shares is regularly traded on one or more recognised stock exchanges;
> d) a person, other than an individual, that:
>   i) is a non-profit organisation of a type that is agreed to by the Contracting Jurisdictions through an exchange of diplomatic notes; or
>   ii) is an entity or arrangement established in that Contracting Jurisdiction that is treated as a separate person under the taxation laws of that Contracting Jurisdiction and:
>   A) that is established and operated exclusively or almost exclusively to administer or provide retirement benefits and ancillary or incidental benefits to individuals and that is regulated as such by that Contracting Jurisdiction or one of its political subdivisions or local authorities; or
>   B) that is established and operated exclusively or almost exclusively to invest funds for the benefit of entities or arrangements referred to in subdivision A);
> e) a person other than an individual, if, on at least half the days of a twelve-month period that includes the time when the benefit would otherwise be accorded, persons who are residents of that Contracting Jurisdiction and that are entitled to benefits of the Covered Tax Agreement under subparagraphs a) to d) own, directly or indirectly, at least 50 per cent of the shares of the person".

This option has been especially popular with developing countries; among jurisdictions that chose to apply it are Argentina, Armenia, Bulgaria, Chile, Colombia, India, Jamaica, Kazakhstan, Kenya, Kuwait, and Senegal.

Due to the numerous choices that the Contracting Jurisdictions have to implement Article 7, their implementation strategies for this article are difficult to systemize. However, an attempt is made below. Thirty-seven jurisdictions implemented the article without reservations/option selection, while 29 territories chose to apply paragraph 7(4) cited above. Denmark, Jamaica, Iceland, and Norway chose to apply paragraph 7(7)(a) which allows application of the Simplified Limitation on Benefits Provision with respect to the granting of benefits under the Covered Tax Agreement by all Contracting Jurisdictions if all of the Contracting Jurisdictions that do not choose pursuant to paragraph 6 to apply the Simplified Limitation on Benefits Provision agree to such application by choosing to apply this subparagraph and notifying the Depositary accordingly. Cote d'Ivoire together with Greece preferred paragraph 7(7)(b), allowing application of the Simplified Limitation on Benefits Provision only by the Contracting Jurisdictions that choose to apply the Simplified Limitation on Benefits Provision, if all of the Contracting Jurisdictions that do not choose pursuant to paragraph 6 to apply the Simplified Limitation on Benefits Provision agree to such application by choosing to apply this subparagraph and notifying the Depositary accordingly.

As implementation choices of various jurisdictions for Article 7 of the MLI Convention differed significantly, the table below presents a simplification thereof.

A jurisdiction chose to apply paragraph 7(4)				
Andorra	Australia	Bahrain	Belgium	Cote d'Ivoire (7(4), 7(7)(b))
Curacao	Cyprus	Czech Republic	Fiji	Gabon
Guernsey	Hungary	Ireland	Isle of Man	Jersey
Liechtenstein	Lithuania	Luxembourg	Malta	Mauritius (Intends to limit SLB)
Netherlands	New Zealand	Papua New Guinea	Seychelles	Singapore
UAE	UK	Ukraine	Uruguay	
A jurisdiction chose to apply paragraph 7(7)(a)				
Denmark	Jamaica (SLB, 7(7)(a))	Iceland	Norway intends to limit SLB	
A jurisdiction chose to apply paragraph 7(7)(b)				
Greece				

Argentina (7(1) NA, SLB NA if already there)	Armenia (SLB)	Bulgaria 17(5)c,SLB NA	Canada intends to limit SLB	Chile 7(1) NA, SLB NA if already there, temporary measure
Colombia (SLB, 7(6)) intends to limit SLB	Germany 7(1) NA if already there	Hong Kong 7(1) NA if already there	India (SLB,7(6)) intends to limit SLB	Italy 17(5)c, SLB NA
Kazakhstan (SLB,7(6))	Kenya (SLB)	Kuwait intends to limit SLB	Mexico 17(5)c, SLB but sometimes NA	Pakistan SLB, 7(6)
Russia 17(5)c, SLB but sometimes NA	San Marino 7(15)b but sometimes NA	Senegal SLB but NA sometimes	Seychelles 7(17)(a) intends to limit SLB	Slovak Republic 7(17)c, SLB
Spain 7(15)b	Sweden 7(17)a: some DTCs not subject to res	Turkey 7(17)a: some DTCs not subject to res	Uruguay SLB, 7(4)	
The article applies / no reservations / provisions already implemented				
Albania	Austria	Barbados	Belize	Bosnia & Herzegovina
Burkina Faso	Cameroon	China	Costa Rica	Croatia
Egypt	Estonia	Finland	France	Georgia
Indonesia	Israel	Japan	Jordan	Korea
Latvia	Malaysia	Monaco	Morocco	Nigeria
North Macedonia	Oman	Panama	Qatar	Romania
Saudi Arabia	Serbia	Slovenia	Portugal	South Africa
Switzerland	Tunisia			

2.6 Article 8: Dividend Transfer Transactions

Article 8 of the Convention aims to amend Contracting Parties DTCs' provisions on taxing dividend transfer transactions. According to the article, "Provisions of a Covered Tax Agreement that exempt dividends paid by a company which is a resident of a Contracting Jurisdiction from tax or that limit the rate at which such dividends may be taxed, provided that the beneficial owner or the recipient is a company which is a resident of the other Contracting Jurisdiction and which owns, holds or controls more than a certain amount of the capital, shares, stock, voting power, voting rights or similar ownership interests of the company paying the dividends, shall apply only if the ownership conditions described in those provisions are met throughout a 365 day period that includes the day of the payment of the dividends."

As with quite a few other articles of the MLI Convention, an absolute majority of jurisdictions—51 out of 95 to be precise—refused to apply provisions of Article 8. Many countries associated with tax avoidance fall into this category. Thirty-four territories implemented the article's provisions fully, and another 10 jurisdictions made some reservations to the article. Armenia, Germany, Norway, Poland, Portugal, and Russia chose not to apply the article entirely to their Covered Tax Agreements to the extent that the provisions described in Article 8(1) already include a minimum holding period. Kenya reserved the right for the entirety of Article 8 not to apply to its Covered Tax Agreements to the extent that the provisions described in Article 8(1) already include a minimum holding period shorter than a 365 day period, while India, Israel, and the Slovak Republic chose not to apply Article 8 to the extent that the provisions described in Article 8(1) already include a minimum holding period longer than a 365-day period.

Implementation strategies of different territories for Article 8 are illustrated in the table below.

A jurisdiction chose to not apply the article entirely				
Andorra	Austria	Bahrain	Barbados	Belize
Bosnia & Herzegovina	Bulgaria	Chile	Croatia	Curacao
Cyprus	Czech Republic	Estonia	Finland	Gabon
Georgia	Greece	Guernsey	Hong Kong	Hungary
Iceland	Isle of Man	Italy	Japan	Jersey
Korea	Kuwait	Latvia	Liechtenstein	Lithuania
Luxembourg	Malaysia	Malta	Mauritius	Monaco
Morocco	Nigeria	Oman	Panama	Papua New Guinea
Qatar	San Marino	Saudi Arabia	Seychelles	Singapore
Sweden	Switzerland	Turkey	UAE	UK
Ukraine				
(i) a jurisdiction chose not to apply the article entirely to its Covered Tax Agreements to the extent that the provisions described in Article 8(1) already include a minimum holding period				
(i) Armenia	(i) Germany	(i) Norway	(i) Poland	(i) Portugal
(i) Russia				
(ii) a jurisdiction reserves the right for the entirety of Article 8 not to apply to its Covered Tax Agreements to the extent that the provisions described in Article 8(1) already include a minimum holding period shorter than a 365 day period				

(ii) Kenya				
(iii) a jurisdiction reserves the right for the entirety of Article 8 not to apply to its Covered Tax Agreements to the extent that the provisions described in Article 8(1) already include a minimum holding period longer than a 365 day period				
(iii) India	(iii) Israel	(iii) Slovak republic		
The article applies / no reservations / provisions already implemented				
Albania	Argentina	Australia	Belgium	Burkina Faso
Cameroon	Canada	China	Colombia	Costa Rica
Cote d'Ivoire	Denmark	Egypt	Fiji	France
Indonesia	Ireland	Jamaica	Jordan	Kazakhstan
Mexico	Netherlands	New Zealand	North Macedonia	Pakistan
Peru	Romania	Senegal	Serbia	Slovenia
South Africa	Spain	Tunisia	Uruguay	

2.7 Article 9: Capital Gains from Alienation of Shares or Interests of Entities Deriving Their Value Principally from Immovable Property

Article 9 of the Multilateral Convention is dedicated to taxation of capital gains from alienation of shares or interests of entities deriving their value principally from immovable property and aims to prevent related manipulations. In particular, the article provides that such capital gains may be taxable in another Contracting Jurisdiction if the relevant value threshold is met within 365 days preceding the alienation, and highlights that the rules of the article apply to shares or comparable interests, such as interests in a partnership or trust (to the extent that such shares or interests are not already covered) in addition to any shares or rights already covered by the provisions.

According to paragraph 4 of Article 9, "... gains derived by a resident of a Contracting Jurisdiction from the alienation of shares or comparable interests, such as interests in a partnership or trust, may be taxed in the other Contracting Jurisdiction if, at any time during the 365 days preceding the alienation, these shares or comparable interests derived more than 50 per cent of their value directly or indirectly from immovable property (real property) situated in that other Contracting Jurisdiction."

As the table below demonstrates, signatories had different approaches to implementation of Article 9 of MLI. Mauritius and Switzerland are the only two jurisdictions that chose not to apply the entirety of Article 9. Six territories, namely Albania, Andorra, Fiji, Gabon, Mexico, and the Netherlands, implemented the article in full without reservations. Forty jurisdictions chose to apply paragraph 9(4) about taxing gains from alienation of shares deriving at least half of their value from immovable property. In addition, three countries—Ireland, Russia, and Slovenia—reserved the right for Article 9(1)(b) not to apply to their Covered Tax Agreements that include a provision of the type described in Article 9(1) that applies to alienation of interests other than shares. Fifty territories chose not to apply paragraph 1 of the article, and Australia decided not to apply paragraph 9(1)(b) as well.

A jurisdiction chose to not apply the article entirely				
Mauritius	Switzerland			
A jurisdiction chose not to apply paragraph 9(1)				
Australia 9(1)(b) NA	Austria	Bahrain 9(1) NA	Barbados 9(1) NA	Belgium 9(1) NA
Belize 9(1) NA	Bulgaria 9(1) NA	Chile 9(1)(a) NA	China 9(1)(a) NA	Curacao 9(1) NA
Cyprus 9(1) NA	Czech Republic	Finland 9(1) NA	Georgia 9(1) NA	Greece
Guernsey 9(1) NA	Hong Kong 9(1) NA	Hungary 9(1) NA		
Iceland 9(1) NA	Isle of Man 9(1) NA	Israel 9(1) NA + 9(4)	Italy 9(1) NA + 9(4)	Jamaica 9(1) NA
Jersey 9(1) NA	Jordan 9(1) NA	Korea 9(1) NA	Kuwait 9(1) NA	
Latvia 9(1) NA	Liechtenstein 9(1) NA	Lithuania 9(1) NA	Luxembourg 9(1) NA	Malaysia 9(1) NA
Malta 9(1) NA + 9(4)	Monaco 9(1) NA	Morocco 9(1) NA	Norway 9(1) NA	Oman 9(1) NA
Panama 9(1) NA	Papua New Guinea 9(1) NA	Qatar 9(1) NA	Romania 9(1) NA	San Marino
Saudi Arabia 9(1) NA	Seychelles 9(1) NA	Singapore 9(1) NA	South Africa 9(1) NA	Sweden 9(1) NA
Turkey 9(1) NA + 9(4)	UAE 9(1) NA	UK 9(1) NA		
A jurisdiction chose to apply paragraph 9(4)				
Argentina 9(4)	Armenia 9(4)	Bosnia & Herzegovina 9(4)	Burkina Faso 9(4)	Cameroon 9(4)
Canada 9(4)	Colombia 9(4)	Costa Rica 9(4)	Cote d'Ivoire 9(4)	Croatia 9(4)
Denmark 9(4)	Egypt 9(4)	Estonia 9(4)	France 9(4)	Germany 9(4)
India 9(4)	Indonesia 9(4)	Japan 9(4)	Kazakhstan 9(4)	Kenya 9(4)

New Zealand 9(4)	Nigeria 9(4)	North Macedonia 9(4)	Pakistan 9(4)	Peru 9(4)
Poland 9(4)	Portugal 9(4)	Senegal 9(4)	Serbia 9(4)	Slovak Republic 9(4)
Spain 9(4)	Tunisia 9(4)	Ukraine 9(4)	Uruguay 9(4)	Ireland *, 9(4)
Russia *, 9(4)	Slovenia *, 9(4)			
The article applies / no reservations / provisions already implemented				
Albania	Andorra	Fiji	Gabon	Mexico
Netherlands				

* A jurisdiction reserves the right for Article 9(1)(b) not to apply to its Covered Tax Agreements that include a provision of the type described in Article 9(1) that applies to the alienation of interests other than shares.

2.8 Article 10: Anti-abuse Rule for Permanent Establishments Situated in Third Jurisdictions

According to Article 10, which aims to introduce an anti-abuse rule for permanent establishments located in third jurisdictions, in cases where:

a) an enterprise of a Contracting Jurisdiction to a Covered Tax Agreement derives income from the other Contracting Jurisdiction and the first-mentioned Contracting Jurisdiction treats such income as attributable to a permanent establishment of the enterprise situated in a third jurisdiction; and
b) the profits attributable to that permanent establishment are exempt from tax in the first-mentioned Contracting Jurisdiction,
tax benefits provided by the Covered Tax Agreement should be denied for any income tax on which in a third jurisdiction would be under 60% of the tax to be imposed in the first-mentioned Contracting Jurisdiction on that item of income if that permanent establishment were situated in the first-mentioned Contracting Jurisdiction.

According to Convention, such provisions shall apply "in place of or in the absence of provisions of a Covered Tax Agreement that deny or limit benefits that would otherwise be granted to an enterprise of a Contracting Jurisdiction which derives income from the other Contracting Jurisdiction that is attributable to a permanent establishment of the enterprise situated in a third jurisdiction."

Out of 95 jurisdictions, information on whose MLI positions was available[5] at the time of writing this chapter, a majority of 66 territories, including majority of enablers of tax avoidance, decided not to apply provisions of MLI Convention Article 10. Thus,

5. Information on signatories' implementation positions is available at the OECD website: https://www.oecd.org/tax/treaties/beps-mli-signatories-and-parties.pdf.

66 out of 95 territories refused to implement an anti-abuse rule for permanent establishments situated in third jurisdictions in their Covered Agreements, while only 29 jurisdictions agreed to do so.

A jurisdiction chose to not apply the article entirely				
Australia	Bahrain	Barbados	Belgium	Belize
Bosnia & Herzegovina	Bulgaria	Burkina Faso	Cameroon	Canada
China	Colombia	Costa Rica	Cote d'Ivoire	Croatia
Curacao	Cyprus	Czech Republic	Egypt	Estonia
France	France	Gabon	Georgia	Greece
Guernsey	Hong Kong	Hungary	Iceland	Indonesia
Isle of Man	Isle of Man	Italy	Jersey	Jordan
Korea	Kuwait	Latvia	Liechtenstein	Lithuania
Luxembourg	Malaysia	Malta	Mauritius	Monaco
Morocco	North Macedonia	Norway	Oman	Panama
Papua New Guinea	Poland	Portugal	Qatar	San Marino
Saudi Arabia	Serbia	Seychelles	Singapore	South Africa
Sweden	Switzerland	Tunisia	Turkey	UAE
UK				
The article applies / no reservations / provisions already implemented				
Albania	Argentina	Argentina	Armenia	Austria
Chile	Denmark	Fiji	Germany	India
Israel	Jamaica	Japan	Kazakhstan	Kenya
Mexico	Netherlands	New Zealand	Nigeria	Pakistan
Peru	Romania	Russia	Senegal	Slovak Republic
Slovenia	Spain	Ukraine	Uruguay	

2.9 Article 11: Application of Tax Agreements to Restrict a Party's Right to Tax Its Own Residents

The article states that a Covered Tax Agreement shall not affect the taxation by a Contracting Jurisdiction of its residents, except with respect to the listed types of benefits granted under provisions of the Covered Tax Agreement, which expressly limit a Contracting Jurisdiction's right to tax its own residents or expressly provide that the

Contracting Jurisdiction where an item of income arises has the exclusive right to tax that item of income.

Sixty-eight jurisdictions out of the 95 territories whose MLI positions were studied made a choice not to apply Article 11 of the MLI in its entirety, refusing to restrict their right to tax their residents, with remaining 27 MLI convention signatories agreeing to implement MLI Convention's Article 11 with no reservations.

A jurisdiction chose to not apply the article entirely				
Albania	Austria	Bahrain	Barbados	Belize
Bosnia & Herzegovina	Bulgaria	Burkina Faso	Cameroon	Canada
Costa Rica	Cote d'Ivoire	Curacao	Cyprus	Czech Republic
Egypt	Estonia	Finland	France	Georgia
Germany	Greece	Guernsey	Hong Kong	Hungary
Iceland	Ireland	Isle of Man	Israel	Italy
Japan	Jersey	Jordan	Kazakhstan	Korea
Kuwait	Latvia	Liechtenstein	Lithuania	Luxembourg
Malaysia	Malta	Mauritius	Monaco	Morocco
Netherlands	Nigeria	North Macedonia	Oman	Panama
Papua New Guinea	Peru	Qatar	San Marino	Saudi Arabia
Seychelles	Seychelles	Singapore	Slovenia	South Africa
Spain	Sweden	Switzerland	Tunisia	Turkey
UAE	Ukraine	Uruguay		
The article applies / no reservations / provisions already implemented				
Andorra	Argentina	Armenia	Australia	Belgium
Chile	China	Colombia	Croatia	Denmark
Fiji	Gabon	India	Indonesia	Kenya
Kenya	Mexico	New Zealand	Norway	Pakistan
Poland	Portugal	Romania	Russia	Senegal
Slovak Republic	UK			

2.10 Article 12: Artificial Avoidance of Permanent Establishment Status Through Commissionaire Arrangements and Similar Strategies

Article 12 of the Multilateral Convention targets situations where Permanent Establishment status is avoided by corporations by claiming that Commissionaire Arrangements and similar strategies do not constitute enough economic presence in a relevant jurisdiction. According to paragraph 1 of the article, as a general rule "… where a person is acting in a Contracting Jurisdiction to a Covered Tax Agreement on behalf of an enterprise and, in doing so, habitually concludes contracts, or habitually plays the principal role leading to the conclusion of contracts that are routinely concluded without material modification by the enterprise, and these contracts are:

(a) in the name of the enterprise; or
(b) for the transfer of the ownership of, or for the granting of the right to use, property owned by that enterprise or that the enterprise has the right to use; or
(c) for the provision of services by that enterprise,

that enterprise shall be deemed to have a permanent establishment in that Contracting Jurisdiction in respect of any activities which that person undertakes for the enterprise … ."

Implementation strategy for this particular MLI article is rather simple and only includes deciding on whether the article's provisions apply to signatory's Covered Tax Agreements or not. Slightly under half (47) of jurisdictions having signed the MLI Convention decided to implement the article's provisions; however, majority of signatories, including many territories highly ranked in the 2021 Corporate Tax Haven Index (Tax Justice Network, 2021) and European countries associated with tax avoidance, refused to implement provisions on avoiding PE status.

A jurisdiction chose to not apply the article entirely				
Andorra	Australia	Austria	Bahrain	Barbados
Belize	Bulgaria	Canada	China	Curacao
Cyprus	Czech Republic	Estonia	Finland	Georgia
Germany	Greece	Guernsey	Hong Kong	Hungary
Iceland	Ireland	Isle of Man	Italy	Jersey
Korea	Kuwait	Latvia	Liechtenstein	Luxembourg
Malta	Mauritius	Monaco	Morocco	Netherlands
Oman	Panama	Poland	Portugal	Qatar
San Marino	Seychelles	Singapore	South Africa	Sweden
Switzerland	UAE	UK		
The article applies / no reservations / provisions already implemented				
Albania	Argentina	Armenia	Belgium	Bosnia & Herzegovina
Burkina Faso	Cameroon	Chile	Colombia	Costa Rica
Cote d'Ivoire	Croatia	Denmark	Egypt	Fiji

France	Gabon	India	Indonesia	Israel
Jamaica	Japan	Jordan	Kazakhstan	Kenya
Lithuania	Malaysia	Mexico	New Zealand	Nigeria
North Macedonia	Norway	Pakistan	Papua New Guinea	Peru
Romania	Russia	Saudi Arabia	Senegal	Serbia
Slovak Republic	Slovenia	Spain	Tunisia	Turkey
Ukraine	Uruguay			

2.11 Article 13: Artificial Avoidance of Permanent Establishment Status Through the Specific Activity Exemptions

Article 13 of the Convention aims to prevent avoidance of Permanent Establishment status via performing specific activities that previously did not meet the economic activity threshold in the jurisdiction to constitute a Permanent Establishment. Countries are given a choice between two options:

Option A

According to this option, the term "permanent establishment" should not include:

> the activities specifically listed in the Covered Tax Agreement (prior to modification by this Convention) as activities deemed not to constitute a permanent establishment, whether or not that exception from permanent establishment status is contingent on the activity being of a preparatory or auxiliary character;
> the maintenance of a fixed place of business solely for the purpose of carrying on, for the enterprise, any activity not described in subparagraph a);
> the maintenance of a fixed place of business solely for any combination of activities mentioned in subparagraphs a) and b),
> provided that such activity or, in the case of subparagraph c), the overall activity of the fixed place of business, is of a preparatory or auxiliary character.

According to Option B, the term "permanent establishment" shall be deemed not to include:

a) the activities specifically listed in the Covered Tax Agreement (prior to modification by this Convention) as activities deemed not to constitute a permanent establishment, whether or not that exception from permanent establishment status is contingent on the activity being of a preparatory or auxiliary character, except to the extent that the relevant provision of the Covered Tax Agreement provides explicitly that a specific activity shall be deemed not to constitute a permanent establishment provided that the activity is of a preparatory or auxiliary character;

b) the maintenance of a fixed place of business solely for the purpose of carrying on, for the enterprise, any activity not described in subparagraph a), provided that this activity is of a preparatory or auxiliary character;
c) the maintenance of a fixed place of business solely for any combination of activities mentioned in subparagraphs a) and b), provided that the overall activity of the fixed place of business resulting from this combination is of a preparatory or auxiliary character.

Implementation of the article by Contracting Jurisdictions is illustrated below.

Out of 95 jurisdictions analyzed, 36 chose not to apply the article, and four territories (Chile, Portugal, San Marino, and the United Kingdom) agreed to implement it with no reservations and did not indicate any optional choices. Option A was by far the most popular implementation strategy, with 49 territories choosing it. Only 6 jurisdictions (Belgium, France, Ireland, Lithuania, Luxembourg, and Singapore) preferred Option B, and no territory indicated selection of Option C. Austria, Germany, Luxembourg, and Singapore chose to not apply paragraph 13(4), while Argentina, Australia, and Kenya reserved the right for Article 13(2) not to apply to their Covered Tax Agreements that explicitly state that a list of specific activities shall be deemed not to constitute a permanent establishment only if each of the activities is of a preparatory or auxiliary character.

A jurisdiction chose to not apply the article entirely				
Albania	Andorra	Bahrain	Barbados	Belize
Bosnia & Herzegovina	Bulgaria	Canada	China	Cyprus
Czech Republic	Estonia	Finland	Georgia	Greece
Guernsey	Hong Kong	Hungary	Iceland	Isle of Man
Jersey	Korea	Latvia	Liechtenstein	Malta
Mauritius	Monaco	Morocco	Oman	Panama
Poland	Qatar	Seychelles	Sweden	Switzerland
UAE				
A jurisdiction chose to not apply paragraph 13(4)				
Austria Option A	Germany Option A	Luxembourg Option B	Singapore Option B	
A jurisdiction reserves the right for Article 13(2) not to apply to its Covered Tax Agreements that explicitly state that a list of specific activities shall be deemed not to constitute a permanent establishment only if each of the activities is of a preparatory or auxiliary character, Option A				
Argentina Option A	Australia Option A	Kenya Option A		
A jurisdiction chose to apply Option A				

Armenia (Option A)	Burkina Faso (Option A)	Cameroon (Option A)	Colombia (Option A)	Costa Rica (Option A)
Cote d'Ivoire (Option A)	Croatia (Option A)	Curacao (Option A)	Denmark (Option A)	Egypt (Option A)
Fiji (Option A)	Gabon (Option A)	India (Option A)	Indonesia (Option A)	Israel (Option A)
Italy (Option A)	Jamaica (Option A)	Japan (Option A)	Jordan (Option A)	Kazakhstan (Option A)
Kuwait (Option A)	Malaysia (Option A)	Mexico (Option A)	Netherlands (Option A)	New Zealand (Option A)
Nigeria (Option A)	North Macedonia (Option A)	Norway (Option A)	Pakistan (Option A)	Papua New Guinea (Option A)
Peru (Option A)	Romania (Option A)	Russia (Option A)	Saudi Arabia (Option A)	Senegal (Option A)
Serbia (Option A)	Slovak Republic (Option A)	Slovenia (Option A)	South Africa (Option A)	Spain (Option A)
Tunisia (Option A)	Turkey (Option A)	Ukraine (Option A)	Uruguay (Option A)	
A jurisdiction chose to apply Option B				
Belgium (Option B)	France (Option B)	Ireland (Option B)	Lithuania (Option B)	
The article applies / no reservations / provisions already implemented				
Chile	Portugal	San Marino	UK	

2.12 Article 14: Splitting-Up of Contracts

Article 14 of the MLI Convention deals with splitting-up of contracts and a point of time when different activities constitute a permanent establishment and taxable economic presence. In particular, according to the article:

a) where an enterprise of a Contracting Jurisdiction carries on activities in the other Contracting Jurisdiction at a place that constitutes a building site, construction project, installation project or other specific project identified in the relevant provision of the Covered Tax Agreement, or carries on supervisory or consultancy activities in connection with such a place, in the case of a provision of a Covered Tax Agreement that refers to such activities, and these activities are carried on during one or more periods of time that, in the aggregate, exceed 30 days without exceeding the period or periods referred to in the relevant provision of the Covered Tax Agreement; and
b) where connected activities are carried on in that other Contracting Jurisdiction at (or, where the relevant provision of the Covered Tax Agreement applies to supervisory or consultancy activities, in connection with) the same building

> site, construction or installation project, or other place identified in the relevant provision of the Covered Tax Agreement during different periods of time, each exceeding 30 days, by one or more enterprises closely related to the first-mentioned enterprise, these different periods of time shall be added to the aggregate period of time during which the first-mentioned enterprise has carried on activities at that building site, construction or installation project, or other place identified in the relevant provision of the Covered Tax Agreement.

While 60 countries decided not to apply the article entirely, eight jurisdictions—Australia, Egypt, Ireland, Lithuania, Netherlands, Norway, Russia, and Serbia—chose for Article 14 of MLI to not apply with respect to provisions of their Covered Tax Agreements relating to the exploration for or exploitation of natural resources, while accepting it for other DTCs. The remaining 27 jurisdictions agreed to implement the article with no reservations.

A jurisdiction chose to not apply the article entirely				
Albania	Andorra	Austria	Bahrain	Barbados
Belgium	Belize	Bosnia & Herzegovina	Bulgaria	Canada
Chile	China	Costa Rica	Croatia	Curacao
Cyprus	Czech Republic	Estonia	Finland	France
Georgia	Germany	Greece	Guernsey	Hong Kong
Hungary	Iceland	Isle of Man	Italy	Jamaica
Japan	Jersey	Korea	Latvia	Liechtenstein
Luxembourg	Malaysia	Malta	Mauritius	Mexico
Monaco	Morocco	North Macedonia	Oman	Panama
Peru	Poland	Portugal	Qatar	San Marino
Seychelles	Singapore	Slovenia	South Africa	Spain
Sweden	Switzerland	Turkey	UAE	UK
A jurisdiction chose for the entirety of this Article not to apply with respect to provisions of its Covered Tax Agreements relating to the exploration for or exploitation of natural resources				
Australia	Egypt	Ireland	Lithuania	Netherlands
Norway	Russia	Serbia		
The article applies / no reservations / provisions already implemented				
Argentina	Armenia	Burkina Faso	Cameroon	Colombia
Cote d'Ivoire	Denmark	Fiji	Gabon	India
Indonesia	Israel	Jordan	Kazakhstan	Kenya

Kuwait	New Zealand	Nigeria	Pakistan	Papua New Guinea
Romania	Saudi Arabia	Senegal	Slovak Republic	Tunisia
Ukraine	Uruguay			

2.13 Article 15: Definition of a Person Closely Related to an Enterprise

Article 15 defines a person as being "closely related to an enterprise" if, based on all the relevant facts and circumstances, one has control of the other or both are under control of the same persons or enterprises. According to the Convention, a person shall always be considered as closely related to an enterprise if one directly or indirectly possesses more than 50% of the beneficial interest in the other (or, in the case of a company, more than 50% of the aggregate vote and value of the company's shares or of the beneficial equity interest in the company), or if another person possesses directly or indirectly more than 50% of the beneficial interest (or, in the case of a company, more than 50% of the aggregate vote and value of the company's shares or of the beneficial equity interest in the company) in the person and the enterprise.

The majority of countries chose to apply Article 15. Fifty-seven jurisdictions implemented it entirely for all their Covered Tax Agreements, while 34 territories decided not to apply the article to the Covered Tax Agreements to which the reservations described in Article 12(4), Article 13(6)(c), and Article 14(3)(a) apply. Italy made a reservation that it assumes "that this Article may operate only as far as paragraph 4 of Article 13 is concerned since Italy has opted out Articles 12 and 14," and San Marino noted that "having made a reservation under Article 12(4) and Article 14(3)(a), the Republic of San Marino assumes that Article 15 shall only apply with respect to Article 13(4)." Andorra, Czech Republic, Panama, and Switzerland refused to apply Article 15 of the MLI Convention entirely.

A jurisdiction chose to not apply the article entirely				
Andorra	Czech Republic	Panama	Switzerland	
A jurisdiction chose not to apply the article to the Covered Tax Agreements to which the reservations described in Article 12(4), Article 13(6)(c), and Article 14(3)(a) apply				
Austria	Bahrain	Barbados	Belize	Bulgaria
Canada	China	Cyprus	Estonia	Finland
Georgia	Germany	Greece	Guernsey	Hong Kong
Hungary	Iceland	Isle of Man	Jersey	Korea
Latvia	Lichtenstein	Luxembourg	Malta	Mauritius

Monaco	Morocco	Oman	Poland	Qatar
Seychelles	Singapore	Sweden	UAE	
The article applies / no reservations / provisions already implemented				
Albania	Argentina	Armenia	Australia	Belgium
Bosnia & Herzegovina	Burkina Faso	Cameroon	Chile	Colombia
Costa Rica	Cote d'Ivoire	Croatia	Curacao	Denmark
Egypt	Fiji	France	Gabon	India
Indonesia	Ireland	Israel	Jamaica	Japan
Jordan	Italy*	Kazakhstan	Kenya	Kuwait
Lithuania	Malaysia	Mexico	Netherlands	New Zealand
Nigeria	North Macedonia	Norway	Pakistan	Papua New Guinea
Peru	Portugal	Romania	Russia	San Marino**
Saudi Arabia	Senegal	Serbia	Slovak Republic	Slovenia
South Africa	Spain	Tunisia	Turkey	UK
Ukraine	Uruguay			

* 'We assume that this Article may operate only as far as paragraph 4 of Article 13 is concerned, since Italy has opted out Articles 12 and 14'.

** 'Having made a reservation under Article 12(4) and Article 14(3)(a), the Republic of San Marino assumes that Article 15 shall only apply with respect to Article 13(4)'.

2.14 Article 16: Mutual Agreement Procedure

Article 16 of the Convention is dedicated to Mutual Agreement Procedure and provides the taxpayers with a right to present their case to the competent authority of either Contracting Jurisdiction if they believe that actions of one or both Contracting Jurisdictions will lead to the taxpayer being taxed not in accordance with the Covered Tax Agreement. The case can be presented to a competent authority within three years from the first notification of the action resulting in taxation not in accordance with the provisions of the Covered Tax Agreement, and the right to present the case does not depend on the remedies provided by relevant jurisdictions. In case the competent authority is unable to resolve the case on its own, it shall resolve the case by mutual agreement with the competent authority of the other Contracting Jurisdiction.

As the table below demonstrates, the majority of signatories, 62 jurisdictions, did not have any reservations regarding the article, while 30 territories chose not to apply its first sentence, and three countries, Mexico, Senegal, and Switzerland chose not to apply the second sentence of Article 16 "on the basis that it intends to meet the minimum standard for improving dispute resolution under the OECD/G20 BEPS

Package." Canada, Chile, and Monaco refused to implement both the 1st and 2nd sentences of the article.

The article applies / no reservations / provisions already implemented				
Andorra	Argentina	Australia	Bahrain	Barbados
Belgium	Belize	Bulgaria	Burkina Faso	Cameroon
Colombia	Costa Rica	Cote d'Ivoire	Cyprus	Czech Republic
Denmark	Egypt	Estonia	Fiji	Finland
France	Gabon	Georgia	Greece	Guernsey
Hong Kong	Iceland	Ireland	Isle of Man	Jamaica
Japan	Jersey	Jordan	Kazakhstan	Korea
Kuwait	Liechtenstein	Lithuania	Luxembourg	Malaysia
Malta	Mauritius	Morocco	Netherlands	New Zealand
Nigeria	Norway	Oman	Pakistan	Panama
Papua New Guinea	Qatar	Russia	Saudi Arabia	Seychelles
Sweden	Tunisia	Turkey	UAE	UK
Ukraine	Uruguay			
A jurisdiction chose for the 1st sentence of the article to not apply to its DTCs				
Albania	Armenia	Austria	Bosnia & Herzegovina	China
Croatia	Curacao	Germany	Hungary	India
Indonesia	Israel	Italy	Kenya	Latvia
North Macedonia	Peru	Poland	Portugal	Romania
San Marino	Serbia	Singapore	Slovak Republic	Slovenia
South Africa	Spain			
A jurisdiction chose for the 2nd sentence of the article to not apply to its DTCs				
Mexico	Senegal	Switzerland		
A jurisdiction chose not to apply both 1st and 2nd sentences of the article to its DTCs				
Canada	Chile	Monaco		

2.15 Article 17: Corresponding Adjustments

Article 17 of the MLI Convention is dedicated to corresponding adjustments which occur in cases of risk of double taxation when the other Contracting State makes a transfer pricing adjustment of taxpayer's transaction. Such requirement was met with caution by developing countries as some of them feel pressured to accept transfer pricing rules and standards developed by the OECD which sometimes fail to deliver adequate pricing in lower-income economies' context.

Jurisdictional positions regarding the article's implementation are as follows. Forty territories agreed to implement the article without reservations. Forty-three jurisdictions chose to apply paragraph 17(3)(a) stating that "the entirety of this Article does not apply to the Covered Tax Agreements that already contain an identical provision." Twelve territories decided to apply paragraph 17(3)(b) which reads as follows: "the entirety of this Article does not apply to the Covered Tax Agreements on the basis that in the absence of such provision:

(i) the Contracting Jurisdiction shall make the appropriate adjustment referred to in paragraph 1; or
(ii) its competent authority shall endeavour to resolve the case under the provisions of a Covered Tax Agreement relating to mutual agreement procedure." Three countries, Canada, Monaco and Senegal, indicated that paragraph 17(3)(c) applies and "in the case of reservation under clause ii) of subparagraph c) of paragraph 5 of Article 16 (Mutual Agreement Procedure), the entirety of this Article does not apply to the Covered Tax Agreements on the basis that in its bilateral treaty negotiations it shall accept a treaty provision of the type contained in paragraph 1, provided that the Contracting Jurisdictions were able to reach agreement on that provision and on the Mutual Agreement Procedure." Canada applied both paragraphs 17(3)(a) and 17(3)(c), Latvia chose to apply paragraphs 17(3)(a) and 17(3)(b) simultaneously, while Monaco implemented both paragraphs 17(3)(b) and 17(3)(c).

The article applies / no reservations / provisions already implemented				
Albania	Andorra	Argentina	Armenia	Austria
Bahrain	Barbados	Belgium	Burkina Faso	Cameroon
China	Colombia	Cyprus	Fiji	France
Indonesia	Israel	Italy	Jamaica	Japan
Kazakhstan	Kenya	Kuwait	Lithuania	Luxembourg
Malta	Mauritius	Netherlands	New Zealand	North Macedonia
Pakistan	Peru	Portugal	Saudi Arabia	Singapore
South Africa	Switzerland	Tunisia	UAE	UK
A jurisdiction chose to apply paragraph 17(3)(a): the entirety of this Article does not apply to the Covered Tax Agreements that already contain an identical provision				

Australia	Bosnia & Herzegovina (17(3)(a))	Bulgaria	Chile (17)(3)(a)	Costa Rica
Cote d'Ivoire	Croatia	Denmark (17)(3)(a)	Estonia (17)(3)(a)	Finland (17)(3)(a)
Gabon (17)(3)(a))	Georgia (17(3)(a))	Germany	Greece	Guernsey
Hong Kong	Hungary (17(3)(a))	Iceland (17(3)(a))	India (17(3)(a))	Ireland (17)(3)(a)
Isle of Man	Jersey (17(3)(a))	Korea (17)(3)(a)	Liechtenstein 17(3)(a)	Malaysia (17(3(a))
Mexico (17(3)(a))	Nigeria (17(3(a))	Norway (17(3)(a))	Oman	Panama
Poland	San Marino	Romania (17(3)(a))	Russia (17(3)(a))	Serbia (17)(3)(a))
Slovak Republic (17)(3)(a))	Slovenia (17)(3)(a))	Spain (17(3)(a))	Sweden 17(3)(a))	Turkey (17(3)(a))
Uruguay (17)(3)(a))				
A jurisdiction indicated that paragraph 17(3)(b) applies: the entirety of this Article does not apply to the Covered Tax Agreements on the basis that in the absence of such provision: i) the Contracting Jurisdiction shall make the appropriate adjustment referred to in paragraph 1; or ii) its competent authority shall endeavour to resolve the case under the provisions of a Covered Tax Agreement relating to mutual agreement procedure				
Belize (17)(3)(b)	Curacao (17)(3)(b)	Czech Republic (17)(3)(b)	Egypt (17)(3)(b)	Jordan (17)(3)(b)
Morocco (17)(3)(b)	Papua New Guinea (17)(3)(b)	Qatar (17)(3)(b)	Seychelles (17(3)(b))	Ukraine (17)(3)(b))
A jurisdiction chose to apply paragraph 17(3)(c)				
Senegal (17)(3)(c*))				
A jurisdiction chose to apply several paragraphs				
Canada (17(3)(a), 17(3)(c))*	Latvia (17)(3)(a), 17(3)(b))	Monaco (17)(3)(b)), (17)(3)(c)*		

* A jurisdiction indicated that paragraph 17(3)(c) applies: in the case of reservation under clause ii) of subparagraph c) of paragraph 5 of Article 16 (Mutual Agreement Procedure), the entirety of this

Article does not apply to the Covered Tax Agreements on the basis that in its bilateral treaty negotiations it shall accept a treaty provision of the type contained in paragraph 1, provided that the Contracting Jurisdictions were able to reach agreement on that provision and on the Mutual Agreement Procedure.

2.16 Article 18: Choice to Apply Part VI (Arbitration)

Article 18 of the Convention provides the Contracting Jurisdictions with an opportunity to apply mandatory arbitration for resolving tax controversies. Here, the countries are expressing (or not) their principle consent to applicability of Part VI of the MLI convention, which is dedicated to arbitration, to their Covered Tax Agreements. Part VI is only applicable where both Contracting Jurisdictions have given their consent to it.

Rather uncommonly, 61 jurisdictions did not mention this article in their MLI positions. Out of those who did, 31 territories decided to apply Part VI of the MLI Convention, and three countries, namely Israel, Kenya, and the Slovak Republic, decided not to implement MLI Convention provisions concerning arbitration. A rather uncommon implementation of the article might be associated with concerns "developing" countries expressed about the Mandatory Arbitration procedure and its ability to provide satisfactory, just results.

A jurisdiction chose to not apply Part VI				
Israel	Kenya	Slovak Republic		
A jurisdiction chose to apply Part VI				
Andorra	Australia	Austria	Barbados	Belgium
Canada	Curacao	Denmark	Fiji	Finland
France	Germany	Greece	Hungary	Ireland
Italy	Japan	Liechtenstein	Luxembourg	Malta
Mauritius	Netherlands	New Zealand	Papua New Guinea	Portugal
Singapore	Slovenia	Spain	Sweden	Switzerland
UK				
The article is not mentioned in jurisdiction's MLI position				
Albania	Argentina	Armenia	Bahrain	Belize
Bosnia & Herzegovina	Bulgaria	Burkina Faso	Cameroon	Chile
China	Colombia	Costa Rica	Cote d'Ivoire	Croatia
Cyprus	Czech Republic	Egypt	Estonia	Gabon
Georgia	Guernsey	Hong Kong	Iceland	India
Indonesia	Isle of Man	Jamaica	Jersey	Jordan

Kazakhstan	Korea	Kuwait	Latvia	Lithuania
Malaysia	Mexico	Monaco	Morocco	Nigeria
North Macedonia	Norway	Oman	Pakistan	Panama
Peru	Poland	Qatar	Romania	Russia
San Marino	Saudi Arabia	Senegal	Serbia	Seychelles
South Africa	Tunisia	Turkey	UAE	Ukraine
Uruguay				

2.17 Article 19: Mandatory Binding Arbitration

Article 19 introduces norms giving an overview of mandatory binding arbitration procedure according to which where a person has reasons to believe that actions of one or both of the Contracting Jurisdictions have resulted in taxation of that person not in accordance with the provisions of the Covered Tax Agreement, such person has a right to present a case to the competent authority of a Contracting Jurisdiction. According to the article, if competent authorities of the Contracting Jurisdictions are unable to resolve the case by mutual agreement within two years, any unresolved issues arising from the case shall, if the person so requests in writing, be submitted to mandatory arbitration, the rules of which are provided in Part VI of the Convention.

A record number of 70 jurisdictions did not mention the article in their MLI positions, while Austria, France, Germany, Greece, Liechtenstein, Portugal, Slovenia, Sweden, and Switzerland implemented it substituting the two-year term for three years. Twenty-one territories reserved the right for the following rules to apply with respect to their Covered Tax Agreements notwithstanding the other provisions of Article 19:

(a) any unresolved issue arising from a mutual agreement procedure case otherwise within the scope of the arbitration process provided for by the Convention shall not be submitted to arbitration, if a decision on this issue has already been rendered by a court or administrative tribunal of either Contracting Jurisdiction;
(b) if, at any time after a request for arbitration has been made and before the arbitration panel has delivered its decision to the competent authorities of the Contracting Jurisdictions, a decision concerning the issue is rendered by a court or administrative tribunal of one of the Contracting Jurisdictions, the arbitration process shall terminate.

Such a modest number of jurisdictions implementing the article might indicate that the Mandatory Arbitration Procedure is an area achieving agreement on which is particularly challenging in present international relations conditions.

The article is not mentioned in jurisdiction's MLI position				
Albania	Argentina	Armenia	Bahrain	Barbados
Belize	Bosnia & Herzegovina	Bulgaria	Burkina Faso	
Cameroon	Chile	China	Colombia	Costa Rica
Cote d'Ivoire	Croatia	Curacao	Cyprus	Czech Republic
Egypt	Estonia	Fiji	Finland	Gabon
Georgia	Guernsey	Hong Kong	Iceland	India
Indonesia	Isle of Man	Israel	Jamaica	Jersey
Jordan	Kazakhstan	Kenya	Korea	Kuwait
Latvia	Lithuania	Malaysia	Mexico	Monaco
Morocco	Netherlands	Nigeria	North Macedonia	Norway
Oman	Pakistan	Panama	Peru	Poland
Qatar	Romania	Russia	San Marino	Saudi Arabia
Senegal	Serbia	Seychelles	Slovak Republic	South Africa
Tunisia	Turkey	UAE	UK	Ukraine
Uruguay				
The article applies with some amendments				
Germany*	Australia**	Ireland**	New Zealand**	Austria*,**
Liechtenstein*	Andorra**	Italy**	Papua New Guinea**	France*,**
Switzerland*	Belgium**	Japan**	Spain**	Greece*,**
Sweden*	Canada**	Luxembourg**	Singapore**	Portugal*,**
	Denmark**	Malta**		Slovenia*,**
	Hungary**	Mauritius**		

* Three years instead of two.

** A jurisdiction reserves the right for the following rules to apply with respect to its Covered Tax Agreements notwithstanding the other provisions of Article 19:

a) any unresolved issue arising from a mutual agreement procedure case otherwise within the scope of the arbitration process provided for by the Convention shall not be submitted to arbitration, if a decision on this issue has already been rendered by a court or administrative tribunal of either Contracting Jurisdiction;

b) if, at any time after a request for arbitration has been made and before the arbitration panel has delivered its decision to the competent authorities of the Contracting Jurisdictions, a decision concerning the issue is rendered by a court or administrative tribunal of one of the Contracting Jurisdictions, the arbitration process shall terminate.

3 CONCLUSION

Analysis demonstrates that some MLI Convention provisions are clearly more effective than others. While there are articles that were accepted by a vast majority of signatories, other Convention provisions or options were not implemented by a single jurisdiction.

As the MLI Convention design remains complex and countries are given multiple options to decide how they would like the Convention provisions to be implemented, identifying the most popular MLI Convention provision is currently impossible, as mechanisms of implementation differ among countries. However, identifying the least popular provision is a little easier.

Article 11 (Application of Tax Agreements to Restrict a Party's Right to Tax its Own Residents) was not implemented by 68 jurisdictions. Sixty-six territories rejected to apply Article 10 (Anti-abuse Rule for Permanent Establishments Situated in Third Jurisdictions), and 65 Convention signatories did not opt for Article 3 on Transparent Entities. However, section IV on Mandatory Arbitration probably remains the biggest concern: consensus on the issue seems to be hard to build, and as many as 70 jurisdictions out of 95 ignored Article 19 on Mandatory Arbitration procedure, for example.

There are some identifiable trends in countries' strategies of implementing the MLI Convention. There are demonstrably "more compliant" and "less compliant" jurisdictions among MLI Convention signatories. What is surprising is that the "less compliant" category consists not only—and not even mainly—of tropical islands and former British colonies, but also rich European jurisdictions (Switzerland being one example), which are also highly ranked in the Corporate Tax Haven Index. The correlation between a jurisdiction's position in the Index and its unwillingness to fully implement the MLI convention is quite strong.

The "more compliant" category usually consists of several developing countries, such as Kenya and India, some Scandinavian jurisdictions supporting transparency and cooperation, such as Denmark and Norway, as well as some "neutral" European jurisdictions such as the Czech Republic and Slovenia.

Future research investigating the differences of MLI Convention implementation strategies between "developed" and "developing" countries would be useful and valuable for a better understanding of the dynamics of international tax policy making.

BIBLIOGRAPHY

OECD Multilateral Convention to Implement Tax Treaty Related Measures to Prevent BEPS // https://www.oecd.org/tax/treaties/multilateral-convention-to-impleme nt-tax-treaty-related-measures-to-prevent-beps.htm.

OECD (2015), Developing a Multilateral Instrument to Modify Bilateral Tax Treaties, Action 15 -2015 Final Report, OECD/G20 Base Erosion and Profit Shifting Project, OECD Publishing, Paris. http://dx.doi.org/10.1787/9789264241688-en.

MLI positions for Albania, Andorra, Argentina, Armenia, Australia, Austria, Bahrain, Barbados, Belgium, Belize, Bosnia and Herzegovina, Bulgaria, Burkina Faso, Cameroon, Canada, Chile, China, Colombia, Costa Rica, Cote d'Ivoire, Croatia, Curacao, Cyprus, Czech Republic, Denmark, Egypt, Estonia, Fiji, Finland, France, Gabon, Georgia, Germany, Greece, Guernsey, Hong Kong, Hungary, Iceland, India, Indonesia, Ireland, Isle of Man, Israel, Italy, Jamaica, Japan, Jersey, Jordan, Kazakhstan, Kenya, Korea, Kuwait, Latvia, Liechtenstein, Lithuania, Luxembourg, Malaysia, Malta, Mauritius, Mexico, Monaco, Morocco, Netherlands, New Zealand, Nigeria, North Macedonia, Norway, Oman, Pakistan, Panama, Papua New Guinea, Peru, Poland, Portugal, Qatar, Romania, Russia, San Marino, Saudi Arabia, Senegal, Serbia, Seychelles, Singapore, Slovak Republic, Slovenia, South Africa, Spain, Sweden, Switzerland, Tunisia, Turkey, UAE, UK, Ukraine and Uruguay / Signatories and Parties (MLI Positions) (oecd.org).

Should Developing Countries Sign the OECD Multilateral Instrument to Address Treaty-Related Base Erosion and Profit Shifting Measures? By Annet Wanyana Oguttu. / CGD Policy Paper 132, November 2018. Available at Should Developing Countries Sign the OECD Multilateral Instrument to Address Treaty-Related Base Erosion and Profit Shifting Measures? | Center For Global Development (cgdev.org).

Corporate Tax Haven Index – 2021 Results // https://cthi.taxjustice.net/en/.

Part III Implementation in Practice: Precedents, Challenges, and Prospects for Uniformity

CHAPTER 8

Domestic and Treaty-Based GAAR and SAAR: Potential Conflicts and Ordering Principles MLI and Argentine Treaty and Domestic Law

Guillermo O. Teijeiro

Guillermo O. Teijeiro analyzes the MLI in light of existing general anti-avoidance regimes (GAARs) and specific anti-avoidance regimes (SAARs). Teijeiro calls the MLI a "new GAAR treaty" and examines its potential collision with domestic GAAR parallels, precedents, and practices from the perspective of Argentina. The chapter outlines the scope of application of the various rules in domestic and international contexts and considers existing conflicts among these various regimes. It then introduces a path to facilitate their harmonious co-existence resolution in the form of ordering principles.

The application of general anti-avoidance rules (GAARs) and special anti-avoidance rules (SAAR), as well as their inter-relationship in a purely domestic and international context, has never been simple nor precise. The situation becomes increasingly complex when GAARs can be applied in a treaty setting to re-characterize taxpayers' transactions or to re-determine the taxpayer to whom an item of income belongs. Moreover, the creation of a new GAAR treaty by the Organisation for Economic Co-operation and Development (OECD) Multilateral Instrument (MLI) and its potential collision with (i) the widespread practice of applying domestic GAAR as a re-characterization and re-determination tool under the treaty umbrella (as is the case in Argentina), and (ii) the pre-existence of a bilaterally agreed-upon GAAR treaty in the Argentine treaty network increases the imperative nature of developing ordering principles for the application of these rules.

The purpose of this contribution consists of: (i) describing the Argentine GAAR and SAAR's scope of application in a purely domestic and international context, (ii) addressing the conflicts between GAAR and domestic and international SAAR, as well as developing ordering principles, (iii) reviewing the administrative and judicial precedents dealing with the application of the domestic GAAR in a treaty context, (iv) analyzing existing treaty GAAR and limitation of benefit clauses (LoB) within the Argentine treaty network, and finally (v) examining the potential overlapping and developing ordering rules between all of the above rules and treaty clauses with the MLI anti-abuse-treaty minimum standard adopted by Argentina, an issue that will become relevant once Argentina (one of the MLI early-bird signatories) ratifies it.

1 BACKGROUND

1.1 Description of Argentine Domestic GAAR and Scope of Application

Argentine GAAR are contained in sections 1 and 2 of the Tax Procedural Law (TPL).[1] Both sections describe the so-called *economic reality principle*, albeit in different contexts. This term is more familiar among Argentine scholars and tax practitioners rather than *substance over form* or other similar terms frequently used in Anglo-Saxon tax circles.

Section 1, TPL, mandates the application of the economic reality principle to the construction of the tax law, while section 2, TPL, provides for the application of the principle to the characterization of the acts and transactions of taxpayers, i.e., to the assessment of facts.

Section 1, TPL, sets forth the principle that tax provisions must be construed in accordance with their purpose and economic meaning; adding that whenever it is not possible to ascertain the meaning or scope of application of a tax rule based on its wording or intent, an interpretation may be made in accordance with private law rules, concepts, and principles.

Section 2, TPL, in turn, leads to the consideration of the acts, situations, and economic relations actually performed, pursued, or created by taxpayers to determine the true nature of the taxable event. Under this rule, whenever a taxpayer's chosen legal form does not coincide with a structure offered or authorized by law to properly shape the actual economic objective pursued, the chosen form may be discarded. In its stead, the law requires the actual economic situation to be considered within the structures provided by private law and the most natural form consistent with the taxpayer's actual economic intention.

GAAR, as defined under sections 1 and 2, TPL, apply to the construction of TPL itself and all other federal tax laws regulating taxes [e.g., income tax, value-added tax

1. Law 11, 683, as amended.

(VAT)] subject to the provisions of TPL,[2] their implementing decrees, and complementary regulations issued by the tax agency (Administración Federal de Ingresos Públicos or AFIP), as well as the assessment of facts in connection with the application of said federal taxes.[3]

Domestic SAAR and treaty GAAR complement the rules aimed at preventing tax avoidance in particular domestic contexts, and in a treaty setting, respectively.

The Argentine Constitution contemplates the reserve or legality principle (section 19 and, particularly, sections 4, 14, 17, 18, 28, and 33, Argentine Constitution). Pursuant to this principle, a legislative enactment by Congress is required to, *inter alia*, create and impose taxes and other contributions in the exercise of taxing powers (sections 4 and 17, Argentine Constitution). Courts have repeatedly and consistently relied on the reserve principle to declare tax rules unconstitutional, and, particularly, counterbalancing GAAR whenever their application results in the levying of taxes beyond the scope of the law (e.g., in cases where the application of GAAR may result in the analogical extension of the taxable event).

1.2 GAAR Applied to the Construction of the Tax Law

Interpreting written tax laws requires addressing two basic questions: What does the law say? What does the law intend to say?

The first question is answered by reference to *textual* or *grammatical interpretation,* which is limited to assessing the plain meaning of the words used in the law. This is the primary method used by the interpreter to determine the meaning and scope of the rule.

The second inquiry (what the law intends to say) is answered by the *logical interpretation* which consists of finding the *ratio legis* or lawmaker's intention, as reflected in the law. This analysis may lead to either a strict, restrictive, or expansive interpretation of the statute.

A strict interpretation follows from a conclusion that the legislator's expression and intent precisely coincide. If that is the case, the result of the logical interpretation matches the result of the textual interpretation. Instead, a restrictive interpretation results if the statutory language is deemed to exceed the deduced intent. Finally, an expansive interpretation prevails whenever the statutory language does not reflect the legislator's intent, since it is expressed in overly narrow terms.

In addition to the methods of interpretation described above, the Argentine Supreme Court has repeatedly applied the so-called *systematic interpretation* of the law, which focuses on the relationship between the scrutinized rule and the remainder

2. The content of TPL exceeds procedural matters to cover substantive tax law topics proper of a tax code, such as the tax agency's organization and functions, definition of taxpayers and other responsible persons, place and date of tax payments, advance payment on account of the final tax liability, allocation of payments, withholdings, interest charges and fines for tax law violations, and statutes of limitations.
3. Unless otherwise noted, GAAR and SAAR will be discussed in the context of the income tax law (ITL). ITL governs the individual income tax, the corporate income tax, and the income tax rules applicable to individual and foreign entities who obtain Argentine source income.

of the legal system. In this sense, the Argentine Supreme Court has declared that rules must be construed to prevent contradictions with other provisions that directly or indirectly govern the subject matter, i.e., without harmonizing the conflicting provisions.[4]

All general interpretative methods apply to the construction of tax statutes, as long as the taxpayers' constitutional rights and other fundamental guarantees are protected. As a consequence of the non-rebuttable principle of reserve or legality, the language used in tax statutes is particularly significant, and the interpretation and application of substantive tax provisions by analogy are forbidden.[5] Analogy clearly contravenes the constitutional principle of reserve or legality, as repeatedly defined by the Argentine Supreme Court.[6]

The economic reality principle contemplated in section 1, TPL, is just an additional interpretative criterion of the tax law which reflects the economic content of the taxable event.

Section 1, TPL, also sets forth the supremacy of tax rules, concepts, and principles over private law rules, concepts, and principles. Only when the interpretation cannot be based on the former, i.e., because the tax law language is clearly predicated on private law terms and principles, may the interpreter resort to private law to resolve an interpretation issue.

1.3 GAAR Applied to the Assessment of Facts

The application of GAAR to the factual matrix has generated significant academic debate and judicial controversy in Argentina. A series of circumstances have fueled the discussion on their scope and limits of application: First, GAAR's own definition, which is based on broadly designed standards, leaves room for potential uncertainty and legitimate differences in interpretation. Second, the tax agency's marked tendency to resort to GAAR to decide complex issues is particularly aggravated due to the frequent lack of adequate quality and precision of the tax legislation. In turn, GAAR is often applied to solve cases more frequently than expected. Moreover, in many instances, the legislator does not promptly react to the dynamics of business transactions. For instance, to maintain revenues, the tax agency is faced with the constant need to broaden the statutory definition of the taxable event by re-characterizing new forms of

4. Argentine Supreme Court Official Collection, Fallos at 307:2053; *id., inter alia*, Fallos 244:129; 255:360; 258:74; 271:7; 278:62; 297:143; 303:248; 1041; 307:993, 2071; 311:193; 316:2499.
5. The current text of Article 1, para. 2. TPL (as amended by law 27,430) reads as follows: *The analogy to expand the scope of the taxable event, exemptions or unlawful tax actions shall not be accepted.*
6. "it is not possible to accept the analogy in the interpretation of substantive tax rules to extend the law beyond what was foreseen by the legislator nor to impose an obligation ... taking into account reiterated doctrine in the sense that, as regards tax obligations, the principle of reserve or legality controls ... " Fallos 312:912; accord, *inter alia*, Fallos 103:155; 180:384; 209:87; 310:290; 316:2329. For a comprehensive analysis, *see also* Teijeiro, *La legalidad y la Seguridad Jurídica en la Jurisprudencia Tributaria de la Corte Suprema de Justicia Argentina*, in Temas de Dereito Tributário, Em Homenagema Gilberto Ulhoa Canto. ABDF/Arraes, Belo Horizonte, 2020, volumen 1, p. 735 ff.

business transactions to match the statutory wording. This is often established by resorting to the economic reality approach contained in section 2, TPL, interpreted in a way that goes far beyond its language and purpose, thus violating the principle of reserve or legality and purportedly transforming legitimate tax planning into tax avoidance. The tax agency's reasoning underlying this position may be summarized as follows: Whenever more than one form or set forms may be used to characterize the taxpayer's economic goal—although all of them may share economic intent—the one that would subject it to the heaviest tax burden should be applied. In other words, regardless of which legal structure or transaction is affected, taxes are due as though the taxpayer has chosen the most unfavorable form.

In its long history—the economic reality principle was first included in Argentine tax legislation in 1946—GAAR's application to the assessment of facts has also been heavily influenced by political and ideological biases. For example, as the Supreme Court's precedents demonstrate, the principle of *maximum taxation* referred to in the preceding paragraph has at times been used in specifically targeted sectors (e.g., transactions entered into by foreign-controlled domestic corporate taxpayers).[7]

Maximum taxation policy ignores that legitimate tax planning efforts to save taxes are not prohibited by the Argentine constitutional and legal system. Indeed, section 19 of the Argentine Constitution states: "No resident of the Nation shall be obliged to perform anything not ordered by law, nor deprived of anything not prohibited by it ...." Coincidentally, in *re I.C.A. Argentina S.R.L.*, the Supreme Court held that "... an honest effort by the taxpayer to keep its taxes as low as legally possible deserves no reproach."[8] This constitutional principle endorses the legitimacy of tax planning efforts and might be deeply undermined if the *maximum taxation* approach to section 2, TPL, ever prevails.

2 GAAR AND SAAR RELATED TO DOMESTIC AND INTERNATIONAL TRANSACTIONS

2.1 Application of GAAR: Content and Scope of Application

Section 2, TPL, allows for deviation from the legal characterization of a transaction whenever taxpayers have used legal forms that are manifestly inadequate to shape the effective economic intent. This means that Argentine GAAR only allow re-characterization when the utilized legal forms are distorted, i.e., they do not conform because of their nature or characteristics (as defined by private law) to the actual economic intention of the taxpayer. In other words, a radical or manifest discrepancy between the legal forms chosen by the taxpayer and the economic essence of the business pursued must exist for section 2, TPL, to apply. Similarly, it has been said that Argentine GAAR only allow discarding the taxpayers' legal characterization of transactions in cases of simulated (sham), indirect, or fiduciary transactions.

7. This was particularly so during the seventies of the 20th century.
8. Fallos 241:210.

As a single, all-embracing rule designed on the basis of a general standard, Argentine GAAR leave considerable room for the tax agency and the courts to determine whether and how they apply to a particular case. In fact, GAAR have been extensively used in several contexts for a number of reasons. Moreover, the negative formulation of the statutory language (i.e., GAAR do not positively define the most appropriate legal form) does not assist with determining which legal form would have been appropriate in a given case to implement the economic intention of the taxpayer. This aspect is an issue in itself since, in essence, re-characterization is a twofold process in which the interpreter must first disqualify the utilized legal form as alien to the economic intention pursued, but then on the basis of facts and circumstances, also identify those others deemed inherent to the stated intention(s) in order to apply the tax treatment afforded to them by the law.

However, GAAR's long history has given the courts ample time to determine the contours of their application, making it possible to predict with reasonable certainty how the courts would decide a particular case with similar issues and facts.

Both the Argentine tax agency and the courts have demonstrated flexibility in applying GAAR to different tax avoidance schemes and transactions. In response, targeted schemes or transactions have changed over time and produced more narrowly drawn statutory SAAR.

As mentioned, one particular area of GAAR's application includes sham transactions, which arise when the legal form used by the taxpayer contradicts the legal reality of the transaction under private law. As a result, the tax should be imposed on the transaction's actual terms and not those simulated by the taxpayer.

While in strict terms the sham concept focuses on legal reality rather than economic reality, sham transactions are challenged through the use of GAAR. Sham transactions may also imply fraudulent conduct leading to tax penalties and criminal persecution, such as when the taxpayer intentionally conceals the true nature of the legal transaction to avoid the tax agency's detection of the actual tax amount owed, or when items of income and/or deductible expenses are artificially shifted to an interposed person or entity for the same purpose.

Other pathologies under GAAR's scrutiny include taxpayers' acts of *fraus legis* (of which the indirect transaction is a species), and the fraudulent use of a legal entity.

The *fraus legis* doctrine prevents taxpayers from exploiting the literal language of the statute for tax avoidance purposes. A transaction is deemed *in fraus legis* when, although valid for private law purposes, its legal form is used to avoid rules that correspond to the economic goal actually pursued. In other words, the legal act or transaction is affected under the umbrella of rules applicable to a different goal or objective in order to avoid the tax.

The indirect transaction is defined as one that fosters a particular objective through an oblique or circular means. Finally, GAAR have been applied in particularly extreme contexts to pierce the corporate veil in the tax field by importing the analogous business law theory. As such, tax law has reacted to the abuse of the legal (separate) corporate personality.

If the legal forms chosen are manifestly inadequate to achieve the intended economic goal, GAAR would apply to reconcile form and intent (substance), even if the taxpayer properly proves that lack of experience or legal knowledge led to choosing the inappropriate form. Conversely, evidence of the taxpayer's intent to save taxes does not per se cause re-characterization under GAAR if the chosen form is deemed adequate to shape the economic goal pursued; in other words, except in the case of an act *in fraus legis*, where by its sole definition the taxpayer's intent matters, use of the most tax-effective legally available type of transaction is beyond the reach of Argentine GAAR, regardless of the taxpayer's intent to save taxes.

The principal consequences of GAAR's application in a given case include re-characterization of a transaction or a series of transactions for tax purposes and/or the re-assignment of income (losses) to the actual beneficiary or beneficiaries in accordance with such re-characterization. Associated consequences are the application of interest on unpaid taxes and fines for tax omission unless certain excepting conditions are met—i.e., those embodied in the concept of excusable error. If the taxpayer's behavior is fraudulent, re-characterization may also lead to criminal prosecution, in addition to interest and higher fines for tax fraud.

Tax re-characterization pursuant to GAAR, however, does not ordinarily project its effects on the legal characterization of the targeted transaction or transactions which remain unaffected from a strictly legal perspective.

As an exception, there might be cases where, through separate and different procedures, transactions are challenged in their own nature under private law (for instance, by applying abuse of law principles) and tax law through GAAR, in which cases the result might be that the utilized legal forms are discarded for legal and tax purposes as well. That could be the case when a legal (paper) entity is artificially interposed in a business transaction and subsequently challenged by disregarding the corporate veil for corporate law and tax purposes. In these types of cases, however, there should be a separate legal challenge to the transaction, so that this feature confirms the principle that re-characterization for tax purposes under GAAR does not, per se, project its effects in the private law field.

GAAR are applied in the domestic and international context as well. There are no domestic constitutional or legal obstacles that prevent their application to international or cross-border transactions. Therefore, sections 1 and 2, TPL, apply to the construction of the Income tax Law (ITL) international rules and to the assessment of facts in connection with international transactions, respectively, only subject to international law limitations on the exercise of tax jurisdiction. In this context, GAAR are applicable with the same meaning and are subject to the same limitations discussed in connection with their application in the domestic context.

As a general rule, section 2, TPL, would allow to re-characterize international transactions for tax purposes if and when such transactions are entered into by: (i) resident individuals and Argentine-domiciled companies, whether generating Argentine or foreign source income/expenses; and (ii) nonresident individuals and entities as long as they generate Argentine source income subject to income tax withholding at source, in which case correlative adjustments to the domestic payer's deductible expenses may also be made.

The tax agency and the courts have applied GAAR as extensively in the international context as in the domestic context. Until 1992, however, the application of GAAR to international transactions was mostly focused on Argentine source-generating transactions by foreigners since, until then, Argentine taxpayers were taxed on a territorial basis only. Within that context, intercompany dealings between foreign-controlled domestic companies and their foreign parent or other foreign-affiliated companies—particularly before the adoption in 1976 of the arm's-length standard currently contained in section 16, ITL—were closely monitored by the tax agency and originated a number of significant judicial decisions.[9]

Domestic GAAR, however, have not proved to be the most efficient tool to fight tax avoidance in an international context. Consequently, SAAR addressed to international transactions have become the norm, as the analysis of the relevant ITL rules demonstrates.

2.2 Domestic SAAR

Domestic SAAR are found in several ITL provisions and are aimed at specific situations that, for different reasons, the legislator has considered inadequately covered by GAAR. In their particular areas of application, SAAR usually describe the targeted transactions in detail and the tax consequences derived therefrom. SAAR may either take the form of mechanical, objective rules that apply to all transactions meeting the statutory definition, or rules whose application depends on a more general standard patterned after GAAR. In the latter case, the law often presumes a specific intent, unless the taxpayer demonstrates the contrary.

Since SAAR are not defined or grouped as such in ITL, a broad, functional approach is followed in this work to encompass them all. Under this view, all ITL rules—whether or not designed as tax avoidance rules and regardless of their nature or characteristics—are deemed SAAR as long as they function as such, i.e., helping ITL taxing or other rules to be applied to their true extent, as originally intended by the lawmaker.[10]

2.3 SAAR Applicable to International Transactions

SAAR applicable to international transactions are ITL rules of a varying nature and function that have developed over time to close legislative loopholes.

Prior to the introduction of the worldwide taxation system for resident individuals and Argentine-domiciled entities, upon enactment of law 25,063 (1998), most SAAR

9. Among others, the Supreme Court's decisions in *re Atkinson Ltda., Refinerías de Maíz, Naarden Argentina S.R.L., Parke-Davis y Cía. de Argentina S.A.I.C., and Kellogg Co. Argentina.*

10. *See* Teijeiro, *Las Normas Anti-elusión en el Derecho Tributario Argentino: su Aplicación y Alcances en el Contexto Internacional,* en Interpretación Ecónomica de las Normas Tributarias, Casás, ed. p. 505 ff., at 541; Editorial Abaco de Rodolfo Depalma, Buenos Aires, 2004.

applicable in the international context were addressed to inbound Argentine source-generating transactions by foreign taxpayers. Within this group, SAAR focused on: (i) reinforcing Argentine tax jurisdiction based on source; (ii) avoiding the erosion of the Argentine income tax basis in the case of foreign beneficiaries doing business with or in Argentina; and (iii) with any one of the purposes stated in (i) and (ii) above, assuring proper tax characterization of targeted cross-border transactions.

Although some long-standing rules in this area have been updated and/or refined in recent years to follow international trends (e.g., the adoption of transfer pricing rules patterned after OECD guidelines to complement the already existing arm's-length transaction standard applicable to cross-border intercompany dealings between related parties), the basic principles behind these rules have remained unchanged.

SAAR aimed at protecting or reinforcing Argentine tax jurisdiction based on source include: (i) a special source rule for technical, financial or similar advice rendered from abroad, which deems fees or other compensation paid therefor as Argentine source income, regardless of the place of performance (section 13, ITL), thus departing from the otherwise generally applicable source rule on service income,; (ii) an exception to the source rule on derivative instruments or contracts, which are generally sourced to where the undertaken risk is situated, in the case of derivatives which are deemed to be substantially equivalent to traditional financial products (e.g., a synthetic loan). In these cases, income source is determined in accordance with the source rules applicable to the actual nature of the income obtained (section 8, ITL); (iii) full allocation to Argentine source of income from exports of goods manufactured, produced, or purchased in Argentina (section 9, ITL); and (iv) a recapture rule on exemptions granted to foreign persons if and when the income is taxable in the beneficiary's home jurisdiction (section 28, ITL).

SAAR geared toward avoiding the erosion of the Argentine income tax basis in the case of foreign persons doing business with or within Argentina (whether applied directly on them or on the domestic counterparty) include: (i) readjustment of prices and reallocation of income in the case of under-invoicing of exports and over-invoicing of imports (section 9, ITL); (ii) establishment of presumed net income bases from Argentine sources in connection with activities carried out partly within and partly without Argentina, as well as activities in which the source of income or expenses associated therewith are difficult to ascertain (sections 9-14, ITL); (iii) departure from the otherwise applicable separate accounting principles to determine PE income on a formulary basis *(*i.e., by arbitrarily allocating to it a portion of the aggregate income of the foreign head office, the co-branches and the domestic branch, considering all of them as an economic unit), if and when the PE lacks accounting records or the same does not accurately reflect net income (section 16, paragraph 2, ITL); (iv) application of arm's-length standards, time matching rules to income/expenses, and transfer pricing rules on intercompany dealings between foreign-owned domestic entities and PEs and foreign related parties [section 16 paragraphs 3, 17 and 18, 24b), last paragraph, ITL]; (v) limitations on the deductibility of interest (thin capitalization rules), compensation for patent and trademark licenses, and royalties/fees for technical assistance paid to foreign beneficiaries [sections 85 paragraphs 4,-8, and 92, e) and m), ITL and regulations thereunder]; and (vi) a system of presumed net income bases for determining effective withholdings on payments to foreign beneficiaries (section 104, ITL). Targeted cross-border transactions subject to proper characterization scrutiny under SAAR also include operating and financial leasing transactions (section 269, ITL implementing decree). Since financial leasing is afforded more favorable treatment, the regulations set forth strict conditions for a transaction to qualify as such.

A number of SAAR addressed to foreign source income or expenses incurred by resident individuals and domestic entities, as well as transactions with tax haven jurisdictions are also included in ITL.

ITL international transparency or anti-tax haven rules includes the following: (i) a much higher effective withholding (35% instead of 15.05%) on interest paid generally under intercompany loans from abroad and loans granted by banks situated in foreign noncooperative jurisdictions (section 104, paragraph c, 2, ITL); (ii) stricter transfer pricing rules for dealings between domestic companies and their foreign related entities or permanent establishments located in noncooperative jurisdictions or low-tax jurisdictions, as defined (section 17, paragraph 2, ITL); (iii) anti-deferral rules on domestic shareholders having an equity participation in foreign entities under certain specified conditions [section 130, paragraph f), ITL]; and (iv) disallowance of the indirect foreign tax credit for domestic shareholders having an equity participation in second-tier foreign subsidiaries held through first-tier entities in noncooperative or low-tax jurisdictions [section 306, b), ITL implementing decree].

According to section 19, ITL, noncooperative foreign jurisdictions are those lacking an exchange of information agreement or a Double Tax Agreement or DTA with an ample clause for exchange of information with Argentina. According to this provision, jurisdictions will also be deemed noncooperative if they have an exchange of tax information or DTA in force and do not effectively provide tax information to Argentina. Low or no-tax jurisdictions are those whose maximum rate of corporate taxation is lower than 60% of the Argentine minimum corporate income tax rate, which currently stands at 25% ((i.e., 60% of 25 or 15%).

3 CONFLICTS OF GAAR WITH DOMESTIC SAAR: ORDERING PRINCIPLES

As anticipated, most SAAR applicable in the domestic context take the form of mechanical, objective rules that assume a potential risk of tax avoidance or abuse in a particular area to define their scope and consequences, with practically no discussion of whether the taxpayers' acts or transactions are described by the respective provisions. In some cases, however, the law allows the taxpayer to prove the contrary, thus escaping the tax consequences described in the rule. That would be the case, *inter alia*, of disbursements lacking proper documentation whenever the payer is able to evidence by other means that the undocumented payments are related to the earning or maintenance of taxable income or the interest presumption unless such interest originates in deferred-payment sales of real estate.

In some other cases, SAAR are more broadly designed (e.g., re-characterization of derivative instruments, or the presumption of interest on the disposition of funds or assets in favor of third persons, when such dispositions are not made in the interest of the business, leaving room for a conceptual discussion of whether the applying conditions of the rules are met in a particular case.

When SAAR are provided for in the tax law, the question arises as to whether GAAR may still be applied in the former particular area of application. This is still an open issue under Argentine tax law.

It may be argued that if specific rules exist, the tax agency and the courts should be precluded from subsidiarily applying GAAR, since the sole existence of SAAR demonstrates that the legislator´s intent was to refine GAAR in a particular area, even with the risk that tax planners may find a loophole that is not covered by the special rule. Since most SAAR are special rules that were developed after the introduction of GAAR into Argentine tax law, the argument would be endorsed by the general legal principle that special subsequent rules supersede prior general rules: *Lex posterior derogat legi priori*, and *Lex specialis derogat legi generali.*

Under a different line of reasoning, however, it might be argued that SAAR merely add another statutory tool to fight tax avoidance and do not prevent the tax agency and the courts from resorting to GAAR, if needed, under the facts and circumstances of a particular case.

In my view, a difference should be made between mechanical (objective), and broadly designed SAAR patterned after GAAR's design elements. The latter appears not to generate actual conflicts, because in designing them, the legislator merely provides for a particular application of the same principle, either based on the significance of the abuse or for other reasons. In any case, the argument would run, the same conclusions might be arrived at by resorting to GAAR in the absence of SAAR. A clear example would be the re-characterization of derivatives when they are substantially equivalent to another transaction having an express treatment in the law (e.g., a synthetic loan).

Among mechanical, objective rules, two sub-groups can be distinctly analyzed. Those permitting the taxpayer to submit evidence to the contrary to escape their application appear to allow the tax agency to resort to GAAR to sustain its own position. For example, a taxpayer may bring evidence in an attempt to prove that a loan was actually intended to be interest-free, thus escaping the application of the interest presumption under the corresponding SAAR; however, the tax agency might sustain the argument based on GAAR that unless such evidence is conclusive, an interest-free loan between companies is inconceivable in principle, since all acts of businessmen are presumably made with consideration under private law.

As regards mechanical objective-type SAAR allowing no evidence to the contrary, the argument could be made that if the taxpayer's transaction does not fall within the scope of the respective rule, GAAR should not be subsidiarily applied. Thus, for example, if directors' fees in a stock corporation do not exceed the statutory 25/40/60%, depending on the case, of accounting profits for the year, it appears that the tax agency would not be able to discuss the reasonableness of the directors' compensation (and corresponding deduction) based on GAAR, nor require the company to prove that such compensation is commensurate with the directors' activities performed during the year.

Based on the foregoing, it appears to be reasonable and in line with the legislator's policy decisions to sustain as general guidance that the more objective and mechanical the SAAR are, the lesser room for GAAR's subsidiary application exists. However, this view has yet to be tested in court.

4 CONFLICTS BETWEEN GAAR AND INTERNATIONAL SAAR: ORDERING PRINCIPLES

As most Argentine SAAR applied in the international context are mechanically based on objective parameters, (i.e., they are of unavoidable application to the taxpayer if the objective conditions to their application are met) GAAR cannot be subsidiarily applied to enlarge the former scope of application.

Nonetheless, in cases where no SAAR have been provided for in the law to fight the use of distorted legal forms in a given context, the Argentine tax system heavily relies on GAAR to re-characterize international transactions in accordance with their economic or legal substance.

GAAR applied to the characterization of international transactions may overlap with objective SAAR, in cases where the taxpayer is allowed to challenge the latter's application by contesting the factual basis for application and proving against the tax agency's fact-finding. Consider the following example: Precise transfer pricing rules apply to intercompany cross-border dealings between related parties, as defined by ITL. Bearing this in mind, assume that an Argentine exporter (i) sells goods (other than commodities to which the Sixth Transfer Pricing Method applies)[11] to a related entity domiciled in a no or low-tax foreign jurisdiction for subsequent resale to final customers in third countries, (ii) conducts sales to the intermediate foreign entity are at below-market prices, and (iii) leaves a margin with the intermediate company because it resells the products at market prices to the final customers. Let's also assume that the intermediate foreign entity lacks substance, i.e., it is a *paper company* and, hence, that the margin earned by it does not compensate for any actual activities (risks and functions) related to the purchase and resale business.

Under a possible approach, the tax agency might attempt to readjust the export price and income of the Argentine taxpayer by resorting to the transfer pricing rules and

11. The so-called Sixth Transfer Pricing Method applies to the export/import of commodities by an Argentine exporter/importer to a foreign related counterparty, channeled through a foreign intermediary entity which is not the final addressee of the goods, in which case, unless the agreements are registered with the tax agency, a non-rebuttable presumption which consists of a deemed transaction price applies: the price to be considered is the prevailing market price as of the date of loading or the actual agreed upon price at the execution date, whichever the highest (accord. s. 17.6, ITL). The rule also applies when the foreign intermediary is a related entity and the final purchaser/seller is unrelated to the Argentine exporter or importer, as the case may be. This is a purely mechanical non-rebuttable SAAR which, as such, excludes any potential application and, overlap with GAAR.

methods provided for in ITL and its implementing regulations. However, under the facts and circumstances of the case, the tax agency might alternatively resort to GAAR, prove that the foreign intermediate entity lacks any substance, that the transaction is, in fact, a sham, and, on that basis, take the position that the intermediate company should be disregarded, and its income fully attributed to the Argentine exporter.

As long as all relevant facts may be properly evidenced by the tax agency, this last approach might be appropriate, and there are no ordering rules under ITL that would prevent the agency from following this approach instead of readjusting the export price pursuant to the transfer pricing mechanism. Moreover, this view is consistent with the interpretation sustained in the case of domestic GAAR and SAAR, in that as long as SAAR allow the taxpayer to escape their consequences by proving otherwise (as would precisely be the case under the transfer pricing rules), the tax agency should be free to counteract any nonconclusive evidence submitted by the taxpayer by resorting to GAAR.

Similar outcomes occurred under prior law with the tax international transparency rules then in force. Until the 2017 tax reform, the scope of application of the international transparency rules was limited to the current attribution to Argentine shareholders of income from passive activities obtained by tax haven corporations. In that scenario, GAAR might have been applied to similar cases not expressly contemplated by the statute, e.g., when the income was obtained through a different foreign vehicle (a foreign trust) if it was proved that no actual transfer of title to the income-producing assets had taken place from the domestic settlor to the foreign trust, as in the case in which the settlor was also the beneficiary of the foreign trust.[12]

5 APPLICATION OF DOMESTIC GAAR TO TREATIES: ADMINISTRATIVE AND JUDICIAL PRECEDENTS

Argentina currently has DTAs in force with the following countries: Australia, Bolivia, Brazil, Belgium, Canada, Chile, Denmark, United Arab Emirates, Germany, Finland, France, Italy, Mexico, the Netherlands, Norway, Russia, Qatar, Spain, Sweden, Switzerland, and the United Kingdom.

With the exception of the DTA with Bolivia (which is patterned after the model tax treaty approved by Decision 40 of the Andean Group) and the DTA with Brazil in its original text (which although structured after the OECD MC allowed both countries to apply their domestic legislation with complete freedom),[13] all other DTAs currently in force are structured along the lines of the OECD MC, with certain modifications.

12. *See*, accord. Ruling 23/00; Tax Court, May 29, 2002, *Julio César Moreno*. This example is no longer valid under current law due to the changes introduced to the international tax transparency regime, and a new SAAR applicable to foreign trusts which somehow codified prior administrative and judicial precedents on the dispossession of assets in trusts.
13. The DTA with Brazil has been amended by an additional amending protocol signed by the contracting parties on July 21, 2017. Among the many changes, those concerning PEs, new withholding ceilings at source on dividends, interest, and royalties, as well as a new LoB provision are worth mentioning.

Deviations from the OECD MC are the result of bilateral negotiations and the acceptance by the contracting foreign state (to varying extents) of variations reflected in the United Nations Model Convention (UN MC). Additional DTAs, not yet in force, have been signed with Austria, China, Japan, Luxemburg, and Turkey, as well as a new Protocol with France.

Before the 1994 constitutional amendment, and according to section 31 of the Argentine Constitution, the Constitution itself, the laws passed by the National Congress, and the treaties with foreign countries were all considered as the supreme law of the Nation. Within this constitutional framework, the legal authority of international treaties was thus equal to that of other federal statutes. Therefore, a treaty might supersede a prior law and a law might supersede a prior treaty, following the principle stating that subsequent law prevails over prior law (*leges posteriores priores contrarias abrogant*).[14]

In *re Ekmekdjian v. Sofovich* (1992),[15] and based on the application of section 27 of the Vienna Convention (ratified by Argentina in 1972), the Argentine Supreme Court substantially changed its former position, stating that conventional international law takes precedence over internal law. This last principle was given constitutional status by the 1994 constitutional amendment. Section 75, 22 of the Argentine Constitution, as amended, sets forth the principle that international treaties approved by Congress prevail over internal laws. As such, a subsequent internal statute (for instance, a domestic income tax amendment) may not override the provisions of an existing DTA.

Regarding the application of GAAR in the context of a DTA, there would be no domestic legal obstacles to apply them in connection with the interpretation of DTAs, or acts or situations of taxpayers subject to DTA provisions.[16]

In addition to the domestic principles and interpretation methods of tax law, principles contained in sections 31-33 of the Vienna Convention also apply to the interpretation of Argentine DTAs.[17] Among these principles, those contained in section 31 of the Vienna Convention deserve particular attention.[18]

14. *See*, Vicchi, (Argentine Report), *Interpretation of Double Taxation Conventions*, LXXVIIIa Cahiers de Droit Fiscal International (1993), pp. 161 ff., at pp. 162-164. The Supreme Court applied these principles *in re S.A. Martin & Cía. Ltda.* (1963) and S.A. *Esso Petrolera Argentina* (1968); Fallos 257:99 and Fallos 271:7, respectively.
15. Fallos 315:1492; *see also Cafés La Virginia*, Fallos 315:1282.
16. Accord. Vicchi, *supra* n. 14, at p. 169, 174; cfr. Díaz Sieiro, *Argentine Report, Form and Substance in Tax Law*, LXXXVIIa Cahiers de Droit Fiscal International, p. 71, at pp. 89-90, and Bugallo, *Compatibilidad de las Cláusulas Antiabuso con los Tratados de Doble Imposición*, Bulletin Argentine Association of Fiscal Studies, March/02, pp. 39 ff.
17. *See* accord. Asorey, *Los tratados internacionales y el ejercicio del poder tributario en América Latina*, RDF 5/07, p.5 ff., Lexis Nexis, November/December 2007. The Vienna Convention was ratified by Argentina through law 19,865 (1972). As regard OECD's position on the issue and the Copernican twist towards allowance of GAAR's application in a treaty setting, *see* Teijeiro, *Abuso o uso impropio de tratados de doble imposición. Medidas unilaterales y bilaterales para prevenirlo. La experiencia en el derecho comparado y en la Argentina*, RDF 5/07, p. 205, ff, at 232/233, Lexis Nexis, November/December 2007.
18. For a detailed discussion of the interpretation provisions of the Vienna Convention, *see* Vogel and Prokisch (General Report), *Interpretation of Double Taxation Conventions*, LXXVIIIa Cahiers de Droit Fiscal International, pp. 55 ff, at pp. 66-74.

As a general rule, and until recently, Argentine DTAs have not contained express anti-treaty shopping rules and have been silent on the possible application, and interpretation of the domestic GAAR of contracting states.[19] Recently established DTAs already in force, however, do contain treaty GAAR and/or LoB provisions (notably the treaties with Spain, Chile, Mexico, United Arab Emirates, and the amending protocol with Brazil).

DTAs can be abused, either by treaty-partner residents or residents of third countries to whom, by their special personal scope, DTA rules are not intended to reach. The issue here is whether a treaty-partner domestic GAAR may apply to its internal treaty interpretation, despite the fact that the DTA is silent on the matter, as was the case with most Argentine DTAs until recently.

The case for the application of these rules in a treaty setting might be supported by the following reasoning: (i) GAAR are an interpretative device aimed at making other rules (whether taxing rules or rules limiting tax benefits) to be applied to the true extent intended for by the legislator or in accordance with the shared expectations of the treaty-partners concerned; (ii) since other states also have an interest in avoiding the unintended application of treaty benefits, the application of such rules would be legitimated by general customary principles of international law; and (iii) to the extent that a DTA recognizes a contracting state's right to tax a particular item of income, general principles would allow the taxing state's domestic rules (including GAAR) to apply when the latter exercises its taxing rights under the DTA unless expressly forbidden thereunder.

Nonetheless, no matter how appealing the preceding reasoning may appear, some connected legal issues should be clarified before risking a definitive answer on the matter. These include: (i) whether the interpretation provisions of the Vienna Convention, to which Argentina is a party, allow sustaining the subsidiary application of GAAR in a treaty setting; (ii) if so, whether the constitutional prevalence of DTAs over domestic law makes a difference, thus potentially preventing domestic GAAR from being applied to DTAs; and finally, (iii) if no authority preventing domestic GAAR's application to DTAs is found, whether some other conditions or limitations are to be considered for the application of domestic GAAR not to be judged by the other treaty-partner as a breach of the DTA itself.

As regards the issue of whether GAAR apply in a treaty setting, Argentine scholars' opinions differ.[20] Contradicting opinions have also been sustained among eminent foreign scholars.[21]

---

19. *See* Teijeiro, *Argentine Anti-Avoidance Rules: Application under Domestic and International Conventional Law*, Tax Notes International, October 2003, pp. 89 ff; *see also* Teijeiro, *The Argentine Tax Treaty Network: A Safe Harbor for Foreign Taxpayers*, Tax Notes International, January 19, 1999, pp. 287 ff. Teijeiro, *LoB Clauses, PPT Standard and the Latin American Treaty Network Choices*, Kluwer International Tax Blog, June 5, 2015; Teijeiro, *Argentine Treaty Network: Will the Schoppable Treaty Soon Became an Extinct Species*, Kluwer International Tax Blog, February 29, 2016. As an exception, limited in scope LoB clauses existed previously under the DTAs with Spain (the old treaty), the U.K. and Sweden.
20. In favor of GAAR's application *see* Vicchi, *supra* n. 14, at p. 174, Tarsitano, *Argentine Report, Tax Treaties and Tax Avoidance: Application of Anti-Avoidance Provisions*, LIXVa Cahiers de Droit Fiscal International, pp. 59 ff. Teijeiro, *Abuso o uso impropio de tratados de doble imposición.*

Assuming that the application of GAAR does not conflict with the Vienna Convention because its clauses do allow deviance from strict textualism when the shared intent of the treaty-partners is not manifest in the text, one may take the position that GAAR might only contradict a particular DTA, depending on its wording and the facts and circumstances under which GAAR are intended to be applied. This position is based on the premise that the rule *pacta sunt servanda* does not solely require a literal interpretation of a DTA.

Moreover, the constitutional prevalence of DTAs over domestic legislation under Argentine law would not be, by itself, a decisive feature that prevents GAAR from being applied in a treaty setting either, as long as that application—generally allowed under a broad construction of section 3, 2 of Argentine DTAs—does not imply a violation of the treaty text and purpose, and/or obligations of the taxing jurisdiction under the DTA.[22]

In addition to the foregoing, it appears reasonable to sustain that a functional harmonization between a DTA's provisions and the domestic tax laws of the contracting parties -the preservation of which should be viewed as forming part of the contracting parties' intent, unless otherwise expressly provided in the DTA–also endorses GAAR application to the same extent as authorized by the parties' domestic rules.

Within this view, it should be clear that the state of residence retains full jurisdiction to take measures if one of its residents makes an abusive use of a DTA. This would be the case, for example, if an Argentine resident channeled back foreign funds to Argentina through an intermediate entity domiciled in a treaty-partner jurisdiction, thus availing himself of treaty-protected income only available to true residents of the other contracting state.[23]

On the contrary, it appears that the source state should be allowed to apply domestic GAAR to deny treaty benefits to a resident of the other contracting state in more limited circumstances. This is the Argentine position, as reflected in the regulations issued by the tax agency, which rely on the other contracting state's competent

Medidas unilaterales y bilaterales para prevenirlo. La experiencia en el derecho comparado y en la Argentina, RDF 5/07, pp. 205, ff, at 232/233, Lexis Nexis, November/December 2007; against GAARs application; Diaz Sieiro, *supra* n. 16, at pp. 89-90, and Bugallo, *supra* n. 18. Díaz Sieiro appears to sustain his opinion on the constitutional prevalence of DTAs over domestic rules according to the 1994 Argentine constitutional amendment.

21. *See, inter alia*, Jeffery, *The Impact of State Sovereignty on Global Trade and International Taxation*, Kluwer, Chapter 4, pp. 102-112; IFA Congress Seminar, *How Domestic Anti-avoidance Rules Affect Double Taxation Conventions*, Seminar Series 19 c, 1994 Congress, pp. 6-9 (Dr. Lowe's opinion), pp. 9-10 (Prof. Laule's opinion), and pp. 10-11 (Mr. Gustasson's opinion) —who express the opinion that a DTA does not affect the application of domestic anti-avoidance rules—, pp. 11-15 (Mr. Katz's opinion, who shares that view within certain limitations). Dr. Lowe also opines that application of domestic anti-avoidance provisions does not conflict with the Vienna Convention (*id.*, p. 23). All these opinions preceded the changes introduced to the Commentaries of the OECD MC in 2003.
22. *See* OECD MC, 2010, Commentary on Article 1, specially paras 22 and 23.
23. Teijeiro, *supra* n. 20, at pp. 238-239.

authority declaration of residence to recognize treaty benefits afforded under a DTA to the residents of the treaty-partner jurisdiction.[24]

However, no similar limitation should apply to the source jurisdiction to re-characterize a transaction under domestic GAAR, unless such a re-characterization is contrary to the DTA's definitions or the parties' shared intent (as reflected in the DTA), in full accordance with section 3, 2 of the OECD MC and similar provisions of Argentine DTAs.

In line with the above-referred position, there are a couple of isolated administrative precedents dealing with inbound transactions. Both deal with the re-characterization of income at source and neither challenge the residency of the treaty-partner beneficiary. One of these precedents was issued by the Tax Agency on January 30, 1996,[25] and addressed the re-characterization of Argentine source income to treaty-partner residents by applying GAAR to the assessment of facts under the DTA with Italy and Spain. In the case at hand, insurance premiums paid by a local borrower to foreign insurers, in connection with money lent to it by foreign banking institutions located in Spain and Italy, were deemed subject to income tax withholdings applicable to interest since, in the tax agency's view, the economic reality showed that through those payments the borrower was, in fact, assuming a higher financial cost equivalent to the insurance cost incurred by the lender to cover the potential insolvency risk of the borrower. The other case is from the Argentine Competent authority (*Dirección Nacional de Impuestos* or DNI) dealing with the reallocation of interest income from DEG to participants under a participated loan agreement governed by the DTA with Germany.[26]

On the contrary, there are numerous precedents of GAAR re-characterization in outbound situations, i.e., affecting Argentine residents' round-tripping investments and income through DTAs.[27]

In Memorandum DNI 64/09, the fact matrix before DNI includes an Argentine resident holding a 99% equity participation in an Austrian holding intermediary company which, in turn, held a 100% participation in a second-tier BVI corporation.

According to the old Austrian DTA, an Argentine resident's holding in an Austrian intermediary and dividends received from that company were not taxable in Argentina by personal assets tax (PAT) and income tax (only a 15% withholding on dividends applied on actual distributions in Austria). Argentine international transparency rules were also circumvented by the interposition of the Austrian holding so that

24. *Id.*
25. Ruling 57/96.
26. DNI Memorandum 3/06.
27. *See, inter alia,* DNI Memorandum 64/09, use of an intermediary (shell) holding company without any economic substance under the old (no longer in force) DTA with Austria. DNI Memorandum 799/10, double non-taxation obtained by using an interposed holding company under the old (no longer in force) Andean Pack-type treaty with Chile. Similarly, Tax Court, *in re Molinos Río de la Plata*, August 14, 2013, affirmed Federal Court of Claims, Court Room I, May 19, 2016. For an analysis of these precedents, *see* Rey, Argentine rapporteur, Main Subject 2, *Planificación transnacional agresiva y abuso de tratados: herramientas de derecho interno y derecho internacional para contrarrestarlos en la era BEPS*, IX Latin American IFA Congress, Buenos Aires, May 31-June 2, 2017.

tax benefits to which the Argentine taxpayer avails itself by routing the investment through the Austrian holding were apparent. DNI's analysis showed that the Austrian holding was a phantom (shell) company without any economic substance.

The decision in DNI 64/09 characterized the situation as an abuse of the treaty and made reference to the possibility of applying GAAR in that context, in accordance with the opinion of the UN Expert Committee on International Tax Cooperation, Subcommittee on Improper Use of Treaties, and the Commentaries to Article 1, OECD MC, 2008. By applying GAAR in that situation, the Argentine competent authority disregarded the interposed company in the treaty-country jurisdiction and treated the holding of the shares and income obtained by the BVI Corporation as though the interposed company did not exist.

In Memorandum 799/10, DNI dealt with a DTA structured after the Andean Pacific Model Treaty and the interposition of a Chilean holding company (Platform Company) by an Argentine ultimate shareholder. The facts, as referred to therein, included the following: (i) an Argentine parent company held equity in second-tier operating subsidiaries domiciled in Latin American countries having no DTA with Argentina through a wholly owned Chilean holding which enjoyed a special (no-tax) holding regime in Chile. The Chilean DTA did not expressly exclude privileged holding companies from the concept of residents; and (ii) by interposing the Chilean holding, the Argentine parent corporation avoided the impact of taxation on dividends in Argentina; dividends that were made up with profits coming from the second-tier operating subsidiaries which, would have otherwise been fully taxable in Argentina (i.e., if paid directly by the operating subsidiaries to the parent Argentina corporation).

On the basis of the facts at hand, the Argentine DNI sustained that: (i) DTAs should not be utilized by taxpayers to ameliorate or eliminate the tax burden through legal forms that would not be adopted but for the tax advantages deriving therefrom; (ii) domestic GAAR may and should be applied to avoid abusive schemes, even in a treaty setting; (iii) considering the Chilean Platform company regime and the DTA rules attributing tax jurisdiction to the parties thereto, the reason to interpose the holding was to deviate dividend income coming from Uruguay and Peru (where the operating subsidiaries were domiciled) that would have otherwise been taxed in Argentina, with the end result of benefiting from a double non-taxation; (iv) double non-taxation obtained by interposing a Chilean Platform company between the Peruvian and Uruguayan subsidiaries, on one hand, and the Argentine Parent on the other hand, contradicted the DTA and implied an abusive conduct which might be challenged under domestic GAAR; (v) from a different perspective, it was also sustained that DTAs are aimed at avoiding double taxation and to that end, treaty-partners should maintain an income tax of general application, and the Chilean Platform company regime was alien to the income system of general application in Chile; and (vi) for that very reason, in the DNI's opinion, the Platform company was beyond the scope of the Chilean DTA; it did not qualify under Article 1 of the DTA (taxes covered), as that article refers to subsequent amendments and replacing taxes using an analogous tax basis to the income tax, and not to subsequent promotional regimes resulting in double non-taxation.

The Competent Authority's opinion in the DNI Memorandum 799/10 gave rise to the *Molinos Río de la Plata* case, first decided by the Tax Court on August 14, 2013.

In line with the previous administrative decision, the Tax Court upheld AFIP's tax claim against the company arguing, *inter alia*, that: (i) there was an abuse of the treaty so that the tax agency (AFIP)'s administrative tax assessment taxing dividends received by *Molinos* in Argentina had to be confirmed; (ii) to find the existence of an abuse, the Tax Court applied domestic GAAR and considered that the Platform Corporation was not the effective beneficiary of the dividend paid out by the operating subsidiaries; (iii) though the effective beneficiary concept was alien to the text and spirit of the DTA (which, as anticipated, was patterned after the Andean Pack Model), the Court found that a deemed "effective beneficiary" concept was built into the applicable GAAR; and, finally, (iv) the Court sustained that a DTA might be used to mitigate or reduce the tax burden, but not to eliminate that tax burden altogether (double non-taxation).

Critics against the Tax Court's decision were widespread and focused on the following considerations: (i) the application of GAAR should not have resulted in a successful challenge of the Platform Company under the fact and circumstances of the case, since there was no apparent distortion of the legal form utilized by the taxpayer. In effect, GAAR consist of a sham-type provision according to which whenever a manifest discrepancy exists between the legal forms used and the economic substance of the transaction, the latter prevails to re-characterize the transaction or redefine the parties thereto for tax purposes. If such a discrepancy exists, the legal forms are to be discarded, regardless of the intention of the taxpayer, i.e., regardless of whether the intention was to avoid taxes or to pursue a legitimate business purpose. On the contrary, if such a discrepancy does not exist, the legal transaction may not be challenged, whatever its purpose, unless it is evidenced that the taxpayer acted *in fraud legis*; (ii) pursuing a tax advantage or benefit under the DTA (e.g., double non-taxation) was not, per se, enough to ignore the intermediate holding, as argued in connection with the Chilean Platform company; (iii) to legitimately challenge the structure under GAAR, the Tax Court should have evidenced that the Chilean holding was not the actual (beneficial) owner of the dividends received from the Peruvian and Uruguayan subsidiaries, and/or lacked economic substance (i.e., it was a paper company which exercised no effective management or administration of the holdings). None of that was undoubtedly evidenced in the case, but the mere fact that dividends received had been immediately redistributed by the Chilean holding to the Argentine Parent Company; (iv) if the preceding conditions were met (the Chilean Platform company used and enjoyed the dividend income without a legal or contractual obligation to pass it over to the Argentine Parent, and managed the equity participations it held), the Chilean holding might not be deemed to have been interposed *in fraus legis,* nor would have failed meeting the substance test. Again, it was not evidenced that dividends received by the Chilean Platform were not its own (i.e., that the holding was constrained to pass the dividends on to the Argentine parent).

In that context, it has been argued that GAAR could not have been resorted to legitimately ignore the Chilean company as a treaty beneficiary, even if, as it appears to be the case, the structure was designed to save taxes (i.e., it was a tax-geared structure).

The Federal Court of Appeals affirmed the Tax Court decision, considering that: (i) the Chilean holding has not been created with the purpose of carrying on the international expansion of the economic group led by the Argentine parent, but with the sole objective of obtaining tax benefits under the Chilean DTA, thus permitting to label it as a mere conduit; (ii) the taxpayer's construction of the DTA contravenes the principle of good faith contemplated in the Vienna Convention; and (iii) the lack of anti-abuse clauses in the DTA allows the application of GAAR.[28]

On November 28, 2018, the Prosecutor before the Supreme Court ruled in favor of the taxpayer, arguing *inter alia* that the honest effort of the taxpayer to limits its taxes to the legal minimum is not reprehensible; that is to say, that a legitimate tax saving in itself is not questionable. In his opinion, the Prosecutor stated that the benefits of the old DTA with Chile were not subject to an "anti-abuse" clause that requires certain minimum substance in the distributing treaty company. In this sense, the opinion stated that the fact that Molinos Chile was a "conduit" company for the tax agency did not violate the DTA. The Prosecutor also rejected the application of GAAR not expressly contemplated in the DTA, since the latter holds a constitutional hierarchy superior to domestic laws. On that basis, the Prosecutor's opinion concluded that even in order to avoid a supposed double non-taxation, the tax administration's assessment could have not relied on Article 2, TPL, i.e., on the principle of economic reality.

A final decision of the case by the Argentine Supreme Court was issued on September 2, 2021, ratifying the decisions of the Tax Court and the Federal Court of Appeals.[29]

6 BILATERAL TREATY GAAR AND LoBs

In June 2008, Argentina unilaterally terminated a number DTAs, including its treaties with Austria, Spain, Switzerland, and Chile. While reasons for termination varied the alleged misuse of the DTAs by Argentine residents through round-trip schemes were at the basis of the DTA terminations with Austria, Spain, and Chile.[30]

In the case of Austria and Chile, a couple of administrative pronouncements from the Argentine Competent authority preceded or followed termination; the decisions set forth application parameters of the DTAs based on GAAR.[31] It is also true that the DTA with Austria, Spain, and Chile provided benefits concerning PAT on the holding of

28. Rey, *supra* n. 27, at p. 27.
29. For a description and commentary of that judgment with my own critical comments, see Teijeiro, A Pre-BEPS, long-expected Landmark Argentine Supreme Court Decision on DTA interpretation and Domestic GAAR Application in a treaty Setting, Kluwer International Tax Blog, September 11, 2021.
30. *See* Teijeiro, *La Terminación Unilateral de los Convenios Internacionales de Doble Imposición: Cuestiones Jurídicas bajo el Derecho Internacional Convencional y el Ordenamiento Constitucional Argentino*, RDF Abeledo Perrot, November/December 2008.
31. The already discussed DNI Memorandum 64/09 and DNI Memorandum 799/10 (with its progeny, the *Molinos Río de la Plata* case).

shares in Argentine companies which were not reproduced in any other Argentine DTA, and there was a decision to cut off this benefit altogether.

Speculation of the reasons for the termination of the Spanish DTA also included the Argentine government's reluctance to afford treaty benefits to Spanish holding companies (ETVEs—*Entidad de Tenencia de Valores Extranjeros*) and to keep recognizing the PAT exclusion on equity holdings in Argentine companies to Spanish residents (including ETVEs).[32] This last benefit under the previous DTA did not have great significance in revenue terms per se, but for the fact that, at least under a possible interpretation, such benefit had a contagious effect: Under the prevailing administrative interpretation until 2006, to the extent the benefit was afforded under a DTA, the same treatment was to be recognized to residents in Latin American states that were members of the Latin American Integration Association (ALADI).[33]

In the case of Switzerland, the main reason for termination was a clause in the Additional Protocol to the DTA which, by equaling the treatment of royalties to that afforded under Swiss law, in practice implied that Argentine-source royalties went fully untaxed, an unparalleled benefit in the Argentine treaty network. Additionally, Argentina wished to correct the treatment afforded to the insurance business and to introduce a wide exchange of information clause, similar to the last OECD version.

Today, Argentina has new DTAs in force with Spain, Switzerland Chile, Mexico, the United Arab Emirates, and an Amending Protocol with Brazil. New treaties not yet in force have additionally been signed with Austria, China, Japan, Luxembourg, and Turkey, as well as an additional Protocol with France.

Section I (persons covered) of the new Spain DTA remains unchanged, so the DTA keeps applying to residents of one or both treaty-partner countries (whether individuals or legal entities) without further qualifications. The DTA application is therefore not conditional upon the resident being taxable or taxed in its jurisdiction of residency; thus, Spanish holding companies (ETVEs) are not subjectively excluded from the new DTA's scope of application.

However, in connection therewith, two clauses in the accompanying Memorandum of Understanding (MoU) are worth mentioning: Clause A, which allows a treaty-partner (e.g., Argentina) to apply domestic GAAR to prevent tax avoidance or evasion; and Clause B, which provides for the application of the beneficial ownership requirement not only in connection with dividends, interest, and royalties (sections 10, 11 and 12) but also in connection with income of any nature received by a treaty-partner beneficiary. Thus, the relevant innovation arising from the new Spanish DTA is the express treaty reference to the application of domestic GAAR.

Additionally, sections C and D of the MoU annexed to the Spanish DTA further provide that the DTA will not disallow the application of domestic rules of fiscal transparency (controlled foreign corporation regime) or thin capitalization rules and that sections 10, 11, 12, and 13 (dividends, interest, royalties, and capital gain provisions) will not apply whenever the primary purpose or one of the primary

32. Section 22, 4 of the old Spanish DTT.
33. DNI Memorandum 1000/02, October 15, 2002; cfr. General Attorney Office (PTN)'s opinion 172/06, June 30, 2006 and AFIP External Note 5/08, July 31, 2008.

purposes of a person related to the origination or assignment of shares or other dividend-generating rights, the origination or assignment of an interest-bearing credit, or the origination or assignment of a royalty-generating right, is to obtain the benefits of such sections. This last rule was a concrete predecessor of MLI's PPT (principal purpose test).[34]

Although perhaps less ambitiously, the new Swiss DTA sets forth an anti-abuse provision aimed at avoiding that residents of third countries may take advantage of the benefits of the DTA by structuring abusive tax planning that leads to double non-taxation.[35]

The new DTA with Chile follows the OECD structure and sets forth strict rules to avoid round-trip treaty shopping schemes. To that end, the Chilean DTA[36] provides (for the first time within the Argentine treaty network) an LoB clause, coupled with a PPT rule patterned after Action 6, BEPS.[37]

Similarly, the treaty with Mexico provides express rules to avoid treaty shopping.[38] The rules consist of an LoB clause and a PPT standard patterned after section 6, BEPS. Moreover, paragraph 6 of section 28 provides that: *The provisions of this agreement shall not prevent any contracting state from applying its provision concerning thin capitalization and controlled foreign corporations (in the case of Mexico, preferential tax regime) or any anti-abuse rule in force in the domestic legislation of the contracting states*. This express reference to the application of domestic GAAR/SAAR, without further qualifications, and leaves open the issue of treaty rules' prevalence and potential overlap with GAAR/SAAR.

Section 16 of the Amending Protocol with Brazil contemplates a PPT rule[39] and an abridged LoB applicable to legal entities based on equity ownership (50%); as an exception, this rule does not apply where the entity carries out business activities different from the mere holding of securities or other assets.[40]

Finally, section 26 of the UAE DTA contains an express LoB and a PPT (paragraph 2) which functions as an escape from the LoB (i.e., as long as it may be evidenced that the establishment of the taxpayer in any of the contracting states, and/or its transactions did not have as one of its principal purposes to benefit from the DTA provisions).

34. *See* Teijeiro, *LoB Clauses, PPT Standard, and the Latin American Treaty Network Choices*, Kluwer International Tax Blog, June 5, 2015.
35. Section 4, 1, Swiss DTA: When defining resident, that provision adds "... This term, however, does not include any person who is liable to tax in that state in respect only of income from sources in that state or capital situated therein."
36. DAT with Chile, s. 24, paras. 1-5 (LoB); para. 6 (PPT); paras. 7-9 (complementary rules).
37. Teijeiro, *Argentine Treaty Network ... .supra* n. 19.
38. DTA with Mexico, s. 28.
39. Brazil Amending Protocol dated July 21, 2017, s. 16 introducing new s. XXVII to the DTA (paras 1 and 2).
40. Amending Protocol, new s. XXVII, para. 3. Paragraph 4 additionally contemplates a rule specifically addressed to income attributable to a PE situated in a third country and exempt in the treaty-partner country where the head office is situated which is aimed at avoiding a double non-taxation.

7 THE OECD MLI AND POTENTIAL CONFLICTS WITH DOMESTIC AND TREATY GAAR/SAAR: A QUEST FOR ORDERING PRINCIPLES UNDER ARGENTINE DOMESTIC AND TREATY LAW

7.1 Background

The Multilateral Convention to Implement Tax-treaty Related Measures to Prevent BEPS (the Multilateral BEPS Convention or MLI) established the implementation of the treaty-based final BEPS outcomes in one single document.

MLI was aimed at providing a framework that could allow amending existing bilateral treaties at once, bringing them in line with BEPS treaty-related minimum standards and recommendations without the need to endeavor complex and lengthy bilateral renegotiations.

Argentina signed MLI in the inaugural ceremony hosted by OECD in Paris on June 7, 2017, where 76 countries and jurisdictions signed or expressed their intention to sign.[41] However, three years later, ratification of MLI by the Argentine Congress is still pending.

In substance, MLI covers the outcomes of BEPS Actions 2, 6, 7, and 14, focusing on how the Convention would need to modify the provisions of bilateral tax agreements in order to implement those measures. As regards Actions 6, it provides a minimum agreed-upon standard.

The Final Report of Action 6 of OECD/G20 BEPS Action Plan, section A, provided for the new treaty anti-abuse rules, with a certain degree of flexibility on implementation. Thus, the following approach was recommended: (i) the inclusion of a clear statement in the DTA, in the sense that parties to the tax treaty intend to avoid creating opportunities for non-taxation or reduced taxation through tax evasion or avoidance (including treaty shopping arrangements); (ii) a specific anti-abuse or LoB rule; and (iii) a more general anti-abuse rule (the PPT rule) aimed at addressing situations that would not be covered by the LoB rule. Moreover, recognizing that LoB and PPT may not be appropriate for all countries and that domestic law may include provisions that make it unnecessary to combine both to prevent treaty shopping, the Final Report set forth a minimum standard of commitment, consisting of (i) a combined approach of LoB and PPT rule, (ii) a PPT rule alone, or (iii) an LoB rule supplemented by a mechanism that would address conduit financing arrangements, not already dealt with in DTAs.

The Final Report also included in this section A changes to the OECD MC aimed at ensuring that DTAs do not inadvertently prevent application of domestic GAAR to fight strategies that seek to circumvent provisions of domestic tax laws.

Section B of the Final Report provided for a reformulation of the Title and Preamble of the OECD MC, clarifying the shared intention of the parties to avoid

41. Teijeiro, *MLI Minimum Standards on Treaty Shopping and Mutual Agreement Procedure. LATAM Countries' Position*, Kluwer International Tax Blog, July 3, 2017.

creating opportunities for tax evasion and avoidance, in particular through treaty shopping arrangements.

In the same line, MLI (Articles 6 and 7) further deals with the minimum standard and optional alternatives to prevent treaty abuse.

The minimum standard requires (i) the inclusion of an express statement in the Preamble stating the common intention to eliminate double taxation without creating opportunities for non-taxation or reduced taxation through tax evasion or avoidance, including treaty shopping arrangements, and (ii) at least a PPT rule, which is the only approach deemed to satisfy the minimum standard by its own. Options include (i) supplementing the PPT rule by the application of a simplified LoB provision (SLoB), or (ii) a standalone detailed LoB provision, used in conjunction with a mechanism dealing with conduit arrangements not already dealt with in tax treaties. MLI does not include a detailed LoB provision so that parties that prefer to use it are allowed to opt out of the PPT and agree to reach a bilateral agreement that satisfies the minimum standard or accept MLI's PPT as an interim rule.

The Preamble text contemplated in paragraph 1 of Article 6 is to be included in place of or in the absence of similar Preamble language in the Covered Tax Agreement, as defined by MLI. Each party must notify OECD on whether each of its Covered Tax Agreements contains Preamble language and the text of the relevant paragraph. When all contracting parties have made such notification, the Preamble language is to be replaced by the text contained in paragraph 1 of Article 6, MLI.

The PPT rule of the MLI applies in place of or in the absence of similar provisions under the Covered Tax Agreements. A party may choose to apply the SLoB to its Covered Tax Agreements, but the provision shall symmetrically apply to a Covered Tax Agreement only where both contracting jurisdictions have chosen to apply it. A SLoB, however, could still be asymmetrically applied by one of the parties to an agreement, if it has decided to do so when the other party agrees to such application notifying OECD accordingly.

Argentina committed itself to amend its Covered Tax Agreements,[42] adopting the text of the Preamble provided for in Part III, Article 6, 1, MLI, and to adopt the minimum standard consisting of a combination of PPT and SLoB.

7.2 MLI and OECD MC

MLI principles (reflecting the conclusions of BEPS Action 6) are now reflected in the Preamble and in the text of the OECD MC 2017, primarily in Articles 1 (Persons Covered) and 29 (Entitlement to Benefits), and their Commentaries. International tax scholars have extensively explored the very nuances of the new treaty anti-abuse rules,

42. Argentine Covered Tax Agreements for MLI purposes, as of the date of MLI execution, were all treaties in force plus Mexico and UAE, but for Brazil and Germany, both under active renegotiation at that time, and Bolivia.

as well as the potential conflicts of said rules with pre-existing domestic GAAR and SAAR.[43]

In this last respect,[44] it is clear that concrete ordering rules or principles must be developed to furnish the new conventional international law with an elemental predictability and certainty. The following comments address this issue in the context of the Argentine domestic and treaty law.

7.3 Ordering Principles: Domestic GAAR/SAAR, Bilateral PPT and/or LoB, and the Anti-abuse MLI Minimum Standard Adopted by Argentina

Once MLI is fully implemented in Argentina through internal ratification and required notification to OECD, the ordering rules from a theoretical point of view will be rather clear: (i) in accordance with the principle that the MLI minimum standard applies in the absence of similar provisions under the Covered Tax Agreements, bilateral PPT/LoB will prevail over the MLI minimum standard adopted by Argentina; (ii) the MLI minimum standard adopted by Argentina (PPT/SLoB) will apply to Covered Tax Agreements lacking similar provisions; (iii) specific bilateral provisions and MLI's PPT/SLoB incorporated to Covered Tax Agreements will prevail over domestic GAAR/SAAR as a tool to fight tax avoidance (including treaty shopping) under the Argentine tax treaty network. In effect, where the application of the provisions of domestic law and those of DTAs produce conflicting results, the provisions of DTAs are intended to prevail.

43. *See*, *inter alia*, Baez Moreno, *GAARs and Treaties: From the Guiding Principle to the Principal Purpose Test. What Have We Gained from BEPS Action 6*, 45 Intertax 6/7, pp. 432 ff. (2017); Chand, *The Principal Purpose Test in the Multilateral Convention: An In Depth Analysis*, 46 Intertax 1, pp. 18 ff. (2018); Chand, *The Interaction of the Principal Purpose Test (and the Guiding Principle) with Treaty and Domestic Anti-avoidance Rules*, 46 Intertax 2, pp. 115 ff. (2018); Danon, *Treaty Abuse in the Post-BEPS World: Analysis of the Policy Shift and Impact of the Principal Purpose Test for MNE Groups*, 72 Bulletin International Taxation 1 (2018); Mosquera Valderrama, Burgers, *Review of Anti-Avoidance Measures of a General Nature and Scope—General Anti-Avoidance Rules and Other Measures*, 73 Bulletin for International Taxation, 10 (2019); Kuźniacki, *The Principal Purpose Test (PPT) in BEPS Action 6 Practical Application*, 10 World Tax Journal 2 (2018); Elliffe, *The Meaning of the Principal Purpose Test: One Ring to Bind Them All?*, 11 World Tax Journal 1 (2019); *Zahra, The Principal Purpose Test: A Critical Analysis of Its Substantive and Procedural Aspects—Part 1*, Bulletin for International Taxation November 2019, pp. 609 ff.; Freedman, The *UK General Anti-Avoidance Rule: Transplants and Lessons*, Bulletin for International Taxation June/July 2019. pp. 332 ff.; van Weeghel, A Deconstruction of the Principal Purposes Test, 11 World Tax Journal 1 (2019), Lang, *The Signalling Function of Article 29(9) of the OECD Model—The "Principal Purpose Test,"* 74 Bulletin for International Taxation 4/5 (2020): Danon, *The PPT in Post-BEPS Tax Treaty Law: It Is a GAAR but Just a GAAR!* Bulletin for International Taxation April/May 2020, pp. 242 ff.: Mithe, *Critical Analysis of the Principal Purpose Test and the Limitation on Benefits Rule: A World Divided but It Takes Two to Tango*, World Tax Journal, (February 2020), 129; Landsiedel, *The Principal Purpose Test's Burden of Proof: Should the OECD Commentary on Article 29(9) Specify Which Party Bears the Onus?* 13 World Tax Journal 1, (2021).

44. *See*, particularly, Chand and Elliffe, *The Interaction of Domestic Anti-Avoidance Rules with Tax Treaties in the Post-BEPS and Digitalized World*, 74 Bulletin for International Taxation April/May 2020, pp. 304 ff.

Application of the ordering rule referred to in subparagraph (i) of the preceding paragraph may require certain previous definitions in particular cases. For example, query whether the anti-abuse rules applicable under the Spanish treaty currently in force may be deemed "similar" to the MLI minimum standard adopted by Argentina, and, hence, prevail over the latter. In this sense, it is worth reminding that there may be some contradiction between both sets of provisions since under the Spanish treaty the PPT rule is limited to Articles 10-13, and this DTA also made expressly applicable the parties' GAAR to situations under the treaty umbrella. In my view, in this case, the MLI provisions, once effective, should supersede the Spanish treaty provisions since the former are of a wider scope and postpone domestic GAAR to the conventional treaty anti-abuse provisions.

A similar analysis would be required when comparing the MLI anti-abuse provisions with some Covered Tax Agreements, such as the LoB provisions under the Chilean Treaty and the Brazilian Protocol, or the Mexican Treaty which, besides adopting a PPT and an LoB, makes domestic GAAR expressly applicable in the treaty setting; not to mention the current treaty with the United Arab Emirates, where the PPT standard functions not to complement the LoB, but rather as a limit against the objective application of the treaty LoB.

In my view, once the MLI becomes effective, the MLI anti-abuse provisions adopted by Argentina (PPT and SLoB), should supersede and prevail over the previously mentioned DTA clauses with their various nuances. In this sense, a decision will bring certainty to the application of anti-abuse rules to the Argentine treaty network.

An additional complexity hinges on whether such a determination should be unilaterally made by Argentina or in conjunction with the treaty-partner jurisdiction. To the extent that the determination might be viewed to affect international commitments undertaken by Argentina with treaty-partner countries, an agreement as to whether the MLI provisions supersede the application of bilaterally negotiated clauses should be required.

Instead, domestic GAAR will remain available wherever Argentine domestic rules might have been circumvented within a treaty umbrella. This position not only arises from MLI itself but is also in line with the status of treaties and their prevalence (pursuant to the Vienna Convention and Argentine Constitutional Law) over domestic legislation. In effect, where the application of the provisions of domestic law and those of DTAs produce conflicting results, the provisions of DTAs are intended to prevail.[45]

In practice, however, it might be troublesome to define whether the treaty and/or domestic rules have been circumvented. Consequently, fine-tuning and prudence would be required to avoid using GAAR as a cure-all subsidiary tool whenever the tax agencies find that the bilateral or multilateral treaty-based anti-abuse rules fall short to apprehend the improper use of a treaty in a given case.

Avoiding GAAR shopping by competent authorities and tax administrations is a great challenge; particularly because these agencies are often inclined to pile up

45. Accord., *contrario sensu* Commentary to Article 1 OECD MC (2017). Paragraphs 77-79.

anti-avoidance rules of a treaty or domestic nature without any hierarchy or prevalence of application to enhance the taxable event and, hence, tax collection.

8 FINAL REMARKS

Anti-abuse measures applicable to international (cross-border) transactions currently proliferate, thereby furnishing tax administrations with efficient tools to fight tax evasion and avoidance in this context.[46]

As a refinement of previously existing domestic GAAR and SAAR, bilateral and multilateral (MLI) treaty anti-abuse responses have established a set of standards for transactions under the treaty umbrella that might create an overlapping effect and hence increase uncertainty among taxpayers unless sound ordering principles are followed in their application.

Some ordering principles are advanced in MLI itself, but others must also be developed to consider the nuances of each jurisdiction's domestic rules and treaty networks, as demonstrated in the preceding discussion focused on Argentina.

46. DAC 6-type rules, such as Argentine AFIP Resolution 4838/20 through which aggressive tax planning schemes using, *inter alia*, DTAs, should be reported, also contribute to ease tax administration's advance notice on this type of transactions.

CHAPTER 9

The DNA of the Principal Purpose Test in the *Multilateral Instrument*

Marcus Livio Gomes

Marcus Livio Gomes examines the content and effect of Article 7 of the Multilateral Instrument (MLI,) namely the anti-abuse provisions and in particular the principal purpose test (PPT). Livio Gomes conceptualises the PPT as a general anti-avoidance rule that in some states will run parallel to domestic rules designed to address the same phenomena. The chapter examines the similarities among the PPT and its domestic general anti-avoidance or anti-abuse rules (GAAR) counterparts in Australia, Canada, South Africa, and the United Kingdom, starting with an exploration of the parameters of the concept of avoidance as it is being developed by the MLI through the PPT.

1 INTRODUCTION

This chapter assesses the future of the anti-abuse provision included in Article 7(1), the PPT, in tax treaties following the entry into force of the MLI. Article 7(1) provides as follows:[1]

> Notwithstanding any provisions of a Covered Tax Agreement, a benefit under the Covered Tax Agreement shall not be granted in respect of an item of income or capital if it is reasonable to conclude, having regard to all relevant facts and circumstances, that obtaining that benefit was one of the principal purposes of any arrangement or transaction that resulted directly or indirectly in that benefit, unless it is established that granting that benefit in these circumstances would be

1. This chapter is based on the article ML Gomes, 'The DNA of the Principal Purpose Test in the Multilateral Instrument', *Intertax*, vol. 47, no. 1, 2019.

in accordance with the object and purpose of the relevant provisions of the Covered Tax Agreement.

The MLI contains a diverse set of provisions, all of which are intended to counter abusive practices that have developed over the years. This section, however, focuses only on the GAARs brought about through the PPT, which specifically addresses the prevention of treaty abuse, relying on the core concept of a 'minimum standard' as envisaged by the *Action 6 Final Report*.[2]

A complete analysis of anti-abuse provisions in a post-MLI world is beyond the scope of this chapter because such an analysis would require a comprehensive assessment of the effects of each provision of the MLI on existing tax treaties. Such a detailed analysis exceeds the confines of this research. For this reason, the content and effect of Article 7 of the MLI is the most prominent theme of this article, despite the interaction of domestic anti-avoidance rules with tax treaties and the interaction of specific anti-avoidance rules SAARs with GAARs, which will not be discussed.

On the other hand, international tax law is in constant flux, as the MLI is still open for signature, thus making it possible for other states to join at any time. This requires periodically updating research to ensure that all of the facts and excerpts are accurate and that none of the cited states or jurisdictions has deviated from their preliminary positions with regard to the MLI.

The subject matter of this chapter is approached systematically, as the research reviews the measures currently available in the *OECD Model Convention* (2017)[3] (the OECD Model) to counter tax avoidance. This is followed by comments on the content of the *Action 6 Final Report* and the relevant provisions of Article 7 of the MLI, especially the PPT. The main differences between primary and secondary elements are highlighted. The author considers the DNA of GAARs to demonstrate which of them has inspired the PPT in the MLI regarding primary elements and secondary elements.

In light of a pattern in the anti-avoidance rule, and as a consequence of the increasing importance of GAARs in both domestic and international settings, the objective of this study is to develop a theoretical framework to scrutinise the GAARs introduced by the PPT and future general tax treaty anti-avoidance rules. As such, this study develops such a framework and determines the structure and elements that can be used to identify and evaluate the PPT as a GAARs. The theoretical framework is based on a thematic analysis of GAARs literature and will be used to identify strengths and weaknesses to offer guidance regarding developing the implementation, application, operation and interpretation of the PPT in the MLI.[4]

The descriptive aspect of this piece aims to provide a framework for comparing solutions to common policy issues by identifying patterns for compatibility or comparison in domestic tax systems and tax treaties concerning GAARs.[5] To accomplish

---

2. OECD, *Action 6 Final Report 2015*.
3. OECD, *Model Tax Convention on Income and on Capital*.
4. D Fernandes and K Sadiq, 'A Principled Framework for Assessing General Anti-Avoidance Regimes', *Brit. Tax Rev.*, no. 2, 2016, ss 1, 3, p. 172.
5. M O'Brien, 'Canada — GAARs: An Emerging Trend in the Tax Landscape', in M Lang, J Owens, P Pistone, A Rust, J Schuch and C Staringer (eds), *GAARs: A Key Element of Tax Systems in the*

this objective, the terms 'scheme, arrangement or transaction', 'purpose, motive and intention', and 'tax benefit, gain or advantage' will be used interchangeably.

Furthermore, there may be different interpretive approaches when comparing common law and civil law jurisdictions. A civil law approach will typically interpret the respective statute based on its written wording, inherent purpose, historical background, and systematic integration within the tax system. In comparison, a common law approach will usually refer to a 'purposive interpretation' of the respective statute.[6] Because of these different approaches, the statutory tax laws of common law countries are typically very detailed in nature, being based on rules rather than principles.[7] Conversely, a typical civil law tax statute tends to be built on principles and is drafted in an open-ended manner.[8] Consequently, legal transplants raise problems[9] as they often do not consider local factors that play a critical role in tax policy design, which is based on tax culture, economic structure and institutional background.[10]

The transplantation of tax laws from one country to another commonly occurs worldwide and the base erosion and profit shifting (BEPS) Project demonstrates this phenomenon, ranging from the wholesale adoption of entire sections of tax law to the importation of a single rule. Such cross-cultural transplantation raises interesting

---

Post-BEPS Tax World, Amsterdam, IBFD, 2016, pp. 151-155; BJ Arnold, 'The Canadian General Anti-Avoidance Rule', in GS Cooper (ed.), *Tax Avoidance and the Rule of Law*, Amsterdam, IBFD, 1997, pp. 230-238; Garbarino 'Comparative Taxation and Legal Theory: The Tax Design Case of the Transplant of General Anti-Avoidance Rules', pp. 765, 767-772; V Thuronyi, *Comparative Tax Law*, Amsterdam, Wolters Kluwer, 2003, p. 460; JF Garner, 'Use of the Comparative Method in University Courses in Law', *J Soc Pub Teachers of L*, vol. 11, 1971, pp. 134-141.

6. In the UK approach, the term 'purposive interpretation' is not used as a synonym for the civil law concept of 'teleological interpretation', but, rather, it refers to a historical or contextual means of interpretation.
7. *See* J Freedman, 'The United Kingdom — GAARs: An Emerging Trend in the Tax Landscape', in M Lang, J Owens, P Pistone, A Rust, J Schuch and C Staringer (eds), *GAARs: A Key Element of Tax Systems in the Post-BEPS Tax World*, Amsterdam, IBFD, 2016, p. 741.
8. Thuronyi, *Comparative Tax Law*, p. 18; J. Prebble, 'Trends in Anti-Avoidance Legislation', *Asian-Pacific Tax and Inv. Bull.* vol. 9, 1991, pp. 57-67.
9. R Krever, 'Chapter 1. General Report: GAARs', in M Lang, J Owens, P Pistone, A Rust, J Schuch and C Staringer (eds), *GAARs: A Key Element of Tax Systems in the Post-BEPS World*, Amsterdam, IBFD, 2016, pp. 1-20; D Pickup, 'In Relation to General Anti-Avoidance Provisions: A Comparative Study of the Legal Frameworks Used by Different Countries to Protect Their Tax Revenues', in J Freedman (ed.), *Beyond Boundaries: Developing Approaches to Tax Avoidance and Tax Risk Management*, Oxford University Centre for Business Taxation, 2008, p. 9, http://eureka.sbs.ox.ac.uk/3563/1/BeyondBoundaries.pdf (accessed 24 June 2020); R Krever, 'Plain English Drafting, Purposive Drafting, Principle-Based Drafting: Does Any of It Matter?', in J Freedman (ed.), *Beyond Boundaries: Developing Approaches to Tax Avoidance and Tax Risk Management*, Oxford University Centre for Business Taxation, 2008, p. 189; Thuronyi, *Comparative Tax Law*, pp. 190-195.
10. MA Livingston, 'Law, Culture and Anthropology: On the Hopes and Limits of Comparative Tax', *Can J L and Jurisprudence*, vol. 18, no. 1, 2005, pp. 121-124, 131-134; J Li, 'Tax Transplants and Local Culture: A Comparative Study of the Chinese and Canadian GAAR', *Theoretical Inquiries in Law*, vol. 11, no. 2, 2010, pp. 655-657 and 670, http://digitalcommons.osgoode.yorku.ca/scholarly_works/430/, (accessed 24 June 2020); Garbarino, 'Comparative Taxation and Legal Theory: The Tax Design Case of the Transplant of General Anti-Avoidance Rules', pp. 767-772; RM Bird, *The BBLR Approach to Tax Reform in Emerging Countries*, University of Toronto, 25 September 2008, https://papers.ssrn.com/sol3/papers.cfm?abstract_id=1273818 (accessed 24 June 2018).

questions about the actual function of seemingly similar rules in countries with different legal systems, as well as diverse institutional and cultural backgrounds,[11] i.e., mainly civil law vis-à-vis common law countries and developed countries vis-à-vis developing countries.[12] Although the GAARs from different countries appear similar on paper, they diverge greatly in terms of the problems addressed, motivations behind their enactment, application and effect.

Ultimately, all these divergences will be reflected in the PPT since indeterminacy allegations are always based on certain formalistic positions violating the principle of legality, as tax avoidance is the result of deficient work by the legislature and it is therefore the responsibility of the legislature and/or courts to counter loopholes in the system.[13]

As mentioned, two main questions will be analysed. First, what are the common requirements or primary elements and the distinguishing requirements or secondary elements of GAARs workable standards as a generic comparative concept for a legal transplant from the PPT (as a GAAR) to tax treaties? Second, given that more discretionary power will be shifted to tax administrations and, as a result, uncertainty could be a consequence of the introduction of the PPT, how can these problems be limited to provide a balance between protecting the tax base and safeguarding taxpayer rights?

2 STATE-OF-THE-ART: WHAT IF TAX AVOIDANCE WERE AN INTERNATIONAL CONCEPT?

This section addresses how difficult it is to define an 'international standard' of avoidance, not only in the domestic approach but also in the actions of international organisations, as was attempted in the *BEPS Action 6 Final Report*.[14] Furthermore, there are misunderstandings regarding translations of concepts from civil law jurisdictions (i.e., *fraude fiscal*, *elisão fiscal*, *evasão fiscal*, *elusión fiscal*, *evasión fiscal* and *evitation fiscal* from French, Portuguese, Spanish and Italian to English) due to the existence of different legal systems such as common law and civil law in the jurisdictions which compose the tax treaty network.

Despite differences in taxpayer aggressiveness and government reactions, tax evasion, tax avoidance, and tax planning are common features of tax systems worldwide and no single response or jurisdiction has provided a complete solution to this issue.[15] Consequently, there is no universal legal or academic definition of

11. Li, 'Tax Transplants and Local Culture'.
12. For an overview concerning legal culture, *see* M van Hoecke and M Warrington, 'Legal Cultures, Legal Paradigms and Legal Doctrine: Towards a New Model for Comparative Law', *Intl & Comparative LQ*, vol. 47, no. 3, 1998, p. 495.
13. C Palao Taboada, 'OECD Base Erosion and Profit Shifting Action 6', *Bull. Int'l Txn*, vol. 69, no. 10, 2015, s. 3.
14. OECD, *Action 6 Final Report 2015*.
15. Krever, 'Chapter 1. General Report'; M Gammie, 'Tax Avoidance and the Rule of Law: A Perspective from the United Kingdom', in GS Cooper (ed.), *Tax Avoidance and the Rule of Law*,

avoidance,[16] which is usually defined negatively[17] or combined with terms such as reasonable, impermissible and unacceptable[18] or aggressive.[19] The terms tax evasion, tax avoidance and tax mitigation, not to mention tax planning and aggressive tax planning, are often used imprecisely, interchangeably or with varying meanings.[20]

There appears to be substantial consensus that the term 'tax evasion' involves an illegal concealment of facts. As such, the term can be considered synonymous with tax fraud, as it requires falsehood of some kind.[21] The 'tax avoidance' concept comes into play with different meanings,[22] deriving from a country's context or, to some extent, in the context of multilateral agreements such as the MLI. Overall, tax avoidance refers to an activity that aims to reduce tax liability that is not criminal.[23] Tax avoidance seems to exist somewhere between tax evasion and tax mitigation, generally understood as a reduction in tax in such a way that falls within the letter of the law but runs counter to its spirit and purpose.[24]

In civil law countries, this concept would be synonymous with abuse of law, abuse of right, *fraus legis*, legal substance, legal form[25] and so on. Courts in civil law countries, and particularly the European Court of Justice (ECJ), have not always been consistent in distinguishing between these Roman law concepts that are used synonymously by the ECJ.[26] In this article, 'tax mitigation' can be considered synonymous with 'acceptable tax planning' or 'tax minimisation'.[27]

The Netherlands, IBFD, 1997, pp. 210-214; V Thuronyi, 'What Can We Learn From Comparative Tax', *Tax Notes*, vol. 103, no. 4, 26 April 2004, p. 463.

16. EC Ribas, *Tax Avoidance: Limits of Legality in Brazil and the United Kingdom: The Aggressiveness of Taxpayers Developing Legal Techniques for Taking Advantage of Weakness in National Tax Systems*, LAP Lambert Academic Publishing, 19 September 2010, pp. 20-25; J Schwarz, 'Abuse and EU Tax Law', *Bull Intl Fisc Doc*, vol. 62, no. 12, December 2008; H Self, 'Acceptable Tax Avoidance', *Tax J* (5 February 2007), p. 221.
17. P Baker, 'Tax Avoidance, Tax Evasion and Tax Mitigation', 2000, p. 12, https://es.scribd.com/document/262173949/Tax-Avoidance-Tax-MitigationPhilip-Baker (accessed 24 June 2020).
18. Thuronyi, *Comparative Tax Law*, pp. 152-153.
19. P Rosenblatt and ME Tron, 'General Report' in *Anti-Avoidance Measures of General Nature and Scope: GAAR and Other Rules*, The Netherlands, Cahiers de Droit Fiscal International, Studies on International Fiscal Law by the International Fiscal Association, 72nd Congress of the IFA, vol. 103A, 2018, p. 15, http://cnkindia.com/uploads/Frontarticles/ifa-cahier-2018-vol103a.pdf (accessed 26 June 2020).
20. Thuronyi, *Comparative Tax Law*, p. 154.
21. Thuronyi, *Comparative Tax Law*, pp. 154-155. Thuronyi states that, in the end, what type of behaviour constitutes tax evasion depends, nonetheless, on the criminal laws of each country.
22. Thuronyi, *Comparative Tax Law*, p. 155.
23. Thuronyi, *Comparative Tax Law*, p. 155.
24. V Chand, *The Interaction of Domestic Anti-Avoidance Rules with Tax Treaties (with Special Considerations for the BEPS project)*, Zurich, Schulthess, 2018; Z Prebble and J Prebble, 'Does the Use of General Anti-Avoidance Rules to Combat Tax Avoidance Breach Principles of the Rule of Law? A Comparative Study', *St Louis ULJ*, vol. 55, no. 1, 2010, pp. 21, 22, https://scholarship.law.slu.edu/lj/vol55/iss1/8 (accessed 28 June 2020); Thuronyi, *Comparative Tax Law*, p. 156; P Lampreave, 'Anti-Tax Avoidance Measures in China and India: An Evaluation of Specific Court Decisions', *Bull Intl Txn*, vol. 67, no. 1, 2013, p. 50; Baker, 'Tax Avoidance, Tax Evasion and Tax Mitigation', p. 9.
25. Thuronyi, *Comparative Tax Law*, pp. 158ff.
26. M Seiler, *GAARs and Judicial Anti-Avoidance in Germany, the UK and the EU*, Series on International Tax Law, vol. 98, Vienna, Linde, 2016, p. 3.
27. Thuronyi, *Comparative Tax Law*, p. 155.

To tackle avoidance, the most popular techniques are, on the one hand, specific or targeted anti-avoidance rules (SAARs/TAARs), characterised by their specificity, detail and reactiveness, and on the other hand, GAARs, which are broader and uncertain.[28] Concerning this issue, Ana Paula Dourado observes:

> Tax avoidance is a legal concept that emanates from the interpretation of either statutory general anti-avoidance rules or general anti-abuse rules (GAARs),[29] sometimes also from targeted and specific anti-avoidance rules, from the judicial creation of GAARs or a principle of abuse, or from the reconciliatory interpretation of all of the mentioned sources.[30]

It follows that GAARs specify and determine in what circumstances tax advantages –specifically, tax benefits – are not intended to be granted by tax systems, thus empowering the tax administration to tackle avoidance where interpretation of the statutory law is not enough, even if courts are supposed to control the application of the GAARs by tax administrations. Ultimately, a grey zone exists in the limits between tax evasion and legitimate or acceptable tax planning, tax mitigation and tax minimisation as synonyms. Conversely, abusive tax planning, illegal tax avoidance or aggressive tax planning as synonyms are not reported as legal concepts.[31] They are misleading and an obstacle to clearly distinguishing or creating a precise international taxonomy among all these various concepts, as they are directly linked to domestic tax systems. In addition, the legal meaning of 'aggressive tax planning' is not clear.[32]

The new concept of aggressive tax planning 'does not aim to be a type of overriding principle to be applied generally (like a soft law GAARs), nor does it aim to

28. Thuronyi, *Comparative Tax Law*, p. 155.
29. The acronym 'GAAR' stands for statutory 'general anti-avoidance rule' or 'general anti-abuse rule'. The UK GAARs follow the latter as a political message that refers to a narrow approach.
30. AP Dourado, 'Tax Avoidance Revisited in the EU BEPS Context', in AP Dourado (ed.), *Tax Avoidance Revisited in the EU BEPS Context*, EATLP International Tax Series, vol. 15, Amsterdam, IBFD, October 2017, p. 3.
31. Dourado, 'Tax Avoidance Revisited in the EU BEPS Context'.
32. AP Dourado, 'Aggressive Tax Planning in the EU Law and in the Light of BEPS: The ECJ Recommendations on Aggressive Tax Planning and BEPS Actions 2 and 6', *Intertax*, vol. 43, no. 1, 2015, p. 42. Dourado states as follows:

> Until the recent movement against BEPS, a distinction has been made, both in international and in European tax law, between tax evasion, tax avoidance (or abuse, in the terms of the European Court of Justice) and tax planning. Whereas tax evasion corresponds to a tax crime or offense as defined by law, tax avoidance implies a difference between the legal form adopted (which is in conformity with the wording of the law) and the substance of the underlying activity or scheme (the substance is not in conformity with the spirit or purpose of the law) and implies recharacterization of the transaction or series of transactions carried out by the taxpayer. Tax planning has not only been considered legal in international tax law, but also compatible with the fundamental freedoms in EU law and even if aimed at reducing the tax burden, it complies both with the purpose of the legislation (main objective test), and the complementary business purpose test (under international tax law) or the genuine economic activity test (under EU law).

constitute a "rule of teleological interpretation" of the regulatory language'.[33] José Manuel Calderón Carrrero and Alberto Quintas Seara point out that its purpose may lie in changing the way the international tax regime is understood, as a new keystone upon which a new tax model, especially the MLI, should be built. Thus, the concept of 'aggressive tax planning' does not constitute a new 'legal concept' for preventing abusive tax practices and cannot be used as a synonymous category for 'illegal tax avoidance' or 'tax abuse'.[34] It should be seen as a 'new tax policy guiding principle'[35] to highlight a paradigm shift and the new way that the OECD and G20 want the international tax regime in the BEPS Project era to be understood,[36] using the PPT as the main tool. Consequently, it is quite difficult to define an 'international standard' of avoidance, deriving from the action of international organisations, such as BEPS Action 6.[37]

This chapter addresses the tax avoidance concept as it is included in the PPT of the MLI only and does not attempt to define the meaning of tax avoidance in a theoretical manner. Broadly speaking, avoidance can be described as an arrangement that leads to tax advantages, the granting of which is not intended by the legal system.[38] This article will circumvent the conceptual dilemma of conceptualising 'tax avoidance' to prevent misinterpretations.

3 SIMILAR FEATURES OF GENERAL ANTI-AVOIDANCE RULES

This section considers similar and inherent features of GAARs to point out the primary and secondary elements that usually constitute the framework of modern counteracting provisions[39] to create a framework for the PPT. Such elements will be used as a

33. JM Calderón Carrrero and A Quintas Seara, 'The Concept of Aggressive Tax Planning Launched by the OECD and the EU Commission in the BEPS Era: Redefining the Border Between Legitimate and Illegitimate Tax Planning', *Intertax*, vol. 44, no. 3, 2016, p. 210.
34. Dourado, 'Aggressive Tax Planning in the EU Law and in the Light of BEPS', p. 43.
35. Calderón Carrrero and Quintas Seara, 'The Concept of "Aggressive Tax Planning" Launched by the OECD and the EU Commission in the BEPS Era'.
36. Gomes, 'Implementation in Practice of the Principal Purpose Test in the Multilateral Convention'. For a comparison of tax abuse and aggressive tax planning between the OECD/G20 BEPS Project and EU Law, *see* P Piantavigna, 'Tax Abuse and Aggressive Tax Planning in the BEPS Era: How EU Law and the OECD Are Establishing a Unifying Conceptual Framework in International Tax Law, Despite Linguistic Discrepancies', *World Tax J.*, vol. 9, 2017; G Ginevra, 'The EU Anti-Tax Avoidance Directive and the Base Erosion and Profit Shifting (BEPS) Action Plan: Necessity and Adequacy of the Measures at the EU Level', *Intertax*, vol. 45, no. 2, 2017, p. 221.
37. OECD, *Action 6 Final Report 2015.*
38. MP Devereux, J Freedman and J Vella, 'Tax Avoidance', *Oxford University Centre for Business Taxation*, 3 December 2012, pp. 1-21; L Hoffmann, 'Tax Avoidance', *Brit Tax Rev*, vol. 197, 2005; Freedman, 'Designing a General Anti-Abuse Rule', pp. 167-173; Freedman, 'The Anatomy of Tax Avoidance Counteraction: Abuse of Law in a Tax Context at Member State and European Union Level, in Prohibition of Abuse of Law' in R de la Feria and S Vogenauer eds, Hart Publishing, 2011, pp. 365-380.
39. Regarding the EU approach, *see* P Piantavigna, 'The Role of the Subjective Element in Tax Abuse and Aggressive Tax Planning', *World Tax J*, vol. 10, no. 2, 2018. Piantavigna points out that:

> The PPT rule also seems consistent with the language of the ATAD, stating that 'a Member State shall ignore an arrangement or a series of arrangements which, having

generic comparison to highlight the framework of the PPT through the analysis of the primary and secondary features that reflect structural and jurisprudential differences between tax systems that call for a different and more targeted system-specific approach.[40] That being said, the validity of these comparative concepts will be analysed, seeking to find workable standards for a legal transplant[41] to the PPT. Considering that a country's experience with GAARs is unique as a product of interactions among its legislative history, the effectiveness of the tax administration, the approach of the courts and the attitude of taxpayers regarding the concept of tax avoidance, this article will consider how these requirements, primary and secondary elements, could be transplanted to the PPT.[42]

Although statutory GAARs are drafted very differently among jurisdictions, it is still remarkable that the structures of common law and civil law systems indicate that they share many similarities.[43] This is because the term 'general anti-avoidance rule' encompasses a diversity of clauses that are broadly drafted and not univocal for addressing tax avoidance,[44] although there are some principles that can be identified in

---

> been put into place for the main purpose or one of the main purposes of obtaining a tax advantage that defeats the object or purpose of the applicable tax law, are not genuine having regard to all relevant facts and,[119] and is also consistent with the GAAR inserted into the EU Parent-Subsidiary Directive (PSD) of 23 July 1990, which was recast in 2011 and revised in July 2014 and January 2015.[...] An anti-avoidance provision is also contained in the original text of the EU Merger Directive,[123][...] In the EU Interest and Royalties Directive, the use of the word 'motive' is interesting:[...].

40. The taxonomy used in this article was mainly inspired by the taxonomy used in P Rosenblatt, *General Anti-Avoidance Rules for Major Developing Countries*, Amsterdam, Wolters Kluwer, 2014. The same taxonomy was used in Rosenblatt and Tron, 'General Report', p. 11. Other scholars have used similar features: Krever, 'Chapter 1. General Report'; N Orow, *General Anti-Avoidance Rules: A Comparative International Analysis*, Bristol UK, Jordan Publishing Ltd, 2000, pp. xxix-xxxix; B Orow, 'Structured Finance and the Operation of General Anti-Avoidance Rules', *Brit Tax Rev.*, vol. 4, 2004, pp. 410-435.
41. R Krever and P Mellor, 'Australia — GAARs: An Emerging Trend in the Tax Landscape', in M Lang, J Owens, P Pistone, A Rust, J Schuch and C Staringer (eds), *GAARs — A Key Element of Tax Systems in the Post-BEPS World*, Amsterdam, IBFD, 2016, pp. 49-51; J Waincymer, 'The Australian Tax Avoidance Experience and Responses: A Critical Review', in GS Cooper (ed.), *Tax the Rule of Law*, Amsterdam, IBFD, 1997, pp. 248-254; D Dunbar, 'Statutory General Anti-Avoidance Rules: Lessons for the United Kingdom from the British Commonwealth', *Bull. Int'l Txn*, vol. 62, no. 12, 2008, p. 533.
42. Krever and Mellor, 'Australia — GAARs: An Emerging Trend in the Tax Landscape', pp. 49-51; BJ Arnold, 'A Comparison of Statutory General Anti-Avoidance Rules and Judicial General Anti-Avoidance Doctrines as a Means of Controlling Tax Avoidance: Which Is Better? (What Would John Tiley Think?)', in J Every Jones, P Harris and D Oliver (eds), *Comparative Perspectives on Revenue Law: Essays in Honour of John Tiley*, Cambridge University Press, 2008, p. 12.
43. Chand, *The Interaction of Domestic Anti-Avoidance Rules*, pp. 60-61; F Zimmer, 'General Report' in *Form and Substance in Tax Law*, The Netherlands, Cahiers de Droit Fiscal International, Studies on International Fiscal Law by the International Fiscal Association, vol. 87A, 2002, pp. 43-46.
44. Krever, 'Chapter 1. General Report', pp. 1-7; Prebble and Prebble, 'Does the Use of General Anti-Avoidance Rules to Combat Tax Avoidance Breach Principles of the Rule of Law?', pp. 21-46; ZA: South Africa Revenue Service–SARS, *Discussion Paper on Tax Avoidance and Section 103 of the Income Tax Act. 1962 (Act 58 of 1962)*, 2005, pp. 27-28.

formulating a statutory GAARs to be applied in any country.[45] The basic design characteristics or elements that are generally regarded as necessary for a representative of what can be considered as an effective statutory GAARs usually share common features, such as 'scheme, arrangement or transaction', 'tax benefit, gain or advantage', and the 'purpose, motive or intent'[46] that are also present in common law and civil law GAARs.[47] The scope and content of these anti-avoidance measures can be diverse due to the constitutional framework, legal system, legal tradition, historical and political context, and tax culture of a specific country.[48]

When drafting modern GAARs, there is an attempt to eliminate and/or reduce the discretionary power of tax administrations by replacing subjective criteria with more objective tests,[49] including secondary tests to characterise a scheme, arrangement or transaction as tax avoidance,[50] inasmuch as they are not essential and have a circumstantial or ancillary nature for the operation of anti-avoidance rules and doctrines.[51] These secondary tests can derive from civil law concepts, such as 'fraud of law', 'abuse of law'[52] and 'abuse of rights', or from common law concepts, such as 'substance over form', 'step transaction' and 'business purpose'. These secondary tests can also produce different results and comparable[53] or incomparable conclusions.[54] Many of such tests were initially developed by judicial doctrines[55] and later changed to a statutory provision or otherwise disapproved by the judiciary in a reading down or bottom-up judicial doctrine, or overruled by the legislature.

45. Krever, 'Chapter 1. General Report', pp. 5-11; Arnold, 'The Canadian General Anti-Avoidance Rule', pp. 225-230.
46. Rosenblatt and Tron, 'General Report', p. 13; N Orow, *General Anti-Avoidance Rules: A Comparative International Analysis*, p. 64; Gammie, 'Tax Avoidance and the Rule of Law', p. 198; Arnold, 'A Comparison of Statutory General Anti-Avoidance Rules'.
47. Krever, 'Chapter 1. General Report', pp. 1-7; Rosenblatt, *General Anti-Avoidance Rules for Major Developing Countries*, p. 27; A van Rooijen, *Anti-Avoidance Techniques: Canada and the Netherlands: An Overview and Comparative Analysis*, McGill University Press, 1994.
48. Livingston, 'Law, Culture and Anthropology', pp. 121-122; Garbarino, 'Comparative Taxation and Legal Theory', pp. 771-772.
49. D de Cogan, 'Tax, Discretion and the Rule of Law', in C Evans, J Freedman and R Krever (eds), *The Delicate Balance: Tax, Discretion and the Rule of Law*, Amsterdam, IBFD, 2011, pp. 9-10.
50. P Gillett, 'The Consultative Document on a General Anti-Avoidance Rule for Direct Taxes: A View from Business', *Brit Tax Rev*, no. 1, 1999, pp. 1-5.
51. Rosenblatt and Tron, 'General Report', p. 17; Rosenblatt, *General Anti-avoidance Rules for Major Developing Countries*, p. 57.
52. Zimmer, 'General Report', p. 42; D Nelken, 'Using the Concept of Legal Cultures', Austral J Legal Philosophy, vol. 29, 2004, pp. 1-3, http://www.austlii.edu.au/au/journals/AUJlLegPhil/2004/11.pdf (accessed 25 June 2020); Livingston, 'Law, Culture and Anthropology', pp. 121-122; Garbarino, 'Comparative Taxation and Legal Theory', pp. 767-772.
53. Rosenblatt and Tron, 'General Report', p. 14.
54. M Gammie, 'The Judicial Approach to Avoidance: Some Reflections on BMBF and SPI', in J Avery Jones, P Harris and D Oliver (eds), *Comparative Perspectives on Revenue Law: Essays in Honour of John Tiley*, Cambridge University Press, 2008, pp. 25-39.
55. J Li, 'Economic Substance: Drawing the Line Between Legitimate Tax Minimization and Abusive Tax Avoidance', *Can Tax J.*, vol. 54, no. 1, 2006, pp. 32-33; BJ Arnold, 'The Long, Slow, Steady Demise of the General Anti-Avoidance Rule', *Can Tax L.*, vol. 52, no. 2, 2004, p. 504, https://www.ctf.ca/ctfweb/Documents/PDF/2004ctj/04ctj2-arnold.pdf (accessed 25 June 2020).

In this analysis, secondary elements can be grouped into three non-exhaustive categories for comparative purposes, namely (i) elements grounded on the 'rationale, reasonableness or appropriateness' for justifying the rational use of indefinite concepts, (ii) elements related to tests intended to explain a transaction or an arrangement by associating form and motive, such as 'business purpose, non-tax purpose and bona fide purpose' and (iii) tests based on the result of the transaction or arrangement in relation to the apparent policy of the legislation, such as 'parliamentary intention (purposive interpretation)' or, for instance,[56] 'abuse of law and fraud of law' in civil law jurisdictions.

There is no hierarchy between primary and secondary elements. There are two main features to highlight and distinguish these two categories. First, primary elements are the most common features of the GAARs, while secondary elements are used in the new GAARs (like the PPT), as a second specialised level of control of tax avoidance that shift more power to tax administrations to investigate the result of the scheme, arrangement, or transaction.

These primary and secondary elements reflect structural and jurisprudential differences between tax systems that call for a different and more targeted system-specific approach.[57] The validity of these comparative concepts will be analysed, seeking to find workable standards for a legal transplant[58] of the PPT into tax treaties. It should be noted that: (a) a country's experience with a GAAR is unique as a product of the interaction between its legislative tradition and history, the effectiveness of the tax administration, the approach of the courts and these requirements will be transplanted from the PPT to a country's tax treaty system;[59] and (b) general anti-avoidance rules and judicial doctrines, especially its scope and content, can be diverse due to the constitutional framework, legal system, legal tradition, historical and political context, and tax culture of the specific country.[60]

The domestic analysis of its elements will address the GAARs introduced by the PPT. To this end, a brief overview is provided, outlining the basic features included in the GAARs and its possible transplant to the PPT. First, the structure of GAARs and the way their main features may be incorporated into some domestic law will be presented. Second, the structure of GAARs and the way their main features can be incorporated into existing tax treaties through the PPT will be analysed. Next, substantive features of the PPT that have been included in the MLI to address BEPS are detailed.

56. Rosenblatt and Tron, 'General Report', p. 25; Rosenblatt, *General Anti-Avoidance Rules for Major Developing Countries*, p. 58.
57. As mentioned regarding s. 3.1, the taxonomy used in this article was mainly inspired by the taxonomy used in Rosenblatt, *General Anti-Avoidance Rules for Major Developing Countries*, p. 27. The same taxonomy was used by Rosenblatt and Tron, 'General Report', p. 15. Others authors have used similar features: Krever, 'Chapter 1. General Report'; B Orow, 'Structured Finance and the Operation of General Anti-Avoidance Rules', pp. 410-435.
58. Waincymer, 'The Australian Tax Avoidance Experience and Responses'; Dunbar, 'Statutory General Anti-Avoidance Rules'.
59. Arnold, 'A Comparison of Statutory General Anti-Avoidance Rules'.
60. Livingston, 'Law, Culture and Anthropology', pp. 121-122; Garbarino, 'Comparative Taxation and Legal Theory', pp. 771-772.

Although interpretation issues will not be addressed, it is nonetheless critical to highlight that Article 2 of the MLI includes definitions of inherent terms such as covered tax agreement, party, contracting jurisdiction and signatory. It also provides that the interpretation of undefined terms in the MLI will be governed by the relevant bilateral tax treaty at the relevant time unless the context requires otherwise. Consequently, the question arises as to whether such terms should be interpreted by reference to domestic law or through contextual interpretation. As a treaty, the MLI is subject to the provisions of the Vienna Convention on the Law of Treaties (VCLT), which is a treaty concerning the international law on treaties between states. The general rules governing the interpretation of treaties are laid down in Articles 31-33[61] of the VCLT, widely recognised as the authoritative guide to the interpretation of treaties.

As highlighted by Yariv Brauner,[62] it can be useful to divide the MLI into two parts, namely (i) the part that encompasses the instrumental rules of the MLI itself, and (ii) the substantive rules that effectively modify bilateral tax treaties. Concerning the instrumental rules, the context and the object and purpose of the MLI will require a standard and coherent interpretation that cannot be different from one bilateral context to the next. Nonetheless, regarding the provisions that impact bilateral tax treaty norms, Professor Brauner[63] pointed out that the 'MLI provisions must be traced back to the MLI and interpreted taking into account their origins, the multilateral context and the standardization, anti-abuse objective.'

This issue gives rise to the question as to whether there would be two types of provisions within a single bilateral tax treaty, namely the original norms and the new MLI norms. Following Professor Brauner, one could say that the application of the MLI should be viewed as a whole to be subject to the MLI context, and its interpretation must consider the MLI object and purpose. For this reason, the well-known debate concerning Article 3(2) of the OECD Model and the question of consideration of the context, object and purpose when undefined terms in a bilateral tax treaty have domestic law meanings should require the application of the normal VCLT rules of interpretation in any event.

Finally, the relationship between GAARs (such as the PPT) and SAARs is not the focus of this research. This issue was addressed by the phrase 'Notwithstanding any provisions of a [covered tax agreement]' in the PPT rule. This inclusion has stressed the

61. The provision reads as follows:

> Article 31 VCLT
>
> General rule of interpretation 1. A treaty shall be interpreted in good faith in accordance with the ordinary meaning to be given to the terms of the treaty in their context and in the light of its object and purpose. 2. The context for the purpose of the interpretation of a treaty shall comprise, in addition to the text, including its preamble and annexes: (a) Any agreement relating to the treaty which was made between all the parties in connexion with the conclusion of the treaty.

62. Y Brauner, 'McBEPS: The MLI — The First Multilateral Tax Treaty that Has Never Been', *Intertax*, vol. 46, no. 1, 2018, p. 6.
63. Y Brauner, 'McBEPS: The MLI — The First Multilateral Tax Treaty that Has Never Been', *Intertax*, vol. 46, no. 1, 2018,

relationship between Article 7 of the MLI and existing provisions of tax treaties to dispel any doubt as to whether the PPT may be used in addition to any specific anti-abuse measures already contained in a tax treaty and the MLI. Based on its literal wording, a transaction or arrangement may be caught by the PPT rule even where the test of other specific or targeted (treaty-based) anti-abuse (SAARs/TAARs) rules has already been passed. To highlight the controversy, some commentators have questioned whether the PPT, as phrased, is limited by the principle of *lex specialis derogat lex generalis.*[64]

4 COMMON REQUIREMENTS OR PRIMARY ELEMENTS OF GAARs: ARE THEY TRULY SUBJECTIVE CRITERIA?

4.1 Characterisation of the Tax Avoidance Scheme, Transaction or Arrangement: The Scheme Requirement

The concept of 'scheme, arrangement or transaction' is a central element of any GAARs, and these circumstances are often referred to in the anti-avoidance provision in varied forms, such as scheme, act or course of action, and so on.[65] This highlights the material and subjective scopes of the anti-avoidance provision.

The PPT emphasises that '[...] obtaining that benefit was one of the principal purposes of any arrangement or transaction that resulted directly or indirectly in that benefit [...]'. This means that the PPT may include any arrangement that gave rise to that benefit, either directly or indirectly. The phrase 'scheme, arrangement or transaction' encompasses the creation, assignment, acquisition or transfer of the income itself, or of the property or right in respect of which the income accrues; as well as

64. Accordingly, in my opinion, considering the PPT as a general anti-abuse treaty rule (tax treaty GAAR), the *lex specialis* principle cannot be applied to let a specific rule (e.g., the MLI's limitation-on-benefits rule) override an application of the PPT to a case covered by both rules. This follows from the fact that written law as stated in the PPT generally prevails over unwritten maxims (*lex specialis* principle) being the explicit and clear message from this statutory provision (MLI). Any other meaning should be pursued through an amendment of the MLI because the supplementary role of the PPT for supporting the limitation-on-benefits clauses of the MLI is clear. The PPT may strengthen the effectiveness of the limitation-on-benefits clause in the MLI by limiting the opportunities to circumvent the objective tests and other means of achieving eligibility to treaty benefits under that provision.

For a similar approach, *see* B Kuźniacki, 'The Principal Purpose Test (PPT) in BEPS Action 6 and the MLI: Exploring Challenges Arising from Its Legal Implementation and Practical Application', *World Tax J.*, vol. 10, no. 2, 2018, pp. 244-245; De Broe and Luts, 'BEPS Action 6: Tax Treaty Abuse' (suggesting that the express language employed in the text of the PPT establishing its application without prejudice reduces the question to somewhat of a non-issue); M Lang, 'BEPS Action 6: Introducing an Anti-abuse Rule in Tax Treaties' (observing that the OECD proposals make it 'much easier for tax authorities to assume an abuse'). Conversely, *see* RJ Danon, 'Treaty Abuse in the Post-BEPS World: Analysis of the Policy Shift and Impact of the Principal Purpose Test for MNE Groups', *Bull Int'l Txn*, vol. 72, no. 1, 2018, p. 52. Danon points out that, '[...] the principle *lex specialis derogat legi generali* continues to apply to the PPT rule'.

65. VR Almendral, 'Tax Avoidance and the European Court of Justice: What Is at Stake for European General Anti-Avoidance Rules', *Intertax*, vol. 33, no. 12, 2005, p. 560, https://e-archivo.uc3m.es/bitstream/handle/10016/9379/tax_ruiz_INTERTAX_2005.pdf, (accessed 28 June 2020).

arrangements concerning the establishment, acquisition or maintenance of a person who derives the income, including the determination of that person as a resident of one of the contracting states. It also includes steps that such persons may take themselves to establish residence.[66] The *Commentary* on the PPT, as found in the 2017 update of the *OECD Model and Commentary*, attempts to encompass a broader interpretation to include any agreement, understanding, scheme, arrangement, transaction or series of transactions, whether or not they are legally enforceable.[67]

Regarding domestic approaches, consider the example of the UK statutory GAARs,[68] which broadly defines 'arrangement' and 'tax arrangements' in a non-exhaustive list under section 214 Interpretation of Part 5. In this Part, 'arrangements include any agreement, understanding, scheme, transaction or series of transactions (whether or not legally enforceable) and would apply to a step or to steps within a wider arrangement as in 207 [...] and 207(3)'. On the other hand, in section 80L, paragraph 1, the South African GAARs[69] states, '[f]or purposes of this Part "arrangement" means any transaction, operation, scheme, agreement or understanding (whether enforceable or not), including all steps therein or parts thereof, and includes any of the foregoing involving the alienation of property; "avoidance arrangement"

---

66. *OECD Model: Commentary on Article 29*, 2017, para 177.
67. *OECD Model: Commentary on Article 29*, para 177.
68. UK: Finance Act 2013, http://www.legislation.gov.uk/ukpga/2013/29/contents/enacted (accessed 25 June 2020). Section 207 states that:

> Arrangements are 'tax arrangements' if, having regard to all the circumstances, it would be reasonable to conclude that the obtaining of a tax advantage was the main purpose, or one of the main purposes, of the arrangements. (2) Tax arrangements are "abusive" if they are arrangements the entering into or carrying out of which cannot reasonably be regarded as a reasonable course of action in relation to the relevant tax provisions, having regard to all the circumstances including – (a) whether the substantive results of the arrangements are consistent with any principles on which those provisions are based (whether express or implied) and the policy objectives of those provisions, (b) whether the means of achieving those results involves one or more contrived or abnormal steps, and (c) whether the arrangements are intended to exploit any shortcomings in those provisions. (3) Where the tax arrangements form part of any other arrangements regard must also be had to those other arrangements. (4) Each of the following is an example of something which might indicate that tax arrangements are abusive [...] (6) The examples given in Subss (4) and (5) are not exhaustive.

Freedman, 'The United Kingdom — GAARs: An Emerging Trend in the Tax Landscape', pp. 741-762.

69. ZA: South Africa Income Tax Act 58 of 1968, section 103(1) amended by the Revenue Law Amendment Act 21 of 2006, s. 6. Current GAARs under ss 80A-80L, https://www.gov.za/documents/income-tax-act-29-may-1962-0000 (accessed 25 June 2020). This section states that '[...] "tax benefit" includes any avoidance, postponement or reduction of any liability for tax'. For a more in-depth analysis of the South African GAARs, *see* ZA: South Africa Revenue Service–SARS, *Discussion Paper on Tax Avoidance*. *See* A Wanyana Oguttu, 'South Africa – GAARs: An Emerging Trend in the Tax Landscape', in Lang, Rust, Schuch, Staringer; Owens and Pistone (eds), *GAARs: A Key Element of Tax Systems in the Post-BEPS Tax World*, Amsterdam, IBFD, May 2016, pp. 611-632; Pickup, 'In Relation to General Anti-Avoidance Provisions', pp. 9-21.

means any arrangement that results in a tax benefit'. Under the Australian GAARs,[70] the term 'scheme' means 'any agreement, arrangement, understanding, promise or undertaking, whether express or implied and whether or not enforceable, or intended to be enforceable, by legal proceedings' and 'any scheme, plan, proposal, action, course of action or course of conduct'.

As such, there is a link among these provisions because they consider any agreement, understanding, scheme, arrangement, transaction or series of transactions, and would apply to a step or to steps within a wider arrangement that result in a tax benefit, broadly defined to consider the whole picture rather than isolated facts and circumstances.[71]

Assuming that the *Commentary*[72] *on the OECD Model* will not bind states involved in the Inclusive Framework[73] on the BEPS Project (whether or not OECD members), as the PPT does not define 'scheme, arrangement or transaction', the issue is whether or not: (i) the absence of a definition will relate simply to the overall transaction, considering the term 'arrangement or transaction'; (ii) it will encompass a series of combined steps or all steps, or a single step within the transaction or a driven part of a broader arrangement ('sub-scheme'); and (iii) it applies to the whole arrangement and/or to a series of transactions, including all steps or parts thereof that will allow the rule to apply to a combination or series of transactions. As the meaning and the concept of 'scheme, arrangement or transaction' are ambiguous, the failure to provide a list of factors and circumstances that characterise tax avoidance only increases the uncertainty.[74] The PPT provision should highlight the necessary connection between these elements and other elements of the GAARs, even though it would, of course, not be feasible to provide a comprehensive definition of these terms and concepts.

---

70. *AU: Australia Tax Laws Amendment Act 2015* (Combating Multinational Tax Avoidance) to widen the dominant purpose test in relation to tax avoidance – Scheme Income Tax Assessment Act 1936, https://www.legislation.gov.au/Details/C2015A00170 (accessed 9 October 2018).
    AU: Australia Tax Laws Amendment (Combating Multinational Tax Avoidance) Act 2015, no. 170, 2015, https://www.legislation.gov.au/Details/C2015A00170 (accessed 25 June 2020). *See* Krever and Mellor, 'Australia — GAARs: An Emerging Trend in the Tax Landscape', pp. 45-64.
71. For a more detailed analysis of the interpretation and application of the Canadian, UK and Indian GAARs, *see* Chand, *The Interaction of Domestic Anti-Avoidance Rules*, pp. 60-61. *See also* Zimmer, 'General Report', pp. 51-60.
72. *OECD Model Tax Convention on Income and on Capital: Commentaries*, 2017.
73. OECD, *Inclusive Framework on BEPS*.
74. As a reference, *see* the Australian Government's Discussion Paper in *AU: Australian Government, Improving the Operation of the Anti-Avoidance Provisions in the Income Tax Law* (The Australian Commonwealth 18 November 2010), https://archive.treasury.gov.au/documents/1901/PDF/dp_anti_avoidance_provisions.pdf (accessed 1 April 2018); D Pickup, 'In Relation to General Anti-Avoidance Provisions: A Comparative Study of the Legal Frameworks Used by Different Countries to Protect their Tax Revenues' in J Freedman (ed.), *Beyond Boundaries: Developing Approaches to Tax Avoidance and Tax Risk Management, OUCBT*, 2008, p. 9; L Zhang, 'Tax Avoidance: Causes and Solutions', *Master's Thesis*, Auckland University of Technology, 2007, https://openrepository.aut.ac.nz/bitstream/handle/10292/13/ZhangLBecky.pdf?sequence=1&isAllowed=y, (accessed 25 June 2020).

In my opinion, as one or a series of transactions or arrangements are covered by the PPT, one transaction alone or a transaction operating in conjunction with a more elaborate series of transactions or arrangements that together result in the benefit, e.g., transactions that are part of so-called stepping-stone schemes (i.e., step transactions), may result in a treaty benefit. In this sense, the PPT is related to an arrangement or transaction, or series thereof, rather than to a taxpayer, implying that this provision has an open personal or subjective scope, even if 'series' may give rise to questions as to whether it requires a sequence in the temporal (pre-planning or pre-ordinance) or logic sense (completion or circularity). Consequently, this provision could be invoked to the detriment of either a taxpayer or whoever is claiming treaty benefits, 'although said taxpayer could merely be a third party that is only "indirectly" involved in an allegedly abusive transaction or arrangement of another taxpayer (which is not claiming treaty benefits)'.[75]

Furthermore, the material scope of the PPT is broader compared to the Guiding Principle, to be extendable to both conduit and abusive restructuring cases, supported by the *2017 Commentary on the OECD Model* that includes the creation, assignment, acquisition or transfer of the income itself, or of the property or right in respect of which the income accrues. This also encompasses arrangements concerning the establishment, acquisition or maintenance of a person who derives the income, including the qualification of that person as a resident of one of the contracting states, besides steps such persons may take themselves to establish residence.[76] The expression 'resulted directly or indirectly in that benefit' is supportive of this analysis,[77] thereby implying that treaty benefits may, for instance, be denied by the source state if these benefits indirectly result from an abusive restructuring.[78]

The modern trend in drafting GAARs is to have a broad, all-embracing and catch-all provision to capture any kind of avoidance.[79] Nevertheless, in practical terms, after analysing the national reports consolidated in the last research concerning GAARs in the post-BEPS world, Richard Krever noted: 'For a variety of reasons, however, there are precious few examples of jurisdictions moving to principle-based drafting or other drafting techniques to overcome the features in their tax laws that given rise to

75. De Broe and Luts, in 'BEPS Action 6: Tax Treaty Abuse', s. 2.2.3., gives the follow example:

> In this respect, the proposed Commentary mentions the example of a transfer of a note receivable by TCo to RCo, because State R has a more beneficial tax treaty with State S, being the Residence State of the debtor, Sco. It is clear that, as it is RCo that will be claiming treaty benefits under the S-R treaty, the PPT (embedded in the S-R) treaty may apply to him if one of the principal purposes (of TCo) in transferring the loan was for RCo to obtain the benefits of the S-R treaty.

See also Lang, 'BEPS Action 6: Introducing an Anti-abuse Rule in Tax Treaties', p. 659.

76. Danon, 'Treaty Abuse in the Post-BEPS World', s. 2.2.3; OECD, *Action 6 Final Report 2015*; *OECD Model: Commentary on Article 29*.
77. Danon, *'Treaty Abuse in the Post-BEPS World'*, s. 2.2.3, p. 132. *See also* Lang, 'BEPS Action 6: Introducing an Anti-abuse Rule in Tax Treaties', p. 659.
78. Danon, *'Treaty Abuse in the Post-BEPS World'*.
79. Rosenblatt, *General Anti-avoidance Rules for Major Developing Countries*, p. 39.

avoidance opportunities.'[80] In this article, 'modern trend' is considered to mean the BEPS Project as a whole and the PPT in particular.

It appears that the PPT is intended to be applied to any 'scheme, arrangement or transaction', by using a comprehensive approach; this is because when drafting the PPT, legislatures failed to define 'tax benefit, gain or advantage' in the provision. Thus, virtually any scheme, arrangement or transaction could be subject to it. Jurisdictions are struggling to define this feature, meaning that the types of conduct to which the anti-avoidance provision may apply cannot be described with certainty – and this is a problematic issue for the PPT as well. In this sense, one issue will be to contrast definitions included in domestic GAARs with those concepts included in the PPT to anticipate how the PPT might be applied; in itself, this could be a problem for the interpretation of tax treaties.

A principle or targeting mechanism, 'reasonableness' was included in the PPT as a secondary or distinguishing element, by applying contrasting attributes used by some countries as a trend, such as 'acceptable or unacceptable', 'permissible or impermissible', 'responsible or irresponsible' and 'appropriateness or inappropriateness'.[81] Nonetheless, this technique is not so straightforward, as it confers even more discretionary power to tax administrations to decide based on these highly indefinite criteria of reasonableness.[82] This issue will be addressed in section 5.1.

4.2 The Identification and Measurement of the Tax Benefit, Gain or Advantage: The Tax Effect Requirement

The concept of 'tax benefit, gain or advantage' is the second common requirement or primary element of GAARs that is useful to delimit or narrow the broader concept of 'scheme, arrangement or transaction' included in the PPT, highlighting the material scope of the avoidance. In the MLI, Article 7(1) declares that: '[...] a benefit under the Covered Tax Agreement shall not be granted in respect of an item of income or capital [...]'. Benefits, gains or advantages are all considered a consequence of and a reason for the tax avoidance scheme, arrangement or transaction.[83] In the PPT, it will be contrasted and will point towards issues such as (i) the meaning of the tax benefit, gain or advantage; (ii) the option for a comprehensive, list-based or hybrid approach;[84] and (iii) the tax benefits that are legitimate and provided by the tax systems.

Regarding domestic approaches, the Australian GAARs[85] tests the existence of schemes by providing a results-based list in section 177C. On the other hand, section

80. Krever, 'Chapter 1. General Report', p. 20.
81. Rosenblatt and Tron, 'General Report', p. 16.
82. Rosenblatt and Tron, 'General Report', p. 18.
83. AU: Australian Government, *Improving the Operation of the Anti-Avoidance Provisions in the Income Tax Law*, p. 1.
84. Rosenblatt and Tron, 'General Report', p. 22.
85. AU: Australia Tax Laws Amendment (Combating Multinational Tax Avoidance) Act 2015. *See* Krever and Mellor, 'Australia — GAARs: An Emerging Trend in the Tax Landscape', pp. 45-64.

245(1) of the Canadian GAARs[86] states that 'tax benefit' is defined to mean a reduction, avoidance or deferral of tax or other amount payable or an increase in a refund of tax or another amount under the Act. The South African GAARs[87] declares that 'tax benefit', 'includes any avoidance, postponement or reduction of any liability for tax'. The UK GAARs[88] states in section 208 that the meaning of 'tax advantage' includes (i) relief or increased relief from tax; (ii) repayment or increased repayment of tax; (iii) avoidance or reduction of a charge to tax or an assessment to tax; (iv) avoidance of a possible assessment to tax; (v) deferral of payment of tax or advancement of repayment of tax; and (vi) avoidance of an obligation to deduct or account for tax.

The link among these laws is to ask what would have happened otherwise if the scheme, arrangement or transaction had not been entered into; in other words, what would be the benefit, gain or advantage. This hypothetical situation, however, is a very difficult task because it can lead to speculation when analysing the scheme, arrangement or transaction in contrast to the rhetorical question as to whether the taxpayer is expected to pay the minimum or maximum amount of tax.[89]

The text of the PPT is silent and only in the *Commentary* is there an indication of its meaning, when it is stated that the term 'benefit' includes all limitations (e.g., a tax reduction, exemption, deferral or refund) on taxation imposed in the source state under Articles 6 through 22 of the *OECD Model*; the relief from double taxation provided by Article 23; and the protection afforded to residents and nationals of a contracting state under Article 24 or any other similar limitations (non-discriminatory clause).[90] This

86. CA: Canada Income Tax Act (RSC, 1985, c 1 (5th Supp)), https://laws-lois.justice.gc.ca/eng/acts/i-3.3/ (accessed 25 June 2020). *See* O'Brien, 'Canada — GAARs: An Emerging Trend in the Tax Landscape', pp. 147-179.
87. ZA: South Africa Income Tax Act 58 of 1968. *See* W. Oguttu, 'South Africa - GAARs: An Emerging Trend in the Tax Landscape', pp. 611-632.
88. UK: Finance Act 2013. *See* Freedman, 'The United Kingdom — GAARs: An Emerging Trend in the Tax Landscape', pp. 741-762.
89. Rosenblatt and Tron, 'General Report', p. 22; *AU: Australian Government, Improving the Operation of the Anti-Avoidance Provisions in the Income Tax Law*, p. 1; Krever, 'Chapter 1. General Report', p. 11; T Murphy, 'Part IVA: From Here to...', *J Austl Txn*, vol. 15, no. 201, 2000; W Barker, 'The Ideology of Tax Avoidance', *Loy U Chi L J*, vol. 40, no. 230, 2009; B Orow, 'Structured Finance and the Operation of General Anti-Avoidance Rules', p. 421. Orow has stressed that:

> The notion of tax advantage presupposes the existence of some benchmark or standard by reference to which liability to taxation, that should have arisen, could be determined. In other words, a tax advantage is not simply a tax saving but rather it necessarily implies a comparison between the tax consequences of the actual arrangement with those of some other hypothetical arrangement which has no existence in fact but which would have resulted in a higher liability to taxation. This conceptual and essentially hypothetical comparison forms the essence and drives the engine of the reconstructive component of statutory general anti-avoidance rules.

90. *OECD Model: Commentary on Article 29*, para 173. *See* Kuźniacki, 'The Principal Purpose Test (PPT) in BEPS Action 6 and the MLI', who comments that:

> It is, however, less easy to understand how the abusive acquisition of a benefit can take place under the equivalent of Article 24 of the OECD Model, since this provision is a non-discrimination clause whose aim is solely to prevent direct and overt discrimination and it cannot be read as a most-favoured nation clause [...] Denying a benefit under

includes, for example, limitations on the taxing rights of a contracting state in respect of dividends, interest or royalties arising in that state, and paid to a resident of the other state as the beneficial owner under Article 10, 11 or 12. It also includes limitations on the taxing rights of a contracting state over a capital gain derived from the alienation of movable property located in that state by a resident of the other state under Article 13. A tax treaty also includes other limitations, such as a tax sparing provision.[91]

The *Commentary on the PPT* does not mention the provisions shaping the scope of treaties (Articles 1 and 2 of the OECD Model) nor definitional clauses (Articles 3-5 of the OECD Model) as rules providing treaty benefits. In my opinion, this omission might seem deliberate, as the foregoing clauses will not normally provide for a treaty benefit on a stand-alone basis, but only in combination with substantive treaty rules. Likewise, it is unlikely that treaty benefits in a treaty abuse scheme would be granted based on the equivalents of Articles 24-31 of the OECD Model.[92] Briefly put, the relevant treaty provisions for the PPT will typically be equivalent to Articles 6-8, 10-22 and 23A and 23B of the OECD Model, even though the *Commentary on the PPT* does not refer to double non-taxation per se.[93]

Chand introduces an interesting issue regarding '...whether a procedural benefit available to a taxpayer, such as access to a Mutual Agreement Procedure MAP or arbitration under Article 25 of the OECD Model, can be denied under the PPT'. Vikram Chand claims that this should not be the case, as such a benefit cannot be considered as 'any other similar limitation' as provided in the *Commentary* on this rule,[94] a remark that does not include the scope of treaties (Articles 1 and 2 of the OECD Model) and definitional provisions (Articles 3 through 5 of the OECD Model) because 'these provisions by themselves do not give any benefits and therefore should be read in conjunction with the other operative provisions'.[95] Moreover, only benefits covered under the relevant tax treaty will fall within the scope of the PPT, but not such benefits

Article 24 of the OECD Model via the PPT would violate the principle of non-discrimination, which has an absolute character from which contracting sates may therefore not derogate.

In the same sense, *see* De Broe and Luts, 'BEPS Action 6: Tax Treaty Abuse', p. 131; A Rust, 'Article 24', in E Reimer and A Rust (eds), *K Vogel on Double Taxation Conventions*, 4th ed, Amsterdam, Wolters Kluwer, 2015, p. 683, 1, mn 4, 1.

91. *OECD Model: Commentary on Article 29*, para. 175.
92. In the same opinion, *see* Lang, 'BEPS Action 6: Introducing an Anti-abuse Rule in Tax Treaties', pp. 656-657; De Broe and Luts, 'BEPS Action 6: Tax Treaty Abuse'.
93. *OECD Model: Commentary on Article 29*, para 173. *Also*, Kuźniacki, 'The Principal Purpose Test (PPT) in BEPS Action 6 and the MLI', who states that 'Such a benefit will fall under a very broad statement contained in paragraph 175 of the Commentary to the PPT, according to which a "treaty benefit" includes all treaty limitations, and thus actual double non-taxation as well'.
94. V Chand, 'The Principal Purpose Test in the Multilateral Convention: An In-Depth Analysis', *Intertax*, vol. 46, no. 1, 2018, pp. 18-44, s. 3.3. *See also* Lang, 'BEPS Action 6: Introducing an Anti-abuse Rule in Tax Treaties', p. 657.
95. Chand, *The Interaction of Domestic Anti-Avoidance Rules*; De Broe and Luts, 'BEPS Action 6: Tax Treaty Abuse'; Lang, 'BEPS Action 6: Introducing an Anti-abuse Rule in Tax Treaties'.

to which a taxpayer may be entitled under domestic law (direct or indirect tax-related benefits) or another tax treaty or EU law.[96]

There is a scholarly debate concerning whether the term 'benefit, gain or advantage' refers to the taxation of one contracting state or to the combined overall tax burden in both contracting states.[97] The concept of 'tax benefit, gain or advantage' could be seen as embracing all limitations on taxation in the source state and relief from double taxation in the residence state, including tax sparing clauses, in pursuit of the effects of double non-taxation or reduced taxation. In my opinion, the term 'benefit' exclusively covers the reduction of domestic taxation that the state applying the tax treaty must accept under the applicable distributive rule, i.e., a reduction of source taxation in the case of dividends, interest and royalties.[98]

Otherwise, the PPT may not be used to deny a benefit stemming exclusively from domestic law, i.e., a participation exemption or a lower domestic corporate income tax in the residence state. As many commentators have pointed out, it consequently follows that the benefit to which the PPT rule refers must be provided 'under this Convention'.[99] The PPT rule is applicable 'in respect of an item of income or capital', meaning that it is a provision requiring an item-by-item income analysis. In this sense, by considering different kinds of income, the PPT rule could lead to a denial of treaty benefits for some income streams, but not for others, following a similar analysis of the beneficial ownership requirement. Otherwise, the analysis of the PPT differs from a limitation-on-benefits provision, which conversely focuses on whether the taxpayer is a 'qualified person or not'.[100]

4.3 Is Finding a Tax Avoidance Purpose, Intent or Motive a Truly Subjective Criterion? The Purpose Requirement or the Subjective Element[101]

After the tax benefit, gain or advantage has been detected and the correspondent scheme, arrangement or transaction has been identified, the third element is to determine whether the taxpayer's purpose, motive or intent in entering into or carrying out the scheme was to obtain that tax benefit, gain or advantage,[102] highlighting

96. Chand, *The Interaction of Domestic Anti-Avoidance Rules*; De Broe and Luts, 'BEPS Action 6: Tax Treaty Abuse'; Lang, 'BEPS Action 6: Introducing an Anti-abuse Rule in Tax Treaties', p. 656.
97. De Broe and Luts, 'BEPS Action 6: Tax Treaty Abuse', p. 208; Lang, 'BEPS Action 6: Introducing an Anti-abuse Rule in Tax Treaties', p. 657.
98. Of the same opinion, Danon, 'Treaty Abuse in the Post-BEPS World', s. 4.2.; De Broe and Luts, 'BEPS Action 6: Tax Treaty Abuse', p. 208.
99. Danon, 'Treaty Abuse in the Post-BEPS World', s. 4.2.1.
100. Danon, 'Treaty Abuse in the Post-BEPS World', s. 4.2.2.
101. Z Prebble and J Prebble, 'Abus de Droit and the General Anti-Avoidance Rule of Income Tax Law: A Comparison of the Laws of Seven Jurisdictions and the European Community', *Working Paper Series No 56 of the Centre for Accounting Governance*, Victoria U of Wellington, 2008, p. 18.
102. Freedman, 'The United Kingdom — GAARs: An Emerging Trend in the Tax Landscape', pp. 748-750; M Cashmere, 'A GAAR for the United Kingdom? The Australian Experience', *Brit Tax Rev.*, vol. 2, 2008, pp. 125-159.

whether there is a truly subjective scope of avoidance. Article 7(1) provides: '[...] if it is reasonable to conclude, having regard to all relevant facts and circumstances, that obtaining that benefit was one of the principal purposes [...]', stressing the purpose test. The ordinary meaning suggests that a court or tax administration would rationally or sensibly reach a judgment or opinion, after considering all the relevant facts and circumstances. The question arises as to whether this is a subjective or objective assessment, and to what extent is it necessary to consider the taxpayer's purpose, intention or motive in undertaking the transaction.

The PPT has two different intertwined concepts, namely (i) the reasonable conclusion that the principal purpose is determined based on objective criteria, and (ii) relating to one of the principal purposes of the arrangement or transaction.[103] This means that to assess whether one of the principal purposes of an arrangement or transaction was to obtain the tax benefit, the tax authority must determine its reasonableness. As noted by many scholars, tax avoidance is a purpose-based notion under which it is necessary to determine a logical connection among all the elements that are aimed at obtaining a tax benefit.[104] Because purpose can be viewed subjectively, many commentators state that it should not be a basic element of a GAARs, given that '[...] whether or not a transaction is taxable should depend on the characteristics particular to the transaction and not be tied to the subjective attitudes of each taxpayer [...]',[105] and it would be impossible to read the minds of taxpayers and obtain evidence of their motives.[106] In spite of much criticism regarding this purposive element of GAARs, Nabil Orow notes that 'the presence of a particular state of mind may be a circumstance which, when combined with the other elements, may indicate that as a matter of construction the arrangement is one for the avoidance of tax to which a GAAR is intended to apply'.[107] In this sense, following Dr Orow, the issue regarding whether and to what extent purpose should apply poses a difficult question of policy.

Nevertheless, purpose, motive or intention can be based on objective considerations (objective assessment) such as reasons, objectives, results, effects and consequences of the scheme,[108] relying on a results-based test instead of an intention-based

103. This approach was highlighted by C Elliffe, 'The Meaning of the Principal Purpose Test: One Ring to Bind Them All?', *World Tax J.*, vol. 11, no. 1, 19 February 2019, https://ssrn.com/abstract=3346660 (accessed 25 June 2020).
104. Rosenblatt, *General Anti-Avoidance Rules for Major Developing Countries*, p. 47; Almendral, 'Tax Avoidance and the European Court of Justice', p. 563; GS Cooper, 'The Design and Structure of General Anti-Tax Avoidance Regimes', *Bull Intl. Fisc Docn*, vol. 63, no. 1, 2009, pp. 26-32; W Schön, 'Statutory Avoidance and Disclosure Rules in Germany', in J Freedman (ed.), *Beyond Boundaries: Developing Approaches to Tax Avoidance and Tax Risk Management*, Oxford University Centre for Business Taxation, 2008, pp. 47-55.
105. B Banoun, 'Tax Avoidance Rules in Scandinavian and Anglo-American Law', *Bull. Int'l Fisc. Docn.*, vol. 56, no. 8/9, 2002, pp. 488-489.
106. M Lang, 'The General Anti-Abuse Rule of Article 80 of the Draft Proposal for a Council Directive on a Common Consolidated Corporate Tax Base', *Eur Txn*, vol. 51, no. 6, 2011, pp. 223 ff.
107. N Orow, *General Anti-Avoidance Rules: A Comparative International Analysis*, pp. 111-112. *See also* Schön, 'Statutory Avoidance and Disclosure Rules in Germany'.
108. Rooijen, *Anti-Avoidance Techniques: Canada and the Netherlands: An Overview and Comparative Analysis*, pp. 42-57.

test to connect the elements of that transaction to the overall context. When applying a results-based approach to investigate the purpose, motive or intention of the scheme, arrangement or transaction, the provision should be based on presumptions that will provide guidelines for applying a GAAR and diminish the level of subjective discretionary power exercised by tax administrations when identifying the purpose, motive or intention of the scheme, transaction or arrangement.[109] As such, this would effectively avoid the discussion as to who has the relevant purpose - whether the taxpayer or any third party connected to the scheme.

To illustrate how this issue is addressed in various jurisdictions, consider the following domestic approaches. The Australian GAARs[110] in section 177D(2) works with a long list of matters, factors and circumstances that must be considered to assess the purpose. In addition, section 177CB(2) highlights the purpose by which, 'A decision that a tax effect would have occurred if the scheme had not been entered into or carried out must be based on a postulate that comprises only the events or circumstances that actually happened or existed (other than those that form part of the scheme).' The Canadian GAARs[111] in section 245(3) works with the reasonableness test and the bona fide purpose test to assess the purpose of a scheme or arrangement. In this sense, an avoidance transaction does not include a transaction that 'may reasonably be considered to have been undertaken or arranged primarily for bona fide purposes other than to obtain the tax benefit'. As a result, the purposes of a transaction are determined not only from the taxpayer's statement of intention but also from all the circumstances of the transaction or transactions. If it can be inferred from all the circumstances that the primary or principal purpose in undertaking the transaction is

109. Rosenblatt, *General Anti-avoidance Rules for Major Developing Countries*, p. 48.

110. AU: Australia Tax Laws Amendment (Combating Multinational Tax Avoidance) Act 2015. *See* Krever and Mellor, 'Australia — GAARs: An Emerging Trend in the Tax Landscape', p. 50. These authors stress that while a taxpayer's purpose appears to be a subjective intention, the legislation sets out eight objective considerations (such as any non-arm's-length relationship between parties) that can be relied on to determine the taxpayer's purpose. For this reason, the taxpayer's purpose should be imputed from external indicators pointed out by the statutory criteria.

111. *See* CA: Canada Income Tax Act. *Also*, O'Brien, 'Canada — GAARs: An Emerging Trend in the Tax Landscape', p. 153. O'Brien stated as follows:

> As of March 2015, the SCC has given judgment in four cases on the interpretation and application of the GAAR. The leading case is Canada Trustco, The Queen v. Canada Trustco Mortgage Company, (2005) 2 SCR. 601 at 608; 2005 SCC 54 (Canada Trustco) at (14). In this leading case the requirements for application of the GAAR were summarized at para. 66: a tax benefit resulting from a transaction or part of a series of transactions (s. 245(1) and (2)); that the transaction is an avoidance transaction in the sense that it cannot be said to have been reasonably undertaken or arranged primarily for a bona fide purpose other than to obtain a tax benefit; [...].

Regarding this notion, from my point of view a transaction will not be an avoidance transaction if the taxpayer establishes that it is undertaken primarily for a bona fide business, investment or family purpose. In making this determination, it is important to distinguish those transactions that may have a business, investment or family effect from those that have a business, investment or family purpose. There are many transactions that have a business, investment or family effect, which may nevertheless be avoidance transactions because the primary purpose of the transaction is to obtain a tax benefit.

one other than to obtain a tax benefit, then the transaction is not deemed to be an avoidance transaction.

Under the Indian GAARs,[112] the provision relies on satisfaction of the primary test (the main purpose is to obtain a tax benefit) along with any one of the secondary tests or the tainted element test listed alongside, such as: creating rights/obligations between unrelated parties at arm's length; resulting in direct/indirect misuse/abuse of tax provisions; lacking (or deemed to lack) commercial substance in whole or in part (section 97); and entered into/carried out for a non-bona fide purpose. Under the South African GAARs,[113] the sole or main purpose of the avoidance arrangement must be to obtain a tax benefit, and section 80G(1) sets forth the 'reasonable test', the objective purpose of which does not refer to the intention of the taxpayer but rather to the purpose of the arrangement (i.e., the objective effect it is seeking to achieve, the end accomplished or achieved). Under the UK GAARs,[114] section 207 states that tax arrangements are deemed to be 'abusive' if they are arrangements that entering into or carrying out of cannot reasonably be regarded as a reasonable course of action in relation to the relevant tax provisions, having regard to all the circumstances.

Considering the domestic laws above, it is easy to see that the rationale of the scheme, transaction or arrangement, in fact, the 'reasonableness requirement' that will be analysed in section 4.1 is the common feature to assess the tax avoidance purpose, intent or motive as a result-based test in an objective way. In the PPT, the phrase concerning the 'purpose' is not superfluous, but is indeed essential, as the 'purpose' involves an additional meaning different from the other tests - the 'result' of the scheme, arrangement or transaction. Ultimately, primary and secondary elements always overlap in a circular way, as it is impossible to segregate their features at all. In this sense, this article is attempting a scholarly classification that unifies the most common features in two main categories. Nonetheless, sometimes the same common feature will appear in other sections to delimit their meanings, confirming that the PPT is really open to more than one interpretation (i.e., the taxpayer's). Consequently, the rule can be invoked against a third party only indirectly involved in the transaction.[115]

112. The Indian GAARs, by the Finance Act 2012, has incorporated anti-avoidance provisions in the form of general anti-avoidance rules under Chapter X-A of the Income Tax Act 1961 (ITA), available at https://www.incometaxindia.gov.in/Pages/Direct-Taxes-Data.aspx (accessed 9 October 2018). *See* NM Kapadia, 'India — GAARs: An Emerging Trend in the Tax Landscape', in M Lang, J Owens, P Pistone, A Rust, J Schuch and C Staringer (eds), *GAARs: A Key Element of Tax Systems in the Post-BEPS Tax World*, Amsterdam, IBFD, 2016, p. 326. Kapadia highlights that the Finance Act 2012 has incorporated anti-avoidance provisions in the form of general anti-avoidance rules under Chapter X-A of the Income Tax Act 1961 (ITA) to point out that this amendment incorporating the 'impermissible avoidance arrangement' aim to codify the substance-over-form approach. The author also states that the Indian GAARs are closest to the GAARs applicable in South Africa.

113. ZA: South Africa Income Tax Act 58 of 1968. *See* W Oguttu, 'South Africa - GAARs: An Emerging Trend in the Tax Landscape', pp. 615-617.

114. UK: Finance Act 2013. *See* Freedman, 'The United Kingdom — GAARs: An Emerging Trend in the Tax Landscape', p. 751. Freedman stresses that the moderate targeted approach can be seen in the 'double reasonableness test' that is the centrepiece of UK GAARs legislation.

115. De Broe and Luts, 'BEPS Action 6: Tax Treaty Abuse', p. 133; Lang, 'BEPS Action 6: Introducing an Anti-abuse Rule in Tax Treaties', p. 659.

The 'purpose test' is not so subjective after all, as the purpose, motive or intention must be inferred from the characteristics of the scheme, transaction or arrangement (e.g., the existence or not of a core commercial activity). Consequently, the scheme, arrangement or transaction itself is fiscally unacceptable, regardless of the parties that might be affected. The abusive nature is not a quality pertaining to the will of the taxpayer, but rather a legal attribute of the scheme, transaction or arrangement itself based on all the surrounding facts and circumstances.

Supporting this assertion, references to 'bona fide' and 'core commercial activity' can be found in the *Commentary on the PTT* rule, specifically in paragraph 6:

> The provision is intended to ensure that tax conventions apply in accordance with the purpose for which they were entered into, i.e. to provide benefits in respect of bona fide exchanges of goods and services, and movements of capital and persons as opposed to arrangements whose principal objective is to secure a more favourable tax treatment.[116]

Similarly, paragraph 13 of the *Commentary on the PTT* rule states that 'where an arrangement is inextricably linked to a core commercial activity, and its form has not been driven by considerations of obtaining a benefit, it is unlikely that its principal purpose will be considered to obtain that benefit'.

The PPT follows a new approach when stating that 'obtaining that benefit was "one of the principal purposes" of any arrangement or transaction that resulted directly or indirectly in that benefit'. It relies on a results-based test instead of an intention-based test, so as to highlight the purpose of the scheme, arrangement or transaction, and not the taxpayers' purpose. There are three main approaches to be considered: (i) the sole purpose (a narrow scope); (ii) a significant, primary, main, paramount, predominant, dominant, ruling, prevailing, decisive, principal or most influential purpose (an intermediate scope); and (iii) one of the purposes or a purpose (a broader scope),[117] the latter of which is followed by the PPT. Regarding the PPT, 'there will necessarily be significant differences of opinion as to what constitutes a dominant purpose,'[118] as this criterion grants great discretionary power to tax administrations, especially because the PPT does not provide any framework concerning the burden of proof of the taxpayer or the tax administration.

Furthermore, this will give rise to the issue of distinguishing between tax and non-tax motives,[119] considering that many transactions have multiple purposes, such

116. OECD, *Action 6 Final Report 2015*, p. 58; *OECD Model: Commentary on Article 29*, para 181.
117. Rosenblatt and Tron, 'General Report', p. 23; Rosenblatt, *General Anti-avoidance Rules for Major Developing Countries*, p. 49.
118. B Orow, 'Structured Finance and the Operation of General Anti-avoidance Rules', pp. 410-435; F Vanistendael, 'Taxation, Tax Avoidance and the Rule of Law', *Asian-Pacific Tax Bull.*, vol. 16, no. 3, 2010, p. 214.
119. As highlighted by Chand in *The Interaction of Domestic Anti-Avoidance Rules*, the term 'non-tax purposes' should be interpreted on a much broader basis than the term 'business purposes', as can be seen in *Canada Trustco Mortgage Co v. Canada*, para 33.

as tax avoidance and/or business purposes that are not mutually exclusive[120] for achieving the same economic results.[121] Taking this into account, it is critical to identify and weigh the multiple purposes of the scheme,[122] particularly because business transactions can usually be arranged in one or a series of several complex, innovative and different ways.[123]

It is unlikely to say that tax costs are not significant to multinational corporations. Thus, at least in part, all operations and businesses consider the effect of tax costs,[124] choosing the option which is most tax-efficient and which will most probably result in the greatest tax saving, even if the arrangement was driven by core commercial activities.[125] Thus, one of the principal purposes of a transaction is to obtain a tax benefit.[126] Luc De Broe and Boris Luts propose to reconcile the PPT with the claim that the PPT should be applied only if a transaction or arrangement was solely or at least predominantly inspired by treaty benefits. For instance, benefits of the treaty should be granted even if there is a tax motive, provided that a genuine economic objective is being pursued.[127]

Nonetheless, the introduction of the PPT has changed the game, since taxpayers must demonstrate that a transaction would have taken place notwithstanding the availability of the tax benefit, gain or advantage.[128] Paragraph 12 of the *Commentary on Article 29* confirms this position, which states that '[t]he reference to "one of the principal purposes" in paragraph 7 means that obtaining the benefit under a tax convention need not be the sole or dominant purpose of a particular arrangement or transaction. It is sufficient that at least one of the principal purposes was to obtain the benefit'.[129] Under paragraph 13 of the *Commentary on Article 29* as stated in the *Action 6 Final Report*, a purpose is not deemed to be a principal purpose when obtaining a benefit was not the main consideration for the transaction and, in particular, where the arrangement is linked to a core commercial activity.[130]

The purpose requirement would be satisfied on the grounds that, from a literal reading of the test, one could argue that 'one of the principal purposes' is to obtain a tax

120. Rosenblatt and Tron, 'General Report', p. 23; Rosenblatt, *General Anti-Avoidance Rules for Major Developing Countries*, p. 48; N Orow, *General Anti-Avoidance Rules: A Comparative International Analysis*, pp. 124-127.
121. Arnold, 'The Canadian General Anti-Avoidance Rule'.
122. Baker, 'Tax Avoidance, Tax Evasion and Tax Mitigation'; N Orow, *General Anti-Avoidance Rules*, pp. 117-124.
123. Rosenblatt, *General Anti-avoidance Rules for Major Developing Countries*, p. 49; V Krishna, *Tax Avoidance: The General Anti-Avoidance Rule*, Toronto, Carswell, 1990, pp. 37, 47.
124. De Broe and Luts, 'BEPS Action 6: Tax Treaty Abuse', p. 132.
125. C Bergedahl, '*Anti-Abuse Measures in Tax Treaties Following the OECD Multilateral Instrument – Part 1*', *Bull. Int'l Taxn*, vol. 72, no. 2, 21 December 2017, s. 3.2.1.3.
126. E Pinetz, 'Final Report on Action 6 of the OECD/G20 Base Erosion and Profit Shifting Initiative', s. 2.2.3.
127. De Broe and Luts, 'BEPS Action 6: Tax Treaty Abuse', pp. 122-146.
128. There is little basis to argue that the OECD intention was geared towards a restrictive PPT. In this sense, *see* Bergedahl, '*Anti-Abuse Measures in Tax Treaties Following the OECD Multilateral Instrument – Part 1*', s. 3.1.1.2.; Palao Taboada, 'OECD Base Erosion and Profit Shifting Action 6', s. 2.2.
129. OECD, *Action 6 Final Report 2015*, p. 58; *OECD Model: Commentary on Article 29*, para 181.
130. *OECD Model: Commentary on Article 29*, 2017; OECD, *Action 6 Final Report 2015*, p. 58.

benefit, gain or advantage, even if the scheme, arrangement or transaction had several 'principal purposes' yet no tax purposes.[131] The same issue arose at the time the guiding principle was introduced into the *2003 Commentary on the OECD Model*[132] when it was suggested that a reference to the 'sole purpose' or to the 'predominant purpose' would have been more appropriate.[133] Having said that, the author claims that if factual analysis demonstrates that 'non-tax purposes' outweigh 'tax purposes', the subjective criterion is not fulfilled,[134] an approach that is supported in paragraph 26 of the *2015 BEPS Action 6 Final Report* (*Commentary* in paragraph 13, at 58), as well as in paragraph 181 of the *2017 Commentary on Article 29 of the OECD Model* (Draft).[135] Therefore, in my opinion, following Dr Chand, when factual analysis leads to the conclusion that the scheme, transaction or arrangement is undertaken for bona fide purposes and pursues genuine commercial or economic objectives,[136] the subjective

131. OECD, *Action 6 Final Report 2015*, para. 26; *OECD Model: Commentary on Article 29*, para 180.
132. *OECD Model: Commentary on Article 1*, 2003, para 9.5.
133. Danon, 'Treaty Abuse in the Post-BEPS World', s. 4.2.2.; De Broe and Luts, 'BEPS Action 6: Tax Treaty Abuse', p. 325.
134. Chand, *The Interaction of Domestic Anti-Avoidance Rules*, pp. 60-61; Zimmer, 'General Report'.
135. OECD, *Action 6 Final Report 2015*, para 26 (Commentary on para 13); *OECD Model: Commentary on Article 29*, para 181, establishes that, 'Where an arrangement is inextricably linked to a core commercial activity, and its form has not been driven by considerations of obtaining a benefit, it is unlikely that its principal purpose will be considered to be to obtain that benefit.' Chand, *The Interaction of Domestic Anti-Avoidance Rules*, s. 3.4.3, points out that:

> This clarification has also been reflected in several examples of the PPT. For instance, refer to the fact patterns that deal with: Investments by a collective investment vehicle (CIV) and direct investment to create a plant (see section 4.3.1); (2) investments by intermediary companies that are owned by third State residents such as entities within a multinational group like operating entities (see sections 4.3.2.1 and 4.3.2.2), entities holding share and patents (see section 4.3.2.3), service entities (see section 4.3.2.4), financing entities (see section 4.3.2.5) and intellectual property licensing entities (see section 4.3.2.6); (3) investments by intermediary companies that are owned/set up by third States non-CIVs such as regional portfolio investment companies (see section 4.3.2.8), securitization companies (see section 4.3.2.9) or real estate companies (see section 4.3.2.10)'. To adds that: 'In the foregoing examples, the non-tax purposes seem to outweigh the fact that obtaining a tax benefit seemed to be one of the purpose (in some examples the tax benefit seems to be an ancillary purpose)[...]'.

136. Although not within the scope of this book, the EU Directives provide that 'arrangements' may be regarded to be genuine if they are put into place 'for valid commercial reasons which reflect economic reality'. *See* Council Directive (EU) 2015/121, 27 January 2015, amending Directive 2011/96/EU, on the common system of taxation applicable in the case of parent companies and subsidiaries of different Member States; OJ L 21/1, 28 January 2015, art 1 and Council Directive (EU) 2016/1164, 12 July 2016, laying down rules against tax avoidance practices that directly affect the functioning of the internal market; OJ L 193/1, 19 July 2016, art 6(2). Moreover, ECJ case law indicates that domestic anti-avoidance rules (such as CFC rules), which constitute a restriction to freedom (such as freedom of establishment), may be justified when they relate to 'wholly artificial arrangements'. In other words, if the domestic anti-avoidance rules apply to arrangements that encompass economic reality, then such rules will be contrary to the freedom of establishment provisions even though the arrangement contains tax motives. *See* UK: ECJ, 12 September 2006, Case C-196/04, *Cadbury Schweppes v. Commissioners of Inland Revenue*, ECLI:EU:C:2006:544, paras 68-69.

element should not be satisfied,[137] as non-tax purposes could be considered fundamental drivers of the transaction exceeding tax purposes.[138]

This does not mean that the purpose requirement should be interpreted in a 'restrictive manner' as some commentators have proposed; on the contrary, it should be analysed by applying a case-by-case approach. The *Commentary on Article 10* (2017)[139] lists ten examples to illustrate a variety of cases demonstrating its understanding of the phrase 'one of the principal purposes'. Nonetheless, most of these examples are self-evident and, regarding the examples provided in the Discussion Draft on non-collective investment vehicle (CIV) examples, too specific.[140]

Having said that, a GAAR should contain criteria to balance different purposes and protect schemes, arrangements or transactions where the tax benefit, gain or advantage is only incidental.[141] Otherwise, judicial and administrative courts must seek a balance during dispute resolution. In the PPT, this condition requires an objective analysis to put the scheme, arrangement or transaction in place,[142] it being a factual analysis of all circumstances surrounding the arrangement or transaction on a case-by-case basis.[143] This means that as usual in modern GAARs, the purpose requirement component of the PPT is also objectified by a 'distinguishing or secondary element', specifically the 'reasonableness' criterion as stressed by the phrase 'if it is reasonable to conclude', which will be analysed in section 4.1. In my opinion, this requirement is complex and will give rise to much controversy, as the text of the PPT rule and the related *2017 Commentary on the OECD Model* could be read as supporting both a broad and a narrow meaning. This is because the phrase 'reasonable to conclude' implies that it is not necessary to find conclusive proof of the purpose, intent or motive of a taxpayer regarding a scheme, arrangement or transaction - which will shift the problem to the burden of proof once again.[144] It has been stated that the most difficult task will be to identify a purpose, intention or motive on the basis of an objective analysis.[145]

---

137. Chand, *The Interaction of Domestic Anti-Avoidance Rules*, pp. 60-61; Zimmer, 'General Report', p. 192; De Broe and Luts 'BEPS Action 6: Tax Treaty Abuse', p. 132.
138. Chand, *The Interaction of Domestic Anti-Avoidance Rules*, pp. 60-61; Zimmer, 'General Report', p. 192.
139. *OECD Model: Commentary on Article 29.*
140. Bergedahl, '*Anti-Abuse Measures in Tax Treaties Following the OECD Multilateral Instrument – Part 1*'.
141. Rosenblatt, *General Anti-avoidance Rules for Major Developing Countries*, p. 54.
142. OECD, *Action 6 Final Report 2015*, pp. 57-58; *OECD Model: Commentary on Article 29*, para 178.
143. OECD, *Action 6 Final Report 2015*, pp. 57-58; *OECD Model: Commentary on Article 29*, para 178.
144. In the same sense, *see* Danon 'Treaty Abuse in the Post-BEPS World', s. 2.2.3. On the other hand, *OECD Model: Commentary on Article 29*, para 178 (2017) establishes that:

    > It should not be lightly assumed, however, that obtaining a benefit under a tax treaty was one of the principal purposes of an arrangement or transaction and merely reviewing the effects of an arrangement will not usually enable a conclusion to be drawn about its purpose.

145. *See*, e.g., Lang, 'BEPS Action 6: Introducing an Anti-abuse Rule in Tax Treaties', p. 658; B Moreno, 'GAARs and Treaties: From the Guiding Principle to the Principal Purpose Test', p. 436.

Briefly put, the purpose, intention or motive is the link between tax avoidance and tax advantage, gain or benefit as a modern trend in GAARs. Instead of modern GAARs based on objective tests (a results-based approach) that rely on presumptions of the purpose, intent or motive (usually defined by the end result of the scheme, arrangement or transaction or its effect), the PPT does not provide any list of the presumptions or objective test. The analysis shows some patterns that form the framework of the modern GAARs referred to as common comparative elements, such as 'scheme, transaction or arrangement', 'tax benefit, gain or advantage', and 'purpose, motive or intention'; when used by common law and civil law jurisdictions, all of them are 'interrelated in a circular way such that it is impossible to explain one of them without referring to the other two,' sometimes expressed as 'in connection with'.[146]

Modern legislative drafting of these rules seeks to make them objective by using two methods. First, by mixing a comprehensive definition (a principle-based approach) with some attributes such as 'reasonableness or unreasonableness, acceptable or unacceptable, permissible or impermissible, responsible or irresponsible, appropriateness or inappropriateness', and so on.[147] even considering that these tests are based on open-textual concepts (and are thus indeterminate concepts), uncertainties may arise.[148] The second method mixes a comprehensive definition (a principle-based approach) with a non-exhaustive list-based approach (a results-based approach is applied for investigating the purpose, intention or motive). In this second method, the provision will be based on presumptions to provide guidance for the application of the GAARs and to diminish the level of subjective discretionary power exercised by tax administrations in identifying the result of the transaction. The PPT applies the first method because it uses a comprehensive definition without a list-based approach.

4.4 Interim Remarks

A tax avoidance 'scheme, transaction or arrangement', 'tax benefit, gain or advantage' and 'purpose, motive or intention' as common requirements or primary elements are all workable standards that function as a generic comparative concept for a legal transplant of the PPT to tax treaties under the form of a comprehensive GAARs. Considering that there is no feasible way to provide a comprehensive definition of these terms and concepts, as they are open and indefinite, the PPT follows the same path as many GAARs and does not define these concepts.

A list-based approach would include the great risk that taxpayers will structure their businesses so as not to fall within any factor mentioned in the list. In addition, including a list in the PPT could prove inflexible when dealing with new developments regarding aggressive tax planning. The treaty and/or MLI would need to be changed any time that the contracting states would like to include a new element or situation

146. Rosenblatt and Tron, 'General Report', p. 25; Rosenblatt, *General Anti-avoidance Rules for Major Developing Countries*, p. 55.
147. Rosenblatt and Tron, 'General Report', pp. 16-17.
148. Rosenblatt and Tron, 'General Report', pp. 16-17.

that has appeared in practice, and this would not be practical or realistic. Nonetheless, these disadvantages may be overcome if the list was accompanied by a catch-all clause allowing for more flexibility, albeit bearing in mind that this would undermine the purpose of the list. The limitation on benefits already follows a list-based approach that should prevent at least some uncertainty and would give countries the possibility to select this option.

Considering that the interconnection of substantive primary elements is not enough to provide a clear distinction between legitimate tax avoidance and aggressive tax planning, other secondary or ancillary elements such as artificiality, contrivance, form and substance, economic substance, misuse and abuse of law will all have to come into play. They are not essential and have a circumstantial or ancillary nature (albeit significant) for the operation of anti-avoidance rules and doctrines. This will be analysed in the following section.[149]

5 DISTINGUISHING REQUIREMENTS OR SECONDARY ELEMENTS OF GAARS: ARE THEY TRULY OBJECTIVE CRITERIA?

5.1 The 'Rationale' of the Scheme, Transaction or Arrangement: The Reasonableness Requirement

Article 7(1) of the MLI states that '[...] a benefit under the Covered Tax Agreement shall not be granted in respect of an item of income or capital if it is reasonable to conclude, having regard to all relevant facts and circumstances [...]'. As noted in section 4.1., the PPT has two distinct, intertwined concepts: the reasonable conclusion that is based on objective criteria, and, in addition, would rationally arrive by reasoning after considering all the relevant facts and circumstances. As previously highlighted, to assess whether one of the principal purposes of the arrangement or transaction was to obtain the tax benefit, the approach of the tax administration must be based on reasonableness.

Aiming to address what is perceived as tax avoidance, some GAARs are drafted with reference to contrasting concepts such as 'reasonable or unreasonable', 'acceptable or unacceptable', 'permissible or impermissible', and 'responsible or irresponsible, appropriateness or inappropriateness,' to name just a few.[150] The test based on reasonableness[151] is a typical concept of the aim of common law jurisdictions[152] to

149. Rosenblatt and Tron, 'General Report', p. 17.
150. Rosenblatt and Tron, 'General Report', p. 16; Dunbar, 'Statutory General Anti-Avoidance Rules'.
151. Rosenblatt, *General Anti-Avoidance Rules for Major Developing Countries*, p. 63, where he stressed that some GAARs, e.g., New Zealand (ITA 1994 s BG1(2)), use the wider and vague term 'appropriate' instead of 'reasonable', as the former has a broader meaning than the latter.
152. Baker, 'Tax Avoidance, Tax Evasion and Tax Mitigation', p. 13; WB Barker, 'The Ideology of Tax Avoidance', *Loyola U Chicago L J*, vol. 40, no. 2, 2009, p. 241; SW Bowman, 'Interpretation of Tax Legislation: The Evolution of Purposive Analysis', *Can Tax J.*, vol. 43, no. 5, 1995, p. 1181, https://www.ctf.ca/ctfweb/Documents/PDF/1995ctj/1995CTJ5_08_Bowman.pdf (28 June 2020); J Braithwaite, 'Making Tax Law More Certain: A Theory', *Working Paper No 44*,

define the hypothetical scheme,[153] arrangement or transaction to uncover the purpose, motive or intention,[154] in turn, be able, if necessary, to quantify the amount of tax benefit, gain or advantage avoided.[155] As this test is built on broad, relative and indefinite concepts, such as 'reasonable or unreasonable', 'acceptable or unacceptable', 'permissible or impermissible', 'responsible or irresponsible' and 'appropriateness or inappropriateness', power is shifted to the tax administration in the first step to apply it, although the result of its application could be reviewed by the courts in a second step.[156]

Under this test, a determination should be made as to what the taxpayer would have normally done had there not been any scheme, arrangement or transaction.[157] On such grounds, the counterfactual would require a hypothetical reconstruction of the events that would have happened, what might reasonably or appropriately be expected to have happened, or which hypothetical state of affairs had the avoidance transaction or arrangement not been entered into, creating uncertainty within multiple reasonable options.[158]

As mentioned in section 3.1.3., the Canadian GAARs[159] in section 245(3) works with the reasonableness test and the bona fide purpose test to assess the purpose of the scheme or arrangement. In this sense, an avoidance transaction does not include a transaction that 'may reasonably be considered to have been undertaken or arranged primarily for bona fide purposes other than to obtain the tax benefit'. Under the South African GAARs,[160] section 80G(1) states that the 'reasonable test' sets out a distinction between 'permissible' and 'impermissible' tax avoidance, describing the latter as tax avoidance practices that extend beyond what is legally acceptable. The permissible test is based on three tests, namely (i) 'abnormality of the transaction', (ii) the lack of commercial substance and (iii) whether the transaction frustrates the legislative purpose.[161]

The Australian National University, Australian Taxation Office, Centre for Tax System Integrity, 2002, p. 5, https://www.anu.edu.au/fellows/jbraithwaite/_documents/Articles/Making_Tax_2003.pdf, (accessed 28 June 2020).

153. N Orow, *General Anti-Avoidance Rules: A Comparative International Analysis*, pp. 94-109.
154. Almendral, 'Tax Avoidance and the European Court of Justice', pp. 560-582.
155. R Edmonds, 'Part IVA and Anti-Avoidance: Where Are We Now?', *Revenue L. J.*, vol. 12, no. 1, 2002, p. 67.
156. J Dácio Rolim, *Normas antielisivas tributárias*, São Paulo, Dialética, 2001, pp. 59-60; J Dácio Rolim, 'Reflexões sobre normas gerais antielisivas na jurisprudência', in D Yamashita (ed.), *Planejamento tributário à luz da jurisprudencia*, São Paulo, Lex, 2007; J Dácio Rolim and P Rosenblatt, 'Dez anos da Norma Geral Antielisiva no Brasil', *Revista Dialética de Direito Tributário*, no. 197, 2012, pp. 83-96.
157. N Orow, *General Anti-Avoidance Rules: A Comparative International Analysis*, p. 174.
158. Rosenblatt and Tron, 'General Report', p. 21; Cashmere, 'A GAAR for the United Kingdom? The Australian Experience', p. 149.
159. CA: Canada Income Tax Act. *See* O'Brien, 'Canada — GAARs: An Emerging Trend in the Tax Landscape', p. 153.
160. ZA: South Africa Income Tax Act 58 of 1968. *See* Oguttu, 'South Africa - GAARs: An Emerging Trend in the Tax Landscape', pp. 615-617.
161. Arnold, 'A Comparison of Statutory General Anti-Avoidance Rules', p. 13.

Under the UK GAARs,[162] section 207 states that tax arrangements are deemed to be 'abusive' if they are arrangements that the entering into or carrying out of cannot reasonably be regarded as a reasonable course of action in relation to the relevant tax provisions, taking into consideration all the circumstances. Nonetheless, the statutory UK GAARs works differently from the Australian GAARs because it provides for an exception to arrangements that 'cannot reasonably be regarded as a reasonable course of action'. The Indian GAARs can be highlighted as well, being mostly based on the South African GAARs and the Canadian GAARs, albeit providing a non-exhaustive list of criteria that may be taken into account to define the counterfactual.

As demonstrated by domestic law, uncertainty can be avoided or diminished by the use of a second reasonableness test to identify the purpose, motive or intention of the scheme, arrangement or transaction (double reasonableness test), which is in fact applied by many jurisdictions. By and large, the main features of the quoted domestic GAARs, namely the 'reasonableness test', are the capacity to (i) interpret and apply indeterminate concepts to determine the counterfactual, (ii) identify and measure the tax benefit, gain or advantage and (iii) find a tax avoidance purpose, motive or intention.[163] It follows that statutory GAARs may have the first reasonableness test to find a tax benefit, gain or advantage, and the second reasonableness test to identify the purpose, motive or intention of the scheme, arrangement or transaction. Consequently, reasonableness is considered an objective test related to the purpose of the scheme, arrangement or transaction (i.e., its effects), and not the taxpayer's purpose, intent or motive.[164] The PPT is based on a double reasonableness test inasmuch as the first is based on the 'reasonableness test' and the second on the 'object and purpose of the relevant provisions of the MLI,' which will be analysed in section 5.3.

The PPT does not use the 'artificiality' criterion to find the nature of the scheme. 'Artificiality' can be used as a synonym for unnaturalness, contrivance, irregularity, complexity, fictitiousness, abnormality and so on. Even though it is not a concept, 'artificiality' can be understood as the lack of a logical and coherent correspondence between the arrangement and the underlying economic reality.[165] In this sense, the concept of artificiality can be used to distinguish less acceptable tax avoidance schemes from more acceptable tax planning schemes.[166] As a reference, 'artificiality' is the criterion used by the ECJ,[167] and it was constantly used as reference in European case

162. UK: Finance Act 2013. *See* Freedman, 'The United Kingdom — GAARs: An Emerging Trend in the Tax Landscape', p. 751. Freedman stresses that the moderate targeted approach can be seen in the 'double reasonableness test' that forms the centrepiece of UK GAAR legislation.
163. Rosenblatt, *General Anti-Avoidance Rules for Major Developing Countries*, p. 64.
164. Arnold, 'The Canadian General Anti-Avoidance Rule'.
165. Almendral, 'Tax Avoidance and the European Court of Justice', p. 563; Thuronyi, *Comparative Tax Law*, pp. 133-205.
166. N Orow, *General Anti-Avoidance Rules: A Comparative International Analysis*, pp. 76-94.
167. The ECJ went on to state as follows in UK: ECJ, *Cadbury Schweppes* (C-196/04):

> In order for a restriction on the freedom of establishment to be justified on the ground of prevention of abusive practices, the specific objective of such a restriction must be to prevent conduct involving the creation of wholly artificial arrangements which do not reflect economic reality, with a view to escaping the tax normally due on the profits generated by activities carried out on national territory....[i]n order to find that there is

law before the BEPS Project.[168] Given that there is no universal legal benchmark or standard for determining what constitutes an artificial scheme, arrangement or transaction, other vague concepts are used in domestic legal systems to analyse the nature of a scheme, arrangement or transaction, such as abnormality, lack of business purpose, non-tax purpose, the deviation of legal form from substance (substance over form) or economic substance (economic reality). As mentioned, this article seeks to group similar features, with the awareness that it is impossible to segregate basic elements that can be interconnected or linked.

The term 'all relevant facts and circumstances' is not defined in the *Commentary on the PPT*,[169] although in my opinion, Examples A-M (on general treaty abuse cases) and A-F (on conduit treaty abuse cases) contained in the *Commentary on Article 29 of the OECD Model*[170] provide some guidelines on how to understand its meaning.[171] These examples suggest that the existence (or absence) of a core commercial activity other than obtaining treaty benefits can be seen as highly relevant facts and circumstances that can be used to determine whether the PPT should be applied.[172]

5.2 The 'Form and Motives' of the Scheme, Transaction or Arrangement

The 'purpose, motive or intention' is difficult to identify as a common requirement or primary element. A presumption is used as a distinguishing requirement or secondary element by contrasting the purposes, motives or intention (business, non-tax and bona fide) and the form of the scheme, arrangement or transaction to classify its end–result as a test based on the 'business purpose', 'non-tax purpose' and 'bona fide purpose'. Of the three tests based on the 'business purpose', 'non-tax purpose' and 'bona fide purpose', the last one is the most interesting formulation because it is broader than the

such an arrangement there must be, in addition to the subjective element consisting of the intention to obtain a tax advantage, objective circumstances showing that, despite formal observance of the conditions laid down by Community law, the objective pursued by the freedom of establishment... has not been achieved... In those circumstances, in order for the legislation of the CFCs to comply with Community law, the taxation provided for by that legislation must be excluded where, despite the existence of tax motives the incorporation of a CFC reflects economic reality. That incorporation must correspond with an actual establishment intended to carry on genuine economic activities in the host Member State... that finding must be based on objective factors that are ascertainable by third parties with regard, in particular, to the extent to which the CFC physically exists in terms of premises, staff and equipment.

168. Another noteworthy issue concerns whether the PPT refers to the current state of affairs or to the time when the arrangement or transaction occurred because there are no guidelines or indicia in the provision as to whether reasonable judgment should consider the current state of affairs or the time when the events took place; this in itself contributes to a lack of certainty. An analysis of this issue is beyond the scope of this book.
169. Kuźniacki, 'The Principal Purpose Test (PPT) in BEPS Action 6 and the MLI'.
170. *OECD Model: Commentary on Article 29*, paras 182 and 187.
171. *OECD Model: Commentary on Article 29*, paras 182 and 187.
172. In the same sense, Kuźniacki, 'The Principal Purpose Test (PPT) in BEPS Action 6 and the MLI' states that 'In these examples, relevant facts are not distinguished from relevant circumstances but seem to be considered together as the source of evidence and factors used for determining an application of the PPT.'

business purpose, as it is not limited to business schemes and could include family or other types of schemes, arrangements or transactions.[173] The tests based on the form and motives of the scheme, arrangement or transaction are intertwined with the tests based on the purpose, motive or intention because tax avoidance is a purpose-based notion where it is necessary to determine a logical connection among all the elements that are oriented toward obtaining a tax benefit, gain or advantage.

This group could also be classified as establishing rules that mandate an interpretation and application of tax law to the economic substance of a transaction (or series of transactions) rather than the legal form.[174] From this perspective, the provision would allow tax administrations to reassess based on a hypothetical legal transaction that better reflects the underlying economic substance. This test is a statutory substance-over-form rule based on the nature of the scheme.[175] The scope of the purpose depends on how it is drafted in a particular GAAR, according to three main approaches, namely (i) the sole purpose (narrow scope); (ii) a significant, primary, main, paramount, predominant, dominant, ruling, prevailing, decisive, principal or the most influential purpose (intermediate scope); or (iii) one of the purposes or a purpose (broader scope). Any of these three approaches requires that different tax and non-tax purposes in a multi-purpose transaction be balanced to decide whether it is tax-driven.

Regarding domestic approaches, the UK GAARs[176] uses the expression 'economic purposes' instead of 'business purpose', 'non-tax purpose' or 'bona fide purpose'. The South African GAARs[177] borrowed the 'bona fide purpose, other than obtaining a tax benefit' test from the Canadian GAARs and also uses the broader concept of 'lack of

173. Rosenblatt and Tron, 'General Report', p. 24; Rosenblatt, *General Anti-Avoidance Rules for Major Developing Countries*, pp. 74-78.
174. Krever, 'Chapter 1. General Report', p. 4.
175. Arnold, 'The Canadian General Anti-Avoidance Rule', p. 225.
176. UK: Finance Act 2013, s. 207(4), catalogues some indicators by which tax arrangement might be abusive in a non-exhaustive list. Cases in this list include 'economic purposes' when considering abusive tax arrangements. Section 207 stipulates the meaning of 'tax arrangements' and 'abusive' as:

> (4) Each of the following is an example of something which might indicate that tax arrangements are abusive – (a) the arrangements result in an amount of income, profits or gains for tax purposes i.e. significantly less than the amount for economic purposes, (b) the arrangements result in deductions or losses of an amount for tax purposes i.e. significantly greater than the amount for economic purposes, and (c) the arrangements result in a claim for the repayment or crediting of tax (including foreign tax) that has not been, and is unlikely to be, paid, but in each case only if it is reasonable to assume that such a result was not the anticipated result when the relevant tax provisions were enacted.

See Freedman, 'The United Kingdom — GAARs: An Emerging Trend in the Tax Landscape', pp. 741-762.
177. ZA: South Africa Income Tax Act 58 of 1968. *See* W Oguttu, 'South Africa – GAARs: An Emerging Trend in the Tax Landscape', pp. 615-617. Oguttu stresses that an avoidance arrangement constitutes an impermissible avoidance arrangement if it exhibits certain tainted elements in the context of business, in a context other than business or in any other context; especially pointing to the bona fide business purpose and the lack of commercial substance to conclude that the South Africa GAARs apply the common law doctrine of substance over form.

commercial substance' or 'commerciality test'. The Canadian GAARs[178] works with the 'reasonableness and bona fide purposes tests', meaning that an avoidance transaction does not include a transaction that 'may reasonably be considered to have been undertaken or arranged primarily for bona fide purposes other than to obtain the tax benefit'. The Indian GAARs[179] also adopts the Canadian GAARs's bona fide purpose. In addition, this law has codified the substance-over-form doctrine borrowed from the South African GAARs based on the lack of 'commercial substance'. The Australian GAARs[180] explicitly states in section 177D that schemes are deemed to be for the purpose of obtaining a tax benefit if the scheme would be concluded, having regard to certain matters, such as (i) the way the arrangement or transaction was entered into or carried out and, mainly, (ii) the form and substance of the arrangement or transaction.

Each domestic law referenced is based on the codification of two main features, namely (i) the lack of commercial substance or business purpose and (ii) the substance over form or form and motives by contrasting the purpose, motive or intention (business, non-tax and bona fide) and the form of the scheme, arrangement or transaction to qualify its end result.

One of the most interesting issues concerns whether the principle of good faith enshrined in Article 26 and/or Article 38(1)(c) of the VCLT can be applied to the PPT. The interpretation of tax treaties laid down in Articles 31 and 32 of the VCLT, and the function of good faith specifically will become even more critical because of the transfer of discretionary power to the tax administrations of states under the MLI. Broadly speaking, there are concerns as to whether the principle of good faith can be considered as an 'inherent anti-abuse rule' existing in tax treaties and if it can counteract treaty abuse (such as treaty shopping or rule shopping) as an unwritten prohibition of abuse of tax treaties.

Both scholars[181] and national courts[182] disagree on the existence and application of such an unwritten anti-abuse rule in tax treaties (the principle of good faith). In my

178. CA: Canada Income Tax Act. *See* O'Brien, 'Canada — GAARs: An Emerging Trend in the Tax Landscape', p. 153; E Mazansky, 'South Africa's New General Anti-avoidance Rule: The Final GAAR', *Bull. Int'l Taxn*, vol. 61, no. 4, 2007, pp. 162-163; T Bowler, 'Countering Tax Avoidance in the UK: Which Way Forward?', The Institute for Fiscal Studies, *TLRC Discussion Paper No 7*, February 2009, p. 165, https://www.ifs.org.uk/comms/dp7.pdf (accessed 28 June 2020).

179. In India, the Finance Act 2012 incorporated anti-avoidance provisions in the form of general anti-avoidance rules under Chapter X-A of the Income Tax Act 1961 (ITA), available at https://www.incometaxindia.gov.in/Pages/Direct-Taxes-Data.aspx (accessed 9 October 20 18). *See* Kapadia, 'India — GAARs: An Emerging Trend in the Tax Landscape', p. 326.

180. AU: Australia Tax Laws Amendment (Combating Multinational Tax Avoidance) Act 2015. *See* Krever and Mellor, 'Australia — GAARs: An Emerging Trend in the Tax Landscape', p. 50.

181. Concurring with the existence of such an unwritten anti-abuse rule, DA Ward, 'Access to Tax Treaty Benefits: Research Report Prepared for the Advisory Panel on Canada's System of International Taxation', *Advisory Panel on Canada's System of International Taxation*, 2008; FA Engelen, *On Values and Norms: The Principle of Good Faith in the Law of Treaties and the Law of Tax Treaties in Particular*, Netherlands, Kluwer, 2006. On the other hand, dissenting with the existence of such an unwritten anti-abuse rule, *see* Chand, *The Interaction of Domestic Anti-Avoidance Rules*, s. 2.1.3.1; Danon, 'Treaty Abuse in the Post-BEPS World', s. 2.3.2.2.

182. As reported by Chand, *The Interaction of Domestic Anti-Avoidance Rules*, s. 2.1.3.1, accepting; the Swiss Supreme Court has endorsed similar reasoning. The Federal Tribunal defined this concept by referring to the 'look-through', 'bona fide' and 'activity' provisions suggested by the

opinion, such a rule does exist because any provision of a tax treaty must be interpreted in light of its purpose, even if the purpose is 'unwritten,' so as to be in line with the whole legal system. Nonetheless, the principle of good faith must be applied to a lesser extent if applied as a distinguishing requirement or a secondary element of the PPT.[183] As a result, if the PPT is included in a tax treaty, the good faith principle would be a supplementary requirement. In this sense, the treaty PPT will prevail over the inherent anti-abuse rule, as it is a written anti-avoidance rule and can be considered a *lex specialis* in comparison to the unwritten anti-abuse rule.[184]

This is significant because the preamble and Article 6 of the MLI establish that tax treaties attempt to eliminate double taxation 'without creating opportunities for non-taxation or reduced taxation ...'. As Article 31(2) of the VCLT states that the context of a treaty includes its preamble, the *BEPS Action 6 Final Report*[185] notes that the foregoing statement and objectives ought to be considered when interpreting and applying the provisions of the relevant tax treaty. The issue that must be considered is whether these considerations (without creating opportunities for non-taxation or reduced taxation) represent a truly stated purpose for their application to bilateral tax treaties *vis-à-vis* the main goal of tax treaties, which is to promote exchanges of goods and services and the movement of capital and persons by eliminating international double taxation. Briefly put, the MLI has given a new dimension to tax treaty interpretation under the principles of Articles 31-33 of the VCLT.[186]

These new treaty terms included in the MLI must be given an 'ordinary meaning' in their 'context' and 'in light of the object and purpose'. This will give rise to an issue regarding the role of the text of the MLI and its *Explanatory Statement vis-à-vis* the *BEPS Action 6 Final Report* and the *2017 OECD Model* and the *Commentary* thereon, which now entail an unprecedented base waiting to be considered. This interpretative material includes not only the MLI itself, the *Explanatory Statement* to the MLI, and the original bilateral agreements with which the MLI will coexist, but also the entire OECD/G20 BEPS Package of which the MLI was created.[187]

There will also be greater importance attributed to supplementary means of interpretation when one considers that the treaty terms in the MLI are new (Article 32 of the VCLT). In this respect, the MLI preamble, when referring to the loss of tax revenue for governments due to 'aggressive international tax planning that has the

---

2014 Commentary on the OECD Model (CH: SC, 28 November 2005, *ApS v. Federal Tax Administration*, 8 ITLR 536, pp. 536-562). In the same sense, IL: DC Tel Aviv-Yafo, 30 December 2007, *Yanko-Weiss Holdings Ltd v. Holon Assessing Office*, 10 ITLR 524, pp. 524-550.

Rejected in *Vodafone International Holdings BV v. Union of India* (Civil Appeal No 733 on 20 January 2012) and CA: *MIL (Investments) SA v. Canada*, 9 ITLR 25, 18 August 2006.

183. In this sense, my analysis is not in line with Chand, *The Interaction of Domestic Anti-Avoidance Rules*, s. 2.1 or Danon, 'Treaty Abuse in the Post-BEPS World', s. 2.3. These are the most recent works analysing these issues.
184. Engelen, *On Values and Norms*; Ward, 'Access to Tax Treaty Benefits'.
185. OECD, *Action 6 Final Report 2015*.
186. Gomes, 'International Taxation and the Challenges for Multilateralism'; Gomes, 'Implementation in Practice of the Principal Purpose Test in the Multilateral Convention'.
187. Gomes, 'International Taxation and the Challenges for Multilateralism'; Gomes, 'Implementation in Practice of the Principal Purpose Test in the Multilateral Convention'.

effect of artificially shifting profits to locations where they are subject to non-taxation or reduced taxation', will play a key role in the interpretation process. Indeed, this is one of the major issues to be discussed.

Commentators, however, have stated that the object and purpose of a tax treaty is only one of the elements that needs to be considered for interpretation purposes and that this cannot override the treaty's clear substantive provisions.[188] In my opinion, the following distinctions should be made. Although it will be clear in the future from the preamble of tax treaties that the latter should not be used to create double non-taxation, this secondary objective must be equally balanced with the primary objective, namely the avoidance of double taxation (which must be analysed on a case-by-case basis). Accordingly, there is no hierarchy between these two objectives in the interpretative process. Nonetheless, the objectives in the preamble should not be used to deny treaty benefits beyond the text or the scope of the potentially applicable treaty anti-avoidance provision.[189] For this reason, the good faith principle must play a key role not only in attributing the appropriate weight to the ordinary meaning of treaty terms but, principally, in taking into account their new context and the new objects and purposes of tax treaties - specifically its function of tempering states in the exercise of the discretionary power by tax administrations (now broader than ever) - to deny treaty application to taxpayers.

The PPT has not been drafted literally based on the 'form and motives' to rely on tests grounded on the 'business purpose', 'non-tax purpose' or 'bona fide purpose nature' of the scheme, transaction or arrangement.

5.3 The 'Purpose of the Legislation': The Purposive Interpretation Requirement or the Objective Element

This approach intends to further the literal meaning of the law to investigate the context by reading the statute as a whole to ascertain its purpose, its motive or the intention of the legislation in order to elucidate the underlying tax policy[190] as a test based on 'the parliamentary intention', 'the underlying policy of a provision' or 'the purposive interpretation'.

188. L De Broe, 'Tax Treaty and EU Law Aspects of the LOB and PPT Provision Proposed by BEPS Action 6', in RJ Danon (ed.), *Rethinking Corporate Tax Policy: OECD/EU Perspectives and Swiss Corporate Tax Reform III*, Kluwer/Schulthess, 2017, pp. 203-204.
189. Danon, in 'Treaty Abuse in the Post-BEPS World', states that there is a hierarchy between these two objectives. In this sense, creating double non-taxation is the primary goal and should supersede the second goal, which is to avoid double taxation.
190. The purposive interpretation may refer to different ideas. In this sense, the meaning used in this work is a simplification just to highlight the PPT approach based on the 'object and purpose of the relevant provisions' of the MLI, as may be read in Article 7.1. For an in-depth analysis of the MLI, the following should be considered: the subjective intention of the parliament, the subjective intent of the legislature, the underlying police, the rationale or justification of parliamentary actions and, finally, a prediction of what the legislature may have intended. *See also* Arnold, 'The Long, Slow, Steady Demise of the General Anti-Avoidance Rule', pp. 496-503; RA Tooma, *Legislating Against Tax Avoidance*, Amsterdam, IBFD, 2008, pp. 44-50, 78.

Article 7(1) of the MLI states that '[...] unless it is established that granting that benefit in these circumstances would be in accordance with the object and purpose of the relevant provisions of the Covered Tax Agreement'. The PPT will not apply if a taxpayer can prove beyond dispute that the granting of the benefit is in line with the object and purpose of the relevant treaty provisions. As the *Commentary on the OECD Model* suggests that it is the taxpayer that must establish or prove this, it appears relatively clear that the burden rests on the taxpayer.[191]

In my opinion, this feature (the purposive interpretation requirement) supports the objective assessment of the principal purposes of the scheme, arrangement or transaction, indicating that the object and purpose of the treaty is to prevent treaty shopping, and suggests that the purpose, motive or intention is the overall objective of the transaction. Other authors, however, level the criticism that this could lead to a risky, speculative tax policy analysis.[192]

Concerning domestic approaches, the UK GAARs[193] has introduced a test based on parliamentary intention whereby the transaction or arrangement must be consistent with the principles on which the provisions are based, expressed or implied, or with their policy objectives. In the South African GAARs,[194] the provision is guided by 'the misuse and abuse tests' borrowing the 'rationale' from the Canadian GAARs provision 'in order to find the meaning that harmonizes the wording, object, spirit and purpose of the provisions of the Income Tax Act'. The Canadian GAARs[195] also works with the concept of 'misuse or abuse,' relying on the object, spirit or purpose of the provision in section 245(4), all of them highlighting a common link, namely a purposive interpretation.

This section states that there is abusive tax avoidance if it cannot be reasonably concluded that a tax benefit, gain or advantage would be consistent with the object, spirit or purpose of the provision relied upon by the taxpayer. In this sense, schemes,

191. OECD, *Action 6 Final Report 2015*, p. 58; *OECD Model: Commentary on Article 29*, para 181.
192. Rosenblatt, *General Anti-Avoidance Rules for Major Developing Countries*, p. 81; Arnold, 'The Long, Slow, Steady Demise of the General Anti-Avoidance Rule'; N Orow, *General Anti-avoidance Rules: A Comparative International Analysis*, pp. 220-222; J Freedman, 'Interpreting Tax Statutes: Tax Avoidance and the Intention of Parliament', *L. Q. Rev.*, vol. 123, 2007, pp. 74-75, https://www.law.upenn.edu/institutes/taxlaw/pastseminars/201011papers/Freedman1.pdf (accessed 25 June 2020).
193. UK: Finance Act 2013, s. 207(2). *See* Freedman, 'The United Kingdom — GAARs: An Emerging Trend in the Tax Landscape', pp. 741-762.
194. ZA: South Africa Income Tax Act 58 of 1968, s. 80. *See* W Oguttu, 'South Africa - GAARs: An Emerging Trend in the Tax Landscape', pp. 615-617; Mazansky, 'South Africa's New General Anti-avoidance Rule', pp. 161-163; Arnold, 'A Comparison of Statutory General Anti-Avoidance Rules', pp. 1-15. *See also* Bowler, 'Countering Tax Avoidance in the UK', p. 165. The provision sets forth:

> Impermissible tax avoidance arrangements 80A. An avoidance arrangement is an impermissible avoidance arrangement if its sole or main purpose was to obtain a tax benefit and [...] or (c) in any context - [...]; or (ii) it would result directly or indirectly in the misuse or abuse of the provisions of this Act (including the provisions of this Part).

195. CA: Canada Income Tax Act. *See* O'Brien, 'Canada — GAARs: An Emerging Trend in the Tax Landscape', p. 153.

arrangements or transactions that rely on specific provisions, whether incentive provisions or otherwise, for their tax consequences or on general rules of Canadian tax law, can be negated if these consequences are so inconsistent with the general purpose, motive or intention of the Act as they could not have been within the contemplation of the legislature. In civil law systems, the purposive approach is often called a 'teleological interpretation,' playing a significant role in the codification of the abuse of law and fraud of law doctrines.[196]

The PPT provision in the MLI focuses on an objective element, namely the issue as to whether the benefit, gain or advantage 'would be in accordance with the object and purpose of the relevant provisions of the Covered Tax Agreement'. Commentators diverge about whether the objective criterion of the PPT should be examined in light of the objective of the applicable treaty provision or by reference to the treaty as a whole.[197] Relying on the text of the PPT provision as found in the MLI,[198] only the objective and purpose of the relevant treaty provision should be taken into account.[199] Nonetheless, this approach poses several practical difficulties, as 'it is generally not obvious to assign a specific purpose to treaty provisions such as the distributive rules whose general objective is simply to allocate taxing rights with a view to eliminating double taxation'.[200] Chand adds: 'In a tax avoidance scheme, a resident taxpayer always respects the formal conditions of tax treaties such as the conditions imposed by the time limit, ownership threshold or the relevant distributive rule.' Consequently, the scheme, transaction or arrangement implemented by a taxpayer must be in accordance

196. Rosenblatt and Tron, 'General Report', p. 25; Freedman, 'Interpreting Tax Statutes: Tax Avoidance and the Intention of Parliament', pp. 82-83; Z Preble and J Preble, 'Comparing the General Anti-Avoidance Rule of Income Tax Law with the Civil Law Doctrine of Abuse of Law', *Bull. Int'l Taxn*, vol. 62, no. 4, 2008, pp. 158-159; GJ Airs, et al., 'Abuse of Tax Law Across Europe (Part II)', *EC Tax Rev.*, vol. 19, no. 2, 2010, pp. 127-133.
197. *See*, e.g., De Broe, 'Tax Treaty and EU Law Aspects of the LOB and PPT Provision Proposed by BEPS Action 6', p. 213; Chand, *The Interaction of Domestic Anti-Avoidance Rules*, s. 3.5.2, pp. 116, 187; B Moreno, 'GAARs and Treaties: From the Guiding Principle to the Principal Purpose Test', p. 435; I Zahra, The Principal Purpose Test: A Critical Analysis of Its Substantive and Procedural Aspects - Part 1', p. 13, s. 3.3.1. Zahra points out:

> In the author's opinion, the reference to the relevant provisions is purposely ambiguous in referring to the tax as a whole, the preamble and the distributive rules on a case-by-case basis. This is somewhat logical and understandable, as it would be very challenging for a court or a tribunal to determine the object and purpose of an individual treaty article, without referring to the context of the tax treaty as a whole.

198. Article 31(1) VCLT.
199. Danon, 'Treaty Abuse in the Post-BEPS World', s. 4.3.2. In the same vein, *see* B Moreno, 'GAARs and Treaties: From the Guiding Principle to the Principal Purpose Test', p. 437; De Broe, 'Tax Treaty and EU Law Aspects of the LOB and PPT Provision Proposed by BEPS Action 6', p. 213.
200. Danon, 'Treaty Abuse in the Post-BEPS World', s. 4.3.2. In the same vein, *see* B Moreno, 'GAARs and Treaties: From the Guiding Principle to the Principal Purpose Test', p. 437; De Broe, 'Tax Treaty and EU Law Aspects of the LOB and PPT Provision Proposed by BEPS Action 6', p. 213.

with the 'object and purpose of the relevant provisions', an approach that would make the PPT provision and its goal redundant.[201]

201. *See* S van Weeghel, 'A Deconstruction of the Principal Purpose Test', *World Tax J.*, vol. 11, no. 1, 2019, s. 4, points out:

> Accordingly, before one applies article 29[9] of the 2017 OECD Model, the relevant provisions of the Convention should be interpreted in accordance with the interpretation rules of the VCLT. [...] Although article 31[1] of the VCLT prescribes that the terms of the treaty should be construed in their context and in light of the object and purpose of the treaty, as stated above, the ordinary meaning of the terms of the treaty is the standing point [...].

In the same article, *see* the interesting example involving Article 10 of the 2017 OECD Model to illustrate this tension:

> A simple example involving article 10 of the 2017 OECD Model may illustrate this tension:
>
> 1. Dividends paid by a company which is a resident of a Contracting State to a resident of the other Contracting State may be taxed in that other State.
> 2. However, dividends paid by a company which is a resident of a Contracting State may also be taxed in that State according to the laws of that State, but if the beneficial owner of the dividends is a resident of the other Contracting State, the tax so charged shall not exceed:
>   5 per cent of the gross amount of the dividends if the beneficial owner is a company which holds directly at least 25 per cent of the capital of the company paying the dividends throughout a 365 day period that includes the day of the payment of the dividend (for the purpose of computing that period, no account shall be taken of changes of ownership that would directly result from a corporate reorganisation, such as a merger or divisive reorganisation, of the company that holds the shares or that pays the dividend);
>
> 15 per cent of the gross amount of the dividends in all other cases.
>
> TCO, a company resident in State T, owns shares of SCO, a company listed on the stock exchange of State S. State T does not have a tax convention with State S, and therefore, any dividend paid by SCO to TCO is subject to a withholding tax on dividends of 25% in accordance with the domestic law of State S. Under the State R-State S tax convention, however, there is no withholding tax on dividends paid by a company resident in a contracting state and beneficially owned by a company resident in the other state. In order to avoid State S taxation in respect of SCO dividends, TCO decides to incorporate a holding company in State R (RCO) and transfers the shares in SCO to RCO. RCO has unrestricted ownership of the SCO shares and is under no obligation to pass on dividends received by it from SCO. RCO's ownership of TCO shares is not merely temporary, but long-term.
>
> In the application of article 10 of the 2017 OECD Model to this simple fact pattern, its terms must be interpreted. Some of these are defined in the treaty (dividends, company, resident, etc.), and others (e.g. paid by, paid to, beneficial owner) are not. If it is assumed that RCO is indeed a treaty resident, the beneficial owner of the SCO dividend, etc., a textual interpretation of article 10 would lead to the conclusion that RCO is entitled to the reduced treaty rate. If one would test this result against the object and purpose of article 10 in a narrow sense, i.e. the avoidance of double taxation in respect of dividends paid by residents of State S to residents of State R, textual and teleological interpretation would align. If one would then test the result against the object and purpose of the treaty as a whole, one may conclude that the conclusion is in line with the principal purpose of the treaty, i.e. the elimination of double taxation, but possibly not with one of the ancillary purposes, i.e. the prevention of tax avoidance, in particular in light of the guiding principle as introduced in the Commentary on Article 1 of the 2003 OECD Model. Regardless of whether the transfer of the SCO shares indeed resulted in tax avoidance, it appears that the application of article 31 of the VCLT results in an interpretation of article 10 to the effect that treaty

Accordingly, such an approach, which focuses on a textual, literal and isolated reading and interpretation of the treaty terms, should be rejected[202] on account of Article 31(1)[203] of the VCLT. The VCLT states that a treaty is to be interpreted in good faith in accordance with the ordinary meaning to be given to the terms of the treaty in their context and in 'the light of its object and purpose'. This statement is supported by Article 31(2)(3) of the VCLT, under which the 'context' of a tax treaty means the entire text of the tax treaty, including its preamble and annexes, taking into account subsequent agreements that might assist in the application and interpretation of a tax treaty – in this case, the MLI. Nonetheless, this implies another issue, namely what is the object and purpose of a tax treaty. One should consider that the 'object and

---

benefits are granted to RCO in accordance with the terms of article 10. In Villiger's words, one of the treaty's objects and purposes may have found its limits in the treaty text itself.

However, if article 29(9) of the 2017 OECD Model is applied in respect of this simple example, it is clear that the first prong of the test, i.e. the subjective part, is met: the principal purpose of the interposition of RCO is obtaining the benefit of the reduced taxation of dividends. The question then becomes whether nevertheless granting treaty benefits would be in accordance with the object and purpose of the relevant provisions of the State S-State R tax treaty. If the tension between the various purposes of the treaty cannot be resolved, treaty benefits will be denied, at least in the system presented by article 29(9). In this example, it becomes clear that article 29(9) does not merely confirm the guiding principle, but adds a dimension to it, and one could argue that article 29(9) reduces the weight of the principal purpose of the tax treaty (the avoidance of double taxation) in favour of an ancillary purpose (the prevention of tax avoidance).

In practice, the facts and the application of a tax treaty provision in respect of the facts are rarely as straightforward as suggested in this example. There may be reasons to question (i) the residence of RCO (if, in fact, its shareholder, TCO, manages the entity and State R would be the loser state pursuant to article 4(3) of the tax treaty between State T and State R); (ii) the reality of the involvement of RCO (perhaps it has no employees, it has no involvement with the ownership of the shares, dividends are paid directly to TCO or it does not record any dividend income in its accounts); or (iii) the beneficial ownership of the dividends (if there is an arrangement between TCO and RCO that effectively renders RCO a nominee for TCO). It would not be inconsistent with the textual interpretation of article 10 of the 2017 OECD Model to deny treaty benefits in the case of any of these circumstances. While that is quite clear with respect to residence and beneficial ownership, it may be less clear when the reality of the involvement of RCO is the issue, but also in that case, if it would be determined that the interposition of RCO amounts to a sham, the denial of treaty benefits seems almost universally accepted if one looks at international case law.

202. Chand, *The Interaction of Domestic Anti-Avoidance Rules*, pp. 193-196; B Moreno, 'GAARs and Treaties: From the Guiding Principle to the Principal Purpose Test', pp. 436-440.

203. Article 31 VCLT on the General Rule of Interpretation:

> 1.A treaty shall be interpreted in good faith in accordance with the ordinary meaning to be given to the terms of the treaty in their context and in the light of its object and purpose. 2. The context for the purpose of the interpretation of a treaty shall comprise, in addition to the text, including its preamble and annexes: (a) Any agreement relating to the treaty which was made between all the parties in connection with the conclusion of the treaty; (b) Any instrument which was made by one or more parties in connection with the conclusion of the treaty and accepted by the other parties as an instrument related to the treaty. 3. There shall be taken into account, together with the context: (a) Any subsequent agreement between the parties regarding the interpretation of the treaty or the application of its provisions; (b) Any subsequent practice in the application of the treaty which establishes the agreement of the parties regarding its interpretation; (c) Any relevant rules of international law applicable in the relations between the parties. 4. A special meaning shall be given to a term if it is established that the parties so intended.

purpose' of tax treaties are multi-fold in the sense that after the BEPS Project, if an amendment is made to the title and preamble of a tax treaty pursuant to Article 6(1) of the MLI, the PPT provision should be interpreted in light of the objectives of allocating taxing rights and eliminating double taxation along with the prevention of tax evasion and tax avoidance.[204]

In my opinion, the purpose of relevant treaty provisions regarding the application of the PPT can be determined by considering the ultimate and operative treaty purposes and their context. This suggestion finds support from Klaus Vogel and Rainer Prokisch,[205] who point out that although the ultimate and operative treaty purposes may not be very helpful in the interpretation of distributive rules (as it is precisely such distributive rules that identify the purpose of the treaty), a possible application of these purposes is critical to address treaty abusive practices.[206] Thus, there is no doubt that it must be ascertained from the text of the treaty itself, especially from the title and preamble.[207] To ascertain the object and purpose of a tax treaty, one should take into account the need to ensure the elimination of double taxation of income and also the non-creation of opportunities for non-taxation or reduced taxation through tax evasion or avoidance (including through treaty-shopping arrangements),[208] being treated equally in case-by-case analyses.[209]

---

204. Chand, *The Interaction of Domestic Anti-Avoidance Rules*, pp. 60-61; Zimmer, 'General Report', p. 195.
205. K Vogel and RG Prokisch, *IFA Cahiers 1993 — Volume 78A. Interpretation of Double Taxation Conventions, General Report*, pp. 69, 70-71; Rust, 'Article 24'.
206. Vogel and Prokisch, *IFA Cahiers 1993 — Volume 78a*, p. 72; Kuźniacki, 'The Principal Purpose Test (PPT) in BEPS Action 6 and the MLI', s. 2.6.
207. Article 6 MLI on Treaty Abuse:

> Purpose of a Covered Tax Agreement 1. A Covered Tax Agreement shall be modified to include the following preamble text: "Intending to eliminate double taxation with respect to the taxes covered by this agreement without creating opportunities for non-taxation or reduced taxation through tax evasion or avoidance (including through treaty-shopping arrangements aimed at obtaining reliefs provided in this agreement for the indirect benefit of residents of third jurisdictions).

208. Chand, in *The Interaction of Domestic Anti-Avoidance Rules*, pp. 193-197, has proposed a two-stage analysis to ascertain the object and purpose of the 'relevant provisions'. In the first stage, the taxpayer has to determine the object and purpose of the 'relevant provisions' in light of the objectives pursued by the tax treaty (legal analysis). Subsequently, in the second stage, taxpayer will have to prove that the transaction/arrangement respects the object and purpose of the 'relevant provisions' at stake (application of the legal analysis to the facts at stake).
209. In the recent Canadian case of Alta Energy (2018) (CA: TCC, 22 August 2018, *alta Energy Luxembourg SARL v. The Queen*, 2018 TCC 152, Case Law IBFD), a Luxembourg resident company claimed an exemption from capital gains taxation on disposal of shares in Canada under Article 13(5) of the Canadian — Luxembourg Income and Capital Tax Treaty (Convention between The Government of Canada and the Government of the Grand Duchy of Luxembourg for the Avoidance of Double Taxation and the Prevention of Fiscal Evasion with Respect to Taxes on Income and on Capital, 10 September 1999, as amended through 2010). One of the issues involved the application of the Canadian GAAR so as to deny the benefit of the exemption. In this interesting case the Tax Court of Canada (TCC) had to start examining the object, spirit and purpose of the relevant rule before determining whether the transaction deviated from that rationale. The TCC held that, though a tax treaty is a multi-purpose legal instrument and its preamble does give an indication of the general purpose of the tax treaty,

5.4 Interim Remarks

The 'reasonableness or appropriateness' and the 'purpose of the legislation or tests grounded on parliamentary intention, the underlying policy of a provision or purposive interpretation' as a distinguishing requirement or secondary element are workable standards that function as a generic comparative concept for a legal transplant of the PPT to tax treaties under the form of a comprehensive GAARs. Nonetheless, as the meaning of these words and concepts are generic, indefinite and open, the delimitation of the objective scope is a difficult task.

Regarding the purpose, motive or intention of the legislation, the PPT is based on an objective element in the sense that the benefit 'would be in accordance with the object and purpose of the relevant provisions of the Covered Tax Agreement'. Indeed, it will provide ample discretionary power to the tax administration and pose difficulties for courts in their attempts to carry out the purposive interpretation. Otherwise, the PPT has not been drafted literally based on the 'form and motives' to rely on tests based on the 'business purpose' of the scheme, transaction or arrangement.

Modern legislative drafting of GAARs is attempting to make them objective using two methods. First, some attributes are usually added to comprehensive GAARs, such as 'appropriateness or inappropriateness, reasonable or unreasonable, acceptable or unacceptable, permissible or impermissible, responsible or irresponsible', where the 'reasonableness' test is the one adopted by the PPT. Considering that these tests are based on open-textual concepts and indeterminate concepts, they could add even more uncertainty, but it is almost impossible to deliver a comprehensive definition.

Second, mixing a comprehensive definition (one of the principal purposes evaluated by reasonableness and purposive interpretation) with a non-exhaustive list-based approach (circumstances, results and concepts) could provide a criterion to be taken into account to identify and define the counterfactual arrangement or transaction, and ultimately a tax avoidance scheme. The PPT uses the first method, adding the 'reasonableness test', whereas the second method (identifying and defining circumstances, results and concepts) is not applied. The PPT resorts to a comprehensive definition without a list-based approach to be used as guidance for identifying and defining the counterfactual scheme, arrangement or transaction, thereby shifting power to tax administrations. Thus, it is difficult to find a balance between protecting the tax base and safeguarding taxpayers. As explained in section 4.4., on account of this absence, it may be susceptible to a top-down or bottom-up approach via domestic judicial interpretation or legislative counteraction, leading to a narrow definition of tax avoidance by national courts. The top-down or bottom-up approach could reduce the scope of the PPT concerning 'one of the principal purposes' to the 'main purpose,' as it was in the 'guiding principle'.

---

this alone remains vague regarding the application of specific distributive rules. It should be noted that this judgment did not took in account the new preamble to the MLI, this new focus on tax avoidance and treaty shopping will have a bearing on similar cases.

6 CLOSING REMARKS

The PPT reflects modern GAARs implying a certain degree of indeterminacy and the transfer of discretionary power to tax administrations, providing flexibility to react to new tax planning and abusive structures, as the concept of tax avoidance cannot be totally formalised or objectified. Therefore, such inevitable indeterminacy is not a conclusive argument against the adoption of the PPT as a GAAR in tax treaties. In fact, achieving absolute certainty in the application of tax law is impossible if one considers the inherent ambiguities of any language.[210] Furthermore, the main feature of the PPT, like other modern GAARs, relies on these indefinite and open concepts to target the widest possible range of treaty avoidance and abusive practices, playing a supplementary role to specific anti-treaty abuse provisions. It was chosen as the most attractive and preferable solution for governments, as the majority of signatories to the MLI intend to implement the PPT as a stand-alone provision to meet the minimum standard required by *BEPS Action 6*.

The common requirements (or primary elements) and the distinguishing requirements (or secondary elements) are workable standards that function as a generic comparative concept for a legal transplant of the PPT to tax treaties under the form of a comprehensive GAAR. Nonetheless, primary and secondary elements should be drafted in more detail to include presumptions, definitions, concepts and results to facilitate the implementation, application and interpretation of the PPT, reflecting a principle-based approach as well as a list-based approach.

A balanced approach could be reached through the doctrine of 'core commercial activity' or 'bona fide purpose', to be constructed by national courts. Ultimately, states might not give the PPT rule an interpretation that exceeds business reality or bona fide tests focused on substance. In this sense, the PPT might apply to both abusive restructurings and conduit situations not 'inextricably linked to a core commercial activity'.

The issue of the binding effect of the *Commentary on the OECD Model* will be amplified in the context of the Inclusive Framework, as most members of the Inclusive Framework are not OECD members. One should bear in mind that several conflicts and disputes will arise due to double taxation of income when a treaty partner follows a different approach that emphasises a textual interpretation of treaty provisions (lenient application) or the business purpose test that emphasises a substantive interpretation of treaty provisions (strict application), between different legal systems as mainly common law and civil law approaches. Ultimately, both extremes are not useful legal solutions. Overall, the current PPT wording (as included in the MLI) does not tend towards a narrow application.

It is impossible to craft an international template, as the MLI will be interpreted from many domestic legal, social and economic perspectives, including different legal

210. C Atkinson, 'General Anti-Avoidance Rules: Exploring the Balance between the Taxpayer's Need for Certainty and the Government's Need to Prevent Tax Avoidance', *J. Austl. Taxn.*, vol. 14, no. 1, 2012, pp. 15 and 18, http://jausttax.com.au/Articles_Free/JAT%20Volume%2014,%20Issue%201%20-%20Atkinson%20Free.pdf (accessed 25 June 2020).

systems. As mentioned, absolute consistency is impossible and tax administrations and domestic courts tend to examine tax treaty concepts (such as concepts of abuse and avoidance of domestic tax law) from the domestic law approach. Domestic GAARs (statutory or judicial doctrine) must be amended to broaden or reduce their scope through domestic legislative procedures. Conversely, from the OECD's perspective, the PPT guidelines are derived from the *BEPS Action 6 Final Report* and the *Commentary on the OECD Model* (2017), which require rounds of negotiations and coordination at the international level, revealing how its implementation is even more complicated. This could indeed lead to uncertainties and increased tax treaty disputes around the globe.

It is likely that courts may be more averse towards interpreting the PPT, as many of them do not consider themselves obliged to follow the *Commentary on the OECD Model*. In addition, the Inclusive Framework is deemed to be just a commitment to follow a 'minimum standard' by more than one hundred countries, many of which do not belong to the OECD or the G20. Nonetheless, it is the judiciary's role to establish interpretation and harmonisation to create consistency among all of these new anti-avoidance provisions worldwide regarding the tax treaty network. Ultimately, after the MLI comes into force, the efficacy of the PPT will depend on the willingness to exercise it by the contracting states, the reaction and response of the courts in the construction of its interpretation, application and implementation, and the commitment shown to the peer-review process established by the Inclusive Framework of the OECD/G20 BEPS Project. Indeed, there is still much to be accomplished.

CHAPTER 10

Virtual PE Concept and the Challenges of a Multilateral Solution

Michell Przepiorka & Gisele Barra Bossa

Michell Przepiorka and Gisele Barra Bossa analyze the impact of the MLI from the perspective of one of the countries that has not signed it, namely Brazil. Przepiorka and Barra Bossa argue that Brazil's recent treaty negotiations evidence an intent to align with the MLI in practice even if Brazil has long sought to safeguard its source tax base by, *inter alia*, adopting lower thresholds to the taxation of non-residents and using fixed margins in its transfer pricing regime in contravention of global consensus norms and standards. The chapter argues there may be room in tax multilateralism for Brazil's unique approach.

The challenges arising from the digital economy pose an opportunity to rediscusses the nexus consensus prevailing since the 1920s. The permanent establishment (PE) joint with the arm's-length principle is probably the cornerstone of international taxation. The present chapter aims to reviews the concept, considering the digitalization of the economy and the potential challenges of a multilateral solution.

1 INTRODUCTION

In 2009, one of the seminars on the International Fiscal Association (IFA) Seminar was "Is there a permanent establishment?" At that time, the general reporters Jacques Sasseville and Arvid Skaar indicated the question as one of the *most frequent tax treaty issues that advisers, government officials, and courts have to deal with. It is also a question that has a large number of ramifications and on which much has already been written.*[1]

Since the 1920s, the concept has been accepted as a fair compromise between source and residence taxation. However, it is well-known that the concept was developed when the only mobile international industry of any significance was international transportation.[2] The economy was physical.[3]

The concept has been disseminated among tax treaties worldwide with a harmonized wording. However, the scenario changed after 2017. The artificial avoidance of the concept of Permanent Establishment (PE) was one of the concerns the Organisation for Economic Co-operation and Development (OECD) addressed in the base erosion and profit shifting (BEPS) project, resulting in several changes in Article 5. The Multilateral Instrument (MLI) has contributed to a "deharmonization" of the treaties.[4]

The progressive dematerialization of the economy raises a new question,[5] is there a future to the PE concept? As Pasquale Pistone points out, *the validity and legitimacy of the PE concept depend on its ability to achieve a fair allocation of taxing powers between the state of residence of the enterprise and that in which it has a non-occasional economic presence,*[6] which cannot be affirmed today.

There is an emergent consensus that *the concept of PE is inadequate for the allocation of taxing jurisdiction over modern, mobile international business because it infringes neutrality and equivalence in taxation,*[7] but there is no clear answer to what nexus would be more suitable to allocate taxing rights on news business models.[8]

1. Sasseville, Jacques & Skaar, Arvid A. 'General Report. International Fiscal Association'. *IFA CAHIERS 2009—Vancouver (Canada)—Is There a Permanent Establishment?* Vol. 94-a, p. 21.
2. Arvid Aage Skaar, *Permanent Establishment: Erosion of a Tax Treaty Principle,* Second Edition, 6.1 The End of the 19th Century: The Relative Immobility of Production Factors.
3. *See* Roland T. Rust & Ming-Hui Huang, *The Physical Economy,* in The Feeling Economy. (Roland T. Rust & Ming-Hui Huang eds., Palgrave Macmillan, Cham. 2021).
4. Arvid Aage Skaar, *Permanent Establishment: Erosion of a Tax Treaty Principle,* Second Edition, at 1.2.2 Hypothesis: No Harmonization Through the OECD PE Definition (2020).
5. The technological inventions leading to the digital economy in the 21st century have increased the pressure on the conventional idea that taxing rights shall be based on the taxpayer's residence or the taxpayer's presence in another country (source of the income). The digital economy has strengthened the view that income does not have one specific "source," but several "sources." Thus, the question has been raised as to whether the location of the consumer (the market state) rather than the location of the taxpayer should be the basis for taxing rights, at least for the digital economy (Arvid Aage Skaar, *Permanent Establishment: Erosion of a Tax Treaty Principle,* Second Edition, at 6.2 the 21st century: mobile production factors and industries without physical presence).
6. Pasquale Pistone, *Permanent Establishment and the Digital Economy,* in New Trends in the Definition of Permanent Establishment (G. Maisto ed., IBFD 2019), at 9.2. Adjusting the PE concept to the challenges of the digital economy. *See also* F.A. García Prats, *OECD—Commentary on Article 5 of the OECD Model,* Global Topics IBFD (accessed May 1, 2021).
7. Arvid Aage Skaar, *Permanent Establishment: Erosion of a Tax Treaty Principle,* Second Edition, at 1.2.2 Hypothesis: No Harmonization Through the OECD PE Definition (2020).
8. Pasquale Pistone states that remote operation of business has changed the way of doing business, first with distance selling and then with the diffusion of e-commerce. Currently, business models are to a major or minor extent digitalized. This allows them to operate remotely by means of a virtual interaction with users and customers, often conducted by algorithms and bots. In such context, physical presence in the market country is optional, or limited to marginal functions of

The present chapter analyzes whether there is still room for the concept of PE as the digital economy progressively turns the brick-and-mortar economy. To do that, topic 1 states how the concept was first developed and why it has lost importance over time.

The subsequent topic states the developments in the concept after the BEPS project started until the issuance of the report on Pillar One and Pillar Two. Following that, the chapter presents the authors' opinions on the taxation of the digital economy. Finally, the paper depicts the Brazilian position on the taxation of the digital economy and the potential challenges of a multilateral solution.

2 THE CONCEPT OF PE: PAST

The concept of "PE" is part of the core of Bilateral Tax Treaties,[9] as Article 7(1) establishes the profits of an enterprise resident in one contracting state are taxable only in that State unless the enterprise carries on business through a PE in the other state. In other words, in the classic model, the source State is only entitled to tax business profits if a PE is characterized. As Schwarz points out, *it constitutes the minimum threshold that must be met before business profit may be taxed in a host country.*[10]

Traditionally, the concept is used to "determine the right of a Contracting State to tax the profits of an enterprise of the other Contracting State."[11] As it is known today, the concept of PE originated in German domestic law in the 19th century, appearing later in the Austria-Hungary-Prussia Tax Treaty signed in 1899.[12] The League of Nations played an essential role in its general use of tax treaties around the world.[13] From the early 1920s up to today, the PE threshold has been commonly used as the main instrument to establish taxing jurisdiction over business profits.[14]

The definition of a PE does not fall within the scope of a distributive rule, but is a "threshold for source State taxation of business profits; it is a criterion reflecting the involvement of a non-resident person in the economy of the source State to a significant degree."[15]

---

the business process, such as in the case of limited risk distributors Pasquale Pistone, *Permanent Establishment and the Digital Economy*, in New Trends in the Definition of Permanent Establishment (G. Maisto ed., IBFD 2019) at 9.1. Introduction.

9. Arvid Aage Skaar, *Permanent Establishment: Erosion of a Tax Treaty Principle,* Second Edition, 1.1 Permanent Establishment: A Commercially Separate But Legally Integrated Entity (2020).
10. Jonathan Schwarz, *Schwarz on Tax Treaties*, (Wolters Kluwer 2017) at 15-000.
11. OECD Commentaries to Article 5. Model Tax Convention on Income and on Capital: Condensed Version, (2017).
12. Brian J. Arnold, *Article 5: Permanent Establishment—Global Tax Treaty Commentaries*, Global Topics IBFD (P. Pistone ed., IBFD 2020), at 1.2.1.1. First references.
13. João Francisco Bianco, *O Estabelecimento Permanente na Legislação do Imposto de Renda*. In: Valdir de Oliveira Rocha (Coord.). Grandes Questões Atuais do Direito Tributário, (2005). at 300.
14. Arvid Aage Skaar, *Permanent Establishment: Erosion of a Tax Treaty Principle,* Second Edition, at 1.1 Permanent Establishment: A Commercially Separate But Legally Integrated Entity (2020).
15. Victor Uckmar, *Double Taxation Conventions,* in International Tax Law (Andrea Amateuci ed. Kluwer Law International), pp. 149-181 (166).

The PE threshold has advantages and disadvantages. Among the first, Brian Arnold enumerates (i) the effectiveness in tax enforceability, considering tax collection as well as the identification of taxpayers doing business in the country; (ii) legal certainty for taxpayers and tax authorities; (iii) limitation of compliance costs; and (iv) guarantee of the source State tax system integrity.[16] On the other hand, some disadvantages may arise from the introduction of any threshold: (i) it means that the source State gives up its tax rights—at least theoretically since, in practice, tax collection cannot be confirmed due to difficulties in tax enforcement; (ii) it induces some avoidance behavior as taxpayers start to organize their activities in such a way as not to reach the threshold.[17]

The acceptance of the concept is justified by the fact that it allows the reconciliation among requirements of international justice (prerogative of source-based taxation)[18] and practical prudence (prerogative of residence-based taxation), as it also simplifies and facilitates taxation of cross-border activities, accomplishing three main objectives: (i) assigning tax revenue to the source State; (ii) maintaining practicability by establishing a minimum threshold); and (iii) providing neutrality between the different forms of a secondary establishment available to foreign investors.[19]

Probably for these reasons, until the 2017 OECD Model Tax Convention, the wording of Article 5 in both the OECD and the UN Model has remained pretty the same since the 1963 OECD Model, providing for three main species of PE: (i) physical or basic-rule PE; (ii) construction PE; and (iii) agency PE. The UN Model also includes a service PE and an insurance PE clause.[20]

Notice that despite no significant changes in the wording, one cannot say the same regarding the commentaries that experienced numerous changes were made during that period, including clarifications and even new interpretations of the definition of PE as expressed in paragraph 1 of Article 5.[21]

The physical PE is defined in Article 5(1) as a fixed place of business through which the business of an enterprise is wholly or partly carried on. Therefore, three

16. Brian J. Arnold, *Article 5: Permanent Establishment—Global Tax Treaty Commentaries*, Global Topics IBFD, at 1.1.2.7.2. Advantages.
17. Brian J. Arnold, *Article 5: Permanent Establishment—Global Tax Treaty Commentaries*, Global Topics IBFD, at 1.1.2.7.3. Disadvantages.
18. Contrariwise, Dornelles sustains that *the "permanent establishment," although generally recognized as an expression of the source principle, is, in reality, much more linked to the principle of domicile than to any other* (Francisco N. Dornelles, *O Modelo ONU para Eliminar a Dupla Tributação da Renda, e os Países em Desenvolvimento*. In A. Toffoli Tavolaro, B. Machado & I.G. da Silva Martins, Princípios Tributários no Direito Brasileiro e Comparado, at 208 (1988).
19. Ekkehart Reimer, *Article 5: Permanent Establishment*, in Klaus Vogel on Double Taxation Conventions, I. Overview and Main Features (Ekkehart Reimer & Alexander Rust eds, Wolters Kluwer 2014).
20. Jean Schaffner also lists: (i) Substantial equipment PE, defined as place of location of the relevant equipment (in certain particular double tax treaties, but not in any of the OECD or UN Models) and (ii) Offshore activities PE, defined as the place where natural resources are explored and/or extracted (e.g., oil and gas extraction) (*The Territorial Link as a Condition to Create a Permanent Establishment*, 41(12) Intertax (2013) at 1.2 Definition of Permanent Establishment).
21. *See* Jan de Joede et al. *Interpretation and Application of Article 5 (Permanent Establishment) of the OECD Model Tax Convention. Response from IBFD Research Staff* (Availabe at http://www.oecd.org/tax/treaties/49782184.pdf, 2012) at p. 2.

conditions must be met: (i) the existence of a "place of business"; (ii) this place of business must be fixed, i.e., it must be established at a distinct place with a certain degree of permanence; and, (iii) the carrying on of the business of the enterprise through this fixed place of business, which usually means that a person conducts the business of the enterprise in the State in which the fixed place is situated.

Each criterion adds layers of complexity to the characterization of a PE.[22] Despite OECD's efforts to clarify those criteria through the presentation of examples in the Commentaries, they are not sufficient to expose every nuance of reality, not to mention its lack of bindingness.[23] It is important to note that for the characterization of a PE, all elements need to be present, which can only be ascertained in the light of a specific case.[24]

The analysis of each criterion would be beyond the scope of this article. However, it seems important to address the definition of "place of business" since the physical presence can be the most challenging one to the adoption of the PE clause as an economic nexus to the digital economy[25] as it is so rooted in the history of the concept[26] and at the same time is so obsolete.[27]

In its turn, the concept of place is associated with tangible assets, whether unity or a collection, excluded the possibility of purely intangible property be qualified in this way.[28] In this sense, addressing the question, the OECD has already confirmed that a server or other automated equipment may be eligible as a place of business under certain conditions.[29]

Notice that the server is necessarily physically stored somewhere; so, this storage must meet the permanency test. On the other hand, under these conditions, a domain name, an IP address, or an internet website does not constitute tangible property and, therefore, does not constitute a PE.[30]

It is noteworthy that despite not being specifically designed to address the digital economy, the service PE clause could be an alternative mechanism to trigger source

22. *See* Jan de Joede et al. *Interpretation and Application of Article 5 (Permanent Establishment) of the OECD Model Tax Convention. Response from IBFD Research Staff* (2012).
23. Michell Przepiorka, *Estabelecimento Permanente à Brasileira*, Revista Direito Tributário Internacional Atual, vol. 02, (2017) at 147.
24. For an overview of these elements *see* Ekkehart Reimer, *Article 5: Permanent Establishment*, in Klaus Vogel on Double Taxation Conventions, I. Overview and Main Features (Ekkehart Reimer & Alexander Rust eds 2014); Brian J. Arnold, *Article 5: Permanent Establishment—Global Tax Treaty Commentaries*, Global Topics IBFD.
25. Alexander Hemmelrath & Elke Wilcox, *AOA, BEPS, E-Commerce—"Permanent Establishment" in Flux*, in: Practical Problems in European and International Tax Law: Essays in Honour of Manfred Mössner (Heike Jochum et al. 2016), at 8.3.6. E-commerce and the digital economy.
26. Vishesh Dhuldhoya, *The Future of the Permanent Establishment Concept*, 724a/(Special Issue) Bulletin for International Taxation (2018), at 1. Introduction.
27. D.W. Blum, *Permanent Establishments and Action 1 on the Digital Economy of the OECD Base Erosion and Profit Shifting Initiative—The Nexus Criterion Redefined?*, 69 Bulletin for International Taxation. 6/7, at s. 2.2. (2015).
28. Ekkehart Reimer, *Article 5: Permanent Establishment*, in Klaus Vogel on Double Taxation Conventions, (Ekkehart Reimer & Alexander Rust (eds)) at B. Article 5(1) OECD and UN MC).
29. Commentaries.
30. Commentaries.

taxation on digital services, partially solving the issue as it would not address online sales.[31]

The lack of a specific rule addressing the sales of goods online allowed multinationals to carry on their business worldwide without triggering the PE clause. International case law shows that tax authorities assessed taxpayers that shaped their business structures to avoid the PE concept.

On the matter, the Dell Case is illustrative. Despite the same clause wording, the National Courts of Spain and Norway reached different interpretations of the term "authority to conclude contracts in the name of the enterprise."[32] This shows not only the legal uncertainty circumventing the PE rules but also one of the firsts reactions against the base erosion due to the insufficiency of concept to deal with the dematerialization of the economy.[33]

3 THE CONCEPT OF PE POST BEPS: PRESENT

It is noticeable that changes in the concept of PE intended to address the digital economy may affect how it applies to the brick-and-mortar economy, leading to a period of uncertainty on its application. The main challenge is not ring-fence the new business structures, maintaining the level playing field.[34]

The question regarding the application of the definition of PEs in the context of e-commerce is not new. In fact, in 2000, the Technical Advisory Group on Monitoring the Application of Existing Treaty Norms for Taxing Business Profits (the "Business Profits TAG") faced the question.[35] However, it concluded at the time that *fundamental*

31. Jean Schaffner, *The Territorial Link as a Condition to Create a Permanent Establishment*, 41(12) Intertax (2013) at 5 Services permanent establishment.
32. *See* Stephane Austry, *Agent PE: The "in the name of" Concept*, in New Trends in the Definition of Permanent Establishment (G. Maisto ed., IBFD 2019).
33. *See* Adolfo J. Martín Jiménez, *The Spanish Position on the Concept of a Permanent Establishment: Anticipating BEPS, Beyond BEPS or Simply a Wrong Interpretation of Article 5 of the OECD Model?*, 70 Bulletin for International Taxation, 8 (2016).
34. In this sense, Jean Schaffner sustains that: the main concern here is to keep a level playing field between all forms of commerce, traditional commerce and e-commerce. The concept of permanent establishment maintains this level playing field. If one were to consider that no permanent establishment is required to create taxation rights in the source country of e-commerce income or if, on the contrary, e-commerce income is always taxed in the country of the provider, the level playing field would no longer be guaranteed. As a consequence, countries could be incentivized either to block e-commerce, as they are not able to get their fair share of profits from these activities, or, alternatively, promote excessively this form of commerce, if they believe that this could maximize their revenue. In other words, the right taxation should not as such be linked to the way in which a certain commerce is conducted (Jean Schaffner, *The Territorial Link as a Condition to Create a Permanent Establishment*, 41(12) Intertax (2013) at 1.2 Definition of Permanent Establishment).
35. Jeroen Kuppens reports that the TAG reached the following consensus (subject to some dissenting opinions of Portugal and Spain): (i) a website cannot, in itself, constitute a permanent establishment; (ii) a website hosting arrangement typically does not result in a permanent establishment for the enterprise that carries on business through that website; (iii) an Internet Service Provider (ISP) does not, except in very unusual circumstances, constitute a dependent agent of another enterprise; (iv) human intervention is not required for the existence of a permanent establishment; and (v) the issue of whether or not computer equipment at a given

changes should only be undertaken if there was a broad agreement that a particular alternative was clearly superior to the existing rules.[36]

Later on, in 2013, the OECD released the Action Plan on Base Erosion and Profit Shifting (BEPS),[37] which indicated the spread of the digital economy as a challenge for international taxation. In this context, the OECD presented 15 Action Plans to address BEPS issues,[38] tackling PE rules in Action Plan 1 ("Address the Tax Challenges of the Digital Economy")[39] and Action Plan 7 ("Prevent the Artificial Avoidance of PE Status").

Action 1 did not provide clear answers as to how the challenges arising from the digital economy should be addressed.[40] The Final Project indicated three types of solutions for future discussion: (i) alternatives to the existing PE threshold; (ii) the imposition of a withholding tax on certain types of digital transactions; and (iii) the introduction of an excise tax or other levy.[41]

BEPS Action Plan 7,[42] in its turn, deals with the artificial avoidance of PE status through (1) the use of commissionaire arrangements; (2) the abuse of the "independent agent" exception in Article 5(6) of the OECD Model; (3) specific activity exception in

location constitutes a permanent establishment depends on whether or not the functions performed through that equipment exceed the preparatory or auxiliary threshold, and this is to be decided on a case-by-case analysis (*Electronic Commerce—Permanent Establishments*, Global Topics IBFD (2021), at 3.2.1.1. General.

36. OECD, *Final report of the Technical Advisory Group on Monitoring the Application of Existing Treaty Norms for Taxing Business Profits* (2004) at 72.
37. OECD, *Action Plan on Base Erosion and Profit Shifting* (2013).
38. *See* Yariv Brauner, *What the BEPS?* 16 Florida Tax Review 2 (2014).
39. Yariv Brauner states that Action item one begins its description of issues with the same PE issue, yet it uses a more general language of "nexus" and taxable presence, not limiting itself to the PE questions of past (What the BEPS? 16 Florida Tax Review 2 (2014) at 72).
40. Jeroen Kuppens lists the main finds of the report: (i) it is not possible to ring-fence the digital economy for tax purposes; (ii) key features and "new" business models that exacerbate BEPS risks have been identified; (iii) certain BEPS risks have been addressed by other work in the actions of the OECD's BEPS Project. The actions that will need to consider specific issues linked to the digital economy are notably: (iii.i) Action 3 "Designing Effective Controlled Foreign Company Rules"; (iii.ii) Action 7 "Preventing the Artificial Avoidance of Permanent Establishment Status"; and (iii.iii) Actions 8-10 "Aligning Transfer Pricing Outcomes with Value Creation"; (iv) the digital economy also raises broader, direct tax challenges (nexus, characterization and data), as well as indirect tax challenges (VAT collection in the destination state for cross-border B2C transactions); (v) the collection of VAT in B2C transactions to be addressed at the end of 2015 through the work of Working Party 9; (vi) potential options regarding direct tax challenges have been refined; and (vii) the economic incidence of VAT and CIT and impact on potential options have been considered (*Electronic Commerce—Permanent Establishments*, Global Topics IBFD (2021), at 4.1. Report on Action 1 "Addressing the Tax Challenges of the Digital Economy").
41. (OECD (2015), *Addressing the Tax Challenges of the Digital Economy, Action 1*—2015 Final Report, OECD/G20Base Erosion and Profit Shifting Project, OECD Publishing, Paris, at 132).
42. *See* Sophie Chatel & Lee Harley, *Article 5 of the OECD Model: Recent Amendments and Upcoming Challenges*, in New Trends in the Definition of Permanent Establishment (G. Maisto ed., IBFD 2019).

Article 5(4), including the fragmentation of activities; (4) the exception in Article 5(3) by splitting of contracts.[43]

In other words, the plan addressed specific loopholes identified in practice and not solved in case law.[44] It has proposed amendments to the definition of a PE and the related Commentary on Article 5 of the OECD Model,[45] broadening its scope.[46]

Those changes were supposed to be broadly introduced through four articles of the Multilateral Convention to Implement Tax Treaty Related Measures to Prevent BEPS (MLI): (i) Article 12 MLI: Artificial avoidance of PE status through commissionaire arrangements and similar strategies; (ii) Article 13 MLI: Artificial avoidance of PE status through the specific activity exemptions; (iii) Article 14 MLI: Splitting up contracts; and (iv) Article 15 MLI: Definition of a person closely related to an enterprise.

However, these provisions are not minimum standards; thus, adhesion was not consistent.[47] More importantly, the new provisions shall still be tested before national courts to define its full extension. Until then, however, such changes will only lead to more uncertainty about applying the PE concept.

---

43. Vishesh Dhuldhoya, *The Future of the Permanent Establishment Concept*, 72 4a/Special Issue Bulletin for International Taxation (2018), at 2.2. Action 7: Preventing the artificial avoidance of PE status.
44. Zimmer, Dell, Amazon, Boston Scientific.
45. Daniel de Paiva Gomes, Eduardo de Paiva Gomes & Gisele Barra Bossa, *Tributação direta dos rendimentos provenientes da computação na nuvem: estabelecimento permanente*. In: Tathiane Piscitelli & Gisele Barra Bossa, Tributação da Nuvem, 2° Ed. (2020), at 113.
46. Beps Action 1 summarized the main changes as follows: 371. The work on Action7 (preventing the artificial avoidance of PE Status) concluded that activities previously considered to be merely preparatory or auxiliary in nature for the purposes of the exceptions usually found in the definition of PE may nowadays correspond to core business activities of an enterprise, particularly in the digital economy. It was therefore agreed to modify the list of exceptions contained in Article 5(4) of the OECD Model Tax Convention to ensure that each of the exceptions included therein is restricted to activities that are otherwise of a "preparatory or auxiliary" character, and a new anti-fragmentation rule was introduced to ensure that it is not possible to benefit from these exceptions through the fragmentation of business activities among closely related enterprises. For example, the maintenance of a very large local warehouse in which a significant number of employees work for purposes of storing and delivering goods sold online to customers by an online seller of physical products (whose business model relies on the proximity to customers and the need for quick delivery to clients) would constitute a PE for that seller.

    372. In addition, it was agreed to modify the definition of PE contained in Article 5(5) and 5(6) of the OECD Model Tax Convention to address circumstances in which artificial arrangements relating to the sales of goods or services of one company in a multinational group effectively result in the conclusion of contracts, such that the sales should be treated as if they had been made by that company. For example, where the sales force of a local subsidiary of an online seller of tangible products or an online provider of advertising services habitually plays the principal role in the conclusion of contracts with prospective large clients for those products or services, and these contracts are routinely concluded without material modification by the parent company, this activity would result in a permanent establishment for the parent company (OECD (2015), Addressing the Tax Challenges of the Digital Economy, Action 1—2015 Final Report, OECD/G20Base Erosion and Profit Shifting Project, OECD Publishing, Paris, at 145).
47. *See* Sophie Chatel & Lee Harley, *Article 5 of the OECD Model: Recent Amendments and Upcoming Challenges*, in New Trends in the Definition of Permanent Establishment (G. Maisto ed., IBFD 2019) at 2.3. Implementation via the Multilateral Convention to Implement Tax Treaty Related Measures to Prevent Base Erosion and Profit Shifting (MLI).

Further developments on the taxation of the digital economy have not been achieved yet. One can say that today countries are struggling between continuing to tweak the old rules and new solutions.[48] Peter Hongler and Pasquale Pistone proposed an amendment to Article 5 to establish the thresholds for deeming the existence of a virtual PE.[49]

However, besides the difficulties of achieving consensus in an internationally acceptable definition of a virtual PE, current proposals have the additional challenge of identifying the attributable profit or enabling formulary apportionment methodologies.[50]

The lack of a cooperative solution regarding the taxation of the digital economy pushed Countries to address the question unilaterally through "Digital Services taxes."[51] In this context, the Members of the European Council issued a statement reiterating *the preference for and commitment to a global solution on international digital taxation,* but not discarding the possibility of moving forward *if the prospect of a global solution is not forthcoming*, anticipating a *proposal on a digital levy, with a view to its introduction at the latest by 1 January 2023 strong.*[52]

In summary, today, Tax Authorities have to challenge Digital Economics via an unfit concept of PE, while Government discusses the viability of a "temporary" digital tax approach simultaneously as the features of a virtual PE or other economic nexus. Notice that the brand new OECD proposal, i.e., Pillar One, does not give away the PE concept, indicated as a "plus factor" to justify source taxation on consumer-facing business.[53]

Meanwhile, countries started adopting unilateral measures to combat avoidance and increase their budget. India, for instance, can be considered the pioneer in this path with the introduction of the equalization levy tax in 2016. More recently, it has also its

48. Yariv Brauner, *What the BEPS?* 16 Florida Tax Review 2 (2014) at 72.
49. The amendment should add the following text to Article 5 of the OECD Model: "If an enterprise resident in one Contracting State provides access to (or offers) an electronic application, database, online market place or storage room or offers advertising services on a website or in an electronic application used by more than 1,000 individual users per month domiciled in the other Contracting State, such enterprise shall be deemed to have a permanent establishment in the other Contracting State if the total amount of revenue the enterprise due to the aforementioned services in the other Contracting State exceeds XXX (EUR, USD, GBP, CNY, CHF, etc.) p.a." (Peter Hongler & Pasquale Pistone, *Blueprints for a New PE Nexus to Tax Business Income in the Era of the Digital Economy* (2015, Journals & Papers IBFD), at p. 25.
50. Sophie Chatel & Lee Harley lists three proposals: (i) The "user participation" proposal; (ii) The "marketing intangibles" proposal; and (iii) The "significant economic presence" proposal (*Article 5 of the OECD Model: Recent Amendments and Upcoming Challenges* New Trends in the Definition of Permanent Establishment (G. Maisto ed., IBFD 2019) at 2.4. Challenges posed by the digitalization of the economy). *See also* Dale Pinto, *E-Commerce and Source-Based Income Taxation*, IBFD Doctoral Series vol. 6, Books IBFD. Available at: https://research.ibfd.org/#/doc?url=/document/esii_chaphead).
51. Andres Báez Moreno & Yariv Brauner propose a withholding tax solution, sustaining its superiority over alternative reforms proposed (*Taxing the Digital Economy Post BEPS ... Seriously*, 58(1) Columbia Journal of Transnational Law (2019).
52. Available at https://www.consilium.europa.eu/media/48976/250321-vtc-euco-statement-en.pdf.
53. OECD, *Tax Challenges Arising from Digitalisation—Report on Pillar One Blueprint: Inclusive Framework on BEPS* (2021) at 3. Nexus.

domestic law to include the concept of "significant economic presence" in the definition of PE.[54-55] In spite of the wording, Indians domestic courts have interpreted tax treaties and national legislation to broaden source taxation.[56]

It is worth mentioning that the US Supreme Court in Wayfair eliminated the physical-presence requirement, allowing the imposition of sales-tax-collection obligations on remote sellers. The case may have open the path to future legislation attributing joint and several liability to domestic taxpayers.[57]

In this sense, marketplaces and payment processors can be the missing link to source taxation. Multinationals can be compelled to formalize their business at the source country to be subject to net income taxation at the risk of gross-income taxations.

All that considered, one may ask if there is a future to the PE concept.

4 THE CONCEPT OF PE AND DIGITAL ECONOMY: FUTURE?

It is still early to identify how the digital economy will be addressed to assure a compromise between developed and developing countries. Recent news indicates that unilateral taxes are the temporary answer while multilateral consensus is not reached.[58] Differences in the scope of unilateral taxes can be exploited by taxpayers or even increase tax competition.

There is a consensus that the traditional PE concept is unfit for the digital economy. It is still based on the necessity of a physical presence. As of 2019, the inclusive framework discusses how digitalization should affect existing nexus and profit allocation rules.[59] Publication of reports on Pillar One and Pillar 2 hint at the partial disregard of the PE threshold to Automated digital services (ADS).[60]

---

54. By expanding the scope of the Levy in Finance Act 2020 w.e.f. April 1, 2020, the Levy shall be charged at 2% of the consideration earned by an e-commerce operator from: Online sale of goods/provision of services; or Facilitation of the sale of goods/provision of services; or Combination of the above activities.
55. The budget has defined significant economic presence to include any: Transaction in respect of goods, services and property by nonresident in India including provision of download of data/software beyond a specific revenue threshold. Systematic and continuous soliciting of business activities or engaging in interaction with specified number of users through digital means. The number of users beyond which this will be triggered is yet to be prescribed (https://mnetax.com/india-budget-advances-virtual-digital-pe-concept-tax-non-resident-business-25849).
56. https://taxguru.in/income-tax/virtual-permanent-establishment-vpe-taxation-electronic-commerce-transactions.html.
57. *See* Ruth Mason, *Implications of Wayfair (July 5, 2018)*, 46 Intertax 810 (2018), Available at SSRN: https://ssrn.com/abstract=3214465 or http://dx.doi.org/10.2139/ssrn.3214465.
58. Elke Asen, *What European OECD Countries Are Doing about Digital Services Taxes*, Tax Foundation, 2021.
59. This range of country views can be broadly divided into three groups: Group 1: Those countries who take the view that the reliance on data and user participation seen in some highly digitalized businesses is a new and unique feature of digitalization that, under the existing international tax framework, leads to a misalignment between the location in which profits are taxed and the location in which value is created. This problem, in the view of these countries, is isolated to certain highly digitalized business models; Group 2: Those countries who take the view that the

At this point, one can ask if there is a future to PE concerns as pillar one indicates that a significant digital presence nexus can be adopted soon.

In Svetlana Buriak's point of view, the scope of the new taxing right for market jurisdictions should be limited to: (i) businesses that cooperate with business users in the market jurisdiction to jointly deliver services or goods to end-users; (ii) businesses that actively engage users in using their services in exchange for data provided by these customers that are ultimately traded, used for targeted advertisement services or other income-generating commercial purposes; and (iii) businesses that target a market and perform business functions like marketing, data collection and sales through digitalized channels and tools (also with the assistance of Artificial Intelligence – AI).[61]

Therefore, in the authors' point of view, the lack of consensus on how the digital economy should be taxed will lead to unilateral measures ring-facing part of the economy to answering public increasing pressure for multinational enterprise fair taxation. Mainly due to the need for revenue to cover COVID-19 expenditure.[62] However, the concept of PE will still serve as a threshold to a relevant part of the

ongoing transformation of the economy, as a result of digitalization and globalization more widely, challenges the effectiveness of the existing international tax framework more generally. For this group, the problem is not specific to highly digitalized business models; Group 3: Those countries who take the view that the BEPS package of measures has addressed the concerns and time should be allowed to assess the impact of these changes. These countries are generally satisfied with the existing international tax framework and do not currently *see* the need for significant further reform (Sophie Chatel & Lee Harley, *Article 5 of the OECD Model: Recent Amendments and Upcoming Challenges*, in New Trends in the Definition of Permanent Establishment (G. Maisto ed., IBFD 2019) at 2.4. Challenges posed by the digitalization of the economy).

60. The report defines ADS as The definition of ADS is comprised of a positive list of ADS activities; a negative list of non-ADS activities; and a general definition. Providing a positive list and a negative list provides certainty to MNEs and tax administrations in respect of existing business models; as well as flexibility for the future, as the lists can be updated from time to time as business models evolve. The general definition ensures that a rule remains in place to address rapidly changing business models not otherwise addressed by the positive or negative list. In practice, businesses and tax administrations will apply the rules by going through the following process. First, they will identify whether an activity is on the positive list (i.e. included); if it is, it is an ADS business. Second, if the activity is not on the positive list, they will need to check whether it is on the negative list (i.e. excluded); if it is on the negative list, it is not an ADS business. Only if an activity is not on either list is it necessary to consider whether it meets the conditions in the general definition (OECD, *Tax Challenges Arising from Digitalisation—Report on Pillar One Blueprint: Inclusive Framework on BEPS* (2021) at 2.1.2. Automated digital services).
61. Svetlana Buriak, *A New Taxing Right for the Market Jurisdiction: Where Are the Limits?*, 48(3) Intertax (2020), at 4.1 The Nexus and Its Scope Under the Unified Approach.
62. In this sense, the OECD stated that: The current context of the COVID-19 pandemic makes the need for a solution even more compelling than when it was first considered. Governments have responded through increased spending on healthcare and by providing unprecedented levels of financial support to both businesses and workers to cushion them from the economic blow of this crisis. However, the time will come when governments will need to focus on putting their finances back on a fair and sustainable footing (OECD, *Tax Challenges Arising from Digitalisation—Report on Pillar One Blueprint: Inclusive Framework on BEPS* (2021).

economy, even though there is still room for some improvements in the current rules to clarify or even encompass other business models.[63]

5 VIRTUAL PE CONCEPT AND THE CHALLENGES OF A MULTILATERAL SOLUTION

After exploring various possible legal options for achieving this goal, Pasquale Pistone sustains that the most satisfactory solution involves an amendment to the BEPS MLI. According to his position, the change is possible in the light of the object and purpose of the BEPS MLI and may take place with a coordinated amendment to the covered tax agreements or a dedicated protocol.

In this regard, maintaining the feet on the ground, it is remembered that almost five years after the Multilateral Convention to Implement Tax Treaty Related Measures to Prevent BEPS (MLI) was released, only 95 countries have signed it.[64] Considering that 139 States are members of the inclusive framework, the low adhesion is evidenced.[65]

Furthermore, the MLI experience demonstrated that there would hardly be harmonization unless the PE provision is considered a minimum standard. Notice that wording harmonization does not mean equal interpretation.

The opt-in/opt-out model adopted eased the instrument's political viability but left open issues. From a practical point of view, the model increased compliance costs and opened up opportunities for tax plannings. Multinationals now have the chance to determine their business structure considering the PE threshold of different states.

Even if consensus is reached on how PE should be changed to address the digital economy, implementation would still cause some issues. Despite the challenges, the authors are convinced that if it is decided that the adaptation of the PE concept is the most suitable option, it shall be introduced by a MLI[66] to avoid timing mismatches among States regarding the provision introduction in their tax treaty networks.

6 THE BRAZILIAN POSITION ON THE TAXATION OF THE DIGITAL ECONOMY

Historically, Brazil has stood for its positions in International Tax Policy. Besides adopting typical transfer pricing and controlled foreign corporation (CFC) rules, limitation on deductibility of royalties rules, the tax treaty policy is well-remarked. Not

63. Svetlana Buriak, *A New Taxing Right for the Market Jurisdiction: Where Are the Limits?*, 48(3) Intertax (2020), at 4.1 The Nexus and Its Scope Under the Unified Approach, 4.2 Service PE Under the UN Model, 4.3 Virtual Permanent Agency.
64. OECD, Signatories and parties to the multilateral convention to implement tax treaty related measures to prevent base erosion and profit shifting—status as of April 20, 2021 <https://www.oecd.org/ctp/treaties/beps-mli-signatories-and-parties.pdf>.
65. OECD, Members of the OECD/G20 Inclusive Framework on BEPS—Updated: February 2021 <https://www.oecd.org/tax/beps/inclusive-framework-on-beps-composition.pdf>.
66. Pasquale Pistone, *Permanent Establishment and the Digital Economy*, in New Trends in the Definition of Permanent Establishment (G. Maisto ed., IBFD 2019), at 9.7. Conclusions.

only from wording deviations and protocol provisions but also their domestic interpretation. All that is to safeguard source taxation.

From a domestic standpoint, the taxation of income according to the place of its production is the general rule under Brazilian law. The first express exception to the source of production located as economic nexus was the taxation of "income of technical services and technical, administrative and similar assistance derived from Brazil and received by individuals or legal entities resident or domiciled abroad, regardless of the form of payment and the place and date on which the operation was contracted, the services performed or the assistance provided" as prescribed by Decree-Law No. 1,418/1975.

Brazil's hyperinflationary period until 1994 with the stabilization of the economy pushed Brazilian lawmakers *to design a tax policy capable of minimizing the risk of loss of taxable income associated with intangible assets. By adopting a mix of profit and turnover taxes on outbound payments of royalty and service fees, Brazilian cross-border taxes already target and are heavily levied on a good part of the digital income paid to nonresidents.*[67]

Nowadays, Article 741 of the Income Tax Regulation (RIR/2018) provides that income of any nature earned from sources located in the country (source of production) is subject to withholding tax, while Article 744 of the RIR/2018 prescribes that income, capital gains, and other income paid, credited, delivered, employed, or remitted to nonresidents are subject to taxation of sources located in the country (source of payment).

Generally, nonresident entities are only subject to withholding income tax for income received from Brazilian sources relating to services, rights, and capital gains on the sale of Brazilian assets. On the other hand, the sale of goods does not suffer the incidence of a withholding tax in Brazil.

Nonresidents are treated as equivalent to legal entities domiciled in Brazil (depending on representations or commissioners), subject to the same rules that apply to those entities. In this regime, nonresidents exercise economic activity in the Brazilian territory through an organization of persons or assets, allowing tax authorities to identify that the foreign company is doing business in Brazil.

In this case, the income earned is subject to taxation under Article 159 of the RIR/2018, according to which: *subsidiaries, branches, agencies, or representations of nonresidents are considered legal entities relating to the results of the operations carried out by their representatives or their commissioners in the country.* Thus, the taxation of nonresident branches, agencies, or representations follows the regulations applicable to other Brazilian legal entities. Brazilian domestic law does not address the characterization of PEs of nonresidents in Brazil.

Brazil also protects its tax basis at a treaty policy level. For instance, with the inclusion of technical and similar services in the scope of articles granting source taxation.

67. Alex de Almeida, *Brazil's Experience with Unilaterally Taxing the Tech Industry Versus International Digital Taxation*, 27(5) International Transfer Pricing Journal (2020) at 1. Introduction.

As a general rule, Brazil also includes its tax treaties protocols the equalization of income related to technical services and technical assistance to royalties, attracting the application of the article equivalent to Article 12 of the OECD Model Convention and, thus, allowing the exercise of tax jurisdiction by the source country.

Not only that, but Brazilian tax treaties also include Article 14 as the wording preserves source taxation in case the service is configured through a fixed base or as long as the service provider remains in the source state for a period equivalent or greater than 183 days. More recently, Brazil has also made use of an article equivalent to Article 12-A of the UN Model Convention.[68]

As Takano and Przepiorka had reported,[69] Brazil formally requested its accession to the OECD on May 20, 2017, indicating that it would comply with the organization standards, BEPS guidelines included. Yet, Brazil surprisingly has not signed the MLI proposed on BEPS Action 15 (from now on MLI),[70] opting to renegotiate its tax treaty network on a bilateral basis. Such decision was justified under the following premises: (i) the complexity of the MLI, which could generate lengthy discussions in Brazilian National Congress, thereby delaying the approval of the MLI for years;[71] (ii) the relatively small tax treaty network, which turns the renegotiation of each tax treaty concluded a feasible possibility.

Despite not having signed the MLI, Brazil has timidly shown signs of compliance with the minimum standards suggested by the OECD. For example, on the occasion of the amendment to the protocol to the Argentina-Brazil double tax convention (1980), signed on July 21, 2017.

In that opportunity, besides limiting the taxation at the source State,[72] it also (i) modified the title and the preamble of the tax treaty to explicitly include the purpose of preventing tax avoidance in accordance with BEPS Action 6; (ii) updated the PE concept according to the new reading propose in the MLI; (iii) replaced the exemption

68. In summary, *Brazil's tax treaty policy relies on a negotiation strategy to legally circumvent the PE rule of article 7 of the OECD Model. The tax authorities have historically negotiated that profits from technical and administrative services and the like should be treated as royalties under Article 12 of the OECD Model, agreeing with the other state to expressly classify services of any nature that would normally fall under article 7 as instead falling under article 12, granting Brazil the right to tax* (Alex de Almeida, *Brazil's Experience with Unilaterally Taxing the Tech Industry Versus International Digital Taxation*, 27(5) International Transfer Pricing Journal (2020) at 3.2. Business profits and the PE rule.
69. Caio Augusto Takano & Michell Przepiorka, *Taxation and Finance in Latin America: Brazil*, 21(3) Finance and Capital Markets (2019), at 2.1. Brazil Treaty Networking and the MLI.
70. "On May 29 the Brazilian Treasury and the Ministry of Foreign Affairs issued a joint letter to the OECD formally requesting that the OECD initiate the accession procedure for Brazil to become an OECD member" (Falcão, Tatiana. *Is Brazil's Tax System Ready for OECD Accession?* Tax Notes International, January 8, 2018, p. 181. Available at: https://s3.amazonaws.com/pdfs.taxnotes.com/2018/89ti0181.pdf. Last access: March 2, 2019).
71. Tomazela, Ramon. *Brazil's Absence from the Multilateral BEPS Convention and the New Amending Protocol Signed Between Brazil and Argentina*. Kluwer International Tax Blog, September 5, 2017. Available at http://kluwertaxblog.com/2017/09/05/brazils-absence-multilateral-beps-convention-new-amending-protocol-signed-brazil-argentina/. Last access: March 1, 2019.
72. The new protocol set up withholding tax limits to dividends, interests and royalties: 15% or 10% for dividends; 15% for interest; and 15% or 10% for royalties.

method in Article 23-A with the credit method in Article 23-B of the OECD Model Convention; (iv) adopted the MLI wording regarding the Mutual Assistance Procedure (from now on MAP), except for the mandatory binding arbitration clause, which was not accepted by Brazilian Tax Authorities; and (v) added a clause containing both the Limitation on Benefits (LoB) provisions and the Principal Purpose Test (PPT).

Accordingly, in 2018, Brazil concluded three new tax treaties with Switzerland, Singapore, and the United Arab Emirates. Such features nevertheless have not been entirely maintained in the tax treaties concluded with Switzerland[73] and Singapore.[74] Although some minor differences, one may affirm that these recent tax treaties are in line with BEPS recommendations.

In general, the Double Tax Treaty (DTT) between Brazil and Switzerland is in line with the Brazilian Fiscal Policy on tax treaties, barely deviating only to include some MLI inputs and a clause specifically dealing with the Fees for technical services. Some other relevant features of this treaty would be the following: (i) the inclusion of the preamble suggested by in the MLI; (ii) the inclusion of entitlement to benefit clause following PPT and LoB provisions suggested in the MLI; (iii) the clarification that the treaty applies to income derived by or through an entity or arrangement treated as wholly or partly fiscally transparent under the tax law of either Contracting State to the extent that the income is treated as income of a resident of that state (for tax purposes by that state); and (iv) specific rules regarding the treatment of collective investment vehicles (CIVs).

However, one may argue that the main innovation vis-à-vis the traditional Brazilian tax treaties negotiation policy (or regarding the Brazilian DTT Model[75]) concerns the possibility of a secondary tax adjustment be allowed in Brazil as a result of a Mutual Agreement Procedure, although absent Article 9(2).[76]

In its turn, the main deviations of the DTT between Brazil and Singapore concerning Brazilian tax treaties policy: (i) resource to Mutual Agreement Procedure to solve residence conflicts of legal persons;[77] (ii) similarly to the treaty with Switzerland, the treaty addresses transparent entities in Article 1 and provides for a clause dealing

73. For more details, *see*: *Brazil; Switzerland—Treaty Between Brazil and Switzerland*—details (May 15, 2018), News IBFD. Available at: https://research.ibfd.org/#/doc?url=/document/tns_2018-05-15_br_1. Last access: March 3, 2019.
74. Carvalho, Lucas de Lima. *A Closer Look at the (New) Brazil-Switzerland Tax Treaty*. Available at https://www.linkedin.com/pulse/closer-look-new-brazil-singapore-tax-treaty-lucas-de-lima-carvalho/. Last access: March 1, 2019.
75. Duarte Filho & Paulo César Teixeira. *Double Tax Treaties Policies of Brazil: The Braziliana Model Taz Convention*. Rio de Janeiro: Lumen Juris, 2018.
76. Protocol to the DTT Brazil-Switzerland: 5. With reference to Arts 9 and 25: It is understood that the absence of a clause providing for an obligation of a Contracting State to make an appropriate corresponding adjustment cannot be construed so as to hinder a Contracting State to make such an appropriate adjustment if it has been agreed to in the course of a mutual agreement procedure.
77. Article 4, 3. Where by reason of the provisions of para. 1 a person other than an individual is a resident of both Contracting States, then it shall be deemed to be a resident only of the State in which its place of effective management is situated. *If its place of effective management cannot be determined, the competent authorities of the Contracting States shall settle the question by mutual agreement.*

with fees for technical services; and (iii) the inclusion of an entitlement to benefit clause based on PPT and LoB provisions.[78]

The treaty concluded with the United Arab Emirates also introduced some relevant innovations: (i) Article 1 adopted the wording of the MLI provision on transparent entities; (ii) Article 4 sets forth that a company that is resident in both States is considered as resident in neither of them for the treaty purpose; (iii) concerning Article 5, probably this treaty is the most prompted by the MLI in the Brazilian Treaty Networking, as Article 5, §3° reflects the exact content of Article 14, § 1° of the MLI, except for references to "supervisory or consultancy activities." Article 5, §4° reproduces Article 13, §§ 2° and 4° of the MLI. At last, Article 5th, § 8 replicates the text of Article 15, § 1°.

It is worth noting that a specific clause to deal with fees for technical services was also included in this treaty and a saving clause for natural resources, and—against all the oddities—a brand new tax sparing provision. At last, the DTT between Brazil and the United Arab Emirates provides an entitlement to a benefits clause based on PPT and LoB provisions, along with the lines of Article 7, § 1°, and Article 10, § 1° of the MLI. Furthermore, the treaty also includes a stricter provision to UAE companies entitled to treaty benefits.

Finally, the protocol signed with Sweden, in the same way, included provisions of the MLI: (i) Article 1 adopted the wording of the MLI provision on transparent entities; (ii) Article 4 established that when a person other than an individual is resident of both States, his residence shall be determined through mutual agreement, but, if the States fail to determine his residence, such person shall not be entitled to the benefits of the treaty, unless the Competent authorities have otherwise agreed; (iii) the tax sparing clause was eliminated, with Article 23 providing for the deduction method as for the new protocol; (iv) it has also updated the Mutual Agreement Procedure, adopting paragraphs 1-4 of the OECD 2017 model Convention drafted in accordance with the MLI; and (v) it included a simplified LoB clause in addition with a PPT clause.

It is worth mentioning that Articles 10, 11, and 12 provided for taxation at source. On the other hand, a most-favored clause was introduced at the protocol limited in scope to treaties and/or protocols signed with Member States of the OECD after March 19, 2019, excluding any State in Latin American. Moreover, the protocol to Article 11 established that interest on equity paid under Brazilian law should be qualified as interest for treaty purposes. It maintained the Brazil policy, including fees for technical services and technical assistance under Article 12, paragraph 3.

Finally, it is important to state that the Brazilian Congressman had presented law projects to introduce a Digital Service Tax (DST) on the domestic legislation. However,

78. The Treaty adopts a combined approach consisting of a simplified U.S.-style limitation on benefits (LoB) rule and a principal purpose test (PPT) rule as a means to prevent treaty shopping. At the time of signing the MLI, Singapore had chosen to apply the PPT rule as part of its commitment to the minimum standard under BEPS Action 6 and this would be the first treaty Singapore has signed incorporating the LoB rule. The Treaty also includes an anti-abuse rule for PEs situated in other countries, the language of which aligns with Article 10 in the text of the MLI (https://www.ey.com/gl/en/services/tax/international-tax/alert--brazil-and-singapore-sign-treaty-for-the-avoidance-of-double-taxation).

it seems more opportunistic free-riding in the international debate to increase tax collection than a real necessity to tackle tax avoidance in the digital economy context.[79]

The arguments in favor of Digital Services Taxes are the same that Brazil always used in favor of its domestic withholding tax. All that leads to the conclusion that Brazil already safeguards its tax basis from a treaty and domestic legislation policy. Perhaps, even beyond all the current discussion on the taxation of the digital economy.

7 FINAL REMARKS

Brazil has always been criticized for its position on international tax policy. However, the challenges arising from the digitalization of the economy showed the insufficiency of the current international tax rules to deal with nonphysical activities, leading to international discussions going around the same positions Brazil has always had.

From the authors' standpoint, withholding taxes on gross income is a good solution to protecting source tax. However, it does not seem more suitable from an international trade perspective as it increases the supply chain costs. An alternative but hard to implement solution is a withholding tax on a net basis considering the exchange of information and mandatory disclosure rules.

Despite being rooted in the international tax policy, the PE concept has always raised uncertainty in its application. Also, it does not seem suitable to address the digital economy as it is today. The current debate can be a chance for a revolution on how taxing rights are allocated between residence and source (or sources depending on the supply chain), even if a complete abandonment of the PE threshold seems improbable.

The concept must be updated to encompass business models that do not require physical presence. In his context, the market must play a role as a relevant factor to determine taxing rights or at least as a factor in the attribution of profits.

Notice that if it is decided that the adaptation of the PE concept is the most suitable option, it shall be introduced by a MLI.[80] Hence, all countries harmonize the way taxing rights should be allocated to avoid double taxation.

79. Daniel de Paiva Gomes & Michell Przepiorka, *As propostas de CIDE digitais: Uma carona indesejada*, Jota (2020).
80. Pasquale Pistone sustains that after exploring various possible legal options for achieving this goal, this chapter has concluded that the most satisfactory solution involves an amendment to the BEPS MLI. This change is possible in the light of the object and purpose of the BEPS MLI and may take place with a coordinated amendment to the covered tax agreements, or a dedicated protocol. The BEPS MLI has the potential of being much more than a multilateral convention in tax matters and should become the global framework treaty on international taxation (Pasquale Pistone, *Permanent Establishment and the Digital Economy*, in New Trends in the Definition of Permanent Establishment (G. Maisto ed., IBFD 2019), at 9.7. Conclusions).

CHAPTER 11

From Bilateralism to Multilateralism: Is This Shift Beneficial for Developing Countries? A Focus on 7(1) MLI

Ricardo García Antón

Ricardo Garcia Anton examines whether the MLI can deliver uniformity of tax norms across states given its hallmark feature, namely, its flexibility. Focusing on the treaty abuse protections laid out in Article 7(1) with a particular eye toward the distinct approaches taken by developed and developing countries, the chapter analyzes a series of gaps and inconsistencies in application and interpretation that will prove challenging to the goal of harmonization. Among these are inconsistencies in the burden of proof standards among MLI and domestic law terms within and across states, incompatible definitions and applications of economic substance rules, and varying hierarchies of legal standards between MLI and domestic law special and general anti-abuse regimes.

1 INTRODUCTION: THE MLI AS A HYBRID INSTRUMENT

The Organisation for Economic Co-operation and Development (OECD) Multilateral Instrument to Implement Tax Treaty Related Measures to Prevent Base Erosion and Profit Shifting (BEPS) (MLI) has been presented as a major achievement in the shift from bilateralism to multilateralism.[1] Such a triumphalist approach contrasts a more

1. On the narrative of the shift, *see* J. Owens, "Tax Transparency: The 'Full Monty,'" (2014) 68 *Bulletin International Taxation*, Issue 9, pp. 512-514; P. Pistone, "Coordinating the Action of Regional and Global Players During the Shift from Bilateralism to Multilateralism in International Tax Law," (2014) 6 *World Tax Journal*, Issue 1, pp. 3-9; V. Averyanova & J. Sampat, "Transfer Pricing Aspects of Intra-Group Financial Guarantees in Light of the BEPS Action Plan," (2015) 22

pessimistic reception of the MLI by several authors, who posit that bilateralism still prevails and very little true multilateralism has been achieved so far.[2] The flexibility of the MLI (opt-ins, opt-outs, reservations) to gain political support enhances the bilateral nature of the MLI and results in an international tax system that is still fragmented.

Rather than endorsing one of the two extreme narratives above, I have defended a conflictual nature of the MLI, in which two competing layers of governance—bilateral and multilateral—lead to a noncoherent legal instrument.[3] The conflictual and hybrid narrative of the MLI has two visible purposes. On one hand, it better accommodates the findings in public international law in which multilateralism traditionally overlaps with bilateral settings, thereby expelling any idea of the prevalence of a form of governance.[4] On the other hand, it serves to assist in the interpretation of several provisions of the MLI, such as Article 30 MLI on the subsequent modification of a covered tax agreement (CTA). For example, a bilateral understating of Article 30 MLI would allow two Contracting States to abolish a minimum standard within a subsequent modification of the bilateral treaty—such as the principal purpose test in Article 7(1) MLI (PPT)—whereas a multilateral understanding of this article would preserve the consensus achieved in the minimum standards by precluding such subsequent modification.[5]

The hybrid nature of the MLI has allowed me to firmly defend the position that the minimum standards in MLI, together with the minimum standards monitored by the BEPS Inclusive Framework, aspire to become customary international law (CIL).[6] The aspiration of any multilateral treaty to forge international customs is supported in public international law literature in areas like the Law of the Sea or the World Trade Organization (WTO).[7] As such, international taxation should not "behave" differently

International Transfer Pricing Journal, Issue 6, pp. 361-368; I. Mosquera Valderrama, "Legitimacy and the Making of International Tax Law: The Challenges of Multilateralism," (2015) 7 *World Tax Journal*, Issue 3, pp. 343-382; P. Pistone, R. Julien & F. Cannas, "Can the Derivative Benefits Provision and the Competent Authority Discretionary Relief Provision Render the OECD-Proposed LoB Clause Compatible with EU Fundamental Freedoms?" in M. Lang et al. (eds), *Base Erosion and Profit Shifting (BEPS)*, (Linde, 2016), p. 212.

2. W.C. Hasslenner, "A Multilateral Interpretation of the Multilateral Instrument (and Covered Tax Agreements)?," (2020) 74 *Bulletin for International Taxation* pp. 4/5, Online IBFD Journal (accessed December 3, 2020); Y. Brauner, "McBEPS: The MLI—The First Multilateral Tax Treaty That Has Never Been," (2018) 46 *Intertax*, Issue 1, pp. 6-17; D.W. Blum, "The Relationship Between the OECD Multilateral Instrument and Covered Tax Agreements: Multilateralism and the Interpretation of the MLI," (2018) 72 *Bulletin for International Taxation* p. 3, Online IBFD Journal; J. Zornoza Perez, "Multilateralism in International Taxation: Is It really the Future?," in Y. Brauner (ed.), *Research Handbook on International Taxation*, (Elgar, 2020), pp. 317-340.
3. R. Garcia Anton, "Multilateral Dynamics in Bilateral Settings: Back to Realpolitik," (2019) 4 *British Tax Review*, pp. 462-486; R. Garcia Anton, "Substantive Multilateralism in the Context of the MLI" in A.P. Dourado (ed.), *The Multilateral Instrument*, (IBFD, 2021).
4. In this regard, *see* J.H.H. Weiler, "The Geology of International Law—Governance, Democracy and Legitimacy," (2004) 64 *Heidelberg Journal of International Law*, pp. 547-562.
5. Further discussion on the potential interpretations of Art. 30 MLI, in Garcia Anton (2019), *supra* n. 3, p. 502.
6. On the embryonic stage of the BEPS minimum standards in the evolution of customary international law in anti-avoidance, *see* in Garcia Anton (2019), *supra* n. 3.
7. On the literature stressing that treaties are a source of CIL, *see* G. Blum, "Bilateralism, Multilateralism, and the Architecture of International Law" (2008) 49 *Harvard International Law*

in international law. For the time being, the minimum standards in the MLI, and especially in Article 7 MLI, are simply embryonic customs still far from being considered CIL.[8]

This chapter aims to analyze whether the shift towards multilateralism benefits developing countries. To accomplish that, I focus on the minimum standard in treaty abuse laid down in Article 7(1) MLI (the PPT rule).[9] If developing countries could derive a benefit from the shift from bilateralism to multilateralism, such a shift would have made sense. Otherwise, the shift would be merely rhetorical without a real impact on the tax policies of developing countries. To determine whether such a benefit exists for developing countries, it is necessary to first monitor the empirical enforcement of Article 7 MLI. I will make the argument that despite the wide implementation of the standard, there are still important asymmetries, loopholes, and inconsistencies that may jeopardize the success of a shift from bilateralism to multilateralism. Such resistance towards implementing the PPT in Article 7(1) MLI could be grounded for two main reasons: (i) preventing tax abuse is truly embedded within the legal culture of every State; (ii) the PPT is not a self-executing norm, and it heavily depends on the burden of proof between the tax administration and the taxpayer, which will eventually be reviewed by the judiciary.

The structure of this chapter is as follows. Section 2 looks briefly at the status of the implementation of the MLI in developing countries in comparison with developed countries. Section 3 explores the aspiration of Article 7 MLI to become a multilateral norm to prevent treaty abuse. Section 4 is devoted to outlining the resistance of countries towards the implementation of the standard in Article 7(1) MLI. Section 5 is devoted to analyzing the Double Taxation Convention (DTC) practice in terms of treaty abuse after the entry into force of the MLI. Section 6 focuses on whether the PPT is beneficial for developing countries. Finally, this chapter will conclude by affirming that the previous asymmetries, inconsistencies, and mismatches may thwart the supposed shift from bilateralism to multilateralism, despite the wide implementation of the PPT.

2 THE IMPLEMENTATION OF THE MLI IN DEVELOPING COUNTRIES

A multilateral treaty has been remarked as beneficial for poorer countries since unitary norms and minimum standards would protect less experienced countries.[10] Indeed, in

Journal, issue 2, p. 329; J.O. McGinnis, "The Appropriate Hierarchy of Global Multilateralism and Customary International Law: The Example of the WTO", (2003) 44 *Virginia Journal of International Law*, pp. 229-284; G.L. Scott & C. Carr, "Multilateral Treaties and the Formation of Customary International Law," (1996) 25 *Denver Journal of International Law and Policy*, issue 1, pp. 71-94; A.D'Amato, *The Concept of Custom in International Law* (Cornell University Press, 1971); R. Baxter, "Multilateral Treaties as Evidence of Customary International Law," (1965) 41 *British Yearbook of International Law*, pp. 275.

8. For the purposes of this chapter, I have skipped the discussion on whether the MLI provisions, and specially the PPT becomes CIL.
9. For the purposes of this chapter, I will indistinctively make reference to Article 29(9) OECD MC (2017) and Article 7(1) MLI to refer to the PPT.
10. Y. Brauner, "Tax Treaty Negotiations: Myth and Reality," (2020), p. 67. Available at SSRN: https://ssrn.com/abstract=3722607 or http://dx.doi.org/10.2139/ssrn.3722607; *see also* my

bilateral treaty negotiations, richer countries could impose their position on poorer countries, which would eventually curtail source taxing rights.[11] Such a scenario would be unlikely to occur in a multilateral negotiation, in which a coalition of poorer countries, supported by regional integration organizations, could pressure rich countries by putting the agreement on standby until their claims are approved.

However, the previous ideal scenario has not yet occurred. The heralded flexibility of the MLI, with opt-in and opt-out provisions, coupled with few minimum standards has not produced the expected results in terms of acceptance of the instrument. States do not usually select their whole DTC network of DTCs as CTAs, thereby revealing a less willing commitment towards multilateral solutions.[12] For example, it is quite striking that a country such as Switzerland, which has key jurisdiction in international tax planning, has only listed 14 DTCs as CTAs of the MLI from a network of 117 DTCs.[13] Also, crucial DTCs for international tax planners, such as the DTC Mauritius–India which helps channel investments to the latter country, have not been listed by Mauritius in the MLI.[14] In addition to the low list of DTCs covered by the MLI, the MLI signatories are quite reluctant to endorse certain optional provisions such as the permanent establishment (PE) provisions derived from BEPS Action 7 (Articles 12, 13, 14, and 15 MLI), and hybrid mismatches (Articles 3, 4, and 5 MLI).[15]

Comparing developed and developing countries, Suranjali Tandon confirms several trends: (i) a higher proportion of developed countries tend to exclude treaties with developing countries from the list of CTAs;[16] (ii) more developed countries than developing countries have opted out of some of the optional articles of the MLI, namely the PE provisions;[17] (iii) more developed countries than developing countries have opted in for Part VI of the MLI (arbitration).[18] This data confirms that the pendulum swings in favor of developed countries, insofar as they do not list their entire treaty network and opt out of key provisions to prevent abusive transactions like the PE. In terms of anti-abuse provisions in Article 7 MLI, commentators stress that the majority of States apply the PPT, and only a few countries decide to supplement the PPT with the simplified Limitation of Benefits (LoB) provision (12 signatories).[19]

---

previous contribution on the interaction of transaction costs and member surplus in multilateral versus bilateral negotiations, R. Garcia Anton, "The 21st Century Multilateralism in International Taxation. The Emperor's New Clothes," (2016) 6 *World Tax Journal*, issue 2; pp. 147-192.

11. M. Hearson, "Measuring Tax Treaty Negotiation Outcomes: the Action Aid Tax Treaties Dataset," (2016) Working Paper 47 ICTP.
12. On a detailed analysis of listed covered tax agreements, *see* S. Tandon, "The Multilateral Legal Instrument: A Developing Country Perspective", (2018) NIPFP Working Paper Series No. 220, Available at https://www.nipfp.org.in/media/medialibrary/2018/03/WP_2018_220.pdf.
13. Tandon, *supra* n. 12, p. 8.
14. Tandon, *supra* n. 12, p. 3.
15. *See* Garcia Anton (2019), *supra* n. 3, p. 504.
16. Tandon, *supra* n. 12, p. 12.
17. Tandon, *supra* n. 12, p. 13.
18. Tandon, *supra* n. 12, p. 14.
19. On the reasons for not a wider acceptance of the MLI's LoB, Kuzniacki sees high complexity and the ineffectiveness of certain tests, *see* B. Kuzniacki, "Implementation and Application of the

3 A LOOK INTO ARTICLE 7 MLI AS A MINIMUM STANDARD TO PREVENT THE IMPROPER USE OF TREATIES

Is it possible to come up with a uniform and consistent rule applicable to all States to prevent abusive arrangements put in place by the taxpayer? In principle, one may answer this question in the negative. The linguistic, conceptual, and practical discrepancies around the concepts of anti-avoidance and tax evasion point to domestic legislation jeopardizing a homogenous meaning of abuse.[20] As Brian Arnold stated: "There is a great deal of confusion about the terms 'tax avoidance' and 'tax evasion.' Obviously, countries often draw the line between tax avoidance and tax evasion and between acceptable and unacceptable tax avoidance differently."[21] Generally speaking, while tax evasion is a criminal offense punishable by fines or imprisonment, tax avoidance involves the reduction of tax by legal means rather than by fraud, nondisclosure, or misrepresentation.[22] To prevent tax avoidance, the typology and scope of the rules considerably differ among jurisdictions. Stef Van Weeghel summarized them as substance over form, sham, abuse of law, *fraus legis*, and general anti-avoidance rule (GAAR).[23] Depending on the country, the previous rules tackling tax avoidance schemes cover cases wherein the parties simulate entering into a contract where, in reality, they have not entered into the transaction at all, or cases wherein the parties entered into a different transaction than the one embodied in the written contract.

The lack of a unique rule to combat anti-avoidance arrangements among different States almost makes speaking about a uniform and consistent approach to abuse audacious. However, if we narrow the topic to the prevention of abuse in the context of DTCs, a more nuanced opinion can be conveyed. The minimum standards in Articles 6 and 7 MLI consolidate a general principle that DTCs aim to foster economic cooperation and enhance cooperation in tax matters without permitting abusive schemes. The minimum standard in Article 7 MLI, coupled with Article 6 MLI, is clearly linked to the guiding principle, which is included in the Commentaries to Article 1 of the OECD MC and UN MC.[24] Since 2003, the guiding principle states that "the benefits

LOB Clause in BEPS Action 6/MLI: legal and Pragmatic Challenges," in A.P. Dourado (ed.), *The Multilateral Instrument*, (IBFD, 2021), pp. 267-292.

20. On the conceptual and linguistic discrepancies on the concepts of anti-avoidance and tax evasion, there is abundant literature. *See* V. Uckmar, "General Report," in *IFA Cahiers, Tax Avoidance/Tax Evasion* vol. 68a., 23 (IFA, 1983); M. Mössner, "Tax Avoidance Concepts and European Tax Education—Professors of Tax Law Hold First Meeting in Osnabrück," (1999) 39 *European Taxation*, issue 3, pp. 92-135; S. van Weeghel, "General Report," in *IFA Cahiers, Tax Treaties and Tax Avoidance: Application of Anti Avoidance Provisions*, vol. 95A, 19-20 (IFA, 2010); P. Piantavigna, "Tax Abuse and Aggressive Tax Planning in the BEPS Era: How EU Law and the OECD Are Establishing a Unifying Conceptual Framework in International Tax Law, Despite Linguistic Discrepancies", (2017) 9 *World Tax Journal*, (Online edition); C. Öner, "Is Tax Avoidance the Theory of Everything in Tax Law? A Terminological Analysis of EU Legislation and Case Law", (2019) 27 *EC Tax Review*, issue 2, pp. 96-112.
21. B. Arnold, *UN Practical Portfolio: Protecting the Tax Base of Developing Countries Through the Use of General Anti-avoidance Rules* (UN, 2019), p. 9.
22. Arnold, *supra* n. 21, p. 9.
23. van Weeghel, *supra* n. 20, p. 22.
24. The guiding principle is currently formulated in the para. 61 of the Commentaries of Article 1 to the OECD MC (2017) and Article 22 UN MC (2017).

of a double taxation convention should not be available where a main purpose for entering into certain transactions or arrangements was to secure a more favorable tax position and obtaining that more favorable treatment in these circumstances would be contrary to the object and purpose of the relevant provisions." This guiding principle, which becomes the basis for the current drafting of the PPT in Article 29(9) OECD MC,[25] imposes a teleological interpretation of a DTC. Applying the DTC to an arrangement where one of the main purposes was to obtain a tax advantage defeats the *telos* of a DTC, whose object and purpose is to foster economic cooperation between the two signatories. The amendment to the DTC Preamble within Article 6 MLI reinforces the previous teleological interpretation of a DTC.

In the 2003 update of the OECD MC, the introduction of the guiding principle put an end to the controversial 1977 OECD's position, which presumed that domestic anti-avoidance rules could not be applicable to the DTC context unless the contracting States expressly agreed to do so.[26] Since 2003, it is clear that treaty abuse can therefore be tackled with domestic anti-avoidance provisions. Both the OECD MC and UN MC point out that there should be no conflict between domestic GAAR and treaty provisions to prevent abuse. In other words, either by a specific GAAR in a DTC or by a domestic GAAR, a State can deny the benefits provided in a DTC if the arrangement was deemed abusive.

In the author's view, to prevent treaty abuse, the joint reading of (i) the guiding principle in the Commentaries of Article 1 of the OECD MC and UN MC, and (ii) the minimum standards in Article 6 and Article 7 MLI, exported to the OECD and UN MC (2017) encapsulates a uniform principle that bilateral DTCs cannot be abused. The MLI has tightened the guiding principle envisaged by the Commentaries to Article 1 of the OECD MC and UN MC. If the DTC does not contain a specific GAAR (i.e., Article 29(9) OECD MC), the domestic GAAR interpreted in line with the guiding principle would entitle the State to deny treaty benefits.[27]

The BEPS Action 6 and Article 7 MLI aimed to prevent the improper use of tax treaties by giving several alternatives to States. The reading of Article 7(15) and 7(6) MLI entitles the signatory States of the MLI to comply with the minimum standard by including one of the following options in their CTAs: (1) a principal purpose test only (PPT—29.9 OECD MC); (2) a PPT and either a simplified or a detailed LoB provision; or (3) a detailed LoB provision, supplemented by a mechanism that would deal with conduit arrangements, in particular conduit financing structures not already dealt with in DTCs.

Whilst abuse is not permitted in the context of DTCs, States have different legal forms to combat abusive practices in Article 7 MLI. The multiplicity of means to combat

25. I will use indistinctively Article 29(9) and Article 7(1) MLI to refer to the PPT.
26. On the introduction of the guiding principle, *see* Arnold, *supra* n. 21, pp. 54; on the criticisms to the OECD's position held in 1977, *see* A. Martin Jimenez, "Las Medidas Anti-Elusivas/Anti-Abuso Internas y los Convenios para la Eliminación de la Doble Imposición," in M. Teresa Soler Roch & F. Serrano Anton (eds.), *Las Medidas Anti-abuso en la normativa española y en los CDIs y su Compatibilidad con el Derecho Comunitario*, (IEF, 2002), pp. 109-162.
27. *See* para. 77 of the Commentaries to Article 1 of the OECD MC (2017) and para. 42 of the UN MC (2017).

treaty abuse is obviously linked to the fact that the definition of abuse is embedded within the domestic legal culture of every country. Therefore, some countries would prefer to include a detailed LoB, rather than a PPT. Even though countries can deny treaty benefits without a PPT or LoB in their DTCs by applying domestic anti-abuse provisions in line with the guiding principle: "thus, many countries are able to deny treaty benefits in abusive cases without the need for a general anti-abuse rule, such as Article 29, paragraph 9, in their treaties. For this purpose, these countries can apply a general anti-abuse rule found in domestic law, judicial doctrines or principles of interpretation found in domestic law or they can interpret the provisions of their tax treaties in order to deny the benefits of a treaty in abusive cases."[28]

4 THE RESISTANCE AGAINST A HOMOGENOUS SHIFT TO PREVENT TREATY ABUSE

Despite the multiplicity of ways to comply with the standard in Article 7 MLI, several commentators observe that over half of the countries worldwide have committed to the PPT.[29] Such evidence is reinforced by the 2018 peer review report of BEPS Action 6, in which the majority of States expressed their preference for the PPT.[30] The fact that many States are endorsing the PPT in their treaty network does not mean that a uniform and consistent result has been achieved worldwide.

The PPT, conceptualized as GAARs, is not a self-executing norm. Putting the GAAR into practice lies in the interpretation of its constituent elements: done first by the tax administration and then ultimately reviewed by the judiciary. Such interpretation of the structural elements of the GAAR (i.e., series of transactions, tax benefit, purpose, saving provision)[31] is heavily dependent on the domestic legal culture of abuse and the burden of proof between the tax administration and the taxpayer. Commentators have observed that the GAAR is a legal mechanism that resorts to an unusual form of interpretation beyond what is normally understood as statutory interpretation, insofar as it denies tax benefits in transactions that contradict the object, spirit, or purpose of the relevant provisions.[32] This unusual form of interpretation does not mean that it yields a breach of the legal certainty principle, provided that the

28. *See* para. 52 of the Commentaries to Article 1 of the UN MC (2017).
29. *See* for example, I. Mosquera Valderrama, "BEPS Principal Purpose Test and Customary International Law," (2020) 33 *Leiden Journal of International Law*, pp. 759.
30. *See* OECD, Prevention of Treaty Abuse—Peer Review Report on Treaty Shopping, (2019) Available at: https://www.oecd-ilibrary.org/docserver/9789264312388-en.pdf?expires = 1615204156&id = id&accname = guest&checksum = 2E500E477C72DB71E268B2093DB5A336.
31. On the structural elements of the GAAR, *see* Arnold, *supra* n. 21, pp. 97 ss.
32. J. Freedman, "The Anatomy of Tax Avoidance Counteraction: Abuse of Law in a Tax Context at Member State and European Union Level," in R. de la Feria & S. Vogenauer, (eds.), *Prohibition of Abuse of Law: A New Principle of EU Law?* (Hart Publishing, 2011), p. 365; D. G. Duff, "The Interpretive Exercise under the General Anti-Avoidance Rule," (2020) Available in SSRN https://ssrn.com/abstract = 3670375. Forthcoming in B. Arnold, ed., *The General Anti-Avoidance Rule—Past and Future* (Canadian Tax Foundation, 2021).

teleological interpretation of the GAAR is supported by evidence.[33] The GAAR is a last resort provision that gives a broad discretion to the tax administration to face the problem of tax avoidance but is subject to the rule of law.[34] The interpretative task would vary depending on the jurisdiction since abuse is clearly embedded within a domestic legal culture.

In the author's view, it is thus unlikely to achieve a homogenous result irrespective of the legal background the interpreter has and the jurisdiction/court in which the anti-abuse standard is applied.[35] Indeed, the PPT in Article 29(9) OECD MC (2017) grants a broad margin of discretion to the tax authorities, which can be translated into an extended fear of uncertainty.[36] The following subsection outlines several inconsistencies and asymmetries which jeopardize a uniform application of the standard: (4.1) Conflicts related to the wording of the standards at the international level; and (4.2) Conflicts related to the interaction of the standard with domestic anti-abuse provisions.

4.1 Lack of Consistency of the Anti-abuse Standard at the International Level

This section focuses on potential conflicts and doubts that may arise between (i) the guiding principle and the PPT; and (ii) the MLI LoB and PPT.

4.1.1 Conflict Between the PPT and the Guiding Principle

While the guiding principle in the Commentaries to Article 1 of the OECD MC and UN MC is drafted as a "main purpose" test, Article 29(9) of the OECD MC (Article 7(1) MLI) is drafted as "one of the main purposes."[37] The latter test is much more favorable to the tax administration insofar as if the transactions or arrangements result in a tax benefit, "it seems unlikely that none of the main purposes for the transaction or arrangement

33. There is abundant literature that stress that the GAAR does not breach the legal certainty principle. *See* in this regard, David G. Duff, "General Anti-Avoidance Rules Revisited: Reflections on Tim Edgar's 'Building a Better GAAR'" (2020), 68 *Canadian Tax Journal,* issue 2, pp. 579.
34. On the usual misconceptions related to the GAAR, *see* B. Arnold, "The Long, Slow, Steady Demise of the General Anti-Avoidance Rule," (2004) 52 *Canadian Tax Journal,* issue 2, pp. 488-511.
35. Due the potential divergences and perils of inconsistencies, some authors have ventured an autonomous common meaning of the PPT C. Elliffe, "The Meaning of the Principal Purpose Test: One Ring to Bind Them All" (2019) *World Tax Journal,* issue 1, (IBFD Online).
36. On the risks of inconsistent and diverse interpretation of the PPT that would potentially undermine the whole system of tax treaty benefits, *see* P. Baker, "The Multilateral Convention to Implement Tax Treaty Related Measures to Prevent Base Erosion and Profit Shifting," (2017) *British Tax Review* 3, pp. 281-284; Kuźniacki referred to a deliberately broad anti-treaty abuse rule which grant a vast discretionary power to tax authorities triggering issues of legal certainty. *See* B. Kuźniacki, "The Principal Purpose Test (PPT) in BEPS Action 6 and the MLI: Exploring Challenges Arising from Its Legal Implementation and Practical Application," (2018) 10 *World Tax Journal* (IBFD Journals Online).
37. On the different wording between the PPT and the guiding principle, *see* R. Danon, "The PPT in Post-BEPS Tax Treaty Law: It Is a GAAR but Just a GAAR!" (2020) 74 *Bulletin for International Taxation,* issue 4/5, (IBFD Online), s. 3(3).

was obtaining that tax benefit." The wording of Article 29(9) lowers the anti-treaty abuse standard defined in the guiding principle in 2003.[38] Conversely, the "main purpose" test is more favorable to the taxpayer. Since transactions or arrangements have multiple purposes, tax authorities and courts must weigh those purposes in order to properly argue that the tax purpose was the most important, among the other possible purposes.[39] If a DTC is not an MLI-CTA and lacks a provision to deny treaty benefits drafted in a similar fashion to Article 7(1) MLI, the interpretation of a domestic GAAR in line with the guiding principle could lead to different results.[40] Consequently, as commentators recently stressed, the guiding principle becomes an interpretative tool based on Article 31 of the Vienna Convention of the Law of the Treaties ("VCLT"), which cannot be equated to the PPT.[41]

Besides the different wording and legal status, in terms of the burden of proof, there are significant differences between the guiding principle and Article 29(9) OECD MC. While in the guiding principle the onus is on the tax authorities, in the latter standard "the tax authorities only have to pass the 'reasonableness' test with respect to the motive ('one of the principal purposes'), and then the onus is on the taxpayer, who has to demonstrate that granting a benefit would be in accordance with the object and purpose of 'the relevant provisions of this Convention."[42] .'" However, Błażej Kuźniacki defends that the tax authorities must also consider the purpose of the relevant provision of the DTC, even if the wording of the PPT does not require them to do so.[43] Perhaps as in many legal systems occur, it is more logical that the tax authorities gather evidence that one of the principal purposes of the transactions was to obtain a treaty benefit, whilst the taxpayer demonstrates the existence of economic substance and business purposes.

The conflict between the different wordings of the PPT is problematic not only between the PPT and the guiding principle but also within the European Union (EU). Member States are obliged to implement a "main purpose test" in the EU GAAR in Article 6 of the Directive (EU) 2016/1164, of July 12, 2016, which lays down rules against tax avoidance practices that directly affect the functioning of the internal

38. On the criticisms to the low threshold for treaty-abuse, *see* Arnold, *supra* n. 21, p. 111; Kuźniacki, *supra* n. 36, s. 2.3.3; L. De Broe & J. Luts, "BEPS Action 6: Tax Treaty Abuse" (2015) 43 *Intertax*, issue 2, pp. 132.
39. Arnold, *supra* n. 21, p. 112; see para. 179 and 180 of the Commentaries to Article 29(9) OECD MC: "All the evidence must be weighed to determine whether it is reasonable to conclude that an arrangement or transaction was undertaken or arranged for such purpose. [...] It is sufficient that at least one of the principal purposes was to obtain the benefit."
40. On the difficulties to apply the guiding principle by courts and tribunals, *see* B. Arnold, "Tax Treaties and Tax Avoidance: The 2003 Revisions to the Commentary to the OECD Model," (2004) 58 *Bulletin for International Fiscal Documentation*. 6, p. 246 Journals IBFD; A. Martín Jiménez, "The 2003 Revision of the OECD Commentaries on the Improper Use of Tax Treaties: A Case for the Declining Effect of the OECD Commentaries?," (2004) 58 *Bulletin for International Fiscal Documentation*. 1, p. 18 (2004), Journals IBFD.
41. R. Danon, D. Gutmann, M. Lukkien, G. Maisto, A. Martín Jiménez, & B. Malek, "The Prohibition of Abuse of Rights After the ECJ Danish Cases," (2021) 49 *Intertax*, Issue 6 & 7, p. 488.
42. S. van Weeghel, A Deconstruction of the Principal Purposes Test, (2019) 11 *World Tax Journal*, issue 1, (IBFD Online), Section 3.
43. Kuźniacki, *supra* n. 36, s. 2.2.

market in the Anti-Tax Avoidance Directive (ATAD). The drafting of the EU GAAR would conflict with the bilateral treaties signed by the Member States and covered by the MLI, which subscribes to the wording "one of the main purposes" Article 7(1) MLI[44]

4.1.2 *The Interplay Between PPT and LoB: Lack of Clarity on the Meaning of Economic Substance*

The examples provided to the OECD in the Commentaries to Article 29(9) open a wide array of interpretative problems linked to the meaning of economic substance. These examples not only lack a sufficient explanation of the economic nexus of a series of transactions but also are quite simplistic and confusing.[45] Commentators are also quite divided on how to determine economic substance within the PPT test. Martin Jimenez argues in favor of re-aligning the "delineation" and "nonrecognition" tests in the OECD Transfer Pricing Guidelines (2017) and Article 29(9) OECD. Therefore, in his view, the transfer pricing substance should be taken into consideration when applying the PPT.[46] Conversely, Robert J. Danon adopts a more formalistic approach to reject the automatic application of the transfer pricing rules to determine whether an economic substance exists within the PPT test.[47] In the area of Intellectual Property (IP) income, Professor Danon posits that transfer pricing rules could be used for guidance of substance, but not in other taxpayers' arrangements.[48]

The lack of precise meaning of economic substance triggers important inconsistencies between the PPT in Article 29(9) OECD MC (2017) and LoB (29(1)-(7) OECD MC (2017). The interplay between the PPT and the LoB in the MLI may provoke inconsistencies since the MLI's LoB can apply asymmetrically.[49] Accordingly, the same taxpayer's scheme could be assessed under the PPT and LoB by one country that elected to apply both standards, and exclusively under the PPT by another country.

In the current OECD MC (2017), the nexus or economic substance that the taxpayer has with its State of Residence for the LoB test does not influence the PPT analysis.[50] As Professor Van Weeghel puts it, "if a resident passes the LOB test, a treaty benefit can still be denied if the arrangement or transaction it entered into had obtained that benefit as one of the principal purposes and it could not be established that granting that benefit would be in accordance with the object and purpose of the

44. On this conflict between the drafting of the EU GAAR and the PPT in Article 7(1) MLI (Article 29(9) OECD MC), *see* Zornoza, *supra* n. 2, p. 329; C. De Pietro, "Beneficial Ownership, Tax Abuse and Legal Pluralism: An Analysis in Light of the CJEU's Judgment Concerning the Danish Cases on Interest," (2020) 48 *Intertax*, issue 12, pp. 1075-1086.
45. On the criticisms to the examples and the need for more nuanced analysis. *See* A. Martin Jimenez, "Value Creation: A Guiding Light for the Interpretation of Tax Treaties?," (2020) 74 *Bulletin International Taxation*, issue 4/5, (IBFD Online), s. 4(2); van Weeghel, *supra* n. 42, s. 8; Elliffe, *supra* n. 35, s. 5.
46. Martin Jimenez, *supra* n. 45, s. 4.2.
47. *See* Danon, *supra* n. 37, s. 3.3.3.
48. *See* Danon, *supra* n. 37, s. 3.3.3.
49. *See* Article 7(7)(b) MLI.
50. *See* paras 172 and 173 of the Commentaries to Article 29(9) OECD MC.

relevant provisions of the convention."[51] It does not make sense that the nexus requirements in the LoB clause that looks for the shareholders behind the resident (ownership test) and for the link between the business conducted and the income in respect of which treaty benefit is claimed (active conduct of a business test) does not count for Article 29(9) OECD MC (2017). In search for reconciliation, Professor Van Weeghel and Professor Danon suggest an amendment of the OECD Commentaries to facilitate that a taxpayer who meets conditions of that LoB provision, in the absence of a LoB clause in the DTC, meets the nexus element of the PPT.[52] Professor Báez Moreno proposes to apply the PPT to rule-shopping cases, whilst treaty shopping strategies should be covered under the LoB provision.[53]

4.2 Lack of Consistency Between PPT and Domestic Law

This subsection explores the conflict in wording between domestic GAARs and the PPT provision. Both the Commentaries to Article 1 of the OECD MC and UN MC presume that such conflict would not exist in most cases, provided that the domestic GAARs are aligned with the guiding principle or Article 29(9) OECD MC.[54]

Several examples show that domestic GAARs are not precisely aligned with the international standard. This is the case of the Spanish GAAR in Article 15 of the General Tax Code (GTC), which is labeled as "conflict in the application of the tax rules:" "A conflict in the application of tax rules will arise when the taxpayer succeeds in total or partially avoiding the taxable event or obtains a tax base or tax due reduction through acts or arrangements in which both the following circumstances occur: (a) Individually considered or, as a group, such acts are clearly artificial or improper for attaining the pursued objective; (b) That no other legal or economically relevant consequences, on the fringes of the tax saving, arise from the adoption of this legal form or arrangement as would have arisen had the normal, proper form be used."[55] In terms of wording, the differences between the PPT and the Spanish GAAR are quite significant.

51. van Weeghel, *supra* n. 42, s. 7.
52. van Weeghel, *supra* n. 42, s. 11; Danon, *supra* n. 37, s. 3.3.2.
53. *See also*, A. Baez Moreno, "GAARs and Treaties: From the Guiding Principle to the Principal Purpose Test. What Have We Gained from BEPS Action 6?," (2017) 45 *Intertax*, issue 6/7, pp. 432-446.
54. *See* para. 77 of the Commentaries to Article 1 OECD MC (2017) and para. 42 of the UN MC (2107).
55. This translation to English can be found in A. Baez Moreno & J. Zornoza Perez, "Spain Report," IFA Cahiers 2018, Vol. 103A, *Anti-avoidance measures of general nature and scope—GAAR and other rules*. The detailed analysis of the Spanish GAAR and the controversies linked to the distinction between *fraus legis* and simulation exceed from the scope of this contribution. On this issue, recent works can be consulted, C. Palao, "En favor de la indispensable claridad y rigor en la reacción frente a la elusión fiscal," (2020) *Nueva Fiscalidad*, n. 2, pp. 23-71; F. García Berro, *Elusión tributaria y cláusulas anti-abuso en la jurisprudencia del TS*, (Fundación Impuestos y Competitividad, 2019); A. Delgado Pacheco, *Las normas generales anti-elusión en la jurisprudencia española y europea, tesis defendida en la Universidad Autónoma de Madrid*, (Universidad Autonoma de Madrid, 2017. Available at:https://repositorio.uam.es/bitstream/handle/10486/679948/delgado_pacheco_abelardo.pdf?sequence=1.

First, the Spanish GAAR places the emphasis on the artificiality of the arrangement, which is missing in the drafting of the PPT rule in Article 7(1) MLI. Second, the Spanish GAAR would apply when the transactions lack relevant effects, compared to the natural or adequate arrangement, other than a tax advantage (business purpose test). Third, the Spanish rule does not provide for a *saving provision* that would apply when obtaining the treaty benefit might be in accordance with the object and purpose of the corresponding treaty provisions unless it is implicit within the meaning of artificiality.[56] The previous differences have led several commentators to conclude that the Spanish GAAR in Article 15 GTC adopts a mainly objective approach.[57]

Reconciling both anti-abuse provisions is cumbersome when artificiality is the core element of the Spanish GAAR, and the PPT designs a purpose test. Delgado Pacheco has been one of the few authors to argue that case law from the Spanish Supreme Court has approached the interpretation of the Spanish domestic GAAR to international standards, particularly the EU GAAR. However, an amendment of the former would be necessary to comply with the ATAD.[58]

As an attempt to assess the Spanish GAAR under the lens of a purpose test, two observations can be made. First, the artificiality can be assessed under the subjective test of the PPT, since the latter is based on objective facts and circumstances, and not the taxpayer's intentions.[59] Second, the "business purpose test" in the Spanish GAAR could be interpreted as a "sole purpose" test.[60] As stated in paragraph (b) of Article 15(1) GTC, the series of transactions have no legal or economic effects other than the tax saving. Notice that "one of the principal purposes" in Article 7(1) MLI means that "it is sufficient that at least one of the principal purposes was to obtain a tax advantage," thereby demonstrating economic and business motives.[61] If this reading is accepted, the scope of the Spanish GAAR is thus much narrower than the PPT, and less favorable to the tax administration. While a "sole purpose test" would require the tax administration to give enough evidence that there was an absence of business and economic reasons behind the arrangements, "one of the principal purposes" would require the tax administration to prove that the tax benefit was the principal goal of the transactions, based on objective facts or circumstances.

Regardless of whether the Spanish GAAR is considered a completely different standard in relation to the PPT, or the Spanish GAAR is framed under a "sole purpose test," a clear conflict would emerge in either scenario. If the DTC does not provide for a specific rule to solve the compatibility conflict, Baez Moreno and Zornoza Perez

56. On a detailed account of the saving provisions in the GAAR, *see* Arnold, *supra* n. 21, p. 113.
57. Baez Moreno & Zornoza Perez, *supra* n. 55, p. 7; C. Palao Taboada, "The Spanish General Anti-Abuse Rule", 70 *Bulletin for International Taxation* 8 (2016), Journal Articles & Opinion Pieces IBFD; A. Ranz, "Principal Purpose Test," in P. Hernández González-Barreda (ed.) *El Plan de Acción sobre Erosión de Bases Imponibles y Traslado de Beneficios (BEPS)*, (Aranzadi, 2017), pp. 195-2006.
58. Delgado Pacheco, *supra* n. 55, p. 331.
59. *See* para. 179 of the Commentaries to Article 29(9) OECD MC (2017); Arnold, *supra* n. 21, p. 90.
60. On the typology of purpose test, Arnold distinguishes between a (i) sole or exclusive purpose test; (ii) "primary or main purpose test"; (iii) "one of the primary or main purpose test". *See* Arnold, *supra* n. 21, pp. 107 and ss.
61. *See* para. 180 of the Commentaries to Article 29(9) OECD MC (2017).

argue that considering that the Spanish GAAR is a completely different anti-abuse from the PPT in the DTCs: "The treaty GAAR will lead to the non-application of the DTC; in its turn, the domestic GAAR will be applicable or nonapplicable on its own terms. Irrespective of the prior result, the conclusion will always be the same: i.e. the treaty is not applicable and therefore the transaction will be taxed according to the domestic law (including the domestic GAAR)."[62]

Nevertheless, another possible interpretation could be held in line with interpreting the Spanish GAAR as a purpose test. In principle, the *pacta sunt servanda* doctrine enshrined in Article 26 of the Vienna Convention on the Law of Treaties (VCLT) would impede that the domestic GAAR supersedes a DTC GAAR. However, tax treaties cannot make a taxpayer worse off than under the relevant domestic law. Applying "one of the principal purposes" is less favorable to the taxpayer than a "sole purpose test." Hence, the domestic GAAR would prevail, and the tax authorities could not apply the broad purpose test.

Such interpretation may cause perplexity since it curtails the power of the tax administration to fight against abusive tax, limiting the wide faculties under 7(1) MLI. The problem of compatibility of domestic GAAR with the PPT in Article 7(1) MLI is not exclusive to Spain. Many countries, namely developing countries, in domestic law adopt a wide panoply of GAARs. Since their domestic GAARs are not identical to the purpose test in Article 29(9) OECD MC, conflicts could arise. It is possible to bundle the countries into the following three categories:

- "Sole purpose test:" In Sri Lanka, its domestic GAAR introduces a "sole or dominant purpose,"[63] as well as the recent GAAR introduced in Mexico. The wording of this type of GAAR is quite narrow insofar as it applies only in case of a complete absence of a business reason.[64] Peru follows the wording of the Spanish GAAR, thereby anchoring its GAAR in the artificiality and a "sole or predominant purpose" test.[65]
- "Main Purpose Test:" In India[66] and Russia, the GAAR is drafted as a "Main purpose test."
- "Substance over form approach:" In Argentina, its domestic law refers to the economic reality principle, which sets forth that the transactions carried by the taxpayers should be determined based on the true economic nature of the

62. Baez Moreno & Zornoza Perez, *supra* n. 55, p. 15.
63. S. Felix, "Sri Lanka Report," IFA Cahiers 2018, Vol. 103A, *Anti-avoidance measures of general nature and scope—GAAR and other rules.*
64. E. Grageda, "Mexico's GAAR: Will the Bullied Become the Bully?," (2021) *International Tax Notes*. Available at: "https://www.taxnotes.com/tax-notes-today-international/tax-avoidance-and-evasion/mexicos-gaar-will-bullied-become-bully/2021/02/18/2l6x0?highlight=mexico%20GAAR."
65. J. A. Fernández Cartagena, "Peru Report," IFA Cahiers 2018, Vol. 103A, *Anti-avoidance measures of general nature and scope—GAAR and other rules.*
66. S. Banwat & V. Math, "India Report," IFA Cahiers 2018, Vol. 103A, *Anti-avoidance measures of general nature and scope—GAAR and other rules.*

transactions.[67] In the absence of a specific GAAR, the recourse to substance over form prevails in Turkey, Uruguay, and Indonesia.[68] The domestic GAAR in Chile and Korea refers to a substance over form principle.[69] In this group of countries, under the economic reality principle, the subjective test is not clearly mentioned.

These examples simply sketch the potential conflicts that jeopardize a consistent and uniform application of a GAAR.

5 THE DTC'S PRACTICE AFTER THE ENTRY INTO FORCE OF THE MLI

After analyzing the previous potential conflicts, inconsistencies, and asymmetries, one may wonder whether the shift from bilateralism and multilateralism is effectively taking place, namely the PPT in Article 7 MLI. The flexibility of the MLI has been heralded as the main feature of the text. The signatory States are entitled to list the number of DTCs, which are CTAs and therefore subject to the MLI provisions, provided that matches exist with the other signatory jurisdiction.[70] But the MLI does not walk alone in the long march towards implementing the minimum standards. The OECD/G20 Inclusive Framework on BEPS (BEPS Inclusive Framework) currently formed by 125 countries aims to ensure the implementation of the BEPS Package, namely the four BEPS minimum standards (BEPS Action 5, Action 6, Action 13, and Action 14).[71] Beyond the abovementioned BEPS minimum standards, the BEPS Inclusive Framework aims to accelerate consensus in BEPS areas, in which the States conveyed different levels of commitment (i.e., BEPS Action 2, BEPS Action 7).[72]

Since the expectation under the BEPS Inclusive Framework is that its members implement the four minimum standards, the OECD will conduct peer review processes

67. G. Teijeiro, "Argentina Report," IFA Cahiers 2018, Vol. 103A, *Anti-avoidance measures of general nature and scope—GAAR and other rules.*
68. C. Oner, "Turkey Report," IFA Cahiers 2018, Vol. 103A, *Anti-avoidance measures of general nature and scope—GAAR and other rules; I. Sukard,* "Indonesia Report," *IFA Cahiers 2018, Vol. 103A, Anti-avoidance measures of general nature and scope—GAAR and other rules; A. Galeazzi & I. Pérez Bessi,* "Uruguay Report," IFA Cahiers 2018, Vol. 103A, *Anti-avoidance measures of general nature and scope—GAAR and other rules.*
69. C. Anguita Oyarzun, "Chile Report," IFA Cahiers 2018, Vol. 103A, *Anti-avoidance measures of general nature and scope—GAAR and other rules;* B. Kim & H. Park, "Korea Report." IFA Cahiers 2018, Vol. 103A, *Anti-avoidance measures of general nature and scope—GAAR and other rules.*
70. *See* Article 2(1) a) MLI.
71. On the BEPS Inclusive Framework, *see* the OECD website https://www.oecd.org/tax/beps/beps-about.htm/; on the involvement of developing countries in the BEPS inclusive Framework, *see* I. Burgers & I. Mosquera Valderrama, "Corporate Taxation and BEPS: A Fair Slice for Developing Countries," (2017) *Erasmus Law Review* 1, pp. 37-38; A. Christians &.L. van Apeldoorn, "The OECD Inclusive Framework," (2018) 72 *Bulletin International Taxation,* issue 4/5, (Journals IBFD).
72. *See* this opinion in L.E. Schoueri & G. Galdino, "Obligations to MLI Non-Signatories within the Inclusive Framework," in A.P. Dourado (ed.) *International and EU Multilateralism: Challenges Raised by the MLI,* (IBFD 2020), pp. 161-196.

to verify that the level of implementation of the standard is adequate.[73] In relation to BEPS Action 6, one may logically presume that the States that commit to submitting their DTC network to the MLI also follows the anti-abuse standards (Article 6 or 7 MLI) in relation to those treaties, which are expressly not covered in the MLI and forthcoming bilateral DTCs. This logical position could be anchored in the need for coherence and prevention of a bad assessment during the OECD peer review process.

However, logic is not always followed in international law. There are several examples in which consistency with the international standard is lacking:

- There are DTCs signed by nonmembers of the BEPS Inclusive Framework and the MLI, which deviate from the wording of Article 7(1) MLI. This is the case of Article 26(3) of the DTC between Monaco and Montenegro (2018),[74] in which the PPT is drafted as a "main purpose test" instead of "one of the principal purposes" and without the objective test. The fact that Montenegro is not a member of the BEPS Inclusive Framework may explain the deviation from the PPT test.
- There are DTCs signed by Members of the BEPS Inclusive Framework, which deviate from the standard. In the 2018 DTC signed between Oman and Sri Lanka[75]—both Members of the BEPS Inclusive Framework—neither the Preamble in Article 6 MLI nor a specific anti-abuse provision in Article 7 MLI appears in the DTC. The explanation could be that DTC negotiation takes many years, so the States prefer to sign the treaty without the standard, rather than starting[76] Another possible explanation is that these DTCs are signed by States[77] The moment they sign the MLI, one may presume that the anti-abuse provisions in Articles 6 and 7 would apply.
- There are new treaties signed by members of the BEPS Inclusive Framework and MLI signatories, which despite not being listed as CTAs within the MLI, deviate from the standard in Article 7 MLI and do not refer to the new Preamble in Article 6 MLI. For example, consider Article 28 DTC Qatar–Ukraine.[78] In this anti-abuse provision, instead of "one of the principal purposes," the wording follows a "main purpose" test and discards the objective test ("in accordance with the object and purpose of the relevant provisions"). The article also does not refer to "having regard to all relevant facts or circumstances." One possible explanation of this deviation is that the DTC was concluded earlier (March 20, 2018) than the signature of the MLI for both countries: December 4, 2018 (Qatar) and December 23, 2018 (Ukraine).[79]

73. *See* OECD, Prevention of Treaty Abuse—Peer Review Report on Treaty Shopping, (2019). Available at: https://www.oecd-ilibrary.org/docserver/9789264312388-en.pdf?expires=1615204156&id=id&accname=guest&checksum=2E500E477C72DB71E268B2093DB5A336.
74. DTC Monaco–Montenegro (2018), Treaties IBFD.
75. DTC Oman–Sri Lanka (2018), Treaties IBFD.
76. This opinion is shared by Schoueri & Galdino, *supra* n. 72, pp. 191; these authors refer to more.
77. DTCs: DTC Paraguay-Quatar (2018), Treaties IBFD; DTC Croatia–Vietnam (2018), Treaties IBFD; DTC Macau–Vietnam (2018), Treaties IBFD.
78. *See* Article 28 of the DTC Qatar–Ukraine (2018). Treaties IBFD.
79. On this explanation, *see* Schoueri & Galdino, *supra* n. 72, pp. 192.

However, the MLI was released in November 2016, so the States already knew how Article 7 MLI looked. Therefore, a deliberate deviation from the standard triggers doubts on the burden of proof, namely the evidence given by the taxpayer that acted in accordance with the object and purpose of a relevant provision.

- In the 2018 DTC between Georgia and Saudi Arabia, the deviation from the PPT standard is more extreme. The fact that both countries are MLI signatories and members of the BEPS Inclusive Framework did not impede the adoption of a totally different anti-abuse provision: "Notwithstanding the provisions of any other Articles of this Agreement, benefits provided under this Agreement shall not be granted to companies of either Contracting State if the purpose of the creation of such companies is to obtain benefits under this Agreement that would not otherwise be available."[80] The provision targets conduit companies, thereby limiting itself to companies and not individuals.[81]
- Countries like Brazil, which is a member of the BEPS Inclusive Framework, but not of the MLI, adopt a very different LoB provision, which cannot be equated to the Simplified Limitation of benefit (SLoB) in Article 7 MLI.[82]

The next question that arises is whether these previous deviations are mere anecdotes or whether they reveal a solid trend of divergence among countries. A quick review of the recent DTCs (2018-2020), signed by member countries of the BEPS Inclusive Framework and MLI signatories, shows that the majority of States endorse the literal wording of the PPT (Article 7(1) MLI)—although these treaties are carved out from the MLI.[83] Even though, countries that do not belong to either the BEPS Inclusive Framework or to the MLI have endorsed the literal wording of the PPT in Article 7(1) MLI in their recent treaties (Ecuador, Uzbekistan, Ghana, Turkmenistan, Iraq).[84]

80. DTC Georgia-Saudi Arabia Income and Capital Tax Treaty (2018), Treaties IBFD.
81. *See* Schoueri & Galdino, *supra* n. 72, pp. 193-194; in the DTC Hong Kong-India (2018), IBFD Treaties, Article 28(2) mixes Article 6 and Article 7 MLI.
82. *See* Article 27(2) DTC Brazil-Peru (2006), Treaties IBFD; Article 28 DTC Brazil-Trinidad and Tobago (2010), Treaties IBFD.
83. *See* Article 28 DTC Cyprus-Egypt (2019), Treaties IBFD; Article 22 of the DTC Ireland-Netherlands (2019), Treaties IBFD; Article 29(2) Japan-Peru (2020), Treaties IBFD; Article 29(1) DTC Liechtenstein-Lithuania (2019), Treaties IBFD; Article 23 DTC Cyprus-United Kingdom (2018) (as amended through 2018), Treaties IBFD; Article 23(1) DTC Guernsey-United Kingdom, Treaties IBFD; Article 28(5) Japan-Uzbekistan (2019), Treaties IBFD; Article 28(2) Croatia-Japan (2018), Treaties IBFD; Article 22(1) Chile-United Arab Emirates (2019, not in force), Treaties IBFD; Article 23 DTC China-New Zealand (2019), Treaties IBFD; Article 29 DTC Cyprus-Kazakhstan Income Tax Treaty (2019), Treaties IBFD; Article 28 DTC Italy-Uruguay (2019), Treaties IBFD; Article 28(2) DTC Angola—Portugal (2018); Article 24 DTC Bulgaria—Pakistan (2019), Treaties IBFD; Article 28 DTC Cyprus-Egypt (2019), Treaties IBFD; Article 27 DTC Armenia-Singapore (2019), Treaties IBFD; Article 25 A of the DTC Guernsey-Isle of Man (2013) (as amended through 2019).
84. Article 28 of the DTC between Ecuador-Japan (2019), Treaties IBFD; Article 28(5) Japan-Uzbekistan (2019), Treaties IBFD; Article 29(1) DTC Ghana-Malta (2019), Treaties IBFD; Article 27(1) of the DTC Singapore-Turkmenistan (2019); Article 26(2) DTC Iraq-Netherlands (2019), Treaties IBFD; Article 28 of the DTC Korea-Turkmenistan (2015) (As amended through 2019), Treaties IBFD.

In the author's view, few deviations may be deemed as anecdotal, since global trends seem to endorse the standards in Articles 6 and 7 MLI. The role of the OECD in enforcing the standards through the peer review process of Action 6 becomes a powerful tool to compel the members of the BEPS Inclusive Framework to apply the standards. The "naming and shaming strategy" provokes States to adhere to the standard: "The Peer Review reveals that a large majority of Inclusive Framework members have begun to translate their commitment on treaty shopping into actions and are now in the process of modifying their treaty network."[85] The OECD expects that in the next peer review exercises, compliance with the standard will increase.

6 IS THE PPT BENEFICIAL FOR DEVELOPING COUNTRIES?

The previous two sections show that the wording of the PPT is widely reproduced in DTCs not covered by the MLI, although many inconsistencies and doubts are still present in the analysis of the standard. The success of the PPT among the MLI signatories may be seen as a way to foster worldwide uniformity and consistency in preventing treaty abuse.[86] One may wonder whether this intended uniformity is beneficial for developing countries. In other words, is the shift from bilateralism to multilateralism, represented by the PPT, a positive goal that ought to be welcomed by developing countries?

Developing countries are at a clear crossroads. On one hand, to attract investment; and on the other hand, to fight against BEPS strategies. Accordingly, commentators and institutions like the UN or the International Monetary Fund (IMF), confirm that the implementation of GAARs in developing countries is a recommended tool to curb unacceptable tax avoidance practices.[87] Due to the broad discretion, they confer to the tax administration to deny tax benefits, awareness has been raised to minimize risks of corruption and uncertainty for taxpayers stemming from the subjective test.[88] I defend that the PPT is a suitable mechanism for developing countries, based on two arguments.

First, the PPT rule does not exclusively represent the interests of rich countries. The anti-avoidance rule broadly equips the tax administrations of developing countries

85. *See* OECD, Peer Review Report on Treaty Shopping, *supra* n. 72, p. 11.
86. Tandon, *supra* n. 12, p. 14; C. Eliffe, "The Meaning of the Principal Purposes Test: One Ring to Bind Them All?", (2019) 11 *World Tax Journal*, issue 1, pp. 47-76.
87. M. Lennard, "Base Erosion and Profit Shifting and Developing Country Tax Administrations," (2016) 44, *Intertax*, Issue 10, pp. 740-745; *see* the IMF Legal Department in C. Waerzeggers & C. Hillier, "Introducing a General Anti-Avoidance Rule (GAAR): Ensuring That a GAAR Achieves Its Purpose," (2016) *Tax Law IMF Technical Note*, 2016/1. Available at SSRN: https://ssrn.com/abstract=2729042; *see* the UN Practical Portfolio to protect the tax base of developing countries, Arnold, *supra* n. 21.
88. Waerzeggers & Hillier, *supra* n. 87, p. 1; Lennard, *supra* n. 87, p. 742; C. Pramasanti & C. Tjen, "Is Indonesia Benefitting from the Multilateral Instrument?" (2019) 25 *Asia Pacific Tax Bulletin* 6 (2019), Online Journal IBFD, s. 2.3.1.2.: "However, the authors believe that although the PPT will empower the DGT to deny tax treaty benefits in the case of tax avoidance, the implementation of the PPT will cause some legal uncertainties. By definition, the PPT implementation will be heavily based on the subjective judgment of tax officials to decide whether or not any avoidance has occurred."

with a powerful tool to deny treaty benefits if abuse is proven. The PPT is not a self-executing norm and the current application depends on the burden of proof between the tax administration and the taxpayer. In the hands of the tax authorities, the PPT would work as a last resort rule to combat abusive schemes whenever domestic Specific Anti-Abusive Rules (SAARs) cannot be applicable in the treaty context. If a DTC does not specifically allow for a domestic SAAR to apply, there would be a potential conflict between the SAAR found in domestic law and the DTC.[89] A conflict under Article 26 VCLT (*pacta sunt servanda*) would lead to the non-application of the domestic SAAR. For these cases, the PPT could play an important role if both tests, subjective and objective, concur.

Second, several commentators have harshly criticized the considerable weight granted to the subjective test within the PPT—which may trigger legal uncertainty and potential arbitrary solutions by the tax authorities. Authors such as Michael Lang and Andrés Báez Moreno have challenged the subjective test to support a more objective interpretation of the PPT.[90] Professor Lang concluded that the PPT emphasizes the necessity for purposive interpretation of a DTC, thereby discarding any relevance afforded to the subjective element (one of the principal purposes). The purposive interpretation of a particular provision of the DTC is sufficient to verify whether "having regard to all relevant facts and circumstances," the taxpayer deviated from the object and purpose of the abovementioned provision. Since the subjective element become meaningless, Article 29(9) does not represent a legal basis for denying treaty benefits, and therefore, its role is simply to reinforce a purposive interpretation.[91] Báez suggests that a PPT test should be built on the notions of artificiality and business purpose: "The design of a material tax rule based upon subjective criteria, be it a domestic one, a distributive rule in a treaty or a domestic or treaty GAAR, might provoke that two taxpayers, in identical objective circumstances (according to the ability to pay or benefit principle), receive a totally different tax treatment only because of their different (proven) intention."[92] Discarding any subjective element in the PPT and returning to an exclusively objective test based on artificiality risks the "automatization" of the GAAR, regardless of the circumstances of the case.

The following example with leveraged acquisitions could shed light on the risks of an approach that is exclusively based on artificiality. Under debt push-down structures, first, higher interest expenses are allocated to a newly set-up holding company that has been constituted to acquire a targeted company, and second, group taxation between the target company and the holding applies to make the higher interest paid by the holding company deductible against the profit individually accrued by the target company. It is not difficult to test artificiality when the set of transactions (i.e., constitution of a holding company, loan granted from the parent company to

89. *See* paras 70, 71, 72 of the Commentaries to Article 1 OECD MC (2017).
90. M. Lang, "The Signalling Function of Article 29(9) of the OECD Model—The 'Principal Purpose Test,'" (2020) 74 *Bulletin for International Taxation*, issue 4-5, (IBFD Online); Báez Moreno, *supra* n. 53.
91. Lang, *supra* n. 90, s. 2.
92. Báez Moreno, *supra* n. 53, p. 436; Lang, *supra* n. 90.

finance the acquisition of the targeted company by the holding and group taxation regime) are oriented to a legitimate business purpose, which is the acquisition of an operative company. What is the checklist to be followed by the tax administration to determine artificiality in this case? If these set of transactions are deemed to be artificial to achieve a tax advantage, a "proper/normal" way of acquiring the target company should also be defined in contrast to the artificiality. Conversely, a subjective test based on factual circumstances—i.e., high-interest deduction through group taxation regime, no real activity in the holding company—could serve as evidence that one of the principal purposes of the transaction was to obtain a tax advantage.

In treaty-shopping cases, the recourse to both tests of the PPT (subjective and objective) could also be relevant to overcome the shortcomings of a purely objective test based on artificiality. In *Alta Energia*,[93] the shares of a Canadian company were transferred first to a new Luxembourg subsidiary constituted in 2012, and subsequently, a sale of the shares to a third buyer took place in 2013. The capital gain was exclusively taxable in Luxembourg due to Article 13(5) of the DTC between Canada and Luxembourg (1999). Given that Luxembourg is well-known for offering tax advantages for holding companies, would all similar transactions similar to those discussed in *Alta Energia* benefit from the benefits provided in Article 13 of the Canada and Luxembourg DTC network? In other words, are all these arrangements/schemes artificial and thus automatically abusive? The reasoning of the Tax Court confirms the compliance with the objective test, meaning that the transaction does not defeat the object and purpose of the treaty: "There is nothing in the Treaty that suggests that a single purpose holding corporation, resident in Luxembourg, cannot avail itself of the benefits of the Treaty."[94] Yet, the subjective test is also crucial to demonstrate the abusive purpose of the set of transactions and prevent automatization in applying the anti-abuse test. In this judgment, however, the tax administration could not convince the Tax Court that one of the main purposes of the series of transactions was to obtain a tax advantage (i.e. no taxation of the capital gain in Canada). Linking the subjective test with the external facts derived from the transactions carried out by the taxpayer is an effective way to combat the potential perils of a purely arbitrary application of the PPT and automatization by tax authorities. Both tests, the subjective and the objective, are needed to combat treaty-shopping cases.

7 CONCLUSION

The fact that the PPT is widely implemented by developed and developing countries shows that a shift from bilateralism to multilateralism is occurring. Although I have shown some divergences in treaty practice by some States, the bulk of treaties in the aftermath of the MLI follow the PPT standard. This tendency is visible in States that are neither signatories of the MLI nor members of the BEPS Inclusive Framework.

93. Canada: Tax Court, August 22, 2018, 2018 TCC 152, *Alta Energy Luxembourg S.A.R.L. v. The Queen*, Tax Treaty Case Law IBFD. This case is still pending at the Canadian Supreme Court.
94. *See Alta Energy Luxembourg*, para. 91.

Despite its wide implementation, I have argued that a homogenous application of the PPT is unlikely since GAARs are not a self-executing norm. Accordingly, the interpretation of the PPT by the tax administration, and subsequently by judicial bodies, is heavily dependent on the domestic legal culture of abuse and the burden of proof between the tax administration and the taxpayer. Apart from these circumstances, there are still asymmetries and inconsistencies at the international and domestic levels, which may thwart the shift towards a homogenous and uniform anti-abuse treaty provision in the long term. Finally, I have argued in favor of implementing the PPT for developing countries; and moving towards a purpose test, as the PPT sets forth, grants the tax administration of these countries a broad margin of maneuverability to combat abusive schemes.

CHAPTER 12

Aggressive Tax Planning and Its Interaction with the MLI

Cristián Billardi

Cristián Billardi asks whether the MLI will truly deliver uniform tax norms, or instead will merely open new avenues of tax avoidance and potentially lead to new cycles of tax negotiation. Billardi analyzes the goals and scope of the MLI in the context of the development of global norms surrounding the codification and sanction of aggressive tax planning, notably in the context of the European Union's Anti-Tax Avoidance and DAC6 Directives. The chapter examines some difficult areas of divergence and asymmetry surrounding the definition of the concept including with respect to the intended scope of coverage, the burden of proof standards, the assignment of responsibilities among taxpayers and their advisers, and coordination across the pluralistic legal regimes and institutions of the international tax system.

1 INTRODUCTION

In the current dynamic transitional context of domestic and global tax law, tax and fiscal systems are dealing with parallel agendas. The so-called global tax law[1] has seen

1. Specially in our Latin American region, these three agendas coexist and are claimed by different players. The global or international agenda is usually imposed by international organizations (mainly the IMF, WB, OECD) based on the needs appearing more or less necessary, urgent or important according to the heterogeneous situation of the different States that follow directly or indirectly its recommendations, guidelines or schemes of "conditional help." Within this last agenda, in turn, there are different times and needs limited not only to the degree of addition of each Latin American Country to the OECD (in particular, Mexico, Chile and Colombia) but also to the degree with which several Countries adopt such Actions.

many new challenges that parallel the "emergency" agenda that has been intensified by effects of the COVID-19 pandemic and permanently postponed structural reforms (e.g., a greater number of taxpayers; informal economy regularization, among others).

The purpose of the analysis of this chapter is framed in the postponed structural reforms, as it addresses the scope of a multilateral solution to the issue of tax base erosion and profit shifting (BEPS) at the transnational level.

Although domestic systems have generally foreseen and incorporated legal concepts aimed at counteracting said phenomenon, they are limited both in territory and timeframe.

From a territorial viewpoint, it is clear that unilateral solutions are powerless to counteract a phenomenon of global reach. In turn, from a temporal viewpoint, the remedies that already exist in the underlying legal system,[2] as well as other tax law concepts that have been introduced on an ad hoc basis to counteract these phenomena,[3] are only employed after the conduct has been effectively implemented and the taxable base erosion has been achieved.

Even if bilateral conventions are signed to avoid double taxation on income and property, Double Tax Conventions (DTCs) have extended the scope of their purposes to take this phenomenon into account (and thus, shifted away from the goal of avoiding double taxation towards fighting against international fraud and eliminating international double non-taxation, etc.). DTCs have incorporated several legal remedies that are already in force in local regimes. However, they certainly do not entirely eliminate the double taxation phenomenon, since they are bilateral solutions. In fact, the possibility of obtaining a benefit from a treaty derives from the asymmetry between the more than 3,600 DTCs in force. Therefore, the introduction of uncoordinated measures appears to contribute more to the problem rather than to the solution.

In this scenario, the vision proposed by the Organisation for Economic Co-operation and Development (OECD) and its BEPS Action Plan (with G20 political support) seeks to resolve both limitations. On the one hand, through the adoption of a mechanism whereby operators (taxpayers and intermediaries) disclose their potentially aggressive tax planning (ATP) structures in due time and/or upon its implementation, and, on the other hand, through the creation of a multilateral instrument (MLI) that receives the contrast measures adopted by the interested States uniformly.

In this sense, both ATP and the MLI can be theoretically perceived as useful instruments to effectively apply measures to counteract taxable base erosion and illegitimate profit shifting.

This report aims to analyze the status of the reach of those objectives in the context of their current evolution.

I am aware that other substantial matters ought to be subject to discussion and prior consensus in the international field. I refer, in the first place, to the attribution of

For a global vision of the phenomenon, refer, among others, to García Novoa, C. in "*De intermediarios, chivatos, impuestos digitales uy otras cuestiones*," at www.politicafiscal.es.

2. For example, measures to counter fraud, abuse of right, simulation, and other compliance issues.
3. For example, measures to counter tax evasion and tax avoidance, such as general anti-avoidance rules (GAAR), limitation of benefits, rules enshrining substance over form, beneficial owner, etc.

a real taxable base and the acknowledgment of an actual tax authority.[4] The discussion on these topics is particularly robust in the current context and the present analysis is instrumental to the advancement of this discussion.

2 ATP: ORIGIN AND STATED PURPOSES OF THE BEPS ACTION 12

There Is No Uniform Concept for ATP

For instance, one of the original documents generally quoted as having conceptualized ATP defines it as "taking advantage of the technicalities of a tax system or of mismatches between two or more tax systems for the purpose of reducing tax liability" [Taxud/2016/DE/319].

This analysis is not intended to expand upon the complex conceptualization of ATP and how it interrelates with other concepts that, even when not uniform, are better known in the fields of domestic and international tax law (i.e., the concepts of evasion, tax avoidance, treaty abuse, lawful tax planning, option economy, etc.). However, it is useful to highlight how doctrinal conceptualizations of ATP seem to focus on one of multiple differential features of this concept. Some authors highlight its political-moral origin: "it is not a juridical concept, but rather political" (García Novoa); others note that we are in the presence of a "new conceptual category of global tax law" (Pasquale Pistone[5]), while others, in turn, note that it is an essentially transactional concept, wherein only the result not admitted by the system, regardless of the intention to act, ought to be considered (Sergio André Rocha).[6]

These qualifications seem to be mutually complementary rather than contradictory. There is certain agreement on the result required for it to arise and of the conflict between substance and form adopted. On the other hand, the irrelevance of the subjective aspect seems to be more arguable.

This disagreement clearly appears when analyzing how the concept has been adopted by different domestic tax law systems.

Before reviewing the reasons why an early disclosure of the fiscal structures by the taxpayer was deemed necessary, it may be useful to briefly assess the background that led to the introduction of the concept both within the scope of the OECD's BEPS Plan, as well as in the European Union rules[7] (in particular, the Anti-Tax Avoidance Directive (ATAD) and its DAC 6[8]).

4. The issue deserves a questioning about: (1) What taxable base? and (2) Who is responsible for exercising the tax power and within what limits?
5. "... Conceptual category of global tax law, consisting on the taking advantage of the transnational mismatches between tax systems for the purpose of obtaining fiscal benefits (or tax benefits) that the States would not have otherwise granted." Pistone, P. "*La PFA e le categorie concettuali del Diritto Tributario Globale*" in Riv. Trimestrale di diritto tributario; 2-2016. Ed. Giapichelli.
6. "Exclusive concept of international taxation that reaches the control of non-intentional tax advantages"; *see*, among other works, Rocha Sergio, A. *Planejamento Tributario na obra de Marco Aurelio Greco*. Ed. Lumen Juris, Brazil, 2019.
7. For a vision of the European perspective, *see* Cachia, F. "Aggressive tax planning: an analysis from an UE perspective" (2017) 5 EC Tax Review 257 et seq.
8. ATAD Anti-tax Avoidance Directive (2016/1164 of 12-07-2016; DAC6 Directive (EU) 2018/822 of 25-05-2018.

Certainly, the anachronism of the OECD and United Nations (UN) solutions has been observed when facing a diverse economic scenario, which evolved from a domestic model of exchange of goods to a global market of services and the digital economy, within an economic globalization context strongly driven by technological change.

In that sense, technological evolution appears as a real change of transversal paradigm to all social relations and, therefore, to tax law relations. Just think about the transformation caused by the digital economy, not only in terms of globalization but also among technology exporter and importer countries. For instance, regarding the agitated field of international distribution of the tax power, it is interesting to see how many European Countries—who are exporters of capital and technology, and consequently defenders of the residency principle—find that their interests are now more closely aligned to those of countries that have historically been importers of technology and defenders of the principle of the source when dealing with "e-tech giants."

This progressive erosion of the bilateral conventions model has led to the need to introduce specific remedies, for example, limitation of benefit clauses (LoB), as well as broadened the purposes of such a convention (from the limitation of double taxation to fighting against international tax avoidance and international double non-taxation). However, while it is far from solving many existing issues, it revealed other concerns related to treaty shopping, treaty abuse, and the proper leveraging of asymmetries derived from the coexistence among domestic systems and over 3,600 bilateral conventions in force.

Early this century, the paradigm change from "tax havens" (low or no taxation with fiscal, banking, and corporate secrecy) to "noncooperative jurisdictions" on information exchange, shows the need for tax authorities to first avail themselves of reliable data regarding the act or business subject-matter of the taxable event. Then, the question shall not lie on the data or fragmented transactions, but on the possibility of their proper processing, until reaching quality, filtered, and reliable information about the entire scheme planned by taxpayers, intermediaries, and tax advisors professionally involved in structuring those schemes. Moreover, the proper information ought to be timely transmitted and before the effects of taxable base erosion that will lead to its implementation.

A brief review of the last decades shows increasing concern for having proper and shared information by the tax authorities involved. It is worth recalling the OECD report on "Harmful tax competition[9]" (1998) that gave way to information exchange agreements—first, bilaterally and upon request—until reaching its current developmental stage, which favors a multilateral automatic exchange and mutual fiscal administrative assistance. It is worth recalling that the United States, in turn, promoted its FATCA[10] model (2010) still in force.

The 2006 OECD Seoul Forum is usually quoted as one of the milestones of the organization regarding cases of transnational breach, which becomes evident in

9. 231998041COV.XPR (Page 1) (oecd.org).
10. Foreign Account Tax Compliance Act (FATCA) | Internal Revenue Service (irs.gov).

conduct ranging "from tax fraud to aggressive tax planning." At this meeting, it was agreed that there was a need for "examining the role of tax intermediaries (e.g., accounting and law firms, other tax advisors and financial institutions) in relation to non-compliance and the promotion of unacceptable tax minimization arrangements ..." (i-ii).

It is also worth mentioning a government's claims when having to face the effects and responsibilities of the so-called subprime mortgage crisis (2008), who blamed the informatics giants and other multinational operators that the low amount they paid in taxes for profit shifting "was not morally fair."[11]

Unilateral actions to face these phenomena multiplied. Consequently, by that same date, the Aaronson Report[12] (2011), tabled by the British Government in the 2012 budget, ended up recommending the introduction of GAAR aimed at artificial and abusive tax schemes, though back then it did not seem to cover tax planning in general, as it will later extend on other subsequent formulations.

We then reach the well-known BEPS Action Plan (2013), whereby Action 12: "requires taxpayers to disclose their aggressive tax planning schemes (2015)"; which was preceded by the OECD document "Co-operative Compliance: A Framework. From Enhanced Relationship to Co-operative Compliance" (2013). Such action must be jointly analyzed with other levels of information *(local, master file, country by country report)* as mentioned above.

In turn, through its set of anti-abuse measures,[13] the European Union (EU) issued the communication Directive on tax intermediaries ("mandatory disclosure" from the Directive of Administrative Co-operation (DAC) 6) that forces Member States to introduce ATP information rules, whereby ATP was understood as the "taking advantage of the technicalities of a tax system or of mismatches between two or more tax systems for the purpose of reducing tax liability" (CE 2012).

As Cesar García Novoa noted, by analyzing the historical evolution of ATP, one might see its marked political-moral origin. In my opinion, the advancement of moral questioning arising in soft law which is then materialized in legal rules, far from deserving qualification as a "new world paradigm" seems to go back to a certain medieval juridical "mannerism." I remember in a different field how the work of Cesare Beccaria "Dei delitti e delle pene" (1764) had as its main purpose and merit to separate

11. *Reino Unido investiga si Starbucks, Google y Amazon pagan suficiente impuesto*—BBC News Mundo (2012) The claim—mainly motivated in political and social pressure towards the unequal assumption of the costs derived from the subprime crisis led to the "fiscal agreement" in 2016, whereby Google acknowledged its aggressive tax planning which at the same time ratified having acted within the British tax law.
12. Independent study on GAAR published—GOV.UK (www.gov.uk).
13. The "set of anti-abuse measures" is expressed in Directive (EU) of 12-05-2017 which amends Directive (EU) 2016/1164 "hybrid mismatches with third countries." It is integrated to Directive 2011/16/UE on the mandatory automatic exchange of information in the tax area and the "anti-avoidance set of measures" (January 2016) "to prevent aggressive tax planning, boost tax transparency and create a level playing field for all businesses in the EU."

    See also Taxation Papers (n° 71-2017) "Aggressive tax planning indicators. Final report," which conceptualize ATP as "taking advantage of the technicalities of a tax system or of mismatches between two or more tax systems for the purpose of reducing tax liability"; Taxud/2016/DE/319; paragraph 2.1.

that which is morally reproachable from the legally condemnable, with special reference to tax law.[14]

Furthermore, from the very moment the ATP enters a particular legal system, its "legal nature" (i.e., its actual function within a certain juridical system) is unavoidable. In effect, legal operators must coordinate ATP legislation with the entire domestic juridical system. Thus, it is important to assess the compatibility of ATP not only with the institutions interested in tax law (taxpayer rights, tax advisors duties, etc.) but also with the entire legal system (*privacy*, contractual freedom, professional secrecy, etc.).[15]

To assess the functionality and efficiency of ATP, it may be useful to recall that the purported objectives of Action 12 of the BEPS Action Plan require that ATP be reported either directly or indirectly, within domestic legal systems.

In this sense, the decision of "requiring taxpayers to disclose their ATP schemes" (Cap. 1) is aimed at: (a) obtaining early information about potentially aggressive or abusive tax avoidances schemes *in order to obtain information for risk assessment*; (b) identifying the schemes, and the users and promoters thereof in a timely manner; and (c) acting as a deterrent to reduce the promotion and use of avoidance schemes.

Thus, there are two stages of the information transfer process: the first stage, which entails the mandatory disclosure by the intermediary and/or taxpayer stated by the rule, and the second stage, which entails the information exchange between the taxpayers involved in the disclosed scheme. The same mechanics of "mandatory disclosure and cooperative compliance" were also adopted by the EU's DAC 6.

There is plenty of criticism to the mandatory survey of ATP structures, either in case of eventual conflict with the rights of taxpayers as well as for the effects it entails regarding tax authority-taxpayer relations, advisor–taxpayer relations, and among the different tax authorities. This chapter will not expand on any doubts as to the effectiveness of the objectives set forth by Action 12. However, one should keep in mind the assessment as to whether: (a) these are the same objectives pursued by tax authorities who have incorporated the concept within their domestic systems; and (b) those objectives are reached through the MLI set forth in Action 15 in its current wording.

14. Chapter XVII of Beccaria's work addresses the issue of "The Tax Authority" (the spirit of the tax authority in its Spanish version), wherein he reports the atrocities of the "offensive process," while at the same time poses several of the principles currently listed as taxpayers' rights and guarantees. *See*, among others, my article "*Cláusula General Antielusiva. Su funcionalidad. ¿Cuál evolución jurídica?*" in the Minutes of the 20th Seminar of the AMDF, México, November 2020.

15. Certainly, this is an analysis that ought to be done on each particular system, based on the legal precept chosen to reach the objectives expected by its introduction to the regulations, and consequently, assess its functionality and efficiency.

3 VERIFIED ASYMMETRIES OF THE INTRODUCTION OF ATP INTO DOMESTIC LEGAL SYSTEMS

Specialized doctrine has commented on the difficulties entailed in the implementation and coordination of the shift "from international fiscal efficiency and neutrality to globalization of national economic and fiscal anti-avoidance policies."[16]

There are two interrelated factors one must analyze when verifying how domestic systems have begun to incorporate the concept of ATP in their domestic tax regimes. On the one hand, it is worthwhile to refer to instances where countries have either achieved uniformity or disagreed when introducing the concept into their different domestic legal systems. On the other hand, it is worthwhile to assess whether the introduction of the ATP information regime to domestic tax regimes is achieved in a manner that is consistent or inconsistent with the objectives and parameters proposed by the BEPS Action Plan.

From this viewpoint, the same objectives may be reached through different regulatory approaches. For example, by identifying the intermediaries or advisors involved according to the naming of one or all the acting intermediaries, or instead, placing this duty on the taxpayer. On the contrary, any differences may be due to interests other than those set by the BEPS Plan (e.g., demand information of fiscal planning both transactional and domestic).

As it may be assumed, those asymmetries may counteract the aim of reaching a uniform and efficient application of the concept globally.

Upon drafting this work, several local tax systems have incorporated the ATP[17] information regime and many others are either currently working towards its regulatory approval or are in the preliminary discussion stage.[18]

In general, the incorporation of the ATP information regime has been achieved through ad hoc rules. Indeed, this is the case among the EU Member States, who have incorporated the community DAC 6[19] into their domestic systems. It is worth recalling that within the context of the EU, the introduction of the ATP information regime also had to be coordinated with the community anti-fraud rules (CICCIS Project, Anti-avoidance Package, DAC 6, CAC 7, etc.). The following states have already incorporated the ATP information regime into their domestic laws: Germany,[20] Austria, Belgium, Bulgaria, Croatia, Denmark, Estonia, Slovakia, Slovenia, Finland, France,[21]

16. According to Amatucci, F. "*L'adeguamento dell'ordinamento tributario nazionale alle linee guida dell'Ocse e dell'UE in materia di lotta alla pianificazione fiscale aggressiva*"; in http://www.rivistatrimestralediritto tributario.it/linee-ocse-ue-pianificazione-fiscale-aggressiva.
17. For example, the regimes set forth in the United Kingdom (DOTA), Canada, South Africa and Portugal, among the first in domestic implementation.
18. This is the case, for example, of the Brazilian system, that is discussing a structural reform. As revealed by S.A. Rocha, the deficiencies of the concept incorporation project in 2015 prevented it from reaching parliamentary agreement for approval.
19. Directive on Administrative Cooperation amended six times Directive 2018/822/UE (25-05-2018) "amending Directive 2011/16/UE as regards mandatory automatic exchange of information in the field of taxation in relation to reportable cross-border arrangements."
20. The incorporation of the DAC 6 was made by the Bundesrat on December 20, 2019.
21. Ordinance No. 2019-1068 of October 21, 2019.

the Netherlands,[22] Italy,[23] Ireland, Lithuania, Malta, and Portugal;[24] additionally, the United Kingdom had adopted it prior to their effective exit from the EU. The following Member States are currently implementing the regime within their domestic laws: Spain,[25] Cyprus, Czech Republic, Luxemburg, Romania, Switzerland, Greece, and Latvia.

The incorporation of an ad hoc measure can also be found in part among Latin American countries. For example, while the Argentine system[26] has incorporated the concept without expressly mentioning the OECD directives as their source, the prevision of the Mexican regime (an OECD Member State) shows certain particularities that are different from its European peers.[27] Other systems, like the Chilean regime, have tackled problems related to the disclosure of planning structures by implying specific information requirements within legal regimes that are already in force.

As one might observe, the lack of a proper definition of the concept, which was noted at the beginning of this work, may reveal a fundamental asymmetry that exists within the characterizing elements of ATP. It is not difficult to see that there is uncertainty or even conceptual confusion[28] that exists in both domestic regulations and in OECD or EU directives concerning ATP. In fact, it is observed how the reproaches of political-moral nature condemning behaviors of tax fraud and ATP, later appeared as *soft law* and were then introduced as juridical rules. However, this progress was not followed by a conceptual precision of the concept.

From a preliminary comparison, it can be noted that the emerging incorporations of ATP within domestic systems has led to multiple divergences, among which the following are particularly worth mentioning:

(1) Asymmetries regarding spatial scope: Does it reach only transactional planning or also domestic planning?
(2) Asymmetries regarding material scope and the reportable schemes: should all planning be informed or only that which *a priori*—according to certain *hallmarks*—appears as potentially "aggressive"? Does it also require the existence of a "tax advantage" and, in such cases, is there a minimum threshold from which the structure must be disclosed?

22. Incorporated by Decree on June 29, 2020.
23. Executive Order 100/2020.
24. Law 26/2020.
25. Approved by the Council of Ministers on June 2020, authorizing to amend the General Tax Law (RD 1065/2017).
26. General Resolution 4838/20.
27. As regards the amendment to Title VI of the Mexican Federal Fiscal Code, *see*, among others: Ortiz, O. "*Esquemas reportables y los asesores de la documentación de Precios de Transferencia*," in https://www.ey.com/es_mx/tax/transfer-pricing-planning-ome/esquemas-reportables-y-los-asesores-de-la-documentacion. On the date of this report, the informative declaration had not been yet published.
28. In effect, it is not unusual to treat evasion and avoidance as synonyms. For example, *see* recitals 4 and 5 of the combination of Executive Orders 232/2000 and 197/2017 that incorporate provisions of Directive EU 218/822; or the Report from the Special Commission TAX3 of the European Parliament (2019) when referring to the investigation about the "Panama Papers" notes that "tax avoidance and tax evasion are related tax crimes and continuously on focus."

(3) Asymmetries regarding pre-qualification of the conduct implemented/to be implemented: is the intermediary obliged to inform about their prior analysis, or does this qualification exclusively lie on the tax authority? In relation to the previous point, is the "erosive" purpose of the taxpayer relevant, or is it sufficient that the result not captured by the rule exists?

(4) Asymmetries regarding the subjective scope: is the main obligor the intermediary's advisor or the taxpayer? If the intermediary includes several parties, are each of the parties involved responsible, or does the report prepared by one of them—in the same or different country—release the others?

(5) Asymmetries regarding its coordination with the institutions already in force within each system: (a) the interaction of ATP with taxpayers' guarantees has not been uniform (in principle, a lack of certainty was reported; there is also an imbalance between the tax authority's powers and the taxpayers' guarantees, inequality between targets and means, and an increase of the burden related to compliance, among other reasons); (b) the interaction with other instrumental tax law remedies is not uniform either (e.g. general anti-avoidance clauses, or "*tax whistleblowing*"[29]); (c) and with the entire legal system in general (e.g. the scope of professional secrecy).

(6) Asymmetries regarding the punishing scope: this aspect is expressly and exclusively reserved to domestic systems, and can range from merely formal sanctions (e.g. breach of information regimes), to other monetary sanctions that consider the intermediaries' fees or the proper basis of the structure that ought to be reported. Other types of accessory sanctions can also be employed, such as the elimination of records linked to its business operation (e.g. State suppliers), obstacles to obtaining fiscal certificates, or having its "recidivism" negatively influence future sanctions.

Even when not making an extensive comparison between these aspects, it is worth highlighting two special issues that show a high degree of divergence in the regulatory admittances, which may compromise the objectives pursued for its incorporation, namely: the structure type that ought to be disclosed and the eventual sanctions in case of breach.
The diverse information that ought to be disclosed to the tax authority influences not only the actions of domestic administration but also the efficiency of ATP disclosure internationally as it is intended.

One of the disputes arising from the lack of determination of ATP lies on whether the structures to be disclosed must state the "purpose" of obtaining tax benefits not expressly consented by the system or, instead, whether it is sufficient that the result may exist without needing to analyze the subjective aspect followed by the planning structure. As it may be observed, the divergence shall condition not only which structure ought to be informed, but also the punishment if a breach occurs.

29. In this regard, *see* Marino, G. "L'evoluzione del Tax Whistleblowing: dal contrasto all'evasione fiscale internazionale alla prevenzione della pianificazione fiscale aggressive," at RDT Atual, 45-2020.

In statutory law, there are two divergent positions: (1) those countries following the DAC 6 (in general, all EU countries) have stipulated that only the planning structures that show certain features or elements (*hallmarks*[30]) that may be potentially erosive of the taxable base must be disclosed; and (2) those countries where the obligor must inform any tax planning scheme upon request from the tax authority (such as Chile). An intermediate stance is one where, although listed transactions are set,[31] the accent is not on its potential "aggressiveness" but directly on the result of obtaining "a tax advantage or any other type of benefit in favor of the taxpayer" (e.g., Argentina and México).

While in the first case, the preliminary risk analysis lies on the acting advisor and/or intermediary, in the second case the qualification regarding its "aggressiveness" lies on the tax authority; thus, in the latter systems—and as it happens with other information regimes—the primary liability lies on the taxpayer, despite some liabilities falling on the acting advisors.

This reflects, to a certain extent, the different domestic goals pursued when introducing ATP rules. In other words, does the rule only seek to "... obtain information for the assessment of risks" or would it use the information for a specific purpose and eventually punish the conduct of the taxpayer and other operators involved in its implementation?

As already observed, the asymmetries on what and how the information should be disclosed have caused much criticism regarding the taxpayer-tax authority-advisor relationship as to which structure should be disclosed and what information is relevant to such end. Critics also cite the increase of juridical uncertainty and the cost of compliance to the taxpayer as shortcomings of current domestic ATP formulations.

Furthermore, it is clear that the information gathered could then be shared with other interested tax authorities. Sometimes, these authorities will have a different material scope of the information they aim to gather. However, the information they have received was subject to a different process of analysis (by different agents: by the liable intermediary and/or by the same receiving tax authority?), which will undoubtedly undermine the objectives of the concept. Thus, for example, the recipient tax authority may receive a lot of irrelevant information to process, amounting to overdisclosure.

A relevant aspect worth considering which is closely related to the topic is whether the international transmission of disclosed information is automatic in accordance with an autonomous ad hoc regulation (as foreseen by the "second step" of

30. In general, hallmarks referred to the structure itself are foreseen (e.g., confidentiality clause by the advisor regarding "custom-made" schemes) and other special hallmarks where, basically, the system has already identified asymmetric sources of erosion (e.g., double deduction of losses, etc.).

31. In the Argentine case ordered by General Resolution RG 4838/20, after stating what is understood by International Tax Planning -ITP- (Article 4), there are a series of situations where "it is specially deemed that there is an ITP, to later conclude with an open clause providing that also a situation" specifically set forth in the microsite "Fiscal Planning Information Regime" (Article 4 item f) is also subject thereto.

the DAC 6, since 2021[32]) or, if the transmission of disclosed information will only be transferred pursuant to the instruments and agreements that the issuing country has in force with the jurisdictions with which the exchange of information had been envisaged and, in principle, do not expect this transmission to be automatic.

"Significant asymmetries also persist in the context of sanctions which are set forth in cases where the ATP disclosure scheme has been breached. This is particularly evident within the EU. This is because the community legal system has left the punishing aspect to the jurisdiction of each domestic system with the only caveat being that those sanctions must be "effective, proportional and deterrent," as repeatedly upheld by the European Court of Justice.

A brief comparative analysis of the sanctions imposed within this scope[33] shows that pecuniary sanctions range from relatively negligible minimums (e.g., EUR 1,000 in the case of the Italian reduced sanction) to maximums that exceed EUR 1 million (e.g., GBP 1 million in the British system).

This "proportionality" asymmetry further increases when analyzing the possible exceptions or inapplicability of the penalty. For instance, the German system provides for a wide framework of circumstances allowing the non-application of sanctions, whereas the French system does not expressly foresee any exception to a breach. Some local projects provided for the quantification of pecuniary sanctions taking as a parameter the fees accrued by the intermediary advisor, or even the same amount of the entire operation structured.

Finally, it is worth noting that in addition to formal pecuniary penalties, other regimes—like the Argentine system—provide for other types of accessory or "improper" penalties that may be even more onerous than the monetary fine. For example, the disallowance of applications or tax certificates, the growth of its risk profile which influences whether or not it shall be audited, or even worsening its other tax penalties,[34] among others. Those "improper" sanctions—particularly when introduced through regulations—have brought about objections by tax advisors as to their constitutionality, which has motivated a preventive action by the judicial power.[35]

32. Thus, for example, Article 9,2 of Italian Executive Order 100/2020 provides for the first information exchange "on April 30, 2021."
33. For a comparative analysis within the European scope, *see* Deloitte Netherland's report "DAC-6 country-specific penalties and penalty mitigation survey" dated March 27, 2020 (https://www.inrev.org/system/files/2020-04/DAC6%20country-specific%20penalties%20and%20penalty%20mitigation%20survey%20%28Deloitte%29.pdf).
34. In effect, this is provided by Articles 13 and 15 of the quoted RG 4838/20. D. Rajmilovich notes precisely the factual or anomalous penalties set forth in the Resolution. Rajmilovich, D. "*El nuevo régimen de informaciones de planificaciones fiscales.*" La Ley on-line publishing house.
35. Thus, for instance, the Professional Council of Economic Sciences (CPCE) of the Argentine Province of Santa Cruz noted that "the rule infringes the principle of typicality and legality, strict in criminal matters because it typifies infringements and in some cases, as in a criminal rule in which the criminal conduct is defined by reference to another non-criminal rule [called '*ley penal en blanco*'] (art. 4 inc. f) sets improper requirements and sanctions in order to keep the subjects bound within certain records, conditioning the issuance of tax acknowledgments, among other measures (art. 13), without any supporting law." Cautionary Judgment from the Federal Court of Río Gallegos dated January 20, 2021 in re "*Consejo Profesional de Ciencias Económicas de la Provincia de Santa Cruz v. AFIP- DGI on autonomous injunction* (docket number 28/2021)."

The sanction for breach of the ATP regime should not be confused with the sanction set forth in case of a tax crime. However, the interrelation between both punishment spheres is narrower when the effective compliance with the ATP disclosure implies a conditioning upon assessing the taxpayer's[36] behavior or, on the contrary, when the breach of the information regime may deserve any other type of criminal treatment, in addition to the administrative sanction set forth by the ATP[37] regime.

Going back to the subject matter of our analysis, it is clear how this difference in sanctions may be found contrary not only to the objectives foreseen upon introducing the ATP but also to the efficiency of the BEPS Plan in general. Furthermore, the difference in sanctions across domestic systems demonstrates how far we are from achieving the harmonization and coordination of ATP regimes across systems in the fight against tax avoidance and unlawful profit shifting. Another effect that may be caused due to the difference in sanctions might be "forum shopping" of jurisdictions depending on juridical certainty, the degree of taxpayer's guarantees (e.g., scope of the exception based on professional secrecy), or even depending on the amount and types of sanctions set by the systems in cases where the "mandatory disclosure" of tax planning is breached.

As a preliminary conclusion of this section, it seems as if the disclosure of ATP structures, as incorporated by domestic systems, suffers from conceptual imprecisions and is motivated by different objectives across administrations that, even when based on different original needs,[38] may be disclosed contrary to the same expected purpose. This is particularly relevant when considering the asymmetries generated by the introduction of ATP to a legal system, and in its application by the tax authority. Ultimately, it is an imprecise tool whose efficiency and effect shall depend on the use of it made by each individual administration.[39]

Such a situation, in turn, may compromise not only the functionality and efficiency of ATP regulations but also the implementation and efficiency of the BEPS Action Plan, where such asymmetries create a new source of tax forum shopping.

36. Thus, for example, when the taxpayer implements the same duly informed planning structure, hardly can the tax authority qualify such acting as "fraudulent concealment or omission" of the income obtained based on such operations (typical conducts generally committing the crime of evasion).
37. The question here is whether said breach (omission) may constitute a "combination" with the crime of international evasion charged on the taxpayer, or if this latter may fall under the concept of concealment when it is construed that said omission "helped to avoid or hinder the investigation."
38. Thus, for example: Do they have data or not, do they have processing and transmission capacity or not? Do they only pursue obtaining qualified information in due time to set risk profile bases or do they have an auditing anticipation or pre-determinant nature? etc.
39. If the administration is efficient, ineffective or inquiring, since it will nevertheless use the ATP tool that will consequently prove efficient, useless, or disrespectful for the rights of taxpayers.

4 THE MULTILATERAL CONVENTION (MLI) AS A SUITABLE INSTRUMENT

4.1 A MLI for a Global Phenomenon

The exceeding of limits implied by any unilateral or bilateral solution to comprehensive issues—like those touched on by the BEPS Action Plan—has been discussed for more than a century by international tax law doctrine. I note here the historical reference of Oliver Bühler, who has referred to how the Treaties signed by Belgium, Luxembourg, the Netherlands, and France in 1843-1845 provided reciprocal administrative assistance.[40]

So far, the few examples of "multilateral" conventions, like the Nordic Convention (Norway, Sweden, Finland, Demark, and Iceland), the Andean Pact (Colombia, Ecuador, Peru, and Bolivia), or the Directives on tax matters issued by the European Union, are regional agreements or provisions limited to certain specific matters (e.g., intra-group transactional dividends).

Even though it is true that "multilateralism" in the last decades has been more prevalent due in part to administrative cooperation and information exchange, the creation of an exclusive MLI with international reach—or at least a regional reach—to replace bilateral DTTs and also act as a source of rules of subjective rights for taxpayers, still appears far off. The adoption of "minimum standards" by the BEPS does not change this situation.

In any case, even if BEPS fails to expand upon the current interpretation asymmetry, it is clear that eventually there will be a need for a uniform ATP interpretation. In this sense, we must recall that the proposal of vesting international jurisdictional bodies with binding decisions for Member States (International Tax Court) has been posited by renowned authors for some time now (Bühler, V. Tanzi, Victor Uckmar, R. Valdez Costa,[41] Fernando Serrano Antón,[42] among others[43]), and although its materialization seems distant, the implementation of a MLI cannot avoid its discussion.

From an international fiscal political viewpoint, the historical context that allowed the advancement of the objectives proposed by the G20 and the OECD must be considered.

To this effect, note that there is a need for further questioning and careful monitoring as to whether the MLI accounts for restructuring objectives of the international tax system or instead, simply puts forward partial remedies to the distortions created by the same system players. Particularly, I refer to the asymmetry evidenced

40. As background of the few multilateral treaties, it is mentioned the attempted treaty of the Austrian-Hungarian monarchy (1899-1922), though it shall find no practical application.
41. *Instituciones de Derecho Tributario*. Ed. Depalma, Buenos Aires, 1992, pp. 20, 27, 35 et seq.
42. Antón, F.S. *La resolución de conflictos en el derecho internacional tributario: procedimiento amistoso y arbitraje*. Thompson Reuters—Civitas, 2010, section 7.2.7 "El Tribunal Europeo de Derechos Humanos," p. 453.
43. Among the most recent, *see* Azzi, J. "Tackling Tax treaty tensions: time to think about an international tax court" (1988) 52 Bulletin for IBFD 344-357.

between the global actions of multinationals and bilateral DTTs that could be used not only to limit international double taxation but also as instruments of treaty abuse or ATP[44] practices.

This chapter will not expand on this topic, though it is necessary to think about whether the MLI allows for a shared objective that implies amending the system's structure to make it "more equal and cooperative," thus offering "real solutions to real people" (in the UN's declared vision);[45] or if it seeks to impose "patch" actions so that States—and particularly members of the OECD[46]—cease to resign tax collection, especially due to the actions of multinationals.

The positions that find in multilateralism "a new principle of international tax law in the articulated solutions"[47] seem to be grouped in the first line. This adds to the classic principles of territoriality and personality of taxation.

In the second case, it would not be a paradigm shift or a new multilateral agreement, but rather a precarious instrument to limit taxable base erosion, without substantially altering the international distribution structure currently in force.

In any case, whether multilateralism is acknowledged as a "de facto principle of global taxation" or a limited functional instrument to adopt the partial remedies undertaken by the BEPS Plan, it is necessary to consider its interaction with the ATP phenomenon and the role international operators must play in this interaction.

4.2 MLI Instrumental in Fighting Against ATP

One ought to consider whether the MLI proposed by the BEPS Action Plan seems, in principle, suitable to face a phenomenon of global magnitude, such as ATP.

---

44. *See*, among others, Zornoza Pérez, J. "Multilateralism in international taxation: it is really the future?"; in Research handbook on international taxation. Ed. Yariv Brauner, December 2020.
45. In his capacity as Secretary-General of the United Nations, Ban Ki Moon spoke about this multilateralism vision in his speech "Working together can take today's major challenge" (2009).
46. The need to recover tax collection is certainly not exclusive in developed Countries. In developing importer Countries, in turn, the objectives seem to focus on the need to have more information for auditing purposes in relation to their residents owners of property abroad and a larger collection source regarding multinationals (mainly, the informatics giants) that operate in their territory (economic presence) without need of a specific organizational or physical presence.

    For an interesting reflection about the supposed "equal footing" regarding discussion and adoption of BEPS Actions among OECD and extra OECD countries, the dialogue of Professor Duran Rojo and Professor Daniel Fuentes may be consulted in GIDIT—Grupo de *Investigación en Derecho Internacional Tributario—DIÁLOGOS TRIBUTARIOS con el profesor Luis Durán | Facebook*.
47. In the absence of a regulatory duty or a duty derived from international custom that forces the States to cooperate in tax determination or collection, the de facto imposition of multilateral measures has been sustained. Thus, it was noted that "... the daily evolution of the measures articulated by the OECD and the EU leads us to conclude on the existence of this international tax law de facto principle, despite its future." materialization into any regulatory body" Sanchez-Archidona Hidalgo; *supra* page 29, 33.

To this effect, the Recitals, in their justification for the implementation of an MLI, recognize "that governments lose substantial corporate tax revenue because of aggressive international tax planning that has the effect of artificially shifting profits to locations where they are subject to non-taxation or reduced taxation." (1st, paragraph)

Consequently, while Action 12 appears to be a suitable tool to fight against practices that result in taxable base erosion and unlawful profit shifting, the MLI foreseen in Action 15 might also act as a suitable instrument.

The MLI appears to support functional multilateralism, with the aim of eliminating distortions caused by the asymmetries of the systems. These asymmetries are mainly derived from the leveraging of the networks of bilateral conventions in force (DTCs) by multinational companies which result in the erosion that is precisely meant to be prevented by the Action Plan.

In other words, the BEPS MLI appears as an instrument that is comprised of measures (actions) aimed at fighting ATP, as ATP can sometimes lead to the erosion of the taxable base and facilitate unlawful profit shifting.

To this effect, the MLI contains several anti-abuse measures: (a) ratification of the fight against treaty abuse and double non-taxation as the subject matter of DTCs (preamble); (b) the prevision of the rule of the principal purpose test (PPT[48]) that may be complemented in turn with the LoB[49] clause; (c) provisions that avoid double deduction; (d) the "salvage" clause to recover taxation to residents exempted in another jurisdiction; (e) specific rules aimed at dividends (e.g., minimum holding term); and (f) rules regarding permanent establishments located in third jurisdictions.

With a different method of analysis, Carbajo Vasco[50] has noted how the international fight against tax fraud "cannot be seen exclusively as a matter of justice, equity or an expedite means to gain income, but also, and mainly, as a tool necessary to facilitate the operation of the economy." Consequently, if this is then another parameter to analyze the MLI's justification and efficiency, then its implementation must also be judged based on its efficiency at market level. First, an assessment should be made as to whether the MLI implies a higher degree of security and legal certainty of juridical acts, which is a basic aspect both in the relations between States and in the investment and maintenance of a proper level of rents collection and public expenditure.

48. Vg. "one of the main purposes" as ad hoc test from the EU perspective and the practice of the Canadian "committee" that restricts its discretional use by the tax authority.
    The issue is far more complex in case of an interaction of domestic anti-avoidance clauses as regards their compatibility, coexistence and use with the conventional PPT; a matter that even if admitted—specially the adoption of double non-taxation as subject matter of the DTT—is far from being peaceful in that sense.
49. Vg. Action 6 of North-American origin and perspective (as limitation clause of access to DTT).
50. Carbajo Vasco, D. "*La lucha contra la planificación fiscal agresiva y las obligaciones de información tributaria.*" Crónica Tributaria, 2016, No. 158, pages 115. In my opinion, it may be taken also as an instrument of market defense by the party conditioning and leading the same market.

4.2.1 *The Role of International Players*

When asserting that ATP is global and that consequently there is a need for a "multilateral" remedy, it is unavoidable to refer to the role of international players in the development of such a phenomenon.

To that effect, the doctrine has revealed the shared liability of governments and multinationals when reporting the increase in avoidance and aggressive structures.

It is widely known that governments have brought forward claims against multinationals regarding their aggressive tax action; these claims have often been made based on political/moral arguments rather than on the juridical base ("it is lawful but immoral"). Let's recall that some of these claims have been accepted by multinationals based on the economic losses that social questioning could entail, particularly in times of crisis when their economic effects seem to be primarily borne by the citizens who cannot "escape" the negative economic effects, nor transfer their losses or benefits.

From a strictly juridical perspective, a persisting line of thought tends to give transnational companies an active role in promoting rights, mainly via international organizations such as the ILO or the OECD, through *soft law* mechanisms and the Corporate Social Responsibility (CSR) movement. For example, *stakeholder theories*[51] imply obligations on corporations that actively have an impact on the conduct of stakeholders, so that these corporations are responsible not only for respecting human rights obligations but also for the general protection and promotion of rights.[52]

According to Elena Pariotti,[53] these obligations are still moral obligations that came into being through voluntary integration and harmonized *soft law* mechanisms, which often assume a legal value.

Despite the limits acknowledged by international law when directly holding companies or other private players liable, it should be noted how a significant subsection of international doctrine posits that companies are deemed subjects of law due to their increasing power and influence on the international framework and on the evolution of international law.[54]

In the fiscal sphere, it is clear how this evolution has caused several reactions, ranging from the "immorality" of not paying taxes to the modification of the suitable legislative mechanisms to counteract the tax avoidance phenomenon (special clauses

51. The definition of the European Union's Green Book of Corporate Social Responsibility (COM/2001(0366) is understood as the concept whereby "companies decide to contribute voluntarily to the achievement of a better society and a cleaner environment." In this sense, the companies are required not only to respect the law and to maximize the benefits to shareholders but also to restrain negative externalities and contribute to the social development of the communities where they are present. By opposition to the term *shareholders*, the term *stakeholders* includes not only workers, clients, suppliers or *partners* of the company but also the environment and the reference community.
52. *See* Billardi, C. *Los derechos del hombre y su tutela jurídica en el derecho tributario y financiero.* Ed. Ad Hoc. Buenos Aires, 2018.
53. Pariotti, E. *I diritti umani: concetto, teoria, evoluzione.* Cedam 2013.
54. As summarized by Pariotti, *supra* page 148, this solution is proposed by Clapham, Dine, Donaldson, Higgins, Jäggers, among others.

and general anti-avoidance clauses) or of ATP (in terms of BEPS) and the enactment of the prohibition of double non-taxation as the very purpose of double international taxation treaties.

However, note that recognizing the "international subjectivity" of multinational companies would not only affect whether the company can be found liable but also potentially lead to the company being granted the right to speak and vote autonomously from the States where they operate or are deemed residents. As it will be understood, this paradigm shift would not only change the international tax system but also the capacities of multinationals as taxpayers.[55]

On a similar note as the liability of multinationals in the implementation of ATP structures, it is also worthwhile to mention the active role of governments in not articulating timely remedies, and deliberately allowing or even promoting the use of tax law loopholes due to internal asymmetries or asymmetries derived from the interaction with other national systems. This complacent role governments sometimes play has been denoted as a "passiveness in the production of rules that has factually favored infringer entities."[56]

To this effect, while States denounce the unlawful practices of multinationals, they themselves adopt "preferential" tax policies whose effects favor ATP, thus increasing harmful tax competition among the same States that tend to justify their action with the need to "recover revenue" and "attract direct foreign investment."[57]

For example, the European Commission recently cautioned against the actions of seven of its Member States which allowed for ATP[58] policies.

The fact that some countries have denounced and renegotiated their DTCs—despite criticism about their form—is concrete evidence that governments have the tools to either resort to the resolution mechanism set forth within the DTC (e.g., mutual agreement procedure or arbitration), or to denounce the bilateral Treaty altogether (e.g., denunciation made by Argentina regarding the agreements signed with Switzerland, Spain, and Chile).

Finally, it is worth mentioning the liability of supranational technical bodies, whose growing influence in designing international tax policy seems ever more relevant in the current context.

---

55. There would be a distinction between, for example, domestic taxpayers and global taxpayers.
56. In that sense, *see*, among others: Sanchez-Archidona Hidalgo, *supra* Serrano Anton, F. "*La era post BEPS o la ejecución de su plan de acción: convenio multilateral vs. implementación unilateral*"; Jimenez, M. & Calderon Carrero, J.J, "*El Plan de acción BEPS de la OECD para eliminar la erosión de la base imponible y el traslado de los beneficios a otras jurisdicciones: ¿final, el principio del final o el final del principio?*" in Quincena Fiscal; 2014; No. 1-2-, pp. 112 et seq.

    In other words, the same Governments have tended to encourage aggressive tax schemes when they found it beneficial to later complain when their consequences are adverse on tax collection terms.
57. It could be held that if the exchange terms are not changed on a global economic-financial level, any modification of the tax system shall be ineffective when not instrumental to deepening the existing inequalities.
58. *La Comisión Europea advierte a siete países por políticas fiscales agresivas que pueden llevar a eludir impuestos* (rtve.es).

To illustrate this, one might look at the actions of the European Fiscal Board and the OECD's Committee on Fiscal Affairs, as well as the growth of *soft law* rules derived from the directives of these organizations (guidelines, recommendations, or even models, etc.), which have been incorporated as sources of international law or embraced, without amendments, within domestic legal systems, including those who are not full members of these organizations.

In particular, the OECD is often seen as the organization that is most capable of influencing domestic tax policy or the subjective rights of taxpayers. One might argue that international tax policy ought to be adopted by a more pluralistic international body that is not only comprised of a few wealthy nations.

Furthermore, it has been noted that in the adoption of OECD directives, consensus is often difficult to achieve and that in practice, States sometimes feel pressured to impose the directive to achieve international unanimity. This practice clearly contradicts the principle of consensus. Certainly, "international unanimity" in fiscal policy is a euphemism that may result in complicit inactivity. However, it should be noted that because of the "instrumental technicality" of coordinating between governments, some substantial decisions that are made regarding the sovereign tax powers of States (and other government levels whose powers have been recognized), and the rights of the citizens-taxpayers, are sometimes kept hidden or confidential.

In the context of ATP specifically, the European Union or the OECD may also exercise a more direct or indirect influence[59] globally. To this effect, these organizations may either significantly influence ATP policies or, instead, may opt to not play an important role in developing a policy.

One such example of the European Commission exercising its influence can be seen through its cautioning of Member States regarding their harmful, discriminatory fiscal policies, or their allowing State aid that might distort the market. Examples of inactivity, in turn, may be found in the OECD's unequal treatment of States in their reporting process regarding "tax havens," or "noncooperative jurisdictions" within some States but not others.

4.3 Efficiency of a Nonexclusive MLI of Asymmetrical Implementation

In "developing a multilateral instrument to modify bilateral tax treaties,"[60] the OECD assumes that the MLI is "desirable and possible." In this sense, we should recall that the BEPS Action Plan provides that "… the goal of Action 15 is to streamline the implementation of the tax treaty-related BEPS measures"; while the "BEPS Summary" (2015) noted that "This is an innovative approach with no exact precedent in the tax world … ."

59. Certainly the austerity or conditional financial aid measures imposed or "suggested" by the multilateral credit bodies become relevant when they comprise fiscal nature provisions.
60. http://www.oecd-ilibrary.org/taxation/developing-a-multilateral-instrument-to-modify-bilateral-tax-treaties_9789264219250-en.

Despite these premises, let's recall that the MLI foreseen by BEPS Action 15 (2013) that came out in June 2017[61] is not a classical, uniform, or exclusive multilateral Convention that substitutes the more than 3,600 bilateral conventions currently in force. Effectively, as mentioned above, the MLI proposed by the BEPS Action Plan does not replace bilateral conventions but rather coexists with them. Presently, there are 1700 DTCs subject to the MLI that have been ratified by 60 countries.[62] The MLI does not cover all the matters found within DTCs but partially expands upon a reduced number of DTCs provisions that entail the implementation of a minimum standard of BEPS Action Plans.

Despite any initial misapprehensions about the MLIs background and introduction to legislation,[63] I have noted elsewhere that the adoption of the MLI proposed by BEPS Action 15[64] has led to criticism. This is particularly true considering the conflicting interaction the MLI has with the DTCs that are currently in force, the asymmetrical implementation of the compatibility clause,[65] the signature and implementation in different phases by different countries (implementation at different times[66]), the difficulty of consensually broadening the "minimum standard," the

61. *See* "Multilateral Convention to implement Tax treaty related Measures to Prevent Base Erosion and Profit Shifting" OECD, 2017. The MLI was adopted on November 24, 2016 and signed on June 7, 2017 by 67 jurisdictions for the first signing ceremony.
62. On December 21, 20, Barbados deposited the MLI ratification instrument. According to OECD's report, at present there are 60 jurisdictions that have passed and ratified said instrument that came into force on January 1, 2021 in more than 600 DTTs signed by these 60 jurisdictions. According to the same OECD report, only 95 out of the 194 OECD member countries have signed the MLI until today. *See* www.oecd.org/tax/treaties/beps-mli-signatories-and-parties.pdf.
63. Regarding its justification, I remember questioning about OECD's orders versus the declared consensus by the national sovereignties.

    It is not suitable to address here its juridical hierarchy or the means of incorporation whereby domestic systems introduce those instruments into their laws. The matter necessarily involves the "Vienna Convention on the Law of Treaties" (in particular, its Article 15). For its domestic introduction, as recalled by Bulit Goñi—for the Argentine system- "... Those agreement or treaties, bilateral as well as plurilateral, according to the National Argentine Court constitute 'a complex federal act ending up with its approval and ratification,' certainly meaning that they are set by the Executive Branch, approved by the Legislative Branch, and executed again by the Executive through its record and deposit. In addition, it was decided both on the direct operability of treaties —international or internal—i.e. that no law—national or local, as the case may be- is necessary to make them valid, for in addition the obligations among signatory States, subjective rights for taxpayers are derived." Bulit Goñi, E. "*Constitución Nacional Argentina y Derecho Internacional Tributario*"; in Treaty, *supra* pp. 287 et seq.).
64. Billardi, C. "*Il Multilateralismo nel BEPS e la sua interazione con le convenzioni per evitare la doppia imposizione*"; in *L'evasione e l'elusione fiscale in ambito nazionale e internazionale*. Dir. F. Amatucci. R. Cordeiro Guerra. Ed. Aracne, Italia 2017, pp. 339-356. *See also* Bosman, A. "General aspects of de Multilateral instrument" in Intertax, vol. 45, I.10; pp. 642 et seq.
65. First of all, the language matter, considering that the MLI's official version languages are English and French, and the DTTs tend to consider different languages (e.g., those entered into in Spanish speaking countries); which matter has strong interpretation relevance by the competent administrative bodies and local courts.
66. Certainly, its effective term depends on the ratification and implementation date of each Country according to its domestic regime of juridical incorporation of the MLI. In addition, the Preamble and Action 6 would have a different effective term. In the end, for the purpose of its real application, it should be verified whether the other Country with which it is related through a specific DTT has also ratified the MLI, if in force and if no reserve was made on the topic in question.

possibility for a party to place a reserve, and the lack of agreement on a uniform controversy resolution instrument (MAP).[67]

Referring to our topic of reflection, this chapter has already noted how the MLI appears as a formal instrument that contains Actions conceived to avoid or alleviate the effects of taxable bases erosion amongst countries who adopt the MLI framework. However, it is legitimate to question whether this goal is hindered by the same peculiarities of the MLI, which has been qualified as "flexible" and as a tool for strengthening "bilateral multilateralism." To this effect, this asymmetric multilateralism of joint implementation with the DTCs in force that allowed its adhesion can strongly inhibit its implementation[68] and runs the risk of fostering treaty shopping.

In effect, a MLI in the abstract seems more efficient than any unilateral or bilateral action to implement the designed policies[69]—among them, the contrast to the ATP—in practice its asymmetrical implementation not only implies a lower degree of juridical certainty but also may encourage forum shopping, where the implementation and interpretation of domestic rules diverge between countries or at the very least, lacks coordination. To date, the MLI is in force in less than 60 jurisdictions and has not been ratified by countries which are typically seen as important players in tax policy in the international context. The issue is still more complex in the Latin American context. This is because there is coordination in fiscal policy between countries who are already members of the OECD and those in the process of adhesion to the OECD (e.g., Chile and México in the first case, and Costa Rica and Colombia in the second)—who are bound by OECD directives—with other jurisdictions that are not associated with the OECD. Further, the timeline for the MLI's incorporation within each of these blocks is not consistent either (for instance, the MLI is already in force in Uruguay as of 2020, while the USA and Brazil have not yet signed).

Certainly, the lack of a supranational jurisdictional instance—despite its political consideration—and the current impossibility of agreeing on a unique dispute resolution procedure does not help to limit the asymmetrical effects herein described and does not foster a uniform interpretation or consistent implementation of the MLI.

Even though it may be held that these obstacles are characteristic of any MLI intermediary implementation stage, it cannot prevent us from critically reviewing the

67. The means of arbitration does not comprise the minimum MLI standard. It should also be borne in mind that the Arbitration has been subject to historical rejection by most of the Latin American countries who tend to deem it an extension of jurisdiction generally incompatible with its domestic jurisdictional system. In addition, it has been objected by doctrine (Figueroa) for it places the "national company" in disadvantage versus the conglomerate of the multinational.

    Carlos Forcada reveals that only 20 out of the 182 DTT signed by Latin American Countries provide for Arbitration, and from these only two refer to non-OECD countries.

    In practice, the DTTs signed after 2008 have not included this mechanism, not even as substitution, within their provisions (e.g., DTTs signed by Argentina with Uruguay or Spain).

68. Stefano Dorigo warns how multilateralism is precisely contradicted by effect of the discretion vested on particular legal systems. Dorigo, S. L'impatto della Convenzione multilaterale BEPS sul sistema dei trattati contro le doppie imposizioni (rivistatrimestralediritttotributario.it).

69. Which was already observed in the incapacity of the unilateral solutions, as well as in the change of objectives of the same DTTs that passed from fighting against double bilateral taxation to fighting against tax havens, international tax avoidance, double non-taxation and now the ATP translationally. Thus the unavoidable need of consented solutions of international reach.

dissimilarities of the MLI's effects compared to the objectives declared when it was first proposed.

To this effect, if in the above analysis we discarded that the purpose of the MLI is to alter the international taxation bases, the effects pronounced at this implementation stage might cause one to doubt that the specific purpose of the MLI was to resolve problems of asymmetries within DTCs. Moreover, this chapter discusses how an asymmetrical implementation with the absence of a supranational jurisdictional body runs the risk of creating new erosions to the taxable base and the ATP.

In other words, there is a risk that the declared goal may be replaced by another more urgent problem, i.e., an increase of the tax administration powers based on the exercise of its auditing and collection power. Despite the legitimacy of this goal, there is a risk that such an urgent problem becomes an end in itself and conspires against the scope of the goals proposed by the MLI and the DTCs. For example, the "recovery" of a certain matter or taxable base by a particular State could hinder the coordination goal pursued by the MLI and even result in double or multiple taxation.

For those who assess the justification of the MLI based on the market, the high degree of juridical uncertainty of the current implementation phase impedes the objective of being a useful tool to ease the management of the economy, while at the same time generates new instances of "harmful tax competition," as already reported by the European Commission in relation to countries whose regimes facilitate ATP.

5 CONCLUSION

Certainly, in a transition stage such as the current one, it is not suitable to seek final conclusions. However, I believe it could be useful to underline certain aspects of the current implementation of the MLI and of domestic ATP regimes that showcase criticisms regarding the objectives declared by the BEPS Action Plan.

To this effect, the ATP schemes disclosure tools, as incorporated by domestic systems, suffer from conceptual inaccuracies and show relevant asymmetries, both in its incorporation to the domestic legal systems and in its stage of application by the national tax authorities. This may compromise not only the functionality and efficiency of ATP rules but also the materialization of the BEPS Action Plan objectives when those asymmetries become a new source of tax forum shopping.

International organizations, multinational companies, and States are jointly responsible for the generation of the ATP phenomenon and its resolution requires a coordinated and shared action by these same players. In turn, the jointly implemented asymmetric multilateralism with the DTCs that are currently in force, which has allowed for the flexible adhesion of the MLI by signatory countries is a feature that may strongly hinder the MLI's effective implementation.

Furthermore, it is observed how in the present transitional stage, the original goals of the MLI stated by the BEPS Plan have shifted to other more immediate and urgent goals, such as the increase of the tax authority's powers in its auditing and collection role.

The current reality of asymmetries and different implementation timelines existing in both instruments (ATP and MLI) impedes the goals brought forward by the BEPS Action Plan and, at the same time, may bring about new ATP scenarios based on the same failure to coordinate created by the MLI. Effectively, at the current stage of evolution, the system does not guarantee that taxes are paid at the place where income is generated; or even that benefits are not transferred to less cooperative jurisdictions, but rather appears as a new source of distortion, which now favors less "aggressive" systems to counteract ATP.

These criticisms are further pronounced when one considers that it is not possible to impose a shared mechanism of dispute resolution that settles asymmetries related to the interpretation and implementation of the MLI.

Finally, these circumstances effect the relationships between tax authority-taxpayer; taxpayer-advisor; and between States; with the resulting risk of increasing harmful tax competition and the exacerbation of juridical-tax uncertainty. As I recall, this was precisely what the BEPS Plan intended to limit.

As it can easily be observed, the present circumstance carries harmful effects not only for the relationship between States or the distortion of foreign investment but also for the scope of taxpayers' rights.

In other words, if this criticism is not addressed, there is a risk that the so-called paradigm shift brought on by the MLI is just a fiscal "gatopardism" where everything is meant to change when in reality, nothing actually changes.[70]

BIBLIOGRAPHY

Amatucci, Fabrizio "L'adeguamento dell'ordinamento tributario nazionale alle linee guida dell'Ocse e dell'UE in materia di lotta alla pianificazione fiscale aggressiva"; in http://www.rivistatrimestralediritttotributario.it/linee-ocse-ue-pianificazione-fiscale-aggressiva

Billardi, C "El Multilateralismo en BEPS y su interacción con los Convenios para evitar la doble imposición" in DPTI 3/2015.

"Il Multilateralismo nel BEPS e la sua interazione con le convenzioni per evitare la doppia imposizione"; in *L'evasione e l'elusione fiscale in ambito nazionale e internazionale*. Dir. F. Amatucci. R. Cordeiro Guerra. Ed. Aracne, Italy 2017, pp. 339-356.

"Origen y evolución del Derecho Internacional Tributario" in Tratado de Derecho Internacional Tributario (Directors: Rubén O. Asorey, Fernando D. García). Book I, pp. 27 et seq. Publishing house: La Ley, Bs.As. 2003.

Bosman, Alexander "General Aspects of De Multilateral Instrument" in Intertax, vol. 45, I.10; pp. 642 et seq.

70. A similar warning is made by Prof. Duran Rojo (Dialogues 8-1-21) when expressing his fear that the MLI as "umbrella multilateralism" ends up limiting to a political type commitment, even far from common rules actually in force.

Bravo, Nathalie "The Multilateral Tax Instrument and Its Relationship with Tax Treaties," in World Tax Journal, October 2016, pp. 279 et seq.

Cachia, Franklin "Aggressive Tax Planning: An Analysis from an UE Perspective" in EC Tax Review 2017/5; pp. 257 et seq.

Dorigo, Stefano "L'impatto della Convenzione multilaterale BEPS sul sistema dei trattati contro le doppie imposizioni," in L'impatto della Convenzione multilaterale BEPS sul sistema dei trattati contro le doppie imposizioni (rivistatrimestralediritt otributario.it)

García, Fernando D. "Fuentes del Derecho Internacional Tributario" in Tratado de Derecho Internacional Tributario (Directores: Rubén O. Asorey, Fernando D. García). Book I, pp. 50 et seq. Publishing house: La Ley, Bs.As. 2003.

Rizzardi, Raffaele "Con la convenzione multilaterale le azioni BEPS entrano direttamente negli accordi dei singoli"; in Corriere Tributario 3/2017.

Rocha Sergio A. Planejamento Tributario na obra de Marco Aurelio Greco. Ed. Lumen Juris, Brasil, 2019.

Rocha Sergio A. Brazil's International Tax Policy, Ed. Lumen Juris, Brasil, 2017.

Pistone, P. "La pianificazione fiscale aggressiva e le categorie concettuali del diritto globale," in Rivista Trimestrale Di Diritto Tributario. Vol. 2. pp. 395-439 (2016).

Pistone, P. "Abuse of Companies and the Prohibition of Abusive Tax Practices"; in Birkmose H.S., Engsig Sorensen K. (eds.) Abuse of Companies in Tax Law pp. 309-328 Alphen aan den Rijn Kluwer Law International (2019).

Pistone, P. "Diritto internazionale pubblico e diritto tributario"; in Diritto E Pratica Tributaria Internazionale -DPTI- pp. 454-502.

Sánchez-Archidona Hidalgo, G. "El multilateralismo frente a los problemas fiscales internacionales del Siglo XXI"; in Rev. RCyT. CEF, number 418 (January 2018)- pp. 5-36.

Sánchez-Archidona Hidalgo, G. "Reflections on Multilateral Tax Solutions in a Poste-BEPS Context," in Intertax, Vol. 45, I. 11; pp. 714 et seq.

Schoueri, Luís E. Planejamento Fiscal através de Acordos de Bitributação: Treaty Shopping. Ed. Revista dos Tribunais. 1995.

Tanzi, V., Taxation in an Integrated World, The Brookings Institution, Washington, DC, 1995.

Uckmar, V. Estudios de derecho tributario constitucional e internacional, Ábaco, Buenos Aires, 2005.

Zornoza Pérez, J. "Multilateralism in International Taxation: It Is Really the Future?"; in Research Handbook on International Taxation. Ed. Yariv Brauner, December 2020.

Index

B

F

G

H

SERIES ON INTERNATIONAL TAXATION

1. Alberto Xavier, *The Taxation of Foreign Investment in Brazil,* 1980 (ISBN 90-200-0582-0).
2. Hugh J. Ault & Albert J. Rädler, *The German Corporation Tax Law with 1980 Amendments,* 1981 (ISBN 90-200-0642-8).
3. Paul R. McDaniel & Hugh J. Ault, *Introduction to United States International Taxation,* 1981 (ISBN 90-6544-004-6).
4. Albert J. Rädler, *German Transfer Pricing/Prix de Transfer en Allemagne,* 1984 (ISBN 90-6544-143-3).
5. Paul R. McDaniel & Stanley S. Surrey, *International Aspects of Tax Expenditures:* A *Comparative Study,* 1985 (ISBN 90-654-4163-8).
6. Kees van Raad, *Nondiscrimination in International Tax Law,* 1986 (ISBN 90-6544-266-9).
7. Sijbren Cnossen (ed.), *Tax Coordination in the European Community,* 1987 (ISBN 90-6544-272-3).
8. Ben Terra, *Sales Taxation. The Case of Value Added Tax in the European Community,* 1989 (ISBN 90-6544-381-9).
9. Rutsel S.J. Martha, *The Jurisdiction to Tax in International Law: Theory and Practice of Legislative Fiscal Jurisdiction,* 1989 (ISBN 90-654-4416-5).
10. Paul R. McDaniel & Hugh J. Ault, *Introduction to United States International Taxation* (3rd revised edition), 1989 (ISBN 90-6544-423-8).
11. Manuel Pires, *International Juridicial Double Taxation of Income,* 1989 (ISBN 90-6544-426-2).
12. A.H.M. Daniels, *Issues in International Partnership Taxation,* 1991 (ISBN 90-654-4577-3).
13. Arvid A. Skaar, *Permanent Establishment: Erosion of a Tax Treaty Principle,* 1992 (ISBN 90-6544-594-3).
14. Cyrille David & Geerten M.M. Michielse (eds), *Tax Treatment of Financial Instruments,* 1996 (ISBN 90-654-4666-4).
15. Herbert H. Alpert & Kees van Raad (eds), *Essays on International Taxation,* 1993 (ISBN 90-654-4781-4).
16. Wolfgang Gassner, Michael Lang & Eduard Lechner (eds), *Tax Treaties and EC Law,* 1997 (ISBN 90-411-0680-4).
17. Glória Teixeira, *Taxing Corporate Profits in the EU,* 1997 (ISBN 90-411-0703-7).
18. Michael Lang et al. (eds), *Multilateral Tax Treaties,* 1998 (ISBN 90-411-0704-5).
19. Stef van Weeghel, *The Improper Use of Tax Treaties,* 1998 (ISBN 90-411-0737-1).

20. Klaus Vogel (ed.), *Interpretation of Tax Law and Treaties and Transfer Pricing in Japan and Germany*, 1998 (ISBN 90-411-9655-2).
21. Bertil Wiman (ed.), *International Studies in Taxation: Law and Economics; Liber Amicorum Leif Mutén*, 1999 (ISBN 90-411-9692-7).
22. Alfonso J. Martín Jiménez, *Towards Corporate Tax Harmonization in the European Community*, 1999 (ISBN 90-411-9690-0).
23. Ramon J. Jeffery, *The Impact of State Sovereignty on Global Trade and International Taxation*, 1999 (ISBN 90-411-9703-6).
24. A.J. Easson, *Taxation of Foreign Direct Investment*, 1999 (ISBN 90-411-9741-9).
25. Marjaana Helminen, *The Dividend Concept in International Tax Law: Dividend Payments Between Corporate Entities*, 1999 (ISBN 90-411-9765-6).
26. Paul Kirchhof, Moris Lehner, Kees van Raad, Arndt Raupach & Michael-Rodi (eds), *International and Comparative Taxation: Essays in Honour of Klaus Vogel*, 2002 (ISBN 90-411-9841-5).
27. Krister Andersson, Peter Melz & Christer Silfverberg (eds), *Liber Amicorum Sven-Olof Lodin*, 2001 (ISBN 90-411-9850-4).
28. Juan Martín Jovanovich, *Customs Valuation and Transfer Pricing: Is It Possible to Harmonize Customs and Tax Rules?*, Second Edition, 2018 (ISBN 978-90-411-6134-5).
29. Stefano Simontacchi, *Taxation of Capital Gains under the OECD Model Convention: With Special Regard to Immovable Property*, 2007 (ISBN 978-90-411-2549-1).
30. Michael Lang, Josef Schuch, & Claus Staringer (eds), *Tax Treaty Law and EC Law*, 2007 (ISBN 978-90-411-2629-0).
31. Duncan Bentley, *Taxpayers' Rights: Theory Origin and Implementation*, 2007 (ISBN 978-90-411-2650-4).
32. Sergio André Rocha, *Interpretation of Double Taxation Conventions: General Theory and Brazilian Perspective*, 2008 (ISBN 978-90-411-2822-5).
33. Robert F. van Brederode, *Systems of General Sales Taxation: Theory, Policy and Practice*, 2009 (ISBN 978-90-411-2832-4).
34. John G. Head & Richard Krever (eds), *Tax Reform in the 21st Century: A Volume in Memory of Richard Musgrave*, 2009 (ISBN 978-90-411-2829-4).
35. Jens Wittendorff, *Transfer Pricing and the Arm's Length Principle in International Tax Law*, 2010 (ISBN 978-90-411-3270-3).
36. Marjaana Helminen, *The International Tax Law Concept of Dividend*, Second Edition, 2017 (ISBN 978-90-411-8394-1).
37. Robert F. van Brederode (ed.), *Immovable Property under VAT: A Comparative Global Analysis*, 2011 (ISBN 978-90-411-3126-3).
38. Dennis Weber & Stef van Weeghel, *The 2010 OECD Updates: Model Tax Convention & Transfer Pricing Guidelines - A Critical Review*, 2011 (ISBN 978-90-411-3812-5).
39. Yariv Brauner & Martin James McMahon, Jr. (eds), *The Proper Tax Base: Structural Fairness from an International and Comparative Perspective— Essays in Honour of Paul McDaniel*, 2012 (ISBN 978-90-411-3286-4).
40. Robert F. van Brederode (ed.), *Science, Technology and Taxation*, 2012 (ISBN 978-90-411-3125-6).

41. Oskar Henkow, *The VAT/GST Treatment of Public Bodies*, 2013 (ISBN 978-90-411-4663-2).
42. Jean Schaffner, *How Fixed Is a Permanent Establishment?*, 2013 (ISBN 978-90-411-4662-5).
43. Miguel Correia, *Taxation of Corporate Groups*, 2013 (ISBN 978-90-411-4841-4).
44. Veronika Daurer, *Tax Treaties and Developing Countries*, 2014 (ISBN 978-90-411-4982-4).
45. Claire Micheau, *State Aid, Subsidy and Tax Incentives under EU and WTO Law*, 2014 (ISBN 978-90-411-4555-0).
46. Robert F. van Brederode & Richard Krever (eds), *Legal Interpretation of Tax Law*, 2014 (ISBN 978-90-411-4945-9).
47. Radhakishan Rawal, *Taxation of Cross-border Services*, 2014 (ISBN 978-90-411-4947-3).
48. João Dácio Rolim, *Proportionality and Fair Taxation*, 2014 (ISBN 978-90-411-5838-3).
49. Paulo Rosenblatt, *General Anti-avoidance Rules for Major Developing Countries*, 2015 (ISBN 978-90-411-5839-0).
50. Gaspar Lopes Dias V.S., *Tax Arbitrage through Cross-Border Financial Engineering*, 2015 (ISBN 978-90-411-5875-8).
51. Geerten M.M. Michielse & Victor Thuronyi (eds), *Tax Design Issues Worldwide*, 2015 (ISBN 978-90-411-5610-5).
52. Oktavia Weidmann, *Taxation of Derivatives*, 2015 (ISBN 978-90-411-5977-9).
53. Chris Evans, Richard Krever & Peter Mellor (eds), *Tax Simplification*, 2015 (ISBN 978-90-411-5976-2).
54. Reuven Avi-Yonah & Joel Slemrod (eds), *Taxation and Migration*, 2015 (ISBN 978-90-411-6136-9).
55. Alexander Bosman, *Other Income under Tax Treaties: An Analysis of Article 21 of the OECD Model Convention*, 2015 (ISBN 978-90-411-6610-4).
56. John Abrahamson, *International Taxation of Manufacturing and Distribution*, 2016 (ISBN 978-90-411-6664-7).
57. Frederik Boulogne, *Shortcomings in the EU Merger Directive*, 2016 (ISBN 978-90-411-6713-2).
58. Angelika Meindl-Ringler, *Beneficial Ownership in International Tax Law*, 2016 (ISBN 978-90-411-6833-7).
59. Andreas Waltrich, *Cross-Border Taxation of Permanent Establishments: An International Comparison*, 2016 (ISBN 978-90-411-6832-0).
60. Sergio André Rocha & Allison Christians (eds), *Tax Sovereignty in the BEPS Era*, 2017 (ISBN 978-90-411-6707-1).
61. Peter Antony Wilson, *BRICS and International Tax Law*, 2018 (ISBN 978-90-411-9435-0).
62. Louise Otis, Brigitte Alepin & Blanca Moreno-Dodson (eds), *Winning the Tax Wars: Tax Competition and Cooperation*, 2018 (ISBN 978-90-411-9460-2).
63. Marta Castelon, *International Taxation of Income from Services under Double Taxation Conventions: Development, Practice and Policy*, 2018 (ISBN 978-90-411-9594-4).

64. D.M. Broekhuijsen, *A Multilateral Tax Treaty: Designing an Instrument to Modernise International Tax Law*, 2018 (ISBN 978-90-411-9872-3).
65. John Abrahamson, *International Taxation of Energy Production and Distribution*, 2018 (ISBN 978-90-411-9101-4).
66. Leopoldo Parada, *Double Non-taxation and the Use of Hybrid Entities: An Alternative Approach in the New Era of BEPS*, 2018 (ISBN 978-90-411-9991-1).
67. Richard Snoeij, *International Tax Aspects of Sovereign Wealth Investors: A Source State Perspective*, 2018 (ISBN 978-90-411-9431-2).
68. Aleksandra Bal, *Taxation, Virtual Currency and Blockchain*, 2019 (ISBN 978-94-035-0103-1).
69. Werner Haslehner, Georg Kofler, Katerina Pantazatou & Alexander Rust (eds), *Tax and the Digital Economy: Challenges and Proposals for Reform*, 2019 (ISBN 978-94-035-0361-5).
70. Eva Escribano, *Jurisdiction to Tax Corporate Income Pursuant to the Presumptive Benefit Principle: A Critical Analysis of Structural Paradigms Underlying Corporate Income Taxation and Proposals for Reform*, 2019 (ISBN 978-94-035-0640-1).
71. Jérôme Monsenego & Jan Bjuvberg (eds), *International Taxation in a Changing Landscape: Liber Amicorum in Honour of Bertil Wiman*, 2019 (ISBN 978-90-411-9234-9).
72. Kasper Dziurdź, *Non-discrimination in Tax Treaty Law and World Trade Law: The Impact of Formal, Substantive and Subjective Approaches*, 2019 (ISBN 978-94-035-0904-4).
73. Félix Daniel Martínez Laguna, *Hybrid Financial Instruments, Double Nontaxation and Linking Rules*, 2019 (ISBN 978-94-035-1074-3).
74. Jan Gooijer, *Tax Treaty Residence of Entities*, 2019 (ISBN 978-94-035-1301-0).
75. John Abrahamson, *International Taxation of Banking*, 2020 (ISBN 978-94-035-1094-1).
76. Richard Krever & François Vaillancourt (eds), *The Allocation of Multinational Business Income: Reassessing the Formulary Apportionment Option*, 2020 (ISBN 978-94-035-0614-2).
77. Ajit Kumar Singh, *Exploring the Nexus Doctrine in International Tax Law*, 2021 (ISBN 978-94-035-3363-6).
78. Galya Savir, *Regulation and Tax in Space*, 2021 (ISBN 978-94-035-3393-3).
79. Rita Julien, *Credit Method Compatibility and Constraints under EU Law: An Analysis of the Case Law of the CJEU*, 2022 (ISBN 978-94-035-2363-7).
80. Sergio André Rocha & Allison Christians (eds), *A Multilateral Convention for Tax: From Theory to Implementation*, 2022 (ISBN 978-90-411-9428-2).

www.ingramcontent.com/pod-product-compliance
Lightning Source LLC
Chambersburg PA
CBHW071237230926
51849CB00001B/132
9789041194282